Dictionary of Literary Biography

Dictionary of Literary Biography Documentary Series

Dictionary of Literary Biography Yearbooks

1980 edited by Karen L. Rood, Jean W. Ross, and Richard Ziegfeld (1981)

1981 edited by Karen L. Rood, Jean W. Ross, and Richard Ziegfeld (1982)

1982 edited by Richard Ziegfeld; associate editors: Jean W. Ross and Lynne C. Zeigler (1983)

1983 edited by Mary Bruccoli and Jean W. Ross; associate editor Richard Ziegfeld (1984)

1984 edited by Jean W. Ross (1985)

1985 edited by Jean W. Ross (1986)

1986 edited by J. M. Brook (1987)

1987 edited by J. M. Brook (1988)

1988 edited by J. M. Brook (1989)

1989 edited by J. M. Brook (1990)

1990 edited by James W. Hipp (1991)

1991 edited by James W. Hipp (1992)

1992 edited by James W. Hipp (1993)

1993 edited by James W. Hipp, contributing editor George Garrett (1994)

1994 edited by James W. Hipp, contributing editor George Garrett (1995)

1995 edited by James W. Hipp, contributing editor George Garrett (1996)

1996 edited by Samuel W. Bruce and L. Kay Webster, contributing editor George Garrett (1997)

1997 edited by Matthew J. Bruccoli and George Garrett, with the assistance of L. Kay Webster (1998)

1998 edited by Matthew J. Bruccoli, contributing editor George Garrett, with the assistance of D. W. Thomas (1999)

1999 edited by Matthew J. Bruccoli, contributing editor George Garrett, with the assistance of D. W. Thomas (2000)

2000 edited by Matthew J. Bruccoli, contributing editor George Garrett, with the assistance of George Parker Anderson (2001)

2001 edited by Matthew J. Bruccoli, contributing editor George Garrett, with the assistance of George Parker Anderson (2002)

2002 edited by Matthew J. Bruccoli and George Garrett; George Parker Anderson, Assistant Editor (2003)

Concise Series

Concise Dictionary of American Literary Biography, 7 volumes (1988–1999): *The New Consciousness, 1941–1968; Colonization to the American Renaissance, 1640–1865; Realism, Naturalism, and Local Color, 1865–1917; The Twenties, 1917–1929; The Age of Maturity, 1929–1941; Broadening Views, 1968–1988; Supplement: Modern Writers, 1900–1998.*

Concise Dictionary of British Literary Biography, 8 volumes (1991–1992): *Writers of the Middle Ages and Renaissance Before 1660; Writers of the Restoration and Eighteenth Century, 1660–1789; Writers of the Romantic Period, 1789–1832; Victorian Writers, 1832–1890; Late-Victorian and Edwardian Writers, 1890–1914; Modern Writers, 1914–1945; Writers After World War II, 1945–1960; Contemporary Writers, 1960 to Present.*

Concise Dictionary of World Literary Biography, 4 volumes (1999–2000): *Ancient Greek and Roman Writers; German Writers; African, Caribbean, and Latin American Writers; South Slavic and Eastern European Writers.*

Dictionary of Literary Biography® • Volume Three Hundred Twenty-Three

South Asian Writers
in English

Dictionary of Literary Biography® • Volume Three Hundred Twenty-Three

South Asian Writers
in English

Fakrul Alam
University of Dhaka

A Bruccoli Clark Layman Book

THOMSON

GALE

Detroit • New York • San Francisco • San Diego • New Haven, Conn. • Waterville, Maine • London • Munich

Dictionary of Literary Biography
Volume 323: South Asian Writers in English
Fakrul Alam

Editorial Directors
Matthew J. Bruccoli and Richard Layman

LIBRARY OF CONGRESS CATALOGING-IN-PUBLICATION DATA

South Asian writers in English / edited by Fakrul Alam.
    p. cm. — (Dictionary of literary biography ; v. 323)
    "A Bruccoli Clark Layman book."
    Includes bibliographical references and index.
    ISBN 0–7876–8141–5 (hardcover : alk. paper)
    1.   South Asian literature (English)—Bio-bibliography—Dictionaries. 2. Authors, South Asian—Biography—Dictionaries. I. Alam, Fakrul. II. Series.

    PR9570.S642S68 2006
    820.9'95403—dc22

                             2005035602

Printed in the United States of America
10 9 8 7 6 5 4 3 2 1

Contents

Contents

Plan of the Series

. . . Almost the most prodigious asset of a country, and perhaps its most precious possession, is its native literary product—when that product is fine and noble and enduring.

Mark Twain*

The advisory board, the editors, and the publisher of the *Dictionary of Literary Biography* are joined in endorsing Mark Twain's declaration. The literature of a nation provides an inexhaustible resource of permanent worth. Our purpose is to make literature and its creators better understood and more accessible to students and the reading public, while satisfying the needs of teachers and researchers.

To meet these requirements, *literary biography* has been construed in terms of the author's achievement. The most important thing about a writer is his writing. Accordingly, the entries in *DLB* are career biographies, tracing the development of the author's canon and the evolution of his reputation.

The purpose of *DLB* is not only to provide reliable information in a usable format but also to place the figures in the larger perspective of literary history and to offer appraisals of their accomplishments by qualified scholars.

The publication plan for *DLB* resulted from two years of preparation. The project was proposed to Bruccoli Clark by Frederick G. Ruffner, president of the Gale Research Company, in November 1975. After specimen entries were prepared and typeset, an advisory board was formed to refine the entry format and develop the series rationale. In meetings held during 1976, the publisher, series editors, and advisory board approved the scheme for a comprehensive biographical dictionary of persons who contributed to literature. Editorial work on the first volume began in January 1977, and it was published in 1978. In order to make *DLB* more than a dictionary and to compile volumes that individually have claim to status as literary history, it was decided to organize volumes by topic, period, or

From an unpublished section of Mark Twain's autobiography, copyright by the Mark Twain Company

genre. Each of these freestanding volumes provides a biographical-bibliographical guide and overview for a particular area of literature. We are convinced that this organization—as opposed to a single alphabet method—constitutes a valuable innovation in the presentation of reference material. The volume plan necessarily requires many decisions for the placement and treatment of authors. Certain figures will be included in separate volumes, but with different entries emphasizing the aspect of his career appropriate to each volume. Ernest Hemingway, for example, is represented in *American Writers in Paris, 1920–1939* by an entry focusing on his expatriate apprenticeship; he is also in *American Novelists, 1910–1945* with an entry surveying his entire career, as well as in *American Short-Story Writers, 1910–1945, Second Series* with an entry concentrating on his short fiction. Each volume includes a cumulative index of the subject authors and articles.

Between 1981 and 2002 the series was augmented and updated by the *DLB Yearbooks*. There have also been nineteen *DLB Documentary Series* volumes, which provide illustrations, facsimiles, and biographical and critical source materials for figures, works, or groups judged to have particular interest for students. In 1999 the *Documentary Series* was incorporated into the *DLB* volume numbering system beginning with *DLB 210: Ernest Hemingway.*

We define literature as the *intellectual commerce of a nation:* not merely as belles lettres but as that ample and complex process by which ideas are generated, shaped, and transmitted. *DLB* entries are not limited to "creative writers" but extend to other figures who in their time and in their way influenced the mind of a people. Thus the series encompasses historians, journalists, publishers, book collectors, and screenwriters. By this means readers of *DLB* may be aided to perceive literature not as cult scripture in the keeping of intellectual high priests but firmly positioned at the center of a nation's life.

DLB includes the major writers appropriate to each volume and those standing in the ranks behind them. Scholarly and critical counsel has been sought in deciding which minor figures to include and how full their entries should be. Wherever possible, useful references are made to figures who do not warrant separate entries.

Each *DLB* volume has an expert volume editor responsible for planning the volume, selecting the figures for inclusion, and assigning the entries. Volume editors are also responsible for preparing, where appropriate, appendices surveying the major periodicals and literary and intellectual movements for their volumes, as well as lists of further readings. Work on the series as a whole is coordinated at the Bruccoli Clark Layman editorial center in Columbia, South Carolina, where the editorial staff is responsible for accuracy and utility of the published volumes.

One feature that distinguishes *DLB* is the illustration policy—its concern with the iconography of literature. Just as an author is influenced by his surroundings, so is the reader's understanding of the author enhanced by a knowledge of his environment. Therefore *DLB* volumes include not only drawings, paintings, and photographs of authors, often depicting them at various stages in their careers, but also illustrations of their families and places where they lived. Title pages are regularly reproduced in facsimile along with dust jackets for modern authors. The dust jackets are a special feature of *DLB* because they often document better than anything else the way in which an author's work was perceived in its own time. Specimens of the writers' manuscripts and letters are included when feasible.

Samuel Johnson rightly decreed that "The chief glory of every people arises from its authors." The purpose of the *Dictionary of Literary Biography* is to compile literary history in the surest way available to us—by accurate and comprehensive treatment of the lives and work of those who contributed to it.

The *DLB* Advisory Board

Introduction

South Asian writing in English has its origins in the British colonization of the Indian subcontinent, a process that began in the eighteenth century, initially under the aegis of the East India Company. A key date in its history was 1757, when a British force under Robert Clive defeated the powerful ruler of Bengal, Siraj-ud-Dawlah, thereby taking effective control of a large part of India. At this time the Mogul Empire was fast disintegrating, a situation the British exploited to their advantage. The expansionist policies of the English also enabled them to conquer all of Ceylon by 1815. By the 1850s most of the region now identified as South Asia—specifically, the areas that now constitute the sovereign states of India, Pakistan, Bangladesh, and Sri Lanka—had become part of the British Empire.

Linguistic colonialism inevitably followed on the heels of the political acquisition of South Asia. Initially, British administrators debated among themselves whether they should impose English on the people of the subcontinent or whether they should retain Persian and Sanskrit for legal and administrative purposes. For a while, British civil servants were made to learn these languages by "orientalists," policy makers of the East India Company who favored the retention of the "native" languages for administrative work. But the "Anglicists," the group in favor of the widespread use of English in offices, had won the day by 1835, the year when the politician and historian Thomas Babington Macaulay produced his famous minutes on law and education as a member of the Supreme Council of India. According to Macaulay, introducing the English language to the subcontinent was essential to "form a class who may be interpreters between us and the millions whom we govern—a class of persons Indian in blood and colour, but English in tastes, in opinions, in morals and in intellect." This verdict was further ratified by Lord William Bentinck, the governor-general of the period, who declared that "the great objects of British [rule in India] ought to be the promotion of European literature and science among the natives of India, and all funds appropriated for the purpose of education would be best employed on English education alone," implying thereby that the process of "civilizing" India

could take place only through the propagation of the English language.

The English language and English literature were thus imported to the subcontinent by the conquerors as part of imperial policy. However, it must be noted that at least a few Indians had acquired proficiency in the language on their own and had started to write in English years before Macaulay's report. In all probability, Sake Deen Mahomet, an Indian who moved first to Ireland, settled in England, and then published *The Travels of Dean Mahomet, a Native of Patna in Bengal, through Several Parts of India* (1794), was the first published Indian writer in English. The first Indian writer in English of note, Rammohun Roy, not only published essays in English on topics such as religion and social reform in the first decades of the nineteenth century but also led a campaign by Indians demanding English education for themselves years before Macaulay's report was published.

Although Indians perceived English chiefly as the language of administration and higher education for most of the nineteenth century, a few Indian writers made it their language of literary activity even in the first half of the century. The verse of the Eurasian poet Henry Derozio, for instance, attracted attention in Bengal, as did his leadership of a group of young Bengalis who embraced Enlightenment ideals and wanted to emulate the literary feats of the English Romantics. Viewed with the advantage of hindsight, however, the works of most Indian authors attempting to write in English creatively at that time appear now to be derivative and undistinguished. In fact, the writers from this period who made a lasting impact on Indian literature later viewed their own English publications as false starts. Michael Madhusudan Dutt, the greatest Bengali poet of the nineteenth century, initially published verse in English, at times attempting to write like Sir Walter Scott or George Gordon, Lord Byron, and at times emulating John Milton. Similarly, Bankim Chandra Chatterji, regarded as the best Bengali novelist of the age, wrote his first novel, *Rajmohan's Wife* (1864), in English before deciding to write fiction in his mother tongue.

Of course, not all nineteenth-century Indian writing in English is undistinguished and of interest now mainly for historical reasons. Feminist scholars have resurrected the reputation of Toru Dutt, who was nineteen when she published a volume of verse translations from the French titled *A Sheaf Gleaned in French Fields* (1876), which was praised by critics such as Edmund Gosse. Her *Ancient Ballads and Legends of Hindustan* (1882), a posthumously published verse collection, confirms that Dutt was a poet of considerable talent. Similarly, the Indian sage Swami Vivekananda wrote elevated English prose of the spiritual life that can still be appreciated. Vivekananda became popular as a speaker in the west in the 1890s for his eloquent speeches and lectures in English.

The earliest writer featured in *DLB 323: South Asian Writers in English* is Rabindranath Tagore. When he received the 1913 Nobel Prize in literature for *Gitanjali (Song Offerings)* (1912), a volume of his own translations of his Bengali-language lyrics, writing in English emanating from the subcontinent won worldwide acclaim for the first time. Tagore went on to publish many more translations of his verse, plays, and fiction and even occasionally wrote poems in English. He also lectured on various topics in English in Europe and America for almost two decades. Many of these lectures were subsequently published. Although Tagore's reputation as a writer began to decline steadily in the West in the 1920s, *Collected Poems and Plays of Rabindranath Tagore* (1936) has always remained in print, testifying to his stature as a South Asian writer in English.

Except for Tagore, the only other writers included in *DLB 323: South Asian Writers in English* whose works span the opening decades of the twentieth century are Ananda Coomaraswamy and Mohandas Karamchand Gandhi. In *A History of Indian English Literature* (1982) M. K. Naik describes the Ceylon-born Coomaraswamy as "[o]ne of the pioneers of a just evaluation of Hindu and eastern art . . . his importance as an ambassador of Indian and oriental art, thought and tradition cannot be overestimated." Initially, Gandhi wrote for English journals and published pamphlets in the language, but he soon switched to writing in his mother tongue, Gujarati. He himself dictated the translation of *Hind Swaraj*, originally published in 1909, into English as *Indian Home Rule*, thereby attracting considerable attention in some Western circles. The most important of Gandhi's later works–for example, his autobiography, *The Story of My Experiments with Truth* (1927, 1929)–were rendered into English by others, but because of their impact on subsequent developments in South Asian politics and culture, and because of the lasting impact made globally by the English versions, they are considered in this volume.

Like Gandhi, Pandit Jawaharlal Nehru represents resurgent nationalism in India articulated effectively in the first half of the twentieth century. Unlike Gandhi, however, Nehru wrote almost entirely in English. His work shows how the colonized can appropriate the colonizers' language to resist them, to reach the widest possible audience, and to seize the initiative in the discourse of power. Nehru's most famous English works are *Jawaharlal Nehru: An Autobiography* (1936) and *The Discovery of India* (1945), both triumphs of Indian English prose. His eloquent wielding of the English language in the service of Indian independence still rings in the ears of people interested in India through his famous speech "A Tryst with Destiny," delivered at the moment of Indian independence in 1947. Not surprisingly, Salman Rushdie and Elizabeth West begin their much-reviewed anthology, *The Vintage Book of Indian Writing, 1947–1997* (1997), published to commemorate the golden jubilee of Independence, with Nehru's speech.

In *The Perishable Empire: Essays on Indian Writing in English* (2000), Meenakshi Mukherjee writes that "Indian writing in English as a recognizable literary phenomenon becomes visible only in the 1930s," the decade when Mulk Raj Anand, R. K. Narayan, and Raja Rao began their long and distinguished careers as Indian novelists. It was no accident that the sudden arrivals of these writers in the South Asian literary scene coincided with the ferment of nationalism and Gandhi's activism against social and imperial injustice. Anand's first novel, *Untouchable* (1933), is about a class of people championed by Gandhi precisely because they were ostracized by mainstream Hindu society at that time. Anand's subsequent novels, such as *Coolie* (1936), *Two Leaves and a Bud* (1937), and *The Village* (1939), continued to focus on the plight of underprivileged people and marginalized communities. Although he kept writing fiction until the 1990s, only his first two novels have had a lasting impact on readers.

In contrast, Narayan continued to develop as a novelist for decades. His earliest novels, *Swami and Friends: A Novel of Malgudi* (1935), *The Bachelor of Arts* (1937), and *The Dark Room* (1938), are portraits of life in small-town southern India in the waning years of the Raj and constitute the prelude to a remarkable career that came to maturity with his great novels of the 1950s and 1960s: *The Financial Expert* (1952), *The Guide* (1958), and *The Man-Eater of Malgudi* (1961). Among Narayan's later works, *The Painter of Signs* (1976) is also a significant achievement. Indisputably one of the most important Indian English novelists of his generation, he was for some years considered a front-runner for the Nobel Prize for his Malgudi novels. (Malgudi is the fictional region Narayan created in the manner of Thomas

Hardy's Wessex, William Faulkner's Yoknapatawpha County, and Gabriel García Márquez's Macondo.)

Rao has written only five novels; the first, *Kanthapura,* was published in 1938, while the last, *The Chessmaster and His Moves,* came out in 1988. *Kanthapura* is an attempt to convey fictionally the transformations wrought by Gandhi and the freedom struggle on Indian consciousness, even in remote and rural regions, but it is also notable as an experiment with form and language. As Rao states in his well-known introduction to the book, he attempted to create his own version of a *sthala-purana* (legendary history), a popular form in the Indian narrative tradition. He endeavored to find an answer to the problems faced by Indian English novelists who felt compelled to tell a story "in a language that is not one's own [in] the spirit that is one's own." Stylistically, he claims, he tried to convey the rhythms of Indian life in his own way. Some critics consider Rao's second novel, *The Serpent and the Rope* (1960), a greater achievement because of its manifold themes and philosophic resonance, but *Kanthapura* is his most seminal book for the way it ushered in a tradition of formal and linguistic experimentation that represented an alternative to the realism forged by Anand and Narayan.

Another novelist of note from the pre-Partition period included in *DLB 323: South Asian Writers in English* is Ahmed Ali, whose *Twilight in Delhi* (1940) evokes the life of the Muslims of colonial India. Ali moved to Pakistan after the creation of the country in 1947 and continued to produce fiction, verse, and translations of some distinction, but he also played an active role in stewarding Pakistani writing in English in its formative period.

The partitioning of the subcontinent into India and Pakistan in August 1947 and the withdrawal of the British from Ceylon in 1948 were, of course, momentous political events. Pakistan itself broke up into the sovereign states of Pakistan and Bangladesh in 1971, and Ceylon was renamed Sri Lanka in 1972. After independence, each of these countries followed its own policy regarding the English language. These varying policies led to marked differences in the quality and the quantity of the literature produced in English in South Asia. Inevitably, the magnitude of India alone ensures that it will continue to play a primary role in South Asian writing in English.

In the case of India, the constitution adopted after Independence stated that the English language would be used for official purposes for fifteen years, but at the end of this period the Indian parliament extended its use indefinitely by making it an "associate official language" of Hindi. In actual practice, however, English has steadily grown in importance in the country, partly as a "link" language between the many different languages spoken in various Indian states and partly because of the nation's increasing involvement in global trade and commerce and the movement of a substantial number of Indians around the world. English is also the preferred language in higher education, the highest echelons of administration, the judiciary, and book and journal publishing. As the Indian writer K. Satchidanandan observes in *Indian Literature: Positions and Propositions* (1999), "India is the third largest English-using nation after the USA and UK [with] about 35 million users of the language . . . about 5 percent of India's population." He goes on to note that in addition to being "an 'associate official language' in the constitution," English "is the state language of four states and of most of the Union territories."

It should come as no surprise, then, that Indian English literature continued to flourish after the Partition. Several noteworthy writers of fiction and nonfiction emerged after Independence. The most idiosyncratic of them is G. V. Desani, who was born in Nairobi, was educated in England, and taught philosophy at the University of Texas at Austin. His *All about Mr. Hatterr* (1948; revised, 1972) is a comic masterpiece, a Rabelaisian and Joycean romp and a dizzying linguistic experiment. Another idiosyncratic writer who emerged shortly after Independence was Nirad C. Chaudhuri. His first and most important work, *The Autobiography of an Unknown Indian* (1951), is an impressive record of the coming of age of an unusual man as well as an erudite assessment of the impact made by Enlightenment ideals on nineteenth-century Indians. The sequel, *Thy Hand, Great Anarch! India, 1921–1952* (1987), as weighty in content as it is massive in size, records Chaudhuri's move from Kolkata (Calcutta) to Delhi and from youth to middle age. He also recounts the increasing disillusionment with his country that took him to England for the last three decades of his life. Both works are controversial, for Chaudhuri was a gadfly, critical of Indian nationalism as well as of the loss of nerves of the British rulers and the decline of England. Khushwant Singh, an early admirer of Chaudhuri, also has a claim in any study of post-Partition men of letters in India. His *Train to Pakistan* (1956) is one of the earliest representatives of the impassioned novels concerned with the trauma of Partition in 1947. Singh has written many other works of fiction but deserves to be considered for his English-language journalism and autobiographical writing as well. Also notable is Ved Mehta, who became blind in boyhood. He studied in schools for blind children, went to Oxford University and Harvard University, and then became associated with *The New Yorker*. In addition to collections of his pieces for that magazine—for example, *John Is Easy to Please: Encounters with the Written and the Spoken Word*

(1971)–he has written several works in the autobiographical vein that make him one of the leading Indian writers of English prose. Other male prose writers who have been excluded from *DLB 323: South Asian Writers in English* but could be studied with profit by anyone considering the period in greater detail are the novelists Sudhindra Nath Ghose, Bhabani Bhattacharya, and Manohar Malgonkar.

In the post-Partition period three women novelists of distinction emerged: Kamala Markandaya, Nayantara Sahgal, and Ruth Prawer Jhabvala. Markandaya's first novel, *Nectar in a Sieve* (1954), deals with the life of the rural poor. Her later novels treat themes such as strains in cross-cultural relationships, tensions created by the introduction of Western values into Indian lives, and the plight of expatriate Indians in England. Of her later books, the most notable are *The Coffer Dams* (1969), a novel about the encounter between the personnel of a British engineering firm building a dam in India and the local people, and *The Nowhere Man* (1972), one of the first fictional studies of Indian immigrants in the West, a theme as popular in South Asian writing in English as the partitioning of the subcontinent. Sahgal, a member of the Nehru family, is fascinated by political themes, as in *Storm in Chandigarh* (1969), a Partition novel, and *Rich Like Us* (1985), a fictional rendering of the consequences of the emergency rule imposed on India from 1975 to 1977 by her cousin Indira Gandhi. Unlike Markandaya and Sahgal, Jhabvala is not Indian by birth. She now lives outside the country, but her marriage to an Indian and subsequent stay in India for more than two decades has enabled her to treat with sensitivity the lives of Indians, especially the women. Another of her favorite themes is the encounter between Westerners and Indians, as is evident in her Booker Prize–winning *Heat and Dust* (1975). Jhabvala is also well known as the screenwriter for several critically acclaimed movies by Merchant Ivory Productions.

The premier Indian woman novelist in English of the post-Partition years is Anita Desai. Her first novel was *Cry, the Peacock* (1963); among her other significant works of fiction are *Fire on the Mountain* (1977), which was awarded the Royal Society of Literature's Winifred Holtby Prize; *Clear Light of Day* (1980); *In Custody* (1984); *Baumgartner's Bombay* (1988); and *Games at Twilight and Other Stories* (1978). Desai is a novelist of delicate perceptions and a chronicler of lonely lives who writes fiction that is quiet but resonant. In the early 1990s she moved to the United States, where she now teaches at the Massachusetts Institute of Technology. With the move to North America, she has broadened her range to include themes such as the South Asian diaspora, as in *Journey to Ithaca* (1995).

Unlike Indian fiction in English, which took off in the 1930s, Indian poetry in English made its presence felt in a considerable way only after Independence, although Sarojini Naidu did publish a few volumes of verse in the first two decades of the twentieth century that attracted some attention. The mystic poet Sri Aurobindo (Aurobindo Ghose) has always had something of a cult following, and his epic poem in English, *Savitri: A Legend and a Symbol* (1950), published in a definitive edition in 1954, has some devotees, but neither the poet nor his epic has had a significant impact on subsequent Indian English verse, and quite a few critics consider the work to be something of a curiosity. The poet who is widely acknowledged as the first major Indian poet writing in English is Nissim Ezekiel. His ability to write poems specifically of his time and place and his often ironic and urbane early verse have left a deep impression on later poets of the subcontinent. Ezekiel began writing in the 1950s; his *Collected Poems, 1952–1988* (1989) is a testimony to his ability to develop in many directions, for the volume includes poems in the confessional mode as well as accounts of spiritual voyaging. Ezekiel also has the distinction of having played a key role in directing Indian English verse toward the modernist idiom. The sprightly and polished essays in his *Selected Prose* (1992) are worth reading, too.

Other pioneering poets who steered Indian poetry in English toward the contemporary world include Jayanta Mahapatra, for although he often focuses on traditional Indian scenes, his tone, idiom, and forms ally him with modernism. A. K. Ramanujan spent most of his working life at the University of Chicago as a professor of linguistics specializing in the Dravidian languages, and it is thus appropriate that he often wrote about memories of India, loss, and transience. He is also widely admired as one of the leading translators of Tamil poetry into English. Arun Kolatkar, a bilingual poet, writes mostly in Marathi, but his English-language *Jejuri* (1976) brought him a Commonwealth Poetry Prize. *Jejuri* is a long poem in thirty-one sections about a pilgrimage, observed wryly but also with sympathy, to a famous temple. Dom Moraes received early international recognition when he was awarded the Hawthornden Prize in England for his first collection of verse, *A Beginning* (1957). In 1966 he published *Poems, 1955–1965*. He resumed publishing poetry in the 1980s that was freer in form and more disillusioned in tone than the earlier verse; *Collected Poems, 1957–1987* came out in 1987. Moraes also published a prose autobiography, *My Son's Father* (1968), which has been widely acclaimed. Other Indian English poets of Moraes's generation not included in *DLB 323: South Asian Writers in English* but who should be studied by students pursuing the subject in greater detail include R. Parthasarathy, Keki N. Daruwalla, Dilip Chitre, Gieve Patel, and Arvind Krishna Mehrota.

Among twentieth-century Indian women poets, the most distinctive voice is that of Kamala Das. Almost as soon as she published her first collection, *Summer in Calcutta: Fifty Poems* (1965), she attracted widespread attention for her bold confessional poems and for speaking out on behalf of all women and rejecting the roles reserved for them in Indian society. Das is just as outspoken in her autobiography, *My Story* (1976). The fact that there is no other Indian woman poet of her generation who approaches her in stature is significant. Conditions were not conducive for women to write verse in the decades before or after Independence, although some women novelists emerged soon after the nation was founded.

Independence brought a new generation of Indian writers, epitomized by Salman Rushdie, the title of whose seminal novel *Midnight's Children* (1981) alludes to the creation of India and Pakistan at midnight between 14 and 15 August 1947 and at the same time heralds a new generation of writers. Before Rushdie, a few Indian English writers had been admired abroad as well as in India, but their sales everywhere had been at best modest and their readership limited mostly to specialists. Rushdie's novel changed all that. Not only did *Midnight's Children* receive enormous worldwide attention, but it was also awarded the 1981 Booker Prize and, in 1993, "the Booker of Bookers" Prize as the best novel to have received the prize in its first twenty-five years. Rushdie became an instant celebrity with the publication of the book and found himself at the head of a new generation of writers from the subcontinent that was more cosmopolitan; more in tune with recent developments in literary theory, such as postcolonialism and postmodernism; more self-assertive; and more given to experimentation with form and language. Many of these writers were part of the diaspora of South Asians to the West that had begun in the wake of decolonization; some had studied there, while others habitually crisscrossed the globe. Even those who stayed at home were in tune with the latest artistic movements in the rest of the world.

Fiction in particular was the genre in which the explosion of Indian writing in English was most clearly felt. Rushdie followed *Midnight's Children* with *Shame* (1983), a novelistic critique of the progress of Pakistan as a nation through the early 1980s. *The Satanic Verses* (1988), a novel covering continents as well as centuries of history, made him extremely controversial, earning him censure from most parts of the Islamic world for its satiric sections on the Prophet of Islam and Ayatollah Ruhollah Khomeini of Iran. The book was ultimately

banned in India, Pakistan, and Bangladesh. The fatwa pronounced on him by the ayatollah has meant that Rushdie has been unable to return to India. Although he continues to write as an expatriate now resident in England, only two of his subsequent works are outstanding: the fairy-tale-like *Haroun and the Sea of Stories* (1990) and *Imaginary Homelands: Essays and Criticism, 1981–1991* (1991).

Among the other novelists of Rushdie's generations, perhaps only Vikram Seth and Amitav Ghosh are of comparable standing. Seth is the ultimate cosmopolitan writer. *The Golden Gate: A Novel in Verse* (1986), his first novel, is set in San Francisco and is reminiscent of Aleksandr Sergeevich Pushkin's *Eugene Onegin* (1833). *A Suitable Boy* (1993), Seth's second novel, is a massive realist narrative of post-Partition India written in the manner of a Victorian triple-decker novel, while his third, *An Equal Music* (1999), is as English and as romantic a work as can be imagined. Seth is also an accomplished poet, having won a Commonwealth Poetry Prize for his verse, and a travel writer of distinction who has received the Thomas Cook Travel Book Award for *From Heaven Lake: Travels through Sinkiang and Tibet* (1983). Ghosh, too, has excelled in many different forms of the novel and is almost as cosmopolitan and widely traveled a writer as Seth. Ghosh's most impressive work is *The Shadow Lines* (1988), a novel about memory and desire, the diasporic consciousness, and the invisible lines that bind people and transcend boundaries. His *In an Antique Land: History in the Guise of a Traveler's Tale* (1992), part travel writing and part quest narrative, also reflects his interest in the "shadow lines" that connect people despite differences in space and time.

Among other Indian novelists who have been singled out for treatment in *DLB 323: South Asian Writers in English,* Upmanyu Chatterjee is notable mainly for his first novel, *English, August: An Indian Story* (1988), a caustic look at small-town India from the perspective of an alienated civil servant. Amit Chaudhuri has published four novels, *A Strange and Sublime Address* (1991), *Afternoon Raag* (1993), *Freedom Song* (1998), and *A New World* (2000), all of them lyrical and impressionistic evocations of places and moods, mostly centered on Kolkata, the city where he now lives. Other novelists of this generation who are worth reading but who have been excluded from this volume for lack of space are I. Allan Sealy, Shashi Tharoor, Mukul Kesavan, Vikram Chandra, and Pankaj Mishra.

Although Shashi Deshpande is nine years older than Rushdie, her first major novel, *That Long Silence* (1988), is part of the explosion of the Indian English novel that has been felt globally. Deshpande writes eloquently about the lot of Indian women and the crises that they habitually negotiate. Bharati Mukherjee, born in Kolkata, moved to America for graduate studies and settled for a while in Canada before deciding to adopt American citizenship. In one phase of her career she wrote fiction about the loneliness of expatriate women, as in the novel *Wife* (1975), and the racism against Asian Americans that she experienced in Canada, as in the short-story collection *Darkness* (1985). Later, however, she celebrated the vibrancy of immigrant lives and the transformation of America by new Asian immigrants in *The Middleman and Other Stories* (1988), a volume that earned her the National Book Critics Circle Award for fiction, and in several other novels.

The continuing vitality of Indian women writers of fiction is evident in the emergence of several talents in the 1990s who garnered important literary prizes. Chitra Banerjee Divakaruni received the American Book Award for her 1995 collection of fiction about the lives of Indian immigrants in North America, *Arranged Marriage,* and has published two other novels and three volumes of poetry that have made her a leading modern Indian writer in American. Sunetra Gupta received the Sahitya Akademi Award, a significant award for Indian literature, for her lyrical evocation of Kolkata life in *Memories of Rain* (1992), although most people have found her subsequent novels too trying. Arundhati Roy's *The God of Small Things* (1997) was an international best-seller and won her the Booker Prize for her sensitive and imaginative treatment of the lives of children, continuing caste prejudice in India, and the vulnerability of women. Unlike Bharati Mukherjee, Divakaruni, and Gupta, all of whom live outside India, Roy is firmly rooted in the country and has become an activist for several causes, as is evident in her polemical essays. Jhumpa Lahiri, in contrast, was born in England and has lived most of her life in the United States, but all of the stories of her Pulitzer Prize–winning debut collection, *Interpreter of Maladies* (1999), are either about Asian Americans of Indian origin in the United States or are set in India and deal mostly with themes such as expatriation and cross-cultural encounters. It is to be regretted that writers as impressive as Gita Mehta, Padma Hejmadi, Githa Hariharan, and Kiran Desai have not been included in *DLB 323: South Asian Writers in English,* but they are certainly noteworthy presences in contemporary Indian fiction in English.

Rushdie's generation did not produce as many accomplished poets as it did novelists. Nevertheless, Agha Shahid Ali must be considered one of the leading poets of the period, and his death in 2001 was a great loss for Indian poetry in English. Originally from the Indian part of Kashmir, he settled in the United States and wrote poetry of exile, loss of home, and the culture he left behind. Meena Alexander, an English professor at the Graduate Center of the City University of New York, has been writing verse since the 1980s about family, the formation of the feminine self, and expatriation. She is the author, too, of the novels *Nampally Road* (1991) and *Manhattan Music* (1997) and a memoir, *Fault Lines* (1993). Alexander has also written a work blending her verse with autobiographical prose and her creative work with her critical expertise, revealingly titled *The Shock of Arrival: Reflections on Postcolonial Experience* (1996). Sujata Bhatt has spent most of her adult life outside India. After pursuing her studies in the United States, she eventually settled in Germany. Like Agha Shahid Ali and Alexander, Bhatt has made expatriation and the ties that bind the expatriate to India themes in her writing. Like Alexander, she explores the role of women in society. Bhatt received a Commonwealth Poetry Prize for her first collection, *Brunizem* (1988). The work of these three poets, as well as Seth's and Divakaruni's verse, indicates that even though not as appreciated internationally as Indian fiction in English, contemporary Indian poetry in English has its standard-bearers. Also worthy of mention are Eunice De Souza, Manohar Shetty, and Melanie Silgardo, although they are not considered in this volume.

The weakest genre of Indian writing in English is drama. Perhaps because of the lack of a tradition of English-language theater and thriving performing companies, the few plays that were written were mostly considered not worthy of staging, although some of Tagore's plays in his own translations were performed when he was at the height of his fame. While the first Indian play in English was Krishna Mohan Banerji's *The Persecuted* (1831), only two dramatists have merited inclusion in *DLB 323: South Asian Writers in English.* Girish Karnad writes plays in his mother tongue, Kannada, but he also translates them into excellent English versions. He is considered one of India's leading dramatists for his historical plays, such as *Tughlaq* (1965) and *Hayavadana* (1972). Karnad draws on the Indian classical tradition to write experimental works on themes such as illusion and reality, imagination and art, and the relevance of the past in present times. Unlike Karnad, Mahesh Dattani writes plays only in English and focuses on the present, treating subjects such as the Indian family and gender perceptions and roles in plays such as *Final Solutions* (1993) and *Tara* (1990). Dattani is the first Indian dramatist to have received the country's prestigious Sahitya Akademi Award for plays written in English.

The course of Pakistani writing in English was to some extent determined when the country made Urdu its sole national language soon after Independence in 1947, even though English continued to be the language of higher administration. The status of English was further eroded in the 1970s and 1980s by governments that pursued a nationalistic agenda, and the language was taught proficiently only in elite schools. This policy contrasts with that of India, where English-language instruction was never seriously undermined and where the language grew steadily in importance. Also, it must be remembered that political power in colonial India centered at first in Kolkata and then in Delhi, while Mumbai (Bombay) and Chennai (Madras) became the other hubs of administrative and commercial activity. Consequently, the English language flourished in these places from the beginnings of the colonial period, and a tradition of Indian writing in English developed around them, unlike in the areas that initially comprised West and East Pakistan, the regions that became Pakistan and Bangladesh after 1971.

In fact, when Pakistani writing in English emerged, its founding figures were Indians such as Ahmed Ali and Shahid Suhrawardy, both of whom immigrated to Pakistan after Partition. The first Pakistani writer in English of distinction born in the area that now comprises Pakistan was the poet Taufiq Rafat, whose status in his country is comparable to that of Ezekiel in India. Rafat became the leading writer of poetry in English resident in his country, writing in a contemporary idiom about city life, love, and the people he knew and becoming a source of inspiration for others. His *Arrival of the Monsoon: Collected Poems, 1947–78* (1985) is considered a landmark in the history of Pakistani literature in English. Readers further interested in the course of Pakistani poetry should also read the poems of Maki Kureishi, Daud Kamal, and Alamgir Hashmi.

The outstanding writer of Pakistani origin writing in English is Zulfikar Ghose. Ghose, however, is truly cosmopolitan, and it must be said that his links with Pakistan are tenuous, for although he was born in a part of British India that is now in Pakistan, he spent his boyhood in Mumbai, left for England in his teens, spent almost two decades there, and then moved to America to teach at the University of Texas at Austin. But his novel *The Murder of Aziz Khan* (1967) is set in post-Independence Pakistan; his first collection of poems, *The Loss of India* (1964), focuses on the loss of identity; and his autobiography, *Confessions of a Native-Alien* (1965) deals with the trauma of the uprooted. Ghose's novels are experimental, ranging from the realistic to the metafictional, while his poems are written in a wide variety of styles and explore many themes but are often concerned with alienation and migration.

The novelist Bapsi Sidhwa has spent most of her life in Pakistan, although, like Ghose, she ended up as an academic in the United States. Sidhwa's first work, *The Crow Eaters* (1978), is a comic novel centering on the

Parsi community to which she belongs. Her second book, *The Bride* (1983), has a feminist theme. Sidhwa's third and perhaps best-known work, published as *Ice-Candy-Man* (1988) in England and as *Cracking India* (1991) in the United States, is a novel about the Partition. The progress of a Pakistani girl in the United States is the theme of *An American Brat* (1993). Sidhwa is undoubtedly the most important Pakistani novelist in English and has received her country's highest literary awards, as well as considerable international recognition for her fiction.

Other promising Pakistani writers in English include Adam Zameenzad, whose first novel, *The Thirteenth House* (1987), won him the David Higham Award, and Mohsin Hamid, whose diasporic narrative *Moth Smoke* (2000) indicates that he may turn out to be a major novelist. Sara Suleri, an English professor at Yale University, has written an important work of criticism on colonial and postcolonial encounters, *The Rhetoric of English India* (1992), but her memoir, *Meatless Days* (1989), represents Pakistani nonfiction prose at its best. In it she writes about her family, memory, exile, and lost ties. The useful compilation *A Dragonfly in the Sun: An Anthology of Pakistani Writing in English* (1997) presents works by other talented Pakistani writers in English, but as Muneeza Shamsie, the editor, observes in her introduction, creative work in English has been considered to be "a somewhat irrelevant activity and a colonial hangover" for so long that it has never had the kind of presence in Pakistan that it has in India.

In Sri Lanka, too, there was a reaction against the language of the colonizer after Independence. The dominant Sinhalese community made Sinhalese the state language in 1956. As in Pakistan and Bangladesh, creative writing in English was increasingly considered an elitist activity until the 1980s. Not surprisingly, when Sri Lankan writing in English surfaced internationally, it was primarily the work of expatriates. Foremost among them is Michael Ondaatje, who immigrated to Canada in 1962. Ondaatje is perhaps most famous for his fiction, although he is more prolific as a poet. He won the Booker Prize for *The English Patient* (1992), his novel set during World War II; in an earlier work, *Running in the Family* (1982), he combines prose, poetry, family memoir, and the theme of the exile's return. *Anil's Ghost* (2000) fictionalizes the experience of a Sri Lankan expatriate female forensic pathologist who returns to her country on an assignment, only to find the island riven by violence.

Another Sri Lankan who has settled in Canada, Shyam Selvadurai, made his name with *Funny Boy* (1994), a novel about the strife encountered by the minority Tamil community on the island in the 1980s and the narrator's increasing awareness of his homosexuality in a society that is hostile to it. Selvadurai followed up this novel with *Cinnamon Gardens* (1998), which also involves homosexuality but focuses on the Sri Lankan community in England and the splintering of a Sri Lankan family. Another important Sri Lankan Tamil writer is Ambalavaner Sivanandan, whose *When Memory Dies* (1997) won a Commonwealth Writers Prize. *When Memory Dies* is also about the ethnic conflict that has been the main feature of Sri Lankan life since the 1980s, but Sivanandan also depicts the way in which the communal harmony that existed previously between the Sinhalese and the Tamil gave way to racism and violence.

Romesh Gunesekera immigrated to London in the early 1970s and has written the novels *Reef* (1994) and *The Sandglass* (1998), as well as a short-story collection, *Monkfish Moon* (1992). He writes as a Sri Lankan fascinated with the beauty of the island but critical about aspects of its violent society, which has not endeared him to Sri Lankan critics, although he is appreciated in the West.

Unlike expatriate writers such as Ondaatje, Selvadurai, and Gunesekera, Sri Lankan writers in English resident in their own country have never received sufficient international exposure, nor have their works been published or written about abroad. Nevertheless, there has been significant creative work in English in Sri Lanka. The verse and fiction of Jean Arasanayagam, the verse of Anne Ranasinghe, the fiction of Carl Muller, and P. B. Rambukwelle's novel *The Desert Makers* (1985) are signs that criticism of South Asian writing in English should pay more attention to Sri Lankan writers. It must be stressed, too, that the English language itself has made a comeback on the island in a way that presages more quality writing in the future.

Most historians of Bangladesh date the origins of the independence movement in the country to 21 February 1952, when students in East Pakistan demonstrating against the imposition of Urdu as the national language and demanding equal status for the Bengali language were shot at by the police. The deaths of some of the demonstrators in the incident sparked off a chain of events that led to the birth of Bangladesh in 1971. Independence and linguistic nationalism, however, also led to the marginalization of English. Bengali replaced English as the language of administration as well as of higher education. As in Sri Lanka, only late in the twentieth century did policy makers reverse their decision and begin stressing the importance of learning English at all levels of education.

For these reasons, there is little quality writing in English in Bangladesh. There are, however, two important exceptions to this generalization. One is the expatriate novelist Adib Khan, who moved to Australia in

1974 and received the Commonwealth Prize for Best First Book for his *Seasonal Adjustments* (1994), which deals with the theme of the expatriate's return to the country he left behind. Since, then, Khan has written two more novels that have also earned him modest fame in Australia. Kaiser Haq teaches English at the University of Dhaka and has published a considerable number of poems in English at home and abroad. The best of his early verse is collected in *A Happy Farewell* (1994) and affiliates him with the contemporary Indian poetry in English associated with Ezekiel. The chapbook *Black Orchid* (1996) marks a departure, in which Haq's verse becomes freer as he celebrates sexuality. *The Logopathic Reviewer's Song* (2002) shows him widening his range further and writing experimental prose poems as well as verse that resembles his ironic, controlled early works and the freer poetry of sexual liberation in *Black Orchid*.

The fate of the English language has differed from country to country in the subcontinent after the British left South Asia, and the literature produced in each of the countries of the region has consequently followed its own course. It must also be acknowledged that the expression "South Asia" is a relatively new construction. Nevertheless, it is feasible now to talk of South Asian writing in English since a body of creative writing has emerged that can be considered as a whole. Certainly, the English writings in these countries share common origins and often deal with similar themes. One cluster of themes has to do with colonization and decolonization, the ferment of nationalism, East-West encounters, and cross-cultural relationships. Additionally, South Asian literature in English often deals with political upheavals and the violence accompanying events such as the Partition and the war leading to the independence of Bangladesh in 1971. The writers of the region also tend to treat religious, class, and caste prejudice, as well as endemic poverty—in short, social injustice—in their writings. Several have focused on the underprivileged and marginalized. The rural poor and life in the small towns and megacities of the subcontinent have all been represented in their writings. The alienated consciousness of the writer using the English language is another recurrent theme.

Since the 1970s, expatriation, the state of immigrant communities in the West, the trauma of being uprooted, the diasporic consciousness, and the loss of "home" and identity have preoccupied many South Asian writers, especially those who have opted to remain in the West. Some expatriate authors have celebrated cultural hybridity and the energy of new immigrants. Ties that are severed or loosened and ties that bind or seem indissoluble are often the obsessions of writers who have emigrated from South Asia or have decided to adopt a cosmopolitan life and become citizens of the world. Another theme of some of these expatriates is that of the exile's return to a country that has changed and the search for roots. The lot of women, whether living in South Asia or as immigrants in the West, is also an important theme.

South Asian writers in English from all parts of the subcontinent share a common fascination with the English language. The early authors used the language primarily as a weapon to "write back" against the colonizers, so to speak, and to address social or intellectual issues, but later writers found inventive ways to make it their own and express their innermost feelings. The ultimate experiment, perhaps, was that of Rushdie, whose "chutnificiation" of the English language in *Midnight's Children* has delighted readers all over the world.

South Asian writing in English is thriving and is well worth reading. Whether studied as a whole or separately as Indian, Pakistani, Sri Lankan, or Bangladeshi literature; considered from the perspective of postcolonial literature; or constituted in new categories, such as Asian American literature, it is increasing in importance as a field of study. It is hoped that *DLB 323: South Asian Writers in English* will be seen as an indispensable research and reference tool for general readers as well as academics and that it will also be considered a testimony to a body of writing that has enriched English literature.

DLB 323: South Asian Writers in English has been several years in the making and has been a collaborative effort on a truly global scale. The editor is deeply grateful to the contributors, who span four continents, and to Babul Prasad, of the English department at the University of Dhaka, who spent long hours preparing the text at the initial stage of the work.

—*Fakrul Alam*

Acknowledgments

This book was produced by Bruccoli Clark Layman, Inc. R. Bland Lawson was the in-house editor. He was assisted by George Parker Anderson, Tracy Simmons Bitonti, Charles Brower, Philip B. Dematteis, and Penelope M. Hope.

Production manager is Philip B. Dematteis.

Administrative support was provided by Carol A. Cheschi.

Accountant is Ann-Marie Holland.

Copyediting supervisor is Sally R. Evans. The copyediting staff includes Phyllis A. Avant, Caryl Brown, Melissa D. Hinton, Philip I. Jones, Rebecca Mayo, and Nancy E. Smith.

Pipeline manager is James F. Tidd Jr.

Editorial associates are Elizabeth Leverton, Dickson Monk, and Timothy C. Simmons.

In-house vetter is Catherine M. Polit.

Permissions editor is Amber L. Coker. Permissions assistant is Crystal A. Gleim.

Layout and graphics supervisor is Janet E. Hill. The graphics staff includes Zoe R. Cook.

Office manager is Kathy Lawler Merlette.

Photography editor is Mark J. McEwan.

Digital photographic copy work was performed by Joseph M. Bruccoli.

Systems manager is Donald Kevin Starling.

Typesetting supervisor is Kathleen M. Flanagan. The typesetting staff includes Patricia Marie Flanagan and Pamela D. Norton.

Library research was facilitated by the following librarians at the Thomas Cooper Library of the University of South Carolina: Elizabeth Suddeth and the rare-book department; Jo Cottingham, interlibrary loan department; circulation department head Tucker Taylor; reference department head Virginia W. Weathers; reference department staff Laurel Baker, Marilee Birchfield, Kate Boyd, Paul Cammarata, Joshua Garris, Gary Geer, Tom Marcil, Rose Marshall, and Sharon Verba; interlibrary loan department head Marna Hostetler; and interlibrary loan staff Bill Fetty and Nelson Rivera.

South Asian Writers
in English

Dictionary of Literary Biography

Meena Alexander

(17 February 1951 –   )

E. Nageswara Rao
Osmania University

BOOKS: *The Bird's Bright Ring* (Calcutta: Writers
    Workshop, 1976);
I Root My Name (Calcutta: United Writers, 1977);
In the Middle Earth (New Delhi: Enact, 1977);
Without Place (Calcutta: Writers Workshop, 1977);
The Poetic Self: Towards a Phenomenology of Romanticism
    (New Delhi: Arnold-Heinemann, 1979; Atlantic
    Highlands, N.J.: Humanities Press, 1980);
Stone Roots (New Delhi: Arnold-Heinemann, 1980);
House of a Thousand Doors: Poems and Prose Pieces (Wash-
    ington, D.C.: Three Continents Press, 1988);
The Storm: A Poem in Five Parts (New York: Red Dust, 1989);
*Women in Romanticism: Mary Wollstonecraft, Dorothy Words-
    worth, and Mary Shelley* (Basingstoke, U.K.: Mac-
    millan, 1989; Savage, Md.: Barnes & Noble,
    1989);
Nampally Road (San Francisco: Mercury House, 1991;
    Hyderabad: Disha, 1991);
Night-Scene, the Garden (New York: Red Dust, 1992);
Fault Lines: A Memoir (New York: Feminist Press/City
    University of New York, 1993; New Delhi: Pen-
    guin, 1993; revised and enlarged, New York: Femi-
    nist Press/City University of New York, 2003);
River and Bridge (New Delhi: Rupa, 1995; Toronto:
    Toronto South Asian Review, 1996);
The Shock of Arrival: Reflections on Postcolonial Experience
    (Boston: South End Press, 1996);
Manhattan Music (San Francisco: Mercury House, 1997);
Illiterate Heart (Evanston, Ill.: TriQuarterly/Northwest-
    ern University Press, 2002);
Raw Silk (Evanston, Ill.: TriQuarterly/Northwestern
    University Press, 2004).

OTHER: *Truth Tales: Contemporary Stories by Women
    Writers of India*, introduction by Alexander (New

*Meena Alexander (photograph © Ram Rahman; from the
back cover of* Manhattan Music, *1997; Jean and
Alexander Heard Library, Vanderbilt University)*

York: Feminist Press/City University of New York, 1990);

Lalithambika Antherjanam, *Cast Me Out If You Will: Stories and Memoir,* translated and edited, with an introduction, by Gita Krishnankutty, foreword by Alexander (New York: Feminist Press, 1998);

Indian Love Poems, edited by Alexander (New York: Knopf, 2005).

SELECTED PERIODICAL PUBLICATION–
UNCOLLECTED: "Sarojini Naidu: Romanticism and Resistance," *Economic and Political Weekly,* 20, no. 43 (1985): 68–71.

Meena Alexander began her literary career as a poet, but she also writes fiction, memoirs, and literary criticism. Whatever the genre, she articulates the anguish of people in different parts of the world in a contemporary idiom. In her writings she has responded to many violent events, including the civil war in Sudan, the rape of a woman by Hyderabad police, and ethnic conflicts in Bosnia and Sri Lanka. Human suffering, whether caused by man or natural calamities, such as the 1977 cyclone that struck Diviseema on the Bay of Bengal, evokes an emotional response in her. Alexander has drawn upon her rich experience in countries as far apart as India, Sudan, England, and the United States to write poems and stories of absorbing interest.

Alexander was born Mary Elizabeth Alexander on 17 February 1951 in Allahabad, India, to George Alexander and Mary Alexander. She was named after her paternal grandmother. Her father, a government employee, was deputed by the Indian government to Sudan, and the family moved there in 1956. She attended Unity High School in Khartoum, graduating in 1964. At fifteen she changed her name to Meena, which was both her nickname and pen name. In school she was exposed to several languages, including French and Arabic. Although her mother tongue was Malayalam, she learned neither to read nor write in that language, instead choosing English as her vehicle for self-expression. Alexander's first poems, written in English while she attended the University of Khartoum, were translated into Arabic by her friends and published in Arabic newspapers. Although she could not read her own poems when they appeared in print for the first time, the sound and sense of both Arabic and Malayalam enabled her, as she writes in *Fault Lines: A Memoir* (1993), to "dissolve and dissipate . . . the canonical burden of British English."

Alexander obtained her B.A. in English and French literature with honors from the University of Khartoum in 1969. On the advice of her examiner, Jim Boulton, she enrolled at the University of Nottingham in England to work on her doctorate in English. She earned the degree in 1973 with a dissertation titled "The Vital Centrality: An Essay in Phenomenological Aesthetics on the Human Self-Image, with Special Reference to Romantic, Symbolist and Modern Poetry," later abridged and published as *The Poetic Self: Towards a Phenomenology of Romanticism* (1979). The study of Romanticism in Khartoum and Nottingham shaped Alexander's interests and attitudes. In *Fault Lines* she writes, "I was deeply attracted to the poetry and prose of the English Romantics, whose intense, even tormented probing into the nature of image and language were underwritten by the call for a revolutionary knowledge. I will never forget the first time I read Coleridge. . . . I carried with me the magical thought of what he, borrowing from Schlegel, developed as the notion of organic form." In the dissertation she identifies the importance of the body in the perception of Romantic poets such as William Wordsworth, who had endowed matter with divinity. Through the interpenetration and overlapping of "inner time," the self is revealed. Alexander also states that Matthew Arnold and Charles Baudelaire had different approaches to "coping with the space around the body in an age that would not imbue matter with divinity." Walt Whitman presented a third alternative through the *I* imaged in poetry; in this way he established "an explicit poetics of embodiment." Alexander's doctoral research, as she explains in *The Poetic Self,* dealt with "the problem of human time and the way in which it is inextricably bound up with both the living bodily 'I' and the poetic self."

On returning to India, Alexander worked in 1974 as a lecturer at Miranda House, the women's college of Delhi University, and in 1975 as a Council of Scientific and Industrial Research (CSIR) Fellow at Jawaharlal Nehru University, in New Delhi. Her sojourn in Delhi coincided with Prime Minister Indira Gandhi's imposition of emergency rule in India, following a court ruling setting aside Gandhi's reelection to Parliament. Emergency rule involved the curtailing of civil rights and provoked nationwide protests, in which Alexander participated.

Alexander moved to Hyderabad in 1975, first to the Central Institute of English and Foreign Languages and then to the University of Hyderabad, teaching for two years at each of these institutions. During this time she established many fruitful friendships with writers, social activists, academics, and feminists. These years were also productive in that she published three volumes of poetry, as well as *The Poetic Self.*

In *The Bird's Bright Ring* (1976) Alexander introduces themes, such as grandmothers, and images, such as a "wounded mouth," that recur in her later writings. This book of poetry was followed by two more, *I Root*

My Name (1977) and *Without Place* (1977). She came to understand the importance of place for a poet through her interaction with Jayanta Mahapatra, whose poetry she admires. She writes in *Fault Lines* that she learned from Mahapatra how the landscape sustains the elegiac voice and how to accept the ravages of time. In *Without Place* Alexander speaks of her realization that "Poetry is place." Some are prose pieces; others are not anchored to a specific place or lack a running theme. Apart from Mahapatra, other writers who have influenced Alexander, as she told interviewer Roshni Rustomji-Kerns in 1998, include Kamala Das, Galway Kinnell, Adrienne Rich, Nawal El Saadawi, Anita Desai, Maxine Hong Kingston, Toni Morrison, and Assia Djebar.

Without Place includes the essay "Exiled by a Dead Script," in which Alexander admits the sense of unreality one has in writing English-language poetry in India: "English in India is a nowhere language." An Indian attempting to write in English finds herself exiled. In order to refuse exile, the writer must transform the English language, break its syntax, and make it serve her purposes. Language is one of the recurring themes in Alexander's verse, as is indicated by poems such as "Veined Words" and "Stained Words," from *I Root My Name*.

In 1979 Alexander upstaged her mother's plans to arrange her marriage by wedding David Lelyveld, an American. The same year, she became a visiting fellow at the Sorbonne in Paris and then immigrated to the United States with her husband. Since then she has taught in New York, initially at Fordham University and later at Hunter College and the Graduate Center of the City University of New York. She has had several visiting teaching assignments at other universities.

In the essay "Sarojini Naidu: Romanticism and Resistance" (1985) Alexander examines a poet and prominent leader of the Indian National Congress who spearheaded the movement for freedom in India. Naidu was a close associate of Mohandas Karamchand Gandhi and a powerful orator based in Hyderabad. Her heirs gifted her residence to the University of Hyderabad, and Alexander worked in the same building when she taught at the university in the late 1970s. According to Alexander, Naidu, who started as a poet following the model of the English Decadents, created "images of exhausted women, hermetically sealed, a double colonization that the interchange of cultures drew her to." Her political voice, however, was impassioned and roused people to action. This "radical cleft" between Naidu's dual roles as poet and politician, between her poetic diction and her persuasive oratory, fascinated Alexander. Like Naidu, she has adopted dual roles as both a creative writer and an activist.

Front cover for Alexander's 1997 novel, about an Indian woman who marries an American and moves to New York but becomes disenchanted with her life in the city (Jean and Alexander Heard Library, Vanderbilt University)

Alexander continued writing both poetry and prose after she moved to the United States, and in 1988 she published *House of a Thousand Doors: Poems and Prose Pieces.* In *The Shock of Arrival: Reflections on Postcolonial Experience* (1996) she describes the title poem as a "dream poem" in which the two figures of her maternal and paternal grandmothers are "dissolved into one." Alexander associates people and places, the past and the present, and ponders over their significance. For instance, in the prose poem "Hotel Alexandria," which she calls her "first American poem in spirit," she describes the demolition of a poor people's home in the heart of New York. She finds it heartbreaking to watch old people carrying their few belongings from the home. As a frequent immigrant, she understands the problems of dislocation. By way of contrast, the poet invokes her childhood memories of Alexandria (which her family visited when they were living in Sudan), where the scene was peaceful. "Hotel Alexandria" and the title poem are described as "portals to my life, entry into a new world."

The Storm: A Poem in Five Parts (1989) and *Night-Scene, the Garden* (1992) are long poems, each published as a chapbook, that together constitute "a part of a poetic autobiography," Aruna Srivastava quotes Alexander as saying. She likens *The Storm* to a palm fan, which is used in the warm season in the Kerala countryside. As a "bits and pieces" narrative (Alexander's favorite phrase in *Fault Lines*), *The Storm* deals with displacement, violence, and ritualized order, all parts of a woman's experience of the world. The poet condemns the violence evident everywhere:

> Let me sing my song
> Even the crude parts of it
> The decrepit seethe of war
> Cruelty inflicted on clear thought

Alexander wrote the companion volume, *Night-Scene, the Garden,* with the experience of the birth of her daughter, Svati, fresh in her mind. As she explains, while writing the work, she was haunted by "ferocious alphabets of flesh." She passionately invokes the "alphabets":

> Come ferocious alphabets of flesh
> Splinter and raze my page
> That out of the dumb
> And bleeding part of me
> I may claim my heritage.

Themes involving Romanticism and feminism have continued to claim Alexander's critical attention in her writings, as in *Women in Romanticism: Mary Wollstonecraft, Dorothy Wordsworth, and Mary Shelley* (1989). The three writers were all "rebels" in their own way, but Alexander finds that they were also "searching for literary knowledge, for a territory shaped by the truths of a female life." She observes that maternity and raising children, both closely allied to the female body, challenged the "presumptions of power" in the Romantic age.

Alexander's first novel, *Nampally Road* (1991), grew out of her life in Hyderabad. The epigraph, a quote from the Buddhist philosopher Nagarjuna, perhaps epitomizes the dilemma of contemporary India: "If fire is lit in water, who can extinguish it?" *Nampally Road* is set in a world of disorder and brutality. These trends are further aggravated by the insensitivity and vulgarity of those in power. Mira Kannadical, the central character and in many ways similar to Alexander, comes to Hyderabad with a doctorate from a British university to teach English literature at the local university. She is soon jolted by news of the gang rape of a woman by the police. She finds the incident indicative of the way the old world is blowing up. This narration of the general collapse of law and order and the vulgar display of pomp by rulers is intercut with the story of Mira's passionate affair with Ramu, a university colleague. Reviewer John Oliver Perry called *Nampally Road* "a major contribution to South Asian-American fiction" (*World Literature Today,* Spring 1991).

Alexander turned autobiographer with her 1993 memoir, *Fault Lines,* written at the request of a friend, Florence Howe, in the United States. In *The Shock of Arrival: Reflections on Postcolonial Experience,* published in 1996, Alexander writes that she thought bringing out the memoir would allow her to claim a place in the United States and shed her marginal existence. The fault lines of the title refer to the "cracks" caused by her multiple migrations across nations. Alexander describes how she was brought up by her mother in the strict belief that women should stay home. As a girl she kept a journal in which she expressed her adolescent agonies: "If you want me to live as a woman, why educate me?" She also found that her sexual desires were essential for her poetry. *Fault Lines* is a candid account of a sensitive woman growing aware of her potential and of the discrimination she suffered because of her complexion and sex. Alexander escaped from a restrictive environment by asserting her independence. The burden of the memoir, and of much of her creative work, is the sense of dislocation. The frequent crossing of borders has made her question where she really belongs. In Manhattan, too, she feels that she is "a fissured thing, a body crossed by fault lines." In a *Booklist* review, Alice Joyce described *Fault Lines* as "an inspiring contribution to feminist literature" (15 March 1993).

The feeling of alienation addressed in *Fault Lines* is also evident in the poetry collection *River and Bridge* (1995). The constant hyphenated references to her bother Alexander: "Everything that comes to me is hyphenated. A woman poet, a woman poet of color." In "Ashtamudi Lake" and "San Andreas Fault," she takes a bird's-eye view of mythology, history, and literature, establishing links in the process. She focuses on the victims of injustice, violence, and cruelty, such as Draupadi, the wife of the five Pandava brothers in the Indian epic *Mahabharata,* who was wronged and humiliated before her husbands in the royal court. Alexander uses Draupadi as a prototype of the wronged woman. Similarly, a Muslim woman killed in Sarajevo, Turks burned alive in New Germany, and a man in Somalia clutching his starving child find sympathy with Alexander. In "Ashtamudi Lake" she writes with anguish,

Arawac or Indian
The names confine
there is nothing for us
in the white man's burden.

    The Shock of Arrival is another collection of poems and prose pieces, some of which were included in earlier volumes. Racist incidents in New York spurred Alexander to write "Art of Pariahs." The pariahs identified in the poem are the queen of Nubia, the rani of Jhansi, and the poet herself. The poem is a plea to rid the world of the limitations of race, color, and sex:

Outcastes all, let's conjure honey scraped from stones,
An underground railroad stacked with rainbow skin,
Manhattan's mixed rivers rising.

The shock of arrival and of crossing borders produces "art that enshrines disjunction." Alexander cannot tolerate the narrow view of "here-there business." She asks poignantly, "How long did one have to live somewhere to make it one's home anyway?" She admits that "to cross a border can be to die a little. And the shock of a new life comes in, tearing up the old skin, old habits of awareness." Rich is quoted on the cover of the book as saying that in *The Shock of Arrival,* Alexander "has written a fierce new complexity into questions of identity, diaspora, tradition, language and community."

    After having lived in Manhattan for eighteen years, Alexander published her second novel, *Manhattan Music* (1997). Like *Nampally Road,* it is a largely autobiographical work and in a way continues the adventures of the heroine of that novel. Sandhya Rosenblum, an Indian woman married to an American Jew, migrates to the United States with her husband, Stephen. He promises her that she will be happy in Manhattan but then leaves her to her own devices. Whenever he commutes to Connecticut for his job, she feels lonely. There is emptiness in Sandhya's life, and she has an affair with Rashid, an Egyptian scholar in New York. She thought that by marrying Stephen she could start a new life in the New World; instead, she hears disturbing reports from Bosnia, Rwanda, and Sri Lanka. She is haunted by the terror of living moment by moment in a war zone. Unable to cope with her emotional situation, she attempts suicide by hanging, but her friend Draupadi rescues her. Sandhya remembers that in her native state of Kerala, young girls who became pregnant through premarital sex attempted suicide by jumping into wells to avoid social scandal. Her cousin Sakhi takes her to a women's meeting in Manhattan so that she can empathize with the problems of others. As Sandhya listens to saxophone music in the city, she regains her faith and feels that there is a place for her, too.

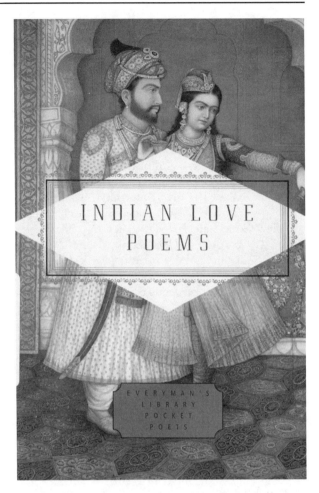

Dust jacket for the 2005 poetry anthology edited by Alexander that includes verse ranging from the Kama Sutra *to selections by contemporary writers such as Kamala Das and Vikram Seth (Richland County Public Library)*

    Manhattan Music is not only a critique of the seamy side of American life from the perspective of a sensitive immigrant woman but also a critique of the larger world outside, which hardly offers better security to women. Dealing with the contradictions in America, Sandhya's cousin comments, "New Yorkers had the Empire State Building and the World Trade Center. Still, what good did it do to live staring down from an immense height at poverty and pain crawling on the ground, human beings drugged out of their minds, stabbing each other, shooting, for absolutely no reason. . . . " Alexander senses the strong undercurrent of resentment, particularly among Arab immigrants. She writes, "What if Manhattan were being bombed by an imaginary nation thousands of miles away?"

    Alexander's *Illiterate Heart* (2002) includes the poem "Fragments," in which she writes, "I start to write fragments / As much to myself as to another." In other poems she speaks of the art of poetic composition. As she explained to Rustomji-Kerns, she writes "to clarify, to bring to the light, to make known, first of all to myself, and so ultimately–or that's the hope–to others, that density, that chaos even, of the emotional life."

Few writers of Meena Alexander's generation can claim her rich multilingual and multicultural experience. Border crossings, both physical and psychological, have molded her personality, her vision, and her writing. She has received several honors throughout her career, including an Altrusa International Award (1973), Professional Staff Congress of the City University of New York Research Foundation Awards (1989, 1990), MacDowell Colony Fellowships (1993, 1998), the New York State Foundation for the Arts Poetry Award (1999), a PEN Open Book Award (2002, for *Illiterate Heart*), and a residency at the Rockefeller Foundation Bellagio Study and Conference Center (2005). Out of the trauma of multiple migrations, Alexander emerged as a significant voice of feminism. With strong roots in rural Kerala and the Malayalam language, and with Das, Mahapatra, Desai, and Rich as literary influences, she has earned a respectable place among South Asian writers in English.

Interviews:

Susie Tharu, "A Conversation with Meena Alexander," *Chandrabhaga,* no. 7 (Summer 1982): 69–74;

Deepika Bahri and Mary Vasudeva, "Observing Ourselves among Others: Interview with Meena Alexander," in *Between the Lines: South Asians and Postcoloniality* (Philadelphia: Temple University Press, 1996), pp. 35–53;

Roshni Rustomji-Kerns, "An Interview with Meena Alexander," *Weber Studies* 15, no. 1 (1998): 18–27;

Erika Duncan, "A Portrait of Meena Alexander," *World Literature Today,* 73, no. 1 (1999): 23–28;

Amy Ling, "Interview with Meena Alexander," in *Yellow Light: The Flowering of Asian American Arts,* edited by Ling (Philadelphia: Temple University Press, 1999), pp. 83–84;

Zainab Ali and Dharini Rasiah, "Meena Alexander," in *Words Matter: Conversations with Asian American Writers,* edited by King-Kok Cheung (Hawaii: University of Hawaii Press/UCLA Asian American Studies Center, 2000), pp. 69–91;

Rajini Srikanth and Esther Y. Iwanaga, "The Voice that Passes through Me: An Interview with Meena Alexander," in *Bold Words: A Century of Asian American Writing,* edited by Srikanth and Iwanaga (New Brunswick, N.J.: Rutgers University Press, 2001), pp. 3–9;

Lopamudra Basu, "Lyric Poem in a Time of Violence: A Conversation with Meena Alexander," *Social Text,* 20, no. 3 (2002): 31–38;

Maureen Fadem, "Translation, an Art of Negativity: A Conversation with Meena Alexander," *Nimrod,* 45, no. 2 (2002): 102–110.

References:

Bruce King, *Modern Indian Poetry in English* (Delhi & New York: Oxford University Press, 2001), pp. 310–311;

Sudeep Sen, "Midnight's (Grand) Children: Post-Independence Indian Poetry in English," in *Trends and Techniques in Contemporary Indian English Poetry,* edited by Rama Nair (New Delhi: Prestige, 2001), pp. 45–72;

Aruna Srivastava, "Meena Alexander," in *Contemporary Poets,* fifth edition, edited by Tracy Chevalier (Chicago: St. James Press, 1991), pp. 10–12.

Agha Shahid Ali

(4 February 1949 – 8 December 2001)

Lawrence Needham
Lakeland Community College

BOOKS: *Bone-Sculpture* (Calcutta: Writers Workshop, 1972);

In Memory of Begum Akhtar (Calcutta: Writers Workshop, 1979);

T. S. Eliot as Editor (Ann Arbor, Mich.: UMI Research Press, 1986);

The Half-Inch Himalayas (Middleton, Conn.: Wesleyan University Press, 1987);

A Walk through the Yellow Pages (Tucson: SUN/gemini Press, 1987);

A Nostalgist's Map of America (New York: Norton, 1991);

The Beloved Witness: Selected Poems (New Delhi & New York: Viking, 1992);

The Country without a Post Office (New York: Norton, 1997); republished as *The Country without a Post Office: Poems 1991–1995* (New Delhi: Ravi Dayal, 2000);

Rooms Are Never Finished (New York: Norton, 2001; Delhi: Permanent Black, 2002);

Call Me Ishmael Tonight: A Book of Ghazals (New York: Norton, 2003).

Collection: *The Final Collections: Call Me Ishmael Tonight: A Book of Ghazals and Rooms Are Never Finished* (Delhi: Permanent Black, 2004).

OTHER: Faiz Ahmed Faiz, *The Rebel's Silhouette,* translated by Ali (Salt Lake City: Peregrine Smith, 1991; Delhi: Oxford University Press, 1992); revised as *The Rebel's Silhouette: Selected Poems,* introduction by Ali (Amherst: University of Massachusetts Press, 1995);

"*The Rebel's Silhouette:* Translating Faiz Ahmed Faiz," in *Between Languages and Cultures: Translation and Cross-Cultural Texts,* edited by Anuradha Dingwaney and Carol Maier (Pittsburgh: University of Pittsburgh Press, 1995), pp. 75–90;

"The Ghazal in America: May I?" in *After New Formalism: Poets on Form, Narrative, and Tradition,* edited by Annie Finch (Ashland, Ore.: Story Line Press, 1999), pp. 123–132;

Agha Shahid Ali (photograph by Neil Davenport; from the dust jacket for Rooms Are Never Finished, *2001; Richland County Public Library)*

"*Ghazals, Qasidas, Rubais,* and a Literary Giant," in *The Poetry of Our World: An International Anthology of Contemporary Poetry,* edited by Jeffrey Paine (New York: HarperCollins, 2000), pp. 407–411;

Ravishing DisUnities: Real Ghazals in English, edited by Ali (Middleton, Conn.: Wesleyan University Press / Hanover, N.H.: University Press of New England, 2000);

"Ghazal: To Be Teased into DisUnity," in *An Exaltation of Forms: Contemporary Poets Celebrate the Diversity of Their Art,* edited by Finch and Katherine Varnes (Ann Arbor: University of Michigan Press, 2002), pp. 210–216.

SELECTED PERIODICAL PUBLICATION–
UNCOLLECTED: *"The Satanic Verses:* A Secular Muslim's Response," *Yale Journal of Criticism,* 4, no. 1
(1990): 295–300.

When speaking of the gifts that were the legacy of
his diverse background, Agha Shahid Ali sometimes
remarked that he was a universe. He was not boasting
but simply indicating that he was the product of unique
historical circumstances, influenced by three cultures–
Western, Hindu, and Muslim–and four literatures:
English, Kashmiri, Persian, and Urdu. At home he listened to Indian and Western classical compositions,
jazz, rock, and Arabic and Carnatic music. With family
members he discussed the works of Mirza Ghalib,
Hafiz, William Shakespeare, Faiz Ahmed Faiz, Johann
Wolfgang von Goethe, and Thomas Mann. By training
and temperament Ali was inclusive and ecumenical; he
did not shrink from the label "cosmopolitan," valuing
cultural and intellectual generosity and insisting that
participation in global communities in no way pre-
cluded a belief in political self-determination. His background and instinctive generosity fed a hope that he
could bring something new to literature in English.
That hope was realized in a body of poems that has
changed the idea of what it means to write poetry in
English.

Ali was born to Agha Ashraf Ali and Sufia
Nomani in New Delhi on 4 February 1949; he grew up
in Kashmir. The second of four children from a progressive, upper-class Muslim family, he inherited his
parents' respect for education and culture. During his
teens, two events shaped Ali's life significantly: his
three-year stay in Muncie, Indiana, where his father
was pursuing a doctorate in comparative education at
Ball State University; and his meeting with Begum
Akhtar, a singer of *ghazals* (a Persian lyric form in
rhymed couplets) and a cultural icon of a disappearing,
syncretic artistic tradition.

Ali graduated from the University of Kashmir in
Srinigar and from Hindu College of Delhi University,
where he taught English literature from 1970 to 1975.
Returning to the United States, he earned a doctorate in
English from Pennsylvania State University in 1984
and an M.F.A. from the University of Arizona in 1985.
While living in Arizona, he met poet James Merrill,
whose advice and example encouraged him to work on
his technique and experiment with a variety of poetic
forms. At heart an educator, Ali taught at Hamilton
College; the University of Massachusetts at Amherst,
where he directed the graduate creative-writing program; and Utah State University. As a visiting writer he
held positions at Princeton University, New York University, Baruch College, and the State University of
New York at Binghamton. Ali received fellowships
from the Guggenheim Memorial Foundation, the Pennsylvania Council on the Arts, the Bread Loaf Writers'
Conference, and the Ingram-Merrill Foundation. He
was also awarded a Pushcart Prize in 1996.

Ali's first two volumes of poetry, *Bone-Sculpture*
(1972) and *In Memory of Begum Akhtar* (1979), published
as chapbooks in India, constitute apprentice works, but
they remain fascinating as indices of subjects and concerns evidenced later in his more accomplished, critically acclaimed volumes. These subjects include a
preoccupation with loss, separation, and death; concern
about the place of multiple traditions–English, Urdu,
Hindu, and Muslim–in the writer's life and art; and
reflections on the relationship of memory and history to
art, and of art to life.

Bone-Sculpture depicts a wasteland beyond redemption, consigned to material corruption and a legacy of
dust and graves. The volume is attenuated, offering little scope for the actualities of lived experience; presented as a "dream-ritual of dead men" within a "dream
landscape" of bones and stones, the text evades any
sustained engagement with life. In the phrase reiterated
in "Bones," the first poem in the volume, there is "no
time" for any of the activities that later form the basis of
Ali's poetics. There is "no time . . . to remember ancestors who know a history of miracles," as Ali does in *The
Half-Inch Himalayas* (1987); "no time" to honor "slaughtered martyrs" in ritual remembrance binding past,
present, and future, as he does in *Rooms Are Never Finished* (2001); and no time to mix memory with the
desire for a better future, as he does in *The Country without a Post Office* (1997).

In the interval between "dying and death," the
poet assumes the posture that he is "waiting for death"
("Autumn in Srinigar"). This attitude is ultimately
revealed as a mask in "Introducing," from *In Memory of
Begum Akhtar:* "I tried being clever. . . . Bones my masks
/ Death the adolescent password." Yet, despite his hesitation to reveal himself in *Bone-Sculpture,* he is prescient
concerning his prospects as a poet, intuiting his future
success abroad, as he confesses in "dear editor": "I have
my hopes / hopes which assume shapes in / alien territories."

The reluctance to draw upon personal experience, the posturing, and the use of masks, as well as the
pervasive influence of English predecessors–particularly the overwhelming presence of T. S. Eliot–betray a
young poet struggling to discover his subject matter,
style, and voice. In contrast with *Bone-Sculpture,* Ali's
next chapbook, *In Memory of Begum Akhtar,* bespeaks a
writer with confidence in his poetic powers and self-
consciousness about his art. In this sense, "Introducing"
is aptly named, bringing Ali before the public as a legiti-

mate poet by the humorous announcement of his literary pedigree: English Romantic poetry at fifteen, Urdu poetry at sixteen, free verse at eighteen, Eliot's *The Waste Land* (1922), and "discipline," leaving him to "slant my way through rhymes, stumbling through my twenties." This self-deprecating litany suggests an increased awareness about his formation as a poet and the resources of his art. For example, "Note Autobiographical–1" and "Note Autobiographical–2" describe the poet's turning from God and Islam to poetry as an article of faith. The death of a pious grandfather and, finally, the theft of shoes at a local mosque crystallize for him a growing sense of the irrelevance of God in an increasingly secular world and trigger his embrace of Urdu poetry: "My voice cracked on Ghalib / and my tongue forgot the texture of prayer" ("Note Autobiographical–2"). Thus, *In Memory of Begum Akhtar* documents Ali's encounter with and immersion in the Urdu poetic tradition, specifically the *ghazals* of Ghalib, Mir Taqi Mir, and Faiz, adapted by the singer Akhtar. Yet, his newfound faith in verse is marked by disquietude, as he questions both its permanence and relevance in the title poem, as well as its ability to sustain and offer refuge in "Thumri for Rasoolan Bai." The singer Rasoolan Bai "built her house with bricks of bhairavi" (a type of Indian raga), only to see it burned down during the 1969 communal riots in Ahmedabad. As Bruce King observes, in this collection Ali sees himself as the belated heir to Bai and Akhtar, who represent for him the rapidly disappearing culture of pre-Partition northern India, "with its rich Muslim culture that had taken Indian roots and developed as Indian culture with shared sources." The viability of such a syncretic art in post-Independence India is questioned in "Learning Urdu" and its revision, "After the Partition of India," in which the poet's preceptor, a victim of the two-nation theory, is unable to teach him Urdu: "he now remembers but / half the lines. . . . History broke the back of poetry." Ali is unable to express this catastrophic loss adequately, just as he is unable, in good faith, to address the social ills of post-Independence India. Despite the fact that *In Memory of Begum Akhtar* includes poems published in Indian periodicals, it ends with the sense that the poet has reached a dead end in India and that, for a time, his future lies elsewhere, as "rare saffron" or an "exotic export" ("A Note on Spices"), collecting a degree in English overseas. That journey abroad resulted in *T. S. Eliot as Editor* (1986), the published version of Ali's 1984 dissertation, and *The Half-Inch Himalayas,* the 1987 book that established his reputation as a poet.

What is experienced as loss in *In Memory of Begum Akhtar*–the dead, poetic power, and tradition–resurfaces in *The Half-Inch Himalayas,* in which Ali is

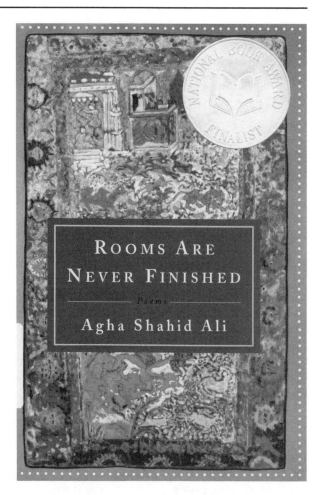

Dust jacket for the collection of poetry inspired by the death of Ali's mother from brain cancer in 1997, published just before his own death from the same disease in December 2001 (Richland County Public Library)

haunted by history and the past. In his backward gaze he recovers particulars missing from his earlier works–India, Kashmir, and the Agha clan–motivated by his physical separation from the subcontinent. Separation from the beloved is both deprivation and opportunity in these poems; the poet suffers in exile but gains in self-knowledge as he inventories his losses, careful, however, to evade the embrace of the past through exercising the re-creative powers of memory. Thus, the title poem from *In Memory of Begum Akhtar* reappears in this volume, placed beside "Homage to Faiz Ahmed Faiz." Akhtar and the poet Faiz are resurrected, and, in lieu of the silence of the departed, the poet now hears "some song" by Faiz, recovering a "memory of musk, the rebel face of hope." The turn from Ghalib in earlier poems to Faiz in these poems is significant, signaling Ali's growing historical and political consciousness. The poet who redefined the archetypal figure of the beloved in traditional Urdu poetry as revolution, Faiz stands inside history "as always . . . witness to a 'rain of stones.'" Following Faiz's example, Ali assumed in his poetry the role of witness, and in Faiz he discovered a model for employing tradition in original ways.

Historical and political awareness infuse many poems in *The Half-Inch Himalayas*. In "After Seeing Kozintsev's King Lear in Delhi," Ali records one detail of the British legacy in India, finding parallels in the careers of Lear and Zafar, a poet and the last Mogul emperor, "led through this street / by British soldiers, his feet in chains, / to watch his sons hanged" by "'men of stone.'" "Dacca Gauzes" notes the passing of an art, the creation of gauzes "known as woven air, running / water, evening dew," halted when "the hands of weavers were amputated, / the looms of Bengal silenced, / and the cotton shipped raw / by the British to England." The success of the poem is owing, in part, to the use of contrast in the evocation of exquisite gauzes juxtaposed with the blunt description of horrific acts. Contrast is an important rhetorical principle in Ali's poetry, particularly in *The Half-Inch Himalayas* and in later collections where the Urdu poetic tradition abuts with poetry in the American tradition.

A Walk through the Yellow Pages (1987) is a chapbook depicting Ali at home in America, comfortable with its idioms, familiar with its terrain—bars, bathrooms, restaurants, and phone companies—and willing to reclaim them as poetic subjects in witty, pointed verse. Much of its writing is of the "found" variety; the poet discovers dead writing—language vitiated by mechanical repetition or abandoned to the streets and bathroom stalls—and recovers it. He brings considerable enthusiasm to the project, discovering new linguistic resources in transforming advertising copy, bathroom graffiti, restaurant menus, and fairy tales. Casual and experimental, *A Walk through the Yellow Pages* features techniques and stylistic approaches—monologue, impersonation, and unusual points of view—that Ali later employed with great effect in *A Nostalgist's Map of America* (1991), a tribute to the primordial, enduring beauty of the American Southwest as well as a critique of the modern American wasteland, disconnected from history and meaningful community.

In *A Nostalgist's Map of America* Ali shows a fascination with moments of change and transition on a grand scale; he is a student of the American sublime, particularly practitioners such as Emily Dickinson and Georgia O'Keeffe, whose voices contribute to the rich texture of the book. Ali's poems are well served by his choice of the Southwest as the predominant subject of his writing. Lost tribes, vanished villages, vast deserts, geological epochs, and cataclysmic changes support a vocabulary of loss and desolation as well as the mythic

subtexts informing poems such as "Medusa," "The Youngest of the Graeae," and "Eurydice." The prefatory poem in the collection, "Eurydice" establishes the motifs—loss, separation, departures, arrivals, infidelity, and hope—that are woven into the four-part arrangement of the book. Set in a concentration camp and evocative of the Holocaust, "Eurydice" flirts with the aestheticizing of violence that it decries in the fascistic culture it depicts; yet, throughout the poem, the value of aesthetics is questioned as Ali self-consciously reflects on the limitations of art and the artist. Orpheus is portrayed as disengaging from life and the living, while his art is shown to be at best ineffectual and at worst escapist or even collusive with an oppressive fascist regime.

Part 1 of *A Nostalgist's Map of America* continues the motif of sudden arrivals and departures established in "Eurydice," as figures wander through landscapes and human "worlds" emptied of life and meaning. Striving "only to connect" in a modern wasteland, these figures—in particular, that of the poet—are betrayed by the fragile shelters and false securities of personal relationships, religion, and the routines of everyday life. The absence of certainties and sureties in part 1 initiates the poet's search for connectedness in part 2. The title poem of the collection testifies to the limits of language and art, which fail to take the measure of human suffering and are powerless and even false before death; yet, the poem also records the poet's fidelity to his subject as he struggles to remember a dead friend without falsity or sentimentality. "In Search of Evanescence," an eleven-part allusive poem, keeps Ali's promise to write his dying friend—albeit belatedly and posthumously—thereby fulfilling his duty to remember and effecting a partial redemption of loss. Titled "From Another Desert," part 3 consists of thirteen poems that, like "In Search of Evanescence," are variations on a theme, in this case the poet's search for the beloved (lover, friend, God, or the revolution) as mirrored in the traditional Arabic story of the love of Quais (also called Majnoon, meaning "mad" or "possessed") for Laila. A translation into a new context of themes and motifs from the first two sections, "From Another Desert" is enriched by and enriches the poems preceding and following it. Part 3 revisits the question, raised in "Eurydice," of the poet's relationship to the political order, most notably in poems 9 and 6. Poem 9 imagines Majnoon excluded from a Persian miniature in which a world of privilege revolves without him. The scene is a royal hunt; riding a tiger, Prince Jehangir, his coat glistening with drops of blood, will not dismount into Majnoon's wilderness of sorrow, a world of keenly experienced injustice. Yet, that wilderness is an inspiration for the poet, who, in poem 6, is "ready to face doom" and write in blood the sorrows of the world, his knowledge gathered from the silences of the victims of history, his art intimating revolution and the end of injustice. Part 4 revisits the desert of the American Southwest, continuing Ali's interest in retelling the stories of victims and recounting narratives of loss, most memorably in "Snow on the Desert," the poet's reckoning of "everything the earth / and I had lost, of all / that I would lose / of all that I was losing."

As Ali was experimenting with the English language in *A Walk through the Yellow Pages* and charting new poetic territory in *A Nostalgist's Map of America,* he was also developing and consolidating his command of the Urdu literary tradition by translating representative poems of Faiz, a poet lionized in major parts of Asia and Africa but little known in the West. The result was *The Rebel's Silhouette* (1991), a book of translations of Faiz's verse completed largely during the summers of 1988 and 1989 with the help of Ali's grandmother Sufia Agha Ashraf Ali. *The Rebel's Silhouette* not only familiarized many Western readers with the works of a world-class poet but also introduced them to the *ghazal,* a poetic form that, through Ali's efforts, became increasingly popular among poets. (He later edited *Ravishing DisUnities: Real Ghazals in English,* published in 2000.) Ali's own poetic achievement was increasingly being recognized on the Indian subcontinent, as evidenced by his inclusion in *The Oxford India Anthology of Twelve Modern Indian Poets* (1992) and by the publication in New Delhi of *The Beloved Witness: Selected Poems* (1992).

Ali's successes as a poet and translator were offset by tragic circumstances in Kashmir, his native region. Ruined worlds and lost paradises are the subjects of *The Country without a Post Office,* published in 1997. Centered on the ongoing Indian-Pakistani conflict in Kashmir, which touched Ali personally as he learned of the death of friends and watched the ruin of his homeland and the culture that sustained it, the collection is his most overtly political work, although the political overtures are not made at the expense of the impassioned poetry. Written in poetic forms such as the *ghazal,* the *pantoum* (a Malaysian verse form in which the second and fourth lines of each quatrain make up the first and third lines of the next), and the villanelle, the poems in *The Country without a Post Office* signal an advance in Ali's craft.

Apocalyptic in tone and elemental in imagery and emotion, *The Country without a Post Office* documents the end of a world Ali loved, the shared Indo-Muslim culture of Kashmir, lost to internecine conflict and warfare. This loss is recorded in "Farewell"; as Ali states in a note to the poem, it is "a plaintive love letter from a Kashmiri Muslim to a Kashmiri Pandit" who are now enemies, the poignancy of their situation underscored by a startling image: "in the lake the arms of temples and mosques are locked in each other's arms." In "I See

Dust jacket for the posthumously published 2003 collection of Ali's poems written in an ancient Persian lyric form that he helped to popularize in the West (Richland County Public Library)

Kashmir from New Delhi at Midnight," the sense of loss deepens when, by the "dazzling light" of Kashmir burning, pandits are shown "removing statues from temples" and inhabitants disappear in the shadows, having fled or been murdered, as the country is consigned to ruin. Yet, while *The Country without a Post Office* documents heartbreaking devastation, Ali also attempts an act of reclamation in poems such as "A Pastoral" and "I Dream I Am the Only Passenger on Flight 423 to Srinigar." As his world is disappearing, he evokes its presence by referencing recognizable places, legends, myths, and material culture, as in "The History of Paisley," a poem of reconciliation.

The creative word capable of redeeming time and reclaiming the past intimates the arrival of a longed-for "blessed word" that will recall Kashmir from the void, as expressed in "The Blessed Word: A Prologue." Wrapped "in the black velvet Void" and as yet unspoken, the blessed word represents the possibility of seeing the homeland and future anew. Yet, because it is unspoken, the blessed word also points to some inadequacy or failure in communication, a theme suggested in *The Country without a Post Office* by unread correspondence and undelivered mail. Failure to respond or adequately address the situation, a source of guilt for the poet, also implicates passive observers who attempt to place themselves outside the conflict. In "The Correspondent," this disengaged stance is epitomized by a newsman, whom the speaker entreats to lend assistance by witnessing the violence, asking, "When will the satellites / transmit my songs / carry Kashmir . . . across seas?" *The Country without a Post Office* is Ali's "letter to the world" soliciting attention, for "to be forgotten is . . . [the] most menacing image of the End" ("After the August Wedding in Lahore, Pakistan").

Following the depiction of ruin in *The Country without a Post Office*, Ali's *Rooms Are Never Finished*, published shortly before his death in December 2001, represents an insistent effort to restore order and value to a shattered world, despite the recognition that cherished things remain broken and the act of restoration will always be "never finished." *Rooms Are Never Finished,* a 2001 National Book Award finalist, concerns the loss of Ali's mother in 1997 to brain cancer, the illness that was also to claim him four years later, presented against the backdrop of hostilities in Kashmir. Prefaced by "Lenox Hill," a brilliant canzone recording the poet's helplessness and unremitting sorrow at the death of his mother, the centerpiece of *Rooms Are Never Finished* is part 1, "From Amherst to Kashmir," an allusive twelve-part sequence depicting the return of his mother's body to Kashmir for burial. Framed by poems depicting the martyrdom of Muhammad's grandson Husayn in Karbala, Iraq, and the mourning of Zaynab, Husayn's sister, Ali's personal loss takes on larger significance, transformed by ritual and art into a stable, recurring pattern of significance. Part 2 of the collection explores other consolations for loss and separation—art, love, and "the temporal order of things"—often with wry humor and the recognition that the magnitude of Ali's subject and the depth of his feeling exceed the bounds of his stanzas. Part 3 consists of "Eleven Stars over Andalusia," a joint translation by Ali and Ahmad Dallal of a poem by the Palestinian writer Mahmoud Darwish depicting the expulsion of the Moors from Spain; it is a lament for all exiles who have lost their homeland. The final part is the moving "I Dream I Am at the Ghat of the Only World," Ali's attempt to reconcile himself to the loss of his mother, of Pakistani writer and political activist Eqbal Ahmad, and of Merrill, who has the last word, or the words that Ali gives him: "THE LOVED ONE ALWAYS LEAVES."

On 8 December 2001 the fifty-two-year-old Ali died at his brother's home in Amherst. His death attracted international notice, garnering tributes from the United States and abroad. In the words of Ellen Bryant Voigt, Ali "was—*sui generis*—among poets, a fractious crew—universally beloved," simply because "he loved the world." *Call Me Ishmael Tonight: A Book of Ghazals* was published posthumously in 2003. Some new, written during his illness, and some old, taken from previous volumes, the *ghazals* pay tribute to the poetry he loved and offer insightful glimpses into his complex personality.

No estimation of Agha Shahid Ali's contribution to literature would be complete without some mention of his role as a cultural ambassador in championing the *ghazal* in the West and translating the poetry of Faiz. For many, this role is his most enduring legacy. Ali was a witness to the rich traditions of Arabic, Persian, and Urdu literatures, which have global significance and must shape any intelligent, honest conception of world literature. At once exacting and good-humored, Ali explored with the best American poets the subtle complexities of the *ghazal,* demanding of himself and others their best efforts with a poetic form that commanded his attention and respect. He was also "witness to 'a rain of stones,'" to quote from "Homage to Faiz Ahmed Faiz." Ali's poetry acknowledges and evokes the voices of the victims of history, as well as the stories of the forgotten and vanished, in Chile; Bisbee, Arizona; Armenia; Chechnya; Bosnia; and, above all, Kashmir. Perhaps as importantly, he brought something new into the English language. Contributing his distinctive voice and particular vision, the product of a unique tricultural heritage, Ali articulated new beginnings and fresh possibilities for poetry in English.

References:

Bruce King, *Modern Indian Poetry in English,* revised edition (Delhi & New York: Oxford University Press, 2001), pp. 257–274;

Ellen Bryant Voigt, "In Memoriam: Agha Shahid Ali, 1949–2001," *Norton Poets Online* (2001) <http://www.nortonpoets.com/ex/aliamemoriam.htm>.

Ahmed Ali

(1 July 1908 – 14 January 1994)

Tariq Rahman
Quaid-i-Azam University

BOOKS IN ENGLISH: *The Land of Twilight: A One Act Play in Verse* (Lucknow: R. R. Sreshta, 1937);

Twilight in Delhi (London: Hogarth, 1940; Bombay & London: Oxford University Press, 1966 [i.e., 1967]);

Mr. Eliot's Penny World of Dreams: An Essay in the Interpretation of T. S. Eliot's Poetry (Bombay: Published for Lucknow University Press by New Book Co., 1942);

Muslim China (Karachi: Pakistan Institute of International Affairs, 1949);

Purple Gold Mountain: Poems from China (London: Keepsake Press, 1960);

Ocean of Night (London: Peter Owen, 1964);

The Failure of an Intellect (Karachi: Akrash, 1968);

Problem of Style and Technique in Ghalib (Karachi: Akrash, 1969);

The Shadow and the Substance: Principles of Reality, Art and Literature (Karachi: Karachi University Press, 1977);

Of Rats and Diplomats (Hyderabad: Sangam, 1985);

The Prison-House: Short Stories (Karachi: Akrash, 1985);

Selected Poems: Ahmed Ali, edited by Klaus Stuckert (Gulbarga, India: JIWE, 1988).

PLAY PRODUCTIONS: *The Land of Twilight,* Lucknow, 1931;

Break the Chains, Lucknow, 1932.

OTHER: *The Flaming Earth: Poems from Indonesia,* edited and translated by Ali (Karachi: Friends of the Indonesian Republic Society, 1949);

The Falcon and the Hunted Bird [anthology], translated by Ali (Karachi: Kitab, 1950);

The Bulbul and the Rose [anthology], edited and translated by Ali (Karachi: Times Press, 1960);

Ghalib: Two Essays, by Ali and Alessandro Bausani, Orientalia Romana, no. 3 (Rome: Instituto Italiano per il Medio ed Estremo Oriente, 1969);

Ahmed Ali (www.thedailystar.net)

The Golden Tradition: An Anthology of Urdu Poetry, edited and translated by Ali (New York: Columbia University Press, 1973);

Al-Qur'an: A Contemporary Translation (Karachi: Akrash, 1984; revised edition, Princeton, N.J.: Princeton University Press, 1988);

Selected Short Stories from Pakistan: Urdu, edited by Ali (Islamabad: Pakistan Academy of Letters, 1988).

Ahmed Ali is one of the pioneers of English fiction and poetry on the Indian subcontinent. His literary career began in British India, and he continued to make his mark as a writer first in undivided India and then in Pakistan. He began writing in Urdu, his mother tongue, but later switched to English. He was one of the first Indian Muslim writers to embrace modernity and to make an impact on Indian English writing. He was also an adept translator of not only Urdu but also Chinese verse and of the Muslim holy book, the Qur'an.

Most sources give the date of Ali's birth as 1 July 1910; however, in a 1985 personal interview, Ali stated that dates were not accurately recorded in schools when he was a pupil, and that the year was probably 1908. In 2005 Ali's son Urooj Ahmed Ali confirmed that although the date had been changed on some papers to 1910, the original date on Ali's passport was 1908.

He was born in Delhi into a family of theologians. His father, Syed Shujauddin Ali, worked in the British civil service, and his mother's name was Ahmad Kaniz Asghar Begum. When his father died in 1919, the eight-year-old Ali and his mother went to live with his uncle in India's United Provinces. His uncle brought him up according to conservative Islamic traditions. After attending elementary school at Gurgaon, Ali went to a missionary school in Azamgarh. At an early age, Ali was interested in Urdu literature, much to the disapproval of his puritan uncle, who considered poetry and fiction immoral.

Ali went on to study science at Aligarh Muslim University from 1925 to 1927. An essay that he wrote attracted the attention of one of his professors, an Englishman, who introduced him to English literature and to Raja Rao, a lifelong friend who eventually became one of the leading Indian English novelists. Ali soon lost interest in studying science and decided to study literature instead.

In 1927 Ali was admitted to Lucknow University, where he earned his B.A. (in 1930) and M.A. (in 1931) in English literature. He seemed to thrive in intellectual circles and became a political activist urging reform and the end of both fatalism in his people and imperialist rule in India. At this stage of his life he succeeded in publishing a few stories in Urdu and published his first story in English in the *Lucknow University Journal*. He also wrote and produced two English plays, *The Land of Twilight* (1931; published 1937) and *Break the Chains* (1932), in which his anti-British and progressive ideas found outlets.

After his graduation in 1931 he became a lecturer in English at Lucknow University and started publishing literary works in both Urdu and English. Along with three friends, Sajjad Zahir, Rashid Jahan, and Sahibzada Mahmudzzafar Khan, he published a literary anthology in 1932 titled *Angaray* (Burning Coals), the radical and inflammatory contents of which angered conservative Muslims. As Ali reminisced in an interview with Muneeza Shamsie in 1990: "We were lampooned. We were abused. There were editorials on the front page and pamphlets written against us. Speeches were delivered in pulpits and mosques and some of the *qassais* [butchers] ran after us with daggers." The British government of India banned the book in 1933 for "hurting the religious susceptibilities of a section of the community." In response, Ali and his friends proposed forming a League of Progressive Authors to articulate progressive ideas and oppose censorship. This group evolved in 1936 to become the All-India Progressive Writers' Association, an organization dedicated to independence, reform, religious harmony, and socialism. However, Ali eventually left the association, since he was not willing to be constrained by the Marxism of many of its members.

In 1934 Ali published *Sholey* (Flames), a collection of short fiction in Urdu. "Our Lane," the English translation of "Hamari Gali," one of the stories of the collection, was published soon after in *New Writing* in London. Partly because of its favorable reception, and partly because he longed for a wider audience to whom he could present his interpretation of Indian Muslim society, Ali began to write increasingly in English. The major consequence of this move was his first and most important novel in English, *Twilight in Delhi* (1940). He managed to finish it at about the time World War II was breaking out. During a trip to England in 1939, he showed the manuscript to novelist E. M. Forster, who helped him find an agent. The novel was eventually sold to Hogarth Press, which published it in 1940.

Twilight in Delhi is set in Delhi and depicts life in an upper-class Muslim family in the second decade of the twentieth century. The protagonist, Mir Nihal, is a successful Muslim merchant who, though past fifty, is still healthy and full of life. He exercises complete control over his extended family and finds pleasure in raising pigeons and making love to his mistress, a beautiful courtesan. The novel, however, records his gradual loss of power. His son Asghar marries despite Mir Nihal's reservations about his choice; a cat kills the pigeons; and the mistress falls ill and dies. In the end Mir Nihal, unable to bear the trauma of another son's death in an influenza epidemic, becomes paralyzed, and readers see the old man "on his bed more dead than alive, too broken to think even of the past."

At the symbolic level, *Twilight in Delhi* shows through the portrait of Mir Nihal's family how the world of the Muslim feudal gentry of North India was coming to an end, defeated by the forces of modernity.

The clash between the traditional values of the old, decaying world and emergent ones are dramatized by the clash between Mir Nihal and Asghar. Mir Nihal is unable to appreciate Asghar and his friends or the changes that he sees around him. However, Asghar is shown to be ineffectual and unclear about his goals in life. Ultimately, the novel is about a moribund society and way of life.

The symbolic aspect of the novel is significant, but the narrative technique of *Twilight in Delhi* is realistic. There are vivid depictions of the visit of George V in 1911 for the Coronation Durbar, an event that displayed the power of the British Empire at its peak and that reminds Mir Nihal of the influence lost by Muslims when they ceded power to the English. Ali also shows the impact of the great influenza epidemic of the period as well as the life of Muslim aristocratic families in the traditional *mohallas* (residential areas) of Delhi with considerable realism. Ali attempts to convey the linguistic nuances of the world of Mir Nihal and the idioms of the Muslim gentry by using Urdu words and then glossing them with the help of footnotes or mixing English and Urdu words to capture the sounds as well as the sights of Delhi life.

Reviewers mostly praised *Twilight in India* when it came out in 1940, and the novel continues to be considered a major work of South Asian writing in English of that period. Bonamy Dobree and Edwin Muir were among those who commented positively when the book came out. In a 1967 article, Lawrence Brander praises the novel for "its fascinating pictures; of the Great Durbar when George V visited India in 1911, of early subversive action against British rule, of the 1914 war as it affected India, of the horrifying influenza epidemic . . . and the serious unrest" in the lives of the residents of the houses of old Delhi. Alistair Niven comments appreciatively on "the epic structure" of the novel and Ali's ability to interweave "public and private affairs" in his narrative.

However, a few critics pointed to weaknesses in the novel. Anniah Gowda, in a comparative study of *Twilight in Delhi* and Chinua Achebe's *Things Fall Apart* (1958), praises the latter writer for showing "tragedy to be consequent on the interaction of social forces and human character" while finding Ali's work to be merely fatalistic. Niven charges Ali's book with two weaknesses: stale diction and ineffective nostalgia. In *A History of Indian Literature* (1982), M. K. Naik notes that while the portrait of Muslim family life is done in "painstaking detail," Ali has not succeeded in connecting domestic history with the larger forces of history and the world outside.

Nevertheless, *Twilight in Delhi* made Ali something of a celebrity. After the novel came out, at the height of

Cover for a 1994 edition of Ali's 1940 novel, in which the decline of an upper-class Muslim family illustrates the defeat of traditional values among the feudal aristocracy by the forces of modernity (Richland County Public Library)

World War II, Ali worked for some time for the Delhi bureau of the British Broadcasting Corporation as a representative and listener-research director who reported to George Orwell in London. In 1941 he published a study of T. S. Eliot's poetry, *Mr. Eliot's Penny World of Dreams*. He brought out three collections of short stories in Urdu in 1944 and 1945. Toward the end of the war he became head of the English department at Presidency College in Calcutta. In 1947, when the partition of India was imminent, Ali became a British Council Visiting Professor of English at the National Central University in Nanking. But when news of the partition and the violence that ensued came to him in China, Ali decided to become a citizen of Pakistan. He joined the Pakistan Foreign Service and held positions in China, Morocco, and the United States. In 1950 he married Bilquis Jahan, whose translation of *Twilight in*

*Cover for Ali's 1985 collection of short fiction, including his translations
of early stories he had written in his native language, Urdu
(Van Pelt Library, Pennsylvania State University)*

Delhi into Urdu in 1963 earned her as well as Ali great acclaim. The couple had three sons and a daughter.

While in China, Ali learned Chinese and, with the Chinese poet Fang Ying-Yang, produced "The Call of the Trumpet," a volume of translations of Chinese verse that remains unpublished. However, his immersion into Chinese poetic traditions was productive in another sense, for in 1960 he published *Purple Gold Mountain: Poems from China,* a collection of verse testifying to his ability to blend Chinese, English, and Urdu poetic traditions. Many of the poems of the volume are essentially imagistic in nature, as is the case with Chinese poetry. In Ali's poems, the image becomes a metaphor, as when in "Loneliness" he describes a pigeon flying and makes the image stand for his sense of loneliness and exile after partition: "Across the vast, unending sky / A pigeon plies its way / Towards the setting sun." In addition to loneliness and alienation, the major themes of the poem are nostalgia and loss; but Eliot as well as the Chinese verse tradition appeared to have

taught Ali to handle these themes impersonally, so that the verse does not become maudlin. These poems make Ali, along with Taufiq Rafat, a pioneer of Pakistani poetry in English.

Ali's second novel, *Ocean of Night,* was conceived as a sequel to his first one, since it continues with the theme from *Twilight in Delhi* of the decadence of the Muslim elite. He began it after the partition of India but eventually published it in 1964. The setting of the novel is pre-Partition Lucknow, and its theme is the ruin of aristocratic feudal families through prostitution. Ali's novel is about a nawab or feudal lord who transfers his property to Huma, his favorite courtesan, but gets involved with another courtesan, Kesari Bai. Eventually, the nawab is ruined and, in a moment of insanity, murders Kesari Bai and commits suicide. Huma, meanwhile, attempts to return the legal documents of his property to him, but he never receives them. After his death, she manages to give the documents to his wife. Huma's consolation is that she finds peace through her selfless deeds.

The novel is on a hackneyed theme, for there were many stories in Urdu fiction about decent courtesans and decadent aristocrats given to drink and debauchery. Niven thus notes the stereotypical plot and "the melodramatic climax" and relates the novel to nineteenth-century English stage productions and Indian popular cinema. Brander finds the treatment of the setting to lack the color and warmth of the earlier novel. The few critics who noticed the work when it was published agreed that it does not attain the artistic level of *Twilight in Delhi,* nor of the other contemporary works in Urdu on similar themes.

Ali followed the unsuccessful second novel with several miscellaneous works, including critical studies of and translations from the Urdu poet Mirza Asadullah Khan Ghalib and *The Golden Tradition: An Anthology of Urdu Poetry* (1973). His last attempt at fiction was his third novel, *Of Rats and Diplomats* (1985). It represents a departure from the realistic mode of narration that he had favored earlier and the theme of decadence in Muslim life that he had made his own. Scholars have described this novel as "magic realist" and connected to the "absurd" tradition of Franz Kafka and Eugène Ionesco. The story is about an army general who is posted as the ambassador of Bachusan to Ratisan. In this new country he is caught early one morning in the garden of another diplomat. Mistaken for a thief, he is recalled. However, he grows a tail and ultimately is transformed into a rat. This tale about diplomacy as observed by a cynic purports to be allegorical and evokes the world of such famous tales as Kafka's *The Metamorphosis* (1915) and Ionesco's play *The Rhinoceros* (1959). Ali's point is that like protagonist General Sourirada Soutanna, everyone in high diplomatic circles has rat-like characteristics and is a repulsive creature. This novel also failed to find favor with the critics, and Ali's reputation as a novelist continues to depend on *Twilight in Delhi.*

In 1985 Ali also published *The Prison-House,* a collection of his short fiction in which he included translations of the stories he had written in Urdu earlier. Ali's short stories belong for the most part to the progressive, realist tradition of Urdu literature, of which Munshi Premchand was the pioneer in Urdu and Hindi fiction; but in some stories, Ali is influenced by modernist narrative technique and uses symbols and events rather than sequential narratives to convey his themes. Among the stories of *The Prison-House,* "Our Lane," "Shammu Khan," and "Two Sides of the Picture" are in the realistic mode. "Our Lane" presents daily life in pre-partition Delhi. In "Two Sides," as in *Twilight in Delhi,* the conflict between tradition and modernity is the focus; but in this case the aristocratic characters support British rule and are not treated sentimentally. Two of the stories, "In the Train" and "The Man Accused," appear to be realistic but have allegorical overtones. The other stories—"My Room," "The Prison-House," "The Castle," and "Before Death"—tend to be surrealistic or have been influenced by the fictional experiments of Virginia Woolf, James Joyce, and Eliot. On the whole, the stories have not impressed the critics and have not earned much attention.

One of Ali's most significant contributions is his translation of the Muslim holy book, *Al-Qur'an: A Contemporary Translation* (1984). Ali uses metrical lines to convey what he characterizes in the preface of the work as "the sonority and rhythmic patterns of the Qur'anic language." The work was revised and republished in 1988 in a "definitive" edition by Princeton University Press and is perhaps the most highly regarded and readable modern translation of the Qur'an in English.

Long before he died on 14 January 1994, Ahmed Ali had earned a preeminent position in Pakistani literature in general and Pakistani writing in English in particular. Certainly, the work he did as a fiction writer, poet, and translator as well as a teacher, scholar, and diplomat made him a distinctive figure in Pakistan. The country conferred on him the Sitara-e-Imtiaz (Star of Distinction) in 1980. He was also awarded an honorary

D.Litt. by Karachi University in 1993. He also had held visiting positions in several American universities. By the time of his death there was no doubt that he would always be considered one of the pioneers of South Asian writing in English.

Interview:

Muneeza Shamsie, "An Interview with Ahmed Ali: Memories of Another Day–Twilight in Karachi," *Newsline* (Karachi), August 1990.

References:

David D. Anderson, "Ahmed Ali and *Twilight in Delhi,*" *Journal of South Asian Literature* (Spring–Summer 1971): 81–86;

Annual of Urdu Studies, 9 (1994);

Lawrence Brander, "Two Novels by Ahmed Ali," *Journal of Commonwealth Literature* (July 1967): 1–8;

Carlo Coppola, "The Short Stories of Ahmed Ali," in *Studies in the Urdu Gazal and Prose Fiction,* edited by Muhammad Umar Memon (Madison: University of Wisconsin Press, 1979);

Anniah Gowda, "Ahmed Ali's *Twilight in Delhi* and Chinua Achebe's *Things Fall Apart,*" in *Alien Voice: Perspectives on Commonwealth Literature,* edited by Avadhesh K. Srivastava (Lucknow: Print House, 1981), pp. 53–60;

Alamgir Hashmi, "Ahmed Ali: the Transition to A Post-Colonial Mode," *World Literature Written in English,* 29, no. 2 (1989): 148–152;

M. K. Naik, *A History of Indian English Literature* (Delhi: Sahitya Akademi, 1982);

Alistair Niven, "Historical Imagination in the Novels of Ahmed Ali," *Journal of Indian Writing in English,* 3 (January–July 1980): 5–11;

Tariq Rahman, "Ahmed Ali," in his *A History of Pakistani Literature in English* (Lahore: Vanguard, 1991), pp. 29–55;

Rahman, "Linguistic Deviation as a Stylistic Device in Pakistani English Fiction," *Journal of Commonwealth Literature,* 25 (1990): 1–11;

Papers:

Ahmed Ali's papers, including the unpublished manuscript "The Call of the Trumpet: An Anthology of Modern Chinese Poetry," are in the possession of his son Urooj Ahmed Ali in Karachi.

Monica Ali

(7 February 1967 –   )

Kaiser Haq
University of Dhaka

BOOK: *Brick Lane* (London: Doubleday, 2003; New York: Scribner, 2003).

SELECTED PERIODICAL PUBLICATIONS– UNCOLLECTED: "Where I'm Coming From," *Guardian,* 17 June 2003;
"Brick Lane," *Jamini: International Arts Quarterly,* 1, no. 2 (November 2003).

Monica Ali created literary history in 2003 when she became the first unpublished author to be included in "Best of Young British Novelists," the decadal list of twenty writers compiled by *Granta.* (The 1983 list included Salman Rushdie and Martin Amis, and the 1993 list featured Hanif Kureishi.) The work that earned Ali the coveted accolade was her first novel, *Brick Lane.* The fifth chapter was published as "Dinner with Dr. Azad" in the April 2003 *Granta,* the issue devoted to the new top twenty, and advance copies of the novel were put on sale at readings. *Brick Lane* was officially launched at the Terrace Bar on the eponymous street in the heart of Banglatown (the London district where many Bangladeshi immigrants have settled) on 2 June 2003 and in New York in September of that year. Laudatory reviews began appearing in newspapers, and Ali was interviewed on television. More than a dozen translators worldwide set to work on the text. *Brick Lane* won the 2003 W. H. Smith People's Choice Award and was short-listed that year for the British Book Awards Literary Fiction Award, the Guardian First Book Award, and, most importantly, the Man Booker Prize in fiction. Ali was also named the 2004 British Book Awards Newcomer of the Year. In the United States, *Brick Lane* was named one of the best books of 2003 by *The New York Times* and was short-listed for the National Book Critics Circle Award and the Art Seidenbaum Award for a first work of fiction, given by *The Los Angeles Times.*

Monica Ali was born in Dhaka on 7 February 1967 to an English mother, Joyce Ali, and a Bangladeshi father, Hatem Ali, who worked as a techno-

Monica Ali (© Robin Matthews; from the dust jacket for Brick Lane, *2003; Bruccoli Clark Layman Archives)*

crat. In the mid 1960s Hatem Ali was a student in the north of England, where he met Joyce, who hailed from the industrial town of Preston, at a dance. He took a job as inspector of technical colleges in Dhaka and found that his family had arranged a match for him, but he declined to follow social custom and rejected the proposal. Instead he married Joyce, who had followed him to Dhaka, even though doing so meant the virtual severance of ties with his family.

Dhaka was then the provincial capital of East Pakistan, but in 1971 it was to become the capital of the People's Republic of Bangladesh, created after a nine-month war of independence. Before the war the Alis led a quiet life in Dhaka and got along well with their neighbors. Monica and her elder brother, Robin (later a professor of genetics at University College, London), lived like other middle-class Bengali children until political cataclysm brought about the family's emigration.

The outbreak of the war on 25 March 1971 prompted Ali's father to send his wife and two children to safety in England. The children's names had not been entered on their mother's British passport, and they spoke only Bengali. Since Bengali was the language of the rebels, it was possible that the Pakistani occupation army personnel on security duty might refuse to believe they were Joyce Ali's children. The anxious mother stuffed her children's mouths with boiled sweets to prevent them from speaking; the trick worked.

England was not welcoming, however. As Monica Ali recalls in "Where I'm Coming From" (2003),

> In London there was no one to meet us. My mother carried us across London on the buses and then got on a train to Manchester. She had no money left. My grandfather, who met us at the station, paid the guard. My grandmother was waiting at home. She was very concerned, she said, about how my mother intended to pay back the fare.

> My father escaped from East Pakistan, over the border to India. From there he finally got permission to join his wife in the UK. It was a temporary situation. When things got sorted out, we would go back. His children settled into school, we stopped speaking to him in Bengali and then we stopped even understanding. The new status quo was accepted. There was no plan, after that, to "go home." Sounding philosophical, my father would say: "I just got stuck here, that's all." And home, because it could never be reached, became mythical: Tagore's golden Bengal, a teasing counterpoint to our drab northern mill town lives.

After the unavoidable difficulties of a transitional period, the Alis settled into a middle-class existence. Joyce and Hatem ran a knickknack shop for some years, selling trinkets and jewelry; he then took a degree in history and taught at the Open University, while she became a counselor in the psychology department of a hospital in Bolton, near Manchester.

As a child of a mixed marriage, Monica Ali felt that she was an outsider, a situation not without positive aspects; she feels it was good training for a writer. After finishing school in Bolton, she entered Wadham College of Oxford University, earning a degree in "Modern Greats" (philosophy, politics, and econom-

ics) in 1988. She worked in the marketing department of two small publishing houses and then at a design and branding agency. An avid reader of novels since childhood, Ali had a vague desire to become a writer, but the urge to begin writing came late, after her marriage to Simon Torrance, a management consultant, and the birth of her son, Felix, in 1999. When Felix was about a year old, she began writing short stories and participated in on-line workshops in which she submitted her stories for criticism. This practice gave her the incentive to write, but she soon felt constrained by the short-fiction genre. As she said in a 2003 interview, " I felt that I didn't have room to breathe. There was something else that I wanted to do. After that it was a question of working up the courage to begin on something larger."

Ali thought of writing an historical novel about Sake Deen Mahomet, whose *The Travels of Dean Mahomet* (1794) was the first book written in English by an Indian, but she abandoned the plan after some time. The idea for *Brick Lane* came to her when, as an editor for the publishing house Verso, she worked on the manuscript of *The Power to Choose: Bangladeshi Women and Labour Market Decisions in London and Dhaka* (2000), a study on garment workers by Naila Kabeer, a Bangladeshi sociologist teaching at Sussex University. Ali then researched London's Banglatown. In "Where I'm Coming From," she claims that she was also inspired to write the book because of her experience of "conflict between first- and second-generation immigrants" and the stories her father used to tell her about village life in his country.

Ali had a second child, a daughter named Shumi, in 2001. When her daughter was five months old, Ali began working on *Brick Lane*. Somehow, writing became a way of finding space for herself and offsetting the pressures of parenting. Another crucial factor in the genesis of the book was the death of Ali's maternal grandmother at this time. As she put it in the 2003 interview, "There's something galvanising about a funeral. I felt the need to not put things off any longer. And I sent my husband outside with the little ones, and I drew the curtains against the sun, and I started then."

After Ali had completed two chapters, she showed them to a friend who was an editor for Doubleday. This contact led to an offer from the firm and an advance that she used to fund child care so that she could have more time to work on the novel. She finished it in eighteen months, having worked "intensively" on it, as she said in 2003, like someone "obsessed."

Brick Lane possesses a dual significance, depending on whether it is considered from a Bangladeshi or

Dust jacket for the British edition of Ali's 2003 novel, about a Bangladeshi woman who struggles to adapt to life in London and keeps in touch with her native country through letters exchanged with her younger sister (Bruccoli Clark Layman Archives)

British perspective. The novel has set a benchmark for Anglophone fiction writers of Bangladeshi origin, overshadowing earlier works, including those of the expatriates Adib Khan and Syed Manzurul Islam. For British readers *Brick Lane* is of interest as the first comprehensive fictional portrayal of Bangladeshis intended for a large audience. The editor of *Granta*, Ian Jack, commended it specifically for bringing "news" from Banglatown.

Brick Lane is the story of Nazneen, born in 1967 in a village near Mymensingh (she shares her birth year and ancestral village, Gouripur, with Ali) and married off at eighteen to a much older man, Chanu, who transplants her to a dismal housing project in the borough of Tower Hamlets in the East End of London, where she slowly and painfully acquires confidence in her own selfhood. Nazneen's only connection with the mother country is through letters from Hasina, her ill-starred younger sister. Strikingly good-

looking (*hasina* means "beautiful" in Bengali) and willful, Hasina elopes with her beau to Khulna, but the romance fades rapidly. The husband turns out to be a wife beater, and she runs away to Dhaka to join the vast army of garment workers. The perils of a pretty sweatshop worker are graphically illustrated: she is slandered, sexually exploited, and sacked. She eventually becomes a domestic and elopes with the cook. Hasina is a survivor. As Nazneen sums up, "She isn't going to give up."

In an interview with Jessica Jernigan, Ali revealed that Nazneen and Hasina came to her "as a pair," sisters "in pursuit of happiness." The difference between them, she stressed, is that "while Hasina's search is externally focused, Nazneen is very much internalized." Ali confessed that she "came to inhabit" Nazneen's "skin more and more as the book went along," which perhaps explains why the portrait of this sister is so memorable. Hasina, in contrast, is conveyed through her letters, in which she communicates strong emotions about a life where she encounters increasingly adverse situations.

Hasina's letters posed a technical problem for Ali. As Hasina has even less education than Nazneen, she is supposed to write imperfect Bengali. But Ali had lost her childhood knowledge of Bengali, so it was impossible for her to imagine the imperfect Bengali and translate it into imperfect English. She circumvented the problem by devising a kind of broken English. The letters provide a disturbing glimpse of Bangladeshi anomie, but many readers found the pidgin English in which they are written unconvincing. Kabeer's *The Power to Choose* makes extensive use of interviews with garment workers conducted in Bengali and translated into simple English. These interviews are more convincing than Hasina's letters, largely because the bland English used does not draw attention to itself, whereas the odd idiom of the letters may cause the reader to stumble. The difference may be seen in a comparison of a few lines from an interview in *The Power to Choose* with Ali's pidgin adaptation:

> The best purdah is the burkah within oneself, the burkah of the mind. . . . You see, if I keep my fingers closed into a fist, you cannot open my hands, can you? Even if you try, it will take you such a long time, it will not be worth your while. Similarly, if I maintain my purdah, no one can take it away from me.

> Pure is in the mind. Keep yourself pure in mind and God will protect. I close my fingers and make fist. I keep my fingers shut like this you cannot open my hands can you? I say like this to her. Even you try it take such long time it not worth it for you. Same thing my modesty. I keep purdah in the mind no one can take it.

Dialogue posed less of a problem for Ali: she used English with a South Asian slant. For instance, the feckless Chanu, the liveliest character in the novel, assuages his sense of personal failure by being dismissive of his friend Dr. Aziz: "He's just a finger blown up to the size of a banana tree." This statement is an effective translation of a Bengali metaphor for an upstart. A little later, Chanu's Bengali speech is rendered in convincing babu English: "Maybe if I get the promotion, then he will be more inclined to extend his hospitality."

A pattern of balances, contrasts, and inversions underlies *Brick Lane*—between Bangladesh and Banglatown, for instance, and between individual characters, such as the two sisters with their contrasting fortunes. There is sadness in two couples, but in one case the wife, Nazneen, is unhappy, whereas in the other the

husband, Dr. Azad, is unhappy. The Azads are affluent, but Chanu and Nazneen are precariously balanced on the lower edge of the lower-middle class. One effect of these contrasts is that the feminism in the novel never becomes doctrinaire.

Nazneen's affair with Karim, although ultimately unsatisfactory, aids her quest for self-realization and introduces her to Banglatown politics. Around 1980, Bangladeshis in the district lived in terror of white gangs. Soon afterward, Bangladeshi youths began putting up organized resistance and eventually secured their territorial rights. After the 11 September 2001 terrorist attacks in the United States, Karim and his friends, the Bengal Tigers, are up in arms against the Islamophobic Lion Hearts, but *Brick Lane* underscores the ultimate futility of religious politics.

The conclusion of *Brick Lane* is open-ended: Chanu is back in Bangladesh, while Nazneen stays back in Banglatown with their daughters, who are sure that their father will soon tire of the chaos in Bangladeshi and return. Meanwhile, there is talk of a vacation in the old country. In the final scene Nazneen's daughters take her ice-skating. When she protests that she cannot skate in a sari, her friend Razia quips, "This is England. You can do whatever you like." Razia's remark is the last sentence in the novel, and one suspects it may be narrowly interpreted by some as a slogan for what the Tories in England once notoriously described as the race-relations industry, but it reveals a significant fact about expatriate Bangladeshis: the men dream of returning but not the women, who, even as second-class citizens, enjoy rights denied them in the mother country.

The critical reception of *Brick Lane* was mixed. Most reviewers hailed the novel as an important work by a promising writer on a subject that was central to contemporary England and the South Asian diaspora. Some reviewers, however, saw the failure of Hasina's letters as symptomatic of Ali's failure to render her subjects convincingly. Still others saw the success of *Brick Lane* in the West and Ali's elevation to the status of celebrity writer on the strength of this one book as the British cultural establishment's attempt to create an icon to represent the sizable Bangladeshi community in the United Kingdom.

Typical of the positive reviews was one in *The Observer* (1 June 2003) in which Harriet Lane praised Ali for fictionalizing a community that was usually overlooked in English letters and for delivering a novel that was "warm, shrewd, startling and hugely readable." Similarly, Elsa Gaztambide praised Ali in *Booklist* (August 2003) for her "extraordinary" power in "capturing the female immigrant experience through her character's innocent perspective." Recommending the book strongly in *Library Journal* (15 June 2003), Ellen Flexman declared that Ali's novel offered "a refreshing glimpse into the everyday lives of families seeking balance between tradition and the demands of the wider world." Although more guarded in his praise, Michael Gorra in *The New York Times* (7 September 2003) noted that Ali displayed a "technical assurance and an inborn generosity that cannot be learned."

In a long review of *Brick Lane* for *The London Review of Books* (9 October 2003), Sukhdev Sandhu, while appreciative of Ali's focus "on the lives of Bangladeshi women" in contemporary England, found the novelist's decision to present Hasina's letters in pidgin English an "odd" one and symptomatic of "the major weakness" of the novel: "its language." Sandhu concluded that *Brick Lane* "is a patchy but promising first novel, strongly indebted to its black and Asian literary antecedents, more interested in character than it is in language or even in the area from which it derives its name." Sandhu also commented on the "ecstatic response to the book and the expectations this has aroused" because of the perception that the novel had "mapped out a new, invisible London."

Brick Lane failed to receive praise from a part of the British Bangladeshi community depicted through the story of Nazneen and Chanu. The Greater Sylhet Development and Welfare Council, an organization that claims to represent expatriate Bangladeshis, wrote an eighteen-page letter to Random House (the publishing group of which Doubleday is now a division) accusing Ali of portraying them negatively and in a distorted manner.

On the whole, though, Monica Ali's debut novel was a success and ensured that the literary public in the English-speaking world and elsewhere would be looking forward to her subsequent books. She set to work on a new novel before the excitement over *Brick Lane* had subsided, informing interviewers that it was on a contemporary theme but revealing no details. Even on the basis of her first novel, it can be safely asserted that Ali has earned a respectable place among those writers who have attracted special attention because they work at the interface between cultures.

Interviews:

Kaiser Haq, "Monica Ali–in an Exclusive Interview," *Daily Star* (Bangladesh), 31 May 2003, p. 5;

Jessica Jernigan, "Nazneen's Voice: Monica Ali on her First Novel," *Borders* <http://www.bordersstores.com/features/feature.jsp?file=ali> [accessed 11 November 2005].

References:

Kaiser Haq, "Jumping Ship: Three Bangladeshi Diaspora Novels in English," *Biblio* (November–December 2004): 29–31; reprinted in *Prince Claus Fund Journal,* no. 11 (December 2004): 58–67;

Naila Kabeer, *The Power to Choose: Bangladeshi Women and Labour Market Decisions in London and Dhaka* (London: Verso, 2000); republished as *Bangladeshi Women Workers and Labour Market Decisions: The Power to Choose* (New Delhi: Vistaar / Dhaka: University Press, 2001).

Mulk Raj Anand

(12 December 1905 – 28 September 2004)

Kamal D. Verma
University of Pittsburgh at Johnstown

BOOKS: *Persian Paintings* (London: Faber & Faber, 1930);

Curries and Other Indian Dishes (London: D. Harmsworth, 1932);

The Golden Breath: Studies in Five Poets of the New India (London: Murray, 1933; New York: Dutton, 1933);

The Hindu View of Art (London: Allen & Unwin, 1933; Bombay: Asia, 1957);

Untouchable, preface by E. M. Forster (Bombay: Kutub-Popular, 1933; London: Wishart, 1935; Harmondsworth, U.K. & New York: Allen Lane, 1940);

Lament on the Death of a Master of Arts (Lucknow, India: Naya Sansar, 1934);

The Lost Child and Other Stories (London: J. A. Allen, 1934; Bombay: Lavanya, 1974);

The Coolie (London: Lawrence & Wishart, 1936; Bombay: Kutub-Popular, 1944); republished as *Coolie* (Harmondsworth, U.K. & New York: Penguin, 1945);

Two Leaves and a Bud (London: Lawrence & Wishart, 1937; Bombay: Kutub, 1946; New York: Liberty, 1954);

The Village (London: Cape, 1939; Bombay: Kutub-Popular, 1960);

Across the Black Waters (London: Cape, 1940; New Delhi: Vision, 1978);

Letters on India (London: Routledge, 1942);

The Sword and the Sickle (London: Cape, 1942; Bombay: Kutub, 1955);

The Barber's Trade Union, and Other Stories (London: Cape, 1944; Bombay: Kutub-Popular, 1959);

The Big Heart (Bombay: Kutub-Popular, 1944; London & New York: Hutchinson, 1945; revised edition, New Delhi: Arnold-Heinemann, 1980);

Indian Fairy Tales (Bombay: Kutub-Popular, 1946);

Apology for Heroism: An Essay in Search of Faith (London: L. Drummond, 1946); republished as *Apology for Heroism: A Brief Autobiography of Ideas* (Bombay: Kutub-Popular, 1957);

Mulk Raj Anand (www.kalakahani.co.uk/13843.html)

The Tractor and the Corn Goddess, and Other Stories (Bombay: Thacker, 1947);

The Bride's Book of Beauty, by Anand and Krishna Hutheesing (Bombay: Kutub, 1949);

Lines Written to an Indian Air: Essays (Bombay: Nalanda, 1949);

Seven Summers, introduction by Saros Cowasjee (London & New York: Hutchinson, 1951; Delhi: Hind, 1970);

The Story of Man . . . (New Delhi: Sikh, 1952);

Private Life of an Indian Prince (London & New York: Hutchinson, 1953; revised edition, London: Bodley Head, 1970);

Reflections on the Golden Bed: and Other Stories (Bombay: Current Book House, 1954);

India in Colour, introduction and text by Anand, photographs by Suzanne Hausammann (London: Thames & Hudson, 1958; Bombay: Taraporevala, 1958; New York: McGraw-Hill, 1958);

The Power of Darkness and Other Stories (Bombay: Jaico, 1959);

The Old Woman and the Cow (Bombay: Kutub-Popular, 1960);

More Indian Fairy Tales (Bombay: Kutub-Popular, 1961);

The Road (Bombay: Kutub-Popular, 1961; London: Oriental University Press, 1987; New York: Facet, 1987);

Is There a Contemporary Indian Civilisation? (Bombay & London: Asia, 1963; Bombay & New York: Asia, 1963);

Death of a Hero: Epitaph for Maqbool Sherwani (Bombay: Kutub-Popular, 1963);

Lajwanti and Other Stories (Bombay: Jaico, 1966);

Morning Face (Bombay: Kutub-Popular, 1968; East Brunswick, N.J.: Book from India, 1986);

Album of Indian Paintings (New Delhi: National Book Trust, India, 1973);

Between Tears and Laughter (New Delhi: Sterling, 1973);

Folk Tales of Punjab (New Delhi: Sterling, 1974);

Confession of a Lover (New Delhi: Arnold-Heinemann, 1976);

Selected Short Stories of Mulk Raj Anand, edited by M. K. Naik (New Delhi: Arnold-Heinemann, 1977);

Seven Little-Known Birds of the Inner Eye (Rutland, Vt.: Tuttle, 1978);

Conversations in Bloomsbury (New Delhi: Arnold-Heinemann, 1981; London: Wildwood House, 1981);

The Bubble (New Delhi: Arnold-Heinemann, 1984; Liverpool: Lucas, 1988);

Little Plays of Mahatma Gandhi (New Delhi: Arnold, 1991).

OTHER: *Marx and Engels on India,* edited by Anand (Allahabad: Socialist Book Club, 1933).

Mulk Raj Anand, a renaissance man, was a novelist, essayist, critic, and thinker. M. K. Naik compares him to an "august and many-branched" banyan tree. The most dramatic moment in the early and sudden recognition of Anand as a novelist came with the publication of two novels, *Untouchable* (1933) and *The Coolie* (1936). *Untouchable* deals with the ignominious problem of caste and untouchability in Indian society and includes a preface by E. M. Forster. Noting Anand's power of sharp observation, objectivity, and directness, Forster remarks, "*Untouchable* could only have been written by an Indian, and by an Indian who observed

from the outside." Forster goes on to observe: "No European, however sympathetic, could have created the character of Bakha, because he would not have known about his troubles. And no Untouchable could have written the book, because he would have been involved in indignation and self-pity." Anand carries over this idea of human exploitation and social injustice in the characterization of Munoo in *The Coolie.* In a larger sense, *untouchable* and *coolie* are interrelated metaphors of universal human degradation, cruelty, and suffering. Anand further developed the metaphor of *coolie* and the sociopolitical issue of class structure in *Two Leaves and a Bud* (1937). Anand's first three novels, which appeared successively within a short period of three years, claimed for him the position of a progressive and unswerving advocate of the lower echelon of society—the oppressed, the victimized, and the dispossessed. In the four novels that followed, Anand persistently showed his preoccupation with man's inhumanity to man.

Anand's career can be divided into two stages: the Anand of the colonial period, who steadfastly critiqued class exploitation, the caste system, colonialism, imperialism, fascism, and racism; and the Anand of the postindependence era, who spread his energies and interests into several directions that became open with the new aspirations of India as a sovereign state. *The Village* trilogy—*The Village* (1939), *Across the Black Waters* (1940), and *The Sword and the Sickle* (1942)—deals with the three stages of growth of Lal Singh, a peasant's son, in the midst of the stormy struggle for India's independence and the various sociopolitical events that faced Europe in the 1930s and 1940s. Whereas *The Village* gives the reader the true picture of Indian village life, *Across the Black Waters* is a representation of Lal Singh's and his friends' experiences of fighting against the Germans in France during World War I. "Anand's achievement in the first two novels of the *Trilogy*," remarks Meenakshi Mukherjee, "has not been surpassed by an Indo-Anglian novelist." The first and only fictional account of the use of Indian troops in World War I, it raises the moral issue of the deployment of Indian troops in a British war. But *The Sword and the Sickle* (the title suggested by George Orwell from one of William Blake's poems) is literally and metaphorically a dramatization between the "sword" (the landlords) and the "sickle" (the peasants). Widely acclaimed as a successful novel, *The Big Heart* (1944) is a dramatic enactment of the conflict between the machine and laborers, the laborers in this case from the community of *thathiars* (coppersmiths), who are threatened with displacement from their hereditary profession. *The Big Heart* also replicates the fierce conflict that took place in Europe between modernity and tradition.

These seven novels of the pre-Independence era—all published in England—have given Anand a well-merited position as a successful and radical novelist. They provide a mirror image of Anand's active interest in the nationalist movement; his understanding of India's social and political problems; his opposition to colonialism, imperialism, and fascism; his uncompromising sympathies with the lowest part of humanity; and his analysis of all forms of social injustice and dehumanization. They also reflect the formation of the early Anand and the evolution of his personality during the pre-Independence era.

Born 12 December 1905 in Peshawar to a Kshatriya family—the second highest caste in the Hindu caste system—Anand was educated mostly in cantonment schools and later at Khalsa College, Amritsar (Punjab University). Anand's father, Lal Chand, began life as a coppersmith but became a military clerk in the British Indian army. His mother, Ishvar Kaur, a peasant girl from a Sikh family, had a religious bent. Mulk Raj was the third of the five children born to the Anands. Anand graduated in 1924 from Punjab University with an honors degree in English and became deeply involved in the nationalist movement. A few important events of the Amritsar period (1921–1924) that left a permanent mark on Anand were his active participation in the Civil Disobedience movement, the death of his nine-year-old cousin Kaushalya, and his love for Yasmin, a married Muslim woman who ultimately committed suicide. Anand enrolled at the University of London in 1925 for a Ph.D. in philosophy under the supervision of G. Dawes Hicks, a famous Kantian. The twenty years Anand spent in England were ones of an impressive intellectual and professional blossoming. By the time he had completed his Ph.D. in 1935, he had developed intimate relationships with prominent English writers and critics. Anand's deep immersion in European intellectual thought and his direct involvement in English politics helped him to understand the British mind, especially in relation to its response to India's nationalistic aspirations. In *Conversations in Bloomsbury* (1981), Anand reproduced from his memory his conversations with writers such as T. S. Eliot, Forster, Leonard and Virginia Woolf, and Aldous Huxley regarding the fundamental issues of freedom and equality for the Calibans of the Empire. During his stay in England, Anand met the English intelligentsia of the Right and the Left. For example, critic Bonamy Dobree, who took great interest in Anand and helped him ungrudgingly, was a professed Tory. Herbert Read, who liked Anand's first important work, *Persian Paintings* (1930), and to whom the work was dedicated, was an anarchist. Dobree greatly admired Anand's essay on Sarojini Naidu included in *The Golden Breath: Studies in*

Front cover for the 1986 edition of Anand's 1933 novel, about India's lowest rung of society, people outside of the Hindu caste system, doomed to servitude (University of South Carolina Upstate Library)

Five Poets of the New India (1933). Read also admired *The Hindu View of Art* (1933), Anand's work that was written under the early influence of Ananda Coomaraswamy and Sarvepalli Radhakrishanan and carries an introductory essay by artist Eric Gill. The two essays "The Religio-Philosophical Hypothesis" and "The Aesthetic Hypothesis" clearly show young Anand's aesthetic sensibility and his early search for philosophical and aesthetic formulation of art based on the religio-philosophical view of the Indian aesthetic of *rasa, bhava,* and *ananda*. Some of Anand's expositions come fairly close to Coomaraswamy's argument, and Anand's philosophical training enabled him to look at history as philosophy of history and at art as philosophy of art.

The publication of *The Lost Child and Other Stories* (1934), Anand's first published work of fiction, was facilitated by Gill's generous efforts. The story "The Lost Child" focuses on the desires of a young boy who gets lost at a festival. (Anand eventually transformed the story into a successful movie, which he himself directed and which was produced by the government of India.) In his autobiographical essay *Apology for Heroism: An Essay in Search of Faith* (1946), Anand revealed that he had undergone a dramatic change between 1934 and 1946. He became greatly involved with the problems of the oppressed people of the world, especially the British working class, but closer to his heart were the poverty of the Indian masses and tyranny of the British in India. Two works that ensued from Anand's encounter with Marxism are *Marx and Engels on India* (1933) and *Letters on India* (1942). The latter was also based on Anand's own experience with the British colonial governance of India and reflects his strong commitment to India's freedom. In his review of *Letters on India,* Orwell defended Anand for his anti-British position, and Read also praised the book, but a few of Anand's English friends were not happy with the radical positions he took in it.

The *Apology for Heroism* is a lucid statement of Anand's social, political, and philosophical thought. His Marxism enabled him to see "not only the history of India but the whole history of human society in some sort of inter-connection." The work is also part of the history of ideas, European and Eastern, that had preoccupied Anand's mind and that enabled him to survive the troublesome and despairing 1930s, the "pink decade." Rejecting the ideas of disinterestedness and escapism in art and aloofness and alienation of the artist in society, Anand boldly embraced Percy Bysshe Shelley's idea of the poet as the "unacknowledged legislator of mankind." The function of art, according to Anand in *Apology for Heroism,* is not to escape from life and society but to communicate "the most intense vision of life." In the postscript to the work Anand clearly and forcefully defines his commitment to humanism based on the "world of values," but not divorced from the world of facts. Believing in the whole man and in his ability to reconstruct a new progressive social order, and admiring the humanity of Rabindranath Tagore, Mohandas Gandhi, and Radhakrishanan, Anand stresses the recognition of human dignity as a directional force in human relationships. He also stresses love, *karuna* (compassion), and *bhakti* (devotion) as central values in the transformation of human conduct and the development of higher consciousness as a basis for the search for the truth of human life. In attempting to strike a synthesis between the world of appearance, illusion, or maya and the world of reality, truth, beauty, and good, Anand concludes the postscript with words from the *Mahabharata* (A.D. 400): "Truth is always natural with the good–Truth is duty. Truth is penance–Everything rests on TRUTH."

Anand's humanism, especially with its central values of love, *karuna, bhakti,* and tenderness, has a spiri-

tual dimension, for it exceeds the structural limits of scientific humanism and combines the developments of head and heart. Anand's socialism, despite its roots in British liberalism and socialism, has a spiritual dimension: "socialism," Anand explains in *Apology for Heroism,* "implies a spiritual change which will evolve its own internal checks, its own standard of values and its own ideals." Significantly, Anand's humanism has tilted toward the depressed, the dispossessed, and the exploited. One might see in it his effort to achieve an eclectic synthesis of various ideologies of social reconstruction, including Marxism, socialism, and humanism. The impact of the Gandhian ideas of moral and social reconstruction can also be seen.

Anand's realism derives its basis from his humanism. His attempt to transfuse history, ideology, and value in his fiction does not in any sense mean a compromise with tradition, nor does it show any slippage in his commitment to revealing human ugliness and depravity. He has stated candidly that the rediscovery of Indian ideals is as meaningful as is the rediscovery of European traditions. In *Apology for Heroism,* Anand undertakes an intellectual analysis of the significant ideas in the two cultural traditions in an attempt to seek a broader basis for his conception of humanism. He rejects fascism, colonialism, imperialism, racism, war, and oppression and prefaces his own concept of humanism with universalism and Indian religious-metaphysical values. Anand's exposure to Western intellectual thought helped him also to see his own heritage somewhat critically and objectively.

Untouchable and *The Coolie* are novels in which the central characters typify suffering humanity. Whereas Bakha is an untouchable, an outcaste in the Hindu caste structure, Munoo, the coolie, and Gangu are laborers of the Kshatriya caste. The untouchables and coolies are poor and impuissant laborers who have unjustly been repressed and victimized by those in society who have the power to control and dominate them. As colonial subjects, Bakha and Gangu are doubly colonized, "slaves of slaves." Bakha's situation in *Untouchable* is much more complex than that of Munoo, because as an untouchable he is permanently denigrated to servitude and placed at the lowest possible rung of society by a tradition against which he cannot rebel. Although a Hindu, he has been placed outside the Hindu caste system. Like all untouchables, he is destined to clean human excrement and sweep dirt and litter from the homes of upper-caste Hindus and public places. Because of his occupation, he must not touch upper-caste Hindus for fear of defiling them. Indeed, no salvation exists for Bakha. That he would remain imprisoned because of a cruel tradition is at the heart of the tragedy. *Untouchable,* compact in structure and inspired by James Joyce's experiment in *Ulysses* (1922), as Naik and Marlene Fisher have noted, is a tragedy in the classic sense, with the exception that Bakha neither rebels nor resorts to incendiary action against social injustice and religious bigotry as classical tragic heroes do.

C. J. George has noted in *Mulk Raj Anand: His Art and Concerns* that Bakha's story is based on Anand's childhood friend, a sweeper boy of the same name, a point also supported by Anand's own essay "The Story of My Experiment with a White Lie." Lakha's three children—Bakha, Sohini, and Rakha—carry on the ancestral profession of cleaning up dung, but Rakha virtually lives in dung. The Brahmin priest's alleged attempt to make advances to Sohini, Bakha's visit to the temple and the alleged pollution of the temple, and the episode of "pollution by touch" all reveal the social and moral injustices of society. Bakha must announce "Posh, posh, sweeper is coming" whenever he is on the move. When Bakha is slapped on the face and his *jalebis* are thrown out, his realization is painfully authentic: "Untouchable! I am an untouchable." A young Brahmin priest accuses Bakha of polluting him but does not hesitate to touch Sohini. Bakha's self-reflective mood helps him to trace the sociohistoric origin of his ancestry to the peasant stock who because of the "serfdom of thousands of years" had changed their occupation. Bakha calmly reflects on the three possible alternatives offered for the eradication of servitude: the Gandhian path of wisdom, sympathy, forgiveness, and pacifism; the teachings of Christianity as interpreted by Colonel Hutchinson of the Salvation Army; and the boon of modern scientific and technological progress. Anand clearly sees the futility of all three positions. The message of Christ, for example, got intermingled with colonialism and imperialism. The assumption that the flush system will eradicate the evil of untouchability is as fanciful and misleading as the Gandhian discipline of self-abnegation and self-sacrifice.

Whereas Bakha is an innocent victim of the old Indian tradition of casteism, the fate of Munoo lies in the hands of the modernist forces—British colonial rule, the capitalistic attitudes of rich mill owners, and the snobbery of the Anglo-Indian community. *The Coolie* deals with the life of an orphan boy from a village in the Kangra Valley. The young boy runs away from abuse and poverty. (The story of the tragic loss of young Munoo's innocence to the world of experience is a common theme in Anand's works.) Leaving his ancestral village, Munoo comes to Sham Nagar and becomes a domestic servant in the house of Babu Nathu Ram. Munoo is beaten, abused, and humiliated. One night he escapes to Daulatpur to work in Seth Prabha Dyal's pickle factory. With the collapse of the bankrupt Seth, Munoo is able to make his way to Bombay, where he

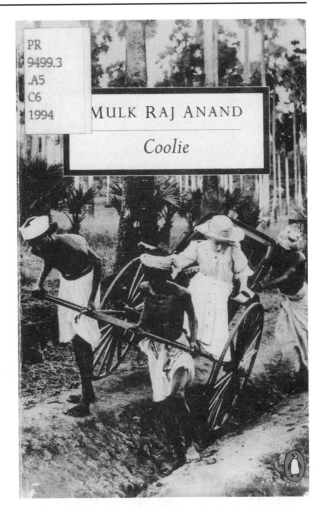

Front cover for the 1993 edition of Anand's 1936 novel about an orphan boy of the laboring caste (University of Missouri–Columbia Libraries)

joins the inhabitants of urban slums. Two important events that change the course of Munoo's life in Bombay are the labor strike in Sir George Cotton Mills and the outbreak of Hindu-Muslim disturbances. Munoo gets hurt in an automobile accident. An Anglo-Indian lady, Mrs. Mainwaring, brings him to Simla, where he works as a rickshaw puller.

Jack Lindsay has maintained that the last chapter, in which Munoo ends up in Simla, is not an integral part of the total structure of the book. While disagreeing with their criticisms about the last chapter of the book, Saros Cowasjee maintains that "it was right of Anand to retrieve his hero from the horrors of Bombay and to help him to regain his identity." Also, bringing Munoo to Simla is consistent with the total design of the book, for it allows Anand to complete his portrait of British India by focusing on the colonial center of power. The portrait of Mr. England is as significant as the portrayal of colonized and dehumanized Indians such as Babu Nathu Ram and the emaciated subaltern, Mrs. Mainwaring. Munoo ends his life, however, not in Simla, the summer capital of the government of India, but in the natural setting of the hills. The village of his birth, Sham Nagar; Daulatpur; Bombay; and Simla are stages in Munoo's journey through the hell of someone who cannot fight the power structures of society. The beautiful Simla Hills remind Munoo of his childhood home in the Kangra Valley, but nature, like society, is of little or no help other than facilitating the final release from life.

In *Two Leaves and a Bud,* Gangu, a peasant from the Punjab, migrates with his family to Assam to work as an indentured laborer on the Macpherson Tea Estate. The novel focuses on the treatment of plantation workers by their colonial masters, the owners of tea gardens. The plantation coolies lead a life of degrading poverty, wretchedness, misery, and despair. Their inhuman working conditions are morally debilitating; the plantation workers are not only poorly paid but also often abused, beaten, and forced to work unusually long hours. Each worker has been promised a piece of land for cultivation, but the plantation owner Reggie Hunt's lust for women must be satisfied to obtain this favor. John de la Havre, the medical officer, and Barbara, colonial official Croft-Cooke's daughter, are the only two humane voices that lament the merciless exploitation of Indian coolies by their compatriots.

The three volumes of the Lalu trilogy portray the life of Lal Singh, the youngest of Nihal Singh's six children. Nandpur, where *The Village* is set, reflects once again Anand's fascination with rural settings. The simplicity, naturalness, vividness, and authenticity of his portrayal of the village; the untainted realism and the long descriptive passages of the novel; and the simple and casual details offered are characteristic of ballad and folklore. "*The Village,*" remarks Alastair Niven, "is perhaps the most rounded portrait of village and rural life that the Indian novel in English offers us." Yet, Nandpur has its unsavory side and problems that are also typical of Indian village life. By placing Nandpur in the historical context of British India, Anand shows that the structure of village life and economy was directly threatened by colonization and modernization. Nihal Singh's poverty, like that of so many other farmers in Nandpur, allows moneylenders such as Chaman Lal to thrive in the village. The collusive role of Sardar Bahadur Harbans Singh is as repugnant as is that of villager Mahant Nandigar. Lalu rebels against religious customs and blind tradition, and the reader knows through Lalu Mahant's hypocrisy and lechery, Sardar's cruel and authoritarian ways, and the moneylender's rapaciousness and cunning. The peasants' lack of awareness of

the self-constricting and cruel tradition that has impeded social progress is also revealing. Finally, Lalu's affection for Maya forces the landlord to file a false charge of theft against him and forces him to escape by joining the army. In the British Indian Army, Lalu gets the affections of Kirpu, Dhanoo, and Lachman Singh—all surrogate father figures. He receives the news of his own father's death on the eve of the Ferozepur Brigade's departure for the war in Europe.

In 1939 Anand married Kathleen Van Gelder, an actress. The following year *Across the Black Waters* was published. It does not have a conventional plot, but the narrative is carefully organized around a series of movements that takes place in France during World War I. In his review of the novel, Dobree observed that Anand's book was the only war book showing "Indian troops in France" but that it was not as "a description of war" that the book achieved its interest, "but as a revelation of what the average Sepoy felt and thought during that strange adventure." The book is not really about World War I but is an account of the feelings and perceptions of the war theater and of Europe by Lalu and other Indian soldiers. Dorothy Figuiera in an essay for *The Indian Imagination* notes Anand's strategy of reversal; instead of a European experiencing the exoticism of the colonial "Other," the Asian subject experiences the exoticism of the European Other. Anand's remarkable strategy of placing Indian soldiers, the simple unsophisticated peasants from the Punjab, in their colonial masters' homeland enables them to see the drama of violent savagery and the meaning and purpose of war, death, and destruction. The Indian soldiers are greatly impressed by the manners and the ideas of the French people. These mercenary Indian soldiers—ill trained, ill equipped, and ill paid, especially when compared to their British counterparts—serve for the most part as cannon fodder. Anand, as Figuiera observes, indicts "the British High Command's incompetence and questions the morality of Indian troops to fight a British war." Anand's main point is that India's right to participate in a global war should be decided not by the colonial regime but by Indians.

Lalu is wounded and taken prisoner by the Germans. He then returns to India to become a revolutionary in *The Sword and the Sickle.* Lalu's hope of being rewarded by the British government for his service in the war is dashed. He finds that his mother is dead and that the family house has been auctioned. Professor Verma recruits him to work as an organizer of peasants. Thus, Lalu and his beloved Maya leave Punjab for Rajgarh, the new locale of the novel. *The Sword and the Sickle* is a sociopolitical novel and combines two major concerns: the social problem of the eviction of peasants by landlords and the political problem of national freedom. Anand's interest in Indian peasantry owes much to Leo Tolstoy, Gandhi, and Jawaharlal Nehru. The novel received laudatory reviews in England from such critics as Orwell. By presenting through Lalu's experience some of the major political ideologies of revolution and social reconstruction–communism, socialism, and Gandhian thought–Anand depicted the various options of bringing about change. With his expanded consciousness, Lalu understands "the need to curb malice, the need for men to stand together as brothers."

The Big Heart shows Anand's effort to portray the conflict between tradition and modernity, and the laborer and the machine. His greatest triumph in the novel is the creation of the tragic figure of Ananta, a coppersmith who is accidentally killed by Ralia, another coppersmith, who, because he is unemployed, is wrecking the machines. The conflict between the two groups of the coppersmith community in Amritsar, the ironmongers who represent the machine and the voice of modernity, and the *thathiars,* the workers who represent tradition, is at the center of the plot. At another level, one finds out that wealth divides the *thathiar* community of the same Kshatriya caste into adversarial classes. Thus, in the class war the socioeconomic category of class gets interchanged with the socioreligious category of caste. Anand's main point in the novel is that in the worker-owner relationship, industrialization without humanistic values represents profitability, greed, and exploitation. One can blame the machine or Ralia for Ananta's death, but Anand the novelist philosophizes about Ananta's death. The philosopher-poet Puran Singh explains to Janki on the eve of Ananta's death the nature of change and social progress: the old order must die in order to make room for the new. (The figure of the poet is a recurring figure in Anand's novels, starting with *Untouchable* and continuing to *The Big Heart.*) The poet's discourse on death, change, and progress is intended to provide some solace to Janki; but in a larger sense Ananta and the poet are two convergent voices of Anand himself. While the poet emphasizes the need for love, compassion, and *bhakti* as a basis for ideal brotherhood, Ananta stands not only for the machine and progress but also for the "big heart."

The critical debate about Anand's achievement as a novelist in the postindependence period is focused on the assumption that independent India would have offered Anand the opportunity to develop new aspirations for his vision and art. Anand returned from England as a well-established writer, but the dissolution of the colonial fantasy did not in any way impede his progress as a novelist. With the dissolution of the British Empire, Anand did not suddenly become bereft of

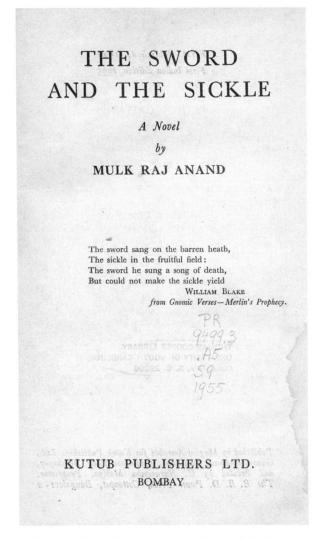

THE SWORD AND THE SICKLE

A Novel

by

MULK RAJ ANAND

The sword sang on the barren heath,
The sickle in the fruitful field:
The sword he sung a song of death,
But could not make the sickle yield
WILLIAM BLAKE
from Gnomic Verses—Merlin's Prophecy.

KUTUB PUBLISHERS LTD.
BOMBAY

Title page for the 1955 edition of Anand's 1942 novel, the third in the Village trilogy, about the stages of growth of Lal Singh, a peasant, *during India's struggle for independence (Thomas Cooper Library, University of South Carolina)*

subject matter for his novels. After India's independence from colonial subjugation, Anand seized the opportunity to reflect on the psychohistorical formation of himself in an attempt to achieve self-consciousness. The mature Anand was a philosopher and historian of culture, but he did not compromise with institutions of social injustice, oppression, and subjugation. He continued his search for a just humanistic order. Anand's "self-search" led to the exploration of the historical and psychological processes that went into the making of himself as a man and as a novelist.

Anand's novel *Private Life of an Indian Prince* (1953) is a dramatic departure from the subject of untouchables, coolies, and peasants, and yet the theme is similar, for Maharaja Ashok Kumar is also a victim. Cowasjee maintains that this novel is Anand's "most

Anand with his unpublished manuscripts, 2000 (www.man-mela.dircon.co.uk/mulkvisitcontent.htm)

impressive work." It has some similarities with Manohar Malgonkar's *The Princes* (1963).

In 1948 Anand and Kathleen divorced. In 1949 he married Shirin Vajifdar, a classical dancer. A few years later, he began a projected seven-novel series.

The novels of the *Seven Ages of Man* series have shown distinct and enduring vitality. Of the projected seven novels, Anand completed four: *Seven Summers* (1951), *Morning Face* (1968), *Confession of a Lover* (1976), and *The Bubble* (1984). He also wrote *Little Plays of Mahatma Gandhi* (1991), the first part of the seven-part volume *And So He Plays His Part*. The remaining two novels were to be "The World Too Large, a World Too Wide" and "Last Scene." In the autobiographical novels of The Seven Ages series, Anand has used memory as a powerful tool for re-creating pictures and images of his own life.

The Seven Ages series is particularly memorable for Anand's creation of Krishan Chander. The treatment of his hero's childhood combines the romantic notion of innocence and experience. The *TLS* reviewer of *Seven Summers* describes Krishan Chander "as a Freudian baby [that] was never born in English fiction of the twenties and thirties." This Freudian characterization of Krishan Chander is more fully developed in

Morning Face, a work in which Anand, influenced by Samuel Butler and George Bernard Shaw, explores fictively the relationship between his father and his family. A proper grasp of Krishan Chander's relationship with his family, especially his father, calls for a grasp of history, psychobiography, and psychoanalysis. Anand has subverted the Krishna myth in the novel, since Krishan Chander is not the Krishna of Hindu mythology but a human Krishna, a hero/antihero. However, his affinity with the mythical Krishna gives Krishan Chander a playfulness, vigor, and freedom not enjoyed by a Butlerian or a Joycean figure. The young Krishan's unreserved involvement with women and his growth as a radical nationalist are further developed in *Confession of a Lover*. During his four years of study at Khalsa College, Amritsar, the young Krishan Chander develops a strong interest in Gandhian ideas, nationalist politics, and poetry. Two notable influences on Krishan are poet Allama Iqbal, who inspires him to write poetry, and Professor Henry, who introduces him to Indian metaphysics. The most painful and probably the most tragic part of the narrative is Krishan's love for Yasmin, who becomes pregnant with his child but dies.

Although the novel *Morning Face* won Anand the prestigious Sahitya Akademy Award, *The Bubble*, the last volume that Anand completed in the proposed series, has been regarded as a greater work. D. Riemenschneider, for example, maintains that *The Bubble* "is perhaps the most ambitious book Anand has written so far because it tells us so much about the author himself." *The Bubble* deals with Krishan Chander's stay in England, his pursuit of a Ph.D. in philosophy, his love affairs, his quest for identity, and his search for the meaning of life. He confronts his own past, examines the sources of his emotional and ideological transformation, assesses the basis of his political thought, seeks validity for his philosophy of humanism, and attempts to redefine his philosophy of art in the larger context of the East-West synthesis. As a young artist in the making, he comes in contact with the important writers of the 1930s. Thus, *Conversations in Bloomsbury* is partly an expanded version of some of the ideas underlying the narrative of *The Bubble*. The two works together show Anand's great disillusionment with those English intellectuals who no doubt championed the cause of liberty but did not support the struggle for Indian freedom. Anand's essay *Apology for Heroism* directly deals with his search for truth and the formation of his intellectual thinking.

Conversations in Bloomsbury is one of the most original and imaginative works in the history of Indian writing in English. It has a complicated structure including confrontations, valuations, and representations of issues of ideology, culture, art, and history. Anand combined in it two perspectives: that of the 1930s, which represents the colonized mind, and that of the 1980s, which stands for the postcolonial mind. The perspective of the 1980s also serves as an intellectualizing principle in his imaginative re-creation of the opinions and attitudes of the Bloomsbury intellectual elite. Anand devotes four chapters to Eliot and focuses on Indian art, religion and metaphysics, and European literary and cultural traditions against the background of Eliot's conversion to royalism, classicism, and Catholicism. In the dialogue with Forster and Leonard Woolf, Anand introduces the metaphor of Caliban for Gandhi. The Prospero-Caliban analogy clearly defines the sociohistorical and sociopolitical contexts of India's struggle for independence. Despite their avowed liberalism, Forster and Woolf do not openly and unreservedly endorse the cause of Indian freedom. At the center of the text of *Conversations in Bloomsbury* is the urbane and civilized discourse in which Anand takes the role of a bold inquirer after truth who hopes that art, ideology, and consciousness can be unified at some point to create a more enduring vision of humanity.

In *Little Plays of Mahatma Gandhi*, Anand presents the portrait of the Mahatma as a saint and a politician. Krishan's ego, his intellectual elitism, is dramatically deflated by the Gandhian moral process of physical labor, of cleaning the latrines.

To assess the career of Anand completely, one must take into account his work as a critic of the arts, especially his work as editor (1945–1981) of the famous elitist journal *Marg* and as chairman (1963–1968) of the Lalit Kala Akademi. Early in this part of his career, Anand came under the influence of Coomaraswamy, Gill, and Read, but later he redefined his aesthetic formulations and was influenced by John Ruskin and William Morris. Following Morris, Anand went to his own ancestors, the *thathiars*—coppersmiths and silversmiths—to affirm that art belonged to the common man and the masses.

Until his death on 28 September 2004, Mulk Raj Anand continued to write tirelessly in a desperate attempt to complete the remaining two volumes in the Seven Ages series. He was also actively engaged in welfare work, even in his nineties. To the end, he remained committed to humanistic ideals of social reconstruction, although in the last phases of his life he placed more emphasis on the development of human consciousness. As he said in an interview with Kamal D. Verma: "The struggle for freedom by each individual is the only way by which the struggle to live a possible existence of calmness may fructify. . . . The struggle for higher consciousness is the only possible way for the good life." This philosophical conception of consciousness remains at the heart of Anand's work and art and makes them distinctive. Anand has staked a claim in Indian writing not only as one of India's leading novelists in the English language but also as a philosopher of culture who, with his expanded consciousness, looks upon history, time, reality, art, and culture as a unified whole.

Interview:

Kamal D. Verma, "An Interview with Mulk Raj Anand," *South Asian Review,* Anand special number, 15 (1991): 31–38.

Letters:

Author to Critic: The Letters of Mulk Raj Anand to Saros Cowasjee, edited by Saros Cowasjee (Calcutta: Writers Workshop, 1973).

References:

Mulk Raj Anand, "The Story of My Experience with a White Lie," *Critical Essays on Indian Writing in English,* second revised edition, edited by M. K. Naik, S. K. Desai, and G. S. Amur (Madras: Macmillan, 1972), pp. 4–18;

G. S. Balarama Gupta, *Mulk Raj Anand: A Study of His Fiction in Humanist Perspective* (Bareilly: Parkash Book Depot, 1974);

Margaret Berry, *Mulk Raj Anand: The Man and the Novelist* (Amsterdam: Oriental Press, 1971);

Saros Cowasjee, *The Coolie: An Assessment* (New Delhi: Oxford University Press, 1976);

Cowasjee, *So Many Freedoms: A Study of the Major Fiction of Mulk Raj Anand* (New Delhi: Oxford University Press, 1977);

R. K. Dhawan, ed., *The Novels of Mulk Raj Anand* (New Delhi: Prestige, 1992);

Marlene Fisher, *The Wisdom of the Heart: A Study of the Works of Mulk Raj Anand* (New Delhi: Sterling, 1985);

C. J. George, *Mulk Raj Anand, His Art and Concerns* (New Delhi: Atlantic, 1994);

S. C. Harrex, "Western Ideology and Eastern Forms of Fiction: The Case of Mulk Raj Anand," in *Asian and Western Writers in Dialogue: New Cultural Identities,* edited by Guy Amirthanayagam (New Delhi: Macmillan, 1996), pp. 142–158;

K. R. Srinivasa Iyengar, *Indian Writing in English,* fifth edition (New Delhi: Sterling, 1985);

Jack Lindsay, *The Elephant and the Lotus: A Study of the Novels of Mulk Raj Anand,* second revised edition (Bombay: Kutub-Popular, 1965);

Meenakshi Mukherjee, *The Twice Born Fiction: Themes and Techniques of the Indian Novel in English,* second edition (New Delhi: Arnold-Heinemann India, 1973);

M. K. Naik, *Mulk Raj Anand* (New York: Humanities Press, 1973);

Alastair Niven, *The Yoke of Pity: A Study in the Fictional Writing of Mulk Raj Anand* (New Delhi: Arnold-Heinemann India, 1978);

Premila Paul, *The Novels of Mulk Raj Anand* (New Delhi: Sterling, 1983);

T. Prabhakar, ed., *The Indian Novel in English: Evaluations* (New Delhi: Phoenix, 1995);

P. K. Rajan, *Studies in Mulk Raj Anand* (New Delhi: Abhinav, 1986);

D. Riemenschneider, *An Ideal Man in Anand's Novels* (Bombay: Kutub-Popular, 1967);

Kamal D. Verma, *The Indian Imagination: Critical Essays on Indian Writing in English* (New York: St. Martin's Press, 2000).

Sujata Bhatt

(6 May 1956 –   )

Premila Paul
American College, Madurai

BOOKS: *Brunizem* (Manchester: Carcanet, 1988; New Delhi: Penguin, 1993);
Monkey Shadows (Manchester: Carcanet, 1991);
Freak Waves: Poems (Victoria, B.C.: Hawthorne Society/ Reference West, 1992);
The Stinking Rose (Manchester: Carcanet, 1995);
Point No Point: Selected Poems (Manchester: Carcanet, 1997);
Augatora (Manchester: Carcanet, 2000); republished as *My Mother's Way of Wearing a Sari* (New Delhi & London: Penguin, 2000);
A Colour for Solitude (Manchester: Carcanet, 2002);
Pure Lizard (Manchester: Carcanet, 2006).

SELECTED PERIODICAL PUBLICATIONS–UNCOLLECTED: "From Gujarat to Connecticut to Bremen," *Skript,* 2 (1988): 7;
"'The Hole in the Wind' from the Author's Point of View," *Connotations,* 10, no. 1 (2000–2001): 99–104.

Sujata Bhatt (photograph by Jutta Golda; from the cover of Brunizem, *1988; Bruccoli Clark Layman Archives)*

Sujata Bhatt is a significant poet of the Indian diaspora who makes sensitive use of her experiences on three continents in her multicultural poetry. She is proud of the different cultures in her background and the plural perspectives that such a situation grants. Bhatt's poetry reflects her ability to convert difficulties into opportunities and to make a home wherever she is.

Born on 6 May 1956 in Ahmedabad, in the Indian state of Gujarat, Bhatt spent her earliest years in New Orleans and in Pune, in the state of Maharashtra, where her father worked in the field of virology. Her paternal grandfather and two maternal uncles are well-respected writers in the Gujarati language. Her father, Pravin N. Bhatt, was a virologist who did postgraduate work in public health and tropical medicine at Tulane University and also studied Ayurvedic medicine (a traditional Indian medical practice) with deep interest. His pioneering work in India in virology and tissue culture led to his being invited to join the comparative-medicine program at Yale University. The family moved to New Haven permanently when Sujata was twelve. Her mother, Indu Pathak Bhatt, had a degree in economics and history. She had also studied Sanskrit, Gujarati, and English literature and worked at Yale as a research assistant. The family was able to make a successful life in the United States without disowning their Indian roots.

At Goucher College in Baltimore, Bhatt initially concentrated on premedical studies but switched majors to earn a B.A. in literature and philosophy in 1980. She received the impetus to continue writing poetry (which she had done since she was eight) from her former professor, the poet Eleanor Wilner, to whom she has dedicated some of her verse. Wilner has continued to exert a great influence on her literary career. Bhatt went on to earn an M.F.A. from the University of Iowa Writers' Workshop in 1986. Here she met the German writer and artist Michael Augustin, who became her husband in 1988. Their daughter, Jenny Mira Swantje, was born on 1 February 1990. The family now lives in Bremen, Germany. Augustin, who is an editor and producer with Radio Bremen, has been supportive of his wife's literary career, contributing illustrations to her poetry collection *Augatora* (2000). Bhatt has worked in the United States and in Canada, where she was the Lansdowne Visiting Writer at the University of Victoria in spring 1992.

Bhatt considers herself an Indian writer who lives outside India. Otherwise, she believes that any further discussions of her identity are futile, for her inner life is complex and private. She does not, however, complain about being uprooted because she can take root anywhere. This ability has given her the refreshing realization that home is not a geographical location but a state of mind. Bhatt has more than one home to miss and more than one to which she can return. In the essay "From Gujarat to Connecticut to Bremen" (1988) she writes, "I feel homesick for both United States and India. . . . I now feel so attached to both the East and the West that I believe I cannot do without either culture."

Bhatt wrote the poems in *Brunizem* (1988) in her twenties, and she refers to the collection as the work of ten years. The volume brought her the 1988 Alice Hunt Bartlett Award and the 1989 Dillons Commonwealth Poetry Prize. Inspired mainly by Bhatt's Indian childhood, *Brunizem* is dedicated to her brother and to the memory of her paternal grandfather. The title of the volume suggests the coexistence of the three worlds in her consciousness: *brunizem,* a word coined from French and Russian elements, refers to the dark brown prairie soil that can be found in Asia, North America, and Europe. Her identity has been forged by her Indian childhood, American education, and European marriage.

Brunizem has three sections: "The First Disciple," "A Different History," and "Eurydice." The landscape depicted in the poems is Gujarat at its vibrant best; the verses are full of sensuous images and childhood memories. In "Go to Ahmedabad," Bhatt recalls and reviews life in that city, her sensitivity toward the sick and the hungry intact. Poems such as "For My Grandmother" and "For Nanabhai Bhatt" reveal her closeness to her grandparents and their association with Mohandas Karamchand Gandhi. "Nachiketa" concerns, among other things, the premature birth of Bhatt's brother. "The Garlic of Truth" brings back the warm memory of her mother's pouring herbal oil carefully prepared with garlic pulp, mustard, and fenugreek seeds into her

ears. *Brunizem* includes poems on growing up and on the awakening of sexuality. "Udaylee" deals with a young woman's experience of being an untouchable when she is menstruating in a room next to a cowshed.

Bhatt's Indian response to life is evident in "Reincarnation," in which the focus is not on the new form of life assumed but on the memory of the old form. In "A Different History" she suggests that gods roam freely, disguised as snakes or monkeys. In Bhatt's writing, animals—small and large, domestic and wild—are as important as human beings. Lizards with tails intact or severed, buffalo in muddy ponds, and a rhinoceros in a Delhi zoo all find their way into her poetry. To her, nature and animals are a part of the human world.

Bhatt does not use poetry as a means of social protest. Her political awareness, however, is evident in poems such as "3 November 1984," about the tragic massacre of Sikhs that was triggered by the assassination of Indira Gandhi. "Written after Hearing about the Soviet Invasion of Afghanistan" records Bhatt's despair and helplessness at distant political events that affected her deeply.

Bhatt revels in the luxury of place-names and languages, and she boldly uses words such as *muliebrity* and *brunizem*. Apart from the lavish use of Gujarati words, she employs the Devanagari script as well. In "Search for My Tongue" she voices the recognition that some sounds cannot be recalled in English words, such as her mother's singing in the kitchen or the voice of a girl at the railway station. On the one hand, the poem expresses the struggle of an immigrant trying to regain the lost tongue, "slippery like the lizard's tail," but on the other, it demonstrates and celebrates Bhatt's multilingualism. In "The Undertow" she recognizes that there are three languages separating her from her lover, but she is certain they understand each other well. She points out in "Marie Curie to Her Husband" that Curie, who continued her husband's work in France and lectured at the Sorbonne, had to count in Polish. "A Different History" shows how grandchildren learned to love the strange English language seen by their ancestors as the oppressor's tongue. Such a language turns out to be an apolitical tool of communication for their generation.

Monkey Shadows (1991) received the Cholmondeley Award and was a Poetry Book Society Recommendation for 1991. The forty-three poems in the collection are arranged in three sections, "The Way to Maninagar," "Angels' Wings," and "Until Our Bones Prevent Us from Going Further." The volume deals with a lesser range of subjects than does

Brunizem, but the depth of treatment of the subjects and the intensity of tone indicate a definite growth in Bhatt's poetry. The verses show a lively interaction between cultures, animals, and humans. The presence of animals shows Bhatt's enduring interest in them, particularly in monkeys and elephants. In "Maninagar Days" she focuses on rhesus monkeys that travel in small groups. Their extended families have feuding brothers, sisters, uncles, aunts, and cousins screaming through the trees, but they always manage "to make peace before every meal." The poet is fascinated by the monkeys' relationship and interaction with humans, particularly children. Monkeys are as "normal and common as dogs," but children do not play with them, seeing them as "children newly arrived from a foreign country unable to speak their language yet." The children see the perfect monkey in a solitary Hanuman langur, who crosses the terrace "with the importance of someone going to the airport." "The Stare" presents a child and a young monkey engaged in nonverbal interaction. The poet perceives a purity and transparence in their innocent gazes, which are free of fear and arrogance.

Bhatt received a childhood connection to elephants through stories she was told. The elephant's mythological association keeps it apart from everyday life. "A Different Way to Dance" is based on the story of the Hindu god Shiva's severing the head of Ganesha, his son, and replacing it with an elephant's head. While driving from Boston, the poet's mother draws her attention to a large elephant chained to a truck. The poet is unable to catch the expression in the eyes of the chained animal, and she imagines the untold aspects of the story of Ganesha. His mother, Parvati, dreams of her son's original human face and what his life might have been like, while the elephant's head dreams of what life might have been like in the jungle among the other elephants. The poet pictures Ganesha's new form, the way he coordinates his tusk and trunk on human knees, and the way his elephant ears guide his human toes.

"What Happened to the Elephant?" is a corollary to "A Different Way to Dance" in which Bhatt adds more details to the story of Ganesha. She points out Shiva's inability to find a nonviolent solution to problems and his meddling with the identity of Ganesha. The newly forged identity of Ganesha, with the coordination of animal and human parts, does not take the carcass of the elephant into account. Nothing is said about the possibility of the elephant body's coming to life or the fate of Ganesha's human head. "What Happened to the Elephant?" raises the question of whether identity lies in the head or the body. A child listening to the story of Ganesha senses the

Front cover for Bhatt's 1988 poetry collection, her first book, which won the Alice Hunt Bartlett Award and the Dillons Commonwealth Poetry Prize (Bruccoli Clark Layman Archives)

callousness of Shiva, who does nothing to set right the life of the elephant. The child's imagination completes the story by making the elephant herd perform the ritual dance of mourning, circling around the headless carcass in a "slow swaying sadness."

Living in Germany has led Blatt to explore the history and culture of that country and other parts of Europe. "Mozartstrasse 18" presents the trauma of Adolf Hitler's Germany. In "Wine from Bordeaux" an eighteen-year-old boy is convinced that his chromosomes have been damaged; he has himself sterilized so that he will not pass on "mistakes" to the next generation. Bhatt's diasporic sensibility is expressed in "Distances," which deals ironically with closeness and accessibility. The ocean in Conil brings her the message that Africa and America are not necessarily continents far apart but could be lands related through waves. The wind and fish could carry messages back and forth. The ocean seems to lie trapped on the page in an atlas, like "a gasping beached whale," but its restlessness helps it to reach out to different continents. Boundaries invite crossing, and enclosures call for breaking.

The Stinking Rose (1995) has five sections: "Freak Waves," "New World Dialogues," "The Stinking Rose," "Old World Blood," and "Riyaj." "Freak Waves" was written during Bhatt's six-month stay at the University of Victoria. Some of the poems in this section explore the myths of the indigenous Haida people of British Columbia. The stinking rose is another name for garlic, which has always fascinated Bhatt. The pungent quality of garlic and its prominence in her childhood account for references to the herb in the titles of many of her poems. Bhatt performed considerable research on garlic and discussed its cultural and mythological associations with the artist Rolf Wienbeck, who contributed illustrations of garlic to *The Stinking Rose.*

"Fate," dedicated to the memory of the poet A. K. Ramanujan, concerns Bhatt's sudden craving for Ramanujan's words; she was engaged in rereading his books in a great rush, unaware that at the time he lay dying in a hospital. The words of Bhatt's mentor, Wilner, open her ruminations of home in "The One Who Goes Away." Bhatt derives strength and sustenance from a home that is always within her: "We weren't allowed to take much / but I managed to hide / my home behind my heart." She is realistic and knows that she cannot retrace her steps to the past or find her first home in the same state that she left it. Her home is therefore not geographically defined or bound. The first departure, accompanied by ceremonies of throwing coconuts into the sea to seek divine blessings, is just the beginning of many more departures and blessings. In another poem Bhatt raises the question "How far east is still east? / And how far west is it still west?" The image of the sea with its changing boundaries becomes the metaphor for the diasporic self of the poet.

In demonstrating that language and food have the ability to defy and cross boundaries, Bhatt resorts to multilingual expression, a method tested and put to use in her earlier volumes. A word becomes an idea, and it is hard to separate the two. Some of her ideas live in her in Gujarati; therefore, the diction and script of the language find their way into her English-language poems. Sometimes Bhatt translates the words, but in other cases the reader is left to conjecture the meaning from the context.

Point No Point: Selected Poems (1997) is a collection of eighty-two of Bhatt's poems from her first three volumes. The title poem is the only new work. Her

2000 collection, *Augatora,* published in India as *My Mother's Way of Wearing a Sari,* was a Poetry Book Society Recommendation and won the Italian Tratti Poetry Prize. The volume is divided into five sections: "Augatora," "History Is a Broken Narrative," "The Hole in the Wind," "The Found Angel: Nine Poems for Ria Eïng," and "Ars Poetica." The cover illustration is a collage by her daughter, Jenny Mira, and her husband, Augustin. The Old High German term *augatora* (eye gate) assumes rich connotations and offers different frames for the perception of life. Bhatt sees a close relationship between the words *window* and *wind,* leading her to *augatora.* She revives a word lost from language to open possibilities for the entry of new cultures and new environments and to reconnect the present with the past.

Memory plays a key role in the bid for interconnection and communion in Bhatt's poetry. *Augatora* includes many memory poems dealing with family relationships. "History Is a Broken Narrative" is a significant memory poem in which the title becomes the refrain. Memory of home brings together images of India and the United States, the lands of her childhood. In New Orleans, at the age of five, Bhatt learned "a whole new alphabet to go with the new world," and in the afternoons her mother refreshed her knowledge of the old alphabet.

Bhatt's concern for the underprivileged and disadvantaged finds expression in several of the poems in *Augatora.* "The Found Angel" brings alive wartime Germany through the experience of an artist who as an infant was abandoned near a German concentration camp in 1945. "A Swimmer in New England Speaks" depicts a polio-stricken girl who refuses to succumb to her situation, hates wheelchairs, moves with crutches, is a strong swimmer, and even thinks of swimming with a boyfriend along with water snakes, until she actually manages to do so. "Voice of the Unwanted Girl" records the angry voice of an aborted female fetus—in formaldehyde—that has been denied entry into life.

"The Hole in the Wind," a poem commissioned by the South Bank Centre in London, forms the third section of *Augatora.* Bhatt was one of eight poets invited to read a fifteen-minute-long poem at the Royal Festival Hall. "The Hole in the Wind" was then read, recorded, and broadcast in 1995 as a BBC radio drama. The title suggests a window, a constantly shifting frame of perception. The poem has elements of different genres and defies classification. The subject is the life of the people on the long, thin, storm-ridden East Frisian Island of Juist, an island deceptively close to the German mainland. The North Sea frequently bites into the island and steals land, causing maps to go out of date. The poem is set in October, when the sea turns rough and sweeps away many people. The main narrative includes the stories of the dead, who narrate their lost lives. It also comments on the fate and conflicting superstitions of the people and on their insecurity because of the constant threat of nature. Human resilience reigns supreme, however, in the survival stories and narratives of loss presented in "The Hole in the Wind." The deft repetitions in the poem serve as refrains and echo the screams of the dead and the dying.

The poems in *A Colour for Solitude* (2002) were written mainly in the form of responses to various paintings by Paula Modersohn-Becker, whom Bhatt first learned about from Rainer Maria Rilke's poem "Requiem for a Friend" (1909). Bhatt had first seen Modersohn-Becker's paintings in the Kunsthalle Bremen in 1985. The experience was so intense that she recorded her reactions in poetry. "Clara Westhoff to Rainer Maria Rilke" and "For Paula Modersohn-Becker," from *Brunizem,* were republished in *A Colour for Solitude* as "No Road Leads to This" and "Was It the Blue Irises?" respectively. "Paula Modersohn Speaks to Herself," from *The Stinking Rose,* was republished as "Self-Portrait on My Fifth Wedding Anniversary" in *A Colour for Solitude.* Most of the poems in the 2002 volume are monologues or dialogues in the words of Modersohn-Becker or of her friend and fellow artist Clara Westhoff, who ended up marrying Rilke. Bhatt spent long hours in museums looking at all the available letters, journals, and manuscripts related to Modersohn-Becker. As she states in the author's note, "facts often free the imagination to probe deeper, to imagine things that otherwise could not have been imagined."

Bhatt admired Rilke as a poet, and she read almost everything he wrote, including his letters and journals. In the process she came to know of his fascination with Modersohn-Becker and his hasty marriage to Westhoff. In *A Colour for Solitude,* Modersohn-Becker and Westhoff appear and reappear like twin protagonists in a narrative, prompting readers to reconstruct the situations in the lives of these artists. The titles of the poems, specific references to the speaker and the addressee, and the author's note all help in this reconstruction. Bhatt uses the titles of Modersohn-Becker's self-portraits as poem titles in most cases. Because she feels that the urge to return to one's original identity is what prompts self-representation in art, she uses the maiden names of the women, Modersohn-Becker and Westhoff, to restore to them their lost identities as artists independent of the relationships that restricted them. The two women in the poems are attracted by Rilke but repulsed by his cal-

Front cover for the Indian edition of Sujata Bhatt's 2000 poetry collection, published in England as Augatora, *in which she explores family memories and expresses her concern for the underprivileged and disadvantaged (Bruccoli Clark Layman Archives)*

lousness. "A Colour for Solitude, PB to RMR" demonstrates the complex relationship between Modersohn-Becker and Rilke.

Modersohn-Becker's paintings displayed a compulsive need for self-representation, and her art became a means of self-assertion. In Bhatt's poems on her art, woman is at times presented as a victim in the hands of man and at other times as a triumphant artist. In "Self-Portrait with Scratches" the twenty-seven-year-old Modersohn-Becker has been reduced to the form of a fourteen-year-old girl, vulnerable and susceptible to hurts. Bhatt uses the image of an assaulted bird and terms such as "clawed," "pulled out," and "snapped off" to render the artist's experience. During Modersohn-Becker's short life she remained a great source of support for Westhoff, despite Rilke's resentment of their closeness. Many poems in *A*

Colour for Solitude, such as "Two Girls in a Landscape," "Two Girls: The Blind Sister," "A Red Rose in November," and "Don't Look at Me Like That," celebrate the value of sisterhood and seem by implication to suggest a sisterly relation between Modersohn-Becker and Westhoff. Bhatt's poems attempt to restore dignity and courage to both of these women and celebrate their art.

During the academic year 2003–2004, Bhatt was a visiting fellow at Dickinson College in Carlisle, Pennsylvania. Another poetry collection, *Pure Lizard,* was published by Carcanet Press in 2006.

Sujata Bhatt's poetry has been widely anthologized and has been translated into more than a dozen European languages as well as two Indian languages. Some of her work is included in the national curriculum in the United Kingdom. She is now considered a major Indian poet who has added a special dimension to diasporic literature. What is seen as displacement by other writers of the Indian diaspora is a rare blessing for her. Her ability to claim her rightful place on three continents adds vitality to her poetry. The sureness of belonging that characterizes Bhatt's consciousness denotes a difference in outlook worthy of celebration.

Interviews:

"Sujata Bhatt in Conversation with Eleanor Wilner," *PN Review,* 19, no. 4 (1993): 34–40;

"Sujata Bhatt in Interview with Cecile Sandten," *Kunapipi,* 21, no. 1 (1999): 110–118.

References:

Vara Neverow-Turk, "Sujata Bhatt," in *Writers of the Indian Diaspora: A Bio-Bibliographical Critical Sourcebook,* edited by Emmanuel S. Nelson (Westport, Conn.: Greenwood Press, 1993), pp. 23–27;

Supriya Sahasrabuddhe, "Indian Consciousness in Sujata Bhatt," *Poiesis,* 2, no. 1 (1993): 27–34;

Cecile Sandten, "Blended Identity: Culture and Language Variations in Sujata Bhatt's 'The Hole in the Wind,'" *Connotations,* 10, no. 1 (2000–2001): 87–98;

Sandten, "In Her Own Voice: Sujata Bhatt and the Aesthetic Articulation of the Diasporic Condition," *Journal of Commonwealth Literature,* 35, no. 1 (2000): 99–119.

Upamanyu Chatterjee

(19 December 1959 –   )

Murari Prasad
Sana'a University

BOOKS: *English, August: An Indian Story* (London: Faber & Faber, 1988; Calcutta: Rupa, 1989);
The Last Burden (London: Faber & Faber, 1993; New Delhi: Viking, 1993);
The Mammaries of the Welfare State (New Delhi & New York: Viking, 2000).

PRODUCED SCRIPTS: *English, August,* by Chatterjee and Dev Benegal, motion picture, Tropicfilm, 1994;
Split Wide Open, by Chatterjee and Farrukh Dhondy, motion picture, Tropicfilm, 1999.

SELECTED PERIODICAL PUBLICATIONS–
UNCOLLECTED: "The Assassination of Indira Gandhi," *London Magazine,* 25, no. 3 (June 1985): 5–17;
"Versus the Godman," *London Magazine,* 25, nos. 9–10 (December 1985 – January 1986): 11–23;
"Desolation, Lust," *London Magazine,* 26, no. 7 (October 1986): 5–26;
"The Killings in Madna," *Festival/The Statesman,* 1 (1991): 98–109.

Upamanyu Chatterjee (photograph by Shanker Chakravarty; The Hindu)

Upamanyu Chatterjee stands out prominently among the Indian writers of English-language fiction whose works appeared in the 1980s in the wake of Salman Rushdie's *Midnight's Children* (1981). *English, August: An Indian Story* (1988) made Chatterjee's reputation. His two other novels, critically acclaimed but not as well received by the public as *English, August,* are *The Last Burden* (1993) and *The Mammaries of the Welfare State* (2000). English-language Indian fiction after Rushdie has been characterized by fantasy, irreverent vocabulary, the confident cadences of Indian English, and sprightly comedy, as well as by subversive and iconoclastic ways of looking at the anarchic post-Independence milieu of India. Chatterjee's works, while representing some of the salient features of this new fiction, are distinctive. For a start, he has based his fiction substantially on his intimate experiences with the Indian Administrative Service (IAS), the civil service left behind by the English. The IAS is the central point around which most of Chatterjee's writing revolves. As a member of the Maharashtra State cadre of the IAS he has largely worked in Bombay, although he has also been posted with the Ministry of Human Resources Development of the union government in New Delhi.

Not much biographical information about Chatterjee is available. Vijay Nambisan, a well-known writer who interviewed him for *The Hindu* in 2001, described him as "weird" in several ways. Nambisan

Front cover for the 2002 Indian edition of Chatterjee's 1988 novel,
about a depressed and introverted civil servant from a privileged
background who is assigned to a post in a backward rural
district (Bruccoli Clark Layman Archives)

including a handful of short stories published in *The London Magazine* and *The Statesman* of Calcutta.

From the mid 1980s to the mid 1990s much new fiction in English coming out of India was written by St. Stephen's graduates who had finished their studies in the 1970s and early 1980s. Their works do not "hang together," as Trivedi would have it, either thematically or aesthetically, but these writers did share the same cultural moment in the exclusive ambience of this northern Indian counterpart of Cambridge University. Humor, a free and unself-conscious use of English, and witty forms of subversion are some of the common features of their works. Most of Chatterjee's characters, with their sheltered and privileged upbringing, colloquial chatter, fads, and jokes, as well as their relaxed attitudes, are traceable to the corridors and classrooms of St. Stephen's.

In Chatterjee's *London Magazine* debut, "The Assassination of Indira Gandhi" (1985), which was included in the first volume of the annual *Best Short Stories,* published by Heinemann in 1986, the young protagonist, Bunny Kairon, represents the malaise and quiet tumult of his generation. The brutal killing of the prime minister of India has shaken the country and triggered widespread violence. Bunny lies paralyzed, mirroring the chaos of his inner and outer worlds. As the corpse of Gandhi lies "remote and cold," Bunny finds the world a "wonderfully unstable place." Even as Manjeet, his brother-in-law, celebrates the event without feeling any guilt at what happened, Bunny feels empty, assailed by the all-pervasive uncertainties around him. He is alienated from his parents and his past and has no sustaining creed, nor is he capable of coming to terms with his vague, existential unease. He sinks into a delirious state following the news of the assassination, visualizing the "blood dyeing the sari and the collapsing, crumbling female form."

In another early story, "Versus the Godman" (1985), the central character, Gangadhar, frets away his time unproductively and despondently. He approaches life with a skeptical and antimetaphysical cast of mind, but he finds the world around him incomprehensible and delusive. The Godman of the title is a charlatan, but his tricks and revelations batter the defenses of Gangadhar's reason and expose him to a world beyond the limits of logic and method. He realizes that humans have no access to the universe of the unknown. The inherent inadequacy of reason forces people to capitulate to fear and accept the inexplicable in the name of faith. Despite his skepticism, Gangadhar keeps a rose given him by the Godman, "for some reason."

added, "Getting literary revelations out of him is like pulling teeth, and this is rare in these days when authors can be packaged and sold like toothpaste and often actively participate in selling." Chatterjee was born on 19 December 1959 in Patna, in the state of Bihar, and was educated at St. Xavier's School in Delhi. Like his contemporaries the writers Amitav Ghosh, Shashi Tharoor, and Allan Sealy, he went to St. Stephen's College in Delhi; attending the college from 1977 to 1980, he majored in English. After obtaining his master's degree in English literature from Delhi University in 1982, he taught at St. Stephen's for a year or so before joining the IAS in 1983. His former teacher and colleague at the college, Harish Trivedi, recalls that Chatterjee was "wonky, witty and silent enough to possibly be a novelist." To be sure, Chatterjee gave early intimations of his literary vocation, and he honed his craft by writing one-act plays for drama festivals at the college and occasional pieces of fiction,

The plot of "Desolation, Lust" (1986) centers on the lack of a meaningful sexual relationship between

Atri and Sheela. A civil servant like Chatterjee, Atri is a trainee in Bombay who has signed up for a job in which he is not interested. As a result, he is passive and quiescent. As love is a euphemism for him, he longs for happiness through lust, which he treats as a biological necessity or "like a part of one's metabolism." Like Bunny, Atri does not want to think; he prays for "the decline of all desire." Typical of his generation, he is plagued by an agonizing rootlessness, so much so that the stages of human existence–from birth to the petty adjustments of marriage to the breeding of children– annoy him. His character prefigures the protagonists in *English, August* and *The Last Burden.*

Faber and Faber published *English, August* in 1988 to positive reviews. Adam Lively declared in *Punch* (17 June 1988) that it "is a marvelously intelligent and entertaining novel, and especially fascinating for any-one curious about modern India." The narrative is built around the experiences of a depressed and intro-verted civil servant from a cosseted background in an imaginary Indian district town, Madna, contiguous to the states of Maharashtra and Andhra Pradesh. Many readers have found the protagonist, Agastya Sen, to be like Chatterjee himself. On an *India Today* talk show (7 December 2000) Chatterjee reacted to readers' percep-tions: ". . . some of it is certainly my own experience, and there is a large part that has been inspired by the things that I have been told, read about etc." In other words, the book is not an exact account of the author's life; he merges his own experience with things he heard or saw in the service, and he looks on the insou-ciant civil servant with irony and affection.

The "August" of the title is an Anglicized corrup-tion of and nickname for Agastya, who comes from an elite background. His upbringing and education have Anglicized him, and he has become partial to sex, alco-hol, and marijuana. Madna, which represents an Indian small town of the 1980s, is unfamiliar to him. Rukun Advani, Chatterjee's fellow St. Stephen's alum-nus and the author of *Beethoven among the Cows* (1994), observes, "Chatterjee's protagonist thinks and speaks the language of St. Stephen's. He is quintessentially the Stephanian graduate extricating himself from the exis-tential dilemmas that made thinking people clench their teeth when faced with the dreariness and mind-lessness of the Indian bureaucracy." In a 1993 inter-view with W. B. Prathima, Chatterjee noted that the book is "about the education of this young twerp from a very urban background." Agastya, as his nickname suggests, is an "English type," eternally bored and indifferent to the realities of Madna. He is out of place amid the illiterate masses and tribals living at the back of beyond. His fellow civil servants, Srivastav, the Madna collector; Kumar, superintendent of police; and

the junior functionaries are pompous, smug, and steeped in the survival strategies of administration. They cling to the privileges and rewards of office while people at the receiving end of the system suffer from deprivation.

Instead of trying to fit into the system, Agastya retreats into a private world of erotic fantasy and mari-juana. His father, also a bureaucrat and now the gover-nor of a state, warns him against taking the "softer options" in life. In order to overcome his restlessness and rise to the occasion, the trainee civil servant reads the *Bhagavadgita* and Marcus Aurelius's *Meditations,* but he fails to arrive at a firm resolution. This inability to find meaning in life seems to be a malaise affecting Agastya's friend Dhrubo, too, despite his well-paying job with an American bank.

Agastya appears to be close to changing his mind-set after a visit to Chipanthi, a drought-stricken tribal village, where he is moved by the plight of hap-less women and children facing an acute shortage of water. For a while he is "recklessly honest" in securing the compliance of his subordinates and in ensuring the supply of water to the villagers. When asked by Pra-thima if Agastya's involvement with the life-affirming medium of water is the turning point in his life, Chat-terjee observed, "The whole water issue is his first out-ward movement. But not in a dramatic way; it is just the hint of looking outward. Even though he is longing to be self-absorbed, events in themselves can pull a per-son out." Agastya slides back into despair, however, and quits Madna.

Chatterjee's narrative mode, Geeta Doctor opined in a review of *English, August* in *Literature Alive* (December 1989), allows for "the careful accumulation of details that produce a powerful image of Madna," which is representative of placid, small-town India. Agastya is a prisoner of frivolous inanities. Meenakshi Mukherjee describes *English, August* as a "zany existen-tial comedy," while Rushdie praises Chatterjee's gift for "elegant social observation."

In *The Last Burden,* published in 1993, Chatterjee moved away from Indian bureaucracy to focus on the complexity of family ties. As he pointed out during an interactive session at the 2002 International Festival of Indian Literature at Hindu College in Delhi, organized by the Indian Council for Cultural Relations (ICCR), "I wrote *The Last Burden* to evince the importance and inevitable friction of filial ties." He revealed in the 1993 interview with Prathima that he had begun "putting things down" for the second novel in 1987, even before he had found a publisher for *English, August,* but he said that it was largely written while he was a writer in resi-dence at the University of Kent in Canterbury.

Front cover for the 1994 paperback edition of Chatterjee's 1993 novel, about an extended Indian family that is riven by discord (Bruccoli Clark Layman Archives)

Unlike *English, August, The Last Burden* has no precise setting. When Chatterjee began writing the novel, he was in Bombay, but he does not name the place where the family spotlighted in the novel lives, nor does he give a surname for the family members. In her review of the book for *Literature Alive* (September 1993), Nilanjana Gupta observed, "The whole family unit seems to have an air of distorted displacement, like the huge cactus they take with them when they leave the small rented flat for a sterile, anonymous house of their own."

The Last Burden is the story of a family that is breaking apart. Chatterjee uncovers multiple strains in the joint but joyless household. The aging couple of the novel, Urmila and Shyamanand, keep grumbling and quarreling even after thirty-seven years of married life but stick to each other. Their sons, Burfi and Jamun, slowly drift apart, and the fondness of the two

brothers for their parents wanes. Burfi; his wife, Joyce; and their sons, Doom and Pista, move away from the joint family. The dying, disintegrating maidservant, Aya, is discarded by the family like a "truss of cast-off clothing." Urmila's critical illness is a cataclysmic episode in the novel. Relationships change further when she is required to undergo expensive medical treatment. Jamun and Burfi seem to be concerned about their mother's health, but they are "in part hatefully callous, in part supportively caring."

Jamun returns from his workplace to look after his ailing mother and lingers on until her partial recovery and eventual death. His piety for his parents is still intact, and Urmila confides her inmost feelings to him. Besides looking after his mother, Jamun, "in a grotesque parody of family life," carries on his affair with Kasturi, his old flame, even after her marriage to Agastya, to whom a passing reference is made toward the end of the novel, and sleeps with Kasibai, his maidservant, and her son. Burfi and Joyce have tense moments, as the latter does not get along in the joint-family setting. Jamun recalls the daily grind of domestic life that his mother has had to cope with in running the family. Shyamanand reminisces about parental care and the affection with which he has raised his sons. He was bitterly resentful when the elder son, Burfi, was wooed away by Joyce. Both sons dislike their father's tantrums, but Jamun is tolerant and treats Shyamanand with deference, whereas Burfi is sulky and defiant.

Money plays an important role in the domestic life and family relations depicted in *The Last Burden.* Shyamanand has saved money by economizing, but Urmila had a tough time meeting household expenses and often had to borrow from her associates. Burfi, although he is well-off, avoids sharing the cost of Urmila's pacemaker. Soon after her death her sons and husband squabble over her will.

The hypocrisy of the middle class in modern India is highlighted in *The Last Burden.* The parents crave a Western education for their children but at the same time adhere to traditional Hindu customs. The positive message, however, is that despite untidy and disingenuous kinship ties between the sons and their ailing, aging parents, and "all the clawing that is happening in the family," the household has to stay afloat and the family has to survive, albeit without familial warmth and affection.

The Last Burden, unlike *English, August,* was poorly received by the reading public. When asked on the 2000 *India Today* talk show why the book "bombed," Chatterjee said, "It did not. It had some good reviews. It simply disappointed those readers who had expected *English, August* (II)." His use of highly wrought language in the novel evoked mixed responses. While Dom Moraes described Chatterjee's bold and innovative use of the English language as "Joycean" and likened the novelist's wit and humor to that of Henry Green and Anthony Powell (*Illustrated Weekly of India,* 28 August – 3 September 1993), James Wood declared in *The Guardian* (17 August 1993) that "Chatterjee's prose is a mad powder of different registers; alas, too often his sentences flake into nothing."

While Chatterjee was working on *The Last Burden,* he was asked to write the screenplay for a motion-picture adaptation of *English, August,* which was released in 1994. Directed by Dev Benegal, who collaborated on the screenplay, the movie was not only a success at the Indian box office but also won the Silver Grand Prix and the Gilberto Martinez Solares Prize for best first movie at the Festival des 3 Continents in Nantes and the Special Jury Prize at the 1994 Torino Film Festival.

Agastya appears again in *The Mammaries of the Welfare State,* published in 2000, but the focus in this novel is different. The new Agastya, according to Chatterjee in his 2001 interview with Nambisan, is an "admirable corrective" to the distracted civil servant of *English, August.* While reading excerpts from the novel at the 2002 International Festival of Indian Literature, Chatterjee said, "*The Mammaries* is written with a view to introducing women in the life of Agastya Sen." Eight years have passed since Agastya joined the IAS, and in the course of time he has mutated from "a malingering probationer" into an honest and clear-sighted civil servant. He is acutely sensitive to the tardy and wasteful bureaucracy in the welfare state that is contemporary India. The vulgarity and venality of politicians and civil servants are treated insightfully in the novel. Agastya defines the unfortunate situation: "In my eight years of service, I haven't come across a single case in which everybody concerned didn't try to milk dry the boobs of the Welfare State." He detests the bureaucratic setup, dominated by hierarchy and statistics, and seeks an outlet for his frustrations in satisfying his keen sexual cravings. In the company of Daya, a savvy, sexy, and talented woman, Agastya has a feeling of release after the leaden treadmill of office life.

In *The Mammaries of the Welfare State,* Agastya is deputy secretary in the secretariat control room in Bombay, having been transferred from the post of joint commissioner of rehabilitation in Delhi. Later, he becomes the collector of Madna, as if to remind readers that this book is a sequel of sorts to *English, August.* Characters and settings from the earlier novel reappear, but *The Mammaries of the Welfare State* is more preoccupied with the financial and sexual shenanigans taking place among the Indian elite, who occupy privileged places but break the law with impunity. The novel is particularly harsh on the self-seeking politicians and avaricious bureaucrats who feed on the dugs of the welfare state.

Nandini Lal noted in her *Biblio* review (January–February 2001) that Chatterjee's lavish gifts for exuberant wordplay and humor, as well as his penchant for depicting the bizarre malfunctions of bureaucracy, made *The Mammaries of the Welfare State* "a plangent criticism of the system." She also felt, however, that the narrative was weighed down by the excess of pompous notes, verbose letters, elaborate circulars, and correspondence replete with official verbiage. Other reviewers, too, found the book funny but less readable than *English, August.*

Chatterjee told Prathima in 1993, "In fact I suspect that my kind of writing is probably more amateurish than professional," but it can be said that his narratives are sufficiently grounded in Indian realities to be authentic and compelling. His wry and ribald humor has also won him many fans. He is essentially a comic novelist who has explored the ugliness and cynicism rife in the world of Indian bureaucracy.

In his 2001 interview with Nambisan, Upamanyu Chatterjee said that he plans to continue writing novels that will carry on the story of the family in *The Last Burden* as well as that of Agastya. As he put it, "The next book will again be a Last Burden kind of book, and then I'll revert to Agastya. I plan to alternate themes . . . I'm fixed for the next 15 or 20 years."

Interviews:

Amitabh Mattoo, "Magic Realism Isn't My Kind of Stuff," *Illustrated Weekly of India* (31 July – 6 August 1993): 28–29;

W. B. Prathima, "Madna, Madras and Beyond: Upamanyu Talks to W. B. Prathima," *Literature Alive,* 6 (September 1993): 52–60;

"My Writing Is Not Scatology; It's Comic," *India Today* (7 December 2000) <http://www.india-today.com/chat/200012/upamanyu.html>;

Vijay Nambisan, "I'm Not Kiran Bedi," *Hindu* (1 April 2001) <http://www.hinduonnet.com/thehindu/2001/04/01/stories/1301129k.htm>.

References:

Rukun Advani, "Novelists in Residence," in *The Fiction of St. Stephen's,* edited by Aditya Bhattacharjea and Lola Chatterji (New Delhi: Ravi Dayal, 2000), pp. 8–17;

Jaya Chakarvorty, "The English Burden Alias the Burden of English," in *Indian Writing in English: The*

Last Decade, edited by Rajul Bhargava (Jaipur: Rawat, 2002), pp. 234–241;

Amitava Kumar, *Bombay London New York: A Literary Journey* (New Delhi: Penguin Books India, 2002);

T. Vijoy Kumar, "I Can't Get No Satisfaction: Upamanyu Chatterjee's *English, August,*" in *The New Indian Novel in English: A Study of the 1980s,* edited by Viney Kirpal (New Delhi: Allied, 1990), pp. 169–178;

Jon Mee, "After Midnight: The Novel in the 1980s and 1990s," in *An Illustrated History of Indian Literature in English,* edited by Arvind Krishna Mehrotra (Delhi: Permanent Black / New Delhi: Ravi Dayal, 2003); republished as *A History of Indian Literature in English* (New York: Columbia University Press, 2003), pp. 318–336;

Meenakshi Mukherjee, "The Anxiety of Indianness: Our Novels in English," *Economic and Political Weekly* (27 November 1993): 2607–2611;

M. K. Naik and Shyamala A. Narayan, *Indian English Literature, 1980–2000: A Critical Survey* (Delhi: Pencraft International, 2001);

Murari Prasad, "Society in Upamanyu Chatterjee's *English, August,*" *Indian Journal of English Studies,* 33 (1994–1995): 68–75;

Prasad, "Upamanyu Chatterjee's *The Last Burden:* A Family Narrative," *Families: A Journal of Representations,* 2, no. 1 (2003): 89–102;

Mohan Ramanan, "*The Last Burden,*" in *Fiction of the Nineties,* edited by Veena Noble Dass and R. K. Dhawan (New Delhi: Prestige, 1994), pp. 98–101;

Meenakshi Raykar, "The Intellectual in a State of 'Anomy': Achebe's *No Longer at Ease* and Chatterjee's *English, August: An Indian Story,*" *New Quest* (March–April 1992): 109–111;

Salman Rushdie, "Damme, This Is the Oriental Scene for You!" *New Yorker,* 73 (23 and 30 June 1997): 50, 52, 54, 56–61;

C. Sengupta, "Upamanyu Chatterjee's *English, August:* Metaphor of Contemporary Youth's Quest for Self-Realization," in *Indian Literature Today,* edited by Dhawan, volume 1 (New Delhi: Prestige, 1994), pp. 110–121;

A. K. Singh, "*English, August:* A Critical Appraisal," in *Recent Indian Fiction,* edited by R. S. Pathak (New Delhi: Prestige, 1994), pp. 82–103;

Pradeep Trikha, "Emotional Bonds in Upamanyu Chatterjee's *The Last Burden,*" in *Indian Literature Today,* volume 1, pp. 122–127;

Harish Trivedi, "Epilogue/Epitaph," in *The Fiction of St. Stephen's,* pp. 207–224.

Amit Chaudhuri

(15 May 1962 –)

Krishna Sen
University of Calcutta

See also the Chaudhuri entry in *DLB 267: Twenty-First-Century British and Irish Novelists.*

BOOKS: *A Strange and Sublime Address* (London: Heinemann, 1991);

Afternoon Raag (London: Heinemann, 1993);

Freedom Song (London: Picador, 1998);

A New World (London: Picador, 2000; New York: Knopf, 2000);

Real Time: Stories and a Reminiscence (London: Picador, 2002; New York: Farrar, Straus & Giroux, 2002);

D. H. Lawrence and "Difference": Postcoloniality and the Poetry of the Present (Oxford: Clarendon Press / Oxford & New York: Oxford University Press, 2003);

Small Orange Flags: On Living during a "State of Emergency" (Calcutta: Seagull, 2003);

Insomniac (London: Aark Arts, 2004);

St. Cyril Road and Other Poems (New Delhi: Penguin Books India / New York: Penguin, 2005).

Collection: *Freedom Song: Three Novels* (New York: Knopf, 1999)—comprises the title novella from *A Strange and Sublime Address, Afternoon Raag,* and *Freedom Song;* republished as *Three Novels* (London: Picador, 2001).

OTHER: "A Small Bengal, NW 3," in *London: The Lives of the City,* edited by Ian Jack, Granta, no. 65 (London: Granta, 1999), pp. 307–310;

"Modernity and the Vernacular" and "The Construction of the Indian Novel in English," in *The Picador Book of Modern Indian Literature,* edited by Chaudhuri (London: Picador, 2001), pp. xvii–xxii, xxiii–xxxi;

"What We Think of America," in *What We Think of America,* edited by Jack, Granta, no. 77 (London: Granta, 2002), pp. 20–23;

"The English Writings of Rabindranath Tagore," in *An Illustrated History of Indian Literature in English,* edited by Arvind Krishna Mehrotra (Delhi: Permanent Black / New Delhi: Ravi Dayal, 2003); republished as *A History of Indian Literature in English*

Amit Chaudhuri (photograph by Jerry Bauer; from the dust jacket for Real Time, *2002; Richland County Public Library)*

(New York: Columbia University Press, 2003), pp. 103–115;

"Oxford," in *Away: The Indian Writer as an Expatriate,* edited by Amitava Kumar (New York: Routledge, 2004), pp. 301–312;

"The Tailor of Gujarat: An Unwilling Icon of Secular India," in *Jubilee,* edited by Jack, Granta, no. 87 (London: Granta, 2004), pp. 259–278;

Arun Kolatkar, *Jejuri,* introduction by Chaudhuri (New York: New York Review of Books, 2005).

SELECTED PERIODICAL PUBLICATIONS–UNCOLLECTED: "The Flute of Modernity," *New Republic* (19 October 1998);

"Slipping into Silence," *Outlook* (4 September 2000);
"A Bottle of Ink, a Pen and a Blotter," *London Review of Books,* 23 (9 August 2001);
"Learning to Write: On V. S. Naipaul," *TLS: The Times Literary Supplement,* 21 September 2001, pp. 22–23;
"Literature: Buddhadev Bose," *Outlook* (19 August 2002);
"Wage a War to Win Your Peace," *Outlook* (27 January 2003);
"Travels in the Subculture of Modernity: East Coast Attitudes to Other Literatures," *TLS: The Times Literary Supplement,* 5 September 2003, pp. 11–13;
"Joyce Remembered," *James Joyce Bloomsday Magazine,* 7 (June 2004);
"In the Waiting-Room of History," *London Review of Books,* 26 (24 June 2004): 3–6;
"Distant Thunder," *Outlook* (2 August 2004).

Amit Chaudhuri belongs to a new generation of Indian writers in English who live and work in India and whose main focus is to depict not the eternal and mythical India traditionally imagined by the West but the complex and cosmopolitan reality of the post-Independence nation of today. As he writes in "Modernity and the Vernacular," from *The Picador Book of Modern Indian Literature* (2001), modern India is a complicated blend of "tradition, history, community and change." The response of India to its colonial past is not a simple narrative of resistance but an intricate process of "self-enquiry and self-redefinition" and of embracing the new while recuperating the old, producing "movements and redefinitions in class and history." The challenge confronting the modern Indian creative artist is to highlight these new cultural variations and altered sensibilities through forms and idioms that reflect their multivalent perspectives.

Chaudhuri observes in "Modernity and the Vernacular" that a major consequence of the social and intellectual churning caused by colonial rule in India was the evolution of a Western-educated Indian middle class that creatively adapted its indigenous ethos to new priorities. What emerged was "a new class structure [that] replaced or inflected, in cities and towns, old hierarchies of caste." As a product of this historical process himself, Chaudhuri has chosen as his special area of "imaginative scrutiny" what he describes in an essay on the English writings of Rabindranath Tagore as the "bafflement, agony and energy of cultural confusion and intermingling [of attitudes and values]" that mark the middle-class Indian of today.

More specifically, Chaudhuri's works focus on the idiosyncrasies and dichotomies of the middle class in his native state of West Bengal in eastern India, bordering Bangladesh. In "Modernity and the Vernacular"

he identifies as his particular themes "the poignance and comedy of the new class tensions, the pathos of the social yearning of the educated lower middle classes, the threatening but exuberant appearance of the new rich." Calcutta, the state capital and the intellectual and emotional heartland of the Bengali community, is to Chaudhuri's oeuvre what the fictional Malgudi was to R. K. Narayan's: the literal as well as the figurative locus of a distinctive culture. Chaudhuri takes a place, Calcutta, and makes of it a world, although it is a world viewed with the gentle irony that comes from the perspective of having spent a considerable part of his life in the more urbane environment of Bombay and in England. Nevertheless, he does more than merely chronicle a particular way of life. Chaudhuri experiments with both the English language and the form of the novel (essentially a Western literary genre) in order to convey a lifestyle and sensitivities that are different from their counterparts in the West.

The best introduction to Chaudhuri's early life and the culture that shaped his sensibility is the reminiscence in free verse titled "E-Minor," from *Real Time: Stories and a Reminiscence* (2002). He was born in Calcutta on 15 May 1962 to Nages Chandra Chaudhuri, a successful corporate executive, and Bijoya Nandi Majumdar Chaudhuri, a homemaker and acclaimed singer. At the age of one-and-a-half he moved with his parents to Bombay, spending summers at his uncle's home in Calcutta. Both aspects of his childhood, the affluent, corporate life of Bombay and the slower and more traditional ambience of Calcutta, are reflected in his work. Floating like a leitmotiv over all these experiences was the voice of his mother, singing devotional hymns and songs by Tagore. Music and the harmony it signifies constitute an important motif in Chaudhuri's work.

In Bombay, Chaudhuri attended the prestigious Cathedral and John Connon School, followed by a year of junior college at Elphinstone College, affiliated with the University of Bombay. He then withdrew from formal schooling to take the British O level and A level examinations by correspondence through Wolsey Hall, in Oxford. By the age of sixteen Chaudhuri had also begun to train seriously in northern Indian classical vocal music under Pandit Govind Prasad Jaipurwale, of the Kunwar Shyam *gharana* (school).

Chaudhuri traveled to England for further studies in 1983, majoring in English at University College, London, and taking his B.A. with first-class honors in 1986. He then entered Balliol College, Oxford University, as a Devorguilla Scholar and began to write and publish. The poetry of D. H. Lawrence, the subject of his 1993 doctoral dissertation, was to have an abiding influence on his entire conception of writing. Contesting an impressive body of Lawrence criticism that judged his poetry, as well as his style in general, as passionate but deficient in form, Chaudhuri invokes several strands of postmodern theory to establish Lawrence as a writer who baffled his critics not because he lacked art but because he espoused a concept of art that was entirely different from mainstream European aesthetics. According to Chaudhuri, Lawrence deliberately emphasized randomness rather than "constructedness" or shapeliness of form as a way of highlighting the totality of life in all its heterogeneity rather than just its significant moments. His apparent formlessness thus projects a vision of life that is holistic rather than selective, one that does not exclude the unheroic and the banal, since these things, too, are intrinsic to life. When Chaudhuri came to write his own novels, he acknowledged his debt to Lawrence by consciously eschewing the conventional architectonics of plot and characterization in favor of the unstructured flow of daily life, which is the normal experience of the average individual.

Chaudhuri's first book, *A Strange and Sublime Address* (1991), comprises the title novella and nine short stories. The novella tells the story of a summer vacation taken by Sandeep, a ten-year-old boy living in Bombay, who visits his uncle's home in Calcutta with his mother. The long, lazy days, the pavements shimmering in the noonday glare, and the cries of itinerant vendors form the backdrop for Sandeep's brief sojourn in the old three-story house in a "middle-middle-class" neighborhood. The days follow one another in trance-like succession, punctuated by the unchanging rituals of daily life—Sandeep frolicking and squabbling with his two younger cousins; leisurely meals with time enough to pick every fish bone clean; evening tea on the balcony; outings in the ancient family car; and the occasional visitor. The only flurry in the even tenor of this daily routine is occasioned by Sandeep's uncle, Chotomama, a large-hearted entrepreneur perpetually dreaming up schemes to strike it rich in business, who suffers and recovers from a minor heart attack. The entire summer is filtered through Sandeep's consciousness, but in a real sense, Calcutta is the protagonist. By a trick of the boy's imagination, the city metamorphoses into a mythic space: "Daily, Calcutta disintegrates, unwhispering, into dust, and daily it rises from dust again." This Phoenix-like vitality makes it the strange and sublime address of Sandeep's childhood recollections. The final moment of the novella distills in a single image the evanescent moods of that magical summer. The three cousins catch sight of a cuckoo, that most elusive of birds. Sensing their gaze, the bird "flew off—not flew off, really, but melted, disappeared, from the material world. As they watched, a delicate shyness seemed to envelop it, and drew a veil over their eyes."

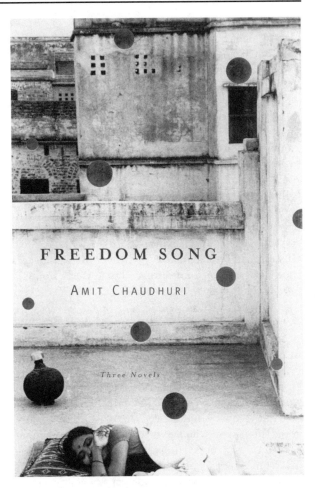

Dust jacket for the 1999 collection comprising "A Strange and Sublime Address," Afternoon Raag, *and* Freedom Song
(Richland County Public Library)

The life portrayed in *A Strange and Sublime Address* is that of the middle and upper-middle echelons of Bengali society, which is Chaudhuri's own background. Chotomama's unglamorous home evokes a securely located heritage: "the photographs and portraits of grandfathers and grandmothers . . . symbolized another world, another order of calm, inviolable existence." The moneyed corporate class of India is portrayed through more-opulent surroundings, such as the apartment in one of the short stories that follows the novella, "The New Maidservant." Seen through the eyes of the disadvantaged young woman of the title, the lavish interior conjures up all the delicacies that she yearns for but cannot afford: "It was a beautiful flat, and to her eyes everything in it seemed to be made either of sugar or pistachio or jaggery or caramel or some fragrant, edible thing. The raised marble platform by the window would be sweet and cool as a mint lozenge if one could possibly taste it, and the dark wooden furniture would have the bittersweet taste of burnt sugar."

The critical response to *A Strange and Sublime Address* signaled the arrival of a striking new talent. The book won the 1991 Betty Trask Award of the Society of Authors for the best first novel by a writer under the age of thirty-five, as well as the Commonwealth Writer's Prize for the best first book in the Eurasian division. In addition, it was short-listed for the 1991 *Guardian* Fiction Prize. The year 1991 closed on a happy note, with Chaudhuri's marriage in December to Rosinka "Rinka" Khastgir, a fellow Bengali and a research scholar. In 1992 he received a Creative Arts Fellowship from Wolfson College, Oxford University, and in 1993 he completed his doctorate on critical theory and the poetry of Lawrence. By this time, the success of *A Strange and Sublime Address* had established Chaudhuri's reputation. In 1993 the BBC produced a short program on him during "India Week" on *The Late Show*.

Chaudhuri was writing his second novel, *Afternoon Raag* (1993), while working on his doctorate. Like *A Strange and Sublime Address,* the book scored notable successes, winning the 1993 Southern Arts Literature Prize and the Encore Award of the Society of Authors, given for the best second novel. *Raag* is the Bengali word for raga, the basis of Indian classical music; fittingly, the book is dedicated to Chaudhuri's music guru, Jaipurwale, who had died shortly before the publication of the novel. Ragas have distinctive moods based on the season and the time of day they are meant to be performed, and afternoon ragas conjure up the meditative rhythms of long, hot summer afternoons in India. *Afternoon Raag* brings together Chaudhuri's experiences of growing up in India and studying in England, dwelling on the sources of his inspiration: his mother, music, literature, and landscape. The protagonist is an unnamed Indian man studying English literature at Oxford whose mental universe effortlessly spans the two poles between which the narrative circles. India is a slow, lyrical cadence of mood and music. Oxford is a bustling world of "men with ear-rings, women wearing gypsy ornaments"; of "a warm kitchen-life of teas and conversations in this country where afternoons come suddenly"; and of cool, muted rooms "that create, in afternoon light or evening shadow, the abidingness of an English interior." *Afternoon Raag* is about the way two contrasting cultures harmonize within the narrator's consciousness like a piece of contrapuntal music.

Early in 1993 Chaudhuri traveled back to Bombay and Calcutta on vacation and was stunned by the changed political scenario in an otherwise tolerant and multicultural country. Militant Hindu fundamentalists had recently demolished a Muslim shrine, the Babri Masjid, in the small northern Indian town of Ayodhya, and Bombay had erupted in virulent religious riots.

Chaudhuri's troubled musings on this new face of Hinduism were the genesis of some of the essays collected in 2003 as *Small Orange Flags: On Living during a "State of Emergency"* (the flags of the title are the insignia of the largest Hindu fundamentalist political party) and also inspired the exploration of the idea of freedom in his third novel, *Freedom Song* (1998). Back in Oxford, Chaudhuri's term as a Creative Arts fellow at Wolfson College ended in 1995. That same year he received a Leverhulme Special Research Fellowship with the English department at Cambridge University, where he taught the Commonwealth and international literature course for the English tripos. Chaudhuri's daughter, Radha, was born in July 1998.

The publication of *Freedom Song* heralded a major change in Chaudhuri's fictional milieu. On the one hand, the novel presents the traumatic effects of the 1947 partition of Bengal from the perspective of a family of Hindu refugees who struggle to maintain a veneer of financial respectability. On the other hand, it chronicles the passionate romance of Bengalis, and especially Calcuttans, since the mid 1970s with the heady Marxist mantra of the redemption of the proletariat. The world depicted in *Freedom Song,* desultory and economically stagnant, is grayer than that in Chaudhuri's previous novels. The gap between the "freedom song" for the downtrodden and the actual realization of those lofty aspirations is presented with sober detachment.

The protagonist of *Freedom Song* is Bhaskar, an insignificant factory worker whose avocation is a utopian involvement with a revolutionary ideology. He spends mornings distributing the party newspaper, *Ganashakti,* to "fellow-travellers of the Communist Party [who] believed in its necessity and its vision" and evenings haunting the shabby local party office. These activities constitute the sum of his radical pursuits. An extended "family" of relatives and friends of relatives—a typically intricate skein of Bengali kinship—eddies around Bhaskar, worrying about his drifting lifestyle and the need to arrange a marriage for him so that he will settle down. He finally marries a woman named Sandhya and adopts a humdrum life far removed from his stirring dreams of social liberation. There are no theatrical climaxes in the life of this average man: "It was difficult to come to terms with how ordinary it was." The novel ends with Bhaskar's Aunt Khuku drowsily reliving memories of childhood, marriage, and friendships, as a stiflingly hot afternoon melts into a light rain that comes "like a merciful gift . . . obliterating as it engenders." *Freedom Song* gestures toward new beginnings and the renewal of hope through simple human situations such as Bhaskar's marriage and Khuku's decision to reestablish contact with her childhood friend Mini, rather than through any dramatic social or political upheaval.

After Chaudhuri's father retired and returned from Bombay to Calcutta, he, too, moved to Calcutta with his wife and daughter in 1999 to become a full-time writer while continuing his musical training under another guru, Pandit A. T. Kanan. That same year, *Freedom Song: Three Novels,* comprising the title novella from *A Strange and Sublime Address, Afternoon Raag,* and *Freedom Song,* was published in the United States by Knopf. The collection was a critical success and a best-seller. *The New York Times* declared it a 1999 Notable Book of the Year. The New York Public Library named it one of the "25 Books to Remember from 1999," and it received the 2000 Book Prize in fiction from *The Los Angeles Times.* That same year Chaudhuri was nominated by the London *Observer* as one of the twenty-one Writers for the Millennium and by *India Today* as one of the Faces of the Millennium.

In his highly acclaimed fourth novel, *A New World* (2000), Chaudhuri returns to the Bengali upper-middle-class milieu and explores the crises of identity experienced by its more cosmopolitan and Westernized members. The irony in the title operates on several levels. Jayojit, an economist and sometime writer, migrated, like many an ambitious Bengali of his generation, to the new world of the United States; he has now returned to the old world of Calcutta for a summer vacation with his ten-year-old son, Vikram (nicknamed Bonny), after a long and messy divorce from Amala, his wife of eleven years. Although he imagined this trip as a return to the security of home, Jayojit finds himself inhabiting the unfamiliar "new world" of the divorced and single parent, who is something of a curiosity in a traditional society. The other main characters are Jayojit's parents, the crusty old Admiral Chatterjee and his diffident and dominated wife, who has always deferred to her husband, as custom demands. Their son's divorce, the result of Amala's infidelity, is for them an unprecedented assault on their deep-rooted cultural norms and conservative family values, an incomprehensible intrusion from some strange "new world." In fact, the only way the elderly couple can deal with the divorce is by refusing to acknowledge or discuss it. The absent Amala looms like a ghostly presence over conversations that carefully skirt the failed marriage, while the admiral's wife smothers Bonny with the excessive attention usually lavished on a motherless child.

Jayojit's parents' stable marriage is not an ideal one, either. Instead of meaningful communication, there is only the bond of habit: the Admiral "behaved with an impatient propriety . . . in relation to his wife, as if someone who mattered to him were watching them," while she, for her part, "had grown used to this

Dust jacket for Chaudhuri's 2000 novel, about a Bengali economist who has made his career in the United States but returns to Calcutta on vacation with his son after a messy divorce (Richland County Public Library)

negligible but returning loneliness." *A New World* juxtaposes the two worlds of the affluent, educated Bengali upper-middle class—the Westernized world of impetuous individualism (Amala's extramarital affair) and cultural hybridity (Vikram's nickname) and the older world of custom and convention—and shows them up for what they are. The patriarchal admiral and his wife are "a mass of confusions," while Jayojit is the rootless modern Indian: "He'd read the Upanishads in English when he was twenty-two, for, despite being a Brahmin, at least in name, he knew no Sanskrit." To quote from Chaudhuri's "E-Minor," the apparently comfortable existence of the family, "refracted / through cut glass, reflected on brass, was, in part, / make-believe."

Jayojit's visit is uneventful. He spends time with his parents, runs minor errands, meets neighbors who are inquisitive about his marriage, and experiences fleeting moments of closeness with an American Salvation Army worker in Calcutta with whom, however, he loses contact. The narrative has all the diffuse, unstructured quality of life itself, its "meaning" hovering somewhere just beyond the line of sight. Jayojit finally returns with his son to their home in the American Midwest on a Bangladesh Biman flight crowded with large Bangladeshi families who all look as though they are "*happy,* and their marriages are working." In the last vignette Jayojit absently listens to a Bangladeshi mother on the plane "exhorting her child to sleep," a simple experience that now eludes his own child. *A New World* captures what Chaudhuri has described in "The Flute of Modernity" (1998), an essay on Tagore, as "the poignancy of the trajectory of Bengali middle-class life, with its *bhadralok* [cultured] propriety, gentility, rationality, and its ironic lack of fulfillment."

A New World received the premier literary prize in India, the Sahitya Akademi Award, in 2002. Chaudhuri edited and provided two introductory essays for the 2001 anthology *The Picador Book of Modern Indian Literature.* He was selected as a judge for the Geoffrey Faber Memorial Prize as well as for the International IMPAC Dublin Literary Award in 2001. Further recognition of his growing stature as a writer came with an invitation to teach Indian literature at Columbia University to students working toward an M.F.A. degree, during the fall 2002 semester.

Real Time: Stories and a Reminiscence, published in 2002, is a collection of fifteen short stories and two free-verse reminiscences. Many of the stories had appeared earlier in *The London Review of Books, The Little Magazine, Civil Lines, Granta, The New Yorker,* and *TLS: The Times Literary Supplement.* Several of them focus on the hybridity of the Bengali middle class, with its distinctive blend of the colonial and the ancestral. Sometimes these contrasting elements coexist without strain. In "Beyond Translation" two sets of young cousins inhabit their mutually exclusive worlds of Bengali and English children's literature with no tension or conflict between their different tastes and worldviews, while in "Portrait of an Artist" the narrative voice finds "a strange connection" between "this small, cold island [Britain] and faraway Bengal," probably because Calcutta was the original seat of British power in India. Sometimes the juxtaposition is comic: in "The Second Marriage" two divorced Bengalis living in England enter into an arranged second marriage in Calcutta, with all the customary rituals. There are times, though, when these diverse orientations are locked in mutual incomprehension: Mr. Chatterjee of "White Lies" oscillates uneasily between the brittle glamour of the "multinational" culture of the company for which he works and the traditional values of his wife's *guruji* (music teacher), without feeling at home in either of these two worlds. Modern

India also has its own brand of indigenous hybridity; the unnamed speaker of "Prelude to an Autobiography: A Fragment" is the child of an intercommunity marriage and therefore says that English is "the only language I have." Moving away from the present, Chaudhuri narrates incidents from Hindu mythology in "An Infatuation" and "The Wedding." The effect of the retelling is to defamiliarize the sacred tales by metaphorically placing them within the bourgeois and post-colonial context suggested by the use of the English language, presenting an epic hero, a god, or a goddess from an unsuspected contemporary perspective.

This use of the English language to demystify the Indian mythical past provides a suggestive point of entry into Chaudhuri's use of language. In the preface to the published version of his dissertation, *D. H. Lawrence and "Difference": Postcoloniality and the Poetry of the Present* (2003), Chaudhuri describes himself as "the kind of writer . . . who believes that language can transform reality." This belief has a bearing on his attitude to English. Indian writers in English from as far back as the nineteenth century have suffered aesthetic crises of conscience for having opted to use the colonizer's tongue. Chaudhuri, however, belongs to a generation that has neither known nor is haunted by the specter of colonialism and accepts the English language with an easy familiarity. As he writes in "The Flute of Modernity," English was "the language that was present at the inception of the Indian middle class and that would always, in one way or another, define its existence." This situation gives the middle-class Indian the privilege of appropriating English from his own historical position of "difference," but it also gestures toward the paradox inherent in this "social-secular-rational-colonial" psyche and its negotiation with "the world of the sub-conscious and the pre-colonial." Thus, Bhaskar, the Marxist hero of *Freedom Song,* submits unhesitatingly to the age-old marriage rites that symbolize the contemporary Indian's "pact with ancestry, caste and divinity." Chaudhuri's comment on Tagore's English writings is revealing: he reads them as indicative of "an Indian bilingual sensibility expressing itself in the English language . . . , a site where categories were mixed up and realigned."

This complexity is important to Chaudhuri. His prose at its best is richly endowed with the qualities he prioritizes in his second introductory essay to *The Picador Book of Modern Indian Literature,* "The Construction of the Indian Novel in English"–delicacy, nuance, inwardness, and irony–but what he suggests as his ultimate aim is to "create a new language by seemingly reproducing the old, a language of altered meanings in which hybridity and post-coloniality reside . . . on the border of absence and recognition." A case in point is the nonitalicized use of the familiar Bengali word *master-moshai* (teacher) in "Portrait of an Artist," from *Real Time*. The English root, *master,* which denotes only a function, is invested with all the associations of hierarchy and deference that reside in the Bengali honorific suffix *moshai.* Chaudhuri contends that this composite English, not the traditional vernaculars, most appropriately projects the urban Indian psyche. That this hybrid and cosmopolitan consciousness characterizes only a small percentage of contemporary Indians does not invalidate the writer's freedom to choose his own terrain.

As with the English language, so with the form of the novel, in which Chaudhuri has sought to evolve his own distinctive mode. His novels are usually described as plotless, but the structured plot has little to do, in Chaudhuri's aesthetic, with the multivalence of life. A character in "Portrait of an Artist" says, "Where our hearts beat, that was secret, or disappointing, or satisfying, or trivial, too trivial for it to become words or a story." Chaudhuri looks for life unfolding "its self-repeating secrets," as he writes in "A Road in Late March," one of the stories from *A Strange and Sublime Address.* In *Freedom Song,* what interests him is not the revolutionary activities of his characters but "the semi-lit, casual backstage and dress rehearsals, the unconscious, helpless putting on and putting off of different selves and incarnations, of their lives." Chaudhuri's realism inheres in the dense clusters of pregnant detail that conjure up the tone of an experience rather than in the elaborate enumeration of scenes and objects.

In "The Construction of the Indian Novel in English," Chaudhuri expresses regret that the enormous variety of contemporary Indian writing, in English and in the indigenous languages, is leveled down in the West to a single template, that of Salman Rushdie. Rather than "big, baggy," complicated narratives, Indian writers have preferred the suggestive: "in their choice of form . . . writers hoped to suggest India by ellipsis rather than by all-inclusiveness." This approach calls for a fluid interface of juxtapositions and discontinuities marked by the same "unfinishedness" that Chaudhuri admires in Lawrence's poetry. He appreciates V. S. Naipaul's rejection of "the closed structure of the conventional novel" in favor of "'unfinished' narratives." In "A Bottle of Ink, a Pen and a Blotter" (2001), a valedictory essay on Narayan, Chaudhuri makes an observation that can be related to his own fiction: "Narayan is less interested in the perfected and self-enclosed novel than he is in the recycling of familiar, used material. . . . Malgudi is not a commodity or a product whose outlines are clear and recognizable–a novel or a place–so much as a web of multiple transactions. . . ."

Dust jacket for Chaudhuri's 2002 collection, which explores the blend of colonial English and traditional Bengali elements in middle-class Bengali society (Richland County Public Library)

Chaudhuri has his own metaphor for this kind of free-flowing, recursive, allusive literary form, a metaphor drawn from Indian classical music, which remains his second love, after writing. (He has recorded a compact disc and two cassettes and has performed at several prestigious venues in India and abroad.) This literary form follows the extemporizing movement of the Indian raga, which apparently meanders aimlessly but actually circles with sureness and logic around dominant moods and tones. In *Afternoon Raag,* Chaudhuri discusses this flow in words that recall his description of Narayan's fictional Malgudi as a "web of multiple transactions": "The greater part of the unfolding of a raag consists of a slow, evasive introduction in which the notes are related to each other by curving glissandos or meends [glides] . . . which, in its unravelling, is a matter of constant erasures and rewritings . . . unlike the notes of Western music, which remain printed upon the page." In "The Flute of Modernity" he detects this movement in the "half-lit" world of the writings of Tagore, who explored, through suggestion and indirection, the "interstitial world . . . of India's extraordinary and often traumatic reinterpretation of itself in this century." Chaudhuri has adopted this kind of probing, elliptical writing as his model.

In 2003 Chaudhuri published *Small Orange Flags: On Living during a "State of Emergency,"* a collection of six essays, two poems, and an interview, with the proceeds from sales of the book to be donated to Peaceworks, a peace initiative for young people in Calcutta. The trigger for these musings on separatism, violence, and the erasure of minority discourses was the resurgence of fundamentalist politics in India in the early 1990s, but Chaudhuri conflates with these incidents other forays into political partisanship: anti-British nationalism in pre-Independence India, racism in the United States, the Cold War, Islamic terrorism, and the American crusade in Iraq. To counterpoint these "states of siege," Chaudhuri returns to the three places that constitute his own spiritual space–Calcutta, Bombay, and England:

> Calcutta used to be a city of the mind, . . . it represented high culture of the modernist kind. Bombay represented a different kind of social upward mobility and the huge possibilities of popular culture. . . .

[M]ulticultural Britain today . . . I don't want to pastoralize it or idealize it, but I do want to be true to my sense of change in it from the seventies when I used to feel deeply discriminated against, to today.

The values these places symbolize–a liberal "high" culture, the energy of the popular and the modern, and an all-inclusive tolerance–sound the dominant notes in Amit Chaudhuri's oeuvre.

Interviews:

Krishna Sen, "In Conversation," *Indian Writing in English* (1993);

Swagato Ganguly and Anjum Katyal, "Space Created," in Chaudhuri, *Small Orange Flags: On Living during a "State of Emergency"* (Calcutta: Seagull, 2003), pp. 42–79.

References:

James Proctor, "Amit Chaudhuri," *Contemporary Writers* <http://www.contemporarywriters.com/authors/?p=auth21> [accessed 22 November 2005];

Sheobhushan Shukla and Anu Shukla, eds., *The Novels of Amit Chaudhuri: An Exploration in the Alternative Tradition* (New Delhi: Sarup & Sons, 2004).

Nirad C. Chaudhuri

(23 November 1897 – 1 August 1999)

Fakrul Alam
University of Dhaka

SELECTED BOOKS IN ENGLISH: *The Autobiography of an Unknown Indian* (London: Macmillan, 1951; New York: Macmillan, 1951);

A Passage to England (New York: St. Martin's Press, 1959; London: Macmillan, 1960);

The Continent of Circe: Being an Essay on the Peoples of India (London: Chatto & Windus, 1965; New York: Oxford University Press, 1966);

The Intellectual in India (New Delhi: Vir, 1967);

To Live or Not to Live! An Essay on Living Happily with Others (Delhi: Hind Pocket Books, 1970);

Scholar Extraordinary: The Life of Professor the Rt. Hon. Friedrich Max Müller, P.C. (London: Chatto & Windus, 1974; New York: Oxford University Press, 1974);

Clive of India: A Political and Psychological Essay (London: Barrie & Jenkins, 1975);

Culture in the Vanity Bag: Being an Essay on Clothing and Adornment in Passing and Abiding India (Bombay: Jaico, 1976);

Hinduism: A Religion to Live By (New York: Oxford University Press, 1979; London: Chatto & Windus, 1979);

Thy Hand, Great Anarch! India, 1921–1952 (London: Chatto & Windus, 1987; Reading, Mass.: Addison-Wesley, 1988);

The East Is East and the West Is West (Calcutta: Mitra & Ghosh, 1996);

Three Horsemen of the New Apocalypse (New Delhi & New York: Oxford University Press, 1997);

From the Archives of a Centenarian, compiled and edited by Dhruva N. Chaudhuri (Calcutta: Mitra & Ghosh, 1997);

Why I Mourn for England (Calcutta: Mitra & Ghosh, 1998).

OTHER: "Kipling," in *Rudyard Kipling: The Man, His Work, and His World,* edited by John J. Gross (London: Weidenfeld & Nicolson, 1972);

"Opening Address," in *The Eye of the Beholder: Indian Writing in English,* edited by Maggie Butcher (London: Commonwealth Institute, 1983), pp. 8–20.

Nirad C. Chaudhuri (photograph by Roger Hutchings; from the dust jacket for Thy Hand, Great Anarch! India, 1921–1952, *1988; Richland County Public Library)*

SELECTED PERIODICAL PUBLICATIONS–UNCOLLECTED: "Universal Darkness," *London Magazine,* new series, 1, no. 3 (August–September 1971): 64–75;

"Why I Write in English," *Kunapipi,* 3, no. 1 (1981): 1–3.

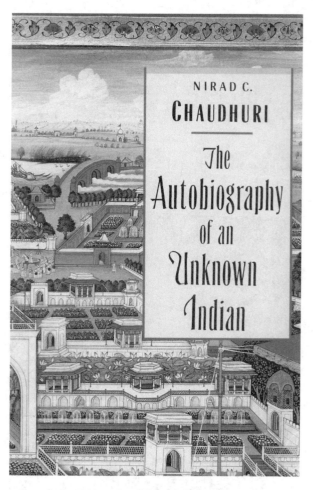

Cover for the 1989 reprint of Chaudhuri's first book, a memoir that describes his life from birth to age twenty-five and charts what he sees as the twentieth-century decline of Indian culture (Richland County Public Library)

When Nirad C. Chaudhuri died in Oxford on 1 August 1999, he was 101 years old and had been recovering from a stroke he had suffered earlier in July of that year. Even in his hundredth year, however, he had published an apology for his work in the May 1997 number of *Granta* magazine that characterizes him well and that indicates what he thought he had achieved in his life. In the piece, "Apologia Pro Scripta Dua," Chaudhuri explains that though he writes because of an "irresistible compulsion" to do so, he was not writing primarily about himself but about the world that he had lived in. He also stresses in the piece the care he took to make his English prose "sound like English to those who were born into the language" and "to get the rhythm and tempo of his prose right." Chaudhuri declares that in a career that extended more than seventy years, in the course of which he had written "fourteen books

in English as well as Bengali" and "had poured out hundreds of articles and broadcasts," he had succeeded in offending Indians who were bent on seeing his works as the product of "an unsuccessful, embittered and soured life" and him as a man who was intent on "denigrating them, their life, and civilization." Chaudhuri leaves no doubt in his "Apologia Pro Scripta Dua" that his intention was never to devalue the independence of his country or lament the British withdrawal from India. He had written as an engagé, someone who was ready to tackle issues others preferred not to confront or acknowledge or tended to elide over. He had taken the risk of being perceived as a controversialist so that he could expose the truth as he saw it. With his countrymen and women, he confesses, he had also adopted the role of a preacher, and if at times he has been seen as someone given to excess, he would at least have liked to be appreciated for his courage and boldness in telling them what they needed to hear.

In *Thy Hand, Great Anarch! India, 1921–1952* (1987), one of his major works, Chaudhuri offers readers a list of the primary ideas that engaged him as a writer: "The nature of ancient and modern Indian Culture; Bengali life and culture, the future of the Bengali people; Hindu-Muslim relations in India; nature of Indian nationalism and finally, Indo-British relations." Earlier on in the book he identifies the chief theme of all his writings as "the impact of western life and civilization" on Indians and "the interaction between the two cultures of which I was a product like thousands of others." He felt that the introduction of Enlightenment values to nineteenth-century India had galvanized Indian culture and resulted in a renaissance that brought out the best in the Bengali mind. Perhaps the later works in English also dealt with one other idea that aroused his passions and that is hinted at in the title of the collection in which the "Apologia Pro Scripta Dua" appeared, *Why I Mourn for England* (1998). This idea is announced explicitly in "Decadence of English Life and Civilization," another essay in the collection. All of his works engage with these ideas one way or the other, but he discusses them most fully in *The Autobiography of an Unknown Indian* (1951), his best-known book, and *Thy Hand, Great Anarch!*, a second volume of autobiography and the culminating work of his career.

Nirad Chandra Chaudhuri was born on 23 November 1897 in Kishoreganj, a small town in what was then East Bengal and is now Bangladesh. In 1910 the family moved to Calcutta, where the education begun at home and continued in a Kishoreganj primary school was completed at Calcutta University. Chaudhuri did well in the first of his two examinations in the university, securing the first place in his B.A. (Honors) examination in history at Calcutta University. Carried away by his success, he became oblivious of the limits to which one has to confine oneself to do well in university examinations. The ambition to take almost all knowledge as his province, as well as ill health during his M.A. examination, resulted in academic disaster, and he left Calcutta University without attaining this degree crucial for getting a secure job.

Chaudhuri stayed in Calcutta until 1941, but up to 1927 he visited Kishoreganj at least once a year. His love for his native town and its environs can be seen in all of his writings. Initially, he considered himself an outsider in Calcutta, but the libraries and museums of the city allowed him to pursue his interests in the arts and history and encouraged him to think independently and creatively. He soon became actively involved in the literary life of Calcutta. He read extensively not only Bengali and English literature but also the literature of France and Germany. He pursued his interest in the arts, history, military science, Western music, anthropology, printing, and typography and cultivated the life of a bibliophile, even while struggling to keep himself and his family afloat. In the 1920s he began to make a name for himself as a literary journalist who wrote both in Bengali and English. His strong views on subjects and penchant for entering into controversies also made him unpopular among many Indians, however.

Chaudhuri failed to find any secure means of employment for a long time and drifted from job to job for almost three decades while in Calcutta. In 1921 he began to work as a deputy controller of war accounts in a job that involved paying the salaries and wages of people engaged in Indian army occupations. The work that he did was uninspiring, but he performed it initially as conscientiously as he could. His interest in literary and cultural issues, though, and his dissatisfaction with the dullness of his duties combined to make him quit his position in 1926. The death of his mother in 1924 also depressed him at this point of his life.

One escape from these frustrations that Chaudhuri was feeling came through his writings. A chance meeting with the Bengali poet Mohitlal Majumdar, one of his former teachers, had led to his first appearance in print when he contributed a piece on a Bengali poet in the November 1925 issue of the *Modern Review,* one of the leading Indian magazines of that period. Soon he became a frequent contributor to literary magazines published from Calcutta in

Bengali as well as in English. He remained unemployed for a while, however, another source of unhappiness for him then. The only thing he looked forward to was a career that he could further by contributing his opinions on some of the major literary issues that were preoccupying intellectuals in Calcutta.

Relief from the ignominy of unemployment came toward the end of 1928 when Chaudhuri became the assistant editor of a Bengali periodical. He continued in this position until 1933. He married Amiya Dhar in 1932 at the age of thirty-four. The couple had three sons: Dhruva and Kirti, both born in 1934, and Prithvi, born in 1939. Toward the end of the 1930s he spent a few years as the private secretary of a leading politician of Bengal. This job allowed him to gain firsthand impressions on the momentous events of the period and the varied personalities who were instrumental in achieving independence for India.

For most of the time that he spent in Calcutta, though, Chaudhuri felt constrained by the income he was receiving and his work environment. When World War II broke out, he broadcast commentaries on contemporary events on Calcutta Radio. His support of the Allied forces, however, and criticism of the Japanese at a time when they were threatening to invade Bengal made him feel vulnerable, especially since this stance made him unpopular in Bengal, where anti-British feelings were running high. Moreover, the politician he worked for was jailed, and he was unemployed again.

In 1942 Chaudhuri left Calcutta for Delhi, where he had found work as a broadcaster with All India Radio. Against the backdrop of the tumultuous events that led to the independence of India, he began work on his first book, *The Autobiography of an Unknown Indian.* He was determined to have the book published in England and succeeded in doing so in 1951.

The Autobiography of an Unknown Indian is the story of Chauduri's life until his twenty-fifth year, written from the perspective of a fifty-year-old man. It is divided into four books, the first of which includes detailed sections on the environment in which he grew up as well as vivid accounts of his birthplace, Kishoreganj; his ancestral village, Banagram; his mother's village, Kalikutch; and the Assamese Hill Station of Shillong, all places that left a deep impression on the growing boy. In this opening section Chaudhuri records the life lived by people in a small town in rural East Bengal. With sensitivity and an eye for detail, he depicts how the landscape,

THE CONTINENT OF
CIRCE

Being an Essay on the Peoples of India by

NIRAD C. CHAUDHURI

'*I will pour out my spirit upon all flesh; and your
sons and your daughters shall prophesy, your old
men shall dream dreams, your young men shall
see visions.*'

Looking up towards the sky . . .

Two Views from the Author's Verandah

Looking down to earth . . .

NEW YORK
OXFORD UNIVERSITY PRESS
1966

Frontispiece and title page for the U.S. edition of Chaudhuri's 1965 work, an interpretation of the history of Indian civilization, in which Chaudhuri argues that the insularity of Hindu Indians led to their enervation (Thomas Cooper Library, University of South Carolina)

seasons, and rituals of the region shaped his consciousness.

In book 2 of *The Autobiography of an Unknown Indian,* Chaudhuri describes the circumstances surrounding his birth in November 1897. He offers sketches of his parents, figures he sees affectionately and with reverence as progressive people. His father was a small-town lawyer but also a cultured man full of reformist zeal and Enlightenment ideals, while his mother, though without the benefit of an English education, knew enough literature to introduce him to William Shakespeare in a Bengali translation. In this section of his autobiography Chaudhuri portrays the environment he grew up in as one where East and West met and where Western ideas had stimulated Indians into what is known as the "Indian Renaissance." In the "Torch Race of the Indian

Renaissance," a chapter that forms the heart of the book, Chaudhuri shows how a dynamic, hybrid culture had resulted in Bengal in the nineteenth century because of the coming together of two civilizations when India came under British rule. As far as Chaudhuri is concerned, this period was the golden age of modern Indian history; during this time as never before, the Hindu middle class "showed greater probity in public and private affairs, attained greater happiness in family and personal life, saw greater fulfillment of cultural aspirations, and put forth greater creativeness in every field than the fifty years between 1860 and 1910."

Chaudhuri's autobiography, however, shows how the glory days of Bengali culture ushered in by the Indian Renaissance were terminated by the advent of nationalism at the turn of the twentieth century. In "Enter Nationalism," the chapter that follows "The Torch Race of the Indian Renaissance," Chaudhuri portrays himself as a product of the last flowering of a distinctive culture, since all that his generation had learned, acquired, or treasured became vulnerable because of Indian nationalistic fervor. The excesses of the movement for Indian independence threatened the attainments of the Indian Renaissance. Anarchist impulses, religious riots, and violence were spreading throughout the land.

What Chaudhuri sees as the disintegration of Indian society because of the political turbulence associated with the nationalist movement coincided with his family's move from Kishoreganj to Calcutta. Book 3 of *The Autobiography of an Unknown Indian* thus deals with his adolescent years in the city. The Calcutta years continue his theme of the decline of Indian culture in the twentieth century. As far as he was concerned, he was recording a major catastrophe: the "degradation of Bengal" was "part of the larger process of the rebarbarization of the whole of India." Although he records fully how the cultural and educational institutions of Calcutta made him a bibliophile and an aesthete, and although the third book shows the artist as a young man in a city that is steeped in culture, the fourth and final book of the autobiography also shows a man increasingly alienated from the events around him and disillusioned by what he saw as the "death of moral consciousness" in his people. As *The Autobiography of an Unknown Indian* comes to a close, Chaudhuri is in despair at the turn of events both in public life and in his own personal history.

The book made Chaudhuri controversial in India itself, at least partly as a result of the dedication of the book, to "the memory of the British Empire in India." This dedication, he explains in his "Apologia Pro Scripta Dua," was meant to be ironic, because he felt that the British had "conferred subjecthood on Indians" without treating them as equals and had molded Indian thought positively without intending to do so or anticipating or appreciating the consequences; but the irony was lost on readers in the newly partitioned subcontinent, who saw Chaudhuri as an uncritical admirer of everything British. As he points out, however, in his account of the reception of *The Autobiography of an Unknown Indian* in *Thy Hand, Great Anarch!*, although Indians were mostly hostile, almost all the major newspaper reviews in London were favorable, and the BBC itself gave the author and his work considerable airtime. Indeed, the BBC invited him to visit England for an extended trip on the basis of its evaluation of his book in 1955.

An outcome of this visit and a few weeks spent in France as part of his European excursion was *A Passage to England* (1959), Chaudhuri's second work in English. The book celebrates "Timeless England," the England he had conjured in his mind through his readings and that was to him a conjuncture of values that transcended time. William Walsh, an English critic who was an early admirer of the author, judged in his *Indian Literature in English* (1990) that *A Passage to England* "is a graceful, unusual travel book but slight by the standards of the Autobiography."

The success of *The Autobiography of an Unknown Indian* as well as the notoriety that it earned him were two reasons that Chaudhuri retired from his job at All India Radio in 1952. From this period he continued to support himself and his family in Delhi through his writings and through editing work. Among the newspapers and periodicals that published his work were *The Times* (London), *Encounter*, the *Atlantic Monthly*, and the Calcutta *Statesman*. It was, on the whole, a precarious existence for him and his wife and three sons, and the only stable source of income he had from 1953 to 1966 was from his work as the editor of the English-language bulletin brought out by the French embassy in Delhi.

Chaudhuri's third book, *The Continent of Circe: Being an Essay on the Peoples of India* (1965), is a provocative and eccentric interpretation of Indian history and civilization, although it testifies to his wide reading and earned him the Duff Cooper Memorial Prize for 1966. The thesis of this book is that after Hinduism came to India when the Aryans moved into the Indo-Gangetic plain, the country became a class- and color-conscious one whose ruling classes closed ranks against subsequent invaders, the Muslims and the English who followed them. A consequence of this insularity was the enervation of Hindu Indians. In effect, they had been lured into India only to be turned into degenerate creatures.

Two other works from this period of Chaudhuri's life are *The Intellectual in India* (1967) and *To Live or Not to Live! An Essay on Living Happily with Others* (1970). Essentially collections of his occasional writing, they were published in India and offered Indians advice on how to live happily in their country. These books were never reprinted in the West. He had by then, however, made a reputation through his first three books as a man of original views, formidable scholarship, and interest in Western civilization and the ways in which Western scholarship had contributed to rewriting the history and civilization of India. This reputation led the family of the famous Indologist Max Müller to request him to write Müller's biography. Since Müller's papers were in the Bodleian Library, Chaudhuri had to come to Oxford in 1970 to work. The decision to leave India permanently was a momentous one for Chaudhuri.

Chaudhuri's work on Müller eventually resulted in the publication of *Scholar Extraordinary: The Life of Professor the Rt. Hon. Friedrich Max Müller, P.C.* in 1974. His knowledge of Indian history and scholarship led to another commission, this time from the publishing firm of Barrie and Jenkins, which wanted him to write a life of Robert Clive, the key figure in the founding of the British Empire in India. The outcome was *Clive of India: A Political and Psychological Essay* (1975). Oxford University Press commissioned him next for another work, published as *Hinduism: A Religion to Live By* (1979).

By the end of the 1970s, Chaudhuri appeared to have no more book commissions and so no more reasons to stay in England. Just when he had decided to return to India, however, an advance from Chatto and Windus to write a sequel to his still popular autobiography ensured that he would remain in England for some more years. Chaudhuri began work on *Thy Hand, Great Anarch!* in the spring of 1979 and had it published in 1987.

At nearly a thousand pages, *Thy Hand, Great Anarch!* is a massive book. It covers the years of his "working life," which began in 1921, and comes to a close at the end of 1952. In the book Chaudhuri continues to juxtapose the story of his life with major events of contemporary India, generalizations about the past of the country, and prophetic pronouncements about its future. The present appears to him a sorry culmination of the decay of values and a continuous slide into anarchy. According to Chaudhuri, the book has three aspects: a record of his "personal life"; his "thoughts and feelings about the public and historical events" he encountered then; and "an account of what happened in India in the political and cultural spheres in the period from 1951 to 1952"—"free," he claims, "from the current myths."

The account of his working life includes a description of his years as a clerk in a military-accounts department of the government of India and his boredom with the job but determination to stick to it, if only to write a great historical work. Nevertheless, he quits after a point and then has to go through years of unemployment and a life led precariously, even as he marries and has children. Similarly to *The Autobiography of an Unknown Indian,* in *Thy Hand, Great Anarch!* Chaudhuri describes how he managed to survive by working for a long time as a literary critic, editor, and literary journalist, all the time preparing himself for the great book that he wanted to write. There is more of his life in this work than in

his earlier volume of autobiography, however, and more of his own immediate family, friends, and mentors. He also provides readers with details of the personal relationships he developed first in Calcutta and then in Delhi.

As a record of an epoch in Indian history, *Thy Hand, Great Anarch!* offers detailed accounts of contemporary politics and cultural figures. In particular, Chaudhuri gives firsthand impressions about "the decline of the political power of Europe in India," which he believes parallels "the decline of modern Indian culture." Chaudhuri sees "putrid decay," and a function of the book is not only to record it but also to warn present-day Indians about the dangers of the rejection of their European heritage. In other words, he sees himself as "a Cassandra giving warnings of calamities to come." He does not spare the British, though, since he is sure that their arrogance, their contempt of Indians imitating them, and their failure to encourage "cultural proselytization" were also responsible for the rejection of all things European that he saw as accompanying nationalism. He feels increasingly alienated from the nationalist consciousness fast developing in India and has apocalyptic forebodings at the precipitous end of British rule in India. Because he worked in the 1930s and 1940s as an editor for the official journal of the Calcutta Corporation and as the private secretary of a famous Bengali politician, Chaudhuri asserts to his readers, he was in a fit position to comment incisively on the politics and public figures of the period.

Thy Hand, Great Anarch! derives its title from the conclusion of Alexander Pope's *The Dunciad* (1728). The title announces the basic thesis of the volume: India for Chaudhuri from 1921 to 1952 was a country sliding steadily into chaos. The decline and fall of the British Empire in India, the decay of the culture created in Bengal when European civilization stimulated a hitherto moribund people into fruitful activity, the apparent end of a generation of men who had become the torchbearers of humanistic values, and the violent emotions set loose by nationalism ensured that the forces of anarchy would have a field day in modern India. Reviewing the moral and cultural wastes he found in the events surrounding the partition of India, he sees himself as Tiresias, suffering it all before the fact, or as Jeremiah, uttering imprecations against his people that would eventually make him an outcast. *Thy Hand, Great Anarch!* is full of apocalyptic pronouncements. At the same time, it chronicles Chaudhuri's own attempts to "pass through an age of decadence without being touched by it." The alienation from his own kind that was in evidence at the conclusion of *The Autobi-*

ography of an Unknown Indian becomes, by the end of the second autobiographical volume, total. He is particularly bitter about his fellow Bengalis, who he felt had abdicated their roles as the standard-bearers of Indian civilization. He depicts himself as looking for a way out of Calcutta: "I was convinced that my people had no future, and I was not prepared to share their fate." Delhi offered him a better place to live not only because of the employment prospects in the capital city but also because to all appearances the "Hindu speaking people of that region had more vitality and therefore promise."

Chaudhuri was disappointed once again, however, when he arrived in Delhi to work as a military analyst for the overseas service of All India Radio from 1942 to 1962. The anarchy let loose during Partition and his experience of Delhi life in the 1940s and 1950s convinced him eventually that North India offered him no better an alternative than Bengal. At the conclusion of *Thy Hand, Great Anarch!* Chaudhuri is contemplating the possibility of leaving his country forever for England. At the time, he recounts, he did not do so because of his concern that his children would be alienated from Indian traditions. It is clear throughout the book, though, that he made the move later, for Chaudhuri assumes the tone of a prophet in exile warning the people he had left of the dangers of complacency and of leading unexamined lives. As the book indicates, his life consisted of a series of westward movements, from Kishoreganj to Calcutta, from Calcutta to Delhi, and from Delhi to Oxford: "My life has always moved west, and once it has done so its direction has never been reversed."

Still, Chaudhuri had ambiguous feeling about his peregrinations. On the one hand, he was acutely aware of being uprooted and of having to lead the life of an extraterritorial writer. Even as he had left Calcutta for Delhi it had occurred to him that "to be uprooted was to be forever on the road." In Oxford, he appeared to be constantly haunted by memories of the beauty of the riverfront of Bengal and the glory days of the Bengali renaissance. The consciousness of being part of the Indian diaspora tormented him as it did other Bengalis, for he knew that they could "never forget their Zion in Calcutta." The city was his Jerusalem even when, or precisely because, Calcuttians attacked him. He notes that a similar fate was the lot of the greatest Bengali of all time, Rabindranath Tagore. Tagore's fate, in fact, prompts him to quote Jesus: "O Jerusalem, Jerusalem, *thou* that killest the prophet, and stonest them which are sent to thee, how often would I have gathered thine children together, and ye would not."

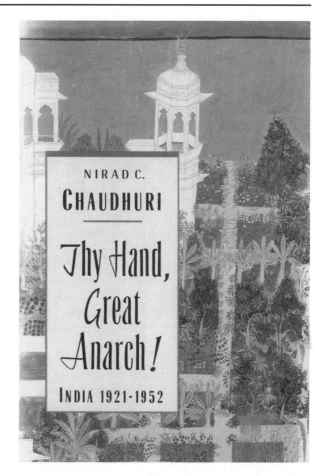

Dust jacket for the U.S. edition of Chaudhuri's second volume of autobiography, which stirred up controversy among Indian readers for its assertions that India had slid into chaos and corruption after the end of British colonial rule (Richland County Public Library)

Like *The Autobiography of an Unknown Indian, Thy Hand, Great Anarch!* received mostly favorable reviews in the West, although Indians continued to be critical of his interpretation of Indian history and characterization of Indian leaders. For instance, writing in the *American Scholar* (Autumn 1988), Edward Shils declares that the work confirms Chaudhuri as "a stylist of the first order, a scholar of great intelligence, learning, and subtlety and a courageous, wise, and honest man." Reviewing this book along with *The Autobiography of an Unknown Indian* in the *New Criterion* (May 1989), David Pryce-Jones observed that Chaudhuri offers in them "a portrait of the slow but triumphant discovery of a powerful writer" who is capable of producing "splendid rhetorical prose" and is something of an "Indian Spengler." At the same time, Pryce-Jones stresses why Indians were so critical of Chaudhuri's work: they see him as a renegade and traitor "to their own kind" who has put himself "beyond the pale by moving to England" and publishing his critiques from there.

In the remaining years of his life, Chaudhuri found a home in Oxford. He wrote mainly in Bengali in the last decades of his literary career, intent on explaining to his countrymen his position on the history of India, his attitude toward the English, the reasons he had decided to stay back, and his feeling of despair at the way the world was shaping. He continued to contribute from time to time on his favorite subjects throughout the 1990s, however, in the Indian English-language newspaper *The Statesman* and English newspapers and periodicals such as the *Daily Telegraph, The Spectator,* and the *New English Review.* He also accepted invitations to speak on the issues that provoked him in various forums. Many of these articles and speeches are collected in *The East Is East and the West Is West* (1996) and *Why I Mourn for England.* The only full-length work that he attempted in English in the 1990s is the monograph-length *Three Horsemen of the New Apocalypse* (1997), a book in which Chaudhuri, then ninety-nine years old, makes his theme the decline and fall of Western civilization and the pervasive decadence he saw all around him in the West and India. Though he had found Oxford a congenial place to retire to, and though he was an admirer of the health-care system of the welfare state, he was put off by the rampant sexuality he saw in the West, the materialism and greed for money that he notes everywhere there. He was convinced that individualism, nationalism, and democracy were taking Europe as well as the rest of the world toward apocalypse. He reveals in the book that he himself has become prey to "inescapable despair" at what was happening. The decadence of India that he analyzes in the two autobiographical volumes is here supplemented by the decadence he witnesses in England and the United States.

Chaudhuri's works reveal a complex and fascinating man. In love with the Enlightenment ideals of the West and the culture spawned by it in India in the nineteenth century, an Anglophile and Francophile, he is also the thoroughly Bengali/Indian babu, particularly proud of the heights Bengali culture reached during the renaissance India experienced at one point of its history. A prude and puritan, he is also revealed in his autobiographical volumes to be romantic, extravagant, and even an "incorrigible Micawberian." Obsessive and fanatical in many ways, he is also someone who champions truth even at the cost of being seen as a pariah by his own people. On a few occasions, he seems quixotic and idiosyncratic in his ideas about history and culture, but he has also mastered many provinces of knowledge and shown impressive analytical skills in his interpretation of events and people on other occasions.

He adopts a variety of roles in his writings: he is an ideologue, a scholar-gypsy, an aesthete, an engagé, and a gadfly who involves himself, as he writes in *Thy Hand, Great Anarch!,* "in every aspect of political, social, and cultural life almost all over the world" but also a lonely, embittered, and alienated figure, misunderstood by his people. Unabashedly egotistical, he also wants his readers to understand that he writes because he cares about his people and their future. He is proud of being a cosmopolitan since he is confident that he has remained "a citizen of the world" even when affirming his identity as "a Bengali, an Indian, an Englishman." Always, his enthusiasm, confidence in himself, and jeu d'esprit offset his jeremiads, his laments, and his moments of pique. At his best, he writes prose that bears the mark of a consummate stylist, and works such as *The Autobiography of an Unknown Indian, A Passage to England,* and *Thy Hand, Great Anarch!* display his mastery not only over the English language but also his ability to structure his ideas carefully and develop his arguments skillfully by juxtaposing personal observations with historical overviews or allusions to the classics of literature and history. He has shaped these works into highly readable works of art, and even the *Continent of Circe,* despite its eccentric thesis, makes for enjoyable reading. In the last analysis, each of these volumes is, like their creator, sui generis. Duncan Fallowell, writing in the *American Scholar* (Spring 1991), described Chaudhuri thus: "affable, lively, a cultural enthusiast, an intellectual, principled, combative, dogmatic, but always immensely interesting." Shils finds in his writings "the activities of an intelligence of very great eminence, of a personality of clear and admirable lineaments in a situation of world-historical significance."

As time has passed, even Indians have begun to appreciate *The Autobiography of an Unknown Indian* for its rich evocation of a world that has gone by and its impressive style, and quite a few Indian scholars now agree that it is one of the few great Indian books that deal with the Indo-English encounter and its consequences. As Swapan Dasgupta observes in the introduction to his centenary collection of essays, *Nirad C. Chaudhuri, the First Hundred Years: A Celebration* (1997), what had prevented many Indians from appreciating Chaudhuri's provocative writings were "two commodities that are pitifully lacking in India: a sense of humor and a sense of history." Dasgupta continues:

There is a strong temptation to dismiss Nirad Chaudhuri as a quaint but inconsequential anachronism who harks back to an ideal age when Empire and Enlightenment blended harmoniously. It should be resisted. Nirad Babu is indeed an oddity, but his exceptional status stems from his readiness to us [*sic*] what we would rather not face up to. . . . it is difficult to find another Indian who can match his grand sweep, his erudition, his accomplishments, and his penchant for having the last laugh.

Among a new generation of postcolonial critics, too, Nirad C. Chaudhuri is being revalued more objectively than before. Sudesh Mishra, writing in a 1988 issue of the *Journal of Commonwealth Literature,* dismisses Chaudhuri's historiography and views him only as a pseudohistorian, but he appreciates Chaudhuri's record of "individual, familial, political, or social events" and acknowledges his ability to write an "imaginative history" of India and calls *The Autobiography of an Unknown Indian* "a masterpiece." As an imaginative witness to Indian history, as one of the finest practitioners of English prose in the subcontinent, as an artificer of words and as someone whose ideas constantly enliven his best works, he is a key figure of Indian English prose writing.

References:

Fakrul Alam, "A House for Mr. Chaudhuri," in *Ideas of Home: Literature of Asian Migration,* edited by Geoffrey Kain (East Lansing: Michigan State University Press, 1997), pp. 45–62;

Swapan Dasgupta, ed., *Nirad C. Chaudhuri, the First Hundred Years: A Celebration* (New Delhi: HarperCollins India, 1997);

Duncan Fallowell, "Nirad C. Chaudhuri: At Home in Oxford," *American Scholar,* 60 (Spring 1991): 242–246;

Sudesh Mishra, "The Two Chaudhuris: Historical Witness and Pseudo-Historian," *Journal of Commonwealth Literature,* 23, no. 1 (1988): 7–15;

David Pryce-Jones, "Remembering India," *New Criterion,* 7 (May 1989): 77–80;

Edward Shils, "Citizen of the World: Nirad C. Chaudhuri," *American Scholar,* 57 (Autumn 1988): 549–572;

William Walsh, *Indian Literature in English* (London & New York: Longman, 1990), pp. 45–53.

Ananda Coomaraswamy

(22 August 1877 – 9 September 1947)

Anthony R. Guneratne
Florida Atlantic University

SELECTED BOOKS: *The Deeper Meaning of the Struggle* (Broad Campden, U.K.: Essex House, 1907);

Mediæval Sinhalese Art (Broad Campden, U.K.: Essex House, 1908; revised, New York: Pantheon, 1956; New Delhi: Munshiram Manoharlal, 2003);

Essays in National Idealism (Colombo: Colombo Apothecaries, 1909);

The Indian Craftsman (London: Probsthain, 1909; New Delhi: Munshiram Manoharlal, 1989);

The Message of the East (Madras: Ganesh, 1909);

Myths and Legends: Hindus and Buddhists, by Coomaraswamy and Margaret E. Noble, as Sister Nivedita (Boston: Nickerson, 1910); republished as *Myths of the Hindus and Buddhists* (London: Harrap, 1913; New York: Farrar & Rinehart, 1934); republished as *Myths and Legends of the Hindus and Buddhists* (Calcutta: Advaita Ashrama, 2001);

Selected Examples of Indian Art (Broad Campden, U.K.: Essex House, 1910; New Delhi: Today & Tomorrow's Printers & Publishers, 1971);

Indian Drawings, 2 volumes (London: India Society, 1910, 1912; Varanasi, Uttar Pradesh: Bharatiya, 1979);

Art and Swadeshi (Madras: Ganesh, 1912);

The Arts and Crafts of India and Ceylon (London & Edinburgh: Foulis, 1913; New York: Farrar, Straus, 1964; New Delhi: Today & Tomorrow's Printers and Publishers, 1971);

Buddha and the Gospel of Buddhism (London: Harrap, 1916; New York: Putnam, 1916; Bombay: Asia Publishing House, 1956; revised by Luisa Coomaraswamy, New York: Harper & Row, 1964);

Rajput Painting: Being an Account of the Hindu Paintings of Rajasthan and the Panjab Himalayas from the Sixteenth to the Nineteenth Century Described in their Relation to Contemporary Thought, 2 volumes (London & New York: H. Milford/Oxford University Press, 1916; Delhi: Motilal Banarsidas, 1976);

Ananda Coomaraswamy, circa 1907 (from Roger Lipsey, ed., Coomaraswamy, vol. 3, 1977; Richland County Public Library)

The Dance of Siva: Fourteen Indian Essays, preface by Romain Rolland (New York: Sunwise Turn, 1918; London: Simpkin, Marshall, Hamilton, Kent, 1924); revised as *The Dance of Shiva: Fourteen Indian Essays* (Bombay: Asia Publishing House, 1948; New York: Noonday Press, 1957; London: P. Owen, 1958);

Twenty-Eight Drawings (New York: Sunwise Turn, 1920);

Catalogue of the Indian Collections in the Museum of Fine Arts, Boston, 6 parts (Boston: Museum of Fine Arts, 1923–1930; Delhi: Bharatiya, 1978);

Introduction to Indian Art (Madras: Theosophical Publishing House, 1923; revised, edited by Mulk Raj Anand, 1956; revised, edited by Alice Coomaraswamy, as Ratan Devi, Delhi: Munshiram Manoharlal, 1969);

History of Indian and Indonesian Art (Leipzig: Hiersemann / New York: Weyhe / London: Goldston, 1927; New Delhi: Munshiram Manoharlal, 1972);

Yaksas, 2 volumes (Washington, D.C.: Smithsonian, 1928, 1931; New Delhi: Munshiram Manoharlal, 1971); revised and enlarged as *Yaksas: Essays in the Water Cosmology,* edited by Paul Schroeder, foreword by Kapila Vatsyayan (New Delhi: Indira Gandhi National Centre for the Arts / Delhi & New York: Oxford University Press, 1993);

An Introduction to the Art of Eastern Asia (Chicago: Open Court, 1932);

A New Approach to the Vedas: An Essay in Translation and Exegesis (London: Luzac, 1933; Delhi: Aparna, 1985); republished as *Essence of the Vedas* (New Delhi: Radha, 1995);

The Transformation of Nature in Art (Cambridge, Mass.: Harvard University Press, 1934; New Delhi: Munshiram Manoharlal, 1974);

Elements of Buddhist Iconography (Cambridge, Mass.: Harvard University Press, 1935; New Delhi: Munshiram Manoharlal, 1972);

The Rg Veda as Land-náma-bók (London: Luzac, 1935; Delhi: Bharatiya, 1979);

Spiritual Authority and Temporal Power in the Indian Theory of Government (New Haven: American Oriental Society, 1942; New Delhi: Munshiram Manoharlal, 1978; revised and enlarged edition, edited by Keshavram N. Iengar and Rama P. Coomaraswamy, New Delhi: Indira Gandhi National Centre for the Arts / Delhi & New York: Oxford University Press, 1993);

Hinduism and Buddhism (New York: Philosophical Library, 1943; New Delhi: Munshiram Manoharlal, 1975; revised and enlarged, edited by Iengar and Rama P. Coomaraswamy, preface by Robert A. Strom, New Delhi: Indira Gandhi National Centre for the Arts/Manohar, 1999);

Why Exhibit Works of Art? (London: Luzac, 1943); republished as *Christian and Oriental Philosophy of Art* (New York: Dover, 1956; New Delhi: Munshiram Manoharlal, 1974);

Figures of Speech or Figures of Thought: Collected Essays on the Traditional or "Normal" View of Art (London: Luzac, 1946; New Delhi: Munshiram Manoharlal, 1981);

Am I My Brother's Keeper? introduction by Robert Allerton Parker (New York: John Day, 1947); republished as *The Bugbear of Literacy* (London: Dobson, 1949; revised and enlarged edition, Bedfont, U.K.: Perennial, 1979);

Time and Eternity (Ascona, Switzerland: Artibus Asiae, 1947; New Delhi: Munshiram Manoharlal, 1988);

The Origin of the Buddha Image (New Delhi: Munshiram Manoharlal, 1972);

Early Indian Architecture: Palaces (New Delhi: Munshiram Manoharlal, 1975);

On the Traditional Doctrine of Art (Ipswich, U.K.: Golgonooza Press, 1977);

Sources of Wisdom (Colombo: Ministry of Cultural Affairs, 1981);

Symbolism of Indian Architecture, introduction by Pramod Chandra (Jaipur: Historical Research Documentation Programme, 1983);

Early Indian Architecture: Cities and City Gates, Etc. (New Delhi: Munshiram Manoharlal, 1991);

Jaina Art (New Delhi: Munshiram Manoharlal, 1994);

The Eight Nayikas (New Delhi: Munshiram Manoharlal, 2000);

Perception of the Vedas, edited by Vidya Nivas Misra (New Delhi: Indira Gandhi National Centre for the Arts/Manohar, 2000);

Writings on Geology and Mineralogy: Scientific Papers and Comments, edited by A. Ranganathan and K. Srinivasa Rao (New Delhi: Indira Gandhi National Centre for the Arts/Manohar, 2001);

Guardians of the Sundoor: Late Iconographic Essays and Drawings of Ananda K. Coomaraswamy, edited, with a preface, by Strom (Louisville, Ky.: Fons Vitae, 2004).

Collections: *The Vedas: Essays in Translation and Exegesis* (Beckenham, U.K.: Prologos Books, 1976)—comprises *A New Approach to the Vedas* and *The Rg Veda as Land-náma-bók;*

Roger Lipsey, ed., *Coomaraswamy,* 3 volumes (Princeton: Princeton University Press, 1977)—comprises volume 1, *Selected Papers: Traditional Art and Symbolism;* volume 2, *Selected Papers: Metaphysics;* and volume 3, *His Life and Work,* by Lipsey; selections from volumes 1 and 2 republished as *The Door in the Sky: Coomaraswamy on Myth and Meaning,* edited, with a preface, by Rama P. Coomaraswamy (Princeton: Princeton University Press, 1997);

The Wisdom of Ananda Coomaraswamy: Being Glimpses of the Mind of Ananda Coomaraswamy: Great Thoughts Selected from His Writings, Letters and Speeches, edited by S. Durai Raja Singam, introduction by Whitall N. Perry (Petaling Jaya, Malaysia: S. Durai Raja Singam, 1979);

What Is Civilization? and Other Essays, foreword by Seyyed Hossein Nasr (Delhi & New York: Oxford University Press, 1989; Ipswich, U.K.: Golgonooza Press, 1989);

Essays in Early Indian Architecture, edited, with an introduction, by Michael W. Meister (New Delhi: Indira Gandhi National Centre for the Arts/Oxford University Press, 1992);

Essays in Architectural Theory, edited by Meister (New Delhi: Indira Gandhi National Centre for the Arts/Oxford University Press, 1995);

Essays on Jaina Art, edited, with an introduction, by Richard J. Cohen (New Delhi: Indira Gandhi National Centre for the Arts/Manohar, 2003);

The Essential Ananda K. Coomaraswamy, edited by Rama P. Coomaraswamy, foreword by Arvind Sharma, prologue by Marco Pallis (Bloomington, Ind.: World Wisdom, 2004).

OTHER: "Report on Thorianite and Thorite," in *Report on the Occurrence of Thorium-Bearing Minerals in Ceylon,* edited by Wyndham R. Dunstan (Colombo, 1904);

Visvakarma: Examples of Indian Architecture, Sculpture, Painting, Handicraft, edited by Coomaraswamy, introduction by Eric Gill, 8 parts (London: Luzac, 1912–1914; New Delhi: Munshiram Manoharlal, 1978);

Stella Bloch, *Dancing and the Drama East and West,* introduction by Coomaraswamy (New York: Orientalia, 1922);

T. G. Aravamuthan, *Portrait Sculpture in South India,* foreword by Coomaraswamy (London: India Society, 1931; New Delhi: Asian Educational Services, 1992);

Nasli M. Heeramaneck, *Loan Exhibition of Early Indian Sculptures, Paintings and Bronzes,* introduction by Coomaraswamy (New York: Heeramaneck Galleries, 1935);

Benjamin Rowland Jr., *The Wall-Paintings of India, Central Asia & Ceylon: A Comparative Study,* introduction by Coomaraswamy, foreword by A. Townshend Johnson (Boston: Merrymount Press, 1938; Delhi: Alfa, 1985);

The Living Thoughts of Gotama, the Buddha, edited by Coomaraswamy and I. B. Horner (London: Cassell, 1948; Bombay: Jaico, 1958; Ann Arbor, Mich.: UMI, 1978); republished as *The Great Thoughts of Gotama the Buddha* (New Delhi: Crest, 1996).

TRANSLATIONS: *Völuspá: Done into English out of the Icelandic of the Elder Edda* (Broad Campden, U.K.: Essex House, 1909);

Muhammad Rida, *Burning and Melting,* translated by Coomaraswamy and Mirza Y. Dawud (London: Old Bourne Press, 1912);

Alice Coomaraswamy, as Ratan Devi, ed., *Thirty Songs from the Panjab and Kashmir,* translated, with an introduction, by Ananda Coomaraswamy, foreword by Rabindranath Tagore (London: Privately printed, 1913; revised and enlarged, edited by Premlata Sharma, foreword by Kapila Vatsyayan, New Delhi: Indira Gandhi National Centre for the Arts/Sterling, 1994);

Vidyapati Thakura, *Vidyapati: Bangiya Padabali: Songs of the Love of Radha and Krishna,* translated by Ananda Coomaraswamy and Arun Sen (London: Old Bourne Press, 1915); republished as *Krishna Purbbaraga* (Varanasi, Uttar Pradesh: Bharatiya, 1979);

The Mirror of Gesture, Being the Abhinaya Darpana of Nandikesvara, translated by Ananda Coomaraswamy and Gopala Kristnayya Duggirala (Cambridge, Mass.: Harvard University Press, 1917; New Delhi: Munshiram Manoharlal, 1970).

SELECTED PERIODICAL PUBLICATIONS–UNCOLLECTED: "The Village Community and Modern Progress," *Ceylon National Review,* 2, no. 7 (1908): 249–260;

"A World Policy for India," *New Age* (24 December 1914): 192–193;

"Love and Art," *Modern Review* (May 1915): 574–584;

"Rajput Painting," *MFA Bulletin,* 16 (1918): 49–62; 17 (1919): 33–43;

"The Philosophy of Mediaeval and Oriental Art," *Zalmoxis,* 1 (1938): 20–49;

"The Iconography of Dürer's Knots and Leonardo's Concatenation," *Arts Quarterly,* 7, no. 2 (1944): 109–128.

Ananda Coomaraswamy's death at the age of seventy brought tributes not only from art historians but also from the same diverse assortment of statesmen, scientists, museum curators, folklorists, philosophers, and students of comparative religion who had either contributed to the festschrift dedicated to him on his birthday less than a month before his death or gathered in celebrations in his honor held concurrently in three countries. At the conclusion of the dinner party at the Faculty Club of Harvard University, he astonished those present by declaring that his practical labors were drawing to an end and that he was preparing to complete his spiritual development in what he now regarded as his homeland, India, newly independent of British rule. These labors are documented by more than nine hundred publications that chart Coomaraswamy's metamorphosis from a scientist into an art historian and political activist and, later, a linguist and philosopher whose theories of iconology and metaphys-

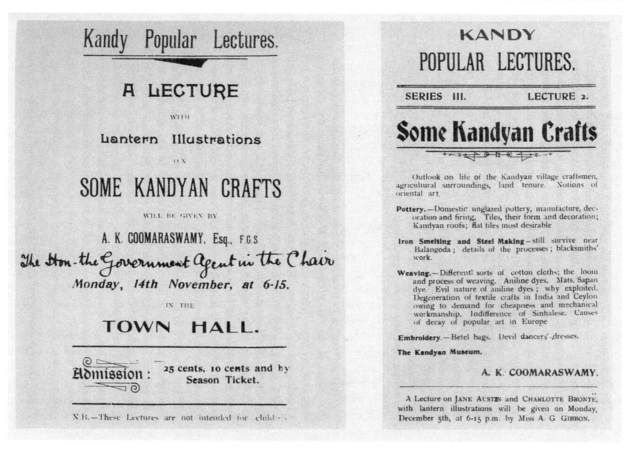

Advertisements for lectures given by Coomaraswamy in Ceylon, circa 1906 (from Roger Lipsey, ed., Coomaraswamy, *vol. 3, 1977; Richland County Public Library)*

ics had an impact on fields as diverse as art history, sociology, religious studies, cultural history, and comparative literature. A political dissident, militant traditionalist, and eloquent adversary of several of the seminal thinkers of his time, Coomaraswamy was the most renowned South Asian philosopher-essayist of the first half of the twentieth century.

Ananda Kentish Coomaraswamy was born in Ceylon (now Sri Lanka) on 22 August 1877. His father, Mutu Coomaraswamy, a linguist who translated into English the ancient Pali epics of Ceylon and Tamil drama, was also famous as a speaker. In 1863, on his first trip to Europe, Mutu Coomaraswamy was called to the bar at Lincoln's Inn, becoming the first Asian-born barrister in England. On his second trip, undertaken in 1874 in his capacity as a member of the legislative council of Ceylon, he was knighted. Shortly thereafter, he met a young woman from Kent, Elizabeth Clay Beeby, who shared his interest in Indian philosophy. The two were married in 1875, and the following year they moved to Ceylon. In 1879 Elizabeth returned to England with her young son. Her husband was to

join her, but he died suddenly on 4 May 1879, the day scheduled for his departure. Although Sir Mutu was a staunch nationalist who sought to ameliorate the excesses of British colonialism, an interesting posthumous tribute to him was made by the equally staunch imperialist Benjamin Disraeli, who cast him as Kusinara, a character given to witty irony, in a novel unfinished at the time of his death in 1881, *Falconet* (1927).

Ananda Coomaraswamy grew up in England; he was close to his mother (who never remarried) and resembled her physically, save for his distinctive complexion. His early education was that of an English gentleman. Nevertheless, as Roger Lipsey observes in *His Life and Work*, volume 3 of *Coomaraswamy* (1977), there is little indication that he identified with English culture. From the late 1890s Coomaraswamy made frequent visits to Ceylon, initially in the company of his mother. While studying for a doctorate in geology at the University of London, he was appointed director of a mineralogical survey of Ceylon and returned there in that capacity in 1902. In the course of crisscrossing Ceylon with his wife, the talented photographer Ethel Mary

Partridge Coomaraswamy, whom he had married in June of that year, he observed many traces of the ancient culture of Ceylon, its continuity in the work of local craftsmen, and the blighting effect of British rule on traditional ways of life. He also began to document the surviving works of art, even while carrying out his scientific duties so conscientiously that in one of his first publications he was able to announce the discovery of a new mineral, thorianite, consisting of a mixture of uranium and thorium ("Report on Thorianite and Thorite," 1904). The impact of his encounters with a vanishing tradition determined the course of his life and the nature of his subsequent writing.

Although Lipsey suggests that Coomaraswamy's works fall into three periods, his prodigious oeuvre probably lends itself more suitably to a four-part division. The first period of his writing might be thought of as his *swadeshi* (native activist) phase. Noting that the British found native mimicry of European customs comical even as they promoted an educational system that encouraged such emulation, he determined to bring about the conditions necessary for self-governance, which he felt was a crucial precondition for a revival of the traditional crafts and culture of Ceylon. From the outset Coomaraswamy assumed that he had inherited his father's mantle. The Ceylon Social Reform Society, which he helped to found and whose journal he edited, declared itself in a January 1906 manifesto; along with the expected call for a revitalization of traditional crafts, it was also concerned with dietary habits and hygiene.

This period of Coomaraswamy's activities culminated in the events following his return to England. Finding a sympathetic audience among the latter-day followers of William Morris, especially the typographers and book illustrators Walter Crane and Eric Gill (whom Coomaraswamy influenced profoundly), he purchased the building then housing Morris's celebrated experiment in book design, the Kelmscott Press, and published a slim volume, *The Deeper Meaning of the Struggle* (1907), and his first major work of art history, *Mediæval Sinhalese Art* (1908). His description of the fifteen-month process of bringing out the latter book as an illustration of East-West symbiosis in reviving craftsmanship echoed Morris's socialism. Nevertheless, several commentators, such as Tanya Harrod and Patrick Brantlinger, have overestimated the extent of Morris's influence on Coomaraswamy. Morris's rejection of the artificial distinction between arts and crafts was a formative influence, but so was the pan-Asianism of the Japanese art historian Kakuzo Okakura, who similarly influenced the leaders of the Indian anticolonial modernist movement, the Tagore family. Aesthetic philosophies deriving from Plato, Meister Eckhart, and the Vedantic and later Sanskritic commentaries on art,

music, and metaphysics held special importance for Coomaraswamy, as did the works of the Scholastics, the Renaissance painters and philosophers under the sway of Neoplatonism, and a few exceptional later figures, notably Johann Wolfgang von Goethe, William Blake, and Henry David Thoreau.

Coomaraswamy spent most of 1909 in India in the company of the Tagore family and returned to India for lengthy periods during the next three years. When he decided to extend a visit there in 1910, his wife returned to England for what turned out to be a permanent separation. The Tagores had, with Auriobondo Ghose, led the resistance to repeated British efforts to partition Bengal along ethnic and religious lines, and perhaps recognizing that the British had had greater success in implementing the divide-and-rule strategy in Ceylon, Coomaraswamy refocused his attention on the art of India and on the more firmly rooted Indian struggle for independence. His last major *swadeshi* works were *Essays in National Idealism* (1909) and *Art and Swadeshi* (1912), the latter including several translations of Rabindranath Tagore's poems, as well as a biographical commentary on the poet.

Before Coomaraswamy had made a profound study of philosophy or expanded on his father's belief that the surest way to end colonial domination was to educate those responsible for it, a dispute known as the Suet Pudding Debate broke out at a meeting of the Royal Society of Arts. The meeting was chaired by one of the champions of Indian craftsmanship and the curator of the Indian holdings in the South Kensington Museum, Sir George Birdwood. By 1910 Indian art had profoundly influenced the painter Gustave Moreau and the French Symbolists, and Indian literature and philosophy had transformed the thinking of Søren Kierkegaard, Arthur Schopenhauer, and Friedrich Nietzsche. In that year the Royal Society of Arts invited E. B. Havell, author of *Indian Sculpture and Painting* (1908), to lecture on arts administration in India. John Ruskin and other British art historians had already expressed disgust with the "unnatural" forms of Indian art while praising Indian craftsmanship, and Havell took as his theme the possibility of Indian fine art. As Lipsey recounts the incident, Birdwood's concluding remarks caused a furor, for he suggested that one of Havell's photographic illustrations, of a Buddha from the Javanese temple of Borobodur seated in meditation, showed the work to be a "senseless similitude, in its immemorial fixed pose," adding that "a boiled suet pudding would serve equally well as a symbol of passionless serenity and purity of soul." Coomaraswamy responded that if Birdwood chose to call the works shown by the Royal Academy of Arts or the Paris Salon "fine" and a figure of the Avalokitesvara (the Buddhist

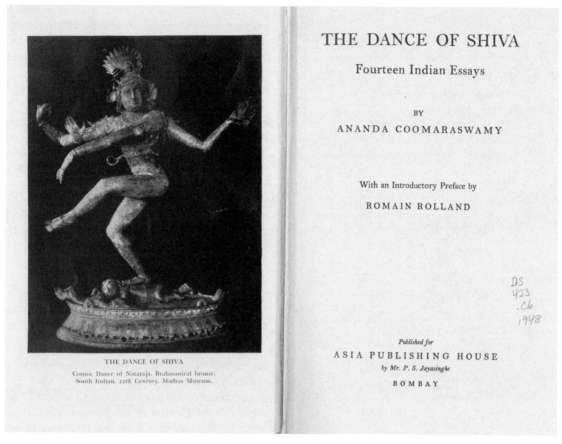

THE DANCE OF SHIVA

Cosmic Dance of Nataraja. Brahmanical bronze.
South Indian. *12th Century*. Madras Museum.

THE DANCE OF SHIVA

Fourteen Indian Essays

BY

ANANDA COOMARASWAMY

With an Introductory Preface by

ROMAIN ROLLAND

Published for

ASIA PUBLISHING HOUSE

by Mr. P. S. Jayasinghe

BOMBAY

Frontispiece and title page for the 1948 Indian edition of Coomaraswamy's influential work on Indian aesthetic theory, originally published in 1918 (Thomas Cooper Library, University of South Carolina)

deity of compassion and mercy) "decorative," then the decorative would be "a profounder revelation, a more living utterance than the fine." If Coomaraswamy had hitherto vacillated between his inherited vocations in art and politics, this encounter confirmed their inseparability and the course of his future writing. Henceforth, he took upon himself the task of defending the artistic inspiration of India, with the result that even his most formal works of art history have a polemical edge, a constant appeal to ancient and traditional values, and an uncompromising rejection of the post-Renaissance sponsorship of art that he came to regard as a departure from the "great tradition" and hence, in his terms, increasingly "provincial" and "sentimental."

The second phase of Coomaraswamy's writing began with the two-volume *Indian Drawings* (1910, 1912) and *The Arts and Crafts of India and Ceylon* (1913). While the second volume of *Indian Drawings,* the most important work on Rajput miniatures up to that time, modified his earlier conviction that all Hindu art had a religious basis (unlike that of the more secular Mogul miniaturists, for instance), by 1913 he had focused his

attention on the fundamentally hieratic nature of classical Indian art. He was beginning to immerse himself in a study of Indian religious philosophy and metaphysics, a preoccupation that was to overshadow art history in the final phase of his career.

Failing to obtain a university post in Benares and unable to create a museum in India for his growing collection of sculptural works and miniature paintings, the dispirited Coomaraswamy was stranded in England on the eve of World War I. His correspondence from this period, partly censored when published, includes some of the most lucid expositions of his philosophical positions and is among the finest epistolary writing by an Asian writer in English. The letters are also the best evidence for his antagonism toward Indian participation in the war effort and suggest that his own refusal to enlist led to repeated harassment by the British authorities. Most of the letters in *Selected Letters of Ananda K. Coomaraswamy* (1988) date from his later years of placid reflection, some of the finest being patient, detailed replies to queries from unknown correspondents. Little personal detail survives from the World War I period, but in the

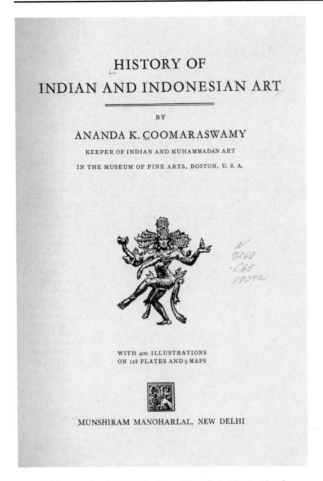

HISTORY OF
INDIAN AND INDONESIAN ART

BY

ANANDA K. COOMARASWAMY

KEEPER OF INDIAN AND MUHAMMADAN ART

IN THE MUSEUM OF FINE ARTS, BOSTON, U. S. A.

WITH 400 ILLUSTRATIONS
ON 128 PLATES AND 9 MAPS

MUNSHIRAM MANOHARLAL, NEW DELHI

*Title page for the 1972 Indian edition of what is considered
Coomaraswamy's most conventional study of art history,
originally published in 1927 (Thomas Cooper
Library, University of South Carolina)*

midst of all the turbulence Coomaraswamy published his first formal work on religious philosophy, *Buddha and the Gospel of Buddhism* (1916), as well as his most important study of a single artistic form of expression, *Rajput Painting* (1916). The latter, the most sumptuously illustrated of all his works, established the serious study of Indian painting in the English-speaking world, transforming purely iconographic study into a systematic cultural exposition. The book marks the beginning of an evolutionary process that led Coomaraswamy to the third phase of his writing. Again, his letters reveal his development, for he wrote in 1939 that his increasing concern with metaphysics was not the result of increasing age but of "maturity": "I was no longer satisfied with a merely descriptive iconography and had to be able to explain the *reasons* for the forms."

By 1916 life in England for Coomaraswamy had become intolerable, and through the intercession of friends he was granted a visa to accompany his second

wife, Alice Richardson Coomaraswamy, whom he had married in 1911, on an American concert tour. Alice was a gifted musician whose performance of ragas under the stage name of Ratan Devi impressed both Tagore and William Butler Yeats; Coomaraswamy used to explain the aesthetics of Indian classical music before she played. The couple had two children: a son, Narada, born in 1912, and a daughter, Rohini, born in 1914. A desperate Coomaraswamy let it be known that his art collection was up for sale, and at this critical moment he made the acquaintance of a Harvard professor of fine arts, Denman Ross. The independently wealthy Ross acquired the collection and had Coomaraswamy installed as curator of the Indian collection at the Museum of Fine Arts in Boston. The museum now had the most extensive collection of Asian art in the United States. The political refugee Coomaraswamy had found a refuge where nothing more was expected of him than cataloguing the holdings of the collection. By this expedient Ross had made one of the singular achievements of twentieth-century scholarship possible.

Coomaraswamy inaugurated this third period of his literary career with one of his most influential works, *The Dance of Siva: Fourteen Indian Essays* (1918), a comprehensive but concise introduction to Indian aesthetic theory. Central to the collection is the idea that beauty and its attributes are not subjective impressions but objectively determined states of being. The aesthetic value of such an image as the Siva Nataraja (Siva, Lord of Dance), once derided by English art historians as a many-armed monstrosity, was part of the fundamental meaning of the image, conveyed properly or poorly according to the skill level of the artist. In Coomaraswamy's view, the artist's freedom to select subject matter is irrelevant, and eccentricities of style are the result of incomplete knowledge of the traditional import of the subject matter. Coomaraswamy's increasing erudition is also much in evidence in *The Dance of Siva*. In an extended passage, the sixth-century Chinese painter and critic Hsieh Ho (Xie He) and Jean-François Millet, separated by centuries and different cultures, are shown to have concordant ideas of beauty.

Most of Coomaraswamy's works of this period were more strictly iconographic and scattered widely among journals. His important writings on the architecture of Hindu temples, for example, were collected much later as *Essays in Early Indian Architecture* (1992). He was also reviewing a spate of publications on South Asian art in French and German that came in the wake of his own popularization of the field, and he wrote his most conventionally historical work, the culmination of this curatorial period, *History of Indian and Indonesian Art* (1927). A sober and encyclopedic study of Indian art and its diffusion in South and Southeast Asia, it remains one of his most-cited works. Only in rare passages (such as a lament that the skill of Sinhalese craftsmen was ill used because the taste of "educated" Ceylonese had "degenerated beyond recovery") is his earlier voice in evidence.

The 1920s were a productive but turbulent time for Coomaraswamy. His marriage to Alice had collapsed in 1917, and his occasional partner from that time onward, Stella Bloch, chose to remain in New York when they married in 1922. Dividing his time between Boston and New York, Coomaraswamy moved in artistic circles, tried his hand at poetry, published his drawings, and invested in a bookstore. This period ended with his divorce from Stella in 1930. Two weeks later he married Luisa Runstein, who remained devoted to him for the rest of his life and with whom he had a son, Rama Poonambulam, born in 1932. He also systematized his activities, dividing them between curatorial duties, writing, and tending his garden.

What followed was the fourth and most controversial phase in Coomaraswamy's development, in which he finally felt himself able to expound on what he termed the "Philosophia Perennis" (Perennial Philosophy). This period began for him with a state of crisis. Recognizing the inadequacy of the translated works on aesthetics and metaphysics on which he had so far relied, he underwent a mental transformation (for which he used the Greek term *metanoia*) and began devoting much of his time to perfecting his Latin and Greek and acquiring a philologically exact knowledge of Pali and Sanskrit. He revised the conclusions he had reached about the Vedic water cosmology in *Yaksas* (1928), a Smithsonian publication. In the second part, published in 1931, he acknowledged even earlier elements of this cosmology. In 1933 he published his first work centered on metaphysics, *A New Approach to the Vedas: An Essay in Translation and Exegesis*. He also began to correspond regularly with others who had come to share the Platonic view that all "true" knowledge is one, or, in Jungian terms, "primal," and preserved in the oldest folk beliefs and religious doctrines. While René Guénon, an expert on Sufi mysticism and a learned popularizer of the "Great Tradition" (a term Guénon preferred to "Philosophia Perennis"), was his peer, many among the younger generation attracted to Coomaraswamy's ideas regarded him as a teacher. Mircea Eliade, the greatest scholar of comparative religion in this younger generation, became a Coomaraswamy convert and referred to him in correspondence as "Cher Maître." Comparative religion was rapidly established as a field of study at major universities in Europe and North America. Joseph Campbell, who specialized in folklore and readily acknowledged his debt to

Coomaraswamy, became its leading American exponent.

Most people came to know Coomaraswamy through the greatest early work of this last period, *The Transformation of Nature in Art* (1934). Drawing on a variety of sources—medieval Christianity, Vedic treatises, Chinese commentaries, works of Islamic mysticism, accounts of folk beliefs, and the works of literary figures such as Dante Alighieri and Jalal al-Din Rumi—Coomaraswamy expounded the Platonic doctrine of the two selves (atman and *jivatman* in Vedic thought) and endeavored to illustrate that ancient and classical theories of art stemmed from a single philosophy. In the years that followed, he continued these researches and produced his most dense and philosophically compact essays, although at times he was more direct, as in the essay collection *Why Exhibit Works of Art?* (1943), in which he insists that museums should not be places to display the fruits of patronage or the spoils of conquest but rather places for research and contemplation. The work of this last period came to fruition with *Figures of Speech or Figures of Thought: Collected Essays on the Traditional or "Normal" View of Art* (1946), in which Coomaraswamy showed that art in its broadest sense functions as a symbolic language with a specific repertoire of images, differing only in the accents given to these images by different ages and different cultures.

Some critics have suggested that Coomaraswamy was antipathetic to all modern art and that he practiced an intolerant traditionalism. His exactitude led to his rejecting much of the work of Carl Jung, because he felt Jung failed to understand the terms *anima* and *animus* properly, and to his chiding Aldous Huxley for his dilettantish attempt to explain "Philosophia Perennis" to a popular audience. Coomaraswamy cited artists such as Paul Cézanne and John Everett Millais, rejecting only art that he believed was affected by commerce and post-Renaissance individualistic patronage, which emphasized stylistic innovation as a means of product differentiation. He recognized that under industrial capitalism the value of most museum holdings lay in the signatures on the works of art, not in the works themselves. Coomaraswamy was an insightful critic of the best modern art, as the artists themselves recognized. Alfred Stieglitz, founder of the Photo-Seccesion group and the person who did the most to introduce European modernism to the United States, was also the first photographer to have his works exhibited at a major museum in the United States when Coomaraswamy arranged to have twenty-seven of his works displayed at the Museum of Fine Arts in Boston. Stieglitz's wife, Georgia O'Keeffe, read Coomaraswamy's works avidly, and artists such as Gill, the French cubist Albert Gleizes,

1934 letter from Coomaraswamy to English illustrator and typographer Eric Gill (from Selected Letters of
Ananda K. Coomaraswamy, *1988; Thomas Cooper Library, University of South Carolina)*

and the American Morris Graves claimed him as an influence.

Coomaraswamy's search for the oldest and most authentic traditions led to criticism from the adherents of beliefs promulgated by those he regarded primarily as reformers, such as Buddha, Jesus, and Martin Luther. His defense of caste (as in a highly uncharacteristic letter to Mohandas Karamchand Gandhi) was based on the premise that, like a medieval guild system, it effected a social division of labor while offering job protection. Likewise, in "Status of Indian Women," an essay from *The Dance of Siva,* he defends arranged marriage, suggests that marriage is both a social ritual and a duty (which, by his description, seems more onerous for women than men), and laments the fact that in the West the end of love leads to the end of marriage. The essay was written during the collapse of his marriage to Alice and his infatuation with Stella. Coomaraswamy did, in fact, make errors when he attempted without sufficient reflection (and as a result of writing too quickly) to subsume all phenomena into the framework of thought that he expounded. The art historian Erwin Panofsky felt moved to insert a refutation in the third edition (1948) of his monograph *Albrecht Dürer* (1943) concerning one of Coomaraswamy's claims about medieval labyrinths.

Even those who disagreed with Coomaraswamy were aware of the extent of his achievement. In the English-speaking academic world there were no departments of non-Western art and little recognition that such art even existed when he began his adult life. He anticipated Panofsky's iconology by more than a decade and virtually established comparative religion and comparative mythology as academic disciplines. In the generation that followed, E. H. Gombrich undertook a defense of Western realism in art that is in many ways a reply to Coomaraswamy's challenge. Coomaraswamy's ideas still reverberate in museum practice: no major museum is today without an Asian section organized along the lines that he proposed. His philosophies even find echoes in such distant fields as the sociology of village communities.

Ananda Coomaraswamy's practice was to write at great speed, generally leaving the process of considered revision until after he had seen his works in print. After his death from a heart attack on 9 September 1947 at his home in Needham, Massachusetts, his widow, Luisa, and, later, his son Rama undertook to collect his scattered works and to release a catalogue raisonné incorporating his revisions. As with the spiritual journey Coomaraswamy envisaged near the end of his life, this task remains incomplete.

Letters:

Alvin Moore Jr. and Rama P. Coomaraswamy, eds., *Selected Letters of Ananda K. Coomaraswamy* (Delhi: Indira Gandhi National Centre for the Arts, 1988; London: Oxford University Press, 1988).

Bibliographies:

Rama P. Coomaraswamy, ed., *Ananda K. Coomaraswamy: Bibliography/Index* (Berwick-upon-Tweed, U.K.: Prologos, 1988);

James S. Crouch, *A Bibliography of Ananda Kentish Coomaraswamy* (New Delhi: Indira Gandhi National Centre for the Arts/Manohar, 2002).

References:

K. Bharatha Iyer, ed., *Art and Thought, Issued in Honour of Dr. Ananda K. Coomaraswamy on the Occasion of His 70th Birthday* (London: Luzac, 1947);

Patrick Brantlinger, "A Postindustrial Prelude to Postcolonialism: John Ruskin, William Morris, and Gandhism," *Critical Inquiry,* 22, no. 3 (1996): 466–485;

James Brow, "Utopia's New-Found Space: Images of the Village Community in the Early Writings of Ananda Coomaraswamy," *Modern Asian Studies,* 33, no. 1 (1999): 67–86;

Tanya Harrod, "Ananda Coomaraswamy: His Ideas and Influence," *Crafts,* no. 143 (November–December 1996): 20–23;

Michael Lind, "Reinventing the Museum," *Public Interest,* 109 (Fall 1992): 22–39;

Vishwanath S. Naravane, *Ananda K. Coomaraswamy* (Boston: Twayne, 1978);

William W. Quinn Jr., *The Only Tradition* (Albany: State University of New York Press, 1997);

S. Durai Raja Singam, ed., *Homage to Ananda K. Coomaraswamy: A Garland of Tributes* (Malaya: Malayan Printers, 1947).

Papers:

Ananda Coomaraswamy's papers are in the Department of Rare Books and Special Collections, Firestone Library, Princeton University.

Kamala Das

(31 March 1934 –   )

Sridhar Rajeswaran

BOOKS IN ENGLISH: *Summer in Calcutta: Fifty Poems* (New Delhi: Rajinder Paul, 1965);

The Descendants (Calcutta: Writers Workshop, 1967);

The Old Playhouse and Other Poems (Madras: Orient Longman, 1973; London: Sangam, 1986);

My Story (Jullundur, Punjab: Sterling, 1976; London & New York: Quartet, 1978);

Alphabet of Lust (New Delhi: Orient, 1976);

A Doll for the Child Prostitute (New Delhi: India Paperbacks, 1977);

Tonight, This Savage Rite: The Love Poems of Kamala Das and Pritish Nandy, by Das and Pritish Nandy (New Delhi: Arnold-Heinemann, 1979);

Collected Poems (Trivandrum: Kamala Das, 1984);

Kamala Das: A Collage, edited by Arun Kuckreja (New Delhi: Vidya Prakashan Mandir, 1984);

Padmavati, the Harlot, and Other Stories (New Delhi: Sterling, 1994);

The Sandal Trees and Other Stories, translated by V. C. Harris and C. K. Mohamed Ummer (Hyderabad: Disha, 1995; London: Sangam, 1995);

Only the Soul Knows How to Sing: Selections from Kamala Das (Kottayam, Kerala: DC Books, 1996);

The Path of the Columnist, as Kamala Surayya (Calcutta: Olive, 2000);

A Childhood in Malabar: A Memoir, translated by Gita Krishnankutty (New Delhi & New York: Penguin, 2003).

Collections: *Kamala Das: A Selection with Essays on Her Work,* edited by S. C. Harrex and Vincent O'Sullivan (Adelaide: Centre for Research in the New Literatures in English, 1986);

The Best of Kamala Das (Kozhikode, Kerala: Bodhi, 1991).

Kamala Das (from the cover of the 2004 edition of Summer in Calcutta; *Bruccoli Clark Layman Archives)*

Kamala Das is one of the most controversial of Indian writers; her achievements as a poet and prose writer have often been counterbalanced by the notoriety she has gained by actions in her personal life. Notwithstanding the negative critique generated by her personal actions and pronouncements in her newspaper columns, her position as a pioneer among postcolonial Indian English poets cannot be denied. Although she has never taken an ideological feminist stand, her poetry has expressed the pain, problems, and personal dissatisfaction of women in a traditional, conventional society such as that of India. Das has contributed significantly to the genres of poetry, prose, fiction, and autobiography in English as well as in her first language, Malayalam. She has won many laurels for her English-language poetry and her prose in Malayalam. Das is also an artist who specializes in the painting of the human figure, usually nudes.

Kamala Das was born on 31 March 1934 in the Malabar district of Kerala to the writers Balamani Amma Nalapat and V. M. Nair. Her mother, Balamani Amma, was the recipient of the Padma Bhushan, the third-highest award conferred on citizens by the Indian government; the Sahitya Akademi Poetry Award (which Das herself earned in later years); and the Saraswati Samman Award, named for the Hindu goddess of learning, Saraswati. Das's uncle Narayana Menon was a Malayalam academic, poet, and philosopher. One of his best-known publications is *Rati Samrajya* (*Rati* is a symbol of sexuality/carnality, and *samrajya* roughly translates as "the reign"), "an academic study based on the writings of Havelock Ellis and the Indian Sexologists," as Das notes in her memoir, *My Story* (1976). She can claim a literary lineage that stretches back even further, for a great-grandmother's sister, Ammalu, and an unmarried aunt, Ammini, were also poets. In *My Story* she reveals how paralysis silenced the poetry in Ammalu, whose vacant eyes testified also to a loss of sensitivity along with loss of the sense of touch. Das writes that when Ammini "recited the love-songs written by Kumaranasan" (an early-twentieth-century Keralan poet), she could sense "for the first time that love was a beautiful anguish and a *tapasya*" (sacrificial suffering).

Das's mother was from the royal Nalapat family, which was part of the Namboodri clan, and her father hailed from the Nair community, which was considered inferior to the Namboodris. At first he seemed to have no real interest in literature or art. He began his life as a car salesman and worked his way up to the position of managing director of Walfords, a British automobile firm. Only toward the end of his life did he return to Kerala and begin to work for the widely circulated Malayalam daily *Mathrubhumi* (Motherland), becoming managing editor. He joined the paper during a tumultuous period, after the end of World War II, the Partition of India, and the assassination of Mohandas Karamchand Gandhi. Das's upbringing reflected a world full of contradictions, as is evident in *My Story*. Also evident in the autobiography and in her poem "The Inheritance" (1973) is the impact on her psyche of the partitioning of India and the anti-Muslim feelings then prevalent.

Such lineages and legacies shaped the growth of Kamala's mind when she was in her early teens and made her more mature than her actual years. She was only fifteen when she was married to the much older K.

Madhav Das, who eventually became the executive director of the Reserve Bank of India and a consultant to the International Monetary Fund. She gave birth to her first son, Monu Nalapat, at age sixteen. Because of the age difference, her husband became a father figure to her, a situation that may have contributed to her later resistance to patriarchy as an entrapment and her decision to pursue unusual paths in life. As Rosemary Marangoly George observes in "Calling Kamala Das Queer: Rereading *My Story*" (2000), this husband-wife relationship could be one of the reasons why the child bride identifies herself as a "youth of sixteen" in Das's most-anthologized poem, the autobiographical "An Introduction," originally published in *Summer in Calcutta: Fifty Poems* (1965). George also provides a useful insight in regard to Das's choice of a pen name for her Malayalam-language publications:

> [W]e need to ponder the issue of Das's choice of the pseudonym, "Madhavi Kutty" [also transliterated as Madhavikkutti or Madhavikkutty]. "Kutty" is a common suffix in Kerala across castes but particularly among upper-caste women. Kutty is also used as an affectionate suffix which is unmarked by gender and religion and best translates as "child" or "small one." Hence, when a child is named after [a] parent or adult, the suffix becomes a way of distinguishing the adult from the child. Madhavi is, however, the feminine form of Madhav, her husband's name.

The name Madhav also refers to Krishna, and the use of the feminine form, Madhavi, also identifies Das as Radha, the eternal consort of Krishna. The relationship of Radha to Krishna is one of unrequited love. The Radha-Krishna strain has pervaded Das's life as an abstraction that she has consistently struggled to concretize in her work, as in "Krishna":

> Your body is my prison, Krishna,
> I cannot see beyond it.
> Your darkness blinds me
> Your Love words shut out the wise world's din.

In spite of the problems related to being the wife of a much older husband, which she has detailed in *My Story*, Das has also acknowledged that Madhav was a great supporter of her writing career. In a 1996 interview with Shobha Warrier she said that she began writing, especially columns for weeklies, to augment the family income, as poetry did not sell. She wrote late at night, after completing her household chores, a practice that she thinks ruined her health.

Das had three sons with her husband, all of whom went on to work for *The Times of India*. The eldest, Monu Nalapat, became the editor of the political pages, and the middle son, Chinnan, became vice president in charge of southern India. After a long career with the paper, the youngest son, Jaisurya, left in 2003 to launch the first Indian communications advisory firm for the print media. Monu Nalapat is also well known as an educational theorist and is a journalist of some standing.

In the course of her life Das has held several important positions. She has served as the poetry editor of *The Illustrated Weekly of India,* president of the Kerala Children's Film Society, chair of the Kerala Forestry Board, and Orient editor of *Poetry Monthly.* She has also received many awards, notable among them the 1963 International PEN Asian Poetry Prize; the 1971 Chaman Lal Award, for her fearless journalism; and the 1985 Asian World Prize and Sahitya Akademi Poetry Award for *Collected Poems* (1984). In 1984 she was shortlisted for the Nobel Prize in literature, along with Marguerite Yourcenar, Doris Lessing, and Nadine Gordimer. Das has also won acclaim for her contributions to Malayalam literature. Her story "Thanuppu" (1967, Cold) brought her the Kerala Sahitya Akademi Short Story Award in 1969. She won the Vayalar Award in 1997 for *Nirmatalam puttakalam* (1993). The Keralan government honored her with its highest award, Ezhuthachan (roughly translated, a person of letters who has been accorded the status of a guru), for her lifetime contributions to Malayalam literature.

Although Das's works have gained much recognition in the form of awards, most critics in India have reacted ambiguously to her writing. Few have taken her seriously, most concentrating instead on what they consider the erotic aspects of her poetry or the socially unconventional elements of her prose. This approach has commodified Das. As Vrinda Nabar notes, critics have become so enmeshed in the novelty of Das's statements about her body that they choose to evaluate her work only at the surface level, without delving deeper into the core of her writings. Considered carefully, however, she emerges as a poet of merit, for she possesses a talent for articulating herself in her verse. So emphatic is her presence in her poetry that the issue of craft does not usually find mention since her uniqueness, as she herself emphasizes, depends on her own life and on a poetics that is merely intuitive in its workings, as in "Stock Taking":

> Do not thrust upon me
> the scriptures compiled by sages
> wise and celibate
> or pacifying philosophies.
> I have held a man
> between my legs. . . .

Das has been accorded an important place in the Indian English poetry canon by only a small group of critics, including Devindra Kohli, E. V. Ramakrishnan, Anisur Rahman, Nabar, and George. For a long time the body of her work was not incorporated into the academic curricula. "Das has been consigned to the rubbish heap of literary history," Nilufer E. Bharucha writes in "Women Poets and Feminist Critics" (1995), conveying the neglect of the writer by the critical establishment and its wariness of her candidness, which makes the reader privy to the poet as a terrorized young bride, an aspiring socialite, and a controversial columnist.

Readers, however, have reacted positively to Das's verse. Even before her first poetry collection, *Summer in Calcutta,* was published in 1965, her poems had appeared in *An Anthology of Commonwealth Verse* (1963), and her works had been widely published in Indian periodicals. Most of the fifty poems in *Summer in Calcutta* are about love and are candid about female sexuality. There is no dividing line between the personal and societal life of the poet. Everything finds its way into Das's poetry, from the streets of Calcutta in "The Dance of the Eunuchs" to a symbolic fire consuming all before it in "Forest Fire." The confessional and sensational elements emerge in this first collection, as is seen in "The Freaks": "I am a freak. It's only / To save my face, I flaunt, at / Times, a grand, flamboyant lust."

In Das's second collection of poetry, *The Descendants* (1967), she focuses almost exclusively on herself and her emotions. In this volume there is a sea change, literarily and figuratively—a shift, as Kohli notes, "from the sun-image of *Summer in Calcutta* to the sea image, from noon to night, from fire to water." The opening poem, "The Suicide," sets the personal tone of the collection:

> Bereft of soul,
> My body shall be bare.
> Bereft of body,
> My soul shall be bare.

The collection is pervaded by a mood of doubt, dejection, and despair typified by the poem "The Doubt." In "The Looking Glass," Das argues that women should be honest with themselves about their physical needs, what she calls the "endless female hungers." Much in this poem shocked contemporary Indian society, especially the references to urination and menstrual blood.

The Old Playhouse and Other Poems (1973) includes poems from Das's two earlier collections and thirteen new poems. Although the tone of the poetry has not changed, there is more analysis of sexual relationships, particularly in the title poem, which concerns incompatibility between males and females. There is also much that is autobiographical in this collection, for instance

"The Swamp," which is based on Das's memory of a swamp in Malabar. "Sunset, Blue Bird" also goes back to the poet's childhood.

Apart from her poetry, Das's 1976 memoir, *My Story*, reveals her inner life and external concerns most directly. It provides the reader with intimate glimpses into her childhood and young adulthood, as well as her involvement with various lovers. In *My Story* she begins with her childhood in Calcutta and describes how she had to cope with feelings of self-abnegation resulting from the consciousness of being someone with "a nut-brown skin, usually branded blackie," whose "blood is red." These childhood events occurred during the colonial period, when race and color were indices of superiority. Such an inferiority complex bred into Das at school was coupled with the inherent superiority of her aristocratic lineage, which in turn was further complicated by the influence on her family of the Gandhian ideology of simplicity. Certain other events in her life, such as her early marriage, marital rape, teen motherhood, and rebellion against the roles imposed on her, led her to seek an outlet in the various homoerotic, autoerotic and heterosexual experiences detailed in *My Story*. These experiences collided with her conventional self, which centered around the roles she had to assume of child, daughter, wife, and mother.

Tonight, This Savage Rite: The Love Poems of Kamala Das and Pritish Nandy (1979) and *Collected Poems*, published in 1984, both feature earlier poems, with only a few new ones. *Only the Soul Knows How to Sing: Selections from Kamala Das* (1996) brings together 142 of Das's old and new poems. As K. Satchidanandan notes in the preface, the poems address Das's old concerns of love, loss, and pain, but there are also new themes of "old age, death and nothingness." A certain distancing is noticeable in the love poetry, lending it a degree of objectivity, as in "An Introduction": "Call / Him not by any name, he is every man / Who wants a woman, just as I am every / Woman who seeks love. . . . " The poems in *Only the Soul Knows How to Sing* also present a spiritual aspect to the search for romantic love. Such a love would make every woman an eternal Radha responding to her Krishna. Krishna is a manifestation of Vishnu, the preserver of the Hindu trinity of Brahma (the Creator), Vishnu, and Shiva (the Destroyer). Radha, Vishnu's beloved in his Krishna form, was a milkmaid, a married woman, and older than Krishna, but she was irresistibly drawn to him. Radha and Krishna are the Hindu symbols of romantic love with divine undertones. Das writes of Radha's obsession with Krishna in "Vrindavan":

Front cover for the 2004 Indian edition of Das's first English-language book, a poetry collection originally published in 1965 (Bruccoli Clark Layman Archives)

> . . . And the flute luring her
> From home and her husband
> Who later asks her of the long scratch
> On the brown aureola of her breast
> And she shyly replies
> Hiding flushed cheeks, it was so dark. . . .

Unlike some of Das's earlier poetry, the verse in *Only the Soul Knows How to Sing* is not overly open or direct. With age has come an awareness that there is much that cannot be comprehended in the middle years, for "The middle is an opaque / glass pane, muddied by fingerprints," and "Life yields its true meaning only / in early youth or in weary / age."

Das's poetry is difficult to categorize, even though it is largely centered on the emotion of love. In his preface to *Only the Soul Knows How to Sing*, Satchidanandan writes, "Kamala's whole *oeuvre* . . . becomes a declaration of the greatness of love that even while being expressed through the body also transcends the body."

Yet, difficult as it is to understand fully the passion, concerns, and even pain in her work, a careful reading allows sensitive readers into a world where, as in "The Looking Glass," they glimpse the honesty and self-realization behind the masks donned by the artist: "getting / A man to love is easy, but living / Without him afterwards may have to be / Faced."

Das was part of the first generation of Indian women who were conscious of their position in society and chafed at the limitations imposed by it. From the perspective of the history of women's lives in the subcontinent, her works can be seen as signaling the beginning of the struggle for women's emancipation. She has adopted a position that makes her a spokeswoman for the unsung other half of the human race. The conditions of her existence have much in common with the issues of women's lives and freedom highlighted in the feminist movement in India. Early marriage, marital rape, and teen motherhood—in short, an ambience of patriarchal suffocation—were the norms during Das's youth.

While some critics have paid attention to Das's poetry, her newspaper columns in *The Blitz* and *The Current* in the 1970s and in *Intimate* in the early 1980s have largely been neglected. Her journalism, however, is also useful in understanding her achievement. The humorous side of Das's personality comes out in her columns. Her sense of humor is wry, and she often uses a mocking tone, which makes it difficult to decide whether she is serious or joking. In her 12 March 1977 column in *Blitz* she comments on the women's movement: "Off and on I too toy with the idea of joining the Women's Lib movement, if only to have the fun of walking around with no bra on. Such a delicious pleasure! But you must do it only when there are several men around to throw admiring glances to your full-blown beauty. Otherwise you might as well wear the wretched thing and forget about the movement." Yet, Das's comments on the women's movement are not always farcical but often reveal the futility of applying Western theoretical or ideological norms to the actual experiences of non-Western women. In her first column for *Blitz* (15 January 1977) she recounts how she had to work on her poetry and prose throughout the night in order to pay the grocer's bills and how doing housework had ruined her hands. When she thought about the women's movement in this context, she writes, "You want to laugh, you want to throw your head up backwards and laugh, but you tell yourself that you must not be hysterical." Das is also honest about her reasons for writing such columns: "If you are rich you will write only poetry, nothing but poetry," adding mischievously, "and when you are not writing you will

rest, see films, take walks, and eat chicken and ice-cream."

Some critics have been angered by the tone of Das's columns; according to Nabar, she is "More a calumnist" than a columnist. The nonchalance with which Das professes her views, the ambivalence that governs her attitude, and the disregard of any sense of consideration for the sensibilities of her readers when she postulates at times deliberately shocking ideas, stand in contrast to her sometimes surprising but always sensitive poetry. Her viewpoints on issues such as the feminist movement may appear naive, for she seems to have no awareness of the reasons behind the positions taken by feminists against male domination, even though they, too, work out of a sense of outrage. Das's views on abortion, bigamy, and an entire range of familial and sexual topics, as well as her advocacy of solutions that pander to the conventional, can at times appear to be reactionary. Perhaps the thing that redeems her columns is the honesty, naiveté and innocence that informs her comments on many issues.

On 16 December 1999, at the age of sixty-five, Das converted to Islam and adopted the name Kamala Surayya. In "Ya Allah," published in *The Week* (26 December 1999), she writes of the "singer / who lost her voice singing"; the "danseuse / whose fatigued limbs tremble" perceives in the face of her beloved, who is also the "beloved of merciful Allah," "the Prophet's features." She declares now that she was seeking refuge in him, believing that none other than "Mohammed would dare / to embrace a sinner and call her / Mother." Das has taken to wearing a veil and has even started writing poetry in basic Arabic.

There was a widespread negative response to Das's conversion to Islam, and articles appeared on the topic in newspapers such as *The Times of India* and *The Hindu*. S. Balakrishnan wrote in *The Times of India* about how Das felt that Islam gave her security and how she did not mind exchanging her hitherto cherished freedom to do what she liked for religious orthodoxy. In "The Histrionics of Kamala Das" (*The Hindu*, 6 February 2000), Havovi Anklesaria placed Das's conversion on a level with her earlier sensational pronouncements regarding feminism and patriarchy in her *Blitz* columns. Yet, even Anklesaria acknowledged that "the impact of Ms. Das's poetry has never been in doubt."

Kamala Das's views may seem contradictory at times and her columns too full of excesses to be accepted seriously, but the searing honesty and originality of her poetry require that it be accorded a high place in South Asian writing in English. Her Malayalam-language poetry and prose provide another reason why she is different from other Indian writers in English, many of whom are not bilingual. Her English-language verse and prose have the flavor of her native tongue, the essence of which has been transliterated, giving a quaintness and freshness to her writing. Das's honest exploration of the female body, physical satisfaction, and women's emotional needs makes her poetry an important contribution to female discourse in post-colonial India. Her writings are central to any assessment of English-language Indian poetry in particular and Indian literature as a whole.

Interview:

Shobha Warrier, "Manipulation Is Not a Bad Word All the Time," *Rediff on the Net* (1996) <http://www.rediff.com/news/1996/3107adas.htm>.

References:

Havovi Anklesaria, "The Histrionics of Kamala Das," *Hindu,* 6 February 2000;

S. Balakrishnan, "I Like Islam's Orthodox Lifestyle: Kamala Das," *Times of India,* 15 December 1999;

Nilufer E. Bharucha, "Women Poets and Feminist Critics," *Indian Horizons,* 44, no. 3 (1995);

A. N. Dwivedi, *Indo-Anglian Poetry* (Allahabad: Kitab Mahal, 1979);

Rosemary Marangoly George, "Calling Kamala Das Queer: Rereading *My Story,*" *Feminist Studies,* 26, no. 3 (2000): 731–763;

Iqbal Kaur, ed., *Perspectives on Kamala Das's Prose* (New Delhi: Intellectual, 1995);

Devindra Kohli, *Kamala Das* (New Delhi: Arnold-Heinemann, 1975);

Manohar Murali, "Kamala Das, Treatment of Love in Her Poetry," *Journal of Indian Writing in English,* 19, no. 1 (1999);

Vrinda Nabar, *The Endless Female Hungers: A Study of Kamala Das* (New Delhi: Sterling, 1994);

Anisur Rahman, *Expressive Form in the Poetry of Kamala Das* (New Delhi: Abhinav, 1981);

E. V. Ramakrishnan, "Kamala Das as a Confessional Poet," *Journal of Indian Writing in English,* 5, no. 1 (1977): 29–34;

P. P. Raveendran, "Text as History, History as Text: A Reading of Kamala Das' *Anamalai Poems,*" *Journal of Commonwealth Literature,* 29, no. 1 (1994): 47–54.

Mahesh Dattani

(7 August 1958 –   )

Ashis Sengupta
University of North Bengal

BOOKS: *Final Solutions and Other Plays* (New Delhi: Manas, 1994)–comprises *Where There's a Will, Dance Like a Man, Bravely Fought the Queen,* and *Final Solutions;*

Tara: A Play in Two Acts (New Delhi: Ravi Dayal / Bangalore: Orient Longman, 1995);

Thirty Days in September (New Delhi: Survivor Communications, 2002);

Bravely Fought the Queen (London: Border Crossings, 2003).

Collections: *Collected Plays* (New Delhi & London: Penguin India, 2000)–comprises *Seven Steps around the Fire, On a Muggy Night in Mumbai, Do the Needful, Final Solutions, Bravely Fought the Queen, Tara, Dance Like a Man,* and *Where There's a Will;*

Collected Plays, Volume Two: Stage, Screen, and Radio Plays (New Delhi: Penguin India, 2005)–comprises *Thirty Days in September, Clearing the Rubble, Dance Like a Man, Mango Soufflé, Seven Steps around the Fire, The Swami and Winston, Morning Raga, Uma and the Fairy Queen, Ek Alag Mausam,* and *The Tale of a Mother Feeding Her Child.*

Mahesh Dattani (photograph by Mahesh Bhat; www.maheshbhat.com)

PLAY PRODUCTIONS: *Where There's a Will,* Bangalore, Chowdiah Memorial Hall, 23 September 1988;

Dance Like a Man, Bangalore, Chowdiah Memorial Hall, 22 September 1989;

Tara (first produced as *Twinkle Tara*), Chowdiah Memorial Hall, 23 October 1990;

Bravely Fought the Queen, Mumbai, Sophia Bhabha Hall, 2 August 1991; revised, London, Battersea Arts Center, 9 April 1996;

Final Solutions, Bangalore, Guru Nanak Bhavan, 10 July 1993;

On a Muggy Night in Mumbai, Mumbai, Tara Theater, 23 November 1998;

Seven Steps around the Fire, Chennai, Museum Theater, 6 August 1999;

Thirty Days in September, Mumbai, Prithvi Theater, 31 May 2001.

PRODUCED SCRIPTS: *Do the Needful,* radio, BBC 4, 14 August 1997;

Seven Circles around the Fire, radio, BBC 4, 9 January 1999;

The Swami and Winston, radio, BBC 4, 3 June 2000;

The Tale of a Mother Feeding Her Child, radio, BBC 3 and 4, October 2000;

Ek Alag Mausam (A Special Season), motion picture, Actionaid India, 2000;

Clearing the Rubble, radio, BBC 4, 26 January 2002;

Dance Like a Man, screenplay by Dattani and Pamela Rooks, motion picture, NFDC and Rooks AV, 2002;

Mango Soufflé, motion picture, Lotus Piktures, 2002;

Uma and the Fairy Queen, radio, BBC 4, 4 August 2003;

Tara Ramaseshan as Lalitha and Veena Sajnani as Dolly in the premiere production of Mahesh Dattani's Bravely Fought the Queen, *in Bombay, August 1991. The play was Dattani's first to be performed abroad, in London in April 1996 (from* Final Solutions and Other Plays, *1994; Gelman Library, George Washington University).*

Morning Raga, motion picture, RK Teleshow/Arka Mediawork, 2004.

OTHER: "Night Queen," in *Yaraana: Gay Writing from India,* edited by Hoshang Merchant (New Delhi: Penguin India, 1999), pp. 57–71;

Madhu Rye, *Tell Me the Name of a Flower; and, The Terrace,* translated by Vijay Padaki, introduction by Dattani (Calcutta: Seagull Books, 2000);

City Plays, introduction by Dattani (Calcutta: Seagull Books, 2004).

SELECTED PERIODICAL PUBLICATION– UNCOLLECTED: "Contemporary Indian Theatre and Its Relevance," *Journal of Indian Writing in English,* 30 (January 2002): 1–4.

Mahesh Dattani became in 1998 the first Indian English-language playwright to receive the Sahitya Akademi Award, the highest national recognition for a writer, for his brilliant treatment of, as the award citation reads, the "tangled attitudes in contemporary India towards communal differences, consumerism and gender." His plays have been published, translated, and staged in India and abroad, including in England and North America. He is a playwright, director, actor, and dancer. His reputation rests mainly on the dozen plays

he has written for the stage as well as for radio productions on the BBC, though he has also been successful in his other roles. His experience as an all-around theater person has, in fact, made him a better playwright. Dattani has directed and starred in several well-known English and Hindi plays, including his own, and has also written or cowritten several Hindi and English screenplays. He defends his writing in English on the grounds that he writes for city people, and all theater in a multilingual and multicultural country is limited by language and region. Moreover, his characters are Indian, and his English is "educated Indian English" spoken in a distinctive manner, as John McRae and Bill Findlay point out in their contribution to *The Oxford Guide to Literature in English Translation* (2000). Prejudice, hypocrisy, guilt, and compromise form the thematic threads of his work. Dattani, in particular, is concerned with the minorities who are forced to live a double life so as to be part of the mainstream. Many of his plays, however, critique Indian middle-class morality and defend the outcasts and potential rebels of society. What is most striking about his plays is the way Dattani brings in the dynamics of choice the individual is faced with while breaking away from traditional roles and the range of emotions it generates. "Society has its concerns about civilization," he says in a 2001 interview with Chitralekha Basu, "and that's why . . . rules are constructed." But at the same time, "the individual shouldn't be thwarted by these norms." His liberal concerns apart, Dattani writes plays for the sheer pleasure of expressing himself through this dynamic medium. His work takes on new forms as he continues to deal with serious but generally unacknowledged issues of contemporary Indian society.

Born on 7 August 1958 into a Gujarati family long settled in Bangalore, Dattani grew up enjoying the affection of his parents, Gokuldas Narandas Dattani and Jaya Gouri Dattani, and two elder sisters. Even as a child he felt drawn toward the exciting world of drama and was impressed by the popular Gujarati plays he saw in Bangalore. It was after reading Edward Albee's *Who's Afraid of Virginia Woolf?* (1962) that Dattani first felt the urge to write. He really began writing, however, only after he saw *Neela Kamra* (Blue Room) in Mumbai in the early 1980s. This play was a Hindi adaptation of Madhu Rye's Gujarati play *Kumarni Agashe* (1972, Kumar's Terrace), which fascinated him for its bold treatment of sexuality and taught him to focus on his own time and place. Dattani's other favorite playwrights have always been Tennessee Williams and Arthur Miller. Interestingly, he was never a student of literature. A graduate in 1981 from St. Joseph's College, Bangalore, in history, economics, and political science, he began his career as an advertising copywriter. Subsequently, he worked with his father in the family business. In 1984, however, he formed his own theater group, Playpen, and concentrated on directing and writing plays. Dattani has turned out one play almost every year, combining this activity since 1997 with scriptwriting for radio, television, and cinema. He has his own studio in Bangalore–Mahesh's Studio–a long-cherished dream realized in 1998. A disciplined and hardworking writer, Dattani also teaches theater courses at the summer sessions program of Portland State University in Oregon.

Where There's a Will (1988), his first play, is a seriocomic portrayal of an Indian upper-middle-class family. A disappointed business tycoon, Hasmukh, takes revenge on his greedy family by virtually cutting them out of his will, something they discover only after his death. The play is neatly divided into two halves, before and after Hasmukh's death, and the piecemeal revelation of the past is largely Ibsenesque. Expectations of inheritance hold his family together during his lifetime, and his will, craftily drafted in favor of his mistress, unites his family members later. The appearance of the man's ghost overhearing unpleasant truths uttered about him by his own people fills the second half of the play with sardonic humor. Power relations in the extended family are at the heart of the dramatic presentation. The play is also an exposé of the fault

lines of patriarchy. A well-received production, it continues to tour occasionally. International performances of the play have included one in Saratoga, California, on 27 June 2003.

In *Dance Like a Man* (1989), which has received rave reviews at home and abroad, Dattani gives up the form and content of drawing-room comedy to explore larger issues and more complex styles. The protagonists are a retired couple, both Bharatanatyam (a south-Indian classical dance form) dancers, and the play depicts their reflections on the past and how it affects their present. Their thwarted ambitions and jealousies outweigh their mutual love and success and ultimately disturb their marriage. Their only common concern is their dancer daughter, whom they want to succeed. As Vivek Benegal wrote in the *Indian Review of Books* (October–December 1994), the play actually critiques "socially sanctioned male-female stereotypes" by exploring the general inhibitions suffered by an Indian man taking dance as a career, especially a dance traditionally performed by women. Further, *Dance Like a Man* goes back to a time when dancing was considered a harlot's pursuit, revealing in the process the duplicity of moral standards in society. In typical Dattani style, the play raises some teasing questions. What makes a man a man? What, after all, constitutes an artiste, male or female? In addition to social and cultural prejudices, the play examines "the unwritten rules of authority"– embodied in Jairaj's autocratic father–that, according to Mithran Devanesen in her introduction to the play for *Collected Plays* (2000), have come to be accepted "as part of the Indian joint family." *Dance Like a Man* is a fine instance of Dattani's fusion of the physical and spatial quality of the Indian theater with the verbal ingenuity of western texts. The thematically unusual play, under Pamela Rooks's direction, was made into a movie of the same name in 2002.

Tara, first performed as *Twinkle Tara* (1990), focuses on another contentious issue–the relative status of girl and boy children in Indian society. Tara and Chandan are Siamese twins, surgically separated after birth. It is later revealed that a decision taken by their mother and grandfather to favor the boy over the girl left Tara crippled for life. Denied the opportunities given to her brother, she eventually dies. The play has multilevel sets that collapse "geographical locations," as Erin B. Mee observed in her introduction to *Tara* for *Collected Plays,* bringing together past and present, interior and exterior. Chandan, who becomes an emergent playwright in London, is writing a play about his own childhood in India, which ends up being his sister's story. Challenged by bitter realities, Tara fights hard to establish her identity before she gives in. *Tara* is also a play about the gendered self. As Mee puts it, it is "about coming to terms with the feminine side of oneself in a world that always favours . . . [the] 'male.'" There are echoes in it, Dattani himself has admitted, of Williams's *The Glass Menagerie* (1944). After its Bangalore premiere, *Tara* had a successful run in Mumbai and Delhi. Still on the Performance Studies curriculum of New York University, it was included in *Drama Contemporary: India,* edited by Mee.

Bravely Fought the Queen (1991) is Dattani's first play to have been performed abroad. Produced by Michael Walling's company, Border Crossings, in London in 1996, it established Dattani as a playwright of international repute. Jointly staged by A'Shore Productions and Vibha in San Francisco in 2003, it won accolades again. Dattani's three-act play shows an India where ancient cultural mores collide with the realities of modern life. The first act provides glimpses of the interior of an Indian joint family. Two sisters, Dolly and Alka, married to two brothers, Jiten and Nitin, live in twin houses on an estate in Bangalore, taking care of their ailing mother-in-law. The second act contrasts the women's circumscribed lives with their husbands' "masculine" world of work, characterized, as it were, by unscrupulous practices and self-indulgent behavior. The women's resistance, followed by revelations of terrible family secrets, culminates in a cathartic confrontation in the final act. The play shows how acting becomes a way of life in a world of hypocrisy, as Walling observes in his prefatory notes for the play in *Collected Plays,* and how the performance mode of the theater, paradoxically, can expose such acting for what it is. Jiten's lechery and violence, which lead to the birth of a crippled child, and Nitin's sense of guilt for his gay nature finally come to the fore and combine with Dolly's frenzied movements and Alka's liberating dance to shatter the fictions all of them had earlier created to shield themselves. As in *Tara,* the Indian woman, though marginalized, emerges as a fighter in this play. The text of *Bravely Fought the Queen* has proved to be flexible enough to allow for improvisation onstage.

Final Solutions (1993), a play about the changing nature of Hindu-Muslim relationships since the Partition of India in 1947, was written for the Deccan Herald Theater Festival in Bangalore in December 1992. Following the demolition of the four-hundred-year-old Babari Masjid by Hindu activists a week before the play was supposed to be performed, it was dropped from the program for fear of a possible escalation of the communal tension building up at that time. It was finally performed the following year in Bangalore and Mumbai. Dattani carefully avoids the kind of melodrama such a story is usually prone to. As C. K. Meena observed in the *Indian Review of Books* (March–April 1999), the theatrical quality of the play lies chiefly in the heightening of tension through small disclosures and in the interweaving of the past and present through the alternation of lines spoken or written by the older and younger selves of a principal character. Contemporary Hindus and Muslims are seen to be influenced by age-old mutual religious and cultural prejudices. The plot once again revolves around a family, reinforcing Dattani's idea of the family as a microcosm of society. Two Muslim youths take refuge in an orthodox Hindu household during a riot that reminds the grandmother of the household, Hardika, of a similar one she had lived through as a young Daksha in August 1947. One of the fugitives is intensely anti-Hindu, while the other feels ambiguous about his Muslim identity. Ramnik, Hardika's son, appears to be a liberal who carries a terrible family guilt that is traced to his father's use of the earlier riot as a ploy to grab a Muslim's property. While Hardika has been misled by her in-laws to disbelieve, if not hate, the Muslims, Aruna, Ramnik's wife, is no less religiously conservative. Smita, their daughter, and Bobby, one of the Muslim youths she may be in love with, deliver a different message, however, by shaking off the oppressive burden of religious practices and yet being tolerant to the believer. For all their "final solutions," the question remains whether the historical wrongs perpetrated by both communities can ever be righted. The solution may also lie, the play ironically suggests, in what director Alyque Padamsee describes as "transferred resentments." In any event, the play confronts Indian audiences with their own hypocrisies and passions. It was translated into Hindi by Shahid Anwar and directed by Arvind Gaur for Asmita Theater in 1998.

The interrogation on different levels of the "normality" of gender and sexual identity in most of the earlier plays becomes more pronounced in *On a Muggy Night in Mumbai* (1998). As Dattani puts it in his preface to *Collected Plays,* the play is "about the travails of gay men and women, some of them strongly anti-heterosexual." McRae writes in his introductory notes for the play in the same volume that it is not simply the first Indian play to handle such a theme, but shows "how society creates patterns of behaviour" to which individuals easily fall victim. The story unfolds in the living room of Kamlesh, an affluent Mumbai-based fashion designer, who has invited his friends, all homosexuals, over to his house. Labeled by Dattani "a metrosexual love story," it nevertheless unravels multiple facets of gay culture. Sharad and Deepali are quite comfortable with their identity as gays. Bunny is a rather more traditional Indian gay who claims to be happily married, publicly denying his sexual nature. The climax comes with the shocking revelation that Prakash, Kamlesh's former love, is about to marry Kamlesh's sister Kiran.

Rooky Dadchanji as Javed and Siddharth Roy Kappor as Bobby in the premiere production of Dattani's play Final Solutions *in Bangalore in July 1993. Production of the play was postponed from the previous year because of fears that it might contribute to tensions between local Hindus and Muslims (from* Final Solutions and Other Plays, *1994; Gelman Library, George Washington University).*

By the end of the play, the anguished Kamlesh exploits others, while Prakash, whose past relationship with Kamlesh now stands exposed to Kiran, becomes a victim of his own sexual uncertainties. Is homosexuality unnatural and therefore a social aberration? Is hypocrisy better than self-expression? *On a Muggy Night in Mumbai* ends with such questions, leaving audiences to find answers for themselves. Dattani creates the impression of a whole society onstage through auditory and visual images of the outer world, thus breaking the bounds of the proscenium. Despite its success in Mumbai, the play is the least produced of Dattani's oeuvre so far—because Indians are still squeamish about sexuality as such, not to speak of alternative sexuality. *Mango Soufflé* (2002), Dattani's first venture as movie director, is based on this play and has already traveled to festivals in Austin, London, and Bangkok.

Dattani's 2001 stage play, *Thirty Days in September,* addresses the issue of child abuse in India. The emphasis is on the dangers of silence maintained by the victim and her or his family to avoid social embarrassment. Based on the real-life experiences of such victims, the play was sponsored by RAHI (Recovering and Healing from Incest), a Delhi-based support center. It is the story of Mala, who when only seven years old is raped by her maternal uncle. The traumatic experience not only leaves her with a sense of guilt but also causes a rift in the mother-daughter relationship since Mala feels she has been betrayed by her mute mother. Later, she drifts from one affair to another, none lasting beyond thirty days. Her self-destructive flight comes to an end with her latest lover, Deepak, who is determined to continue their relationship. Mala narrates her story to Deepak, and in so doing she confronts her horrid past and redefines her present. Finally, the mother also relates her own story of helplessness and discovers her inner strength. The telling in either case is seen as a metaphor for personal healing, and what seem like compelling reasons for suppression are presented as social hypocrisy that stunts the development of the abused. *Thirty Days in September* depicts several places and times, the action moving back and forth on multiple sets. The play has enjoyed full houses in India and abroad ever since its premiere.

With his powerful dialogue and deft use of music, Dattani is at equal ease with writing for the radio. He has had five plays aired on BBC Radio 4. The first two were subsequently adapted for stage and also included in his *Collected Plays. Do the Needful* (1997) was produced as part of a program marking fifty years of Indian independence. As Sally Avens, who directed the play for BBC Radio Drama, says in her notes in *Collected Plays,* the British audience found it easy to empathize as much with a gay man being forced to live within the norms of a traditional "arranged marriage" as with a young woman who fights for her independent love life. Following the successful broadcast of *Do the Needful,* Dattani was commissioned to submit another play. The result was *Seven Circles around the Fire* (1999)—later staged and published as *Seven Steps around the Fire*— which introduces Uma Rao, a researcher-sleuth and wife of Bangalore's police superintendent, to the British listening audience. While uncovering the truth behind a murder in the *hijra* community (a group of castrated Indian males assuming a female gender-role identity) of the city, she finds enough material for her dissertation on class-gender-related violence in Indian society. The listener response was so encouraging that Dattani wrote two sequels to the play: *The Swami and Winston* (2000) and *Uma and the Fairy Queen* (2003). *Clearing the Rubble* (2002), another radio play that came in between the other two, centers around the lives of the victims of the earthquake that devastated Bhuj, in the Indian state of Gujarat, in 2001. The episode of a homebound English journalist, who is searching for a boy whom he had met during the catastrophe, lends a tender touch to the story.

Dattani is an original, vibrant voice in Indian English theater. He addresses issues that confront modern Indian urban society but are seldom acknowledged as real ones. While conscious of the rich tradition of India and its advantages, he challenges the construction of "Indian" that conveniently ignores the problematic present. Theater, according to him, must honestly reflect the playwright's time and place so as to start a dialogue that may eventually help people discover their true identity. His plays, however, are far from didactic. Besides, his desire for popularity does not mean that he is out to appease his audiences or compromise the quality of his work. He accepts all criticism as a means to perfection, as he points out in his preface to *Collected Plays,* although not the "open hostility" he sometimes encounters in parochial universities and literary circles. In 2004 Dattani released *Morning Raga,* his second motion picture.

Indian authors writing in English now have a global reach and acceptance. While the novelists have been conspicuously successful, however, Indian play-wrights have yet to emerge with equal strength. Modern Indian drama came of age in the 1960s, either as adaptations of Western classics or as indigenous works written in vernaculars and later translated into English. Of the plays originally written in English, few have found wider audiences for lack of all the paraphernalia of a successful theatrical production. In this context, Mahesh Dattani stands out. He not only writes about contemporary Indian themes in a language that is, according to Anjum Katyal in *Seagull Theatre Quarterly* (December 1999), "as Indian as any of the . . . vernaculars," but he is also a complete man of the theater, familiar with all aspects of stagecraft. Alka Tyagi's review of Dattani's *Collected Plays,* published in *Indian Literature* (July–August 2000), sums up the general spirit of the critical reception of his work: "this collection is as refreshing [a] treat for the reader as his performances are to the spectator with the innovative use of theatrical space and other elements." Dattani can be regarded as the most important Indian English-language playwright to date.

Interviews:

Anjum Katyal, "Of Page and Stage: An Interview with Mahesh Dattani," *Seagull Theatre Quarterly,* 24 (December 1999): 3–33;

Chitralekha Basu, "Of Marginalised Men," *Statesman Literary Supplement* (Calcutta), 15 July 2001, p. 3;

Lakshmi Subramanyam, "A Dialogue with Mahesh Dattani," in *Muffled Voices: Women in Modern Indian Theatre,* edited by Subramanyam (New Delhi: Shakti, 2002), pp. 128–134;

Ranjita Biswas, "Morning Glory," *Statesman* (Calcutta), 23 October 2004, Lifestyle and Entertainment section, p. 3.

References:

Sara Adhikari, "Stage of Transition," *Literature Alive,* 1 (October 1995): 34–38;

Subir Dhar, "*Where There's a Will* and *Bravely Fought the Queen:* The Drama of Mahesh Dattani," in *Drama: Literature and Performance,* edited by Srobona Munshi and Jharna Sanyal (Calcutta: University of Calcutta, 2002), pp. 207–225;

John McRae and Bill Findlay, "Varieties of English," in *The Oxford Guide to Literature in English Translation,* edited by Peter France (Oxford & New York: Oxford University Press, 2000), pp. 34–38;

Angelie Multani, "On Mahesh Dattani's *Dance Like a Man:* The Politics of Production and Performance," *Seagull Theatre Quarterly,* 11 (September 1996): 58–60.

Anita Desai

(24 June 1937 –   )

Radha Chakravarty
Gargi College, University of Delhi

See also the Desai entry in *DLB 271: British and Irish Novelists Since 1960.*

BOOKS: *Cry, the Peacock* (Calcutta: Rupa, 1963; London: Peter Owen, 1963);

Voices in the City: A Novel (New Delhi: Orient Paperbacks, 1965; London: Peter Owen, 1965);

Bye-Bye, Blackbird (Delhi: Hind Pocket Books, 1971);

Where Shall We Go This Summer? A Novel (Delhi: Vikas, 1975);

Fire on the Mountain (Bombay: Allied, 1977; London: Heinemann, 1977; New York: Harper & Row, 1977);

Games at Twilight and Other Stories (Bombay: Allied, 1978; London: Heinemann, 1978; New York: Harper & Row, 1978);

The Peacock Garden (London: Heinemann, 1979);

Clear Light of Day (Bombay: Allied, 1980; London: Heinemann, 1980; New York: Harper & Row, 1980);

The Village by the Sea: An Indian Family Story (London: Heinemann, 1982; New Delhi: Allied, 1983);

In Custody (London: Heinemann, 1984; New York: Harper & Row, 1984);

Baumgartner's Bombay (London: Heinemann, 1988; New York: Knopf, 1989);

Journey to Ithaca (London: Heinemann, 1995; New York: Knopf, 1995);

Fasting, Feasting (London: Chatto & Windus, 1999; New York: Houghton Mifflin, 1999);

Diamond Dust and Other Stories (London: Chatto & Windus, 2000); republished as *Diamond Dust: Stories* (Boston: Houghton Mifflin, 2000);

The Zigzag Way (London: Chatto & Windus, 2004; Boston: Houghton Mifflin, 2004).

PRODUCED SCRIPT: *In Custody*, motion picture, adapted by Desai and Shahrukh Husain from Desai's novel, Merchant Ivory Productions, 1993.

OTHER: "Ideas in Action," by Desai, Eduardo H. Galeano, and Charles Mungoshi, in *The State of*

Anita Desai (photograph © Jerry Bauer; from the dust jacket for The Zigzag Way, *2004; Richland County Public Library)*

the World's Children 1984 (New York: UNICEF, 1983), pp. 106–136;

"The Indian Writer's Problems," in *Perspectives on Anita Desai,* edited by Ramesh K. Srivastava (Ghaziabad: Vimal Prakashan, 1984), pp. 1–4;

Rabindranath Tagore, *The Home and the World,* translated by Surendranath Tagore, introduction by Desai (Harmondsworth, U.K.: Penguin / New York: Viking Penguin, 1985);

Mitch Epstein, *In Pursuit of India,* introduction by Desai (New York: Aperture, 1987);

Attia Hosain, *Phoenix Fled and Other Stories,* introduction by Desai (London: Virago, 1988; New York: Penguin, 1989);

Hosain, *Sunlight on a Broken Column,* introduction by Desai (London: Virago, 1988; New York: Penguin, 1989);

Anne Brontë, *Agnes Grey,* introduction by Desai (London: Virago, 1990);

"A Fire Had to be Lit," in *The Writer on Her Work: New Essays in New Territory,* volume 2, edited by Janet Sternburg (New York: Norton, 1991), pp. 97–103;

Krishna Dutta and Andrew Robinson, eds., *Noon in Calcutta: Short Stories from Bengal,* preface by Desai (London: Bloomsbury, 1992; New Delhi & New York: Viking, 1992);

Mary Wortley Montagu, *Turkish Embassy Letters,* edited by Malcolm Jack, introduction by Desai (Athens: University of Georgia Press, 1993; London: Pickering, 1993);

'Ismat Cughta'i, *The Quilt & Other Stories,* translated by Tahira Naqvi and Syeda S. Hameed, preface by Desai (Riverdale-on-Hudson, N.Y.: Sheep Meadow Press, 1994);

Salman Rushdie, *Midnight's Children,* introduction by Desai (New York: Knopf, 1995; London: David Campbell, 1995);

Vanessa Baird, ed., *Eye to Eye, Women: Their Words and Worlds. Life in Africa, Asia, Latin America and the Caribbean as Seen in Photographs and in Fiction by the Region's Top Women Writers,* introduction by Desai (Oxford: New Internationalist, 1996; London & New York: Serpent's Tail, 1997);

Tagore, *The Post Office,* translated by Krishna Dutta and Andrew Robinson, introduction by Desai (New York: St. Martin's Press, 1996);

Krishna Dutta, *Calcutta: A Cultural and Literary History,* foreword by Desai (New Delhi: Lotus Collection, 2003; Oxford: Signal, 2003);

E. M. Forster, *Arctic Summer,* foreword by Desai (London: Hesperus, 2003);

D. H. Lawrence, *Daughters of the Vicar,* foreword by Desai (London: Hesperus Classics, 2004);

Carlo Levi, *Words Are Stones: Impressions of Sicily,* translated by Anthony Shugar, foreword by Desai (London: Hesperus, 2005).

SELECTED PERIODICAL PUBLICATIONS–
UNCOLLECTED: "Tea with the Maharani," *Envoy,* 4 (January–February 1959): 22–23, 32;

"Grandmother," *Miscellany,* 1 (August 1960): 1–10;

"The Rage for the Raj: How the Festival of India Lost India," *New Republic,* 697, no. 3 (1985): 26–30;

"Indian Fiction Today," *Daedalus,* 118, no. 4 (1989): 207–231;

"A Secret Connivance," *TLS: The Times Literary Supplement,* no. 4563 (1990): 972;

"Women and Fiction in India," *Toronto South Asian Review,* 10 (Winter 1992): 23–29;

"Tagore," *Brick: A Literary Journal,* 48 (Spring 1994): 39–45.

Along with R. K. Narayan, Raja Rao, and Kamala Markandaya, Anita Desai is a member of a generation of writers who carved out a niche for Indian fiction in English–today a burgeoning literary arena teeming with new writers from across the world. Her novels chart the emotional lives of people struggling to find meaning and stability within the framework of a society in transition. Through sensitive psychological probing and sharp social critique, Desai offers in her earlier novels a spectrum of responses to the situation of India after independence: she addresses the lives of women caught between tradition and modernity, the disintegration of the joint family, cultural differences in encounters between East and West, and the politics of language in a multilingual society. Her later fiction takes a more international perspective, showing India as seen by outsiders. The protagonists of her novels are often caught in the struggle between desire for freedom and the call of duty or responsibility. As a stylist, Desai is known for her intense and suggestive use of imagery.

Anita Mazumdar was born on 24 June 1937 in the hill resort of Mussoorie in northern India to Dhiren N. Mazumdar, a businessman, and his German wife, Antoinette Nime Mazumdar. Her earliest memories are of the home in Old Delhi where she grew up with her brother and two sisters; of the "dozens of houses" she has lived in, Desai told Lalita Pandit in a 20 October 1990 interview (published in 1995), she remembers this one the most vividly: "I think children experience their homes in a way adults do not. Adults may think of the rooms and the furniture, but children actually experience them." Because of her mixed parentage, Mazumdar learned German, English, and Hindi. At this stage she did not experience her hybrid identity as a clash of cultures. Desai told Feroza Jussawalla and Reed Way Dassenbrock in 1992: "As a child, I did not see any conflict in our location in India. Everyone considered my mother very well-adjusted to Indian life and not as a foreigner or an outsider. It was only later, with hindsight, that I began to see her as one and understand her situation." The mother lent a European element to the family's otherwise "very, very Indian home": she told the children German fairy tales, sang and played "O Tannenbaum" on the piano at Christmas, and played recordings of the music of Ludwig van Beethoven,

*Dust jacket for the U.S. edition of Desai's 1977 novel, in which an old
woman's self-chosen isolation in her hilltop home is disrupted
by the arrival of her great-granddaughter
(Richland County Public Library)*

Wolfgang Amadeus Mozart, and Edvard Grieg on the
gramophone. Books by Johann Wolfgang von Goethe,
Friedrich Schiller, and Heinrich Heine were on the
bookshelves. The parents' friends included Germans,
Hungarians, French, Russians, and Britons.

As a German married to an Indian, Desai wrote
in response to an unpublished 2002 questionnaire,
Antoinette Mazumdar was "twice removed from the
English raj," which both she and her husband hated.
She rejected the English practice of sending children
away to boarding schools at "home" in England, and
Anita was educated by the Grey Sisters of the Cambridge Mission at Queen Mary's Higher Secondary
School. At first about half of the girls in the school were
from Muslim families, most of the remainder being
Hindu, and the Urdu language, a repository of Islamic
culture in India, became familiar to Mazumdar through
her exposure to this environment. Desai's novel *In Custody* (1984) testifies to her lingering affection for Urdu

culture, which was soon eroded by the dominance of
Hindi.

Mazumdar wrote her first story at seven. Her
early scribblings were viewed with some amusement by
her family. Later, when she began to publish, amusement gave way to pride. Responding to the 2002 questionnaire, Desai wrote that she was labeled "the writer
in the family," a role she accepted because she "really
never considered another."

Mazumdar was a voracious reader of the books
on her parents' bookshelves, including the works of the
Brontë sisters, Jane Austen, Charles Dickens, Thomas
Hardy, Fyodor Dostoevsky, Marcel Proust, and Rainer
Maria Rilke. Gradually she gravitated toward poetry,
which became a major influence on her work. From
Japanese and Chinese poetry she absorbed the art of
fine detail and subtle description. Sufi poetry, especially
that of Rumi, and the work of modern Russian poets,
including Boris Pasternak, Anna Akhmatova, and Osip
Mandel'shtam, figure in her list of favorites. In the
interview with Pandit, Desai described these writers as
the "gurus" from whom she learned the art of writing.
As for Rabindranath Tagore, she confessed to Pandit:
"I had the usual Indian child's response to Tagore, that
he was something I had to read in school and not for
any great interest or pleasure."

On 15 August 1947 the subcontinent became
independent of British rule and was partitioned into
two countries along religious lines: mainly Hindu India
and mainly Muslim Pakistan. All of the Mazumdars'
Muslim neighbors fled across the border to Pakistan,
and every Muslim girl in the school was gone. "It
seemed to me completely unnatural and an abnormality
that there should be a society so divided," Desai told
Jussawalla and Dassenbrock. Of postpartition India she
said, "It disturbs me immensely to think that it's a country with a monolithic religion, a monolithic society. It's
no longer the composite society I knew."

After completing her schooling at Queen Mary's,
Mazumdar attended Miranda House, a women's college on the campus of Delhi University. She published
occasional pieces in the college magazine, and in 1957
her short story "Circus Cat, Alley Cat" appeared in the
New Delhi periodical *Thought*. That year she obtained a
bachelor's degree with honors in English literature and
won the Pershad Memorial Prize for English. For the
next year she worked at Max Müller Bhavan, the German cultural institute in Calcutta (now known as Kolkata). On 13 December 1958 she married Ashvin
Desai, a business executive; they have four children:
Rahul, Tani, Arjun, and Kiran. Over the next few years
the family moved frequently, living in Calcutta, Bombay (now known as Mumbai), Kalimpong, Chandigarh, Delhi, and Pune. "The world I entered on

marriage was completely uncomprehending of a life of literature," she wrote in response to the 2002 questionnaire. "I continued to write but almost in secret, without anyone observing me at work at my desk so as not to create an open conflict." "Tea with the Maharani" appeared in the London magazine *Envoy* in 1959, and "Grandmother" in *Miscellany* in Calcutta in 1960. On the unpublished questionaire Desai recalled that her children thought that their mother's books appeared "as if by magic," since nobody was aware of her writing them.

Desai's first novel, *Cry, the Peacock* (1963), is clearly influenced by the writings of Virginia Woolf. It is the interior monologue of Maya, the pampered daughter of a rich Brahmin, who marries the lawyer Gautama. Obsessively attached to her father, she expects her husband to be a father substitute; but he is a cold, rational man who does not understand her. Morbid thoughts plague her, because an albino astrologer had predicted during her childhood that four years after her marriage, she or her husband would die: "In the shadows I *saw* peacocks dancing, the thousand-eyes upon their shimmering feathers gazing steadfastly unwinking upon the final truth–Death. I heard their cry and echoed it. I felt their thirst as they gazed at rain-clouds, their passion as they hunted for their mates. . . . Agony, agony, the mortal agony of their cry for lover and for death." She finally kills Gautama by pushing him off a parapet, then commits suicide.

Critics saw the work as marking an important phase in the development of the Indian novel in English: a shift away from the recording of external realities to a focus on the inner world of the protagonist. The poetic quality of Desai's prose also drew critical attention. Reviewers noted her use of symbols such as the peacocks, the moon, a dust storm, and Toto, Maya's dog. They also pointed to her use of myth, from the predictions of the astrologer to Gautama's discussions of the philosophy of the *Bhagavad Gita*. The mythic mode was taken to provide a counterpoint to the harsh realities propelling Maya toward neurosis, murder, and suicide. More-recent studics, however, focus on Desai's refusal to conform to traditional structures of belief. Fawzia Afzal-Khan, for instance, describes *Cry, the Peacock* as the product of a struggle between the romantic aesthetics of mythmaking and the critical-realist insistence on the writer's commitment to reality.

In a 1979 interview with Yashodhara Dalmia, Desai claimed that she seeks to construct "characters who are not average but have been driven into some extremity of despair and so turned against, or made a stand against, the general current." Such despair is experienced by the four protagonists of Desai's second

novel, *Voices in the City* (1965): Nirode, a young man; his sisters, Monisha and Amla; and their mother, Otima. The work is divided into four sections; each is named for one of the main characters and records the anguish he or she suffers. The three siblings resent their mother's negligent attitude toward them and her affair with Major Chadha. Nirode's artistic sensibility rebels against the routine of his journalistic work; unable to find professional stability, he becomes a drifter, moving through relationships with a vacuum at the heart of his existence. The novel evokes the milieu of the Indian urban elite in the 1950s, a modern society that clung to traditional views on women's roles. Equally estranged from her mother and her husband, Monisha commits suicide. Taking up commercial art to earn economic independence, Amla remains alienated from her work. Through Monisha the novel questions the ideology of the Hindu family, and through Amla it reveals the fragility of the apparent independence of the emancipated New Woman. Otima, who is associated with the powerful, destructive Hindu goddess Kali, explodes the myth of motherhood by rejecting her children and retreating to her childhood home in Kalimpong. The Kali myth also symbolizes the suppressed but potent sexuality of the women in the novel.

The most powerful element in the work is the city of Calcutta, with its landmarks Howrah, Chowringhee, the Grand Hotel, Fort Williams, the Victoria Memorial, and Cathedral Park. In *Anita Desai: The Novelist* (1981), Madhusudan Prasad describes the novel as "an epic on Calcutta." Desai evokes the sights, sounds, and smells of Calcutta, but her focus remains psychological: the city is a force that controls the mental states of its inhabitants.

In *Bye-Bye, Blackbird* (1971), Desai moves away from the existential angst of her first two novels to explore the clash of Eastern and Western cultures in an English setting. Dev, a newcomer to England, is traumatized by his experiences of racial discrimination but eventually becomes an Anglophile. At the opposite end of the spectrum is Adit Sen, who is married to an Englishwoman: at first well adjusted to life in England, he begins to feel disillusioned and alienated; he decides to return to India, where he hopes to reconnect with a life free of false pretenses. A third perspective is provided by Sarah Sen, who seeks a balance between the two halves of her identity as a secretary in an English school and as the wife of an Indian. To accompany Adit on his journey of repatriation she must relinquish the English part of herself and grant primacy to her Indian side.

Bye-Bye, Blackbird received a mixed response from critics, who had come to expect intense psychologizing and rich, poetic prose from Desai. In *Perspectives on Anita*

Desai in 1977 (from the dust jacket for Fire on the Mountain, *1977; Richland County Public Library)*

Desai (1984), edited by Ramesh K. Srivastava, Prasad complains that the novel lacks dense imagery, while in the same volume Vinod Bhushan Gulati finds the transformation of Dev and Adit unconvincingly abrupt. Others, however, including S. Krishnamoorthy Aithal in the Srivastava volume, recognized that the novel places Desai within the ranks of postcolonial writers impelled to explore the politics of the Indo-British cross-cultural encounter.

Vacationing on the island of Manori, off the coast of Bombay, Desai chafed under the everyday duties that could not be shaken off even on holiday. She jotted down a note that began: "A long short story about a woman packing up, shutting the house and going off with her three children to spend a holiday in their shack on Manori. Her husband, busy with his own life, seems hardly to notice their departure, leaving her frozen with anger at her neglect and loneliness." The woman wanders about the beach until her loneliness "burns away, burns her up, leaving a cool, grey detachment like a flake of ash where her heart had been." When the husband arrives unexpectedly to confess how much he has missed them, she is furious with him for shattering her calm; but eventually she "relents, admits to a continuation of the agonies of living."

When Desai returned to this idea long afterward, it outgrew the limits of a short story and became the novel *Where Shall We Go This Summer?* (1975). Sita is a sensitive, introverted woman so overwhelmed by the violence in the world that she is reluctant to give birth to the child in her womb. Already a mother of four, she also feels trapped in her marriage to the worldly, practi-

cal Raman. Taking two of her children, Sita abandons her home and escapes to Manori. Sita's dead father was a charismatic leader who had tried to set up a utopian primitivist community on Manori; shorn of his presence, the island of his dreams has lost its magic and appears as a bleak and difficult terrain where sheer survival is a challenge. Suggestions of incest lurk beneath descriptions of the father's relationship with Sita's older sister, Rekha. Disillusionment sets in, and Sita returns to her husband.

Desai wrote her fifth novel, *Fire on the Mountain* (1977), while living in Bombay. Overwhelmed, she says in "A Fire Had to be Lit" (1991), by "the onslaught of a great and abrasive city, its unrelieved ugliness, squalor, and noise," she tried to recapture the sights, sounds, and smells of Kasauli, a hill resort where she had spent the summer as a child. "To do that, I had to send my eight year-old self out into the hills again." Nanda Kaul is an old woman who lives in self-chosen seclusion in a haunted house called Carignano on a hilltop in Kasauli. Her solitude is disrupted when her great-granddaughter, Raka, comes to stay with her. Raka describes herself as "shipwrecked and alone." A bond develops between the old woman and the solitary child. A third figure enters the narrative: Ila Das, the welfare officer whose arid life and violent death shatter the apparent calm of Carignano, exposing the turbulent emotions that lurk beneath the surface of this mountain idyll. (The character of Ila Das is based on a woman who occasionally visited Desai's mother in Delhi. Her shrill voice and odd behavior amused the children. Later, in Kasauli, they heard that she had been raped and murdered in a nearby village.) *Fire on the Mountain* brought Desai international fame. The British Royal Society of Literature awarded her the Winifred Holtby Prize for the novel in 1978, and the work won the National Academy of Letters Award in India the same year.

In 1978 Desai published *Games at Twilight and Other Stories*. The title story uses children's games to suggest the aggression and competitive self-assertion that often underlie adult behavior. In "Studies in the Park" Suno, a student under family pressure to perform well in his examinations, has an epiphany that transforms his attitude to life. Parental insensitivity is also the theme of "Pineapple Cake," in which a child resents being forced to participate in events organized by adults. "A Devoted Son" reverses the perspective, presenting a father's protest against the tyrannical dietary regime prescribed by his doctor son. "Sale" and "The Farewell Party" expose the materialism of the privileged classes. "Surface Textures" and "Pigeons at Daybreak" suggest that happiness has a different definition for each person. Violence lurks in all of the stories, thinly concealed beneath a veneer of innocence and decency.

Games at Twilight and Other Stories was well received in the United Kingdom. Hermione Lee in *The Observer* (13 August 1978) described the stories as "absolutely first rate," while Mary Hope in *The Spectator* (22 July 1978) found them "delicately composed." Indian reviewers were less impressed. Shiv K. Kumar in *The Humanities Review* (July–December 1981) criticized Desai's "overzealous concern with the medium of communication, regardless of the nature of experience embodied in each story." In 1979 Desai won the Sahitya Akademi award for *Fire on the Mountain*.

In 1980 Desai published *Clear Light of Day,* perhaps her most autobiographical work to date. Many of the characters are based on her memories of her neighbors in Old Delhi, and the house in which much of the novel is set is modeled on her childhood home there. In 1992 Desai told John Clement Ball and Chelva Kanaganayakam about the inception of the novel: "the image I began with was one of a tunnel. I thought it would be interesting for my characters in their old age to start digging this hole in their past and to tunnel backwards . . . in order to uncover the very roots of their lives." Sisters Tara and Bim are reunited after a long separation. Tara is married to Bakul, a diplomat, and takes pride in being a wife, mother, and hostess. Bim is single and teaches at a women's college in Delhi. The sisters relive their childhoods, evoking the ethos of Old Delhi before, during, and after the partition. They remember life in the old house with their brothers, Raja and Baba; the negligence of their invalid mother; the dominance of their father; the loving care of Mira Masi, the widowed aunt who became their substitute mother; and Hyder Ali, a Muslim who lived across the street. After the deaths of their parents, the siblings drifted apart. Tara married Bakul and went abroad. Raja, nursed back to health by Bim after suffering from tuberculosis, left for Hyderabad. Mira Masi committed suicide, leaving Bim to take care of the autistic Baba. Bim is filled with rage and frustration at her circumstances until, in a final epiphany, she recognizes the bonds of love that connect her with all those who share her past: "Bim could see as well as by the clear light of day that she felt only love and yearning for them all, and if there were hurts, these gashes and wounds in her side that bled, then it was only because her love was imperfect and did not encompass them thoroughly enough."

Desai has insisted that she deliberately avoided writing a partition novel, because too many books had already been written on the subject. But *Clear Light of Day* is haunted by the shadow of the partition, especially in the description of Hyder Ali's move from Delhi to Hyderabad, a city with a larger Muslim population, in 1947. The decaying house in Old Delhi becomes a

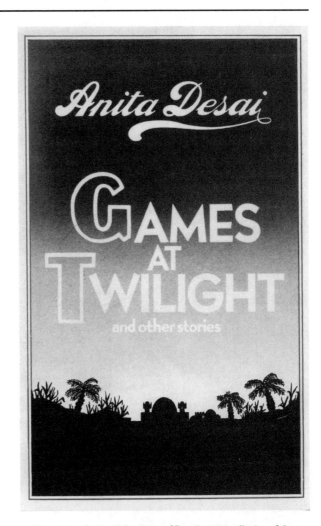

Dust jacket for the U.S. edition of Desai's 1978 collection of short stories, several of which deal with parent-child relationships (Richland County Public Library)

symbol of the passing of an older way of life to make room for a new and changing world. The novel was short-listed for the prestigious British Booker Prize.

Change is also the theme of *The Village by the Sea: An Indian Family Story* (1982), a novel for children set in the fishing village of Thul, outside Bombay. Hari and his sister Lila bear the burden of supporting their poverty-stricken family, which consists of their drunken father, ailing mother, and two younger sisters. Near their hut is the vacation home of Sayyid Ali, a rich Bombay businessman. While Hari and Lila struggle with the scarcity of food, the rising price of medicine, and their father's alcoholism, Sayyid Ali indulges in his hobby of bird-watching. Hari goes to Bombay with a group of villagers to protest a government plan to convert their village into an industrial complex for the production of chemical fertilizer. The villagers are afraid of losing their livelihood; Sayyid Ali supports their cause,

Dust jacket for the U.S. edition of Desai's autobiographical 1980 novel, in which two sisters reminisce about their family's life in Bombay before, during, and after the partition of the subcontinent in 1947 (Richland County Public Library)

though for a different reason: he wants to prevent the pollution of the village. In Bombay, Hari learns to repair watches, a skill he hopes to use when Thul acquires a new population of engineers. He also hopes to start a poultry farm to cater to the needs of the expected newcomers.

Desai's novel highlights the importance of adapting to change but also draws attention to the gap between rich and poor in contemporary Indian society—between Hari's efforts to evolve survival strategies in a rapidly changing world and Sayyid Ali's romantic desire to preserve the old, agricultural way of life. In the dedication Desai claims that the story is entirely factual. In the interview with Jussawalla and Dassenbrock she described her sense of an altered India: "It seems to me a place of increasing violence and of tremendous change. . . . It's an economic revolution, of course, more than a political one at the moment. My sense of it is a place where life has become extremely difficult to

endure." *Village by the Sea* won the *Guardian* Prize for Children's Fiction in 1983 and was adapted for television by the British Broadcasting Corporation in 1992.

One of the stories in *Games at Twilight and Other Stories* is "The Accompanist," about a man who accompanies a sitar maestro on the tanpura. Desai develops the idea of a disciple's self-effacing devotion to his master in more depth in her novel, *In Custody,* in which she moves away from her earlier woman-centered narratives to write from a male point of view. Deven, a mediocre college teacher in the small town of Mirpore, has romantic ideals about the greatness of poetry and becomes obsessed with preserving for posterity the life and works of Nur, the greatest living Urdu poet. He travels to Delhi to meet Nur and is devastated to find the poet living in squalor and self-indulgence. He clings to his ideals, however, and struggles to complete his project. In the process he incurs the resentment of his wife, Sarla, and is taunted, deceived, and exploited by his friend Murad, his colleague Siddiqui, and the great Nur himself. The novel addresses the politics of language in postcolonial India, where the dominance of Hindi threatens the Urdu language and culture with extinction. Backward, decaying, and dreary Mirpore functions as an image of contemporary India. *In Custody* was short-listed for the Booker Prize.

The Bengali writings of Tagore had not interested Desai when she was a child, but in the 1980s she grew better acquainted with his work. In 1985 she wrote the introduction to *The Home and the World,* Surendranath Tagore's translation of his uncle's 1920 novel *Ghare-baire.* That same year she published the article "The Rage for the Raj," a critique of the tendency in the 1980s to romanticize British rule in India in ways that reinforce false stereotypes about Indian culture.

Desai was the Helen Cam Fellow at Girton College of the University of Oxford in 1986–1987 and the Elizabeth Drew Visiting Professor at Smith College in Northampton, Massachusetts, in 1987–1988. In 1988 she became Purington Professor of English at Mount Holyoke College in South Hadley, Massachusetts. Up to this point her published work had expressed the Indian aspect of her identity, but for years she had wanted to write a book that would bring to the fore her associations with German culture. In Bombay she observed an old man who shuffled around feeding stray cats on the streets. An acquaintance informed her that the man was German and was quite wealthy. When he died, Desai was asked to translate a packet of letters in German that were among his effects. Though the letters were bland and uninformative, their stamps identified them as having been sent from a Nazi concentration camp. (Desai said in the Pandit interview, "I read that Jews in concentration camps during the Holo-

Dust jacket for the U.S. edition of Desai's 2004 novel, about an American student's search for his roots in a Mexican ghost town (Richland County Public Library)

Several of Desai's favorite themes are reworked in *Diamond Dust and Other Stories:* youth, age, and death; the minutiae of human relationships; art and life; illusion and reality; time and change; cultural differences; and the pressures of survival in an increasingly difficult world. The stories set child's-eye perspectives against the perceptions of old age. They are permeated by a sense of people's alienation from each other and from their environments, their need for love, and their encounters with small but significant experiences that open the windows to wisdom. Most noticeable is the internationalism of Desai's subject matter, signaling her refusal to remain pigeonholed within convenient definitions of what constitutes "Indian" writing.

Desai assumed emeritus status at MIT in 2002. Her refusal to be pigeonholed as an Indian writer is borne out by *The Zigzag Way* (2004), which is set in Mexico. Seen through the eyes of Eric, a visiting student from Boston, Mexico appears vibrant, mysterious, and full of contradictions. Drawn into a search for his roots, Eric learns about his Cornish grandfather, who

had come to Mexico in search of his own roots, and his grandmother, who died in childbirth. The history of Mexico, its colonial past challenged by the gradual rise of the spirit of revolution, forms the backdrop for Eric's quest for his identity. His journey takes him to a ghost town once inhabited by gold miners. He reads in the library of the town's study center, which is presided over by the formidable Doña Vera, the "Queen of the Sierra" and champion of the indigenous Huichols. Past and present alternate in the three narratives that intertwine in the novel: Eric's, Doña Vera's, and that of Eric's grandmother, Betty. The strands come together on the Day of the Dead, when Eric encounters the swirling, fluid reality of Mexican culture. An aura of the supernatural hangs over the story, becoming explicit when Eric sees figures from the past conversing with the spirit of his grandmother. His journey into the past leads to no certitudes, but through his Mexican experience Eric learns a great deal about himself.

Reviewers agreed that *The Zigzag Way* is more about Mexico than about any specific character or characters. According to Claire Messud in the *New Statesman* (6 September 2004), "Desai's primary interest is manifestly the country itself, its landscape and the curious details of its history, rather than the individuals with whom she has peopled it." According to Melissa Dene in *The Guardian* (2 September 2004), "*The Zigzag Way* is an unfashionably quiet, subtle book, in which history and landscape are more important than character and denouement." The descriptive brilliance of Desai's narrative led Liz Hoggard to speculate in *The Observer* (29 August 2004) about a movie version of the novel: "At her best, Desai approaches the Mexican landscape like a master cinematographer."

Early in her career Desai was compelled to write in secret to avoid conflict with her husband's family; today her daughter Kiran is also a novelist. In responding to the 2002 questionnaire Desai noted that her daughter "must have imbibed the discipline of writing without being aware of it; her working habits are almost exactly like mine. This makes for a great intimacy and companionship between us, the first I have ever experienced."

Desai is a fellow of the British Royal Society of Literature, an honorary member of the American Academy of Arts and Letters, and a member of the New York chapter of the writers' organization PEN. In addition to her creative and academic pursuits, she has undertaken sociological projects that reflect her humanitarian concerns. They include a report for the United Nations Children's Fund (UNICEF) on family welfare in Indonesia (1983); a report for the United Nations Decade of Women in Norway; and a report on the

caust were allowed to write a certain number of letters during the early years at least. These letters were stamped with the numbers they bore in the camps.") Desai felt compelled to imagine a history for their sender. Drawing on her mother's bedtime stories about prewar Germany, on her own extensive reading of Holocaust literature, and on accounts of camps in England and Canada where Germans were interned during World War II, she wrote *Baumgartner's Bombay* (1988). Alex Aronson, a professor at Haifa University in Israel who had been interned in India, shared his memories with her and read and commented on her manuscript.

Hugo Baumgartner, a Jewish fugitive from the Nazi camps in Germany, is captured in India and incarcerated for six years in a British internment camp; German Jews were held in the camps, because the British considered all Germans enemies. After the war comes the partition, and Baumgartner's Muslim business partner is ousted by the dominant Hindus. The death of his Hindu partner leaves him once more vulnerable in a postcolonial nation that looks askance at Europeans. In his struggle for survival Baumgartner is supported by his German friend Lotte. After he is murdered by a young German, she discovers some letters near his body. The messages are brief, uninformative, and repetitious; for instance, "Are you well? I am well. Do not worry. I have enough. Have you enough?" Their significance lies in what they do not say; their very existence bears silent witness to horrors that they do not describe. Their impact depends on the reader's historical knowledge of the Holocaust. The dates on the letters stop abruptly in February 1941.

Desai had already received considerable acclaim in India and the United Kingdom, but *Baumgartner's Bombay* brought her recognition in the United States: India was of limited interest to American readers, but the Jewish material in the novel appealed to the literary establishment. The novel was awarded the Hadassah Prize in New York City in 1989.

In 1989 Desai was the Gildersleeves Professor at Barnard College in New York City and the Ashby Fellow at Clare Hall at the University of Cambridge, and she received the Taraknath Das Award for Contributions to Indo-American Understanding. That year she published the essay "Indian Fiction Today," in which she seeks to identify the distinguishing features of contemporary Indian literature and notes the newfound confidence of Indian writers in English after the publication of Salman Rushdie's *Midnight's Children* (1981). In the essay "A Secret Connivance" (1990) she dismantles the myth of the Mother Goddess, which, she says, dominates the Indian public imagination and obscures the actual oppression of women in contemporary

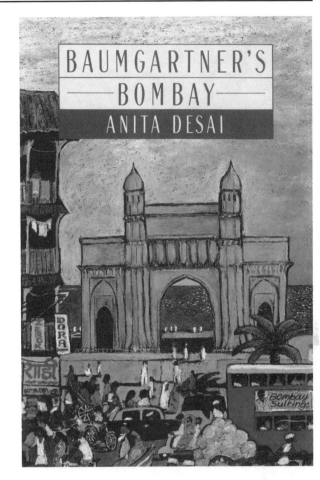

Dust jacket for the U.S. edition (1989) of Desai's 1988 novel, about a German Jew incarcerated in a British internment camp in India during World War II (Richland County Public Library)

Indian society. In the same year she gave a talk at the University of Toronto in which she traced the tradition of women's writing in India from ancient times to the present; the talk was published in 1992 as "Women and Fiction in India."

In 1990 Desai received the Padma Shri, one of the highest national awards in India. In 1992 she was a visiting scholar at the Rockefeller Foundation in Bellagio, Italy, and Distinguished Visiting Professor at the American University of Cairo. In 1993 the New York Public Library honored her with the Literary Lion Award. In 1993 she became the John E. Burchard Professor of Writing at the Massachusetts Institute of Technology (MIT). The Scottish Arts Council awarded her the Neil Gunn Prize for International Literature in 1994.

In her essay "Tagore" (1994) Desai assesses the continued relevance of the Bengali poet. Describing Tagore as a tormented personality who "never thought that his life measured up to his ideal of perfection,"

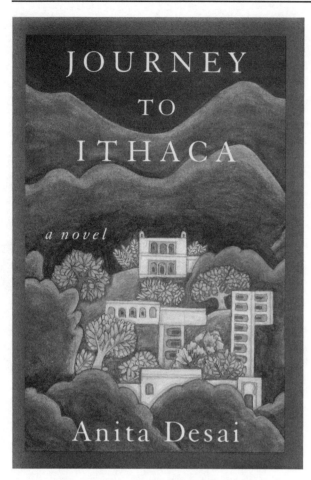

*Dust jacket for the U.S. edition of Desai's 1995 novel, about a
woman's attempt to expose the leader of an ashram as
a fraud during the "hippie invasion" of India in
the 1970s (Richland County Public Library)*

Desai says: "his ghost is still a restless one as if it were in search, in true ghostly tradition, of something that had been mislaid and needed to be found again, or remained unfinished and sought fulfillment."

Desai's move to the United States brought a change in her perspective. *Baumgartner's Bombay* had shown her renewed interest in the international themes she had ignored since *Bye-Bye, Blackbird;* in *Journey to Ithaca* (1995) the shift to an international perspective is even more pronounced. The narrative spans three continents and traces the lives of protagonists from Egypt, Europe, and India. Desai told Jussawalla and Dassenbrock that her interest in cross-cultural identities "coincided with my own leaving India for large portions of the year and living much more abroad now. In a way, that intervenes with my Indian life. It's like a screen that has come between me and India. I can't simply ignore this experience abroad–it's too overwhelming, it demands to be dealt with, somehow grappled with."

Journey to Ithaca is set during the hippie influx into India in the 1970s. Sophie, a German woman, accompanies her Italian husband, Matteo, on his journey to India in search of peace. The Mother, the charismatic head of an Indian ashram, casts her spell on Matteo. Jealous, Sophie sets out to trace the Mother's life story and expose her as a fraud. Sophie's journey takes her to Egypt and Paris and back to India, but the quest for the Mother's true identity turns out to be a search for self-knowledge for Sophie. At the end of the novel she sets out on one more journey: to find Matteo, who has disappeared.

Journey to Ithaca is a richly allusive novel that draws on Indian and Western literatures and mythologies. In spite of the overt internationalism of the text, however, the focus remains on India as the place of self-discovery. But India is presented through Western eyes, a perspective Desai has increasingly adopted in her writings. Responding to the 2002 questionnaire, she wrote: "I remain Indian; I carry my Indian background, upbringing and memories with me wherever I go. I do travel a good deal and am certainly interested in the views foreigners have of India and have written of them. Now that I live abroad much of the time, this has become my subject."

The novel received mixed reviews. In *The New York Times* (30 August 1995), Richard Bernstein praised Desai's "remarkable eye for substance, the things that give life its texture. Nothing escapes her power of observation, not the thickness of the drapes that blot out the light in a bourgeois Parisian home, or the enamel bowl in the office of an Indian doctor." On the other hand, Gabriele Annan complained in *TLS: The Times Literary Supplement* (2 June 1995) that "The narrative is full of gaps and improbabilities, as well as clichés . . . the dialogue is stagey and unconvincing." Bhaskar Ghose, however, argued in *Biblio* (December 1996) that the elegance of Desai's craft "ultimately gives a definition to the story which could have been diffuse, or drearily familiar in the hands of a weaker artist. Within the body of her work, this novel must rank as one of the most ambitious and most tightly crafted works that Anita Desai has undertaken."

Desai's next novel, *Fasting, Feasting* (1999), approaches the cross-cultural theme through a two-part narrative charting the divergent experiences of a young woman in India and her brother in the United States. In the first part the central character is Uma, the plain and awkward older daughter in an Indian household. Unable to bring off an arranged marriage, Uma remains trapped in the family home, dominated by her parents and under the shadow of her attractive and ambitious sister Aruna, who is able to capture a "suitable" groom in the marriage market. Uma is forced to

abandon her studies to help take care of her baby brother, Arun, and, later, to look after her aging parents. All of her attempts at self-expression are frowned on, including her childhood escape to the ashram with her aunt Mira Masi, her outing with her charming but "wild" cousin Ramu as an adult, and her desire to accept a job offer. Outwardly compliant, Uma nurses an inner rage that is expressed in angry silence and in fits in which she collapses, frothing at the mouth. She finds solace only in the hymns sung by nuns at the convent school she attends as a child, the rituals performed by Mira Masi, and the poetry of Ella Wheeler Wilcox.

The second part of the novel is set in Massachusetts, where Uma's brother Arun goes to pursue his education. Though he feels an alien in the United States, he also relishes his solitariness as an escape from the stifling attention of his parents. Spending the summer with the Pattons in their suburban home, he finds the atmosphere extremely cool and detached in contrast to the overwhelming pressures of a traditional Indian family. He discovers that freedom, affluence, and small luxuries coexist strangely with self-denial and psychological power games. Her cooking rejected by her own husband and children, Mrs. Patton showers her affection on Arun, developing an obsessive determination to feed him her own versions of vegetarian food and dragging him to the supermarket on shopping expeditions. Mr. Patton, meanwhile, eats meat, ignoring the reactions of the other members of the family. There is little communication between parents and children: the son, Rod, trains compulsively for football, while his sister, Melanie, manifests her anger and loneliness in sullenness and bouts of bulimia.

In this overwrought atmosphere Arun grasps the underlying similarity between family dynamics in the apparently different cultures of India and the United States. He finds Uma's silent rage replicated in Melanie's behavior and muses: "How strange to encounter it here, . . . where so much is given, where there is both license and plenty." Desai is unsparing in her critique of family values and social customs in India and the United States, using a transnational narrative to highlight both cultural differences and invisible parallels between "East" and "West." *Fasting, Feasting* was her third novel to be short-listed for the Booker Prize. In 1999 she won the Moravia Prize for Literature in Rome.

Desai's *Diamond Dust and Other Stories* (2000) is dedicated to her students in the Program in Writing and Humanistic Studies at MIT. The settings of the stories range from Canada to India to Latin America, and the characters are of various nationalities. The title piece, subtitled "A Tragedy," is set in a staid neighborhood of New Delhi: Mr. Das's grief for his lost dog

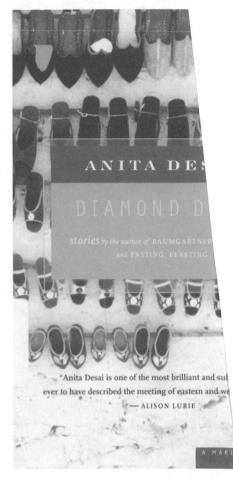

*Cover for the U.S. edition of Desai's collection of shor[t]
set in India, Mexico, Canada, Latin America,
United States (Richland County Public Lib[rary])*

shows that tragedy today resides in the everyday, and the unheroic. In "Royalty" [a liv]ing dilettante from Oxford, revives romanti[c] in the middle-aged Sarla until disillusionm[ent] with it an acceptance of her advancing age a[nd] tion of the stability of her relationship with band. Age and isolation are also the t "Winterscape," in which a pair of old ladies f[rom] disturb the equilibrium of an intercultural m[arriage] Canada. The clash of tradition and modernit[y] lies "Tepoztlan Tomorrow," set in a backward Mexico. A hint of the supernatural animates "[The Man] Who Saw Himself Drown." The link between reality and the artist's struggle to create beauty ugliness and squalor are explored in "The Artist in the context of racial tensions in Massachusetts Rooftop Dwellers" describes the attempted rebel Moyna, a young woman determined to live in[depen]dently in the hostile environment of a colony in [ur]ban New Delhi.

effect of foreign aid on culture and civilization for the UN in Denmark.

In the course of her long career Desai has evolved from chronicling the inner lives of her characters to an awareness of the links between individual psychology and the social and cultural environment. She told Pandit: "It is the confrontation of the inner and the outer that interests me as a novelist. The outer world is dominated by certain forces, the individual's force is enigmatic, variable, an imponderable." The forces beyond the individual's control include society, tradition, history, and culture. "In the Indian society, tradition takes precedence over the individual," she told Pandit. Speaking of her craft in the 2002 interview, Desai emphasized her treatment of time: "Time (history) is the fourth dimension. . . . The present makes little sense unless one looks into the past and considers the future." In Desai's novels time is both personal and historical–an interior awareness as well as an exterior force beyond individual control.

Desai's distinctive literary style evokes internal states of mind while recording sharply detailed impressions of social interactions, using imagery to create a sharply defined concrete reality that suggests more-abstract possibilities. At times the imagery lends a poetic quality to her prose. In *Perspectives on Anita Desai,* Prasad remarks that her novels have a "mosaic textual density" because "Desai's imagery is wedded to her rich lyricism." Images recur with cumulative effect as Desai uses suggestion rather than overt statement to highlight thematic issues or to make rhetorical points.

Among the issues highlighted in Desai's fiction are family relationships and the impact of family dynamics on the individual psyche. She also explores the problems faced by women in contemporary India, particularly middle-class women expected to lead lives of quiet domesticity in a rapidly changing world. Many of Desai's female protagonists rebel against their circumstances, only to compromise in the end. Asked about this point in the 2002 questionnaire, Desai noted that most of her novels describe the lives of women before the feminist movement gathered momentum in India and added: "Of course I have written largely–although not exclusively–about women and women's worlds, simply because that is what I know best. But it is not all that interests me or that I deal with in my writing." Desai also disclaims any overt preoccupation with the politics of postcolonialism, because, as she told Ball and Kanaganayakam, "For the most part I've lived in India, in a home where cultures combined rather than clashed." Desai is also unwilling to be considered a writer of the Indian diaspora, she said in response to the 2002 questionnaire, because it "is not my theme and I'm not very interested in what I read of it." Never-

theless, exile is a major theme in Desai's fiction from Nirode's alienation from the culture of his own city to Baumgartner's loneliness in Bombay and the cultural isolation suffered by Arun in the United States.

In a response to the 2002 questionnaire Anita Desai claimed that "it is my intention, when I write fiction, to explore and reveal the nine-tenths of the truth that lies submerged beneath the one-tenth visible tip of the iceberg." Throughout her fiction she searches for imaginative ways of constructing realities that are too complex to be depicted directly. For her, she wrote in response to the questionnaire, the writer's role in the world is "observing that world, searching for ways to comprehend and understand it, explore it and reveal what you perceive as truth."

Interviews:

Yashodhara Dalmia, "An Interview with Anita Desai," *Times of India,* 29 April 1979, p. 13;

Atma Ram, "Interview with Anita Desai," in *Interviews with Indian Writers* (Calcutta: Calcutta Writers' Workshop, 1983), pp. 21–33;

Ramesh K. Srivastava, "Anita Desai at Work: An Interview," in *Perspectives on Anita Desai,* edited by Srivastava (Ghaziabad: Vimal Prakashan, 1984), pp. 208–226;

John Clement Ball and Chelva Kanaganayakam, "Interview with Anita Desai," *Toronto South Asian Review,* 10, no. 2 (1992): 30–41;

Feroza Jussawalla and Reed Way Dassenbrock, "Anita Desai," in their *Interviews with Writers of the Post-Colonial World* (Jackson: University Press of Mississippi, 1992), pp. 157–179;

Lalita Pandit, "A Sense of Detail and a Sense of Order: Anita Desai Interviewed by Lalita Pandit," in *Literary India: Comparative Studies in Aesthetics, Colonialism, and Culture,* edited by Pandit and Patrick Colm Hogan (Albany: State University of New York Press, 1995), pp. 153–172.

References:

Fawzia Afzal-Khan, *Cultural Imperialism and the Indo-English Novel: Genre and Ideology in R. K. Narayan, Anita Desai, Kamala Markandaya, and Salman Rushdie* (University Park: Pennsylvania State University Press, 1993), pp. 59–96;

Shyam M. Asnani, "Anita Desai's Fiction: A New Dimension," *Indian Literature,* 24, no. 2 (1981): 44–54;

Joy Rosemary Atfield, *Students' Guide to* The Village by the Sea (Thornhill, U.K.: Tynron, 1990);

Usha Bande, *The Novels of Anita Desai: A Study in Character and Conflict* (New Delhi: Prestige, 1988);

Shirley Chew, "Searching Voices: Anita Desai's *Clear Light of Day* and Nayantara Sahgal's *Rich Like Us*," in *Motherlands: Black Women's Writing from Africa, the Caribbean and South Asia,* edited by Susheila Nasta (London: Women's Press, 1991), pp. 43–63;

Kamini Dinesh, ed., *Between Spaces of Silence: Women Creative Writers* (New Delhi: Sterling, 1994), pp. 95–112;

Alamgir Hashmi, "A Reading of Anita Desai's *Clear Light of Day*," *International Fiction Review,* 10, no. 1 (1983): 56–58;

S. Indira, "The Nowhere Men: A Comparative Study of Anita Desai's *Baumgartner's Bombay* and Kamala Markandaya's *The Nowhere Man*," *Indian Journal of English Studies,* 30 (1991–1992): 5–12;

Jasbir Jain, *Stairs to the Attic: The Novels of Anita Desai* (Jaipur: Printwell, 1987);

Asha Kanwar, *Virginia Woolf and Anita Desai: A Comparative Study* (New Delhi: Prestige, 1989);

Viney Kirpal, "An Image of India: A Study of Anita Desai's *In Custody*," *Ariel,* 17, no. 4 (1986): 127–138;

Kirpal, ed., *The New Indian Novel in English: A Study of the 1980s* (New Delhi: Allied, 1990), pp. 67–71, 73–81, 187–199, 213–227, 271–278;

Francine E. Krishna, "Anita Desai: *Fire on the Mountain*," *Indian Literature,* 25, no. 5 (1982): 158–169;

Harveen Sachdeva Mann, "'Going in the Opposite Direction': Feminine Recusancy in Anita Desai's *Voices in the City*," *Ariel,* 23, no. 4 (1992): 75–92;

M. Mani Meitei, "Anita Desai's *Where Shall We Go This Summer?*: A Psychoanalytical Study," *Language Forum: A Half-Yearly Journal of Language and Literature,* 18, nos. 1–2 (1992): 48–58;

Rajeswari Mohan, "The Forked Tongue of Lyric in Anita Desai's *Clear Light of Day*," *Journal of Commonwealth Literature,* 32, no. 1 (1997): 47–66;

Arun P. Mukherjee, "Other Worlds, Other Texts: Teaching Anita Desai's *Clear Light of Day* to Canadian Students," *College Literature,* 22, no. 1 (1995): 192–201;

K. Ayyappa Paniker, ed., *Indian Literature since Independence* (New Delhi: Indian Association for English Studies, 1991), pp. 44–48;

Ujwala Patil, "Sexual Violence and Death in Anita Desai's *Fire on the Mountain*," in *Studies in Indian Fiction in English,* edited by G. S. Balarama Gupta (Gulbarga: JIWE, 1987), pp. 61–67;

K. J. Philips, "Ambiguous Tragic Flaw in Anita Desai's *Fire on the Mountain*," *International Fiction Review,* 17, no. 1 (1990): 3–8;

Madhusudan Prasad, *Anita Desai: The Novelist* (Allahabad, India: New Horizon, 1981);

M. Rajeshwar, "The Dynamics of Attachment and Non-attachment: Maya and Karma Yoga as Aspects of Technique in Anita Desai's *Cry, the Peacock*," *Journal of Indian Writing in English,* 24, no. 2 (1996): 16–23;

Geetha Ramanathan, "Sexual Violence/Textual Violence: Desai's *Fire on the Mountain* and Shirazi's *Javady Alley*," *Modern Fiction Studies,* 39, no. 1 (1993): 17–35;

B. Ramachandra Rao, *The Novels of Anita Desai: A Study* (New Delhi: Kalyani, 1977);

Vimala Rao, "*Where Shall We Go This Summer?* An Analysis," *Commonwealth Quarterly,* 3, no. 9 (1978): 44–50;

R. S. Sharma, *Anita Desai* (New Delhi: Arnold-Heinemann, 1981);

Sharma, "Anita Desai's *Where Shall We Go This Summer?* An Analysis," *Commonwealth Quarterly,* 3, no. 10 (1979): 50–69;

Sunaina Singh, *The Novels of Margaret Atwood and Anita Desai: A Comparative Study in Feminist Perspectives* (New Delhi: Creative Books, 1994);

Avadhesh K. Srivastava, *Alien Voice: Perspectives on Commonwealth Literature* (Lucknow: Print House, 1981), pp. 84–100;

Ramesh K. Srivastava, ed., *Perspectives on Anita Desai* (Ghaziabad: Vimal Prakashan, 1984);

Alladi Uma, "'I Have Had My Vision': Virginia Woolf's *To the Lighthouse* and Anita Desai's *Where Shall We Go This Summer?*" *Literary Criterion,* 22, no. 3 (1987): 73–77.

caust were allowed to write a certain number of letters during the early years at least. These letters were stamped with the numbers they bore in the camps.") Desai felt compelled to imagine a history for their sender. Drawing on her mother's bedtime stories about prewar Germany, on her own extensive reading of Holocaust literature, and on accounts of camps in England and Canada where Germans were interned during World War II, she wrote *Baumgartner's Bombay* (1988). Alex Aronson, a professor at Haifa University in Israel who had been interned in India, shared his memories with her and read and commented on her manuscript.

Hugo Baumgartner, a Jewish fugitive from the Nazi camps in Germany, is captured in India and incarcerated for six years in a British internment camp; German Jews were held in the camps, because the British considered all Germans enemies. After the war comes the partition, and Baumgartner's Muslim business partner is ousted by the dominant Hindus. The death of his Hindu partner leaves him once more vulnerable in a postcolonial nation that looks askance at Europeans. In his struggle for survival Baumgartner is supported by his German friend Lotte. After he is murdered by a young German, she discovers some letters near his body. The messages are brief, uninformative, and repetitious; for instance, "Are you well? I am well. Do not worry. I have enough. Have you enough?" Their significance lies in what they do not say; their very existence bears silent witness to horrors that they do not describe. Their impact depends on the reader's historical knowledge of the Holocaust. The dates on the letters stop abruptly in February 1941.

Desai had already received considerable acclaim in India and the United Kingdom, but *Baumgartner's Bombay* brought her recognition in the United States: India was of limited interest to American readers, but the Jewish material in the novel appealed to the literary establishment. The novel was awarded the Hadassah Prize in New York City in 1989.

In 1989 Desai was the Gildersleeves Professor at Barnard College in New York City and the Ashby Fellow at Clare Hall at the University of Cambridge, and she received the Taraknath Das Award for Contributions to Indo-American Understanding. That year she published the essay "Indian Fiction Today," in which she seeks to identify the distinguishing features of contemporary Indian literature and notes the newfound confidence of Indian writers in English after the publication of Salman Rushdie's *Midnight's Children* (1981). In the essay "A Secret Connivance" (1990) she dismantles the myth of the Mother Goddess, which, she says, dominates the Indian public imagination and obscures the actual oppression of women in contemporary

Dust jacket for the U.S. edition (1989) of Desai's 1988 novel, about a German Jew incarcerated in a British internment camp in India during World War II (Richland County Public Library)

Indian society. In the same year she gave a talk at the University of Toronto in which she traced the tradition of women's writing in India from ancient times to the present; the talk was published in 1992 as "Women and Fiction in India."

In 1990 Desai received the Padma Shri, one of the highest national awards in India. In 1992 she was a visiting scholar at the Rockefeller Foundation in Bellagio, Italy, and Distinguished Visiting Professor at the American University of Cairo. In 1993 the New York Public Library honored her with the Literary Lion Award. In 1993 she became the John E. Burchard Professor of Writing at the Massachusetts Institute of Technology (MIT). The Scottish Arts Council awarded her the Neil Gunn Prize for International Literature in 1994.

In her essay "Tagore" (1994) Desai assesses the continued relevance of the Bengali poet. Describing Tagore as a tormented personality who "never thought that his life measured up to his ideal of perfection,"

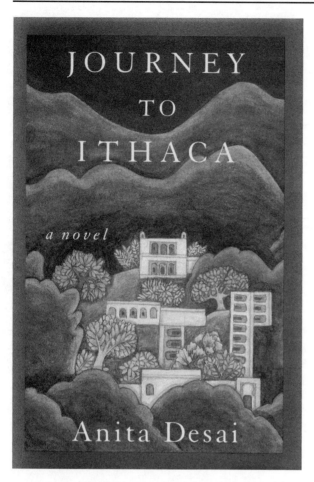

Dust jacket for the U.S. edition of Desai's 1995 novel, about a woman's attempt to expose the leader of an ashram as a fraud during the "hippie invasion" of India in the 1970s (Richland County Public Library)

Journey to Ithaca is set during the hippie influx into India in the 1970s. Sophie, a German woman, accompanies her Italian husband, Matteo, on his journey to India in search of peace. The Mother, the charismatic head of an Indian ashram, casts her spell on Matteo. Jealous, Sophie sets out to trace the Mother's life story and expose her as a fraud. Sophie's journey takes her to Egypt and Paris and back to India, but the quest for the Mother's true identity turns out to be a search for self-knowledge for Sophie. At the end of the novel she sets out on one more journey: to find Matteo, who has disappeared.

Journey to Ithaca is a richly allusive novel that draws on Indian and Western literatures and mythologies. In spite of the overt internationalism of the text, however, the focus remains on India as the place of self-discovery. But India is presented through Western eyes, a perspective Desai has increasingly adopted in her writings. Responding to the 2002 questionnaire, she wrote: "I remain Indian; I carry my Indian background, upbringing and memories with me wherever I go. I do travel a good deal and am certainly interested in the views foreigners have of India and have written of them. Now that I live abroad much of the time, this has become my subject."

The novel received mixed reviews. In *The New York Times* (30 August 1995), Richard Bernstein praised Desai's "remarkable eye for substance, the things that give life its texture. Nothing escapes her power of observation, not the thickness of the drapes that blot out the light in a bourgeois Parisian home, or the enamel bowl in the office of an Indian doctor." On the other hand, Gabriele Annan complained in *TLS: The Times Literary Supplement* (2 June 1995) that "The narrative is full of gaps and improbabilities, as well as clichés . . . the dialogue is stagey and unconvincing." Bhaskar Ghose, however, argued in *Biblio* (December 1996) that the elegance of Desai's craft "ultimately gives a definition to the story which could have been diffuse, or drearily familiar in the hands of a weaker artist. Within the body of her work, this novel must rank as one of the most ambitious and most tightly crafted works that Anita Desai has undertaken."

Desai's next novel, *Fasting, Feasting* (1999), approaches the cross-cultural theme through a two-part narrative charting the divergent experiences of a young woman in India and her brother in the United States. In the first part the central character is Uma, the plain and awkward older daughter in an Indian household. Unable to bring off an arranged marriage, Uma remains trapped in the family home, dominated by her parents and under the shadow of her attractive and ambitious sister Aruna, who is able to capture a "suitable" groom in the marriage market. Uma is forced to

Desai says: "his ghost is still a restless one as if it were in search, in true ghostly tradition, of something that had been mislaid and needed to be found again, or remained unfinished and sought fulfillment."

Desai's move to the United States brought a change in her perspective. *Baumgartner's Bombay* had shown her renewed interest in the international themes she had ignored since *Bye-Bye, Blackbird;* in *Journey to Ithaca* (1995) the shift to an international perspective is even more pronounced. The narrative spans three continents and traces the lives of protagonists from Egypt, Europe, and India. Desai told Jussawalla and Dassenbrock that her interest in cross-cultural identities "coincided with my own leaving India for large portions of the year and living much more abroad now. In a way, that intervenes with my Indian life. It's like a screen that has come between me and India. I can't simply ignore this experience abroad—it's too overwhelming, it demands to be dealt with, somehow grappled with."

abandon her studies to help take care of her baby brother, Arun, and, later, to look after her aging parents. All of her attempts at self-expression are frowned on, including her childhood escape to the ashram with her aunt Mira Masi, her outing with her charming but "wild" cousin Ramu as an adult, and her desire to accept a job offer. Outwardly compliant, Uma nurses an inner rage that is expressed in angry silence and in fits in which she collapses, frothing at the mouth. She finds solace only in the hymns sung by nuns at the convent school she attends as a child, the rituals performed by Mira Masi, and the poetry of Ella Wheeler Wilcox.

The second part of the novel is set in Massachusetts, where Uma's brother Arun goes to pursue his education. Though he feels an alien in the United States, he also relishes his solitariness as an escape from the stifling attention of his parents. Spending the summer with the Pattons in their suburban home, he finds the atmosphere extremely cool and detached in contrast to the overwhelming pressures of a traditional Indian family. He discovers that freedom, affluence, and small luxuries coexist strangely with self-denial and psychological power games. Her cooking rejected by her own husband and children, Mrs. Patton showers her affection on Arun, developing an obsessive determination to feed him her own versions of vegetarian food and dragging him to the supermarket on shopping expeditions. Mr. Patton, meanwhile, eats meat, ignoring the reactions of the other members of the family. There is little communication between parents and children: the son, Rod, trains compulsively for football, while his sister, Melanie, manifests her anger and loneliness in sullenness and bouts of bulimia.

In this overwrought atmosphere Arun grasps the underlying similarity between family dynamics in the apparently different cultures of India and the United States. He finds Uma's silent rage replicated in Melanie's behavior and muses: "How strange to encounter it here, . . . where so much is given, where there is both license and plenty." Desai is unsparing in her critique of family values and social customs in India and the United States, using a transnational narrative to highlight both cultural differences and invisible parallels between "East" and "West." *Fasting, Feasting* was her third novel to be short-listed for the Booker Prize. In 1999 she won the Moravia Prize for Literature in Rome.

Desai's *Diamond Dust and Other Stories* (2000) is dedicated to her students in the Program in Writing and Humanistic Studies at MIT. The settings of the stories range from Canada to India to Latin America, and the characters are of various nationalities. The title piece, subtitled "A Tragedy," is set in a staid neighborhood of New Delhi: Mr. Das's grief for his lost dog

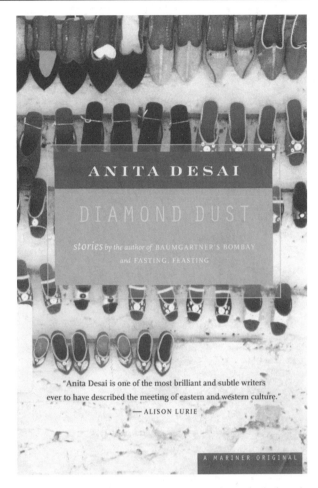

Cover for the U.S. edition of Desai's collection of short stories (2000) set in India, Mexico, Canada, Latin America, and the United States (Richland County Public Library)

shows that tragedy today resides in the minute, the everyday, and the unheroic. In "Royalty" Raja, a visiting dilettante from Oxford, revives romantic memories in the middle-aged Sarla until disillusionment brings with it an acceptance of her advancing age and recognition of the stability of her relationship with her husband. Age and isolation are also the themes of "Winterscape," in which a pair of old ladies from India disturb the equilibrium of an intercultural marriage in Canada. The clash of tradition and modernity underlies "Tepoztlan Tomorrow," set in a backward town in Mexico. A hint of the supernatural animates "The Man Who Saw Himself Drown." The link between art and reality and the artist's struggle to create beauty out of ugliness and squalor are explored in "The Artist's Life" in the context of racial tensions in Massachusetts. "The Rooftop Dwellers" describes the attempted rebellion of Moyna, a young woman determined to live independently in the hostile environment of a colony in suburban New Delhi.

*Dust jacket for the U.S. edition of Desai's 2004 novel, about
an American student's search for his roots in a Mexican
ghost town (Richland County Public Library)*

Several of Desai's favorite themes are reworked in *Diamond Dust and Other Stories:* youth, age, and death; the minutiae of human relationships; art and life; illusion and reality; time and change; cultural differences; and the pressures of survival in an increasingly difficult world. The stories set child's-eye perspectives against the perceptions of old age. They are permeated by a sense of people's alienation from each other and from their environments, their need for love, and their encounters with small but significant experiences that open the windows to wisdom. Most noticeable is the internationalism of Desai's subject matter, signaling her refusal to remain pigeonholed within convenient definitions of what constitutes "Indian" writing.

Desai assumed emeritus status at MIT in 2002. Her refusal to be pigeonholed as an Indian writer is borne out by *The Zigzag Way* (2004), which is set in Mexico. Seen through the eyes of Eric, a visiting student from Boston, Mexico appears vibrant, mysterious, and full of contradictions. Drawn into a search for his roots, Eric learns about his Cornish grandfather, who

had come to Mexico in search of his own roots, and his grandmother, who died in childbirth. The history of Mexico, its colonial past challenged by the gradual rise of the spirit of revolution, forms the backdrop to Eric's quest for his identity. His journey takes him to a ghost town once inhabited by gold miners. He reads in the library of the town's study center, which is presided over by the formidable Doña Vera, the "Queen of the Sierra" and champion of the indigenous Huichols. Past and present alternate in the three narratives that intertwine in the novel: Eric's, Doña Vera's, and that of Eric's grandmother, Betty. The strands come together on the Day of the Dead, when Eric encounters the swirling, fluid reality of Mexican culture. An aura of the supernatural hangs over the story, becoming explicit when Eric sees figures from the past conversing with the spirit of his grandmother. His journey into the past leads to no certitudes, but through his Mexican experience Eric learns a great deal about himself.

Reviewers agreed that *The Zigzag Way* is more about Mexico than about any specific character or characters. According to Claire Messud in the *New Statesman* (6 September 2004), "Desai's primary interest is manifestly the country itself, its landscape and the curious details of its history, rather than the individuals with whom she has peopled it." According to Melissa Dene in *The Guardian* (2 September 2004), "*The Zigzag Way* is an unfashionably quiet, subtle book, in which history and landscape are more important than character and denouement." The descriptive brilliance of Desai's narrative led Liz Hoggard to speculate in *The Observer* (29 August 2004) about a movie version of the novel: "At her best, Desai approaches the Mexican landscape like a master cinematographer."

Early in her career Desai was compelled to write in secret to avoid conflict with her husband's family; today her daughter Kiran is also a novelist. In responding to the 2002 questionnaire Desai noted that her daughter "must have imbibed the discipline of writing without being aware of it; her working habits are almost exactly like mine. This makes for a great intimacy and companionship between us, the first I have ever experienced."

Desai is a fellow of the British Royal Society of Literature, an honorary member of the American Academy of Arts and Letters, and a member of the New York chapter of the writers' organization PEN. In addition to her creative and academic pursuits, she has undertaken sociological projects that reflect her humanitarian concerns. They include a report for the United Nations Children's Fund (UNICEF) on family welfare in Indonesia (1983); a report for the United Nations Decade of Women in Norway; and a report on the effect of foreign aid on culture and civilization for the UN in Denmark.

In the course of her long career Desai has evolved from chronicling the inner lives of her characters to an awareness of the links between individual psychology and the social and cultural environment. She told Pandit: "It is the confrontation of the inner and the outer that interests me as a novelist. The outer world is dominated by certain forces, the individual's force is enigmatic, variable, an imponderable." The forces beyond the individual's control include society, tradition, history, and culture. "In the Indian society, tradition takes precedence over the individual," she told Pandit. Speaking of her craft in the 2002 interview, Desai emphasized her treatment of time: "Time (history) is the fourth dimension. . . . The present makes little sense unless one looks into the past and considers the future." In Desai's novels time is both personal and historical—an interior awareness as well as an exterior force beyond individual control.

Desai's distinctive literary style evokes internal states of mind while recording sharply detailed impressions of social interactions, using imagery to create a sharply defined concrete reality that suggests more-abstract possibilities. At times the imagery lends a poetic quality to her prose. In *Perspectives on Anita Desai,* Prasad remarks that her novels have a "mosaic textual density" because "Desai's imagery is wedded to her rich lyricism." Images recur with cumulative effect as Desai uses suggestion rather than overt statement to highlight thematic issues or to make rhetorical points.

Among the issues highlighted in Desai's fiction are family relationships and the impact of family dynamics on the individual psyche. She also explores the problems faced by women in contemporary India, particularly middle-class women expected to lead lives of quiet domesticity in a rapidly changing world. Many of Desai's female protagonists rebel against their circumstances, only to compromise in the end. Asked about this point in the 2002 questionnaire, Desai noted that most of her novels describe the lives of women before the feminist movement gathered momentum in India and added: "Of course I have written largely—although not exclusively—about women and women's worlds, simply because that is what I know best. But it is not all that interests me or that I deal with in my writing." Desai also disclaims any overt preoccupation with the politics of postcolonialism, because, as she told Ball and Kanaganayakam, "For the most part I've lived in India, in a home where cultures combined rather than clashed." Desai is also unwilling to be considered a writer of the Indian diaspora, she said in response to the 2002 questionnaire, because it "is not my theme and I'm not very interested in what I read of it." Never-

theless, exile is a major theme in Desai's fiction from Nirode's alienation from the culture of his own city to Baumgartner's loneliness in Bombay and the cultural isolation suffered by Arun in the United States.

In a response to the 2002 questionnaire Anita Desai claimed that "it is my intention, when I write fiction, to explore and reveal the nine-tenths of the truth that lies submerged beneath the one-tenth visible tip of the iceberg." Throughout her fiction she searches for imaginative ways of constructing realities that are too complex to be depicted directly. For her, she wrote in response to the questionnaire, the writer's role in the world is "observing that world, searching for ways to comprehend and understand it, explore it and reveal what you perceive as truth."

Interviews:

Yashodhara Dalmia, "An Interview with Anita Desai," *Times of India,* 29 April 1979, p. 13;

Atma Ram, "Interview with Anita Desai," in *Interviews with Indian Writers* (Calcutta: Calcutta Writers' Workshop, 1983), pp. 21–33;

Ramesh K. Srivastava, "Anita Desai at Work: An Interview," in *Perspectives on Anita Desai,* edited by Srivastava (Ghaziabad: Vimal Prakashan, 1984), pp. 208–226;

John Clement Ball and Chelva Kanaganayakam, "Interview with Anita Desai," *Toronto South Asian Review,* 10, no. 2 (1992): 30–41;

Feroza Jussawalla and Reed Way Dassenbrock, "Anita Desai," in their *Interviews with Writers of the Post-Colonial World* (Jackson: University Press of Mississippi, 1992), pp. 157–179;

Lalita Pandit, "A Sense of Detail and a Sense of Order: Anita Desai Interviewed by Lalita Pandit," in *Literary India: Comparative Studies in Aesthetics, Colonialism, and Culture,* edited by Pandit and Patrick Colm Hogan (Albany: State University of New York Press, 1995), pp. 153–172.

References:

Fawzia Afzal-Khan, *Cultural Imperialism and the Indo-English Novel: Genre and Ideology in R. K. Narayan, Anita Desai, Kamala Markandaya, and Salman Rushdie* (University Park: Pennsylvania State University Press, 1993), pp. 59–96;

Shyam M. Asnani, "Anita Desai's Fiction: A New Dimension," *Indian Literature,* 24, no. 2 (1981): 44–54;

Joy Rosemary Atfield, *Students' Guide to* The Village by the Sea (Thornhill, U.K.: Tynron, 1990);

Usha Bande, *The Novels of Anita Desai: A Study in Character and Conflict* (New Delhi: Prestige, 1988);

Shirley Chew, "Searching Voices: Anita Desai's *Clear Light of Day* and Nayantara Sahgal's *Rich Like Us*," in *Motherlands: Black Women's Writing from Africa, the Caribbean and South Asia,* edited by Susheila Nasta (London: Women's Press, 1991), pp. 43–63;

Kamini Dinesh, ed., *Between Spaces of Silence: Women Creative Writers* (New Delhi: Sterling, 1994), pp. 95–112;

Alamgir Hashmi, "A Reading of Anita Desai's *Clear Light of Day*," *International Fiction Review*, 10, no. 1 (1983): 56–58;

S. Indira, "The Nowhere Men: A Comparative Study of Anita Desai's *Baumgartner's Bombay* and Kamala Markandaya's *The Nowhere Man*," *Indian Journal of English Studies,* 30 (1991–1992): 5–12;

Jasbir Jain, *Stairs to the Attic: The Novels of Anita Desai* (Jaipur: Printwell, 1987);

Asha Kanwar, *Virginia Woolf and Anita Desai: A Comparative Study* (New Delhi: Prestige, 1989);

Viney Kirpal, "An Image of India: A Study of Anita Desai's *In Custody*," *Ariel,* 17, no. 4 (1986): 127–138;

Kirpal, ed., *The New Indian Novel in English: A Study of the 1980s* (New Delhi: Allied, 1990), pp. 67–71, 73–81, 187–199, 213–227, 271–278;

Francine E. Krishna, "Anita Desai: *Fire on the Mountain*," *Indian Literature,* 25, no. 5 (1982): 158–169;

Harveen Sachdeva Mann, "'Going in the Opposite Direction': Feminine Recusancy in Anita Desai's *Voices in the City*," *Ariel,* 23, no. 4 (1992): 75–92;

M. Mani Meitei, "Anita Desai's *Where Shall We Go This Summer?*: A Psychoanalytical Study," *Language Forum: A Half-Yearly Journal of Language and Literature,* 18, nos. 1–2 (1992): 48–58;

Rajeswari Mohan, "The Forked Tongue of Lyric in Anita Desai's *Clear Light of Day*," *Journal of Commonwealth Literature,* 32, no. 1 (1997): 47–66;

Arun P. Mukherjee, "Other Worlds, Other Texts: Teaching Anita Desai's *Clear Light of Day* to Canadian Students," *College Literature,* 22, no. 1 (1995): 192–201;

K. Ayyappa Paniker, ed., *Indian Literature since Independence* (New Delhi: Indian Association for English Studies, 1991), pp. 44–48;

Ujwala Patil, "Sexual Violence and Death in Anita Desai's *Fire on the Mountain*," in *Studies in Indian Fiction in English,* edited by G. S. Balarama Gupta (Gulbarga: JIWE, 1987), pp. 61–67;

K. J. Philips, "Ambiguous Tragic Flaw in Anita Desai's *Fire on the Mountain*," *International Fiction Review,* 17, no. 1 (1990): 3–8;

Madhusudan Prasad, *Anita Desai: The Novelist* (Allahabad, India: New Horizon, 1981);

M. Rajeshwar, "The Dynamics of Attachment and Non-attachment: Maya and Karma Yoga as Aspects of Technique in Anita Desai's *Cry, the Peacock*," *Journal of Indian Writing in English,* 24, no. 2 (1996): 16–23;

Geetha Ramanathan, "Sexual Violence/Textual Violence: Desai's *Fire on the Mountain* and Shirazi's *Javady Alley*," *Modern Fiction Studies,* 39, no. 1 (1993): 17–35;

B. Ramachandra Rao, *The Novels of Anita Desai: A Study* (New Delhi: Kalyani, 1977);

Vimala Rao, "*Where Shall We Go This Summer?* An Analysis," *Commonwealth Quarterly,* 3, no. 9 (1978): 44–50;

R. S. Sharma, *Anita Desai* (New Delhi: Arnold-Heinemann, 1981);

Sharma, "Anita Desai's *Where Shall We Go This Summer?* An Analysis," *Commonwealth Quarterly,* 3, no. 10 (1979): 50–69;

Sunaina Singh, *The Novels of Margaret Atwood and Anita Desai: A Comparative Study in Feminist Perspectives* (New Delhi: Creative Books, 1994);

Avadhesh K. Srivastava, *Alien Voice: Perspectives on Commonwealth Literature* (Lucknow: Print House, 1981), pp. 84–100;

Ramesh K. Srivastava, ed., *Perspectives on Anita Desai* (Ghaziabad: Vimal Prakashan, 1984);

Alladi Uma, "'I Have Had My Vision': Virginia Woolf's *To the Lighthouse* and Anita Desai's *Where Shall We Go This Summer?*" *Literary Criterion,* 22, no. 3 (1987): 73–77.

G. V. Desani

(8 July 1909 – 15 November 2000)

Manju Sampat
University of Mumbai

BOOKS: *All About Mr. Hatterr* (London: Aldor, 1948); republished as *All About H. Hatterr: A Gesture* (London: Saturn Press, 1949; New York: Farrar, Straus & Young, 1951; revised edition, London: Bodley Head, 1970; New York: Farrar, Straus & Giroux, 1970; revised edition, New York: Lancer, 1972; revised edition, London: Penguin, 1972);

Hali (London: Saturn Press, 1950; Bombay: *Illustrated Weekly of India*, 1952);

Hali and Collected Stories (Kingston, N.Y.: McPherson, 1991).

SELECTED PERIODICAL PUBLICATION–
UNCOLLECTED: "India For the Plain Hell of It," *New Yorker* (23–30 June 1997): 62–66.

Edition: *All About H. Hatterr* (New Paltz, N.Y.: McPherson, 1986).

G. V. Desani (from the dust jacket for All About H. Hatterr, *1986; Richland County Public Library)*

Although he wrote only one major novel, G. V. Desani is one of the pioneers of Indian English writing. He belongs to the generation of writers such as R. K. Narayan, Raja Rao, and Mulk Raj Anand. Desani is not as well known or as widely read as the other three writers, but his influence over contemporary Indian English writers is apparent. In a 1997 article for *The New Yorker* on Indian writing in English, Salman Rushdie mentions that he "learned a trick or two" from Desani. Rushdie also credits Desani with being the first Indian writer to go "genuinely beyond the Englishness of the English language." While Anand's style had been influenced by Marxist works, and Rao's by Sanskrit literature, and while Narayan had been content to infuse his fiction with local color, Desani's muse was clearly Laurence Sterne's *Tristram Shandy* (1760–1767). His dazzling prose and semantic pyrotechnics definitely have the Shandean touch. Nevertheless, after the much acclaimed novel *All About Mr. Hatterr* came out in 1948 (republished as *All About H. Hatterr: A Gesture*, 1949), Desani's body of work consisted only of a play, some short stories, and a few philosophical papers.

Govindas Vishnoodas Desani was born on 8 July 1909 in Nairobi, Kenya, to Vishnoodas Manghirmal and his wife, Rukmani. When Desani was four years of age, his father, a merchant, took the family to Sind, which was then in India but is now a part of Pakistan. A highly intelligent child, Desani took charge of his own education. At the age of seventeen he ran away from home and migrated to England, where he was admitted as a reader in the British Museum. He spent the next twenty-five years in Britain working as a broadcast journalist and a newspaper correspondent for the Associated Press, *The Times of India,* and Reuters. During this period he also made frequent trips to India in order to lecture on antiquities for the Central India Railways. Throughout World War II, he worked as a lecturer with the Imperial Institute and the Royal Empire Society, and he was known to be an excellent speaker.

Desani's novel *All About H. Hatterr,* which he wrote in 1948, is a cult classic. It is perhaps the earliest example of fantastical and allegorical writing in the genre of Indian fiction in English. Its wild and extraordinary prose makes it an experiment with the English language. Stylistically, the novel derives inspiration from ancient Indian writings, but the novel also has affinities with works based on magic realism. It has autobiographical elements as well and often alludes to William Shakespeare's plays. It uses the freedom of the oral narrative while simultaneously destabilizing and parodying many conventional notions of fiction writing. In his introduction to the 1970 edition of this book, Anthony Burgess refers to its language as one that combines "the colloquialisms of Calcutta and London" and notes that these "seethe together" with "Shakespearean archaisms." Indeed, the tone of the book ranges from sheer farce to subtle philosophic exchanges and all kinds of swapping of experiences between the protagonist, Hatterr, and his sidekick/alter ego, Banerrji. The latter misquotes Shakespeare and spouts *babu* English, or the smattering of English of the semiliterate clerks of the colonial Indian bureaucracy. Hatterr also declares that he uses "rigmarole English, staining your goodly, godly tongue, maybe."

Desani's preface to this book gives the reader many insights to his theme and technique, one of them being that the novel is highly autobiographical. Desani notes that he wrote the book for "Kumari, the most loyal and trusted of friends." Apparently, he had toyed with the idea of marrying this woman, but refrained from doing so because a palmist had predicted his death by assassination, and he wished to spare Kumari from certain widowhood. Desani attributes the dazzling and dizzying prose to the possibility that there are two people writing the book, "A fellow called H. Hatterr and I." Many of the events that transpire in the book are certainly conjecture, as Desani refers to the possibility of "induced experience." He claims to be a worshipper of beauty, but pursuing it costs "expense and effort," so he believes that a better alternative is "to dream instead." All that is required, then, is to sit in an

armchair and induce the experience of seeing a beautiful Himalayan sunset or other visions of "Beauty and Beauty-experience." The book is replete with other examples of such flights of fantasy, and this imaginative exuberance is what makes *All About H. Hatterr* so distinctive.

The preface also makes it abundantly clear that Hatterr's search for answers to existentialist concerns such as the meaning of life, truth, and beauty is based on the author's own spiritual quest for a viable philosophy of life. Writing the book was thus a cathartic experience for the author, and he expresses his hope that as a result of this exercise, he can solve some of the mysteries about the absurdity of existence and simultaneously forge a union between the philosophy of the West and the mysticism of the East.

All About H. Hatterr is an account of the fantastical self-education of the antihero title character, who claims to be "fifty-fifty of the species," as one of his parents was European, while the other was Malay. Shortly after his birth, the family moved to India from Malaysia, and soon thereafter, his "old man kicked the bucket." Subsequently, the court makes him a ward of an English Missionary Society, rather than leave him under the "heathen influence" of his illiterate mother. Hatterr decides to "bolt" from there, and henceforth decides to make his education "his own business." He tries hard to fight off the gnawing feelings of motherlessness, rootlessness, and insecurity. He styles himself H. Hatterr, "H for the nom de plume *Hindustaniwalla,*" or Indian person, and "Hatterr" for the large hat worn by the reverend in charge of the English Missionary Society.

The book begins with Hatterr confiding to his friend Banerrji about the amorous advances of his washerwoman, or *dhobin.* Though he "loathes the very sight of her," he feels "compelled to put her in good humour by a sundry kiss or two," as he owes her some money. However, she chooses to betray him and decides to make a scene outside his club, telling all present about the money he owes her. The club authorities take umbrage at this incident and summarily dismiss Hatterr from the club, since his club dues have not been paid either. Deeply hurt about being thrown out, Hatterr decides to forsake all things European and to "go Indian" instead.

With Banerrji's help, Hatterr gets a job as a reporter with a newspaper run by Mr. Chari-Charier, who has "high regard for struck-off gentlemen," as he too has been debarred from All Soul's College in Oxford. Hatterr interviews the "Sage of *Calcutta*" for his newspaper, but like the *dhobin,* the sage also manages to fool the gullible Hatterr as he strips him of all his clothes. It turns out that the sage is a mere tailor turned con man because his legitimate business is not faring too well. Hence, he has devised an easier method of making profits: he prefers stealing clothes and selling them secondhand.

Hatterr next meets the "Sage of *Rangoon*," and at this point his libido seems to need some taming. Banerrji suggests that Hatterr meet Bill Smythe and his wife, Rosie, who are both circus artists. Hoping to satisfy his libido, Hatterr becomes enamored of Rosie, but once again he falls prey to deception. Rosie inveigles him into becoming their lion tamer, and in return she makes some "immoral promises." He accepts her offer and convinces himself into believing "You seek a woman in a medical libido way. She denies. But she promises, though post-dated, to give all, provided you accept her lion!" The deal is that Hatterr has to lie still in the lion's cage while the lion eats a steak off his chest. On the day that Hatterr performs this daring act, the villainous Smythe switches off all the circus lights. In a scene reminiscent of an absurdist play, the terrified Hatterr envisions his own death while the lion merrily uses him as a human plate. Hatterr "bolts" from there as well, and decides to "keep away from the libido!"

The subsequent chapters of the novel relate his meetings with other sages, whom he approaches reverentially for guidance and knowledge about life. These meetings with the Sages of *Madras, Delhi, Bombay, Mogalsarai-Varanasi,* and *All India* chronicle Hatterr's self-search. However, in all of them, Hatterr is systematically deceived. To each of these sages he asks a question, which forms a "Digest" or message at the beginning of each chapter. Then the rest of the chapter presents what actually transpires at the meetings. Each of these encounters is divided into three stages: "Instruction," "Presumption," and "Life Encounter." The incidents with the seven sages thus mimic the oral narrative conventions of storytelling of ancient Indian scriptures such as the Vedas, the Upanishads, and the fables from the *Panchatantra*. Hatterr's questions to these sages range from subjects such as youth, chance, and women to fate and the polarities of good and evil. Eventually, he does manage to get a few tangible answers to these questions as he comes closer to understanding the discrepancy between appearance and reality. The book ends with a "critique" of Hatterr's life by Yati Rambeli, who is also Y. Beliram, an absentee character in the novel, whom Banerrji often has to consult on Hatterr's behalf. Thus, one of the characters apparently steps out of the fictional world to comment on the novel. Though ultimately Hatterr makes no gains materially, he finally appears to have received an insight into the riddles of existence. Despite the number of times the protagonist has been duped, the final message of the novel is an optimistic one. Hatter's closing lines are, "I am not fed up with Life . . . . I carry on," and he ends

Dust jacket for a 1986 edition of Desani's only major novel, first published in 1948 as All About Mr. Hatterr, *a fantastical allegorical tale about the self-education of the title character as he encounters various sages (Richland County Public Library)*

by advising his audience "Carry on, boys, and continue like hell."

Desani's next work was *Hali* (1950), a short allegorical play that is the antithesis of *All About H. Hatterr* in its philosophical approach. While the latter advocates selfishness as a universal goal, the former elaborates on selflessness and love. *Hali* is written in a high, exalted prose style that includes many exclamations and archaic analogies. It therefore makes for difficult reading. The work is a series of invocations that express the author's views on divinity, destruction, attachment, and the attainment of the true meaning of life.

In the preface of this play, reference is made to the many facets of the goddess Durga. In her benign and giving form, she is beautiful and serene. However, in her vengeful and cruel form she is the destroyer, the slayer who holds lethal weapons in seven of her eight hands. In her eighth hand the goddess holds a mountain lily that is hidden from everyone except those that she chooses to bless. Being able to see the mountain lily and the benevolent side of Durga is also a metaphor for attaining salvation and discovering the true meaning of existence. The various forms of the goddess can be viewed as the different polarities of good and evil, death and rebirth, destruction and renewal. Or, as Desani writes, the forms are suggestive of the "many faces or facets of a contemporary person." In his preface, the author claims to be able to conjure up his own personal "imagined, beautiful and beloved angel Durga." He carries this metaphor forward to create Rooh, the beloved wife of Hali, the protagonist of the play.

Hali is a story of ethereal love, and its essential message is that all of God's creations are destined to die. Hali lives with his beautiful mother, Mira, in the northern hills of India. Hali is also beautiful, in fact so lovely that his mother and the other village women cannot stop gazing at him. However, the gods decree an ordeal for Hali: he sees Mira climb a high mountain and then fall to her death. Mira's entreaties to Isha the Lord to preserve her son are answered; Maya, "a good woman from the plains," finds him and looks after him until he attains manhood. One day, as he walks through the temple, Hali sees the radiant Rohini, who has beautiful jasmine garlands around her neck. He falls in love with her at first sight and eventually marries this "most beloved being God ever made." Rooh, as Hali affectionately calls Rohini, is surely an incarnation of the goddess Durga—the spirit, the formless one. Soon afterward, however, Rooh dies. Hali meditates beside her funeral pyre, and what follows is a series of invocations made to Hali by Mira and Rooh, by Hali to Rooh and Isha the Lord, and by Dwarka, a past incarnation of Hali, to everyone at large. Through these sections readers learn that there has been a prophecy of war and of Hali being cursed so that he will end up despising his fellow brethren. He is cursed to thirst for the blood of his loved ones, and the shock of this discovery is what killed Rooh, for she died of fear, with "her horrored heart torn, torn of terror." Hali the beautiful now becomes the cruel and sacrifice-exacting incarnation of Durga, as he is doomed to a life in which his "heart is no longer a cradle of love." Finally, Isha the Lord hears Hali's invocations and releases Hali from his pain. Hali dies and becomes one with the Lord and thus finally finds peace. *Hali* essentially portrays its author's search for salvation, and in the epilogue the reader learns that ultimately Hali does find "precious treasure lovingly entrusted."

Desani returned to India in 1952 and spent the next several years in seclusion, living in various Buddhist monasteries in India and in Burma. He utilized this time to learn yoga and study Hindu and Bud-

dhist religious scriptures. From 1962 to 1967 he was a special contributor to *The Illustrated Weekly of India,* which was published by *The Times of India.* Many of his short stories were published in this magazine during this period.

In his short stories Desani continues his verbal pyrotechnics as he leads the reader from one fantastical situation to another. These stories are not as difficult to read or understand as *Hali* or *All About H. Hatterr,* nor are they as complicated, but they are farfetched, highly imaginative, and even grotesque at times. Most of them were written in the oral tradition of storytelling.

"Mephisto's Daughter" is about Mephisto, a peasant leader who "wants to conquer all mankind." He lives with his seventeen-year-old daughter, who seems to be in constant fear of him. The protagonist of the story befriends her and attends one of Mephisto's discourses. His main message to his bizarre followers (they all have tails) is that the only reality in life is the "Self," and all else is "Unreal." Mephisto is the "Sly One" who wants his people to be content. If they are content, they will not seek to make enemies and thus will become "immobilized," as they will no longer have any desires and wants. Mephisto dreams that he will then be able to "conquer all mankind."

In "The Fiend Screams '*Kya Chahate Ho,*'" the reader experiences Desani's inclination toward black humor. This story is about the initiation of a boy named Muglai into supernatural rites. Aamil Mia, the boy's father, is convinced that his son has some "devilish stuff" in him, as he can catch live snakes with his bare hands. As a result of reaching this conclusion, Aamil Mia wants to initiate Muglai into a secret rite to invoke the "she-devil," a practice he had inherited from his magician ancestors, but which he himself lacks the courage to try. He teaches Muglai the necessary rites to conjure up the she-devil, and tutors him to ask her for "kabza" (control) if she asks "kya chahate ho" (what do you want). However, when she does appear to him, Muglai chooses to stay quiet in "sheer villainy." This silence so incenses the evil spirit that she destroys all their belongings and again asks him what he wants. Finally he answers, "Ask *abba,*" which she promptly does. Ever since then she has been asking Aamil Mia what he wants. Not to be outdone, he too seems to have an ace up his sleeve, as the next time she asks "kya chahate ho," he plans to tell her to castrate Muglai.

In "With Malice Aforethought" the protagonist, a tour operator in East Africa, discovers that the true meaning of life lies in "self realization" and that it is useless being preoccupied with others. The Truth, he believes, lies in realizing that "all service must be for self." There follow some lengthy conversations between the Lord and the author, as he makes a reference to treason by "G. V. Desani . . . the publishing of his most secret commerce with the Master." This story is imbued with black humor, and it stresses the ephemeral aspect of life.

"The Last Long Letter" is in the form of a series of unmailed letters written by a daughter to her father while she has gone to stay with her fiancé, a prince. The prince has killed himself, and as a good Hindu bride-to-be, the girl is also contemplating *sati* or self-immolation by burning herself at his funeral pyre. Through these letters she tells her father about her desire to become one with her partner and join him in another dimension, for they have been together in other lives as well. The letters also relate the philosophic exchanges she had with the prince before he died. These discussions encompass topics as varied as man's desire to be released from worldly tensions and become one with God, the frailty of life, death and rebirth, and the power and mysteries of the universe and of existence. Thus, this story can also be read as an allegory of life and the meaning of existence and an attempt to understand the many paradoxes of life.

The affinities with the magic realist writers seem apparent in "The Second Mrs. Was Wed in a Nightmare." However, unlike some of the South American writers, who attempt to anchor phantasmagoria in realism at times, Desani makes no attempt to do so in his writing. In this story, the narrator/protagonist seems to have chanced upon "the fifth dimension," where he sees Eric, an ape, playing the music of Johann Sebastian Bach, while all manner of "forms" and "shapes" are passing by. It seems that the ape has been playing this music on his organ "for centuries before J. S. Bach was born." Eric becomes the narrator's spiritual guide and introduces him to his ape-daughter, whom the protagonist ultimately marries. Desani continues with an oblique approach to reality, and he writes in a style that is often astonishing and about situations that are bizarre. The reader either believes or "suspends his disbelief" at his own risk.

Although most of Desani's short stories first appeared in *The Illustrated Weekly of India,* a couple were first published in other journals. "Down with Philosophy" (1979) was initially published in the *Boston University Journal,* while "The Merchant of Kisingarh" appeared in the *Westerly Magazine* of the University of Western Australia.

Because of his deep interest in philosophy, Desani agreed to join the University of Texas in Austin in 1968, when he was appointed as a Fulbright-

G. V. DESANI

HALI

AND

COLLECTED STORIES

McPherson and Company

Title page for Desani's 1991 volume, which includes Hali, *an allegorical play first published in 1950, about a man who turns vengeful after his beloved wife dies of fear upon discovering that he has been cursed by the gods to hate his loved ones (Jean and Alexander Heard Library, Vanderbilt University)*

Hays lecturer in their Department of Philosophy. He taught Buddhist and Samkhya-Yoga philosophy. He worked there for the next eleven years, and in 1979 he became an emeritus professor and also took on American citizenship. He continued to live in Texas until his death on 15 November 2000.

One of Desani's last publications was "India For the Plain Hell of It," an article that appeared in *The New Yorker* in June 1997. It is a travelogue of a visit that Desani made to India in 1952. Unlike most of his other works, this piece of writing is banal and unimpressive, as it merely encapsulates his experiences and impressions of this visit in a simple, factual manner. He stays with a couple of millionaires in Bombay and also meets their partner, who is "twice millionaire." Juxtaposed against this wealth is his encounter with a beggar lady and with the poverty and squalor of Bombay. In recounting this visit, Desani manages to convey the extreme diversity and contrasts prevalent in the city. The article then gives a detailed account of his visit to Aurangabad to view the famous caves and temples of Ajanta and Ellora. He recounts his meetings with other pilgrims and priests and also describes the guided tour of the caves.

Though G. V. Desani's works received much initial critical acclaim, they appear to be fading fast from literary memory, and Desani is no longer a widely read author. In fact, his works still await intensive critical analysis. Perhaps Desani is best described as a "writer's writer," as some of the best-known modern South Asian authors, such as Salman Rushdie and Amitav Ghosh, acknowledge being influenced by his writings. His works are thematically complex and often make for difficult reading; however, his use of language is distinctive and outrageous. More than fifty years after it was written, *All About H. Hatterr* continues to intrigue the discerning reader.

References:

A. L. McLeod, "G. V. Desani (1909–)," in *Writers of the Indian Diaspora: A Bio-Bibliographical Critical Source Book,* edited by Emmanuel S. Nelson (Westport, Conn.: Greenwood Press, 1993);

M. K. Naik, *Studies in Indian English Literature* (New Delhi: Sterling, 1987);

Sheela Reddy, "An Oriental Gent," *Outlook India* (18 December 2000) <http://www.outlookindia.com>;

Salman Rushdie, "Damme, This is the Oriental Scene for You!" *New Yorker* (23–30 June 1997): 50–62;

C. Vijaysree, "Maya/Parody/Metafiction: A Reading of G. V. Desani's *All About H. Hatterr,*" in *Critical Responses: Commonwealth Literature* (New Delhi: Sterling, 1994).

Shashi Deshpande

(19 August 1938 –)

Nilufer E. Bharucha
University of Mumbai

BOOKS: *The Legacy: And Other Stories* (Calcutta: Writer's Workshop, 1978);

A Summer Adventure (Bombay: India Book House, 1978);

The Dark Holds No Terrors: A Novel (Ghaziabad: Vikas, 1980);

The Hidden Treasure (Bombay: India Book House, 1980);

The Only Witness (Bombay: India Book House, 1980);

If I Die Today (Ghaziabad: Vikas, 1982);

The Narayanpur Incident (Bombay: India Book House, 1982);

Come Up and Be Dead: A Novel (New Delhi: Vikas, 1983);

Roots and Shadows: A Novel (New Delhi: Orient Longman, 1983);

It Was Dark: Stories (Calcutta: Writer's Workshop, 1986);

The Miracle and Other Stories (Calcutta: Writer's Workshop, 1986);

It Was the Nightingale (Calcutta: Writer's Workshop, 1986);

That Long Silence (London: Virago, 1988; New Delhi & New York: Penguin, 1989);

The Dark Holds No Terrors (New Delhi: Penguin, 1990);

The Binding Vine (New Delhi: Penguin Books India, 1993; London: Virago, 1993; New York: Feminist Press at the City University of New York, 2002);

The Intrusion: And Other Stories (New Delhi & New York: Penguin, 1993);

A Matter of Time (New Delhi: Penguin, 1996; New York: Feminist Press at the City University of New York, 1999);

Small Remedies (New Delhi & New York: Viking, 2000);

The Stone Women (Calcutta: Writer's Workshop, 2000);

Writing from the Margin and Other Essays (New Delhi & New York: Penguin, 2003);

Moving On (New Delhi: Viking/Penguin India, 2004; New York: Penguin, 2004).

Collection: *Collected Stories,* 2 volumes (New Delhi & London: Penguin, 2003, 2004; New Delhi & New York: Penguin, 2003, 2004).

Shashi Deshpande (photograph by Pratibha Nandakumar; from the dust jacket for A Matter of Time, *1999; Richland County Public Library)*

OTHER: "On the Writing of a Novel," in *Indian Women Novelists,* edited by R. K. Dhawan (New Delhi: Prestige, 1991), pp. 31–36;

Ranjana Harish, *The Female Footprints,* foreword by Deshpande (New Delhi: Sterling, 1996).

SELECTED PERIODICAL PUBLICATIONS–
UNCOLLECTED: "Language No Bar," *Sunday Times of India* (Ahmedabad), 23 April 1995, p. 10;

"Of Concerns, Of Anxieties," *Indian Literature* (September–October 1996): 103–110;

"Midnight's Orphans," *Outlook* (25 February 2002).

For Shashi Deshpande there has been no found-ing of dynasties in the mode of Salman Rushdie with *Midnight's Children* (1981). From 1978, when her first collection of short stories, *The Legacy,* was published, until the publication of *Small Remedies* in 2000, recogni-tion has come slowly. Deshpande's collections of short stories, novels, crime novels, and children's books have only recently begun to bring her the recognition she should have received much earlier. Her books have now begun to appear in Western editions and reprints, and some have been translated into European and Indian languages. Although Deshpande has won a few Indian literary awards, international awards still have not come her way.

The reasons for Deshpande's slow rise to fame are not far to seek. One is that her books began to appear around the time Rushdie's *Midnight's Children* made its spectacular appearance. Another is that they were published when markedly feminist texts were making their presence felt everywhere. Deshpande's texts were neither focused on fractures induced by colonialism nor designed to be alternative narratives. Moreover, her women characters were not militant enough to attract critics of feminist literature. In addition, Deshpande did not want to be labeled as a woman writer and had no intention of being per-ceived as a writer with a feminist agenda. As she says in "Of Concerns, Of Anxieties," in *Indian Literature* (September–October 1996), to be "put into the slot of woman writer" is to feel that one has been "denied the place and dignity of a writer who is dealing with issues that are human issues, of interest to all humanity." Human issues, especially human dignity, are at the heart of all her writing. Whether her women characters are breaking their "long silences," or her male charac-ters—fathers, husbands, brothers, friends—are recogniz-ing the self in the other, or the children of her books are initiated into life, her concern is always with the human condition.

Deshpande was born on 19 August 1938 in Dhar-wad, India. Her father was the noted Kannada writer and Sanskrit scholar Adya Rangacharya, whose pen name was Sriranga. Her mother was Sharada Adya, née Chandrachud. Her father was from Bijapur in Kar-nataka, and her mother from Pune in Maharashtra. Although Kannada and Marathi were both languages of home, Deshpande was sent to English medium schools, first St. Joseph's and then the Basel Mission Girls' School. She completed her schooling and appeared for the Secondary School Leaving Certificate (SSC) examination in 1952. Deshpande completed her B.A. (Honors) in Economics from the Elphinstone Col-lege, Bombay University, in 1956. Twenty-eight years later, in 1984, she earned an M.A. in English literature from the Mysore University.

Deshpande was married in 1962 and lives with her pathologist husband, D. H. Deshpande, in Banga-lore. They have two sons—Vikram, born in 1962, and Raghunandan, in 1964.

Deshpande took up writing seriously only after her marriage and the birth of her sons, when she was thirty years old. After a few of her articles were pub-lished in newspapers and magazines, she also studied journalism. In a private conversation with Nilufer Bharucha in 1997, she has said that her husband, although a nonliterary person, is supportive of her work and is her first reader. Initially, Deshpande wrote when she could get some time in between rearing her children and doing her household work. When she started, she wrote in longhand, but after her short sto-ries began to find publishers, she began using the type-writer in her husband's office after it was closed for the day. Popular women's magazines in India published her early stories. Her first published story was "The Legacy," which appeared in the *Onlooker Annual* of 1972. Only after she wrote the story "Intrusion," which was published in *Femina* in 1974, did she feel that she had found her own voice. She used it to articulate the intri-cacies of human relations within the complex Indian family structure. Her voice eventually attracted atten-tion because it was clear, honest, compassionate, and yet strong and devoid of sentimentality. In spite of her subsequent successful career as a novelist, Deshpande has continued to write short stories. Many of her stories were first published in women's magazines such as *The Eve's Weekly* and *Femina* in India and only much later anthologized. The themes and core concerns of these short stories are not much different from those found in her novels—that is, women trying to find their own voices. Often these voices arise out of silences.

Female silences are at the core of almost all of Deshpande's texts—silences on unhappy marriages, silences on marital rape, silences of stifled daughters, silences of oppressed wives, silences imposed on women in a male-dominated world. Deshpande's women are rarely strident feminists, but most of them in their own ways try to break these silences and seek to be heard.

The Dark Holds No Terrors (1980) won the Nanjan-gud Thirumblamba Award. In this novel (which Desh-pande has declared to be her favorite), the female protagonist, Saru, is a doctor who is better paid than her husband, Manu, a college lecturer. Manu's attitude toward his professionally and socially more successful wife is full of ambiguities. He likes the creature com-forts her money brings them but resents her superior status. This resentment is generally expressed only within the privacy of their home; outside it he puts on the mask of a proud and indulgent husband. Manu's resentment finds expression in the manner in which he savages Saru's body. In this most intimate aspect of the husband-wife relationship he humiliates Saru. She maintains a silence on the perverse punishment the act of love has become between her and Manu. She even tries to tell herself that perhaps it is her own fault and that her success is to blame for her husband's behavior. She further tries to convince herself that she should defer to her husband: "If he's an M.A., you should be a B.A. If he's 5'4" tall, you shouldn't be more than 5'3" tall."

Apart from the dominant and vicious Manu, Saru has to contend with a resentful mother who has never forgiven her daughter for her role in the death of her brother, the cherished male child. Saru's brother, Dhruva, had drowned when the two children were playing in a pool, and their mother cannot forget this episode. As the critic Usha Tambe puts it, in Indian society "a son is much more welcome than a daughter. So Saru is unwelcome." Saru has to come to terms with these vitiated relationships and move beyond the silences of unarticulated resentments, pain, and hurt to wider worlds where she can develop other relationships that might allow her to be revitalized.

Deshpande's women do not, however, move away completely from husbands and families into autonomous feminist spaces. Instead, they tap their inner resources to arrive at positions of strength. In the words of Kamini Dinesh: "The wife, in the end, is therefore not a rebel but a redeemed wife—one who has broken that long silence, one who is no longer afraid of the dark." This reaction might appear a sign of weakness and capitulation to some readers, but within the Indian social context, Deshpande's texts are realistic expressions of the spaces women might be able to wrest for themselves after much effort. Even in Deshpande's detective novels, *Come Up and Be Dead* (1983) and *If I Die Today* (1982), works inspired by Agatha Christie, women quest for independent identities.

Roots and Shadows (1983)—the first novel Deshpande wrote (published second)—was awarded the Thirumaathi Rangammal Prize in 1984. Indu, the protagonist, is another professional woman. She is a journalist with a less than happy marriage who in the course of the novel returns to her ancestral home in a journey that can be compared to a return to the womb, a movement that happens to woman after woman in Deshpande's novels. The sticky walls of the womb-like home of the mother provide many of Deshpande's heroines with the opportunity to rethink their marriages and reconcile their ambitions and aspirations with reality. At the beginning of this narrative, Indu is frightened

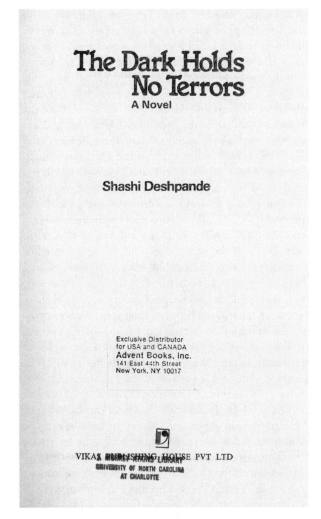

Title page for Deshpande's favorite of her novels, which was published in 1980 and depicts a female doctor whose husband sexually abuses her because he resents her success (J. Murrey Atkins Library, University of North Carolina at Charlotte)

of her love for her husband Jayant as she thinks that her feelings make her terribly dependent on him. Jayant is not always responsive to her devotion, and his lack of response hurts her. Like Saru of *The Dark Holds No Terrors*, Indu is an intelligent woman who feels she has to pay the price for being brighter than her husband. By the end of the novel, Indu has traveled far on the road to self-discovery and decided that she will go back to Jayant, but to a more honest relationship, to see if their home can "stand the scorching touch of honesty." She refuses to touch her dead aunt's money, as that would compromise her independence and integrity.

Jaya in *That Long Silence* (1988) is yet another woman who overcomes silence. According to Cicley Palser Havely, Deshpande "does not overtly invite comparisons with Western equivalents, and certainly does not take any comfort from Western solutions"; this comment is applicable to Jaya's progress in the novel. Unlike Saru, Jaya is not a working woman, and yet she has to face the same spoken and unspoken resentments from the husband that the protagonist of the first novel did. Jaya is an educated, middle-class woman who has subordinated herself to Mohan, her husband. Like the mythical Gandhari in the Indian epic *Mahabharata* (circa 400 B.C.), Jaya never questioned anything her husband did: "Mohan had managed to get the job. I never questioned him how he did it. If Gandhari, who bandaged her eyes to become blind like her husband, could be called an ideal wife, I was an ideal wife too. I bandaged my eyes too." However, this ability to avoid issues becomes difficult when Mohan is indicted on charges of corruption and she has to deal with the outcome while renegotiating her relationship with him and looking after their teenaged children.

As a result of the charges brought against Mohan, the couple have to move out of their comfortable corporate flat and into her family's old flat. Moving into the old flat releases for Jaya long-suppressed memories of her childhood and youth and reminds her of her relationships with people such as Kamat, relationships that had been supplanted by marriage. *That Long Silence* was the first book by Deshpande to attract the attention of Western feminist critics and the first of her works to be published in the West. Although well established by then as a writer in India, Deshpande had not before experienced dealing with a Western publishing house—in this case, Virago Press. The first acknowledgment of her writing talent came from a feminist press, despite her resistance to being labeled a woman writer. But as Adele King has noted, "the work of Shashi Deshpande lends itself particularly well to feminist themes. Her characters are not exemplary feminist heroes, but women struggling to find their own voice." Although Jaya is not a feminist, as the text progresses, she finds her own voice—the voice of a woman as well as a writer, although she still feels some hesitation in the voicing of both. *That Long Silence* marks Deshpande's movement into more-complex narrative forms. In this work Jaya shows much self-reflexivity.

Through Jaya, Deshpande also explores the subject of sex. Although Deshpande is never sexually explicit, her fiction has never shied away from the matter of female sexuality. While many of her heroines are subjected to marital rape, others take pleasure in their sexuality. Several of them have extramarital relationships or are at least physically attracted to men other than their husbands. Jaya is attracted to Kamat, but at the end of the narrative she realizes that she has to sort out her marriage and not "escape" into an affair. She tries to come to terms with conflicting identities, that of

a wife, mother, woman, and writer. Her writing has made her unafraid. She now knows the true meaning of Krishna's sermon to Arjuna on the battlefield in the *Mahabharata—Yathecchasi tatha kuru* (Do as you Desire). She is no longer angry with herself or with her husband and decides that, "I will have to speak, to listen, I will have to erase the silence between us." The text thus ends on a positive note as Jaya moves from silence to speech, from anger to understanding, from despair to hope.

That Long Silence won Deshpande the prestigious Sahitya Akademi Award in 1990. Her father had received the same award in 1970, and in a conversation with Bharucha in 1997, Deshpande said that she had thought of him a great deal when she received this award, as he would have been very happy for her to have received it too. Her father did share her joy of an earlier award, though, as she had been at his home when she had received the notification of the Thirumaathi Rangammal Award in 1984.

In the 1990s, Deshpande became the subject of several dissertations. Indian students wrote most of these, but some were by scholars from universities in the West who interviewed her for their work. By this time, too, much secondary critical material, including full-length studies, had become available on Deshpande, as her texts found their way into courses on Indian literature in English and courses on feminism in India and abroad. This recognition has led to the proliferation of critical material on her books. The tropes of silence, as well as those of the home and the family and the contemporary Indian woman's place in them and in the workplace, are some of the themes treated in these works.

Deshpande also treats the theme of silence and the ancestral home in *The Binding Vine* (1993) and *A Matter of Time* (1996), her subsequent novels. These are also tales of female bonding, especially the bonding between mothers and daughters. Deshpande does not sentimentalize this bond, preferring to explore it in all its complexities and problems. *The Binding Vine* is also a story about silences imposed upon women in an androcentric world and the manner in which women's texts need to be excavated in order that their voices be heard. Linked to this excavation of female voices are narratives of loss and death. At the center of this novel is Urmi and the piercing feeling of emptiness and sorrow she feels at the death of her little daughter, Anu. Kishore, Urmi's husband, works for the Merchant Navy and is away for long periods, so she lives with her mother, Inni. The Urmi-Inni relationship is fraught with problems since as a child Urmi had been sent away to her grandmother's home. She had resented this exile all her life, and it had vitiated her relationship with her mother, until her mother revealed to her that Urmi had been sent away by her father to punish his wife, as he thought she had not fulfilled her motherly duties toward her daughter. This revelation makes Urmi realize that the father she had idealized all her life had not only been unjust to Inni but created a rift between mother and daughter that had taken decades and several more losses to bridge. Urmi's childhood in her grandmother's home had provided her with her best friend, Vaana, and in Vaana's stepbrother, Kishore, she had found a husband. The bonds between Urmi and Vaana, Vaana and her daughters, and Vaana and her mother, called Akka by Urmi, are female bonds that support and endure. Through these strong bonds the hidden story of Kishore's mother, Mira, is revealed. Mira's story also recalls the issues of marital rape and the suppression of female identity. Mira, once a bright and creative girl, was married against her wishes to Kishore's father. She secretly wrote poetry and maintained journals. These were found in a trunk by Akka, who became Kishore's stepmother. Akka reads out these poems to Urmi and Vaana. As they hear the voice of Akka reciting the pain-ridden verse of her husband's first wife, they realize the trauma Mira must have undergone in her marriage—"But tell me friend, did Laxmi too, / twist brocade tassels round her fingers / and tremble, fearing the coming / of the dark-clouded, engulfing night?" Urmi is fascinated by how Mira had linked herself with the goddess Laxmi and had related her displeasure in the conjugal relations of the supposedly ideal cosmic couple Laxmi and Vishnu, thereby challenging the societal stereotypes of ideal marriages based upon supernatural models.

Urmi finds herself being drawn toward her long-dead mother-in-law, and the vine of love sprouts one more tendril. Yet, for Deshpande loving comes at a cost. Urmi knows that to love is to let down one's defense, since love makes one vulnerable. She guards against this possibility even to the extent of not letting her husband, Kishore, come too close. When her infant daughter, Anu, dies, she withdraws from Kishore and instead seeks comfort in her old female bonding with Vaana. Anu also reaches out to other women in need of solace, such as Sakutai.

In the story of Sakutai and her daughter, Kalpana, Deshpande ventures into uncharted territory by focusing on the urban poor. Sakutai seeks to hide Kalpana's rape, as it would bring shame to her family if people knew that Kalpana had been physically abused. The silence on the issue of Kalpana's rape by her sister's husband is linked to the silence about Mira's rape. Kalpana's diaries reveal that she had experienced her husband's physical attentions as rape. In a conventional society the onus of guilt and shame for rape lies on the

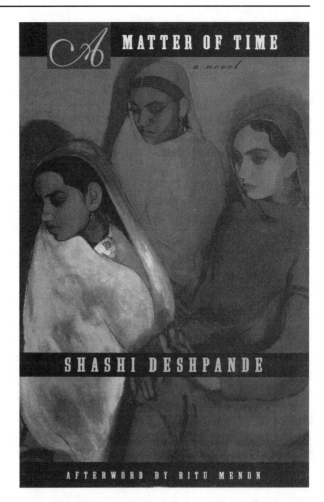

Dust jacket for the 1999 American edition of Deshpande's 1996 novel, in which two generations of women return to their ancestral home to recover from failed marriages (Richland County Public Library)

victim rather than the perpetrator. Texts such as Deshpande's open doors on musty secrets and internalized shames, thereby making possible the victims of physical abuse coming to terms with their predicament.

In *A Matter of Time* the female bonding takes place within the enclosure of an ancestral home—the Big House. The house becomes a metaphor for the enclosed spaces of the womb, a space that restricts as much as it protects. The return of women to the ancestral home can thus be seen as a move that provides protection from a male-dominated world and oppression within marriage. But such a home can also become an enclosure. This novel tells the story of two generations of women who returned to the Big House to seek shelter from unhappy marriages.

The Big House is called Vishwas, named not for the abstract quality of trust but after an ancestor, the man who came down south with the Peshwa's invading army and established the family there. Kalyani's father built it, and she returned to it with her children after her husband Shripati deserted her. He had returned to her, but only to live in an upstairs room, refusing to talk to his wife. His relationship with his daughters, Sumi and Premi, is also strange. As an adult Premi remembers that he had hardly ever spoken to her when she was a child. Premi also feels that Sumi is better than she is. But with Sumi's husband Gopal having deserted her, Premi feels more in control of the situation. Gopal's desertion is seen as a mystery and is mainly narrated through the voice of his young daughter, Aru. Aru is suddenly catapulted into the adult world by his leaving and takes charge of her mother and younger sisters. She learns bitter lessons about the hurt that love can cause.

Aru's father, Gopal, however, is not demonized in the text. Instead, he is seen as weak, the sort of man who should never have married, since he only manages to bring pain and trauma to the lives of his wife and daughters. The lines from the Brhad-aranyaka Upanishad, one of the sacred texts of Hinduism that preface this novel, provide a clue to Gopal's actions—"'Maitreyi,' said Yajnavalkya, 'Verily I am about to go forth from this state [of householder].'" Trying to unravel the mystery of her father's desertion of his family, the young Aru stumbles upon the story of her grandfather's estrangement from her grandmother. The story of how Kalyani had lost her son, a boy only a little younger than Sumi, at a railway station and how this loss had resulted in her husband's ceasing all communication with her, makes a deep impression on Aru. The novel ends with a tragedy that draws Aru and her grandmother together—two women who are joined together across time by pain and loss, yet are strong.

In both *The Binding Vine* and *A Matter of Time,* Deshpande experiments with the form of the novel. She blurs time and space boundaries and juxtaposes the lives of women as well as their past and their present. The poems of Mira, the female poet famous for her devotional lyrics, in *The Binding Vine* provide an element of intertextuality in the novel as well, giving it a postmodernist touch.

With *That Long Silence,* Deshpande had become visible in the West. *The Binding Vine* heightened this visibility, and Deshpande's reputation in India and in the West is today that of a serious writer of women's issues. She also has a presence on the Indian and international conference circuit and is a much sought after speaker.

Small Remedies, the novel Deshpande published in the year 2000, continues the novelist's exploration of female loss and pain. It also continues the Deshpande tradition of strong women who fight societal oppression and identity elision to find themselves. The three women at the center of this narrative are Madhu, Savitribai, and Leela. In this work the postmodernist element is even stronger, as Deshpande juxtaposes time past and time present and intersperses the jumps in time with intertextual elements. Also, micronarratives unfold the smaller stories of the secondary characters, such as Munni and Lata. These stories give voice to the "unsaids" of histories—stories of suicides and unacknowledged illegitimate daughters. *Small Remedies* is also one of Deshpande's most philosophical books. It is full of reflections and musings on most of the themes present in her earlier work—loss, pain, hurt, violence, and death. Additionally, this text includes a self-reflexive element in which narrative frames are found within narrative frames. The story of Madhu is framed within the story of Joe and Leela, which in turn brings in the tales of Lata and Hari. Savitribai's story is set within the loop of Madhu's childhood—a childhood she shared with Savitribai's daughter, Munni.

The titular "small remedies" are the devices and stratagems human beings use to make life bearable in the face of loss, pain, and betrayals—the cosmic blows dealt by the gods in spite of having the "Ganeshas in niches, the decorated thresholds, the mango leaf torans, the Oms, the Swastikas, the charms and amulets," the symbols of good luck with which Indian women decorate their thresholds. These decorations are also supposed to help ward off the evil eye. Yet, "It doesn't help; nothing does. It's always a losing battle such small remedies, these, to counter the terrible disease of being human, of being mortal and vulnerable." Madhu's own small remedies to cheat the gods lie in emotional and physical distancing from the sources of past pain. Work, usually considered an antidote to pain, does not help Madhu. She is sent to the small town of Bhavanipur to write the biography of famous classical singer Savitribai. Her close circle of friends and relatives manufacture this assignment for her in the hope that work will help her overcome the loss of her son, Aditya, who was killed in the serial blasts that rocked Bombay in the wake of the pulling down of the mosque in Ayodhya by Hindu militants in 1992. Madhu's sojourn involves her in the lives of the young couple Lata and Hari, who invite her into their home. Hari's relationship with Leela, Madhu's aunt, provides yet another thread that links the characters in the book into complex patterns of emotional relationships.

Motherhood in *Small Remedies,* as in *The Binding Vine,* is an important strand in the macronarrative. Madhu's existence seems validated to her when she gives birth to Aditya. "A child's birth is a rebirth for a woman, it's like becoming part of the world once again. The first time you emerge through someone else's pain and blood; this time it's your own." This close mother-child bonding is what devastates Deshpande's women when they lose their children–the other of the self. The mother-child, especially mother-daughter, relationships in this book are not always happy. Madhu's mother dies in her girlhood, and Lata's mother commits suicide, while Savitribai and Munni are hardly conventional mother-daughter types. Leela, although childless herself, becomes a mother to her orphaned niece, Madhu, and her stepchildren, Paula and Tony. Leela is unusual, as she is a socially committed woman with strong communist views who had been active during the Emergency imposed upon India by Prime Minister Indira Gandhi in 1975. To Madhu, Leela as the comforting aunt and emotional anchor is important, not Leela the political/feminist icon.

Shashi Deshpande's earlier texts did not have a feminist agenda or aim at postcolonial objectives such as magic realism or the repossession of history. Nor were they focused on contemporary politics. Although Deshpande still does not have an overt agenda on these issues, her texts have progressively shown a greater awareness and interest in all these areas. Yet, for her the personal, the woman, is still at the center of all her texts and her concern with women is at the heart of her endeavors as a writer. As she has said in an interview to the BBC World Service, she does feel that "over the years . . . my books have been very empowering for women. . . ." In another interview, with bangalore-buzz.com, she has expressed her satisfaction with her work as a writer and said, "As long as I have something to say, I will say it."

References:

R. K. Dhawan, ed., *Indian Women Novelists: With a Focus on Feminist and Women Studies: Anita Desai, Shashi Deshpande, Bharati Mukherjee, Shobha De* (New Delhi: Prestige, 1991);

Kamini Dinesh, "Moving Out of the Cloistered Self: Shashi Deshpande's Protagonists," *Margins of Erasure: Purdah in the Subcontinental Novel in English,* edited by Jasbir Jain and Amina Amin (Delhi: Sterling, 1995), p. 204;

Cicley Palser Havely, "Dancing with an Old Flame: The Postcolonial Legacy in Sahgal, Deshpande and Markandaya," in *Mapping Cultural Spaces: Postcolonial Indian Literature in English,* edited by Nilufer E. Bharucha and Vrinda Nabar (Delhi: Vision, 1998), p. 235;

Jasbir Jain, *Gendered Realities, Human Spaces: The Writing of Shashi Deshpande* (Jaipur: Rawat, 2003);

Adele King, "Feminist Criticism & Indian Women Writers," *Bombay Literary Review* (1989);

R. S. Pathak, *The Fiction of Shashi Deshpande* (New Delhi: Creative Books, 1998);

Sarabjit Kaur Sandhu, *The Image of Woman in the Novels of Shashi Deshpande* (New Delhi: Prestige Books, 1991);

Seema Suneel, *Man-Woman Relationship in Indian Fiction: With a Focus on Shashi Deshpande, Rajendra Awasthy and Syed Abdul Malik* (New Delhi: Prestige Books, 1995);

Usha Tambe, "Shashi Deshpande as a Feminist and A Novelist," in *Indian English Fiction 1980–1990: An Assessment,* edited by Nilufer E. Bharucha and Vilas Sarang (Delhi: B. R. Publishers, 1994), p. 125;

"World Service," articles on Shashi Deshpande <http://www.bbc.co.uk/> [accessed 6 January 2006].

Papers:

Shashi Deshpande has given her manuscripts to SCILET; they are housed in the American College, Madurai.

Chitra Banerjee Divakaruni

(29 July 1956 –)

Somdatta Mandal
Visva-Bharati University

BOOKS: *Dark Like the River* (Calcutta: Writers Workshop, 1987);

The Reason for Nasturtiums (Berkeley, Cal.: Berkeley Poets Workshop and Press, 1990);

Black Candle: Poems about Women from India, Pakistan, and Bangladesh (Corvallis, Ore.: Calyx, 1991);

Arranged Marriage (New York: Anchor, 1995; London: Black Swan, 1997);

Leaving Yuba City: New and Selected Poems (New York: Anchor, 1997);

The Mistress of Spices (New York & London: Doubleday, 1997);

Sister of My Heart (New York & London: Doubleday, 1999);

The Unknown Errors of Our Lives (New York: Doubleday, 2001; London: Abacus, 2001);

The Vine of Desire (New York: Doubleday, 2002; London: Abacus, 2002);

Neela: Victory Song (Middleton, Wis.: American Girl, 2002);

The Conch Bearer (Brookfield, Conn.: Roaring Brook, 2003; Frome, U.K.: Chicken House, 2004);

Queen of Dreams (New York: Doubleday, 2004; London: Abacus, 2005).

PLAY PRODUCTION: *Clothes*, Amherst, Mass., New World Theater, Amherst College, 1998.

OTHER: "At Muktinath," in *The Forbidden Stitch: An Asian American Women's Anthology*, edited by Shirley Geok-Lin Lim and Mayumi Tsutakawa (Corvallis, Ore.: Calyx, 1989), p. 29;

"Yuba City School" and "Sondra," in *Looking for Home: Women Writing about Exile*, edited by Deborah Keenan and Roseann Lloyd (Minneapolis, Minn.: Milkweed, 1990);

"Tourists," in *Encountering Cultures: Reading & Writing in a Changing World*, edited by Richard Holeton (Englewood Cliffs, N.J.: Prentice Hall, 1992);

"Childhood," "Outside Pisa," "Indigo," "The Brides Come to Yuba City," and "Yuba City School," in

Chitra Banerjee Divakaruni (photograph by Dru Ariel Banerjee; from the cover of Leaving Yuba City: New and Selected Poems, *1997; Richland County Public Library)*

The Open Boat: Poems from Asian America, edited by Garrett Hongo (New York: Anchor/Doubleday, 1992), pp. 70–80;

Multitude: Cross-Cultural Readings for Writers, edited by Divakaruni (Boston: McGraw-Hill, 1993);

"Making Samosas" and "Visit," in *No More Masks! An Anthology of Twentieth-Century American Women Poets*, revised and enlarged edition, edited by Florence Howe (New York: HarperPerennial, 1993), pp. 457–460;

"Restroom," "Indian Movie, New Jersey," "The Brides Come to Yuba City," and "Yuba City School," in *Unsettling America: An Anthology of Contemporary Multicultural Poetry,* edited by Maria Gillan (New York: Viking, 1994), pp. 21–22, 53, 209–210;

"The Founding of Yuba City" and "Yuba City Wedding," in *Living in America: Poetry and Fiction by South Asian American Writers,* edited by Roshni Rustomji-Kerns (Boulder, Colo.: Westview Press, 1995), pp. 47, 96–99;

"Lalita Mashi," in *Under Western Eyes: Personal Essays from Asian America,* edited by Hongo (New York: Anchor, 1995), pp. 71–90;

"Women with Kite," in *Diverse Voices of Women,* edited by Susan Frank Ballentine and Jessica Barksdale Inclan (Mountain View, Cal.: Mayfield, 1995), pp. 139–140;

"We the Indian Women in America," in *Contours of the Heart: South Asians Map North America,* edited by Sunaina Maira and Rajini Srikanth (New York: Asian American Writers' Workshop, 1996), pp. 268–270;

We, Too, Sing America: A Reader for Writers, edited by Divakaruni (Boston: McGraw-Hill, 1998);

"The Princess in the Palace of Snakes," in *Mirror, Mirror on the Wall: Women Writers Explore Their Favorite Fairy Tales,* edited by Kate Bernheimer (New York: Anchor, 1998), pp. 96–99;

"The Arranged Marriage," in *Asian-American Literature: An Anthology,* edited by Lim (Lincolnwood, Ill.: NTC, 2000), pp. 78–80;

"The Secret of Spices," in *A Matter of Taste: The Penguin Book of Indian Writing on Food,* edited by Nilanjana S. Roy (New Delhi & New York: Penguin, 2004), pp. 199–212;

California Uncovered: Stories for the Twenty-First Century, edited by Divakaruni, William E. Justice, and James Quay (Berkeley, Cal.: Heyday, 2005).

SELECTED PERIODICAL PUBLICATIONS–
UNCOLLECTED: "Dissolving Boundaries," *Bold Type,* no. 3 (May 1997) <www.randomhouse.com/boldtype/0597/divakaruni/essay.html>;

"Common Scents: The Smell of Childhood Never Fades," *Salon.com* (26 June 1997) <www.salon.com/june97/mothers/chitra970626.html>;

"The Disappointment of Aloneness," *Salon.com* (10 July 1997) <www.salon.com/july97/mothers/chitra970710.html>;

"Of Fame and Stomach Flu," *Salon.com* (24 July 1997) <www.salon.com/july97/mothers/chitra970724.html>;

"His First Heartbreak," *Salon.com* (7 August 1997) <www.salon.com/aug97/mothers/chitra.html>;

"Indian, Born in the USA," *Salon.com* (21 August 1997) <www.salon.com/aug97/mothers/chitra970821.html>;

"Blood Brothers," *Salon.com* (4 September 1997) <www.salon.com/sept97/mothers/chitra970904.html>;

"The Common Enemy," *Salon.com* (18 September 1997) <www.salon.com/sept97/mothers/chitra970918.html>;

"Why Don't They Just Leave?" *Salon.com* (2 October 1997) <www.salon.com/mwt/diva/1997/10/02diva.html>;

"Live Free and Starve," *Salon.com* (16 October 1997) <www.salon.com/mwt/diva/1997/10/16diva.html>;

"Giving Life and Taking It Away," *Salon.com* (29 October 1997) <www.salon.com/mwt/diva/1997/10/29diva.html>;

"Talking to Strangers," *Salon.com* (13 November 1997) <www.salon.com/mwt/diva/1997/11/13diva.html>;

"Not an Easy Love," *Salon.com* (11 December 1997) <www.salon.com/mwt/diva/1997/12/11diva.html>;

"My Fictional Children," *Salon.com* (28 January 1998) <www.salon.com/mwt/diva/1998/01/28diva.html>;

"What Women Share," *Bold Type,* 2, no. 10 (January 1999) <www.randomhouse.com/boldtype/0199/divakaruni/essay.html>;

"Do South Asian Women Need Separate Shelter Homes?" *Rediff on the Net* (6 July 1999) <www.rediff.com/news/1999/jul/06us2.htm>;

"Uncertain Objects of Desire," *Atlantic Monthly,* 285 (March 2000);

"Wheat Complexions and Pink Cheeks," *Rediff on the Net* (2 April 2001) <ushome.rediff.com/news/2001/apr/02usspec.htm>;

"Power Goddess," *India Today,* 4 April 2005, pp. 31–33.

Belonging to the group of young Indian writers that emerged on the literary scene with a postcolonial diasporic identity after Salman Rushdie, Chitra Banerjee Divakaruni's position as a South Asian writer in English is distinct and well established. As someone who has spent more time outside India than in it, she has been accepted as an Asian American writer, living with a hybrid identity and writing partially autobiographical work. Most of her stories, set in the Bay Area of California, deal with the experience of immigrants to the United States, whose voice is rarely heard in other writings of Indian writers in English. She has been published in more than fifty magazines, including the *Atlantic Monthly* and *The New Yorker,* and her writing has been included in more than thirty anthologies. Her works have been translated into eleven languages, including Dutch, Hebrew, Portuguese, Danish, German, and Japanese.

Chitra Banerjee was born in Calcutta on 29 July 1956 and spent the first nineteen years of her life in India. Her father, Rajendra Kumar Banerjee, an accountant by profession, and her mother, Tatini Banerjee, a schoolteacher, brought up their four children in modest middle-class ambience. As the second-born

Dust jacket for Divakaruni's first collection of short fiction, published in 1995, comprising mostly stories in which the author dramatizes the changes that modern living and immigration to the United States have wrought on traditional Indian marital life (Richland County Public Library)

child and only girl among three brothers, Partha, Dhruva, and Surya, Chitra spent her childhood days in sibling rivalry and camaraderie. She studied at Loreto House, a convent school run by Irish nuns, from where she graduated in 1971. In 1976 she earned her bachelor's degree in English from Presidency College, University of Calcutta. At the age of nineteen she moved to the United States to continue her studies as an English major and got her master's degree from Wright State University in Dayton, Ohio, in 1978. Working under Stephen Greenblatt on the topic "For Danger Is in Words: A Study of Language in Marlowe's Plays," she received her Ph.D. in English from the University of California at Berkeley in 1984. She held different kinds of jobs to pay for her education, including babysitting, selling merchandise in an Indian boutique, slicing bread at a bakery, and washing instruments at a science lab. She did not begin to write

fiction until after she graduated from Berkeley, when she came to realize that she loved teaching but did not want to do academic writing: "It didn't have enough heart in it. I wanted to write something more immediate." In 1979 in Dayton she married Murthy Divakaruni, an engineer by profession. Her two sons, Anand and Abhay, were born in 1991 and 1994.

Divakaruni and her husband moved to Sunnyvale, California, in 1989. For several years she was interested in issues involving women and worked with Afghani women refugees and women from dysfunctional families, as well as in shelters for battered women. In 1991 she became founder-member and president of Maitri, an organization in the San Francisco area that works for South Asian women in abusive situations. She also associated herself with Asians against Domestic Abuse, an organization in Houston. Her interest in these women grew when she realized that there was no mainstream shelter for immigrant women in distress—a place where people would understand their cultural needs and problems—in the United States. Because of the experience she gathered from counseling sessions, the lives of Asian women opened up to her, revealing unimaginable crises.

For all the years Divakaruni lived in the Bay Area, she taught at Foothill College in Los Altos Hills. She turned to writing as a means of exploring the cultural differences she encountered as a newcomer to the United States. Initially, she started writing for herself, and during the mid 1980s she joined a writer's group at Berkeley University. She wrote poems during that time, and, as she told Roxanne Farmanfarmaian in *Publishers Weekly* (14 May 2001), her venture into serious poetry writing began after she received the news of her grandfather's death in her ancestral village in India: "Poetry was closest to my psyche. Poetry focuses on the moment, on the image, and relies on image to express meaning. That was very important to me, that kind of crystallization, that kind of intensity in a small space."

As he has been with the publications of many Indian writers in English, Professor P. Lal of the Writers Workshop in Calcutta was instrumental in publishing Divakaruni's first book of poetry, *Dark Like the River* (1987). She had already established herself as a poet by the time she published *The Reason for Nasturtiums* (1990), her first verse collection published in the United States. The subtitle of the volume explains her primary interest and indicates that her main focus is the immigrant experience and South Asian women. She shows the experiences and struggles involved in Asian women's attempts to find their own identities, as her poem "The Arranged Marriage" illustrates:

The night is airless-still, as
before a storm. Behind the wedding drums,
cries of jackals from the burning grounds.
The canopy gleams, color
of long life, many children.
Color of bride-blood . . .

. . . The groom's father
produces his scales and in clenched silence
the dowry gold is weighed. But he smiles
and all is well again. Now it is godhuli,
the time of the auspicious seeing.
Time for you, bride of sixteen,
mother, to raise the tear-stained face
that I will learn so well,
to look for the first time into
your husband's opaque eyes.

As the title suggests, Divakaruni's volume of poems *Leaving Yuba City: New and Selected Poems* (1997) includes new poems as well as ones from *Dark Like the River, The Reason for Nasturtiums,* and *Black Candle: Poems about Women from India, Pakistan, and Bangladesh* (1991). These poems draw on similar subject matter to her fiction: womanhood, family life, exile, alienation, exoticism, ethnicity, domesticity, love, and romance. *Leaving Yuba City* is a collection that explores images of India and the Indian experience in the United States, ranging from the adventures of going to a convent school in India run by Irish nuns to the history of the earliest Indian immigrants in the United States. The opening poem, "How I Became a Writer," describes an abusive father ("the gorilla with iron fingers") and the suicide of a mother who puts the poet to bed and locks her in "so I would not be the first to discover her body hanging from the ceiling." The poem concludes, however, with the ironic affirmation "I *know* I'm going to be / the best, the happiest writer in the world."

Leaving Yuba City comprises six sections of interlinked poems. Although they feature many of the same characters, they explore a variety of themes. Divakaruni is particularly interested in how different art forms can influence and inspire each other. The series of poems based on paintings by the American artist Francesco Clemente is of particular interest. In a section devoted to his "Indian Miniatures" series, Divakaruni's words enter into Clemente's dreamscapes and reveal moments of startling visual clarity. She also takes equal inspiration from other artists' interpretations of her native land—photographs by Raghubir Singh and Indian motion pictures, including Mira Nair's *Salaam Bombay!* (1988) and Satyajit Ray's *Ghare-Baire* (1984). As with all of her writing, these poems deal with the experiences of women and their struggle for identity. Her persistent concern with women's experience often deepens as it is arrayed

against varying cultural backgrounds. As Meena Alexander, another poet of Indian origin, states: "Chitra Divakaruni's *Leaving Yuba City* draws us into a realm of the senses, intense, chaotic, site of our pleasures and pain. These are moving lyrics of lives at the edge of the new world."

The group of poems about the immigrant experiences of the Sikhs is especially poignant. Because of immigration restrictions, most of the original Sikh farmers who settled in Yuba City, California, could not bring their families with them or, in the case of single men, go back to get married until the 1940s. As a result, in the 1920s and 1930s several men married local women from Mexico. This section imagines the lives of the farmers who arrived in 1910 and takes on their voices in lush, novelistic prose poems: "I lay in bed and try to picture her, my bride, in a shiny gold salwar-kameez, eyes that were black and bright and deep enough to dive in." The poem "The Brides Come to Yuba City" describes the reunion of the long-separated lovers:

Red-veiled, we lean to each other,
press damp palms, try
broken smiles. The man who met us at the ship
whistles a restless *Angrezi* tune
and scans the fields. Behind us,
the black wedding trunks, sharp-edged,
shiny, stenciled with strange men-names
our bodies do not fit into:
. . . .
He gives a shout, waves at the men, their slow
uneven approach. We crease our eyes
through the veils' red film, cannot breathe. Thirty years
since we saw them. Or never,
like Harvinder, married last year at Hoshiarpur
to her husband's photo,
which she clutches tight to her
to stop the shaking. He is fifty-two,
she sixteen. Tonight—like us all—
she will open her legs to him.

This volume of poetry won a Pushcart Prize, an Allen Ginsberg Prize, and a Gerbode Foundation Award.

After three books of poetry, Divakaruni realized that there were things she wanted to say that would be better expressed in prose. "My poetry was becoming more and more narrative," she admitted to Farmanfarmaian, "and I was becoming more interested in the story element, and the nuances of character change." In 1992 she enrolled in an evening fiction-writing class at Foothill College, where she had started teaching twentieth-century multicultural literature the year before. In 1993 she edited *Multitude: Cross-Cultural Readings for Writers,* an anthology she uses in her own classroom; it is also used at many major universities

Front cover of Divakaruni's 1997 collection of poems about Indian women's struggles for identity (Richland County Public Library)

in the United States. Her criterion for selection, as quoted by Elizabeth Softky in her article "Cross-Cultural Understanding Spiced with the Indian Diaspora" (1997), was "quality, but also stories that focused on problem solving, not just how terrible things are." The anthology includes stories about communication across cultures, expectations of friendships, the 1992 Los Angeles riots, and prejudice against gay people. The book includes works by a variety of authors, some of them her own students. Divakaruni's first volume of short stories, *Arranged Marriage* (1995), explores the cross-cultural experiences of womanhood through a feminist perspective, a theme that continues to inform her work. "It was while I was at Berkeley that I became aware of women's issues and the need for me to do something for them," she has said. Although her outlook has softened and her interest has shifted to more general human themes of memory and desire, at that time she felt militant: "I really wanted to focus on women battling and coming out triumphant."

How changing times affect the cherished Indian institution of arranged marriage is the theme of the eleven stories of *Arranged Marriage*. Most of the stories are about Indian immigrants to the United States from the author's native region of Bengal and are told by female narrators in the first-person-singular point of view, often in the present tense, which imparts to the stories a sense of intimacy. They capture the experience of recent immigrants, mostly from professional classes, such as electronic engineers and businesspeople, but also a few from the working class, such as auto mechanics and convenience-store clerks. There are several immigrant brides who "are both liberated and trapped by cultural changes," as Patricia Holt puts it in her "Women Feel Tug of Two Cultures" (1995), and who are struggling to carve out an identity of their own. Though references to local attractions, postgraduate education, and her Bengali culture are sprinkled liberally throughout the tales, Divakaruni says the stories themselves—which deal with issues such as domestic violence, crime, racism, interracial relationships, economic disparity, abortion, and divorce—were the result of her own imaginings and the experiences of others.

Arranged Marriage received considerable critical acclaim and the 1996 American Book Award, the Bay Area Book Reviewers Award, and the PEN Oakland Award for fiction. Only two of the stories of this collection had been published previously: "The Bats" appeared in *Zyzzyva* (Spring 1993), and "Clothes" in the anthology *Home to Stay: Asian American Women's Fiction* (1990). Some critics have accused Divakaruni of tarnishing the image of the Indian community and reinforcing stereotypes of the "oppressed" Indian woman, but as Julie Mehta quotes the author in "Arranging One's Life" (*Metro*, 3–9 October 1996), her professed aim was to shatter stereotypes: "Some just write about different things, but my approach is to tackle these sensitive topics. I hope people who read my book will not think of the characters as Indians, but feel for them as people."

At once pessimistic and filled with hope, Divakaruni creates contradictory as well as connected fictional worlds through the stories in *Arranged Marriage*. In "Silver Pavements, Golden Roofs," the protagonist—a graduate student newly arrived in the United States, which she considers a land of illusion—is brought face to face with harsh reality when she is assaulted on the mean streets of Chicago. "The Ultrasound," which deals with the issue of female feticide, was later enlarged into the novel *Sister of My Heart* (1999). In "Affair" two temperamentally ill-matched Indo-American couples, whose marriages had been arranged on the basis of their horoscopes having matched "perfectly," divorce after many years of affluent living in Silicon Valley. In "Doors" the character Preeti, after moving to the United States, has come to love the western idea of privacy. She faces a dilemma when her husband's cousin wants to come to live with them. She expresses her discontent with the situation, which shows her newfound decisiveness and her determination to oppose her husband's view of the traditional Indian wife. In "Clothes" the husband of the narrator, Sumita, dies, and she is faced with deciding whether to stay in the United States or to go back to India to live with her in-laws. Sumita calls widows who are serving their in-laws "doves with cutoff wings."

One common theme that runs through all the stories is that Indian-born women living new lives in the United States find independence a mixed blessing that involves walking a tightrope between old beliefs and newfound desires. Though the characters vary, the themes of the short stories are essentially the same—exploration of the nature of arranged marriages as well as the experience of affirmation and rebellion against social traditions.

Divakaruni's first novel, *The Mistress of Spices* (1997), is distinct in that it blends prose and poetry, successfully employing magic realist techniques. Its heroine, Tilo (short for Tilottama), is the "mistress of spices." Born in India, she is shipwrecked on a remote island inhabited by women. Here she encounters an ancient woman who imparts instruction about the power of spices. Ordained after a trial by fire, each new mistress is sent to a far-off land. Tilo heads for Oakland, California, disguised as an old woman, and sets up a shop where she sells spices. While she supplies the ingredients for curries and *kormas,* she also helps her customers to gain a more precious commodity: whatever they most desire. The chapters of the novel are named after spices such as cinnamon, turmeric, and fenugreek, common ingredients of Indian cuisine. Here, however, they have special powers, and Tilo practices her magical powers of healing through them. Through those who visit and revisit her shop, she catches glimpses of the local Indian expatriate community, which includes an abused wife, a naive cabbie, a sullen teen, a yearning young woman, and an old man clinging to dignity, all of whom lack balance. To each, Tilo dispenses wisdom and the appropriate spice, for the restoration of sight, the cleansing of evil, the pain of rejection. When a lonely American ventures into the store, however, a troubled Tilo cannot find the correct spice, for he arouses in her a forbidden desire—which if she follows will destroy her magical powers. Conflicted, she has to choose whether to serve her people or to follow the path leading to her own happiness. Tilo has to decide which part of her heritage she will keep and which part she will choose to abandon.

The Mistress of Spices has a mystical quality to it, and, as Divakaruni puts it in "Dissolving Boundaries," an essay for the on-line journal *Bold Type* (May 1997), "I wrote it in a spirit of play, collapsing the divisions between the realistic world of twentieth century America and the timeless one of myth and magic in my attempt to create a modern fable." She drew on folktales of her childhood memories such as that of a sleeping city under the ocean and speaking serpents, but she changed them almost completely. "The speaking serpents are a different kind of magic that I only partially understand. They represent the grace of the universe, and by that, I mean they are not governed by logic but come to us mortals as a blessing we cannot understand." Unlike in her short stories, the immigrant experience in the novel is dealt with obliquely. Her own immigrant experience in Ohio helped her express the feelings of loneliness and cultural separation that suffuse the novel. Thus the book also becomes a kind of metaphor for the struggle between social responsibility and personal happiness. When asked by Morton Marcus, in an interview for *Metro* (8–14 May 1997), why she had taken the risk of plunging into fantasy when she had already secured a large following and critical praise with the realistic *Arranged Marriage,* Divakaruni replied candidly: "First, I believe a writer should push boundaries, and I wanted to try something new, take risks. But more to the point, the risk-taking came of a near-death experience I had two and a half years ago with the birth of my second child, Abhay, who was born of a Caesarian operation that went wrong." That experience inspired her to create Tilo, who moves back and forth between one existence and another. As she explained to Marcus, "Looking at this question from another perspective, you could say that I took three 'literary risks' in the book. I bridged the purely realistic world and the mythic one; I extended my subject matter from dealing exclusively with the Indian-American community to include three other ethnic groups living in the inner city—Latinos, African Americans and Native Americans—and finally, I tried to bring together the language of poetry and prose so the idiom of the book has a lyric quality appropriate to the genre of magic realism." The concept of boundaries falling away leads the reader to the main theme of the novel, that "happiness comes from being involved in our human world."

The Mistress of Spices is also a love story, the outcome of which keeps the reader in suspense. Interestingly, when Tilo makes her decision, she changes her name to Maya, the Hindu term that defines the every-

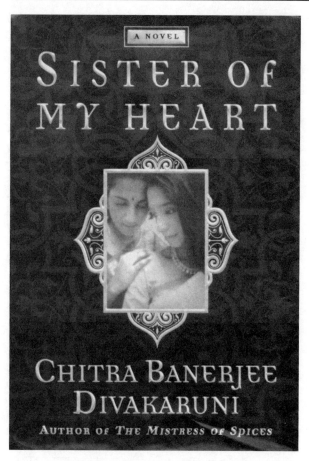

Dust jacket for Divakaruni's 1999 novel, in which cousins Sudha and Anju, raised together in a household of women, are separated by the marriages their family arranges for them (Richland County Public Library)

day world of desire, pain, and joy as the world of illusion, a place of inevitable sorrow from which one is trying to escape. The novel was named one of the best books of 1997 by the *Los Angeles Times* and one of the best books of the twentieth century by the *San Francisco Chronicle,* and was nominated for the Orange Prize in England in 1998.

From mid 1997 to early 1998, Divakaruni also wrote a regular column, "Spice of Life," for the on-line magazine *Salon,* in which she focused upon the issues she knows best. In a column titled "My Fictional Children" (28 January 1998) she notes that everything she ever tried to write about her children has been a failure but that the fictional mothers in her stories have become much more complex and full:

> My writing is made more complicated by the fact that I'm exploring the experience of being Indian, of being brought up in a culture where many still consider motherhood a woman's supreme destiny, and the inability to get pregnant her supreme failure. This is

one of the major themes of the novel I'm working on right now. I think I'm not exaggerating when I say . . . that I wouldn't be writing this book had I not had children myself.

In 1998, commissioned by the New England Foundation, Divakaruni also wrote a play called *Clothes,* which was performed by the New World Theater at Amherst College and at the International Drama Festival, Athens, Greece, in 1999.

Unlike her first novel, *Sister of My Heart* is written in the realist mode and describes the complicated relationships of a family in Bengal. Born in a big, old Calcutta house on the same night when both their fathers mysteriously disappeared, Sudha and Anju are distant cousins and are brought up together. Closer than sisters, they share clothes, worries, and dreams. The Chatterjee family fortunes are at a low ebb, as there are only widows at home—the girls' mothers and their aunt. The forty-two chapters of the novel comprise a sort of extended, multitiered dialogue. The chapters themselves are alternately titled "Anju" and "Sudha" and utilize techniques that are epistolary and exclamatory, with transcultural settings, a tone that is adjectival and highly lyrical, italicized stream-of-consciousness passages, and a romantic style. Slowly the dark secrets of the past are unveiled and test the cousins' mutual loyalty. A family crisis forces their mothers to start the serious business of arranging the girls' marriages, and the pair is torn apart. Sudha moves to her new family's home in rural Bengal, while Anju joins her immigrant husband in California. Although they have both been trained to be perfect wives, nothing has prepared them for the pain, as well as the joy, that each will have to face in her new life. In the novel Indian discrimination against women stands exposed: the cousins consider themselves inferior beings because they are female. Feminist views—both overt and covert—are present in many passages of the novel. The story line, however, becomes predictable. Anju saves Sudha from the machinations of her husband and in-laws, who want to kill the girl child she has conceived, and brings her to the United States.

Reception of *Sister of My Heart* was overwhelmingly positive. For most western readers, the novel provided a new look at female bonding. Divakaruni's impetus was to write about a female-centric theme in a South Asian setting. The novel is her perception of an utter lack of emphasis on women's independence in South Asian literary genres. She identifies the novel as ultimately about storytelling. Influenced by her grandfather, who told stories from South Asian epics, she has woven those childhood folktales into her novel. She explains that the "aloneness" of epic heroines seemed strange to her even as a child. In a 28 February 1999 *San Francisco Examiner* article, she declares that in South Asian mythological stories, "the main relationships the heroines had were with the opposite sex: husbands, sons, lovers, or opponents. They never had any important friends. Perhaps in rebellion against such thinking, I find myself focusing my writing on friendships with women, and trying to balance them with the conflicting passions and demands that come to us as daughters and wives, lovers and mothers." Divakaruni shares the emotions of her protagonists and finds in them a mode of feminist expression. "In the best friendships I have had with women, there is a closeness that is unique, a sympathy that comes from somewhere deep and primal in our bodies and does not need explanation, perhaps because of the life-changing experiences we share." She has denied in interviews, however, that she has attempted to create a comprehensive picture of South Asian family life, likening such an assumption to the idea that one can understand all Americans by reading Flannery O'Connor.

Though *Sister of My Heart* is set in Calcutta, Divakaruni admits that the rest of the story is far from autobiographical and is based on observation and imagination. Around the time the novel was published, she also over the course of about a year wrote a column for the magazine *India Today*. Titled "Stars and Spice," the column dealt with immigrant issues.

Apart from her poems and fictional writing, Divakaruni has also established a reputation for herself with her nonfiction pieces. In "Foreign Affairs: Uncertain Objects of Desire," which appeared in the March 2000 issue of the *Atlantic Monthly,* she sifts through several hundred carefully categorized matrimonial advertisements in *The Times of India,* surmising that in India, a country that straddles the old and the new, they are a good place to look for signs of shifting values. Usually the ads and responses are handled by parents—proof that the practice of arranged marriage is alive and well in India. Reading between the lines of two ads typical of their eras, one from 1969 and one from 1999, she concludes that a great deal about the nature of desired partners, and the protocol for finding them, has changed. Apart from other factors, Divakaruni suggests that perhaps "this echoes a larger pattern of social movement in which the Indian woman's role is changed more rapidly than the Indian man's." In a short article she wrote for the Internet site *Rediff on the Net,* "Wheat Complexion and Pink Cheeks" (2 April 2001), she deplores the Indian obsession for fair-skinned women.

The female protagonists of eight of the nine stories in Divakaruni's sensuously evocative collection *The Unknown Errors of Our Lives* (2001) are caught between the beliefs and traditions of their Indian heritage and those of their, or their children's, new homeland, the United States. Seven out of the nine stories collected in the anthology had been published earlier in various journals and anthologies. The diverse range of the stories of this volume is noteworthy. Most of them depict life in East and West perceptively. The problem of acculturation is deftly dealt with in "Mrs. Dutta Writes a Letter," a story in which a widow discovers that her old-fashioned ways are an embarrassment to her daughter-in-law. A young American woman's pilgrimage in Kashmir is the subject of "The Lives of Strangers." Miscommunication and distancing in a brother-sister relationship is the theme of "The Intelligence of Wild Things." Ruchira, the protagonist of "The Unknown Errors of Our Lives," while packing up in preparation for her forthcoming marriage, discovers her childhood "book of errors," a teenage notebook in which she wrote down ways of improving her life.

"The Names of Stars in Bengali" is the nuanced story of a San Francisco wife and mother who returns to her native village in India to visit her mother, in which each understands afresh the emotional dislocation caused by stepping into "a time machine called immigration" that subjects them to "the alien habit of a world they had imagined imperfectly." All of the stories in *The Unknown Errors of Our Lives* are touching tales of lapsed communication, inarticulate love, and redemptive memories. They illuminate the difficult process of adjustment for women in whom memory and duty must coexist with a new, often painful, and disorienting set of standards. In an interview with Esha Bhattacharjee published in *The Sunday Statesman* on 2 February 2003, when asked what she felt she was—an Indian, an American, or an Indian living in the United States, she confessed: "I have to live with a hybrid identity. In many ways I'm an Indian, but living in America for 19 years has taught me many things. It has helped me look at both cultures more clearly. It has taught me to observe, question, explore and evaluate."

In 2002 Divakaruni moved to Houston, Texas, where she began to teach in the creative-writing program at the University of Houston. In that same year she published *The Vine of Desire,* a novel of depth and sensitivity that can be seen as a sequel to *Sister of My Heart.* It continues the story of Anju and Sudha, the two cousins of the earlier book. The young women now live far from Calcutta, the city of their childhood, and after a year of living separate lives, are rekindling their friendship in the United States. The deep-seated love they feel for each other provides the support they

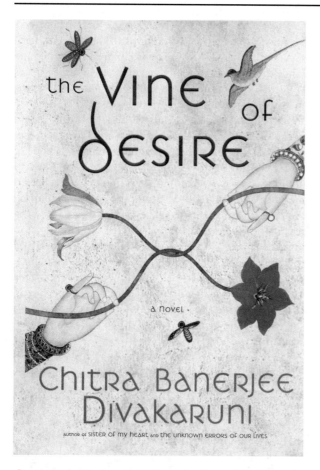

Dust jacket for Divakaruni's 2002 sequel to Sister of My Heart, *in which Sudha and Anju adapt to life among the immigrant Indian community in the United States (Richland County Public Library)*

need: it gives Anju the strength to survive a personal tragedy and Sudha the confidence to make a life for herself and her baby daughter, Dayita, despite not having her husband. The unlikely relationships they form with men and women in the world outside the immigrant Indian community as well as their families in India profoundly transform them, especially when they must confront the deep passionate feelings that Anju's husband has for Sudha. Sudha, seeking a measure of self-worth and trying to assuage loneliness, succumbs to Sunil's need for her and then flees from home to be a nursemaid to an old and ailing man. Sunil also moves out and away. Anju sticks to studies and makes it to the dean's list. The novel ends with her metaphorical declaration, "I've learned to fly." Divakaruni deals with a new facet of immigrant experience in the sense that the movement is not necessarily a physical one or from East to West. By making Sudha decide that she is not interested in the United States anymore and would like to go home, the author treads new ground. Through the eyes of people

caught in the clash of cultures, Divakaruni reveals the rewards and the perils of breaking free from the past and the complicated, often contradictory emotions that shape the passage to independence. *The Vine of Desire* was named one of the best books of 2002 by the *San Francisco Chronicle* and the *Los Angeles Times*. Also in 2002, Divakaruni was also chosen as a literary laureate by the San Francisco Public Library.

Divakaruni's versatility as a writer was confirmed by her first children's book, *Neela: Victory Song* (2002). Part of the "Girls of Many Lands" series, featuring books and dolls based on young girls from various historical periods and cultural traditions, it is the story of a twelve-year-old girl caught up in the Indian Independence movement. In 1939, while her family is preparing for the wedding of her older sister, Neela Sen becomes interested in the world around her. When her father is jailed following a march against British rule, Neela takes matters into her own hands and goes to Calcutta to find him.

Published in September 2003 and chosen as one of the best books of the year by *Publishers Weekly,* Divakaruni's second book for children, *The Conch Bearer,* blends action, adventure, and magic in a kind of quest fantasy. The story opens in a poor section of Kolkata, as Calcutta was renamed in 2001, where twelve-year-old Anand is entrusted with a conch shell imbued with mystical power. Anand's task is to return the shell to its rightful home high in the mountains. Accompanied by a mysterious stranger and a resourceful street urchin, he encounters good and evil both in himself and in those around him.

Divakaruni's sixth novel, *Queen of Dreams* (2004), again utilizes the magic realist mode. Like Tilo of *The Mistress of Spices,* who uses spices to help customers solve their problems, in *Queen of Dreams* Mrs. Gupta is an Indian immigrant who dreams the dreams of others so she can help them in their own lives. This gift of vision and ability to foresee and guide people through their fates fascinates her daughter, Rakhi, who as a young artist and divorced mother living in Berkeley, California, is struggling to keep her footing with her family and with a world in alarming transition. Rakhi also feels isolated from her mother's past in India and the dreamworld she inhabits, and she longs for something to bring them closer. Burdened by her own painful secret, Rakhi finds solace in the discovery, after her mother's death, of her dream journals. "A dream is a telegram from the hidden world," Rakhi's mother writes in her journals, which open the long-closed door to Rakhi's past.

As Rakhi attempts to divine her identity, knowing little of India but drawn inexorably into a sometimes painful history she is only just discovering, her life is shaken by new horrors. In the wake of the terrorist attacks of 11 September 2001 she and her friends must deal with dark new complexities about their acculturation. The ugly violence visited upon them forces the reader to view those terrible days from the point of view of immigrants and Indian Americans whose only crime was the color of their skin or the fact that they wore a turban. As their notions of citizenship are questioned, Rakhi's search for identity intensifies. Haunted by her experiences of racism, she nevertheless finds unexpected blessings: the possibility of new love and understanding for her family.

Divakaruni's journey from being a young graduate student to a mature writer seems to have come full circle. She believes that there are both pluses and minuses to belonging to the growing body of Asian American writers. The interest in Asian American literature makes it easier to get published now than ten or fifteen years ago, as she told Neela Banerjee of *AsianWeek.com* (27 April – 3 May 2001): "The best part is that your writing is now available to so many people, both within and outside of the community. Young South Asians have come up to me and said, 'I really relate to this story. This story has helped me understand my mother, helped me understand my culture.' That's a really good feeling." Divakaruni also admits, however, that being pigeonholed as an Asian American writer can be stifling: "You are expected to be a spokesperson for the community, and that is just an unfair kind of burden. I always try to make it clear that I am presenting one vision about what is true about the Indian American community. It is a very diverse community, and mine is just one angle of looking at it."

As Divakaruni has changed, her style of writing has changed accordingly. For example, *Arranged Marriage* includes a detailed glossary of Bengali and Hindi words, which were italicized in the stories. In *The Vine of Desire* she not only does away with italics and glossaries but uses many Bengali and Hindi words within the text. Through this means she seems to be attempting to get the reader to accept these as a natural part of the characters' world and of their language. When asked by Bhattacharjee as to how she has matured as a writer, she replied that with each new book, she found a "new challenge." Whatever the narrative technique of each of her books might be, she hoped it would connect with the readers.

The critical acclaim and increasing recognition that Chitra Banerjee Divakaruni has received has established her as a promising writer interested in the immigrant experience, not simply that of those who move from East to West. It is a cross-cultural scenario

Dust jacket for Divakaruni's 2004 novel, a work of magic realism that depicts an Indian American woman's relationship with her clairvoyant mother, as well as the hostility that Indian Americans faced after the terrorist attacks of 11 September 2001 (Richland County Public Library)

where, through her writings, the diversity of Indian writing in English is revealed.

Interviews:

Morton Marcus, "Sunnyvale Novelist Chitra Divakaruni Talks about 'The Mistress of Spices' and the Illusory Power of the Material World," *Metro,* 8–14 May 1997;

Roxanne Farmanfarmaian, "Chitra Banerjee Divakaruni: Writing from a Different Place," *Publishers Weekly,* 14 May 2001;

Esha Bhattacharjee, "I Have to Live with a Hybrid Identity," *Sunday Statesman,* 2 February 2003, p. 3;

Robbie Clipper Sethi, "'They Forgive My Fiction': Interview with Chitra Banerjee Divakaruni," Welcome to Little India <www.asanet.com/achal/archive/apr99/fiction.htm> [accessed 28 November 2005].

References:

Janice Albert, "How Now, My Metal of India?" *English Journal,* 4 (September 1997): 99–100;

Debjani Banerjee, "'Home and Us': Re-defining Identity in the South Asian Diaspora through the Writings of Chitra Banerjee Divakaruni and Meena Alexander," in *The Diasporic Imagination: Asian American Writing,* volume 2, edited by Somdatta Mandal (New Delhi: Prestige, 2000), pp. 9–43;

Neela Banerjee, "Mistress of Self," *AsianWeek.com* (27 April – 3 May 2001) <www.asianweek.com/2001_04_27/ae1_chitradivakaruni.html>;

Urbashi Barat, "Sisters of the Heart: Female Bonding in the Fiction of Chitra Banerjee Divakaruni," in *The Diasporic Imagination: Asian-American Writing,* volume 2, edited by Mandal (New Delhi: Prestige, 2000), pp. 44–60;

"Chitra Banerjee Divakaruni," *San Francisco Chronicle,* 24 December 1995, p. A10;

Patricia Holt, "Women Feel Tug of Two Cultures," *San Francisco Chronicle,* 1 August 1995, p. E5;

A. P. Kamath, "Women Writers of Indian Diaspora Create a Big Impact," *Rediff on the Net* (23 August 1999) <www.rediff.com/news/1999/aug/23us1.htm>;

Julie Mehta, "Arranging One's Life," *Metro* (3–9 October 1996) <www.metroactive.com/papers/metro/10.03.96/books-9640.html>;

Arthur J. Pais, "Spice Girl has a Fresh Recipe for Women," *India Today,* 25 January 1999, p. 73;

Elizabeth Softky, "Cross-Cultural Understanding Spiced with the Indian Diaspora," *Black Issues in Higher Education,* 18 (September 1997): 26+.

Nissim Ezekiel

(16 December 1924 – 9 January 2004)

Kaiser Haq
University of Dhaka

BOOKS: *A Time to Change and Other Poems* (London: Fortune Press, 1952);

Sixty Poems (Bombay: Privately printed, 1953);

The Third (Bombay: Privately printed, 1959);

The Unfinished Man: Poems Written in 1959 (Calcutta: Writers Workshop, 1961; edited by Eunice de Souza, Thompson, Conn.: InterCulture, 1969);

Cultural Profiles: Bombay-Poona, edited by Rekha Menon (New Delhi: Inter-National Cultural Centre, 1961);

A New Look at Communism: Papers Read at the Seminar Convened by the Indian Committee for Cultural Freedom at Bombay, August 30–September 1, 1963, by Ezekiel and Amritlal B. Shah (Bombay: Indian Committee for Cultural Freedom, 1963);

The Exact Name: Poems, 1960–1964 (Calcutta: Writers Workshop, 1965);

Two Dozen or So: Selected Poems, edited by Delmar Bogner (New Paltz, N.Y.: State University College, 1967);

Three Plays (Calcutta: P. Lal, 1969);

Hymns in Darkness (Delhi & New York: Oxford University Press, 1976);

Latter-Day Psalms (Delhi & New York: Oxford University Press, 1982);

Collected Poems 1952–1988 (Delhi & Oxford: Oxford University Press, 1989; enlarged, edited by John Thieme, 2005);

Selected Prose (Delhi: Oxford University Press, 1992);

Don't Call It Suicide: A Tragedy (Madras: Macmillan, 1993).

OTHER: *Indian Writers in Conference: The Sixth P.E.N. All-India Writer's Conference, Mysore, 1962,* edited by Ezekiel (Bombay: P.E.N. All-India Centre, 1964);

Ralph Waldo Emerson, *An Emerson Reader,* edited by Ezekiel (Bombay: Popular Prakashan, 1965);

Writing in India: The Seventh P.E.N. All-India Writers' Conference, Lucknow, 1964, edited by Ezekiel (Bombay: P.E.N. All-India Centre, 1965);

Nissim Ezekiel (from <www.geocities.com/varnamala/nissim.jpg>)

Gieve Patel, *Poems,* published by Ezekiel (Bombay: Ezekiel, 1966);

Mario de Miranda, *A Little World of Humor,* preface by Ezekiel (Bombay: Pearl Books, 1968);

Martin Luther King Jr., *A Martin Luther King Reader,* edited by Ezekiel (Bombay: Popular Prakashan, 1969);

Saratkumara Mukhopadhyaya, *The Face: Poems,* translated by Meenakshi Mukherjee and others, edited by Ezekiel (New Delhi: Aavesh Forum, 1971);

Indira Sant, *Snake-skin and Other Poems,* translated by Ezekiel and Vrinda Nabar (Bombay: Nirmala Sadanand, 1975);

20th Century Kannada Poetry, edited and translated by Sumatheendra Nadig, foreword by Ezekiel (Bangalore: Viswa Kannada Sammelana, 1983);

Artists Today, edited by Ezekiel and Ursula Bickelmann (Bombay: Marg, 1987);

Another India: An Anthology of Contemporary Indian Fiction and Poetry, edited by Ezekiel and Mukherjee (New Delhi & New York: Penguin, 1990).

SELECTED PERIODICAL PUBLICATION–
UNCOLLECTED: "Two Poems," *Form: A Magazine of the Arts* (Dhaka), no. 4 (Spring 1986): 17–18.

Nissim Ezekiel is the first poet of the postindependence phase of Indian poetry in English both chronologically and in significance. By absorbing the lessons of modernism and making his poetic debut in an idiom that has retained its freshness, he set an example for his younger contemporaries and for subsequent generations of Indian poets. Ezekiel's position among contemporary Indo-Anglian poets is that of a patriarch, admired by some but resented by others. Ezekiel and his followers have created a body of verse that evinces the naturalization of the English language to the Indian situation, which earlier Indo-Anglian poets did not do.

Nissim Moses Ezekiel was born in Bombay (today Mumbai) on 16 December 1924, the third child of the three sons and two daughters of Moses and Diana Ezekiel. His father was a professor of biology at Wilson College, and his mother a schoolteacher who later started her own school. The family lived in a *chawl* (tenement) at the time of Ezekiel's birth but soon moved to an apartment. They belonged to the oldest of India's three Jewish communities, the Bene Israel, who sailed from Galilee and settled in rural Maharashtra after being shipwrecked off the Indian subcontinent around 150 B.C. In one of his best-known poems, "Background, Casually" (1976), which is his most comprehensive autobiographical piece in verse or in prose, Ezekiel says:

My ancestors, among the castes,
Were aliens crushing seed for bread
(The hooded bullock made his rounds).

In a footnote Ezekiel says that Bene Israel tradition has it that their ancestors took up oil pressing soon after they arrived in India. In a humorous reversal they became known as *Shanwar-teli* (Saturday oil pressers) because they would *not* work on the Jewish Sabbath. (Rural Maharashtra also had "Friday oil-pressers," who were Muslims, and "Monday oil pressers," who were Hindus.) In the late eighteenth century, members of the

Bene Israel began migrating to the fast-growing metropolis of Bombay and soon made a middle-class niche for themselves. Ezekiel's grandfather, Haskelji Israel, became an army officer, fought in the Boer War, then returned to Talkar and taught school:

One of them fought and taught,
A Major bearing British Arms.
He told my father sad stories
Of the Boer War. I dreamed that
Fierce men had bound my feet and hands.

Ezekiel's schooling began at the convent of Jesus and Mary. In 1934 he transferred to another Catholic institution, the Antonio D'Souza High School. He was an introvert and physically unprepossessing, and although he participated enthusiastically in sports and games, he never made it onto the class teams. He turned to dramatics but forgot his lines onstage, provoking laughter from the audience. "Background, Casually" captures the tenor of his high-school days:

I went to Roman Catholic school,
A mugging Jew among the wolves.
They told me I had killed the Christ,
That year I won the scripture prize.
A Muslim sportsman boxed my ears.

The students read poetry by William Wordsworth; John Keats; Percy Bysshe Shelley; George Gordon, Lord Byron; and Alfred Tennyson. Ezekiel started scribbling verse of his own, which was brought to the notice of the teacher by a fellow student. The teacher sarcastically exclaimed: "Ah, ha, listen, all of you, we have a poet in class." Ezekiel "decided at that moment, whatever happens, I am going to write poetry, good, bad or indifferent."

Ezekiel recalled to his biographer, R. Raj Rao, how reading *The Bhagavad Gita* in 1939 startled him because it conveys a morality different from the Judeo-Christian one. He notes in "Background, Casually" that this experience was the beginning of his lifelong interest in the Indian spiritual tradition:

At home on Friday nights the prayers
Were said. My morals had declined.
I heard of Yoga and of Zen.
Could I perhaps be rabbi-saint?
The more I searched, the less I found.

In 1941 Ezekiel entered Wilson College; he was on a scholarship throughout his four years there. His poems appeared in *Thought,* a periodical edited by K. M. Munshi that paid for poetry–Ezekiel's first earnings as a writer. Under the dual influence of his friend Abraham Solomon and M. N. Roy, the charismatic leader of the Radical Democratic Party, he weaned himself away from religion and stopped going to the synagogue. Ezekiel, like most students, had nationalist sympathies; but unlike most he was critical of the Indian National Congress party. Not even Congress leader Mohandas Karamchand Gandhi, he thought, was above hypocrisy.

Ezekiel graduated in 1945 with a first class in English literature and studied for his M.A. at Bombay University on a two-year fellowship from Wilson College; during one term he taught in a school. He received his M.A. in 1947, winning the top student's prize, and took a job as a lecturer at Khalsa College in Bombay. While there, he put into practice Roy's "principle of cooperative social or community living" by residing for a time in the office of the Radical Democratic Party with other party members; later, he lived in a slum with cadres of the Municipal Workers' Union, of which he was the secretary. He ran unsuccessfully in a municipal election. Ezekiel's attitude to the way independence came about in 1947 was equivocal. He was critical of Gandhi's strategy of noncooperation; he was also distressed at the partition of the country into India and Pakistan, which he thought could have been avoided if congress leader Jawaharlal Nehru had not been so eager to become prime minister of an independent India.

Ezekiel resigned from his lectureship after a year, then led a somewhat footloose existence tutoring; writing poems and prose pieces for *The Times of India, The Free Press Journal,* and *The Bharatiya Vidya Bhavan Journal;* and working for the Radical Democratic Party. He also found a new mentor, Ebrahim Alkazi, the scion of a wealthy Arab family in Bombay. Alkazi had two passions, painting and the theater, which Ezekiel soon came to share. When Alkazi went to study at the Royal Academy of Dramatic Arts (RADA) in London in November 1948, he invited Ezekiel to accompany him. Alkazi paid for Ezekiel's passage and let Ezekiel live in his apartment in London. Ezekiel found a job as a clerk in charge of a weekly newsletter at the Indian High Commission, took courses in Chinese and Western philosophy and art appreciation at the City Literary Institute, and enrolled at Birkbeck College for a B.A. in philosophy but did not complete the course. After a year he gave up the High Commission job to write full-time; but his contributions to such periodicals as *The Strand* and *The Illustrated Weekly of India* brought little remuneration, requiring him to take various odd jobs and borrow from his brother Joe. He recalls in "Background, Casually" that

> . . . Philosophy,
> Poverty and Poetry, three
> Companions shared my basement room.

Cover for Nissim Ezekiel's 1976 collection of twenty-seven poems, which was criticized for two pieces that make fun of "Indian English" (Thomas Cooper Library, University of South Carolina)

Meanwhile, Alkazi finished his three years of training at RADA and returned to India without offering to pay Ezekiel's way back. Ezekiel stayed in London for another year, leading a precarious existence. He wrote prolifically, and seven of the twenty-five poems he sent out were accepted for publication. Before long he had completed the manuscript for his first book. An Indian friend paid the £10 required by Fortune Press, a small vanity, to cover the cost of publishing *A Time to Change and Other Poems* (1952). The poems deal with sin and corruption, women, male-female relationships, pedants, and what Bruce King calls the "quest for physical, social and spiritual integration of the self." He uses rhyme and meter for the most part, but the voice is contemporary and clear. King believes that because it moved away from artificial diction and vague and mystical effusions, the volume marks the true beginning "of the canon of modern Indian English poetry."

After four years in London, Ezekiel returned to India in March 1952 by working as a sailor. When he reached Marseilles, copies of *A Time to Change and Other Poems* had arrived from the publisher, with whom he had left the ship's itinerary. He was interviewed by a journalist for a local newspaper. After forty-eight days, he disembarked at Colombo, Ceylon (today Sri Lanka), and made his way to Bombay. He sums up the experience in "Background, Casually":

> The London seasons passed me by.
> I lay in bed two years alone.
> And then a Woman came to tell
> My willing ears I was the Son
> Of Man. I knew that I had failed.
> In everything, a bitter thought.
> So, in an English cargo-ship
> Taking French guns and mortar shells
> To Indo-China, scrubbed the decks
> And learned to laugh again at home.

"When I returned from England, I became philosophical," Ezekiel told Rao. "That meant being very critical of all ideologies, including one's own. I was prepared to make allowances for all kinds of faults from the highest levels to the lowest, facing the reality, as it were." Within days of his arrival in Bombay, he was hired as a subeditor at the *Illustrated Weekly of India*. His responsibilities included the literature section of the magazine. In November 1952 he married Daisy Jacob Dandekar, also from the Bene Israel; he later described the relationship to Rao as a "semi-love marriage." They had two daughters, Kavita and Kalpana, and a son, Elkana.

In 1953 Ezekiel published his second collection of verse, *Sixty Poems,* and distributed it through Bombay's Strand Bookshop. It consists of poems he had written both before and after those included in *A Time to Change and Other Poems.* King comments that the poems written in the 1950s "express a complex modern mind attempting to integrate and order experience through an appropriate style in which imagery and allusion are part of thought."

Ezekiel resumed his friendship with Alkazi, and the two worked together in the Theatre Group—Alkazi directed plays, and Ezekiel assisted—until a dispute with the other members led them to set up a new group, the Theatre Unit. Alkazi began to display an authoritarian aspect of his personality, and the situation remained unpleasant until he left Bombay to teach at the National School of Drama in Delhi.

Ezekiel tired of his subeditor's job after two years and joined an advertising firm as a copywriter. Sent to New York City for six months' training, of which six weeks were spent visiting cities such as Los Angeles and San Francisco, he learned more about art and poetry than about advertising. Ezekiel held the job until 1959, when he was given a bad evaluation and three months' notice. He then worked for a couple of years as manager of a picture-frame factory, whose owner he persuaded to open an art gallery. He describes the period after his return to India in "Background, Casually":

> How to feel at home, was the point.
> Some reading had been done, but what
> Had I observed, except my own
> Exasperation? All Hindus are
> Like that, my father used to say,
>
> When someone talked too loudly, or
> Knocked at the door like the Devil.
> They hawked and spat. They sprawled around.
> I prepared for the worst. Married,
> Changed jobs, and saw myself a fool.
>
> The song of my experience sung,
> I knew that all was yet to sing.

Ezekiel published his third volume of verse in 1959; titling it simply *The Third,* he distributed it, as he had the previous volume, through the Strand Bookshop. The thirty-six poems, written between 1954 and 1958, include musings on the division between the heart and the intellect, some humorous poems, and poems on love and marriage and on animals.

Much of the poetry in Ezekiel's first three collections is prosodically heavy-footed. He is desperately holding out against the lure of a freer style such as that of William Carlos Williams, to whom he writes, in a parody of the latter's free verse, in "For William Carlos Williams" (in *Sixty Poems*):

> I do not want
> to write
> poetry like yours
> but still I
> love
> the way you do it.

Ezekiel's reputation as an Indian poet writing in English was growing steadily. He found time to talk to young poets about their work, many of whom went on to make significant contributions to poetry. Dom Moraes had been taken by his father to see Ezekiel when the latter was on the staff of the *Illustrated Weekly* and recalled that Ezekiel had impressed on him the importance of technique. Gieve Patel, R. Parthasarathy, Adil Jussawalla, Kamala Das, Eunice de Souza, Saleem Peeradina, Santan Rodrigues, Menka Shivdasani, Tara Patel, Charmayne D'Souza, and Ranjit Hoskote were among those who benefited from Ezekiel's mentorship over the years.

Soon after his return from London, Ezekiel had begun assisting Sophiya Wadiya, head of the Indian chapter of the authors' organization PEN, in editing the organization's newsletter, *Indian PEN,* and the magazine *Aryan Path,* which was not a PEN publication. Ezekiel also served as secretary-treasurer of PEN for several years in the 1950s. From 1955 to 1957 he edited *Quest,* an influential journal of ideas and letters.

In 1958 the publisher P. Lal set up the Writers Workshop in Calcutta. The workshop's Indo-Anglian poetry list is the largest in the subcontinent and includes Ezekiel's next two collections. *The Unfinished Man: Poems Written in 1959* (1961) includes autobiographical poems and poems about Bombay. As the title of the volume indicates, the autobiographical pieces show Ezekiel to be aware of his failings. The penultimate poem in the book, "Case Study," depicts him as mired in an unhappy marriage. King notes that Ezekiel refrains from romanticizing himself, depicting himself with irony and wit as well as with seriousness. He finds the volume "remarkable in its self-scrutinizing psychology and polished craft" and says that it moves from "generalization towards the personal, from complaint to decision and ideal."

In 1961 Ezekiel was briefly manager of *Design* magazine, resigning when he found out that his subordinates were not being paid on time. He then became literary and reviews editor of the literary journal *Imprint.* That same year G. D. Parikh, the registrar of Bombay University and an old Royist, arranged Ezekiel's appointment as lecturer and head of the English department at the newly founded Mithibai College of Arts; he later became vice principal of the college. Around this time he and his wife separated, but they never obtained a divorce. In 1964–1965 Ezekiel was a visiting professor at Leeds University in England, and from 1964 to 1966 he published art criticism in *The Times of India.*

The Exact Name: Poems, 1960–1964 (1965), Ezekiel's fifth collection of verse, marks a change in his style toward free verse and the spoken voice. The volume includes "Night of the Scorpion," which illustrates Ezekiel's mastery of free verse. The matter-of-fact opening ("I remember the night my mother / was stung by a scorpion"), use of repetition ("his poison moved in Mother's blood, they said. / May he sit still, they said. / May the sins of your previous birth be burned away tonight, they said"), and gentle comedy ("My father, skeptic, rationalist, trying every curse and blessing") of the poem make it a favorite of anthologists.

The Exact Name is dedicated to Parthasarathy, who taught at Mithibai College, and Jussawalla who became one of his closest friends. Ezekiel had helped Jussawalla

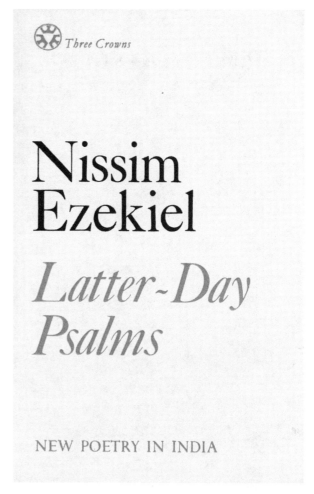

Cover for Ezekiel's final collection of new poems, published in 1982 (Thomas Cooper Library, University of South Carolina)

place his first collection, *Land's End,* with Writers Workshop in 1962. In 1966 Ezekiel published Gieve Patel's first collection, *Poems,* and launched the quarterly *Poetry India,* which ran for six issues before ceasing publication in the spring of 1967.

The most successful of Ezekiel's attempts at conventional forms are "Urban," "Enterprise," and "Marriage," in *The Unfinished Man,* "Philosophy" and "Poet, Lover, Birdwatcher, in *The Exact Name.*" A relaxed lyric grace, subtle imagery, and irony come together in "Poet, Lover, Birdwatcher" in the manner of the poets of "The Movement" in Britain (Philip Larkin, D. J. Enright, and Donald Davie):

> To force the pace and never to be still
> Is not the way of those who study birds
> Or women. The best poets wait for words.
> The hunt is not an exercise of will
> But patient love relaxing on hill
> To note the movement of a timid wing.

SELECTED PROSE

NISSIM EZEKIEL

with an Introduction by
ADIL JUSSAWALLA

PR
9499.3
.E9
A6
1992

DELHI
OXFORD UNIVERSITY PRESS
BOMBAY CALCUTTA MADRAS
1992

Title page for a collection that includes Ezekiel's essay that criticizes V. S. Naipaul's An Area of Darkness *(1964) for its unrelentingly negative view of India (Thomas Cooper Library, University of South Carolina)*

Hess, an American specialist on the works of the Hindu mystical poet Kabir, whom he met when she visited India in 1966. The affair continued the following year when Ezekiel lectured on Indo-Anglian literature at the University of Chicago and lasted until the mid 1970s. Ezekiel claimed that his experience with drugs in the 1960s led him to recognize a divine presence in the universe. Thenceforth, this recognition qualifies his rationalistic skepticism. His dramas *Nalini: A Comedy in Three Acts, Marriage Poem: A One-Act Tragi-Comedy,* and *The Sleepwalkers: An Indoamerican Farce* were collected as *Three Plays* in 1969. The plays are preoccupied with ideas rather than character or action, which is one reason they have not been particularly successful. Ezekiel retired from teaching at Mithibai College in 1972. That same year *Indian Pen* became a full-fledged journal, and Ezekiel and Urmilla Rao were made joint executive editors. In 1973 he presented an art series on Bombay television. He traveled in the United States under the American State Department's International Visitor Leadership Program in 1974 and was a Cultural Award Visitor to Australia in 1975.

In 1976 the Indian branch of Oxford University Press launched a new poetry series, and Ezekiel's Oxford collections *Hymns in Darkness* (1976) and *Latter-Day Psalms* (1982) made his work available to a much wider readership. Most of the twenty-seven poems in *Hymns in Darkness* were written while Ezekiel was teaching at Mithibai College. They include one of his most popular poems, the hilarious "Goodbye Party for Miss Pushpa T. S.," based on his jotting down of the imperfect English of Gujratis—among them the principal of the college. This poem and "The Railway Clerk," in which he also uses "Indian English," were criticized for making fun of Indians. There are also found poems, derived from newspaper reports, and poster poems, which are collections of aphorisms. Like his previous collections, the volume offers poems about love and relationships, such as "The Couple" and "Poem of the Separation"—the latter marking the end of his relationship with Hess—and about Bombay. It also includes poems on religious themes, such as "Guru," "Tribute to the Upanishads," and the long title poem that concludes the volume: it is a prayer, modeled on an Old Testament form, of a "skeptical seeker." The autobiographical "Background, Casually" is also found in this collection; its final lines reveal that Ezekiel had decided to cast his lot irrevocably with the city of his birth:

From the same period comes "In India," in *The Exact Name,* with its insistent three or four beats to a line and mixture of metrical and free verse. King observes in *Three Indian Poets: Nissim Ezekiel, A. K. Ramanujan, Dom Moraes* (1991) that Ezekiel "often likes four iambic feet to a line." He is particularly successful in using the form with satiric intent, as in "Marriage":

> I went through this, believing all,
> Our love denied the Primal Fall.
> Wordless, we walked among the trees,
> And felt immortal as the breeze.

After his separation from his wife, Ezekiel's lifestyle changed in a way characteristic of the time: he began using marijuana and LSD and had many love affairs. The most serious relationship was with Linda

> I have made my commitments now.
> This is one: to stay where I am,
> As others choose to give themselves
> In some remote and backward place.
> My background place is where I am.

Rao notes that by the time *Hymns in Darkness* was published, Ezekiel had become "a star" in the Indian poetic scene. Similarly, King comments that Ezekiel had become "an example" to young Indian poets writing in English and that they began imitating his "secular prayers, confessional autobiographies, poems of the urban landscape" and poems that were "argumentative yet conversational."

Latter-Day Psalms is the final volume of new verse that Ezekiel published. It includes a sequence of ten poems ironically treating biblical Psalms; other poems have Indian settings and situations and make humorous use of Indian English. "Jewish Wedding in Bombay" recalls his marriage ceremony, and the sequence "Nudes" deals with his affairs. *Latter-Day Psalms* won the prestigious Sahitya Akademi Award.

From 1980 to 1983 briefly edited *Freedom First*, a political journal. In 1985 he was a delegate to a United States Information Service–sponsored American Studies conference in Lahore. The following year he attended the Commonwealth Writers Conference in Edinburgh. After Wadiya's death in 1986 he took over as editor of *Indian PEN*. In 1988 he received the Padma Shri, India's highest civic honor. Oxford University Press published his *Collected Poems 1952–1988* in 1989. In 1990 Ezekiel visited Glasgow, Europe's "Cultural Capital" of the year. His *Selected Prose* was published by Oxford University Press in 1992. It includes the masterly "Naipaul's India and Mine," a complex, richly textured essay that will enhance any reader's understanding of the complexities of South Asian reality. Macmillan of India published his play *Don't Call It Suicide* in 1993.

In May 1994 Ezekiel told his biographer, Rao, that he had put together a new collection that he would send to Oxford University Press in a week; nothing more was heard of it. By this time Ezekiel was displaying early signs of Alzheimer's disease. In August 1998 he collapsed at a meeting and was rushed to a hospital, where the diagnosis of Alzheimer's was made. He died on 9 January 2004.

Nissim Ezekiel was the first major figure in Indo-Anglian poetry to find a resonant and authentic Indian voice. His position in the postcolonial canon is secure. K. R. Srinivasa Iyengar commends him for his lucidity, "careful craftsmanship," and ironic vision. M. K. Naik declares him "easily one of the most notable post-independence Indian writers of verse" and notes that at his best he is able to create "something more than minor verse" out of his "sense of alienation" from his surroundings and his self-doubt. Naik also praises Ezekiel for "technical skill of a high order" and a "mastery of the colloquial idiom" that is "matched by a sure command of rhythm and rhyme." William Walsh calls his poetry "lucid, rhythmically subtle, scrupulously honest in its effort to be accurate, calm, deliberate." In *Modern Indian Poetry in English* (1987) King sums up Ezekiel's importance: "Of the group of poets attempting to create a modern English poetry in India, Nissim Ezekiel soon emerged as the leader who advised others, set standards, and created places of publication. . . . Ezekiel brought a sense of discipline, self-criticism and mastery to Indian English poetry. . . . The opening up of Indian poetry to reality in its many guises is perhaps Ezekiel's most significant influence."

Biography:

R. Raj Rao, *Nissim Ezekiel: The Authorized Biography* (Delhi: Viking, 2000).

References:

Bruce King, *Modern Indian Poetry in English* (Delhi & Oxford: Oxford University Press, 1987, pp. 91–109);

King, *Three Indian Poets: Nissim Ezekiel, A. K. Ramanujan, Dom Moraes* (Delhi: Oxford University Press, 1991);

P. N. Lal, *The Poetry of Encounter: Dom Moraes, A. K. Ramanujan and Nissim Ezekiel* (New Delhi: Sterling, 1983);

Dom Moraes, *My Son's Father: An Autobiography* (London: Secker & Warburg, 1968);

M. K. Naik, *A History of Indian English Literature* (Delhi: Sahitya Akademi, 1982);

Saleem Peeradina, ed., *Contemporary Indian Poetry in English* (Bombay: Macmillan, 1972), pp. xiv, 1–4;

Anisur Rahman, *Form and Value in the Poetry of Nissim Ezekiel* (New Delhi: Abhinav, 1981);

K. R. Srinivasa Iyengar, *Indian Writing in English,* fifth edition (New Delhi: Sterling, 1985), pp. 657–660;

William Walsh, *Indian Literature in English* (London: Longman, 1990), pp. 127–136.

Mohandas Karamchand Gandhi

(2 October 1869 – 30 January 1948)

Christel R. Devadawson
University of Delhi

SELECTED BOOKS IN ENGLISH: *Mahatma Gandhi: His Life, Writings and Speeches* (Madras: Ganesh, 1917; enlarged, 1918, 1921);

Speeches and Writings of M. K. Gandhi, introduction by C. F. Andrews (Madras: Natesan, 1918; enlarged, 1922); enlarged as *Speeches and Writings of Mahatma Gandhi* (Madras: Natesan, 1933);

Indian Home Rule (Madras: Ganesh, 1919; revised, 1922); republished as *Hind Swaraj, or, Indian Home Rule* (Madras: Natesan, 1921; revised, Ahmedabad: Navajivan, 1938);

Freedom's Battle, Being a Comprehensive Collection of Writings and Speeches on the Present Situation (Madras: Ganesh, 1921);

Young India, 1919–1922, introduction by Rajendra Prasad (Madras: Ganesan, 1922; New York: Huebsch, 1923; revised, Madras: Ganesan, 1924);

Young India, 1924–1926, introduction by Prasad (Madras: Ganesan, 1927; New York: Viking, 1927);

The Story of My Experiments with Truth, 2 volumes, translated by Mahadev Desai and Pyarelal (Ahmedabad: Navajivan, 1927, 1929); republished in one volume as *An Autobiography; or, The Story of My Experiments with Truth* (Ahmedabad: Navajivan, 1940); republished as *An Autobiography: The Story of My Experiments with Truth* (London: Phoenix Press, 1949; Boston: Beacon, 1957); abridged as *Autobiography* (Bombay: Hind Kitabs, 1950);

Satyagraha in South Africa, translated by Valji Govindji Desai (Madras: Ganesan, 1928; revised, Ahmedabad: Navajivan, 1950; Stanford, Cal.: Academic Reprints, 1954);

From Yeravda Mandir: Ashram Observances, translated by Valji Govindji Desai (Ahmedabad: Navajivan, 1932);

India's Case for Swaraj, edited by Waman P. Kabadi (Bombay: Yeshanand, 1932);

My Early Life, 1869–1914, edited by Mahadev Desai (Bombay: Oxford University Press, 1932);

Mohandas Karamchand Gandhi
(AP World Wide)

Selections from Gandhi, edited by Nirmal Kumar Bose (Calcutta: Navavidhan Publication Committee, 1934; enlarged, Ahmedabad: Navajivan, 1957);

Young India, 1927–1928, edited by Prasad (Madras: Ganesan, 1935);

The Unseen Power, edited by Jag Parvesh Chander (Lahore: Free India, 1937);

Christian Missions, Their Place in India (Ahmedabad: Navajivan, 1941; revised, 1957);

Constructive Programme, Its Meaning and Place (Ahmedabad: Navajivan, 1941; revised and enlarged, 1945);

Economics of Khadi (Ahmedabad: Navajivan, 1941);

The Indian States' Problem (Ahmedabad: Navajivan, 1941);

My Appeal to the British, edited by Anand T. Hingorani (New York: John Day, 1942);

Quit India, edited by R. K. Prabhu and U. R. Rao (Bombay: Padma, 1942);

Women and Social Injustice (Ahmedabad: Navajivan, 1942);

Non-Violence in Peace & War, by Gandhi, Mahadev Desai, and Pyarelal, 2 volumes (Ahmedabad: Navajivan, 1942, 1949; New York: Garland, 1972); selections republished as *Gandhi on Non-Violence,* edited by Thomas Merton (New York: New Directions, 1965);

Ethics of Fasting, edited by Chander (Lahore: Indian Printing Works, 1944);

The Mind of Mahatma Gandhi, edited by Prabhu and Rao (London, Bombay & New York: Oxford University Press, 1945; revised and enlarged, Ahmedabad: Navajivan, 1967);

Delhi Diary: Prayer Speeches from 10-9-47 to 30-1-48 (Ahmedabad: Navajivan, 1948);

Ashram Observances in Action, translated by Valji Govindji Desai (Ahmedabad: Navajivan, 1955).

Collections: *Mahatma Gandhi: His Own Story,* edited by C. F. Andrews, introduction by John Haynes Holmes (London: Allen & Unwin, 1930; New York: Macmillan, 1930)—comprises selections from *The Story of My Experiments with Truth* and *Satyagraha in South Africa;* revised and enlarged as *Mahatma Gandhi at Work: His Own Story Continued* (London: Allen & Unwin, 1931; New York: Macmillan, 1931)—includes a selection from *Indian Home Rule;*

The Mahatma and the Missionary: Selected Writing of Mohandas K. Gandhi, edited by Clifford Manshardt (Chicago: Regnery, 1949);

Satyagraha: Non-Violent Resistance, edited by Bharatan Kumarappa (Ahmedabad: Navajivan, 1951); republished as *Non-Violent Resistance* (New York: Schocken, 1961);

Selected Writings of Mahatma Gandhi, edited, with an introduction, by Ronald Duncan (London: Faber & Faber, 1951; Boston: Beacon, 1951); republished as *Gandhi: Selected Writings* (New York: Harper & Row, 1972);

The Wit and Wisdom of Gandhi, edited, with an introduction, by Homer A. Jack, preface by Holmes (Boston: Beacon, 1951);

Sarvodaya: The Welfare of All, edited by Kumarappa (Ahmedabad: Navajivan, 1954);

The Gandhi Reader: A Source Book of His Life and Writings, edited by Jack (Bloomington: Indiana University Press, 1956; London: Dobson, 1958);

Economic and Industrial Life and Relations, 3 volumes, edited by V. B. Kher (Ahmedabad: Navajivan, 1957);

All Men Are Brothers: Life and Thoughts of Mahatma Gandhi, edited by Krishna Kirpalani (New York: Columbia University Press / Paris: UNESCO, 1958); republished as *All Men Are Brothers: Autobiographical Reflections* (New York: Continuum, 1980);

The Collected Works of Mahatma Gandhi, 100 volumes (New Delhi: Publications Division, Ministry of Information and Broadcasting, Government of India, 1958–1994);

In Search of the Supreme, 3 volumes, edited by Kher (Ahmedabad: Navajivan, 1961);

The Essential Gandhi: An Anthology, edited by Louis Fischer (New York: Random House, 1962; London: Allen & Unwin, 1963);

The Selected Works of Mahatma Gandhi, 6 volumes, edited by Shriman Narayan (Ahmedabad: Navajivan, 1968);

Gandhi: Essential Writings, edited by V. V. Ramana Murti (New Delhi: Gandhi Peace Foundation, 1970);

The Words of Gandhi, edited by Richard Attenborough (New York: Newmarket Press, 1982);

The Quintessence of Gandhi in His Own Words, edited by Shakti Batra (New Delhi: Madhu Muskan, 1984);

The Moral and Political Writings of Mahatma Gandhi, 3 volumes, edited by Raghavan Iyer (Oxford: Clarendon Press, 1986–1987)—comprises volume 1, *Civilization, Politics, and Religion;* volume 2, *Truth and Non-Violence;* and volume 3, *Non-Violent Resistance and Social Transformation;*

Gandhi in India, in His Own Words, edited by Martin Green (Hanover, N.H.: University Press of New England, 1987);

A Gandhi Reader, edited by K. Swaminathan and C. N. Patel (Madras: Orient Longman, 1988);

The Essential Writings of Mahatma Gandhi, edited by Iyer (Delhi & Oxford: Oxford University Press, 1991);

The Penguin Gandhi Reader, edited by Rudrangshu Mukherjee (New Delhi & New York: Penguin, 1993);

Mahatma Gandhi: Selected Political Writings, edited, with an introduction, by Dennis Dalton (Indianapolis: Hackett, 1996);

Hind Swaraj and Other Writings, edited by Anthony J. Parel (Cambridge & New York: Cambridge University Press, 1997);

Mohandas Gandhi: Essential Writings, edited by John Dear (Maryknoll, N.Y.: Orbis, 2002).

OTHER: *Songs from Prison,* translated by Gandhi, edited by John S. Hoyland (London: Allen & Unwin, 1934; New York: Macmillan, 1934);

R. P. Masani, *Dadabhai Naoroji: The Grand Old Man of India,* foreword by Gandhi (London: Allen & Unwin, 1939);

The Gospel of Selfless Action, or, The Gita according to Gandhi, translated, with an introduction, by Mahadev Desai (Ahmedabad: Navajivan, 1946);

Shriman Narayan, *Gandhian Constitution for Free India,* foreword by Gandhi (Allahabad: Kitabistan, 1946);

John Ruskin, *Unto This Last: A Paraphrase by M. K. Gandhi,* translated by Valji Govindji Desai (Ahmedabad: Navajivan, 1956).

Mohandas Karamchand Gandhi's anxiety that he might be the first person in twentieth-century India to undertake an autobiography unintentionally obscures the fact that he came to write about his life after a career in journalism in South Africa and India. He translated from and into Gujarati and English—and occasionally Hindi as well—in the journals that he edited. He developed his own theory and practice of combining journalism, translation, and autobiography to suit the exigencies of the moment and to further his ongoing philosophical revolution.

In *Mahatma Gandhi: Political Saint and Unarmed Prophet* (1973) Dhananjay Keer describes Gandhi as "a perfect blend of a *bania* [a merchant by caste], a barrister, and a *bairagi* [a wandering mendicant and holy man]." Gandhi was born on 2 October 1869 into a family that seemed equally likely to offer an opening into these different ways of life. He was the youngest of the six children of Karamchand "Kaba" Gandhi and his fourth wife, Putlibai Gandhi. Kaba Gandhi was the *diwan* (chief minister) successively of Porbandar, Rajkot, and Vankaner, former princely states of Kathiawar, all of which were absorbed into the state of Gujarat in independent India. In his autobiography, *The Story of My Experiments with Truth* (1927, 1929), Gandhi suggests the kinds of experience to which he had access, stating that his father's "rich experience of practical affairs stood him in good stead in the solution of the most intricate questions and in managing hundreds of men. . . . The outstanding impression my mother has left on my memory is that of saintliness."

Gandhi's marriage at the age of thirteen to Kasturbai Poddar (also thirteen at the time), his mediocre education, and the death of his father in 1886 seemed to dim his prospects. The plan put forward by some of

his acquaintances, however, that he should study law in England, seemed to him to suggest a bright future. In "Why He Went to England" (*The Vegetarian,* 13 August 1891) he recalled, "I thought to myself, if I go to England, not only shall I become a barrister . . . but I shall be able to see England, the land of philosophers and poets, the very centre of civilisation."

Apart from Gandhi's early misadventures in London as a hesitant man-about-town, the years from 1888, when he enrolled as a student at the Inner Temple, to 1891, when he was called to the bar and returned to India, were uneventful. They earned him only the status of a "briefless barrister," as he writes in his autobiography. The offer of a post as legal adviser to a firm of traders of Indian origin in South Africa seemed providential. In 1893 Gandhi sailed for Natal, leaving behind his wife and first two sons, Harlal, born in 1888, and Manilal, born in 1892.

Despite his involvement in the affairs of his client and his efforts at general social uplift for the inward-looking Indian community in South Africa, Gandhi's most strenuous efforts at writing at this time were devoted to working on a guide to London for the overseas student likely to be overwhelmed by the city, as he had once felt himself to be. In retrospect, an extract from this manuscript seems comically out of character for Gandhi, who was later dismissed by Winston Churchill as a "fakir . . . striding half-naked up the steps of the Viceregal Palace":

> The white shirts have been left out [of a list compiled for the reader] because they swell the weekly washing bill. . . . If the fashion goddess is to be adored as it ought to be more or less . . . use the white collars and cuffs and you would lead others to believe that you have white shirts on. This trick is resorted to by thousands in London . . .

While Gandhi's concern for detail and the symbolic fitness of dress resurfaced later in a radically different world, the writing here is pure comedy. It offered an escape from the ugly realities of the world in which he found himself.

In South Africa, Gandhi learned to interpret different kinds of discrimination, including the sullen anger felt by the Boers toward the British (chiefly the administrative class), the superiority both felt in regard to the Indians (primarily traders and indentured laborers), the religious divisions within the Indian community, and the contempt everyone showed toward the indigenous peoples of southern Africa. Biographers such as Raja Rao have seen the change of life these tensions generated in Gandhi as centering on an episode in Pietermaritzburg, where he was ejected from a first-class railway carriage despite his possession of a valid ticket.

The stages in Gandhi's transformation were slow but deliberate. In 1894, at a farewell party organized for him by Dada Abdulla, head of the firm for which he had worked successfully, he learned that the South African government was planning to deny Indians the franchise so as to marginalize and ultimately expel them. Most Indians had immigrated to South Africa as laborers and remained after the expiration of their indenture to become successful traders. The Indian community asked Gandhi to prolong his stay to help secure them the vote. The immediate action he took was to set up the Natal Indian Congress in order to educate public opinion. As honorary secretary, he drew up its constitution. The objectives of the congress suggest the importance Gandhi attached to the need to sensitize people if they were to be changed from a faction into a community: "to do everything that would tend to put the Indians on a better footing morally, socially, intellectually and politically."

From 1895 to 1914 Gandhi developed strategies of resistance to South African authority and deployed these strategies as part of a liberation movement. His third and fourth sons, Ramdas (1897) and Devadas (1900), were also born during this period. In 1895 Gandhi launched a campaign against the reindenture clause in the Indian Immigration Bill. The campaign included a general strike, a series of mass meetings, the implementation of satyagraha (pressure for reform through passive resistance), the establishment of the Phoenix Settlement near Durban as an experiment in an alternative way of life, and a protest march from Durban to Volksrust. In 1903 Gandhi established *Indian Opinion,* the first of a series of periodicals in which he set out his ideals before the constituency he wished to influence. The journal, based in Durban, was divided into Gujarati, English, Hindi, and Tamil sections.

Gandhi attempted to create a society based on values other than the orthodoxies of a religious past or a political present. This aim can be seen in the use he made of his correspondence with Leo Tolstoy, which he translated into Gujarati. He reminded his readers of the values Tolstoy upheld, such as love, nonviolence, and independence of spirit. Gandhi hammered home the doctrine of passive resistance advocated by Tolstoy, who urged Indians to refuse to cooperate with the British government. It is hard to believe that the following words from the preface to Tolstoy's "Letter to a Hindoo" (*Indian Opinion,* 25 December 1909) are Gandhi's judicious selections from Tolstoy rather than Gandhi speaking in his own voice: "Do not resist evil, but also yourselves participate not in evil. . . . A commercial

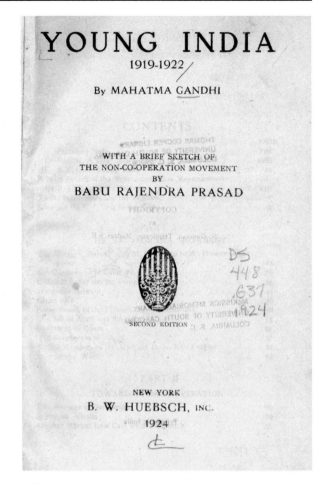

Title page for the second American edition of the 1922 compilation of Gandhi's articles from the English-language weekly he began editing in 1919 (Thomas Cooper Library, University of South Carolina)

company enslaved a nation comprising 200 millions. . . . Do not the figures make it clear that not the English but the Indians have enslaved themselves?" Gandhi used Tolstoy's message to the people of India to sensitize Indians in South Africa. When he wrote later in his autobiography of the social responsibility of a leader to build up a relationship between himself and his community through his writings for them, he referred to the centrality of *Indian Opinion:*

Week after week I poured out my soul in its columns, and expounded the principles and practice of *Satyagraha* as I understood it. . . . The readers looked forward to it for a trustworthy account of the *Satyagraha* campaign as also of the real condition of Indians in South Africa. For me it became a means for the study of human nature in all its casts and shades, as I always aimed at establishing an intimate and clean bond between the editor and the readers.

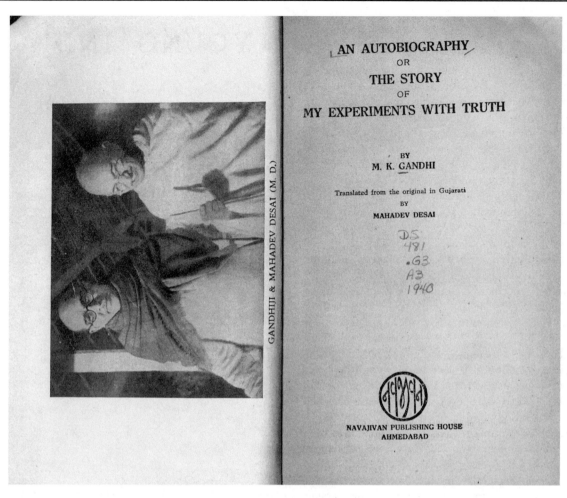

GANDHIJI & MAHADEV DESAI (M. D.)

AN AUTOBIOGRAPHY
OR
THE STORY
OF
MY EXPERIMENTS WITH TRUTH

BY
M. K. GANDHI

Translated from the original in Gujarati
BY
MAHADEV DESAI

DS
481
.G3
A3
1940

NAVAJIVAN PUBLISHING HOUSE
AHMEDABAD

Title page for the 1940 edition of Gandhi's autobiography, originally published in two volumes as The Story of My Experiments with Truth *in 1927 and 1929 (Thomas Cooper Library, University of South Carolina)*

Gandhi concerned himself with making texts originally in English available to this same constituency. For example, he translated John Ruskin's *Unto this Last* (1862) into Gujarati. In championing equality of opportunity, Ruskin seemed to Gandhi to offer an alternative to utilitarianism, which merely sought the good of the greatest number. Gandhi's preface to his translation suggests his attitude to Ruskin's text and his philosophy of adaptation: "We present therefore only the substance of Ruskin's work. We do not even explain what the title of the book means, for it can be understood only by a person who has read the Bible in English. But since the object which the book works towards is the welfare of all—that is, the advancement of all and not merely of the greatest number—we have entitled these articles 'Sarvodaya.'" Gandhi's Gujarati adaptation was translated into English by Valji Govindji Desai and published posthumously as *Unto This Last: A Paraphrase by M. K. Gandhi* (1956).

Gandhi's most sustained effort to raise public awareness during the early phase of his activism was a report on the condition of India that he wrote during a return voyage to Natal from London, where he had gone to argue the case for the Indian community in South Africa. The report, originally published in *Indian Opinion* (11 and 18 December 1909), was titled *Hind Swaraj*. In March 1910 the British government in India seized the Gujarati version, now a booklet, claiming it included seditious matter. Gandhi dictated the English translation, titled *Indian Home Rule* (1919), the following month to Herman Kallenbach, his partner in the Phoenix Settlement.

Hind Swaraj takes the form of a dialogue between an editor who analyzes India under colonial rule and an anxious reader. The underlying principle is that India and England alike were enslaved by commerce. This premise was radical, dispelling two powerful myths: that colonization was a civilizing mission and that British strength sustained the empire. Gandhi writes, "The English have not taken India; we have given it to them. They are not in India because of their strength, but because we keep . . . the English in India for our base self-interest." He suggests that this compulsive materialism was the product of industrialization, which shaped Europe and was beginning to shape India. Machinery was the motive and symbol of a civilization based on material greed. As Gandhi recounts in his autobiography, Indian politician Gopal Krishna Gokhale (a moderate on the question of British rule) sensed the doctrinaire quality of *Hind Swaraj*, stating, "After you have stayed a year in India, your views will correct themselves." Yet, Michael Edwardes's claim in *The Myth of the Mahatma: Gandhi, the British, and the Raj* (1986) that "anglophobia spews out" of the text seems unjustified. *Hind Swaraj* presents the consequences not of a clash of civilizations but of complicity between them, leading to the injury of both.

Gandhi left South Africa for India just before the outbreak of World War I. He spent the year 1915 largely in familiarizing himself with the state of affairs in the country. In 1917 he led agitation in Champaran on behalf of indigo farmers, and the following year he organized a campaign of satyagraha in Ahmedabad in support of mill workers. In April 1919 he launched an all-India satyagraha campaign for freedom, along with a nationwide *hartal* (strike). The government sought to suppress agitation, and martial law was declared after troops opened fire on unarmed civilian protesters in Jallianwala Bagh. Gandhi suspended the satyagraha to atone for his mistaken belief that the public could have resisted provocations to violence.

Gandhi did not abandon satyagraha, but he realized that, as in South Africa, he needed to educate public opinion. In the fall of 1919 he was offered the editorship of *Navajivan*, a Gujarati monthly, and of *Young India*, an English-language weekly intended to replace *The Chronicle*, which had been suppressed. Gandhi shifted both journals to Ahmedabad so that they could be published from his own press, independent of the need for advertising revenue. His writing continued to play an integral part in his political work. In both fields he responded to a particular situation (the imposition of martial law) and to a general philosophical imperative, to explain his commitment to nonviolence as an instrument of political and moral change. As he recalls in his autobiography, "Through these journals I now commenced to the best of my ability the work of educating the reading public in *Satyagraha*. . . . [They] helped me also to some extent to remain at peace with myself, for whilst immediate resort to *Satyagraha* was out of the question, they enabled me freely to ventilate my views and to put heart into the people."

Gandhi's ideology and practice in his writings for *Navajivan* and *Indian Opinion* are powerful because they are indirect. An example may be found in the two-part article "Living on the Past" (*Navajivan,* June 1920), in answer to the suspension of satyagraha. A condemnation of the government might have been almost a reflex response. Instead, Gandhi denounces those who claim a golden age for Indian culture located safely in the distant past. He censures this view as an instance of national inertia and escape from public commitment, asking why cultural stereotypes continue to be marketed. Gandhi quotes various claims—for example, "It was the Hindus who perfected the science of grammar. The *Ramayana* and the *Mahabharata* still remain unrivalled"—and replies, "I do not know how far these statements are true, but this I know, that, if the late Justice Ranade [Mahadev Govind Ranade, jurist, historian, and social reformer with a special interest in women's rights] were alive today and heard such talk of India's past glory, he would certainly have asked, 'So what?'" In the second part of the article Gandhi excoriates national hypocrisy: "we are always pointing out their faults to the British and will continue to do so. . . . [Yet we] make some self-sacrifice in family matters, but very little of it for national work." Gandhi used *Navajivan* to create a sense of shared nationhood in order to facilitate political change rather than merely demand it.

Gandhi's flexibility of thought in his journalism may be seen in the conversation with a student recorded in *Young India* (13, 20 November 1924). Gandhi counters the quintessential undergraduate query on the platonic trinity of beauty, truth, and goodness with a firm reminder of contemporary reality:

> I must think in terms of the millions. And to the millions we cannot give that training to acquire a perception of Beauty, in such a way as to see Truth in it. Show them Truth first, and they will see Beauty afterwards. Orissa [an Indian state devastated at that time by famine] haunts me in my waking hours and in my dreams. Whatever can be useful to those starving millions is beautiful to my mind.

Regardless of the route he took to reach it, Gandhi's goal in his writing was always the same: to shape the nation in terms of a particular kind of ideology and commitment.

The clearest definition of Gandhi's ideology appears in *Satyagraha in South Africa*. In 1922 the noncooperation movement was suspended throughout India because of outbreaks of violence, and Gandhi was imprisoned. He began writing this work in jail, as he realized that it was important for him to define the compulsions of satyagraha to the public. It was published first in *Navajivan* in Gujarati, and Desai then translated it into English for *Current*

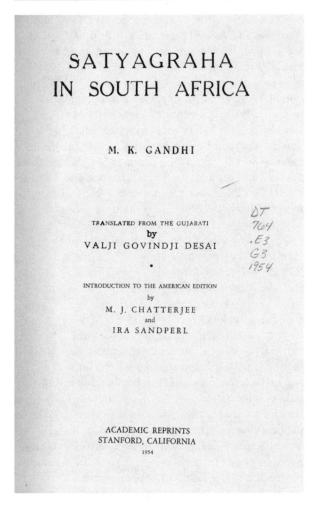

SATYAGRAHA
IN SOUTH AFRICA

M. K. GANDHI

TRANSLATED FROM THE GUJARATI
by
VALJI GOVINDJI DESAI

•

INTRODUCTION TO THE AMERICAN EDITION
by
M. J. CHATTERJEE
and
IRA SANDPERL

ACADEMIC REPRINTS
STANFORD, CALIFORNIA
1954

*Title page for the American edition of Gandhi's 1928 account of his
struggles on behalf of the Indian community in South Africa
(Thomas Cooper Library, University of South Carolina)*

Thought. The translation was published in book form in 1928. Gandhi wanted to explain that nonviolence was not a synonym for cowardice but a weapon of moral force. In *Hind Swaraj* he had used the condition of India to motivate the Indian community in South Africa. In *Satyagraha in South Africa* he recalled the crises of the Indian community in the Transvaal in order to inspire the people of India at a difficult point in the freedom struggle. In 1906 a meeting of Indians had been convened in Johannesburg to oppose anti-Asiatic legislation. The meeting had adopted Gandhi's resolution supporting nonviolent direct action as a means of opposition to government. In *Satyagraha in South Africa* he retells this experience to educate public consciousness in India. Satyagraha, he explains, is an instrument of opposition, which depends on the conscience of the individual for the success of the community: "Every one must only search his own heart, and if the inner voice assures him

that he has the requisite strength to carry him through, then only should he pledge himself. . . ."

Gandhi began writing his autobiography, *The Story of My Experiments with Truth,* in Gujarati in 1925, the year in which he completed *Satyagraha in South Africa.* The English translation was prepared under Gandhi's supervision and serialized in *Young India.* The first volume was published in 1927 and the second in 1929. A single-volume edition was published in 1940 as *An Autobiography; or, The Story of My Experiments with Truth.* Gandhi speculates at first on the relationship between culture and modes of expression: "Writing an autobiography is a practice peculiar to the West. I know of nobody in the East having written one, except amongst those who have come under Western influence." He had reservations about autobiography as a form because of its Western heritage and thought the sense of permanence in such a work obstructed the development of both the subject and his readers. He negotiates these difficulties by pointing out that while his public life was known throughout the world, he alone knew the spiritual life that complemented it. This spiritual life comprised a series of experiments. Although conducted in the public domain, they were continuing applications of a personal understanding of what constituted truth. According to Gandhi, since the personal and the political are expressions alike of attempts to realize the truth, they have to be considered together as part of a single record.

In *The Story of My Experiments with Truth,* Gandhi discusses his decision to commit himself to a life of *brahmacharya* (celibacy). He asserts that self-denial in one's private life is essential for a life of significant public action: "In a word, I could not live both after the flesh and the spirit." He does not indicate the feelings of his wife, who died in 1944, on this issue. Gandhi's musings on the perils of being considered a mahatma (great soul) are ironic and therefore more revealing. He wonders whether fame is less or more helpful than anonymity: "I felt as though I was between the devil and the deep sea. Where no one recognised me, I had to put up with the hardships that fall to the lot of the millions in this land. . . . Where I was surrounded by people who had heard of me I was the victim of their craze for *darshan* [audience]." Confession, however, soon becomes commentary. Gandhi's public life terminates the autobiography. He reminds the reader that after 1921 he lived entirely in the public arena. The history of his life after this time became increasingly that of the Indian freedom struggle. The 1930 march to Dandi to oppose the tax on salt; the second Round Table Conference in London in 1931; the 1942 dismissal of Stafford Cripps's proposal of dominion status for India after the conclusion of the war as "a post-dated cheque on a failing bank"; the launching of the Quit India movement in 1942; and Gandhi's assassination on 30 January 1948 were defining moments in the movement toward independence and beyond.

Gandhi attempted another kind of writing as well: a history of life lived in religious communities. He wrote this account in Gujarati, working on it in installments throughout his jail term in 1932. He gave the manuscripts to Kakasaheb Kalelkar on his release but said they needed revision. In 1948, after Gandhi's assassination, they were published in Gujarati as *Satyagrahashramno Itihas.* Desai translated the text into English, and in 1955 it was published as *Ashram Observances in Action.* It traces the development of different communities set up by Gandhi, including the Phoenix Settlement (1904) and Tolstoy Farm (1910) in South Africa, as well as the Satyagraha (or Sabarmati) Ashram (1915) and Sevagram (1936) in Gujarat. The text sets out and interprets ashram rules and observances. Gandhi analyzes the right kind of life in community. One of the more complicated subjects of the book is the division of Indian society based on *varna* (caste). On the one hand, Gandhi insists that the caste system is no protector of hierarchy and must operate in a world cleansed of untouchability. On the other, he advocates a hereditary choice of occupation so long as no one earns more than a living wage. Later, he makes clear that only marriages between untouchables and caste Hindus could be celebrated in his presence. While *Ashram Observances in Action* is a record of these tentative exercises, they are difficult to explain or follow.

Some facts should be remembered when considering the writings of Gandhi. The first is their combination of bulk and ephemera. The standard set is the hundred-volume *Collected Works of Mahatma Gandhi* (1958–1994), published by the Indian government. Yet, a great deal of this collection is taken up by Gandhi's daily correspondence. According to Raghavan Iyer in his introduction to volume one of *The Moral and Political Writings of Mahatma Gandhi* (1986–1987), "Despite the vast amount of proliferating literature on Mahatma Gandhi, there has yet been no accessible and coherent record of his essential writings. . . . [Gandhi's] actual books were few, short and somewhat inconclusive. . . . His unfinished autobiography and several popular biographies remain the chief–and rather misleading–sources of public knowledge about the personality and impact of Gandhi."

Translation is another concern. Gandhi's original writings in English are to be found in the columns of his journals; he wrote all of his book-length works in Gujarati. Some were originally published serially in his journals. They were translated into English not by Gandhi but by others under his supervision. *Hind Swaraj,* for which he dictated the English version, is the only possible exception. Gandhi's own attitude to translation is complicated, as is seen in regard to Ruskin. To Gandhi, the importance of a translation was the sum of its ability

Front cover for the 2002 compilation that includes autobiographical, political, and spiritual writings as well as speeches and letters (Richland County Public Library)

to communicate the social message of the original text. As he states in "Higher Education" (1938),

> India has to flourish in her own climate, and scenery, and her own literature, even though all the three may be inferior to the English climate, scenery, and literature. We and our children must build on our own heritage. If we borrow another, we impoverish our own. . . . Why need I learn English to get at the best of what Shakespeare and Milton thought and wrote?

This statement raises issues such as cultural protectionism, the definition of a good translation, and the relationship between literature and nation building. As far as Gandhi was concerned–despite his reservations concerning English language and literature–most readers were familiar only with his writings in English. They might keep in mind the value he set on translation, which he saw as a vehicle for the communication of a social or ideological message and not something with literary value in itself.

Finally, there is the question of Gandhi's representation of himself and the social and political revolution he spearheaded. He depended on two principles for his writing. One was that his private life was lived entirely in the public domain. The other was that his writing was an extension of his public life. History, biography, fiction, and cinema attest to the transformational quality of his public life. A suggestion has been made, however, that this quality is better seen through the epic rather than through any other medium. As Rao writes in *The Great Indian Way: A Life of Mahatma Gandhi* (1998), "Facts have to flow into event—there has to be *rasa*, flavour, to make facts melt into life. . . . Thus to face honesty against an Indian event, an Indian life, one's expression has to be epic in style or to lie." While this point may be arguable, it is at least certain that Gandhi's writing about his life needs to be considered against a range of representations of his life and the freedom struggle.

Letters:

Gandhiji's Correspondence with the Government, 2 volumes (Ahmedabad: Navajivan, 1945, 1959);

Famous Letters of Mahatma Gandhi, edited by R. L. Khipple (Lahore: Indian Printing Works, 1947);

F. Mary Barr, ed., *Bapu: Conversations & Correspondence with Mahatma Gandhi* (Bombay: International Book House, 1949);

Bapu's Letters to Mira, 1924–1948 (Ahmedabad: Navajivan, 1949); republished as *Gandhi's Letters to a Disciple* (New York: Harper, 1950);

Selected Letters, edited and translated by Valji Govindji Desai (Ahmedabad: Navajivan, 1949);

Letters to Sardar Vallabhbhai Patel, edited and translated by Valji Govindji Desai and Sudarshan V. Desai (Ahmedabad: Navajivan, 1957);

Letters to Rajkumari Amrit Kaur (Ahmedabad: Navajivan, 1961);

Letters from Gandhi, Nehru, Vinoba, edited by Shriman Narayan (London, Bombay & New York: Asia Publishing House, 1968);

Mahatma Gandhi and Leo Tolstoy: Letters, edited, with an introduction and notes, by B. Srinivasa Murthy,

foreword by Virginia Hartt Ringer (Long Beach, Cal.: Long Beach Publications, 1987);

The Mahatma and the Poet: Letters and Debates between Gandhi and Tagore, 1915–1941, edited, with an introduction, by Sabyasachi Bhattacharya (New Delhi: National Book Trust, 1997).

Bibliographies:

Jagdish Saran Sharma, *Mahatma Gandhi: A Descriptive Bibliography* (Delhi: S. Chand, 1968);

Mohandas Karamchand Gandhi: A Bibliography (New Delhi: Orient Longman, 1974);

April Carter, *Mahatma Gandhi: A Selected Bibliography* (Westport, Conn.: Greenwood Press, 1995);

Ananda M. Pandiri, *A Comprehensive, Annotated Bibliography on Mahatma Gandhi* (Westport, Conn.: Greenwood Press, 1995).

Biographies:

Pyarelal, *Mahatma Gandhi: The Last Phase,* 2 volumes (Ahmedabad: Navajivan, 1956, 1958);

Pyarelal, *Mahatma Gandhi: The Early Phase* (Ahmedabad: Navajivan, 1965);

Pyarelal, *Mahatma Gandhi: The Discovery of Satyagraha—On the Threshold* (Bombay: Sevak Prakashan, 1980);

Raja Rao, *The Great Indian Way: A Life of Mahatma Gandhi* (New Delhi: Vision, 1998).

References:

Judith M. Brown, *Gandhi and Civil Disobedience: The Mahatma in Indian Politics, 1928–34* (Cambridge: Cambridge University Press, 1977);

Brown, *Gandhi's Rise to Power: Indian Politics, 1915–1922* (Cambridge: Cambridge University Press, 1972);

Michael Edwardes, *The Myth of the Mahatma: Gandhi, the British, and the Raj* (London: Constable, 1986);

Dhananjay Keer, *Mahatma Gandhi: Political Saint and Unarmed Prophet* (Bombay: Popular Prakashan, 1973).

Papers:

Mohandas Karamchand Gandhi's papers are in the National Gandhi Museum, Rajghat, New Delhi.

Zulfikar Ghose

(13 March 1935 –   )

Chelva Kanaganayakam
University of Toronto

BOOKS: *The Loss of India* (London: Routledge & Kegan Paul, 1964);

Statement Against Corpses, by Ghose and B. S. Johnson (London: Constable, 1964);

Confessions of a Native-Alien (London: Routledge & Kegan Paul, 1965);

The Contradictions (London: Macmillan, 1966);

The Murder of Aziz Khan (London: Macmillan, 1967; New York: John Day, 1969; Karachi: Oxford University Press, 1998);

Jets from Orange (London: Macmillan, 1967);

The Violent West (London: Macmillan, 1972);

The Incredible Brazilian: The Native (London: Macmillan, 1972; New York: Holt, Rinehart & Winston, 1972; New York: Overlook, 1983);

Crump's Terms (London: Macmillan, 1975);

The Incredible Brazilian: The Beautiful Empire (London: Macmillan, 1975; New York: Overlook, 1984);

The Incredible Brazilian: A Different World (London: Macmillan, 1978; New York: Overlook, 1984);

Hamlet, Prufrock and Language (London: Macmillan, 1978; New York: St. Martin's Press, 1978);

Hulme's Investigations into the Bogart Script (Austin: Curbstone, 1981);

A New History of Torments (London: Hutchinson, 1982; New York: Holt, Rinehart & Winston, 1982);

Don Bueno (London: Hutchinson, 1983; New York: Holt, Rinehart & Winston, 1984);

The Fiction of Reality (London: Macmillan, 1983);

A Memory of Asia: New and Selected Poems (Austin: Curbstone, 1984);

Figures of Enchantment (London: Hutchinson, 1986; New York: Harper & Row, 1986);

Selected Poems (Karachi & Oxford: Oxford University Press, 1991);

The Art of Creating Fiction (London: Macmillan, 1991);

The Triple Mirror of the Self (London: Bloomsbury, 1992);

Shakespeare's Mortal Knowledge: A Reading of the Tragedies (Basingstoke, U.K.: Macmillan, 1993; New York: St. Martin's Press, 1993);

Zulfikar Ghose (photograph by Helena de la Fontaine; from the dust jacket for Don Bueno, *1984; Richland County Public Library)*

Veronica and the Góngora Passion: Stories, Fictions, Tales and One Fable (Toronto: Tsar, 1998).

SELECTED PERIODICAL PUBLICATION–
UNCOLLECTED: "Going Home," *Toronto South Asian Review,* 9, no. 2 (1991): 15–22.

Zulfikar Ghose, an Indo-Pakistani writer with dual American and British citizenship, remains outside the "canon" of postcolonial literature. Despite the urgency of the political context that inspired contemporary writers to take up explicitly political themes in their writing, Ghose remains skeptical about the value of literature as a vehicle for political protest or social reform. In his own work he has resisted addressing contemporary issues in ways that are tendentious or even referential. His ongoing concern has been with form, language, and the function of literature as artifice. Consequently, as a writer and critic he has remained something of an enigma, working outside conventional classifications of commonwealth and postcolonial literature. Until *The Review of Contemporary Fiction* brought out a special issue in 1989 dedicated jointly to Ghose and to Milan Kundera, not more than a handful of critics had heard about him; even fewer had written about his work. Since then the amount of critical attention that has been paid to his work has been scant, although he has continued to write fiction, poetry, and criticism. Ghose remains an author who does not fit into established categories, and his refusal to be bound by labels remains a significant aspect of his work. Ghose maintains that "one's nationality is an irrelevance," although his novel *The Triple Mirror of the Self* (1992) marks at least a partial departure, as it deals with colonial and postcolonial India.

The desire to maintain a measure of distance from nation-centered ways of writing is partially a consequence of Ghose's biographical circumstances. He was born on 13 March 1935 to Khwaja Mohammed Ghose and Salima Virk Ghose in Sialkot, which was then a part of India and is now in Pakistan. He has three sisters. He spent seven years of his youth in Sialkot and ten years in Bombay (now Mumbai), a cosmopolitan city where his neighbors and friends included Hindus, Sikhs, Parsis, and Christians. His father changed the family name from the Muslim "Ghaus" to the more common and easier to pronounce "Ghose," a Hindu name; thus, the name "Zulfikar Ghose" is part Muslim and part Hindu. The duality reflects his marginal status as a Muslim in a predominantly Hindu city, which became heightened during the partition of India in 1947 (the division of the subcontinent into independent India and Pakistan). His autobiographical work, *Confessions of a Native-Alien* (1965), provides a detailed account of his early years in Sialkot and Bombay, including anecdotes about his parents, his extended family, his school, and his teachers, although the book is intended to be a fictive reworking of facts. Having become an exile in the land of his birth after the Partition of India, he left for England in 1952, despite his awareness that migration to England was only going to reinforce his predicament. About his departure with his family, Ghose says in *Confessions of a Native-Alien:*

> When we left Bombay in 1952 for England, we were leaving two countries, for in some ways we were alien to both and our emigration to a country to which we were not native only emphasized our alienation from the country in which we had been born. This distinc-

tion between the two countries of my early life has been the schizophrenic theme of much of my writing: it created a psychological conflict and a pressing need to know that I do belong somewhere, and neither the conflict nor the need has ever been resolved.

Since 1952, Ghose's contact with Pakistan and India has been minimal. He has visited as a reporter and invited guest on a few occasions but has not returned on a regular basis. He continues to think of himself as Indo-Pakistani, although his travels take him to South America more often than to South Asia.

In England he studied at Sloane School in Chelsea and took a degree in English and philosophy at the University of Keele in 1959. He then worked as a correspondent for *The Observer,* served as a teacher, and wrote literary reviews for *The Western Daily Press, The Guardian,* and *The Times Literary Supplement.* He became actively involved in the literary scene and counted among his close friends the British experimental novelist B. S. Johnson. He also met regularly with the poets known as the Group. In 1964 he married Helena de la Fontaine, a Brazilian artist. In 1969 he left for the United States to accept a teaching appointment at the University of Texas at Austin, where he works as a professor of English and teaches creative writing.

Identity, or the predicament of the "native-alien," is central to Ghose, whose movement from one place to another has reinforced his status as an exile. Critics such as Tariq Rahman in *A History of Pakistani Literature in English* (1991) consider Ghose a Pakistani writer, although it would be equally valid to claim that he is Indian, or British, or American. Regardless of his nationality, a sense of loss is always evident in his work. His early collection of poetry, *The Loss of India* (1964), includes several poems that relate directly to the experience of migration and the consequent longing for home. Many of the poems in this collection deal with the predicament of being an outsider in England and reiterate his longing for a home that was no longer available to him.

The same year in which he brought out *The Loss of India,* he also wrote his first collection of short stories, *Statement Against Corpses* (1964), together with Johnson. The preface to the book refers to a dissatisfaction with prevailing conventions and norms that shaped the short story as a genre. Referring to the short story as a moribund form, the authors claim that "the short story deserves, but seldom receives, the same precise attention to language as that given normally only to a poem." The stories themselves reveal a preoccupation with language and form that later became a defining feature of Ghose's work. Among Ghose's stories in this collection, "The Zoo People" is the most complex in its structure and depth of understanding.

Colonial India, which is the subject matter of "The Zoo People," also becomes the concern of Ghose's first novel, *The Contradictions* (1966). The narrative offers a series of contradictions by juxtaposing East and West, India and Britain. One of the major objectives of the novel is to show the fragility of the British presence in India. The central characters discover that values and relationships that were nurtured in the West cannot easily be sustained in India.

In terms of typology it is possible to claim that *The Contradictions* is in the tradition of the Anglo-Indian novel, while Ghose's next work, *The Murder of Aziz Khan* (1967), aligns itself with the mode of Indo-Anglican fiction and is written along the lines of the Victorian novel. The structure of *The Contradictions* is synchronic, while the movement of *The Murder of Aziz Khan* is diachronic. The latter novel traces the life and suffering of the title character, a farmer whose family is destroyed by rapacious industrialists who are determined to claim his land. Notions of land, dislocation, economic exploitation, the nuclear family, exile, and related issues are worked into a traditional agrarian novel that has to do with the downfall of a family that did not have the economic means or power to resist the ruthless businessmen of postcolonial Pakistan. As realistic fiction, the book rings true, and even in retrospect it retains its place as an important novel in Ghose's corpus. In fact, it is the only novel in his entire corpus that is set entirely in Pakistan. This novel is also the only work in which Ghose makes no attempt to depart from the conventions of nineteenth-century realism.

The next ten years or so were productive ones for the author, as he published fiction, poetry, and criticism in a manner that indicated that all three genres were part of a holistic process. His poetry collections *Jets from Orange* (1967) and *The Violent West* (1972) include poems that are set in India, but for the most part they work with a much broader canvas. *Jets from Orange* includes several poems set in Europe, while *The Violent West*, written after his move to Texas, deals with the United States. Ghose was writing *Jets from Orange* during a period when he was teaching at a school in Ealing, west London, close to the Heathrow airport. The familiar sight of planes landing and taking off provided the imaginative drive for many of the poems in this volume. Both collections, however, reflect the impulse in Ghose to locate his writing in places other than South Asia and to experiment with forms that signal a departure from realism. From this point in his career Ghose became an experimental writer, moving from one mode to another in order to find a form that would express the experience of exile. Over the next twenty years,

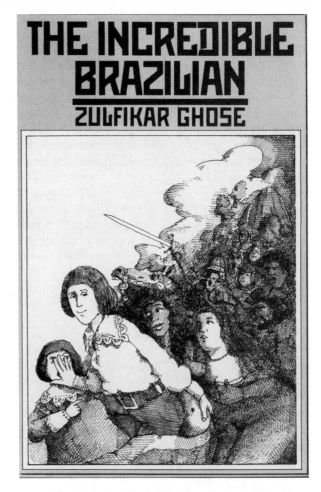

Dust jacket for the American edition of Ghose's 1972 novel, the first in an historical trilogy that depicts the picaresque adventures of the narrator, Gregorio, as he is reincarnated in eighteenth-, nineteenth-, and twentieth-century Brazil (Richland County Public Library)

Ghose's writing recapitulated the various forms that characterize the evolution of fiction in the West.

His next novel, *The Incredible Brazilian: The Native*, which appeared in 1972, was the first part of a trilogy set in Brazil; the others are *The Incredible Brazilian: The Beautiful Empire* (1975) and *The Incredible Brazilian: A Different World* (1978). Ostensibly, these novels belong to the tradition of realistic writing. However, the major challenge of the trilogy is its refusal to conform to any easy typology. The most conspicuous feature, and the most misleading one, is the narrative strategy of knitting together a string of incidents by the simple expedient of making the protagonist the focal point of all of them. The narrator, Gregorio, carries the narrative thread with him as he moves through all three novels, encountering one adventure after another. Gregorio belongs to the company of a long line of illustrious picaresque figures; Ghose is reverting to a mode that not only predates nineteenth-century realism but also is perhaps the earliest mode of fiction, namely, the picaresque mode.

The author is meticulous about documenting historical events that relate to Brazil, with the consequence that the novels convey the impression that their concern is the historical reality of Brazil. The constant sense of verisimilitude and the obvious parallels between Brazil and India lead to the assumption that the novels, in the process of looking closely at Brazil, also reflect on India. The parallel is intentional; however, the novels ultimately subvert the expectations of the realistic novel. Often, the reader is pulled into the world of Brazil only to be abruptly alerted to its fictionality. The deliberate flaws in the logic, for example, are a reminder that a realistic reading of the novels would be counterproductive. In the final analysis, Brazil provides the backdrop to a narrative that is concerned with colonial exploitation, marginality, exile, and loss of identity.

Metaphor is central to Ghose's practice as a writer, and a central one that he uses consistently throughout his novels is the image of a woman to depict the multiplicity of the land. Particularly in the trilogy, the trope is used extensively to explore the ideas of conquest, violation, and destruction. In "Going Home," an essay written in 1991, Ghose explains his fascination with the image by drawing specific attention to the Punjabi women:

> The simpler Punjabi clothes disguise and obscure the female form but cannot suppress the suggestion of her beauty as she walks with a slightly swaying gait that sends minute undulations over her agitated flesh, transforming her, the peasant woman who is a sentimental and partial image in my mind, into a symbol for the land.

Such motifs not only fuse realism with fantasy but also indicate the underlying preoccupations of the narratives. For instance, the "Interlude" and the "Coda" in *A Different World,* which stand apart spatially and temporally from the text and which are subtitled "Soliloquy of the Alien Heart in its Native Land" and "The Undiscovered Country" respectively, provide a microcosm of the author's concerns. The "Interlude" conjures up a variety of images in carefully structured, metaphorical language, while the "Coda," with its oxymorons and images of arrival and departure, builds up a gradual sense of people looking and not perceiving, of arriving and not comprehending, until a sense develops that "the country is still undiscovered and is only a secret dream in your soul."

Much of the complexity of the trilogy comes from the fact that the author is at pains to create in meticu-

lous detail the ethos of three centuries of Brazilian history, and it is not surprising that attention is drawn to the historicism and teleology of the novels. During the time he was writing the trilogy Ghose acquired a fascination with the imagery of Brazil, and he also discovered a seminal work, Gilberto Freyre's *The Masters and the Slaves* (1964). These interests explain the wealth of realistic detail in the novels.

Despite the affinities with the realistic novel and the traditional picaresque, the trilogy refuses to fit comfortably into either of these molds. Often the details provide an insight into the world of Brazil only to move away from it. While the three novels encapsulate a long period of Brazilian history, they also flaunt a circular structure that subverts the value of a linear reading.

Crump's Terms (1975), which was written three years after the first Brazilian novel, belongs to a different tradition, locating its action in England and depicting characters who are either British or European. It deals primarily with Crump, a cynical and disillusioned teacher in London, whose frustrating attempts to impose a sense of order and discipline at the Pinworth School are juxtaposed with the memories of his former wife, Frieda, with whom he spends several vacations in Europe but who finally deserts him to seek asylum in East Germany. The title of the novel refers to the terms within which Crump is expected to organize his life and also the terms that regulate his academic career.

It is possible to seek out autobiographical elements in this novel, as Ghose was for some time a teacher in England and did spend several vacations in Europe; but this line of inquiry leads to no particular illumination. The impulse behind the novel is a desire to escape the hindering presence of historical context and referentiality and to probe alienation not merely as physical displacement but as a state of mind. Objective reality is not jettisoned entirely, but its validity is rendered suspect by patterns of repetition, disruption of time and space, and devices of artifice. It is the only novel in Ghose's corpus that is recognizably in the stream-of-consciousness mode.

A distinctive feature of Ghose's writing is the awareness that language creates its own reality rather than reflecting the conditions in the real world. Using language becomes a way of playing games that construct a world of artifice rather than depict the referent. Ghose does not abandon the real world; he returns obsessively to it. But the preoccupation is juxtaposed with the notion that the relationship between language and reality is deeply problematic. His critical work *Hamlet, Prufrock and Language* (1978) is devoted to an exploration of the relation between language and reality in William Shakespeare's *Hamlet* (circa 1600–1601) and in T. S. Eliot's "The Love Song of J. Alfred Prufrock"

(1915). Having set out the argument, Ghose states: "If we could only hear or speak or arrive at the words which explained, we would know; and having the illusion that there is a necessary correspondence between language and reality, we are driven to despair when our words seem to reveal nothing." This awareness of the hiatus between language and reality explains his constant experimenting and his movement from one mode to another.

Having exhausted the possibilities of the picaresque mode with the Brazilian trilogy, Ghose moved on to a more self-consciously experimental work titled *Hulme's Investigations into the Bogart Script* (1981). This novel, at first sight, has greater affinities with *Crump's Terms* than with the trilogy, but there are major differences. *Hulme's Investigations into the Bogart Script* is predominantly a metafictional work that needs to be seen as a verbal construct that flaunts its language and its artifice. The novel itself is difficult to summarize, for it lacks teleological movement. The nine scripts that make up this postmodernist novel are linked tenuously, sometimes through a repetition of scenes and sometimes through intratextual references. While certain chapters seem more partial to linearity, others are decidedly discontinuous. The novel is a collage of sorts that includes everything from detective thrillers to soap operas.

In Ghose's total corpus, *Hulme's Investigations into the Bogart Script* stands apart as an overtly experimental text. As a bridge between the trilogy and Ghose's subsequent magic realistic novels, *Hulme's Investigations into the Bogart Script* plays an important role. Antireferential writing is pushed to its limit in this novel, to the point that the relation between the narrative and the author's ongoing quest becomes problematic. But it remains a necessary phase, one that leads seamlessly to the next one. In thematic terms, this novel continues the quest for identity that is pervasive in Ghose's writing.

The Fiction of Reality (1983), also written during this phase, is an important critical work. In this book he discusses several authors in his analysis of the scope of fiction and its capacity to deal with reality. The book reads like a series of meditations rather than a conventional critical work. Language and artifice emerge as central preoccupations in Ghose's thinking, and fidelity to empirical realities is seen as less important than a constant struggle with language and form. The critical readings that make up this work serve the dual purpose of revealing Ghose's opinions about contemporary writing while indirectly shedding light on his own work. The three novels that precede and follow the publication of this critical work are a reflection of the thoughts that find expression in it.

These three novels—*A New History of Torments* (1982), *Don Bueno* (1983), and *Figures of Enchantment* (1986)—represent a high point in Ghose's career as a writer. For want of a better term, the novels can well be called magic realist, and certainly some of the contemporary influences were Latin American authors. In a later story titled "Lila of the Butterflies and her Chronicler" (which appears in *Veronica and the Góngora Passion: Stories, Fictions, Tales and One Fable,* 1998), even as he pays tribute to the elder statesman of magic realism, Gabriel García Márquez, Ghose implies that magic realism is far more inclusive and broad than contemporary criticism would suggest. In fact, Machado de Assis is a writer Ghose admires more than García Márquez. However, the dominant mode of the novels is predominantly magic realist in ways that mark a point of departure from the Brazilian trilogy.

Ghose calls this period in his career "a phase of pure imagination," thus implying a distance from reality, although the novels themselves read much like realistic fiction set in South America. The novels do not self-consciously negate the conventions of realism. Interestingly, the realism is preserved by the pervasive use of myth, ritualized behavior, superstitions, seers, and cyclical patterns. The mythology is important, but it is woven into a narrative that accepts and insists on the nonreal. In these works, Ghose attempts to present a ceaseless and compulsive movement toward a void that must be discovered before the possibility of liberation. The quest motif has striking similarities with the work of the Guyanese writer Wilson Harris, whose characters also tend to undertake an archetypal journey into the unknown. The comparison with Harris is an important one, for Harris is one of the few authors to write about Ghose's work, particularly on Ghose's impulse to seek mythical patterns that keep surfacing despite changes in time and space.

The three texts are in some ways symbolic narratives, filled with characters who are hardly aware of the roles they must play in their tragic destinies. Regardless of the vagaries of plot, and despite the conscious efforts of the characters, there is relentless movement toward the completion of a predetermined end. In that sense, the approach to myth in these three novels is essentially Jungian. A tragic sense of closure operates in all three novels, and, as the title of the first one suggests, the history of individual characters, driven by forces they can neither understand nor control, is often nothing other than a history of torments.

Despite the tragic overtone of all three novels, the preoccupation with diaspora is not necessarily negative. The alternative to quest is stagnation, loss of freedom, and a failure to realize one's potential. Departures are necessary and important, even if arrival is uncertain or

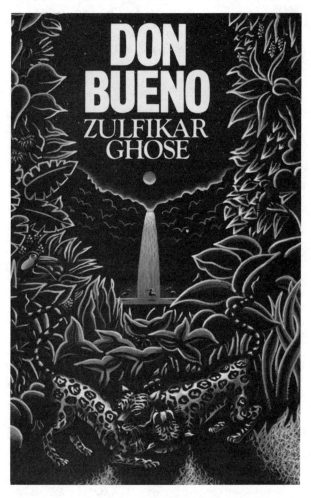

Dust jacket for the American edition (1984) of Ghose's 1983 novel,
which is set in South America and depicts three generations of
abandoned sons who grow up and unwittingly kill their fathers
(Richland County Public Library)

prone to disharmony. A memorable instance of this phenomenon occurs in *Figures of Enchantment* when Federico, a typical inhabitant of Ghose's world, stands outside a magician's shop, wondering if the latter's "magic" would reverse the circumstances that torment him. Unknown to Federico, from within the shop, the magician appraises the boy:

> The boy had a haunted look, the kind he had seen on people who had the compulsion to flee, an anxiety to be leaving some place, without knowing what they were running from, and, in the majority of cases, not even knowing that they were engaged in flight. He himself had known that demon that could suddenly possess the soul and draw it to some landscape as if it were a bird migrating from a dusty scrubland, where it had twittered and warbled, that can discover the full range of its singing voice only when it finds itself after a journey forced by blind instinct, in a cool, dark forest that

is unlike its native habitat as is the terrain of the moon from that of the earth.

The syntax of this neo-Romantic passage leads the reader away from the immediate and the referential context of the novel into yet another world that attempts to focus on the complexity of the native-alien experience. The obsessive memory of home, the inevitability and pain of the quest, and the awareness that a satisfying re-creation of home can only be a construct of the mind are all aspects that keep recurring in Ghose's work.

For Ghose the loss of a sense of home is everpresent, and he confesses in one poem in *A Memory of Asia: New and Selected Poems* (1984) that he longs to "see again what [he has] seen / to confirm former convictions and to know / that a certain vision is a continuing truth." *A Memory of Asia* is a collection of poems that go back to India and Pakistan, but often in a manner that implies a recognition of the limitations of memory. *A Memory of Asia,* coming after a long poetry hiatus, marks yet another turning point. As the title poem indicates, the memory of Asia refuses to disappear, regardless of how much the mind tries to divert itself. Asia is thus an obsessive concern, and all the allegorical structures become a way of dealing with Asia while preserving an aesthetic distance.

A Memory of Asia is equally preoccupied with remembered landscapes, although the perspective is filtered through a consciousness that insists on the fictiveness of memory. In the title poem, the poet describes in detail a roadside temple dedicated to Ganesh, and then wonders whether the descriptive language is really a collection of phrases borrowed from elsewhere and put together in order to create the illusion of reality:

> There was a temple opposite the bus stop
> beside the anachronistic house with its
> trumpet vine and flowering acacias and hibiscus bushes
> surrounded by blocks of flats without gardens,
> and there, while waiting for the bus, one saw
> pot-bellied Ganapati, the Hindu god, garlanded
> with marigolds and jasmine and with
> his elephant head painted the red they used
> post boxes, small brass bells hanging from
> the ceiling to his shoulders and at his feet
> brass trays heaped with mangoes, papayas and jackfruit.
> . . . .
> But this is a revision; I've put some
> of these phrases before. . . . .
> hypotheses first accepted as provisional truths
> becoming certainties by repeated narration.

Several of the poems in this collection acknowledge the presence of India and speak candidly about the urge to relive the world that has been left behind.

The yearning does not translate into essentialist or exotic formulations. The pictures generated by the mind have almost a clinical accuracy. But Ghose is quick to point out that these wonderful images may well be fictions. Often what another author has written may become the basis of the present poem. In short, the relation between the object and the language that is used to describe it is suspect. The reader is thus made aware of the process by which memory creates fictions.

The sense of alienation that comes across in his poetry is equally poignant. The complexity arises from the fact that the pain of being uprooted coexists with an awareness that the imagination creates fictions to substantiate a predetermined truth. And that is not only an aspect of forgetting and reinventing landscapes in one's mind. Even when he visits "home" he is less impressed by what he sees than what he does not see. In "Going Home" he writes about the experience in ways that reflect more than the loss of a remembered landscape:

> At the Peshawar Museum I was struck by the power of the incomplete statue of the fasting Buddha to fix the itinerant self in the timeless and bodiless space. The missing parts of the statue appear to have a vital presence: the starve [sic], absent organs—shrunk, withered, annihilated—throb bloodily in the imagination; that which is not there startles the mind with the certainty of its being; it is an image of amazing contradictions, and illustrates the essential ambiguity of all perception: reality can be composed of absent things, the unseen blazes in our minds with shocking vividness.

The pursuit of verisimilitude is for him thwarted by circumstances. In *The Art of Creating Fiction* (1991) he demonstrates that the kind of realism that struggles to reproduce the referent is, paradoxically, likely to fail, whereas the artifice that works with unlikely material has a much greater chance of success:

> Commissioned to create the illustrations for a novel, a comedy of manners concerning the English nobility, the artist-narrator of Henry James's short story "The Real Thing" is forced to choose between two couples as his models for the principal protagonists: a genteel pair, Major and Mrs Monarch, fallen on hard times, who present themselves by chance at the artist's studio as the real thing . . . and another, incongruous couple, the man an Italian ice-cream vendor whose street business has collapsed and a cockney girl, both obviously the very antithesis of English upper class society. But as he works, the artist realizes that the Monarchs, the real thing, won't do. They simply don't come out right. The only way he can get at believable representation of the noble features of the upper class is by using as his models the comparatively dwarfish Italian and the "freckled" cockney girl.

The idea of multiple perspectives and the significance of artifice appear again in the novel *The Triple Mirror of the Self*. This novel is, arguably, one of Ghose's most accomplished works. In it one sees the need to return to the land he left early in life and fiction. *The Triple Mirror of the Self* begs an immediate comparison with *The Murder of Aziz Khan:* in the latter, the referential canvas is Pakistan; in *The Triple Mirror of the Self* the movement to India constitutes one portion of the entire work. The relation between the two novels points to the author's larger concerns with form, with diction, and with the function of fiction itself. The realism of *The Murder of Aziz Khan* and the artifice of *The Triple Mirror of the Self* have the same ostensible function: to explore the longing for home from the perspective of exile. *The Murder of Aziz Khan* creates a world that is recognizably Pakistan and engages with issues that are often associated with neocolonialism: the fragmentation of land, the exploitation of the poor, the march of capitalism, and the disintegration of the nuclear family. *The Triple Mirror of the Self* does not begin in India: it ends there. And while the larger political context of the Partition is part of the background, the concern is with archetypal structures rather than individual lives. A mythical structure, together with a quest motif, underpins the novel, linking widely different spaces and time periods. It is almost as if the present is yet another manifestation of a timeless myth that gets reenacted. In the second part of the novel, the two characters Shimmers and Isabel, after a journey that has all the trappings of a mythical quest, recognize both their "lostness" and their need for location in a village called Kailost. The incident itself is insignificant until the reader realizes that Kailost is an anagram of Sialkot, the place where the author was born.

In 1993 Ghose published *Shakespeare's Mortal Knowledge,* a critical work that provides a close reading of four tragedies. The chapter on *Hamlet* is a revised version of the reading that appeared in his 1978 critical volume; the new material consists of essays on *Othello* (circa 1604), *King Lear* (circa 1606), and *Macbeth* (circa 1606). All four essays reflect a personal response to the plays and also draw attention to the preoccupations that run through Ghose's own work.

After the publication of *The Triple Mirror of the Self,* Ghose continued to write short stories sporadically; some of them were collected, together with unpublished material, in *Veronica and the Góngora Passion*. Ghose's concerns with myth, ritual, and identity resurface in these tales. The stories are set in India and elsewhere, but again the setting is less important than the constant struggle with language and form to gain access to a body of experience. The term "camouflage" appears in a story titled "Arrival in India," reinforcing not only the

FIGURES OF ENCHANTMENT

A NOVEL BY

ZULFIKAR GHOSE

Dust jacket for the American edition of Ghose's 1986 magical-realism novel, a re-imagining of William Shakespeare's The Tempest *(Richland County Public Library)*

artifice but also the transformation made possible through disguise. Within the context of the story, the term makes perfect sense, since the central character needs to flee from one form of persecution after another, and the capacity to camouflage himself ensures his survival.

But camouflage goes beyond pretense. It suggests a mode of reading and understanding literature. As a trope it describes the unity among the stories that make up this collection. One of the stories, "The Savage Mother of Desire," offers a perfect example of the kind of artifice that distinguishes Ghose's work. Ostensibly, the story is a revenge tale, occasioned by the violation (and impregnation) of a woman, Kalpana, by a doctor. The brother of the woman, outraged by the conduct of the doctor, forces his way into the doctor's apartment and castrates him. It is not difficult to make a connection between the doctor's zeal for sterilizing men and Indira Gandhi's leadership in the 1970s, when there was a determined effort to control India's population

through a sterilization program. The story almost demands a referential reading; but there is more to it than originally appears.

The plot may well account for the teleology of the story, but that is secondary to the working out of myth as the characters act out a predetermined course of events. Events that seem random trigger primordial memories as the central character takes on the role of the savage mother of desire. A combination of the goddess Kali and a Yogi, the savage mother embodies birth and death, sensuality and repulsion, fertility and death. It is thus inevitable that the doctor who causes sterility but is responsible for impregnating Kalpana must pay a price for his role in the re-creation of myth. The story is hardly about cause and effect; it certainly does not make a great deal of sense about moral conduct and punishment. These attributes remain secondary to the ritualistic quality of the story that insists on re-creating itself in the most unexpected of times.

The story is remarkable for its depth and nuance. It also raises fundamental questions about the place of Ghose as a postcolonial or South Asian author. The labels that are often used to describe postcolonial authors such as Ghose are almost always implicated in the historical process of colonialism and the narrative of neocolonialism. To read Ghose in historicist terms would lead to a dead end—which might well explain why he remains largely unknown in postcolonial circles. To read his texts ideologically could well lead to the conclusion that he is guilty of appropriating native culture. It is perhaps true that the absence of context in his work must announce the presence of allegory as a major preoccupation. Ghose's work, however, is neither allegorical nor marginal. It insists on its autonomy as art without forsaking its commitment to the conditions that shaped his sense of exile.

Ghose's most significant literary contribution lies in his fiction, although it is possible to argue that the four collections of poetry he has published provide a template for understanding his fiction. Unlike writers who have remained within a particular frame, Ghose has created a career of experiment as he moves from one form to another in his search for a form that best encompasses the complexity of experience that he strives to express.

Harris is among the few scholars who have consistently praised Zulfikar Ghose's achievement. For the most part, Ghose has not received much critical attention. An exception is *A Dragonfly in the Sun* (1997), an anthology of Pakistani writing in English, edited by Muneeza Shamsie. Not only does this collection pay special attention to Ghose, but also it uses a phrase from one of his poems for its title. In general, apart from the articles in the special issue of *The Review of Con-*

temporary Fiction in 1989, there is little by way of rigorous criticism. Reviews have been laudatory, but they do not generally offer comprehensive analysis. Postcolonial criticism often tends to work within a taxonomy that includes place, author, and text; Ghose's refusal to be bound by such a classification accounts for his marginality.

References:

Ewing Campbell, "Encountering the Other in The Fiction of Reality," *Review of Contemporary Fiction,* 9, no. 2 (1989): 220–224;

Wilson Harris, "A Note on Zulfikar Ghose's 'Nature Strategies,'" *Review of Contemporary Fiction,* 9, no. 2 (1989): 172–178;

Alamgir Hashmi, "Tickling and Being Tickled a la Zulfikar Ghose," *Commonwealth Novel in English,* 1, no. 2 (1982): 156–165;

Chelva Kanaganayakam, *Structures of Negation: The Writings of Zulfikar Ghose* (Toronto: University of Toronto Press, 1993);

Kanaganayakam, "Unreal Reel and the Unreeled Real: *Hulme's Investigations into the Bogart Script,*" *Journal of Indian Writing in English,* 16, no. 2 (1988): 178–190;

Bruce King, "Ghose's Criticism as Theory," *Review of Contemporary Fiction,* 9, no. 2 (1989): 204–208;

Shirley Geok-lin Lim, "A Poetics of Location: Reading Zulfikar Ghose," *Review of Contemporary Fiction,* 9, no. 2 (1989): 188–191;

W. H. New, "Structures of Uncertainty: Reading Ghose's 'The Zoo People,'" *Review of Contemporary Fiction,* 9, no. 2 (1989): 192–197;

Tariq Rahman, *A History of Pakistani Literature in English* (Lahore: Vanguard, 1991);

Rahman, "Zulfikar Ghose and the Land of His Birth," *Review of Contemporary Fiction,* 9, no. 2 (1989): 179–187;

Robert Ross, "The Murder of Aziz Khan," *Review of Contemporary Fiction,* 9, no. 2 (1989): 198–203;

William J. Scheick, "Fictional Self and Mythic Art: *A New History of Torments* and *Don Bueno,*" *Review of Contemporary Fiction,* 9, no. 2 (1989): 209–219;

Muneeza Shamsie, ed., *A Dragonfly in the Sun: An Anthology of Pakistani Writing in English* (Karachi: Oxford University Press, 1997).

Papers:

A collection of Zulfikar Ghose's papers, including poetry typescripts and correspondence with Anthony Smith, Thomas Berger, and B. S. Johnson, is housed at the Harry Ransom Humanities Research Center at the University of Texas at Austin.

Amitav Ghosh

(11 July 1956 –   )

Krishna Sen
University of Calcutta

BOOKS: *The Circle of Reason* (New Delhi: Roli Books, 1986; London: Hamilton, 1986; New York: Viking, 1986);

The Shadow Lines (Delhi: Ravi Dayal/Permanent Black, 1988; London: Bloomsbury, 1988; New York: Viking, 1989);

The Slave of Ms. H. 6 (Calcutta: Centre for Studies in Social Sciences, 1990);

In an Antique Land: History in the Guise of a Traveler's Tale (Delhi: Ravi Dayal, 1992; London: Granta Books, 1992; New York: Knopf, 1993);

The Calcutta Chromosome: A Novel of Fevers, Delirium and Discovery (New York: Avon, 1995; Delhi: Ravi Dayal, 1996; London: Picador, 1996);

Dancing in Cambodia, At Large in Burma (Delhi: Ravi Dayal, 1998);

Countdown (Delhi: Ravi Dayal, 1999);

The Glass Palace (New Delhi: Ravi Dayal, 2000; London: HarperCollins, 2000; New York: Random House, 2000);

The Imam and the Indian: Prose Pieces (Delhi: Ravi Dayal/Permanent Black, 2002);

The Hungry Tide (Delhi: Ravi Dayal, 2004; London: HarperCollins, 2004; Boston: Houghton Mifflin, 2005);

Incendiary Circumstances: A Chronicle of the Turmoil of Our Times (Boston: Houghton Mifflin, 2005).

SELECTED PERIODICAL PUBLICATIONS–
UNCOLLECTED: "The Human Comedy in Cairo: A Review of the Work of Naguib Mahfouz," *New Republic,* 202 (7 May 1990): 32–36;

"Petrofiction," *New Republic,* 206 (2 March 1992): 29–34;

"The Global Reservation: Notes Toward an Ethnography of International Peacekeeping," *Cultural Anthropology,* 9, no. 3 (1994): 412–422;

"The Fundamentalist Challenge," *Wilson Quarterly,* 19 (Spring 1995): 19–31;

"The Ghosts of Mrs. Gandhi," *New Yorker* (17 July 1995): 35–41.

Amitav Ghosh (photograph © Jerry Bauer; from the dust jacket for The Glass Palace, *2001; Richland County Public Library)*

Amitav Ghosh, a leading postcolonial writer in English, is Indian by birth but global in his vision. The central concern of his work is the relationship of the individual to culture and history. He believes, as he wrote in a 14 December 2001 e-mail to Dipesh Chakraborty, the author of *Provincializing Europe* (1999), that "history is never more compelling than when it gives us insights into oneself and the ways in which one's own experience is constituted" (<www.amitavghosh.com>). For Ghosh, history is closely related to fiction and is more about people and their responses than about events and their causes and effects. A character in Ghosh's second novel, *The Shadow Lines* (1988), could be speaking for the author when he remarks, "everyone lives in a story." Looking back on that novel in *The Imam and the Indian: Prose Pieces* (2002), Ghosh reflects on writing about British colonialism, World War II, and the Partition of India: "It became a book not about any one event but about the meaning of events and their effects on the individuals who lived through them."

Ghosh embeds the historical event within a network of relationships, most significantly the relationships of the family. In his e-mail to Chakrabarty, Ghosh explains his rationale: "Two of my novels (*The Shadow Lines,* and my most recent *The Glass Palace*) are centred on families. I know that for myself this is a way of displacing the 'nation'–I am sure that this is the case also with many Indian writers other than myself. In other words, I'd like to suggest that writing about families is one way of not writing about the nation (or other restrictively imagined collectivities)." In *The Imam and the Indian,* Ghosh asserts that "one of the paradoxes of history is that it is impossible to draw a chart of the past without imagining a map of the present and the future." He also contrasts memory, "haunted always by the essential inexplicability of what has come to pass," with history, the business of rationalizing or making sense of the past. Writing about family experience through successive generations allows Ghosh to explore such insights.

Ghosh is known as a postcolonial writer because of his condemnation of imperialism and its consequent violence and prejudice. He believes that art has a special role to play in opposing forces that alienate people and communities. In his acknowledgments to *The Imam and the Indian* he states, "in the circuitry of the imagination, connections are of greater importance than disjunctions." One of the ways of making connections and promoting empathy and understanding is through the act of remembering and narrating stories about human endeavor and suffering. The duty of the artist is to ensure that such stories are not forgotten. Alluding to the Bosnian writer Dzevad Karahasan's essay "Literature and War," Ghosh writes, "It is when we think of the world that the aesthetic of indifference might bring into being, that we recognize the urgency of remembering the stories we have never written."

Ghosh's formative experiences involved travel and encountering cultural differences. Born in Calcutta on 11 July 1956, Ghosh was the son of Shailendra Chandra Ghosh, an officer in the British Indian army who became a diplomat in independent India, and Anjali Ghosh, a homemaker. He spent his childhood with his sister, Chaitali, in Calcutta as well as Dhaka, Colombo, and Iran, followed by a stint in a boarding school at Dehra Dun in Northern India. He graduated with a B.A., with honors in history, from St. Stephen's College, University of Delhi, in 1976 and an M.A. in

sociology from the University of Delhi in 1978. While in college, between 1974 and 1978, he worked as a reporter and editor for the *Indian Express.* In *Countdown* (1999) he vividly recalls covering Prime Minister Indira Gandhi's suspension of constitutional processes during the state of emergency she declared in 1975–1976 and her shocking defeat at the polls the following year.

In 1979 Ghosh earned diplomas in social anthropology from Oxford University in England as well as in Arabic from the Institut Bourguiba de Langues Vivantes in Tunisia. He then completed a Ph.D. in social anthropology from Oxford in 1982, doing a considerable amount of fieldwork in Egypt. He drew directly on his experiences in Egypt for *In an Antique Land: History in the Guise of a Traveler's Tale* (1992) as well as some of the essays in *The Imam and the Indian,* while his academic interests in history, sociology, anthropology, and the history of culture permeate all his books.

From 1982 to 1983 Ghosh was a visiting fellow at the Centre for Development Studies at Thiruvananthapuram (Trivandrum) in Kerala, India. Between 1983 and 1987 he taught in the Department of Sociology at the Delhi School of Economics, University of Delhi, first as a research associate and then as a lecturer. During this period he was associated with the Subaltern Studies Collective, a university group conducting important research into the history of contributions made by the "subaltern" or underprivileged sections of society to India's national culture. Radically departing from the traditional notion of history as a record of the activities of the elite, the group promoted an understanding of history that equally valued the handiwork of millions of nameless people whose influence on the course of events had gone unrecorded because of their perceived social inconsequence. The forgotten histories of such people are an important element in Ghosh's work, as is evident in his first novel, *The Circle of Reason* (1986), which was published while he was still teaching at Delhi.

The Circle of Reason, a picaresque tale set partly in the India of the British Raj and partly in the Middle East and North Africa, is about a young boy nicknamed Alu or "Potato" because his head resembles a large, irregularly-shaped tuber. Orphaned at an early age, Alu is raised in the village of Lalpukur near Calcutta by his childless uncle Balaram and aunt Toru-debi and becomes a master weaver. Balaram's immense enthusiasm for Western rationalism is matched only by his visceral hatred of British sovereignty in India. When the "School of Reason" that he sets up at his home is firebombed on the suspicion of its being a terrorist camp, Alu, the lone survivor, flees to the Middle East and then to North Africa. Pursued as a terrorist, he blends into the densely multicultural societies of the

Dust jacket for the American edition of Ghosh's first novel (1986), in which a young weaver falsely accused of terrorism is pursued through the societies of the Indian Ocean rim (Richland County Public Library)

tions titled "Reason," "Passion," and "Death"—as another quest for truth, and Alu explores ancient Indian culture and philosophy as sources of wisdom and self-knowledge. Although Anthony Burgess in his review in the 6 July 1986 issue of *The New York Times Book Review* simplifies the allegorical implications of Ghosh's book as a binary opposition between traditional and modern or technological societies, Ghosh is more interested in exploring the problems and tensions that arise from the confrontation of East and West. His novel portrays the rich but forgotten past of the East even as it depicts its decline under the onslaught of Western modernity.

Ghosh's postcolonial recuperation of a precolonial past extends beyond the content of his novel to its narrative form. He abandons the traditionally linear plot of the Western novel for an exuberantly digressive and allegorical collage of episodes that recalls *The Arabian Nights,* the Buddhist *Jataka* tales, and the Hindu *Panchatantra. The New York Times* voted *The Circle of Reason* "Notable Title of the Year" in 1987 for its bold experimentation with content and form, and the novel has since been translated and published in Swedish, Italian, Dutch, German, Danish, Finnish, Spanish, and French.

Two years after the success of his first novel Ghosh published *The Shadow Lines,* the title of which recalls Joseph Conrad's 1917 coming-of-age novella *The Shadow-Line: A Confession.* One of Ghosh's most acclaimed novels, *The Shadow Lines* is again experimental and postmodern in its treatment of history and the self. Written as a free-flowing nonchronological memory-narrative, the book spans two world wars, three countries (India, Britain, and what was earlier East Pakistan and is now Bangladesh), and three generations belonging to two interconnected families, one Indian and the other British. The device of filtering the momentous incidents of the first six decades of the twentieth century, during most of which India was still a colony, through the consciousness of a nameless Bengali boy from Calcutta has the effect of reversing the conventional stance on history, recording events not from the imperial center but from the subjugated periphery and showing what it was like to be shaped by, rather than to be in control of, those events.

Ghosh creates a complex vision of history in which apocalyptic violence is leavened by many small individual gestures of compassion and goodwill through counterpoint: the traumatic events of the Partition of India by her British colonial masters in 1947 on the one hand and the close emotional bonds linking the British and the Indian families on the other. The contrast between the divisive political confrontation and the warm personal relationship of the families provides

Indian Ocean rim, gaining a greater understanding of himself and his world. He learns that his Oriental heritage is in no way inferior to that offered by the Occident. He perceives his identity in part as the legacy of a vast precolonial network of historical and economic ties linking the ancient civilizations of Asia and Africa. Through "the flow of centuries of trade," involving "Persians, Iraqis, Zanzibari Arabs, Omanis and Indians," a sophisticated and self-sufficient cosmos evolved that had no need of the West. Ghosh depicts these older cultures, not in stereotypical terms of spirituality or tradition, but in all their bustling materiality and wealth. In his reverse mapping of the world, India, the Middle East, and Africa hold center stage, while Europe huddles on the periphery.

Alu's real name is Nachiketa, the name of a mythological Hindu sage who in the *Katha Upanishad* traveled to the underworld in search of truth. The Nachiketa analogue positions *The Circle of Reason*—with its three seca critique of man-made notions of difference that set up borders and exacerbate distinctions of class and culture. With the narrator moving from childhood to adulthood in the course of the action, the novel is a bildungsroman in which the protagonist learns to recognize the falsity as well as the tragic persistence of "shadow lines."

The story encompasses the negative movements of forcible dispersal and exile and the positive movements of reciprocity and travel. The two parts of the story, "Going Away" and "Coming Home," suggest the integration of all these cultural crossings through the consciousness of the narrator, who belongs to a highly educated, sophisticated, and well-traveled family of Hindus that fled to Calcutta from their ancestral home in predominantly Muslim Dhaka during the riots following the Partition of 1947. The refusal of the narrator's elderly grandmother Tha'mma to come to terms with her permanent banishment from the family home compels her to return to Dhaka in 1964 with a nephew, Tridib, who is tragically killed by a Muslim mob in the communal violence that flares up all over the subcontinent following the theft of a sacred Islamic relic from the Hazratbal mosque in Kashmir. The shadow lines of religious strife and cultural antagonism are thus seen to continue even in postimperial times, and Ghosh clearly wants his readers to consider the ways in which every individual is complicit in engendering hostility and mistrust.

The other main characters in the novel teach the narrator how to negotiate the shadow lines of his world. His chief mentor is his uncle Tridib, a Ph.D. student in archaeology, who helps him to connect the past with the present and find commonalities in difference: "Tridib had given me worlds to travel in and he had given me eyes to see them with." Cousins Robi and Ila are as cosmopolitan as Tridib but lack his imagination and sensitivity and so cannot share his "longing for everything that was not in oneself . . . that carried one beyond the limit of one's mind to other times and other places." From the example of his grandmother Tha'mma the boy discovers the consequences of ignoring reality and indulging a sentimental desire to turn the clock back. Most in tune with Tridib's pragmatic idealism are his British friend May Price and her father, Lionel Tresawsen; their relationship proves that breadth of vision and generosity of spirit can transcend dissimilarities in language and culture. Through his experiences in Calcutta and London the narrator comes to understand that official history is a construct of imperial or national self-interest, the exigencies of politics, the demands of the media, the pressures of racism and religious conflict, and various kinds of vested interests with their rumors and falsehoods. To counteract this fabricated history that stereotypes people and events as

good or bad, it is necessary, the narrator learns, to construct one's own history based on the truth of experience because, as Tridib remarks, "if we didn't try ourselves, we would never be free of other people's inventions."

In 1989 *The Shadow Lines,* which has been translated into several languages, earned India's highest literary honor, the Sahitya Akademi Award. The next year brought Ghosh more recognition–*The Shadow Lines* won the Ananda Puraskar Award and *The Circle of Reason* was honored in France with the prestigious Prix Medici Etrangere–and a major change in his life, as he married Deborah Baker, a senior editor at Little, Brown. The couple made their home in Brooklyn, New York, where they have raised two children, Lila and Nayan.

Even as Ghosh's literary career flourished in the 1990s, he remained active as an academic. He was a Fellow at the Centre for Studies in Social Science in Calcutta from 1990 to 1992. Between 1990 and 1994 he was visiting professor at the University of Virginia and on more than one occasion at Columbia University. He also lectured at the American University in Cairo as Distinguished Visiting Professor in 1994. He became a frequently invited speaker on social anthropology and literature at international conferences and writers' festivals, often giving readings from his works

Ghosh's third major book, *In an Antique Land: History in the Guise of a Traveler's Tale,* is a mainly nonfictional work that mixes history, biography, autobiography, ethnography, travel narrative, and fiction. His narrative moves back and forth between two stories: one based on Ghosh's experiences in Egypt as he was doing research for his doctoral thesis, and the other set in the distant past. Ghosh's research led him to his second story by way of the Cairo Geniza, an archive that contained documents belonging to the Egyptian Jewish community dating back for centuries. His attention was drawn to the life of a wealthy Jewish merchant of North African origin, Abraham Ben Yiju, who traveled from Egypt to the southern coast of India sometime in the twelfth century, following the prosperous Indian Ocean trade. Ben Yiju had an Indian wife, and his trusted slave and "business agent," Bomma, was Indian as well. The role that Bomma played in Ben Yiju's commercial ventures, a proletarian trace in the annals of the rich, fascinated Ghosh. The connection established through trade and family ties between an Egyptian and Indians in the medieval period becomes for Ghosh the symbol of an era in which culture, not conquest, braided societies together. In that world a saint with an Islamic name, Sadi Abu-Hasira, was actually a Jew venerated by Jews and Muslims alike. Language was another marker of cultural connections, as the Arabic word for "sugar"

Dust jacket for the American edition of Ghosh's second novel (1988), in which he traces the lives of two families—one English, one Bengali—as they are shaped by Bangladesh's partition in 1964 (Richland County Public Library)

(*sukkar*) was derived from Sanskrit, while the Hindi word for the term, *misri,* came from "Masr," the old Arabic name for Egypt. Such intercommunity transactions flourished entirely beyond the influence of the West and were in fact destroyed by Western imperialism. As Ghosh notes, "The remains of those small, indistinguishable, intertwined histories, Indian and Egyptian, Muslim and Jewish, Hindu and Muslim, had been partitioned long ago."

Like his predecessor Bomma, Ghosh also traveled from India to Egypt, where he lived in villages in the Nile delta while tracking down the history of that bygone African-Indian connection. The stories of Ghosh and Bomma, of modern Egypt and Ben Yiju's Egypt, coil in and out of each other like a double helix, to use the author's metaphor, structurally replicating the ways in which the past impinges upon the present. Ghosh's interactions with his rustic neighbors, briefly

recounted also in the title essay of *The Imam and the Indian,* provide some of the most exuberantly comic material in all his work. To his surprise he finds contemporary Egyptian culture more insular and materialistic, and, especially during the Gulf War, more fragile with respect to its traditions and values, than Ben Yiju's world, which seems to him to be more ecumenical and urbane. The modern Egyptian fails to understand Ghosh's Hindu beliefs and rituals, labeling them barbaric, while Ben Yiju, a Jew of Arab origin, had Hindu family and friends.

The blend of anthropology and autobiography in *In an Antique Land* aroused considerable interest among anthropologists as well as literary critics. In a review titled "A Passage to India" in the 23 August 1993 issue of *New Republic,* ethnologist Clifford Geertz praised Ghosh's ability to capture the dynamics of the medieval Indian Ocean trade and culture, a "mobile, polyglot and virtually borderless region, which no one owned and no one dominated." The book was the subject of a forty-minute television documentary on BBC Channel 3 in 1992 and listed as a "Notable Book of the Year" by *The New York Times* in 1993.

Ghosh's next book, *The Calcutta Chromosome: A Novel of Fevers, Delirium and Discovery* (1995), is part historical novel, part science fiction, and part medical thriller that transgresses conventional boundaries between fact and fiction and science and the paranormal. The events of the novel unfold along three time settings, the 1890s, 1995, and the early twenty-first century, and in two countries, the United States and India. The result is a cryptic, metafictional story-puzzle that won the Arthur C. Clarke Award for science fiction in 1997.

The novel begins in the twenty-first century when Antar, a low-level Egyptian American computer programmer, finds his ultrasophisticated terminal stalling when it comes across a damaged identification card belonging to Murugan, an eccentric former colleague of Indian origin who disappeared in Calcutta in 1995. Antar's investigations reveal that Murugan had gone to Calcutta to research the "secret history" behind the discovery of the malarial parasite by Colonel Ronald Ross, who won the Nobel Prize in medicine in 1902. Antar eventually learns that an unlikely trio of investigators—Murugan, along with a young journalist, Urmila Roy, and an actress-turned-socialite, Sonali Das—had unearthed a sinister mystic cabal that had planned to use the research done by British scientists to produce a malaria-altered human chromosome (the "Calcutta chromosome") that could be used to carry the genetic imprint of one human being to another, thereby assuring continuity of the self through several transmigrations.

The initiators of this project, the ruthless priestess Mangala Bibi and her acolyte Laakhan, had learned of the malarial parasite through divination long before Ross's "discovery." Murugan infers that they used paranormal means to propel Ross toward his discovery to confer scientific validity on their occult "counter-science"–their use of Ross inverting the expected colonial relationship of the exploiter and the exploited. Wasted by syphilis, Murugan urgently desires to replicate his psychic being through the Calcutta chromosome. Having transgressed beyond permissible limits in this quest, he, like others before him who had interfered in the supernatural processes, loses his mind, ostensibly to syphilitic degeneration. Antar, whose curiosity leads him to decode Mangala's mysteries, also crosses too many boundaries.

In the novel Ghosh plays with the belief that well before science identified its cause and remedy, malaria was successfully treated by indigenous methods in tropical countries but that such "unscientific" cures were dismissed as "fevers" and "delirium." Mangala and Laakhan represent non-Eurocentric, non-Anglophone knowledge that is not credited because it is not articulated in terms acceptable to the West. As an exploration of the bases of knowledge, *The Calcutta Chromosome* does not endorse empirical observation alone or intuition; knowledge and truth are shown to be beyond the sole possession of either the East or the West.

Ghosh's next work, *Dancing in Cambodia, At Large in Burma* (1998) is a nonfictional ethnographical travelogue comprising three short prose pieces–"Dancing in Cambodia," "Stories in Stones," and "At Large in Burma"–in which he again demonstrates the dichotomy between history as recorded and history as emotionally experienced. "Dancing in Cambodia" is framed by descriptions of two performances of the traditional classical dance of that country: beginning with the exhibition of the troupe of Royal dancers who moved Rodin to tears when King Sisowath visited France in May 1906 and ending with the performance of a dance troupe, assembled from among the survivors of the devastating carnage wrought by the Khmer Rouge during the Cambodian Cultural Revolution, in a shattered theater in Phnom Penh. While Rodin's tears had been for the exquisite beauty of an exotic oriental artifact, the packed Cambodian audience for the latter performance wept because the dance symbolized the survival of their culture against all odds. In "Stories in Stones," Ghosh visits the monumental twelfth-century Cambodian temple complex of Angkor Wat, which he calls "a monument to the power of the story," and discusses the sometimes contrary purposes to which the story of the temple is told by priests, politicians, colonial explorers, Western tourists, and ordinary Cambodian citizens.

In "At Large in Burma," Ghosh considers the significance of activist Aung San Suu Kyi for the Burmese people oppressed by a dictatorial government.

From 1999 until 2003 Ghosh was Distinguished Professor in the Department of Comparative Literature at Queen's College, City University of New York. In 1999 his essay "The March of the Novel through History: The Testimony of my Grandfather's Bookcase," a witty, empathetic sketch of the idiosyncratic literary sensibilities of the cultured middle-class Bengali, won the Pushcart Prize, and his article on the political brinkmanship in the confrontation of India and Pakistan over the development of nuclear weapons, which was published separately as a book (1999) and in the 19 October 1998 issue of *The New Yorker*, made the final list for the American Society of Magazine Editors' Award for reporting on a contemporary event. During his years at the college he also brought to press the highly acclaimed *The Glass Palace* (2000) and *The Imam and the Indian* (2002).

More epical in scope than *The Shadow Lines*, *The Glass Palace* is a saga about three generations of two closely linked families in Burma, India, and Malaya from 1885 to 1956 that is also an historical novel about the British colonization of Burma. Arjun, a twentieth-century anti-imperialist character, states the terrible legacy of the colonial experience: "We rebelled against an Empire that has shaped everything in our lives. . . . It is a huge, indelible stain which has tainted all of us. We cannot deny it without destroying ourselves." Yet, while imperialism divides and partitions and sets limits to freedom, the characters in the novel spill so easily over national and family boundaries through friendship and marriage that it becomes difficult to pinpoint a character's affiliation as exclusively Indian or Burmese or Chinese or Malay. *The Glass Palace* is more than merely a revisionary rewriting of a portion of the history of the British Empire from the perspective of the colonized subaltern–it is a paean to the human instincts for bonding and survival.

The primary thrust of the novel is epistemological, as Ghosh explores the process of the making and recording of history and questions whether history, in the sense of a consistent and causal concatenation of events, is at all possible. Ghosh shows that history changes if the viewer's perspective is altered and suggests that fiction, as a transcript of experience rather than of fact, is a viable alternative to the story told by official history. The "Glass Palace" of the title stands not only for the royal palace at Mandalay, the seat of Burmese power before colonial rule, but also for the idea that there are as many "histories" as there are tellers of the tale. History is like the mirrored central hall from which the Glass Palace takes its name: "you could

*Dust jacket for the American edition of Ghosh's 1993 book, which
combines his own experiences in Egypt in the 1980s and his
historical reconstruction of a twelfth-century relationship
between an Egyptian master and an Indian slave
(Richland County Public Library)*

So far as I can determine, *The Glass Palace* is eligible
for the Commonwealth Prize partly because it was
written in English and partly because I happen to
belong to a region that was once conquered and ruled
by Imperial Britain. Of the many reasons why a book's
merits may be recognized these seem to me to be the
least persuasive. That the past engenders the present is
of course undeniable; it is equally undeniable that the
reasons why I write in English are ultimately rooted in
my country's history. Yet, the ways in which we
remember the past are not determined solely by the
brute facts of time: they are also open to choice, reflection and judgment. The issue of how the past is to be
remembered lies at the heart of *The Glass Palace* and I
feel that I would be betraying the spirit of my book if I
were to allow it to be incorporated within that particular memorialization of Empire that passes under the
rubric of "the Commonwealth."

Ghosh's novel did win the Grand Prize for Fiction of
the 2001 Frankfurt eBook Award and was named
among the notable books of the year by *The New York
Times* as well as the *Los Angeles Times* and the *Chicago Tri-
bune.*

In 2002 Ghosh brought out *The Imam and the
Indian: Prose Pieces,* a collection of his published articles.
The first fourteen pieces offer valuable insights into
Ghosh's major literary concerns. The book also
includes "Hungry Stones," Ghosh's sensitive translation of Rabindranath Tagore's Bengali short story
"Kshudita Pashan." The two most moving pieces are
"The Greatest Sorrow: Times of Joy Recalled in
Wretchedness," an essay on diaspora as doomed dispersal rather than hopeful exodus, and "The Ghat of
the Only World: Agha Shahid Ali in Brooklyn," a tribute to the Kashmiri poet of the diaspora. In the range of
its themes and topics, *The Imam and the Indian* offers one
of the best introductions to Ghosh's work.

Ghosh in 2003 became a visiting professor at
Harvard University and the following year published
his fifth novel, *The Hungry Tide* (2004), set in the Sunderbans, the "tide country" of southern Bengal, in the
deltas of the Ganga and the Brahmaputra Rivers. The
novel portrays the stark struggle to survive on the
islands in the Bay of Bengal, an area subject to raging
cyclones and the habitat of tigers, crocodiles, and
snakes. It is the first book in which Ghosh presents a
character, like himself, with both Indian and American
affiliations: one of its protagonists is Piyali Roy, an
American cetologist of Bengali origin who has come to
the Sunderbans to study a rare species of dolphin.
Although she does not at first recognize her ulterior
motive, Piya is also in search of her roots.

Piya meets Kanai Dutt, a suave Delhi-based Bengali businessman visiting his aunt Nilima, a respected
social worker who has dedicated her life to building a

see yourself everywhere," and every image was
refracted in multiple ways.

The Glass Palace was submitted by Ghosh's publisher for the Commonwealth Prize without his knowledge. When he learned that his novel was among the
finalists for the award, he wrote to the administrators of
the prize on 18 March 2001 to withdraw his book from
the competition:

As a grouping of nations collected from the remains
of the British Empire, the Commonwealth serves as an
umbrella forum in global politics. As a literary or cultural grouping however, it seems to me that "the Commonwealth" can only be a misnomer so long as it
excludes the many languages that sustain the cultural
and literary lives of these countries (it is surely incon-
ceivable, for example, that athletes would have to be
fluent in English in order to qualify for the Commonwealth Games).

school, a hospital, and other facilities on one of the most remote of the islands, Lusibari. Kanai has come to collect a packet of papers left for him by his uncle Nirmal, an idealistic Marxist who died under mysterious circumstances. Piya also meets a local boatman, Fokir, whose intimate knowledge of the tidal waters and their traditional lore leads her to the dolphins. Confident in his knowledge of nature but poor, ragged, and unlettered, Fokir is the antithesis of the urbane Piya and the sophisticated Kanai. When Kanai acts as Piya's interpreter with Fokir and the crew of her hired boat, the interaction between the three is socially and psychologically complex. The novel ends with Fokir's death in a fierce cyclone and Piya and Kanai returning to Lusibari to participate in Nilima's welfare work, perhaps to share a future together.

Despite Ghosh's use of a romantic triangle, *The Hungry Tide* is not a conventional love story. The violent confrontation between Kanai and Fokir on a deserted island is not so much over Piya as it is about antagonisms fueled by differences in class, culture, and worldview. Thus, on one level Ghosh presents a story of self-realization, of confronting one's inner demons on the part of Fokir no less than of Piya and Kanai, and of Piya's and Kanai's recognition that the illiterate subaltern Fokir is as much of an individual as themselves. A second strand of the story revolves around Nirmal's manuscript—an account of his clandestine involvement in a people's movement that broke out in 1979 on the island of Morichjhampi—that Kanai reads as he goes about his work, thus setting up a counterpoint to the main action. Kanai learns of the massacre at Morichjhampi, which occurred when the Marxist government of West Bengal forcibly evicted thousands of refugees along with other landless people who had set up a commune there following the 1947 Partition of India. Set off against Nirmal's account is the little-known story of how Englishmen, led by Sir Daniel Hamilton, reclaimed the tidal land and established settlements with names such as Emilybari (Emily's Home) and Annbari (Ann's Home). The pioneering spirit of the elite is celebrated as history, but the accomplishments of the subaltern populace are erased.

The trackless wilderness of the Sunderbans, where all geographical signposts and human settlements are wiped out time and again by tides and storms, is the antithesis of an established civilization with its chronicled continuity. The cavalcade of tempests that Ghosh describes, with place-names and dates and tallies of casualties and the regular reshaping of the face of the land, matches any account of changes wrought by wars and revolutions. In his evocation of the "tide people," whose lives are forever at the mercy of nature and beasts of prey, Ghosh yet shows that they

Dust jacket for the American edition of Ghosh's 2000 novel, a saga of two families that covers more than a century of history following the British takeover of Burma in 1885 (Richland County Public Library)

have created a rich oral culture of tradition, song, and legend. *The Hungry Tide* thus stands at last as proof of Ghosh's inclusive vision of human worth through the stories of one of the least known communities in the world.

Amitav Ghosh has evolved a style and approach to his material distinctively his own. His fictional and nonfictional work mixes history, philosophy, science, literature, ethnography and folk culture on the one hand, and the picaresque narrative, travelogue, the novel of social commentary, fable, folktale, and popular culture genres such as detective fiction on the other. A postmodern writer in many respects, Ghosh is also a humanist. An insightful comment on his work comes from one of his own characters, Daw Thin Thin Aye, who is a creative writer in *The Glass Palace:* "Going into a house, intruding, violating, . . . I feel a kind of terror—and that's when I know I must keep going, step on, past the threshold, into the house." Ghosh's achievement is to take the reader into the edifice of history, discover those forgotten within, and lay bare the feelings that are obscured by facts.

Interview:

N. Silva and A. Tickell, "Amitav Ghosh in Interview," *Kunapipi*, 19, no. 3 (1997): 171–177.

References:

N. Bagchi, "The Process of Validation in Relation to Materiality and Historical Reconstruction in Amitav Ghosh's The Shadow Lines," *Modern Fiction Studies*, 39, no. 1 (1993): 187–202;

R. Basu, 1994, "Amitav Ghosh's Action: Turning the Full Circle," in *Indian-English Fiction 1980–1990: An Assessment*, edited by N. E. Bharucha and V. Sarang (New Delhi: B.R. Publishing, 1994), pp. 151–160;

Basu, "The Novels of Amitav Ghosh," *London Magazine*, 37 (August–September 1997): 159–161;

K. C. Beliappa, "Amitav Ghosh's *In an Antique Land*: An Excursion into Time Past and Time Present," in *The Postmodern Indian Novel: Interrogating the 1980s and 1990s*, edited by V. Kirpal (Bombay: Allied Publishers, 1996), pp. 59–66;

S. Chew, "Texts and Worlds in Amitav Ghosh's *In an Antique Land*," in *Re-Constructing the Book: Literary Texts in Transmission*, edited by M. Bell, S. Chew, S. Eliot, L. Hunter, and J. L. W. West III (Aldershot: Ashgate, 2001), pp. 197–209;

S. Dayal, "The Emergence of the Fragile Subject: Amitav Ghosh's *In an Antique Land*," in *Hybridity and Postcolonialism: Twentieth-Century Indian Literature*, edited by M. Fludernik (Tübingen, Germany: Stauffenburg, 1998), pp. 103–133;

R. K. Dhawan, ed., *The Novels of Amitav Ghosh* (New Delhi: Prestige Books, 1999);

R. Dixon, "'Travelling in the West': The Writing of Amitav Ghosh," *Journal of Commonwealth Literature*, 31, no. 1 (1996): 3–24;

L. James and J. Shepherd, "Shadow Lines: Cross-Cultural Perspectives in the Fiction of Amitav Ghosh," *Commonwealth Essays and Studies*, 14 (Autumn 1991): 28–32;

R. Kamath, "Memory and Discourse: On Amitav Ghosh's *In an Antique Land*," in *The Poetics of Memory*, edited by T. Wagenbaur (Tübingen, Germany: Stauffenburg, 1998), pp. 205–213;

N. Kapadia, "Imagination and Politics in Amitav Ghosh's 'The Shadow Lines,'" in *The New Indian Novel in English: A Study of the 1980s*, edited by V. Kirpal (New Delhi: Allied Publishers, 1990), pp. 201–212;

J. Majeed, "Amitav Ghosh's *In an Antique Land*: The Ethnographer-Historian and the Limits of Irony," *Journal of Commonwealth Literature*, 30, no. 2 (1995): 45–55;

P. Mongia, "Postcolonial Identity in Amitav Ghosh's *The Shadow Lines*," *College Literature*, 20, no. 1 (1993): 225–228;

G. J. V. Prasad, "The Unfolding of a Raga: Narrative Structure in *The Circle of Reason*," in *The New Indian Novel in English: A Study of the 1980s*, edited by V. Kirpal (New Delhi: Allied Publishers, 1990), pp. 101–108;

N. Rao, "Cosmopolitanism, Class and Gender in *The Shadow Lines*," *South Asian Review*, 24, no. 1 (2003);

A. Roy, "Microstoria: Indian Nationalism's 'Little Stories' in Amitav Ghosh's *The Shadow Lines*," *Journal of Commonwealth Literature*, 35, no. 2 (2000): 35–49;

A. Sen, "Crossing Boundaries in Amitav Ghosh's *The Shadow Lines*," *Journal of Commonwealth and Postcolonial Studies*, 5 (Fall 1997): 46–58;

The Shadow Lines, with critical essays by A. N. Kaul, Suvir Kaul, Rajeswari Sunder Rajan, and Meenakshi Mukherjee (New Delhi: Oxford University Press, 1995);

S. Singh, "Inventing London in Amitav Ghosh's *The Shadow Lines*," *Kunapipi*, 21, no. 2 (1999): 15–22;

J. Thieme, "The Discoverer Discovered: Amitav Ghosh's *The Calcutta Chromosome*," in *The Literature of Indian Diaspora: Essays in Criticism*, edited by A. L. McLeod (New Delhi: Sterling Publishers, 2000), pp. 274–290;

Thieme, "Passages to England," in *Liminal Postmodernisms: The Postmodern, the (Post-) Colonial, and the (Post) Feminist*, edited by T. D'haen and H. Bertens (Amsterdam: Rodopi, 1994).

Romesh Gunesekera

(26 February 1954 –)

Chelva Kanaganayakam
University of Toronto

See also the Gunesekera entry in *DLB 267: Twenty-First-Century British and Irish Novelists.*

BOOKS: *Monkfish Moon* (New Delhi & London: Granta/ Penguin / New York: Penguin, 1992);

Reef (London: Granta / New York: Penguin, 1994);

The Sandglass (New York: New Press, 1998; London: Granta, 1998; New Delhi & London: Viking, 1998);

Heaven's Edge (London: Bloomsbury, 2002; New York: Grove Press, 2002).

Edition: *Reef* (New York: New Press, 1995).

By the time Romesh Gunesekera started writing, at least two trends were becoming increasingly apparent in Sri Lanka: first, Sri Lankan writing in English, which for the previous three decades was a relatively marginal activity, was becoming more prolific and more confident in representing the realities of the nation; second, the political turmoil involving the minority Tamils and the majority Sinhalese had taken on a sustained presence. Particularly after the major ethnic conflict of 1983, the politics of ethnicity overshadowed all other national concerns. The burgeoning of literature in English was evident in the many writers who were gaining a reputation in Sri Lanka and the West—among them, Michael Ondaatje, Shyam Selvadurai, Chitra Fernando, Rienzi Crusz, Rajiva Wijesinha, Yasmine Gooneratne, Jean Arasanayagam, Chandani Lokuge, and Carl Muller. Taken together, they created a literary culture that was not only diverse in its narrative forms but also different in its preoccupations. To varying degrees, all of these writers were aware of and responsive to the forms of armed conflict that were destroying the country. Even the most apolitical writers found creating their narrative worlds in ways that did not reflect the presence of conflict almost impossible. Together with conflict came displacement and diaspora, both of which brought home the problematic nature of identity. As in the narratives of Gooneratne

Romesh Gunesekera (photograph by Barbara Piemonte; from the dust jacket for The Sandglass, *1998; Richland County Public Library)*

and Lokuge, the complexity of exile began to take on a new resonance.

The work of Gunesekera is written against this political backdrop of ethnic conflict. Himself a cosmopolitan writer who grew up in Sri Lanka and the Philippines and then settled down in England, Gunesekera was not unaware of the magnitude of the conflict or the price that the country had to pay for containing the turmoil. Born in Colombo on 26 February 1954, Gunesekera, the second son of Douglas and Miriam Gunesekera, and his family lived in Sri Lanka before moving in 1960 to the Philippines, where his father worked for the Asian Development Bank. In 1972 Gunesekera moved to England, attended the University of Liverpool, where he studied English and philosophy, and has remained in England ever since. Although his first book did not come out until much later, he won the Liverpool College Poetry Prize in 1972. His writing becomes a way of addressing the issues that confront contemporary Sri Lanka without necessarily making politics the subject of his writing. In that sense, his work is distinct from that of Wijesinha or Arasanayagam, who are insistently concerned with the political scene. In the novels and one collection of short stories that make up his corpus, Gunesekera has attempted to create fictive spaces that insist on artifice without abandoning the referential realities of Sri Lanka. As Paula Burnett rightly points out in relation to the short stories, "Gunesekera is typically interested in the shaping of narrative, the craft of writing: and the short story form always foregrounds its own artifice." This duality has played a significant role in determining the different responses of readers to his fiction.

Gunesekera does not always avoid a direct engagement with politics. In stories such as "Batik" in *Monkfish Moon* (1992), in which the concern is to foreground the ethnic conflict by depicting the marriage between a Tamil man and a Sinhalese woman, the intention to confront the political scene directly is more evident than in his later work. The Tamil husband in particular, as he changes during the story from a liberal to a Tamil nationalist, becomes a vehicle for expressing commonplace sentiments about ethnic conflict and primordial affiliation. The conflict in the story results from the different viewpoints about the ethnic conflict held by the husband and wife, who are Tamil and Sinhalese. The story drives home the idea that human relationships cannot lie outside the political context. Such stories sacrifice the complexity of human relationships in order to make a political point. "Batik" is a story in which the main interest lies in the force of metaphor rather than the message. "A House in the Country" is similar in addressing the destructive potential of militant movements, but the story is complemented by a complex treatment of land and entitlement. The notion of ownership and the relation between land and landscape provide a counterpoint to the violence that shapes human relations. Thus, the actions of the militants, including the killing of a businessman, become one element in a larger discourse. In a conversation with Rocio G. Davis published in *Miscellanea* in 1997, Gunesekera makes the observation that "people who read the book and are looking for the big events of life . . . are in a sense looking for sociology or political history. But you should be looking for an imaginative life."

"Captives"—a story that has little by way of plot, but which is more concerned with structures that imply layers of meaning—is a contrast to these two stories. Ethnicity is never mentioned. The story traces the relation between the manager of a hotel and a western couple who visit the rock fortress in Sigiriya. One can read the entire story as a western couple's experience of Sri Lanka. For the manager, Horniman, the woman becomes the object of an intense and futile lust, as he offers to take the couple to the mountain and takes every opportunity to stay close to the woman. The manager is too preoccupied with his quest to worry about anything else.

The central motif of the story—one that serves as a framing device—is the tale of Kassyappa, the parricide king whose thirst for power becomes a source of aesthetic creation and remorse. The sensuality of the paintings stands in contrast to his ambition and his downfall. The "public" narrative becomes a way of understanding the "private" tale in which the tourists are "captive" in a deserted hotel. What could well have been a romantic tale, or a Gothic one, becomes neither, as the manager's lust remains unexpressed. Burnett gives the story a postcolonial reading, identifying the plot as a metaphor for the internalized sense of the exotic "other," which refuses to disappear even after political freedom. Having referred to the ideological premise of tourism, she adds that "to the extent that the manager intends to make a living from the Europeans, the economic relationship is an inversion of the essence of empire, but in that he is their servant still, held . . . on the margins of their fulfilled lives, he could be an image from colonial days." In that sense the story functions along the lines of a chronotope (time/space relativity), creating its own spatial and temporal dimensions linked to but separate from historical realities. Such stories appear to be simple on the surface, but their success in large part results from the way in which several motifs are brought together to create a complex structure. The story operates at different levels and can be interpreted as a realistic tale or as an allegory.

In some ways, Gunesekera's views are those of a writer about diaspora. He does not deal with some aspects of Sri Lankan life in great detail. The way in which ritual and space, for instance, intersect in human relationships, lies outside his work. Differences among regions or among religious groups do not engage his interest. His vision is that of the onlooker, and that position enables him to focus on the artifice. Often his emphasis is on fragility—in human relationships, in politics, and in identity. In such instances, the stories provide clusters of images that lead to an epiphany. When stories move toward a climactic moment, often within the framework of the Gothic or adventure or quest, the moment of epiphany turns out to be quite different.

In "Monkfish Moon" the intertextual framework is that of F. Scott Fitzgerald's *The Great Gatsby* (1925) with Peter taking the role of the host who entertains lavishly, all the while being conscious of the emptiness of his ritual. He is the conscientious host who is also detached from the festivities. The narrator, like the narrator of *The Great Gatsby,* tries to find meaning in a confusing sequence of events. The moment of awareness is partial, but that is at least a consequence of the failure of language. Carefully structured and deliberately ambivalent, "Monkfish Moon" comes across as the kind of story in which the author offers many anecdotes that may appear unrelated to the central plot but ultimately combine to create multiple layers of meaning.

In most all of Gunesekera's stories, language serves as an ambivalent medium that functions with its own logic. Often, the language prompts a movement outside the plot to historical context. In "Captives," for instance, the constant dialogue almost always becomes a mode of evasion, and moments of awareness are seen as moments of silence. Thus, when the manager asks the woman several tactless questions, her response is a polite smile. At such moments, the absence of language communicates the complexity of the experience. The juxtaposition of English and Sinhala and the manner in which they intersect is yet another aspect of the preoccupation with language evident in this work. Gunesekera's language is hardly ever opaque, but its transparency is often selective in order to express levels of abstraction.

Gunesekera's first novel, *Reef* (1994), reiterates many of the preoccupations that surface in his collection of short stories, including the idea of fragility and the need to preserve a paradisal world that in countries such as Sri Lanka are on the verge of destruction. The central image of the reef underlines the idea that if certain structures, human or natural, are subject to wanton destruction, the end result will be the collapse of a way of life. The novel begins in London and moves back to Sri Lanka before returning to London. It is the narrative of a cook, Triton, who begins as a helper in the household of Salgado and becomes an extraordinary chef—an accomplishment that later enables him to open a restaurant in London. The dominant metaphor is the reef, which becomes a way of drawing together the multiple themes that run through the novel. Whether in the mingling of different ethnic communities or the coexistence of different lifestyles, something of the richness of a culture is dependent, much like the reef, on a delicate balance based on acceptance and mutual understanding. The reef is also a symbol for memory, which confers identity and also provides the rationale for greed and destruction.

Graphic images of rapacious sharks and dolphins, later framed by murderous insurgents and ethnic groups, underscore the potential for violence in Sri Lanka. The play on "erosion" with notions of "eros" and the "erotic" demonstrate how easily one slides into another, as good-natured banter becomes vulgarity, and the love between Ranjan and Nili turns into suspicion

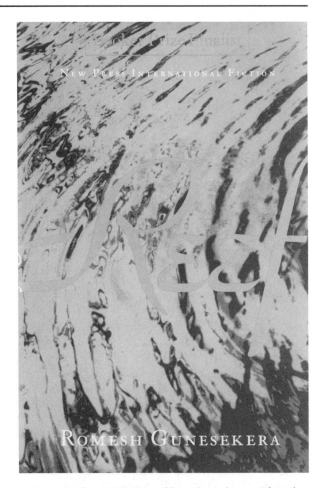

Dust jacket for a 1995 edition of Gunesekera's first novel (1994), which is set in Sri Lanka and London and chronicles the rise of a young man from aristocrat's houseboy to professional chef (Richland County Public Library)

and accusations of adultery. The sensuous descriptions of the sea as sanctuary and as the source of all life serve as motifs in the novel as Salgado tries to keep at bay everything that threatens to destroy it. Salgado's house becomes a metonym for the novel, as its generosity is transformed, first by the ugly presence of Joseph, who sexually abuses Triton, and then by the visitors who exploit the magnanimity of Salgado, and finally the presence of Nili, whose role remains ambivalent throughout the novel. She embodies the dualities that characterize the novel—she is both the embodiment of love and the temptress. Among the critics who have written on the novel, Walter Perera is particularly critical of the author's depiction of women, especially of Nili. According to Perera, "*Reef* is very much written from a man's perspective, a perspective which does not flatter Sri Lankan womanhood." Nili may also be seen as a symbolic figure whose various actions are necessary moments in a narrative about rites of passage. The ending of the novel may be deliberately ambivalent.

The political background of the novel, as of the short stories, is the insurgency of 1971 and the ethnic conflict starting in 1983. In 1971 the Sinhala youth, disillusioned with the political structures of the previous two decades, attempted to overthrow the government. The ill-fated attempt was crushed quickly by the government. In 1983 the conflict between the Sinhalese and the Tamils escalated into brutal violence; the ethnic conflict continued for the next two decades, claiming more than sixty thousand lives. Both are mentioned and contextualized in ways that do not intrude into the narrative. Minute details about the conflicts are avoided in favor of larger generalizations about destruction and animosity. The impulse to destroy and the will to power are manifestations of a land and a people who have forgotten the basis of harmony. Gunesekera's main concern continues to be the more abstract issue of balance. The materiality of the text is clearly less of a concern. In his conversation with Davis, Gunesekera observes that "a book is about itself. We like to think that books are about places, so if we are going to, say, Singapore, then we might want to read a Singapore story. But that doesn't work because if you actually go to Singapore, and want to know how to get from A to B, or where to buy a camera or something, you do not read a novel." The manner in which the landscape is dealt with, particularly the way in which space is used, suggests a clear distance between the text and the world in which it is located. Social relations, for instance, are carried out in a manner that implies a cosmopolitanism that is removed from the family structures, the extended families, or the social network of Sri Lankan society. The characters tend to be relatively isolated from social contexts, and rituals that would link the text with the cultural context of the country are lacking.

Some critics, such as Perera, have suggested that the author has a penchant for exoticizing the country, and by the same token, essentializing the different facets of society. Some of the characters who are part of *Reef* are reminiscent of the fictional creations of Ondaatje, another well-known writer of Sri Lankan descent, who, like Gunesekera, has spent the better part of his life outside Sri Lanka. Perera is emphatic about the deliberate "otherness" flaunted by the author. "A critical engagement with the text discloses that despite some memorable representations of Sri Lankan culture and seascape, *Reef* is guilty of recuperating and perpetuating certain myths and stereotypes about Sri Lanka." Perera provides details to demonstrate the exoticism in the novel. Exoticism, however, may well be a narrative strategy for Gunesekera, who uses the trapping of the exotic to reinforce the sense of artifice in the novel. The novel is, in some senses, about the real Sri Lanka and its political turmoil. But sociological precision is not Gunesekera's

intention. Rather, he imagines the country in a real sense, and the novel owes much of its power to its image-making impulse. The house, the reef, the garden, and the road are some of the recurring images that make up the novel.

Food is also central to *Reef,* as it is to Gunesekera's writing in general. Several pages in the novel are devoted to minute descriptions of varieties of both Sri Lankan and Western food. The choice of a cook as narrator is an important strategy. The novel is replete with ritualized behavior, and that complements the pervasive motif of food. People visit each other, meet at parties, go on trips, or make food an integral part of domestic relations. In each of these instances, Triton's culinary expertise consists of a curious eclecticism that is a result of having learned his lessons from a range of people—from the more traditional servant to the master of the house. Even Nili provides the occasion for more experiment; that she gives Triton a book of recipes as a gift for Christmas underscores his eclecticism. The novel ends with Triton's opening a restaurant in England—yet another instance of food in a changing culture. In Sri Lanka, the food that Triton provides is a curious mix of the East and West. Strangely enough, Salgado eats little, but he pays for all the expensive meals that Triton cooks for others. The food is a hybrid mix—no different from the people who surround Salgado—love cake, patties, seeni sambol, and string hoppers. The Tamils, Sinhalese, and Burghers of different religious persuasions who come to Salgado's house are a reminder of the virtues and limitations of the culture's hybrid nature. Triton's food is not burdened by the past. He makes up the food as he goes along, always open to new ideas and concerned only with pleasing his guests. The newness occupies an interstitial space in the novel that looks at the past and the future. Much like the reef, food remains both metonymy and metaphor in the novel, drawing attention to specificities of landscape and culture while suggesting more-abstract and general concerns about identity.

Reef is probably Gunesekera's most controversial novel. It established him as an important young writer and drew considerable praise in the West. Davis and Burnett, for instance, are extremely warm in their praise for the novel. Both of them are aware, however, that Perera is skeptical about the achievement of the novel. Where Davis and Burnett find "authenticity," Perera finds appropriation and distortion. According to Perera, "Had Gunesekera's failing been merely that of sacrificing depth for breadth the consequences would have been serious but not totally debilitating; what jeopardizes the entire novel, however, is his blinkered attitude to Sri Lanka. . . ." The dichotomy is central to how readers have responded to the author. Even the notion of a lost paradise, which keeps recurring as a significant motif in his works, lends itself to the duality of belonging and otherness.

The notion of a lost Eden, which appears in *Reef,* continues more explicitly in *The Sandglass* (1998), with the major difference that the plot is far more convoluted and the narrative more preoccupied with social interaction. The plot has a familiar element, the doomed attempt by the Ducals to create Arcadia—the name implies sadness—and the destructive presence of the Vatunas, constantly involved with schemes that undermine any attempt to create a paradise. Chapters with headings such as "midnight" and "dawn" are self-explanatory. The novel won the BBC Asia Award for Achievement in Writing and Literature in 1998.

Structured in the form of a quest, the novel traces the history of a family. Many characters appear at various times, while certain ones, such as the father figure, receive more attention than others. Little attention is given to the specifics of the political backdrop. The rivalry between the two families makes up the complex plot of the novel. In addition, the novel is about diaspora, as characters move back and forth from Sri Lanka to England. Particularly in the person of Pearl—a significant name, given the concerns of the novel—a binary is set up between the opulence of Arcadia and the frugality of London. Both involve alienation and despair. All the other characters, including the narrator, Prins, and Naomi, straddle both worlds, and their individual stories contribute to the notion of diaspora as an aspect of the quest for paradise.

Memory and time are equally crucial to the novel. In the conversation with Davis, published at the time that Gunesekera was finishing the draft of *Sandglass,* the author claims that "all writing is about memory." He went on to say that "our imagination is fed by the past, by the impressions we remember, the things we've heard and seen."

A major aspect of *Sandglass* is the social frame, which involves many characters. The narrator, Chip, does not advance the plot but functions as a sympathetic listener who connects events and enables the plot to unfold. The characters are highly individualized, each one contributing to the overall movement of the narrative. The language also moves beyond the referent to a level of abstraction. Thus, in the following passage, the referent is less important than the quality of the language:

> He [Jason] likes to come to this spot from time to time because of its utter darkness. If the moon is veiled, then the tracks only gleam under his feet. To his right and to his left they vanish into black holes. He is faced with the silhouettes of dead trees, shadows without light,

Dust jacket for Gunesekera's 1998 novel, in which the narrator tries to piece together what happened between two warring Sri Lankan families, including the possible murder of a patriarch (Richland County Public Library)

and the roar of an invisible sea. It is a place where vision could fail but the senses come alive: the smell of the sea, the roar of water and wind. The fronds of dead and dying trees. But after a little while the eye begins to learn to see again. To discern shapes out of the darkness, tell the sea from the sky and entrap the imagination. *The imagination is our most molested flower,* he wrote, *so easily crippled in a heartless paradise.*

Gunesekera's novel *Heaven's Edge,* published in 2002, is also his most enigmatic and perhaps his most experimental work. Akash Kapur, reviewing the book for *The New York Times Book Review* (3 February 2003), calls it "Gunesekera's most accomplished work yet." In this novel the familiar markers are kept to a minimum, and the fictional world is barely recognizable as Sri Lanka. Science fiction, magic realism, and realism seem to be woven together in a quest novel. The novel con-

Dust jacket for the American edition of Gunesekera's 2002 novel, a quest narrative that blends science fiction, magic realism, and realism in a war-torn setting resembling Sri Lanka (Richland County Public Library)

myth, with a "hero," a quest, a demon figure, and a possible boon at the end. As in traditional myths, the hero's task is to remove the evil that has tormented a community. The character of Uva is both the reward waiting at the end and a symbol of a land that is being devastated. She is a goddess, lover, and the nation. Uva in this novel has the same effect that Nili has on Salgado in *Reef,* with the one major difference that she is an allegorical figure.

On the other hand, the novel combines these elements within a discourse that gives the myth a contemporary relevance. The novel self-consciously avoids the markers that would identify the forces that oppress the people. The general climate of fear and the pervasive violence that creates a sense of foreboding, rather than the people, are responsible for the killing. No one, however disinterested, is able to escape the violence, and the soldiers finally destroy even Samandia, a kind of pastoral ideal. The novel begins along the lines of a referential work, as Marc goes to the Palm Beach Hotel to rest and to learn about the land. Even the close proximity of Maravil gives a sense of veracity. The initial pages of the novel are in the tradition of realistic writing. Gradually, the realistic presentation is abandoned, although the reality of the novel is never dissipated. All the four elements—earth, fire, air, and water—appear at different times, performing different functions. The novel is a version of a myth and, like all myths, belongs to a discourse in which an ideology expresses its power while masking its hegemonic intentions.

Heaven's Edge marks a turning point in Gunesekera's writing and a watershed in Sri Lankan literature; it attempts to come to terms with the kind of anxiety that appears to have plagued writers who choose to write in English. In this novel, the return to nature is carefully orchestrated to a stage much more complex than the form of agrarian escapism evident earlier in Sri Lankan fiction. Certain patterns begin to emerge as the novel progresses, and these patterns establish self-sufficient structures of meaning. For instance, Uva has a concern for birds. Her farm is also a sanctuary for a wounded nature. Later, Marc shows similar concern when he decides to give shelter to a wounded monkey. Anxiety about human violence is displaced through a preoccupation with animals and birds. Marc's pet monkey takes on so many human characteristics that when the soldiers finally butcher it, the act becomes a form of cannibalism. Such images resonate in the novel, recalling other incidents, such as Kris's murder of the caretakers and Marc's revulsion in thinking that when Kris pours wine into glasses he is in fact filling the goblets with blood. Ethics, violence, and love are central markers that frame the novel and shape its structure.

cerns a young quest figure whose parents are dead and whose association with Sri Lanka draws the narrator to that world. The novel is situated in the war-torn Sri Lanka of recent memory. Gunesekera seems unwilling to insert the markers that made his previous novels recognizably "Sri Lankan." Names of characters and places suggest that the backdrop is Sri Lanka, and the armed conflict is equally reminiscent of the events in the country, but nowhere does the novel claim that the events take place in Sri Lanka.

In terms of structure, the novel operates at the level of myth. The idea of myth as a framing device has always been present in Gunesekera's work. Davis devoted a whole article to the use of the child figure as part of the mythical structure in *Reef.* Davis thinks of myth in Jungian terms and links the mythical framework to the presence of archetypes. In *Heaven's Edge* the use of myth is more traditional and closer to the sense in which Joseph Campbell defines myth. The novel has, on the one hand, all the trappings of conventional

The novel ends in Samandia—a fabled place where myth and nature merge. It is a world to which Marc descends on his mythical bird, and here Uva appears, as she rises from the water. The realism of the novel offers a plausible explanation for a confusing sequence of events, but the narrative also takes on a mythical quality. The intertextual references make this place both timeless and modern. Marc is a Robinson Crusoe figure, determined to survive but resolved to merge with the harmony of nature. What is important, however, is not the linear plot so much as the evocation of a glimpse at an unsullied world. The anxiety of looking for causes, assigning blame, and identifying the enemy are no longer issues in a novel such as *Heaven's Edge*. The violent image with which the novel ends drives home both the national and allegorical aspects of the work. As Kapur observes, "Gunesekera's story may be dreamlike, but his prose is resolutely grounded, and the result . . . is a story that uses realism to transcend reality."

One of the major strengths of Romesh Gunesekera's work—one that sets it apart from much postcolonial literature—is that it hardly ever depends on plot. Certain patterns continue to define his work, but each work marks a new attempt, a fresh way of giving expression to the diaspora. Both in his short stories and in his novels, the author offers a vision that accommodates the objectivity of the outsider and the subjectivity of the insider. Starting with a collection of stories that are predominantly referential, the author moves to modes that are more experimental. The least that can be said about him is that he is among the handful of writers who, in the last ten years, have given renewed interest in Sri Lankan literature in English.

Interview:

Rocio G. Davis, "We Are All Artists of Our Own Lives: A Conversation with Romesh Gunesekera," *Miscellanea: A Journal of English and American Studies,* 18 (1997): 43–54.

References:

Paula Burnett, "The Captives and the Lion's Claw: Reading Romesh Gunesekera's *Monkfish Moon*," *Journal of Commonwealth Literature,* 32, no. 2 (1997): 3–15;

Rocio G. Davis, "'I am an Explorer on a Voyage of Discovery: Myths of Childhood in Romesh Gunesekera's *Reef*," *Commonwealth,* 20, no. 2 (1998): 14–25;

Walter Perera, "Images of Sri Lanka through Expatriate Eyes: Romesh Gunesekera's *Reef*," *Journal of Commonwealth Literature,* 30, no. 1 (1995): 63–78.

Sunetra Gupta

(15 March 1965 –   )

Somdatta Mandal
Visva-Bharati University

BOOKS: *Memories of Rain* (New Delhi: Penguin, 1992; New York: Weidenfeld, 1992; London: Orion, 1992);

The Glassblower's Breath (New York: Grove, 1993; New Delhi: Penguin, 1993; London: Orion, 1993);

Moonlight into Marzipan (London: Phoenix House, 1995; New Delhi: Penguin, 1995);

A Sin of Colour (New Delhi: Penguin, 1999; London: Phoenix House, 1999); republished as *A Sin of Color: A Novel of Obsession* (Naperville, Ill.: Sourcebooks Landmark, 2001).

SELECTED PERIODICAL PUBLICATIONS– UNCOLLECTED:

FICTION

"Strangers & Other Ghosts," *Kunapipi,* 16, no. 1 (1994): 288–295;

"Mother," in *VOX: New Indian Fiction,* edited by Jeet Thayil (Bombay: Sterling, 1996), pp. 52–62.

NONFICTION

"Why I Write," *Kunapipi,* 16, no. 1 (1994);

"A Victim of Truth," *Nature,* 407 (2000): 677;

"Avoiding Ambiguity," *Nature,* 412 (2001): 589.

Sunetra Gupta (photograph by Jerry Bauer; from the cover for A Sin of Color: A Novel of Obsession, *2001; Richland County Public Library)*

A reader in the epidemiology of infectious diseases at the Department of Zoology, Oxford University, is an unlikely profession for a talented novelist whose first novel won her the coveted Indian literary Sahitya Akademi Award in 1996. But Sunetra Gupta has bridged writing and research effectively. Born in Calcutta 15 March 1965 to Dhruva Gupta, a professor of history at the University of Calcutta, and Minati Gupta, a schoolteacher, Gupta is a diasporic Bengali who spent much of her childhood in places such as Ethiopia, Zambia, Liberia, and Birmingham—wherever her father's contractual jobs took the family. She then returned with her parents to live for some time in Calcutta and studied at Patha Bhavan School and La Martinere School—both reputed English medium institutions of the city. Sunetra's father introduced her to the work of Bengali Nobel Laureate Rabindranath Tagore,

and the influence of Tagore's work is evident in her first novel, *Memories of Rain* (1992), which she wrote many years later.

As a teenager in Calcutta, she started by writing science fiction and had Satyajit Ray, a friend of her father, take the time to read her stories. She cherishes the fond memory of how while commenting on her work, among other things, movie director Ray had stressed the use of correct grammar. The fiction he read was in Bengali, stories published in local science-fiction journals such as *Fantastic* and *Samatat.* The exact dates and titles of the pieces have been forgotten by both Gupta and her parents; the only thing they remember is that Adrish Bardhan, the editor of *Fantastic,* encouraged Gupta as a child prodigy. Only after she went to study biology at Princeton University did Gupta switch from writing in her mother tongue to English.

In 1987 Gupta graduated from Princeton University and moved to London to pursue her doctoral studies in biology at Imperial College. While undertaking her research, she ventured into fiction writing, and her debut novel, *Memories of Rain,* was published the year that she received her Ph.D. degree. Revealing her attachment to places she felt she belonged to, especially Calcutta and Oxford, Gupta brings together Anthony and Moni, two characters from disparate worlds, in a Calcutta rainstorm. Anthony is English; he is also intelligent and artistic. Assured and mysterious, Moni is a bright but young Bengali woman who has led a sheltered life. She is steeped in cultural protocol, sensitive to taboos, and fond of Jane Austen and the songs of Tagore. She finds herself both repelled and fascinated by this classmate of her brother's, a visitor from the Europe of her fevered and literary imagination. They fall in love, apprehending unconsummated passion and years of unsatisfying, sorrowful memories. Instead, they are able to marry and make their home in London, where Moni–intense but silent–soon meets disappointment. Once in London, she encounters prejudices, sexism, and betrayal by the husband who had seemed so captivated by her beauty and virginal purity. His blatant disrespect for her shocks her. Her emotions are heightened and accentuated by the gray British weather, the drab buildings, and the bewildering pace of life in a new country. Gupta contrasts masterfully the fecund, languid beauty of faraway home with the bleak internal and external circumstances in which Moni now finds herself. When Anthony begins to stray–even when his mistress becomes practically a member of the household–Moni believes his divided heart will accommodate her, but she cannot bear the hurt when his manner changes to kindness and indifference. The main action of the novel takes place during a single weekend, when Moni, despondent over Anthony's infidelity, secretly plans to take their child and return to India on her birthday. Tension builds as she weighs the consequences and finally makes her decision.

Writing *Memories of Rain* was a profound experience for Gupta. "Suddenly you come to touch a part of yourself," she said to the anonymous Rediff.com interviewer in 1996. Steeped in Bengali culture, especially the Calcutta of the 1950s and 1960s that she nostalgically re-creates in her novel, her writing reveals that she cannot forget the city that she left behind. Also, she had known the city in both good and bad times, and even at a distance has been loyal to it, unlike so many who leave and just remember the heat and dust, the pollu-

tion and noise. An acute Bengaliness pervades this novel, especially the expression of Moni's anguished passion and dark thoughts, articulated through Tagore's songs. In the same interview, Gupta emphasized that her exposure to literature and writing had been conditioned by her father, a major influence on her life.

Unlike the binaries of Calcutta and London, where the first novel was set, the characters in Gupta's second novel, *The Glassblower's Breath* (1993), live in transnational spaces that are "somewhat outside of being anywhere." The plot details a single day in the lives of a butcher, a baker, and a candle maker and the woman all three love. The protagonist of this novel is a young Indian woman in search of ideal love and companionship. Though the settings move between London, Calcutta, Paris, and New York, none of these cities can be considered the true "home" of any of the characters. Like true postcolonial migrants, the characters themselves, though born in one of these cities or somewhere else, wander through these urban settings, living in each one at some time or the other and yet always detached from them. When an acquaintance replies that he hates London, the narrator's response is simply, "When I get tired of London, I go to Paris." The landscapes of these three great cities, full of urban menace, thus form an almost surreal backdrop for this unsettling tale of a young, intelligent Indian woman who struggles but fails to conform to society's blueprints for marriage, family, and friendships.

The heroine of *The Glassblower's Breath* is caught between her own almost limitless capacity for experience–emotional, intellectual, and sexual–and the desire of the men in her life to capture and define her. In spite of her education, freedom, social position, and the privileges she enjoys, she is still condemned to repeat her gendered functions–that is, her role as daughter or wife. Though educated, she becomes the quintessential Indian woman, experiencing emotional and intellectual deprivation. Her desire not to succumb to the patriarchal authority is not so much a manifestation of her libidinous self as it is a form of protest against the traditional norms and values that she had encountered both in Calcutta and in London. She is unable to forget her sister's death from cancer and has frequent nightmares in which she sees the rotting body of her sister that reminds her how the past keeps intruding upon her private space. Gupta's poetic language depends on free association and is allied to continuous time shifts that are reminiscent of Virginia Woolf's stream-of-consciousness mode of narration. Gupta never uses direct speech or dialogue in any of her novels.

As Sandra Ponzanesi points out, the protagonist in *The Glassblower's Breath* is addressed by the second-

Dust jacket for the American edition of Gupta's first novel, published in 1992, the story of a Bengali woman debating whether to leave her unfaithful English husband and return to India (Richland County Public Library)

person pronoun "you" because her identity can never be fully grasped. The reader has to reconstruct her personality through the different narrations associated with her. As in a house full of mirrors, her image is viewed through different perspectives, none of which is satisfactory or permanent. The possibility of authentic knowledge of the self is lost, as lost as the possibility of returning home. All the dislocations of life in the story are articulated by multiple narrators, who trace the adventure of the unnamed female character. In this way she moves continuously through space and through narration in a perpetual process of negotiation of the self: "You have come a long way, my love, a long way from home, you have found your way into a houseful of mirrors, that each tell you a tale, but none as well as you might have." Perhaps the most ironic instance of her dispossession is the omniscient narrator's appropriation of her voice. This male voice decides her life for

her, forms her, and finally destroys her. It is as if she existed only in somebody else's imagination.

Gupta's third novel, *Moonlight into Marzipan* (1995), is a complex and arduous novel that does not follow a regular chronological order of events but shifts backward and forward in time and space, leaving the task of reassembling the fragments of a life to the readers. *Moonlight into Marzipan* is a story of a marriage and its ultimate betrayal. Promothesh and Esha, two promising scientists who were classmates at Calcutta University, find their relationship changing after marriage. In keeping with Indian cultural expectations, Esha turns into a dedicated and submissive wife, but Promothesh collapses under her dedication and feels incapable of living up to her grand expectations. He resumes his research in their Calcutta garage and steps into celebrity status when a chance experiment turns grass into gold. Proceeding to England for further scientific investigations, he initiates the breakup of their relationship.

Promothesh's discovery promised to bring him fame and riches; instead, it triggers a chain of events that begins with his arrival in London and ends with Esha's death, leaving him marooned and confused. His astonishing discovery is forgotten in the process. Into this morass of ambition and self-pity slips love, in the form of his biographer, Alexandra Vorobyova, and "the devil's own apprentice," in the form of Yuri Sen. As in Dante's journey, he encounters Lucifer in the person of Yuri Sen, also an Indian researcher, whose project is a mysterious one. Yuri Sen subverts the narrative by using italics and telling readers that Promothesh is incapable of writing to them. He is, in fact, the one who verbalizes Promothesh's failure with an expression that becomes the title of the novel: "For five years now, he has been kept in this chintz dungeon on the promise of turning moonlight into marzipan and all he has managed to make is molasses out of his life." The dream of creating paradise on earth turns into an irreversible voyage into hell.

Though the novel is divided into four sections—"Prologue," "The Book of Iron," "The Book of Brass," and the "Epilogue"—the major device used by Gupta is to deprive the narration of a reliable narrator. From the opening pages, the readers have to struggle to locate the central character(s) and identify the perspective from which these character(s) are viewed. These characters are not representative of a particular culture and essentially explore various issues that cut across geographical boundaries.

When Alexandra goes away and abandons the text, Promothesh is left with only the pieces of his life he had scribbled down in notes—the results of his long conversation and confessions with the dismissive narrator. The novel takes the form of a dialogue between

Promothesh and the absent narrator. In the process, the novel plays with the ambiguity and confusion between the subject and the object of narration, between the narrator and the narratee. The personal pronouns *I* and *You* are peppered into the text in the attempt to reconstruct the trajectory of Promothesh's life, which remains unfulfilled and is never fully reconstructed.

When she was asked to describe her "growth" from the first novel to her third, Gupta told the Rediff interviewer, "My concerns have become more and more spiritual and there is an obvious effort—a religious dedication if you may say so—to come closer to the truth." The initial self-consciousness and the desire to present India or Bengal in her own work and to be included in a certain community of writers was now over, she said. As she stated, "My work is more 'free' now." Writing for her is a kind of spiritual exercise, in which she is not involved in any political movement but tries to uncover human conditions.

In 1993 Gupta joined the Department of Zoology, Oxford University, as a reader in epidemiology of infectious diseases; she continues to teach there. In 1994 she married an Irish colleague, Adrian Hill, a professor in the Department of Medicine. Their first daughter, Urmila, was born on 16 August 1996, and the second, Nisha, on 19 April 1999. Dividing her time between her family, researching infectious diseases, and writing, Gupta published her fourth novel, *A Sin of Colour,* in 1999.

A Sin of Colour is about the choices made by its two main protagonists, Debendranath Roy and his niece Niharika, during two different time periods, when both are in the last phase of youth. The narrative moves between Oxford and the United States and Calcutta and rural Bengal, but most of the action takes place in Oxford and Calcutta, the two places that Gupta knows best. Both characters are victims of unrequited love, a fact that colors their lives profoundly, eventually leading Niharika to adultery with Daniel Faraday, who is married and a friend of Morgan, the last man to have seen Debendranath alive.

Through seven sections named after seven colors, starting with "Amethyst" and then moving through "Indigo," "Azure," "Jade," "Saffron," "Ochre," and "Crimson," Gupta tells the story of three generations and of a house in Calcutta called Mandalay. Built by a British officer, it passes into the hands of the wealthy Roy family. Debendranath's father brings his clever but child-like bride to Mandalay after their wedding. Many years later, Debendranath's brother brings his own wife, the woman with whom Debendranath is fated to fall in love, to the house. The family's fortunes fluctuate. Independence and partition rob them of much of their wealth, and Debendranath flees the house, his

Dust jacket for Gupta's 1993 novel, which depicts the struggles of an educated Indian woman to escape confining gender roles and find ideal love (Richland County Public Library)

family, and his hopeless love to find a new life in England. The multiple sins, each associated with a color, all concern the one sin that forms the basis of the book—Debendranath's retirement from this world, his ultimate withdrawal from the clutches of human relationships and escape from the demands that are foisted on an individual by society. His desire for true freedom, to run away from all ties, makes the story take a curious turn when a man in his late thirties is last seen entering a punt on the Cherwell in Oxford. When no further trace of him is found, Debendranath Roy is presumed drowned. He leaves behind a pale and languishing widow in Oxford and a mystery that takes twenty years to unfold. By the time Debendranath returns from the dead, Mandalay is in ruins, all but abandoned by the next generation, a house full of ghosts.

A Sin of Colour won the 2000 Southern Arts Literature Award. The narrative unfolds like a conversation, picking one thread and jumping back and forth into the

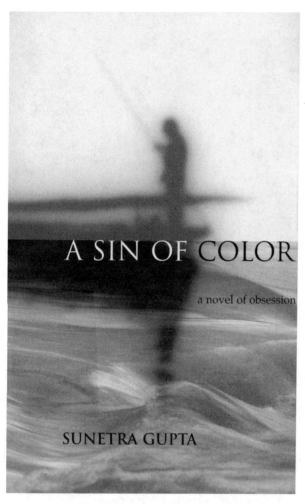

Cover for the 2001 American edition of Gupta's 1999 novel, set mainly in Calcutta and Oxford, about a man who flees from his desire for his brother's wife (Richland County Public Library)

past and future, sometimes taking off on tangents and then returning to the present to initiate another thread that unfolds similarly. Gupta's long sentences, some going on for almost half a page, are filled with adjectives, descriptions, and double metaphors, and they meander through different thought processes and come to a halt abruptly. The repetition does not affect the intent of the book. Despite little action, the dialogues are all without quotes and blend into the general narrative.

Gupta's short story "Mother" (anthologized first in 1996, although the publication date has been forgotten by the author herself) also deals with fraught relationships. The unnamed protagonist of this story is a young and lonely man who lives alone in a shack next to the sea. Things change when his mother, who had left home twenty years ago, comes back to their sprawling and deserted villa on the seashore and tries to bring back stability and normalcy to their lives. The story begins with her project of writing a biography of her dead husband, the young man's father, but this work is ultimately aborted when the woman decides to go back to the city. Loneliness engulfs the young man once again when he returns to his only refuge–the shack by the sea.

Gupta's work defies categorization, and she does not fit into the prevalent fictional modes adopted by other diasporic writers, such as the widely used form of autobiographical fiction, or the historical novel, or magic realism. She believes that market forces have come to affect contemporary writing and for her this phenomenon is disturbing. She has emphasized to the Rediff interviewer: "A readership is being created by offering them exotic tid-bits to titillate them. This is not obvious as something like pornography but the reader is fed a bit of China, bits of India, of this and that and everything is handed over to him on a platter. The reader does not have to work at all and this is something very dangerous." In her writing, Gupta fuses different genres and languages, experimenting continuously with the English language and creating her own personal literary idiom. She is not concerned whether a foreigner understands the nuances of the world that she presents in her books. Although a woman writer, she does not highlight feminist issues in her novels. Though she does not belong to any movement, some of her characters–such as Esha in *Moonlight into Marzipan*–are quite strong. She depicts women with strength of character and dignity but not necessarily as feminists. But, at the same time, characters such as Esha are juxtaposed with other women in her work who represent a consumerist approach to life and have an appetite for exotica but lack the strength to get to the root of matters.

The poetic meandering of language and stylistic innovations that are found in all her novels have made critics repeatedly call her a successor to Woolf. Her play with language is to be found even in her nonfiction. How she manages to juxtapose her scientific career with her literary endeavors is described, for instance, in an article about mathematics in the popular press, "Avoiding Ambiguity." In it she compares mathematical and poetic metaphors, notes the powers and limitations of the language of mathematics, and laments how this language has been misappropriated by some in the social and biological sciences: "The language of mathematical reasoning is no less beautiful for the lack of concealment of meaning. What makes mathematics special is its promise of prophecy, the promise that it will help us understand all mysteries and all knowledge. Without a humble awareness of its limitations, such prophecies can have a very hollow ring."

She has confided to Mithu C. Banerji, "I know I'm here to stay in Oxford." What Gupta said to her interviewer Bronwyn T. Williams (1996) underscores her position as a true postcolonial, as well as a diasporic writer:

> I think one has to be comfortable with the notion that one has one's cultural identity and that one doesn't necessarily have to be at "home," so to speak. But having had that cultural identity, or whatever else it is that is established for you, wherever you are rooted, whatever you are rooted in . . . I think we have to accept that we are going to be perpetually wandering. We are bound to, I think. That's the kind of crisis that we're in now, that we're forced to be in a state of perpetual wandering. I mean we can't be at home. Even if we sit at home, we are forced to travel, just because of what is going on around us.

That Sunetra Gupta is not as popular as the other women novelists of the Indian diaspora may be ascribed to her unusual and demanding style. Unlike others, she does not tend to re-create India through the lens of nostalgia, writing about "imaginary homelands" (to use Salman Rushdie's phrase). Concentrating primarily upon social realism, their best work deals with Indian immigrants, the people they know firsthand. Gupta's densely textured language, piling of words upon words, and transnational characters attract only serious readers to her work.

Interviews:

"A Readership Is Being Created by Offering Them Exotic Tid-bits to Titillate Them," "On the Net" interview (1996) <http://www.rediff.com/news/Feb/21women.htm> [accessed 11/30/05];

Mithu C. Banerji, "Never Far from Home," *Sunday Statesman,* 13 August 2000, p. 3.

References:

Nilufer E. Bharucha, "Charting of Cultural Territory: Second Generation Postcolonial Indian English Fiction," in *The Postmodern Indian English Novel,* edited by Viney Kirpal (Bombay: Allied, 1996), pp. 355–367;

Monika Fludernik, "Colonial vs. Cosmopolitan Hybridity: A Comparison of Mulk Raj Anand & R. K. Narayan with Recent British & North American Expatriate Writing (Singh Baldwin, Divakaruni, Sunetra Gupta)," in *Hybridity & Postcolonialism: Twentieth-Century Indian Literature. ZAA Studies: Language, Literature, & Culture,* edited by Fludernik (Tubingen: Stauffenburg, 1998), pp. 261–290;

Debjani Ganguly, "Of Dreams, Disgressions and Dislocations: The Surreal Fiction of Sunetra Gupta," in *The Postmodern Indian English Novel,* edited by Kirpal (Bombay: Allied, 1996), pp. 311–322;

Sandra Ponzanesi, "In My Mother's House: The Mobilization of Home in Women Writers of the Indian Diaspora," in *The Literature of the Indian Diaspora,* edited by A. L. McLeod (New Delhi: Sterling, 2001), pp. 239–251;

Ponzanesi, "Voyage to Hell: Sunetra Gupta, *Moonlight into Marzipan,*" *Wasafiri,* 26 (Autumn 1997): 73–75;

Bronwyn T. Williams, "A State of Perpetual Wandering: Diaspora and Black British Writers," in *Jouvert: A Journal of Postcolonial Studies,* 3, no. 3 (1999);

Gina Wisker, "Writing by Women from the Indian Sub-Continent," in *Post-Colonial and African American Women's Writing: A Critical Introduction,* edited by Wisker (Houndmills & London: Macmillan, 2000), pp. 179–201, 359–360.

Kaiser Haq
(7 December 1950 –   )

Syed Manzoorul Islam
University of Dhaka

BOOKS: *Starting Lines: Poems, 1968–75* (Dhaka: Liberty, 1978);

A Little Ado: Poems, 1976–77 (Dhaka: Granthabithi, 1978);

A Happy Farewell (Dhaka: University Press, 1994);

Black Orchid (London: Aark Arts, 1996);

The Logopathic Reviewer's Song (London: Aark Arts / Dhaka: University Press, 2002).

OTHER: Shamsur Rahman, *Selected Poems of Shamsur Rahman,* translated and edited, with an introduction, by Haq (Dhaka: BRAC, 1985);

Contemporary Indian Poetry, edited, with an introduction, by Haq (Columbus: Ohio State University Press, 1990);

Rabindranath Tagore, *Quartet,* translated by Haq (Oxford: Heinemann, 1993);

Mirza Sheikh I'tesamuddin, *The Wonders of Vilayet: Being the Memoir, Originally in Persian, of a Visit to France and Britain,* translated by Haq (Leeds: Peepal Tree, 2002);

Ajeet Cour and Pankaj Bhan, eds., *Shamsur Rahman, a Witness of His Times,* poems by Rahman translated by Haq and Kabir Chowdury (New Delhi: Foundation of SAARC Writers and Literature, 2003).

Kaiser Haq (courtesy of Kaiser Haq)

With the publication of two volumes in 1978– *Starting Lines: Poems, 1968–75* and *A Little Ado: Poems, 1976–77*–Kaiser Haq announced his arrival on the Indo-Anglian poetic scene. (The term *Indo-Anglian* is a problematic one. The earlier and more persistent usage, Anglo-Indian, favored Anglo over Indian; the new term reverses the order and privilege, but it is still limited.) Haq's poems range easily across boundaries to claim a place in the mainstream of contemporary English poetry. One notices his indebtedness to William Shakespeare, Robert Herrick, John Donne, Gerard Manley Hopkins, T. S. Eliot, Ezra Pound, W. H. Auden, and Philip Larkin. "My soul is with Shakespeare, my sensibility is / Like Prufrock's tie pin," Haq writes in "Brown, Powerless" (1978). One must also

consider him alongside other poets of his generation writing in English anywhere–not simply South Asia– for a proper understanding of his art. Haq likes the challenge of crossing frontiers and exploring the hidden spaces between cultures and between history and tradition as he ruminates on the nature of language and the art of writing. The experimental poems that he has written turn to Eliot, Pound, Archibald MacLeish, and E. E. Cummings, but their rhythm, syntax, and tropes are in his own style.

As Haq himself proclaims in "Growing Up," from *A Little Ado,* he is a citizen of the world who does not easily slip "between two silly / stools in a proverb." With his "western know-how / and eastern wisdom" he is claimed by both worlds, but Samuel Beckett, Pound, Octavio Paz, and Robert Lowell have as much relevance for him as do Michael Madhusudan Dutt and Rabindranath Tagore. In "On a Road Less Travelled By–Kaiser Haq's Poetry" (1995) Fakrul Alam writes, "the first poem of [Haq's] recent collection, *Black Orchid,* alludes to Samuel Beckett's terminal vision in his works in its opening lines: 'Imagination dying / imagine love,' although the poem ends with an affirmation of sorts." Indeed, Haq's reworking of Beckett's preoccupation with beginning and ending in *Black Orchid* (1996) is just one example of how he accesses the ideas of his forebears only to understand better his own reality. Beckett in this instance functions only as an echoing well, but the voice that it throws back is not diluted by Beckettian dystopia and emptiness but grows strong as it reverberates across cultural spaces. In the end, the first poem in the collection, "Imaginary Love," draws its own demarcation line and strives for a personal solution–as is always the case in Haq's poems. The solution is that poetry, like love, can revive a dying imagination: "Love dying / imagine / a poem / And love, / old Lazarus, / rises again." The solution may seem forced, but it is not facetious. Poetry and love have been two most persistent themes in Haq's writing. His treatment of them has nothing regional about it, except for occasional references to place, time, and mood that are distinctly Bangladeshi or Indian.

Haq works within three traditions–Bangladeshi, Indian, and English–that shape his imagination and constitute his ethos. On the surface, there may be little to distinguish him from an Indian poet, but a closer examination reveals that, despite his indebtedness to Nissim Ezekiel and his unfolding of a subcontinental flavor and mood, Haq's poems have not only a Bangladeshi flavor but also Bangladeshi content as well. In his poetry collections the many references to monsoons and his evocative suggestion of the appeal of the long wet months are indications of his distinct style. In a brief article on Haq in *Sunday* (18–24 November 1990) Khushwant Singh quotes from his "Peasant's Lament" (1994)–"Your name on granny's lips / mumble / put me to sleep / sang in my dreams / Allah . . ."–and concludes that "what distinguishes Kaiser Haq from his Indian contemporaries is the essential Bangladeshiness of some of his poems." This "Bangladeshiness," however, is not a carefully constructed identity that finds reassurance in difference from others but rather a function of Haq's poetic self that is formed out of diverse–often contradictory–influences deriving from place, history, and culture. Thus, like Lowell, he writes to escape from the confusion of living. If part of the confusion

Front cover for Haq's first poetry collection, published in 1978. It includes "Bangladesh '71," about the war leading to the independence of Bangladesh (Center for Research Libraries, Chicago).

can be sorted out by "rubbing long / pages like bandage rolls . . . to wrap around the wounds your [Lowell's] lines point out like finger-posts," then Lowell can function as a priest/poet to whom Haq can bare his soul for a confessional.

Haq's poetry has to be read on three levels. On an intimate level, feelings are conveyed in deft touches, while the mind seeks reassurance and warmth and moves beyond depression and despair. On a deeper level, complexities arise from a feeling of disquiet and dislocation. In this stage, as Alam notes in a different context, "the landscape the poet inhabits is more often than not a desolate one, and only the act of writing or a willed insouciance or love offer routes of escape." On a third level, Haq's poems are self-engrossed and involved with their own sense of being and becoming. The world he portrays in the poems has been willed into being by the poet–it exists as long as he wills it.

There is, however, no obscurity in these poems: one notices rather a coherence of imagery and a balance of emotion and imagination.

Haq is at times an intensely personal poet, strewing personal references (including references to his earlier works) along the way. Speaking about himself, however, he can be deceptive. A poem that functions as a first-person narrative may recall an instance of life by actively seeking out the significance of certain objects and people that are judged meaningful. Often, the self that emerges in the poems is an individual shaped by no time- or place-bound sensitivities and experiences. In "Pop Portrait of a Poet," Haq sketches the portrait of an artist at odds with the world, a poet with sensibilities so fine as to become insubstantial in the end. He wanders about "in filthy, floppy trousers, / hair anarchic, / eyes out of focus," a scarecrow figure to disturb one's dreams. Yet, to Haq, he looks great; he is "groovy." The artist is neither Haq himself nor the poet he would like to be but a personification of an idea: the poet gone wrong or out of tune. In the end, "Pop Portrait of a Poet," from *Starting Lines,* is a seriocomic description of a poet, while the real Haq is a product of history and time, an heir to middle-class values that he often tries to flout but that will not go away easily, thereby creating a tension in his poems that is hard to escape.

Kaiser Mohamed Hamidul Haq was born in 1950 in Dhaka, Bangladesh, to Mohamed Azharul Haq, who worked in textbook publishing, and Hamida Begum. In a 1997 interview with M. A. Quayum for *World Literature Written in English,* Haq admitted that he would not have tried "creative writing in English" if he had not been "an English-medium boy." He started writing poems as he was finishing secondary school. He received undergraduate and graduate degrees from the University of Dhaka and then went to the University of Warwick in Coventry, England, as a Commonwealth scholar to earn his doctorate. After returning home, he joined the English faculty at the University of Dhaka, occasionally traveling to the United States and England on visiting fellowships. He married his first wife, Dipa, in 1976. In the words of another interviewer, Asad Latif (*Straits Times* [Singapore], 16 September 1995), Bangladesh has remained Haq's "terrain of engagement, with himself and the world." Haq told Latif, "I could function creatively elsewhere. I could be myself somewhere else," but in Dhaka he is able to "experience the seasons."

The title of the 1978 collection *Starting Lines* refers to Haq's beginning his studies at the University of Dhaka in 1968. The volume opens with the poet's urge to explain himself, as a quotation from Walt Whitman that forms the motto suggests: "It is time to explain myself—let us stand up." The poems spell out the themes and preoccupations that have stayed with Haq through the years—some losing their weight or urgency along the way but never quite fading out, while others have been reworked into newer ideas. Time, change, the natural world, the seasons, love, poetry, and the self recur again and again in the poems. The world of *Starting Lines* is just beginning to lose its greenness and its freshness, as the urban jungles rise, smothering even the last remaining pastoral greenery and innocence. Nature appears to be on a leash in "Park," a disturbing poem because of the dystopian picture it draws of the world: "All around cars like hounds growl / on dead asphalt." The denizens of the city—"a few derelict humans / figures like bare winter trees"—make "the park their parlour / far from wretched homes." The poem, apparently at odds with the opening mood of "Pastoral" ("A horizon of green hamlets receives the sun") actually complements it, since the world in "Pastoral" turns out to be as unwholesome or dysfunctional as the one described in "Park." The mood continues in "Rain": "Dawn lay smothered in cradle. / Its carcass bloated, spreading / universal grey. . . ." Despite the sharply imagistic picture of "raindrops pricking nipples of water," the poem ends with a mock-pastoral dream of "calm lands bristling with crisp sunshine." "Rain" emphasizes the grayness and boredom of life and forecloses any possibility of release. Rain is not life-giving; the first two lines of the poem establish the finality of death in the image of a bloated carcass.

Barren cityscapes as images of personal dystopia, dislocation, and decay were in literary vogue at the time Haq was writing the poems in *Starting Lines.* Haq took the unreality concept a step further, juxtaposing the bright with the dark and dismal. In "Aubade," the opening line unveils a "clear cool morning green and grey." The uneasy juxtaposition of green and gray is thrown into further confusion by the picture of "paintless whores" plodding "slumward to wash." The gray world of evening calm has been replaced by the returning fever of morning, so that the modern day elegy sings out in tearless moans, ending with images of "inert flesh" and "common dark."

In *Starting Lines,* Haq sometimes arranges his poems as a storyteller arranges his tales—in an anecdotal fashion that broaches major themes (change, loss, and the processes of diminishment) in an unobtrusive way. In "Two Trees and Time," for example, the poet discovers his "oldest picture postcard / in the hip pocket of the pre-faded jeans of memory." The tree is "just about dead," and an admonishing grandmother is also dead: "her hair has long since / stopped growing in her grave." Struggling with change that seems to have no purpose, the poet settles on a study of "changing chiaroscuro," alternating between light and darkness. Perhaps in such a mood of contemplation the poet receives Krishna, who is to be taken around the city. "Krishna in Dacca" is a funny poem, with one incredible happening after another, leading up to the disappearance of the visitor through a manhole. The poet's "senseless mirth" at the end undercuts any pretense at the serious and sublime, but the poem also deals with a diminishment that is, in the end, all too human:

> No, no, no, I flute no more
> my lungs squeak with timeless age.
> I sleep long hours, arrange the flowers
> I receive, Japanese fashion. . . .

There is a sense of genuine wonder in "Hill Station Murree," which recounts Haq's first sight of mountains. The pace of the poem is breathless as it recounts his slow climb up an elevation. The short one-or-two-word lines of the second section come to a temporary halt atop a precarious ledge; the poem then resumes at a more labored pace until the poet reaches the top and turns back to descend.

"Bangladesh '71" is the lone poem on the war leading to the independence of Bangladesh that Haq has written, which is surprising since he fought in the conflict. (He received his commission during the war and resigned in 1972 to return to his studies.) "Bangladesh '71" is not a war poem in the conventional sense; the poet agonizes over death and destruction—"Blood of the doomed stain our sleep"—but the agony is all the more piercing because in time of war, the pen cannot write anything and hangs over the paper like a question mark. Indeed, the question "How, and with what, shall one create art?" looms large over the blood-soaked land as the speaker's fumbling fingers "miss flesh they look for."

The poems in *Starting Lines* are marked by a deep sensitivity to sound and nuances of meaning. Haq's words are well chosen, and his images and metaphors are carefully constructed. There is a masterful mingling of the laconic and pared-down with the delicately embellished and clipped. Haq's distinctive style is an adjustment of technique to purpose, but this adjustment has nothing imposed or artificial about it.

The 1978 collection *A Little Ado,* which features twenty-seven poems written in 1976 and 1977, continues the mood of dislocation and exhaustion in *Starting Lines,* but now the poems gaze more inwardly, attempting to locate the source of disquiet. Outwardly, the poems register ennui, pointlessness, and exhaustion, but there is an unmistakable movement toward a still center where some respite will come and some meaning will emerge. Talking about himself, looking for his roots, or trying to fix a location for his wandering self

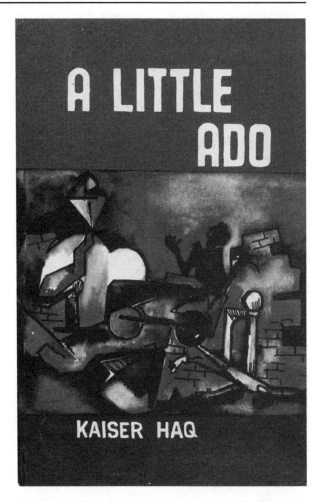

Front cover for Haq's second poetry collection, published in 1978, which continues the mood of exhaustion and dislocation found in the poems of Starting Lines (Center for Research Libraries, Chicago)

provide the poet a way out, but a more central solution appears to be love. In "Season's Greetings" a tentative arrival of spring arouses an equally tentative and joyless response, but in the end, the poet affirms: "Yet spring to me is more: Your kissing mouth." Love is both simple and complex; it is, to quote the short poem "Love," "simple as a sum of addition / done on two fingers, / and complex as a computer's / binary calculations." In "Letter from Hyderabad" the poet sits in the "sweaty, desolate . . . granite wastes": "I look at a lone flaming / gul-mohur and think of you." (The Gulmohur, or Gulmohur, is a flowering ornamental tree.) This epiphany contrasts sharply with moments of depression. In "Rain in the Subcontinent" the poet finds no pleasure in rain, which is a surprise, since monsoon is one season Haq really looks forward to. In this case, monsoon is an oppression that leads to hellish anguish: "Only / the most fearful of Allah / go to mosques" in

Front cover for Haq's third poetry collection, published in 1994, which features new and uncollected poems dating from 1978 to 1993 (Walter Royal Davis Library, University of North Carolina at Chapel Hill)

the rain; but this sacred journey is undercut by the irony in the next line: "with wet patches showing on bottoms raised in prayer."

A Little Ado is full of tales of loss ("A Myth Reworked," in which a boy falls to his death, Icarus-like), boredom and fatuousness ("Street Incident"), urban pathos ("Master Babu"), and irony ("From a Travel Diary"). But there are also moments when the poet feels whole again, even for a brief period. Thus, a woman's "bright arms" hold him steady and stop his headlong fall into an abyss. Waking up from a long nap, he hears children shouting in a field and exclaims, "Oh yes! Its spring once again."

The most engaging poem in *A Little Ado* is "Brown, Powerless," a Caliban-like survey of the poet's own predicament. In the end, the action is ironized by the conclusion: "And if I imagine a banner to raise into the sky, I see a tricolor, yellow, brown and black." In Haq's subsequent poetry collections this quest for iden-

tity is put to rest as a surer, more certain individual emerges in place of a color-doomed man from what he has called elsewhere the "Third Class World" ("More in Water than in Air," *London Magazine,* April–May 1986).

In the years following the publication of his first two books, Haq was involved in various literary projects. He edited and translated *Selected Poems of Shamsur Rahman* (1985), a collection by perhaps the most famous contemporary poet writing in the Bengali language. He served as editor of *Form,* a short-lived magazine of the arts that was published in Dhaka in the 1980s. Haq also edited an anthology, *Contemporary Indian Poetry* (1990), and translated Tagore's novel *Chaturanga* (1916) as *Quartet* (1993).

A Happy Farewell (1994) features new and uncollected poems dating from 1978 to 1993, including four poems written in a regional dialect known as subcontinental English; there are also selections from Haq's first two collections. The title poem records a personal kind of exhaustion: the speaker states that he has "run out of poems." Only "aggravations" rummaged from old notebooks are left, enough "to ruin the morning half way through breakfast." It is time to step out, he feels, from the made-up interior and false security of poetry and confront the "heat and stench in the streets." It is a happy, public farewell to poetry.

The poems in *A Happy Farewell* build on some of Haq's earlier themes. In "Baby Talk," language is seen as a "life sentence": a pampered baby, coaxed to utter a toothless word, is inadvertently caught in the net of language, from which there is no escape. *A Happy Farewell* takes the theme of love a step further to explore erotica. Singh remarks, "there is nothing strait-laced about Kaiser Haq when it comes to erotica," and he quotes from "Abortive Sketch for Erotica" to prove his point. The last line, "a stiff cobra in her hand," has identifiable subcontinental roots, as the cobra and the phallus were combined in ancient cults of Kama, the god of love, to bring out the agony and ecstasy that lead to death—all intermingled in the final act of release. Haq deals with erotica more centrally and metaphysically in his 1996 collection, *Black Orchid.*

A Happy Farewell locates Haq's "Bangladeshiness" in the context of the peasantry, rituals, landscapes, and seasons of the country. "Peasant's Lament," "My Village and I," and "Cousin Shamsu, Darzi" are rooted firmly in Bangladeshi soil. In a sense they mark off the latitude and longitude of the poet's personal geography. There are also poems that record a sudden revelation or a surrealistic vision, such as "On a Street," "Ephemera," "Surreal Morning," and "Disturbance."

The four poems in subcontinental English show a clear indebtedness to the works of Ezekiel ("Civil Service Romance" is dedicated to him). In his introduction to *Contemporary Indian Poetry,* Haq maintains that "the sustained use of Indian English, unlike the use of Caribbean Creole or African pidgin, is possible only in a comic mode." In "In the Indo-Anglian Tradition: Kaiser Haq" (1998) Niaz Zaman writes,

> Nevertheless, when Kaiser Haq uses Indian English, or more specifically, "Banglish," as an ELT [English Language Teaching] specialist terms the English used by Bengalis, the result is far from simply comic. Thus Haq's "Welcome, Tourist Shahib"—a tourist guide spiel—not only reveals the peculiarities of Bangladeshi-English, but also the character of the tourist guide, and perhaps, most importantly, gives an insight into the Bangladeshi ethos, a composite of many heritages and many contradictions.

The tour guide's perspective on life, as Alam notes, "is a mixture of the venal and the patriotic, but disquieting, too." The guide's view of his society is funny but sobering: "Our culture is rich / like television, cinema, dances and songs. . . ." He echoes the easy wisdom of guidebooks, but the picture he paints of middle-class desire is more pathetic than comic.

Haq reversed his "happy farewell" to poetry with *Black Orchid,* published in 1996 and dedicated to the "votaries of Kama and Rati." It is a slim volume, with only nine poems, which are notable for their vitality and their celebration of the power to create. Identity is reshaped out of nothing or chaos through love and erotic abandon. "Yesterday I went digging / for my roots in the library," begins "Nirvana," and it ends with "And I grew speechless. Your buttocks filled my / inward eye. As they do now." *Black Orchid* is also important for the simple reason that Haq celebrates his indulgence in the pleasures that life offers, including those of Kama and Rati (Kama's wife, representing desire). The overtly erotic tone of some of the poems reinforces the sensual rhetoric found in a few of Haq's earlier poems. In *Black Orchid* he refrains from reifying his experiences (as he does in *A Happy Farewell,* by focusing on the processes by which experience is interpreted): his emphasis is rather on reliving experiences and, better still, re-creating them. The poems are essentially "pagan" pieces of pleasure and abandon.

After the death of his wife, Dipa, from cancer in 1999, Haq married Syeda Zinath in 2001. They have a daughter, Raina, born in 2003.

The Logopathic Reviewer's Song (2002) shows Haq taking a new turn. He still has some of his earlier preoccupations—the act of writing poetry, the meaning of poetry in a world increasingly drifting toward meaninglessness, and the agency of love in regenerating the spirit—but they are now expressed in a new, reworked style that is ironic, self-reflexive, philosophical, and matter-of-fact in turn. The word *logopathic* in the title is a "nonce word," which the poet himself defines as a sensitivity to words, the condition of diseased or morbid words, or a term for the treatment of diseased words. The word not only marks out the leading theme of the poems but also suggests the direction of Haq's inventiveness and experimentation.

Some of the poems in *The Logopathic Reviewer's Song* are autobiographical, although one has to negotiate the dispersed identities and personas Haq assumes before the elements that go into the making of his identity can be put together. Thus, the title poem reveals a playful side of the poet as he takes on the persona of a critic ("I'm the greatest / the one / and only logopathic / lit and run critic"), only to damn the chicanery that most critics practice in the name of professional criticism. The last poem in the collection, "Dear Reviewer," shows a more relaxed but nevertheless impish poet ready to face the world for praise or censure but plainly determined not to be moved by it. In "Weekend," one of the most tender poems in the book, the speaker compares himself with an ordinary, *lungi*-clad gardener whose delicate act of gardening becomes a metaphor for writing poetry. But while the happy gardener "bestows a lover's caress / on a plump gourd" before leaving his vegetable patch, the poet feels his inadequacy and his inability of writing "a single poem" he would "care to treat like that." In other poems Haq's cultivated and urbane self takes on the experience of living in different cities and among different groups of people (almost all the poems in *The Logopathic Reviewer's Song* and *A Happy Farewell* are dedicated to friends at home and abroad, suggesting the range of his acquaintance and interactions). He alludes to, compares himself with, and makes use of poets of past and present, such as Shakespeare, William Carlos Williams, Stéphane Mallarmé, and F. T. Prince. He carefully works out each of these poets into the markedly cosmopolitan ethos that *The Logopathic Reviewer's Song* builds up. Yet, Haq never allows his poems to become mired in the niceties of stylistic sophistication. Side by side with "international" content (for example, in "Writer's Retreat"), there is also unabashed "deshi" or local content, serving as a reminder that Haq's roots are firmly planted in the soil where he grew up. Indeed, urban life in overcrowded and chaotic Dhaka provides much of the fun and irony in many of the poems. He makes humorous references to urban habits such as relieving oneself by the side of the road, but in the end, one realizes that these references are merely a means of arriving at a deeper understanding of life.

In addition to appearing in his own collections, Haq's poems and essays have been regularly published in journals such as *London Magazine* (to which he has also contributed essays and reviews), *Chapman, Wasafiri, Acumen, The Journal of Commonwealth Literature, The Cambridge Review, World Literature Written in English, New Quest,* and *Literature Alive.* His works have been anthologized in *The Worlds of Muslim Imagination* (1986), *Stories from South Asia* (1988), *The Arnold Anthology of Post-Colonial Literatures in English* (1996), *Post Independence Voices in South Asian Writings* (2001), and *Masala: Poems from India, Bangladesh, Pakistan, and Sri Lanka* (2005). In 2002 his translation of the memoirs of an eighteenth-century Indian traveler to Europe, Mirza Sheikh I'tesamuddin, was published as *The Wonders of Vilayet: Being the Memoir, Originally in Persian, of a Visit to France and Britain.* Haq is a member of the editorial boards of *Six Seasons Review,* a literary journal, and *Jamini,* an arts magazine, both published in Dhaka.

Kaiser Haq has proved that it is possible for a Bangladeshi poet to use English with sustained liveliness and to register the peculiar pressures—social, economic, and political—that characterize his country. At the same time, his work is related to the broader traditions of South Asian and world literature in a way that should ensure for him a lasting place in the postcolonial canon.

Interviews:
Asad Latif, "Scholar Sees Cultural and Literary Possibilities in Change," *Straits Times* (Singapore), 16 September 1995;

M. A. Quayum, *World Literature Written in English,* 36, no. 1 (1997).

References:
Fakrul Alam, "On a Road Less Travelled By–Kaiser Haq's Poetry," *Daily Star* (Dhaka), 14 December 1995, p. 4;

Carlo Coppola, "Kaiser Haq," in *Contemporary Poets,* seventh edition, edited by Thomas Riggs (Detroit: St. James Press, 2001);

Mohammed Shahriar Haque and Zachary Malik, "Humour in Haq: Poems in Sub-Continental English," in *Beyond Barriers, Fresh Frontiers: Selected Readings on Languages, Literatures and Cultures,* edited by Rosli Talif and others (Serdang, Selangor: Universiti Putra Malaysia Press, 2005), pp. 105–111;

Alamgir Hashmi, "Kaiser Haq," in *Encyclopedia of Post-Colonial Literatures in English,* edited by Eugene Benson and L. W. Conolly, volume 2 (London & New York: Routledge, 1994);

S. M. Islam, "Kaiser Haq," in *The Oxford Companion to Twentieth-Century Poetry in English,* edited by Ian Hamilton (Oxford & New York: Oxford University Press, 1994);

Khushwant Singh, "A Bard from Bangladesh," *Sunday* (Calcutta), 18–24 November 1990, p. 7;

Niaz Zaman, "In the Indo-Anglian Tradition: Kaiser Haq," *Spectrum,* no. 1 (June 1998): 37–40.

Ruth Prawer Jhabvala
(7 May 1927 –)

Ralph J. Crane
University of Tasmania

See also the Jhabvala entries in *DLB 139: British Short-Fiction Writers, 1945–1980,* and *DLB 194: British Novelists Since 1960, Second Series.*

BOOKS: *To Whom She Will* (London: Allen & Unwin, 1955); republished as *Amrita* (New York: Norton, 1956);

The Nature of Passion (London: Allen & Unwin, 1956; New York: Norton, 1957);

Esmond in India (London: Allen & Unwin, 1958; New York: Norton, 1958);

The Householder (London: Murray, 1960; New York: Norton, 1960);

Get Ready for Battle (London: Murray, 1962; New York: Norton, 1963);

Like Birds, Like Fishes and Other Stories (London: Murray, 1963; New York: Norton, 1964);

A Backward Place (London: Murray, 1965; New York: Norton, 1965);

The Householder [screenplay] (Delhi: Ramlochan, 1965);

A Stronger Climate: Nine Stories (London: Murray, 1968; New York: Norton, 1968);

An Experience of India (London: Murray, 1971; New York: Norton, 1972);

A New Dominion (London: Murray, 1972); republished as *Travelers* (New York: Harper & Row, 1973);

Savages: A Film, by James Ivory, from a Screenplay by George Swift Trow and Michael O'Donoghue; and Shakespeare Wallah: A Film, from a Screenplay by R. Prawer Jhabvala and James Ivory (London: Plexus, 1973; New York: Grove, 1973);

Autobiography of a Princess, also Being the Adventures of an American Film Director in the Land of the Maharajahs (New York: Harper & Row, 1975; London: Murray, 1975);

Heat and Dust (London: Murray, 1975; New York: Harper & Row, 1976);

How I Became a Holy Mother, and Other Stories (London: Murray, 1976; enlarged edition, New York: Harper & Row, 1976);

Ruth Prawer Jhabvala (photograph by Mary Ellen Mark; from the cover for East into Upper East: Plain Tales from New York and New Delhi, *1998; Richland County Public Library)*

In Search of Love and Beauty (London: Murray, 1983; New York: Morrow, 1983);

Three Continents (London: Murray, 1987; New York: Morrow, 1987);

Poet and Dancer (London: Murray, 1993; New York: Doubleday, 1993);

Shards of Memory (London: Murray, 1995; New York: Doubleday, 1995);

East into Upper East: Plain Tales from New York and New Delhi (London: Murray, 1998; Washington, D.C.: Counterpoint, 1998);

My Nine Lives: Chapters of a Possible Past (London: Murray, 2004; Washington, D.C.: Shoemaker & Hoard, 2004).

Collections: *How I Became a Holy Mother, and Other Stories* (Harmondsworth, U.K. & New York: Penguin, 1981)—comprises the stories published in *An Experience of India* and *How I Became a Holy Mother, and Other Stories* (1976);

Out of India: Selected Stories (New York: Morrow, 1986; London: Murray, 1987).

PRODUCED SCRIPTS: *The Householder,* motion picture, Merchant Ivory Productions, 1963;

Shakespeare Wallah, motion picture, by Jhabvala and James Ivory, Merchant Ivory Productions, 1965;

The Guru, motion picture, by Jhabvala and Ivory, Merchant Ivory Productions, 1969;

Bombay Talkie, motion picture, Merchant Ivory Productions, 1970;

Autobiography of a Princess, motion picture, Merchant Ivory Productions, 1975;

The Place of Peace, television, Granada, 4 May 1975;

Roseland, motion picture, Merchant Ivory Productions, 1977;

Hullabaloo over Georgie and Bonnie's Pictures, television, Merchant Ivory Productions/London Weekend Television, 1978;

The Europeans, motion picture, Merchant Ivory Productions, 1979;

An Experience of India, television, BBC, 27 April 1980;

"Jane Austen in Manhattan," television, *South Bank Show,* London Weekend Television, 6 July 1980;

Quartet, motion picture, by Jhabvala and Ivory, Merchant Ivory Productions/Lyric International, 1981;

The Courtesans of Bombay, television, by Jhabvala, Ivory, and Ismail Merchant, Merchant Ivory Productions/Channel 4 Television Corporation, 1983;

Heat and Dust, motion picture, Merchant Ivory Productions, 1983;

The Bostonians, motion picture, Merchant Ivory Productions, 1984;

A Room with a View, motion picture, Merchant Ivory Productions, 1985;

Madame Sousatzka, motion picture, by Jhabvala and John Schlesinger, Universal, 1988;

Mr. and Mrs. Bridge, motion picture, Cineplex-Odeon/Merchant Ivory Productions, 1990;

Howards End, motion picture, Merchant Ivory Productions, 1992;

The Remains of the Day, motion picture, Merchant Ivory Productions, 1993;

Jefferson in Paris, motion picture, Merchant Ivory Productions, 1995;

Surviving Picasso, motion picture, Merchant Ivory Productions/David L. Wolper, 1996;

A Soldier's Daughter Never Cries, motion picture, by Jhabvala and Ivory, Merchant Ivory Productions, 1998;

The Golden Bowl, motion picture, Merchant Ivory Productions, 2000;

Le Divorce, motion picture, by Jhabvala and Ivory, Merchant Ivory Productions, 2003.

SELECTED PERIODICAL PUBLICATIONS—UNCOLLECTED:

FICTION

"Before the Wedding," *New Yorker* (28 December 1957): 28–32;

"Better than Dead," *New Yorker* (24 May 1958): 30–36;

"The Elected," *New Yorker* (30 April 1960): 40–45;

"Wedding Preparations," *Kenyon Review,* 23 (1961): 408–422;

"Of Love and Sorrow," *Writers Workshop Miscellany,* 10 (1962): 31–35;

"Light and Reason," *New Statesman,* 19 July 1963, pp. 73–74;

"Foreign Wives," *London Magazine,* new series, 7, no. 10 (1968): 12–22;

"A Very Special Fate," *New Yorker* (29 March 1976): 27–35;

"Commensurate Happiness," *Encounter,* 54, no. 1 (1980): 3–11;

"Grandmother," *New Yorker* (17 November 1980): 54–62.

NONFICTION

"Cakes and Ale," *Writers Workshop Miscellany,* 8 (1961): 53–54;

"Open City: Letter from Delhi," *Encounter,* 22, no. 5 (1964): 40–44;

"Living Abroad–III," *London Magazine,* new series, 10, no. 5 (1970): 41–50;

"Writing for Films," *Illustrated Weekly of India* (21 March 1971): 24–27;

"Moonlight, Jasmine and Ricketts," *New York Times,* 22 April 1975, I: 35;

"Disinheritance," *Blackwood's Magazine* (July 1979): 4–14;

"Writers and the Cinema," *TLS: The Times Literary Supplement,* 18 November 1983, pp. 1287–1288.

Ruth Prawer Jhabvala's position under the banner of Indian or South Asian writing in English is problematic. Indian writing in English is a category that necessarily includes such writers as Sashi Deshpande, who was born in India and still lives and writes there; Salman Rushdie and Rohinton Mistry, who were born in India but who live and write in the West; Anita

Desai, who divides her time between India and the West; and Jhumpa Lahiri, who was born in England and raised in the United States. Migration is part of the postcolonial condition; for all these writers India remains the fixed point of the compass.

Jhabvala's position is entirely different from that of any other Indian writer. Her life has been a series of migrations, including migrations to and from India. She is not and never has been Indian, however. As she explained in an interview with Ramlal G. Agarwal for the magazine *Quest* a year before the publication of *Heat and Dust* (1975): "I write differently from Indian writers because my birth, background, ancestry, and traditions are different." Nor is she simply British, though she is a British citizen, and thus while her work may fit alongside that of such writers as E. M. Forster and Lee Langley, she cannot comfortably be labeled an Anglo-Indian writer (in the Raj sense). Yet, for Jhabvala, too, India is the central point around which her writing revolves.

Ruth Prawer was born in Cologne, Germany, on 7 May 1927, the second child of Marcus Prawer, a Polish-Jewish lawyer who had come to Germany to escape military service, and Eleanora Cohn, who, though she was born in Cologne, was of Russian background. Her brother, Siegbert Salomon Prawer, two years her elder, later became professor of German at Oxford University and an authority on the work of Heinrich Heine, a German poet of Jewish origin.

Prawer grew up in what she describes in "Disinheritance," the text of her 1979 Neil Gunn Memorial Lecture, as "a well-integrated, solid, assimilated, German-Jewish family," which, while being proud of its place in German society, also identified strongly with its Jewish heritage. Her happy early childhood in Cologne came to an abrupt end in 1933, the year Adolf Hitler came to power in Germany. At the age of six Prawer began her education in a segregated Jewish school. Her memories of the period 1933–1939 are of the anti-Semitism she faced on her way to and from school each day, of signs outside shops and cinemas barring Jews, and of gangs of youths breaking the windows of Jewish-owned shops. She also remembers her first composition at school: "The subject: a hare—in German, *der Hase*. I wrote the title, 'Der Hase.' At once I was flooded with my destiny; only I didn't know that's what it was. I only remember my entire absorption, delight, in writing about—giving my impression of—*der Hase*. To think that such happiness could be!"

Although her parents were arrested in 1934, it was some years before Prawer's mother could be persuaded to leave the country with which she proudly identified. When the Prawer family did eventually leave, in April 1939, they were among the last Jewish families to escape Hitler's Germany. In 1948 the knowl-

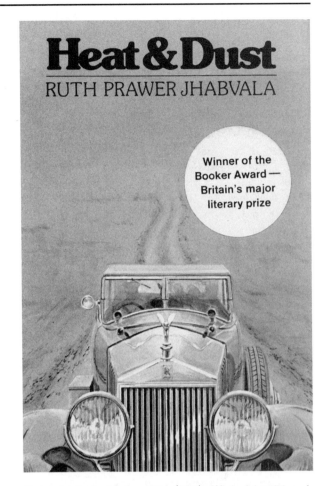

Dust jacket for the American edition (1976) of Jhabvala's 1975 novel, which tells the parallel stories of a woman's experiences in contemporary India and those of her grandfather's first wife fifty years earlier (Richland County Public Library)

edge that his entire family—more than forty people—had died in the Holocaust caused Marcus Prawer to commit suicide.

For Jhabvala, Germany is a country that, as she explained to Bernard Weinraub in a 1983 interview for *The New York Times Magazine,* "smell[s] of blood"; she rarely talks about her childhood there, nor has she ever written about it. From the age of twelve she has been forever an outsider, displaced from the land of her birth.

Following their escape from Germany the Prawer family had hoped to immigrate to the United States, but the outbreak of World War II prevented that, and instead they settled in England. Their first home in England was in Coventry in the Midlands (from where Prawer and her brother were evacuated to Leamington Spa during the war), and from there they moved to the London suburb of Hendon, which had a large Jewish population. Here her parents bought a house, and Marcus Prawer set up a clothing business.

Jhabvala has rarely written about the type of life that the Prawer family and others like them must have experienced in their early years in Britain. Of all her novels and short fictions, only three stories deal with the German-Jewish community in North West London between 1939 and 1951: "A Birthday in London," included in her first collection of short stories, *Like Birds, Like Fishes and Other Stories* (1963); "Two Muses," published thirty-five years later in *East into Upper East: Plain Tales from New York and New Delhi* (1998); and "Refuge in London," from her 2004 work, *My Nine Lives: Chapters of a Possible Past*.

Prawer attended Hendon County School (a local grammar school), and between 1945 and 1951 she read English literature at Queen Mary College, London. In 1951 she graduated with an M.A. degree, having successfully submitted a thesis titled "The Short Story in England, 1700–1750." Looking back in "Disinheritance," she sees this period, during which she read many of the great English and European classics, including George Eliot, Charles Dickens, and Thomas Hardy, as "the great gift, the inheritance, that England gave me: my education which became my tradition—the only tradition I had: that of European literature. It became my equipment, my baggage for the journey I didn't know I had to make: the journey to India."

In 1948 Prawer became a naturalized British citizen, and at a party the following year she met Cyrus S. H. Jhabvala—the son of a trade-union leader and a women's-rights activist—who was in London to study architecture. Shortly after her graduation, on 16 June 1951, they were married at the Burnt Oak registry office, and later the same year, at the age of twenty-four, Jhabvala moved to India with her Parsi husband.

Compared to the Germany Jhabvala fled as a girl and the dour postwar Britain she left as a new bride, the recently independent India must have seemed like a land of plenty. As she previously had done in England, Jhabvala immediately immersed herself in her newly adopted country, and she lived a reasonably typical middle-class Indian life in Delhi, where her three daughters, Renana, Ava, and Firoza, were born and grew up.

This immersion in India gave her the time to write seriously, and within two years of moving to Delhi, Jhabvala had completed her first novel, *To Whom She Will*. The book was published by Allen and Unwin in 1955 to positive reviews. Jhabvala was seen as an important new novelist, and her work was compared favorably with that of writers such as Jane Austen.

Both *To Whom She Will* and her second novel, *The Nature of Passion* (1956), are gentle comedies of manners

that, like all her first six novels, revolve around the domestic and social lives of two or three middle-class Delhi families. The plot of *To Whom She Will*—encapsulated in the British title, which is part of the epigraph taken from the *Panchatantra*—centers on the discordant lovers Amrita and Hari, who plan to marry despite the strong objections of Amrita's family and Hari's impending arranged marriage. Harmony is restored before the end of the novel when Amrita falls in love with a suitable boy and Hari marries the girl his family has chosen for him. In *The Nature of Passion* (which borrows its title from the epigraph taken from the *Bhagavad Gita*) a similar pattern is followed. Here Jhabvala focuses on the lives of Viddi and Nimmi, whose desire to lead independent lives places them in conflict with their father, Lalaji, a wealthy Punjabi contractor. In the course of the conflict that follows, Jhabvala provides her western readers with a sensitive portrait of a Hindu extended family—the type of family she got to know through her husband's Punjabi business partner. Again, harmony is achieved before the end of the novel when Nimmi falls in love with the boy her parents want her to marry, and Viddi gives up his dream of going to England and joins the family business as his father wishes.

To Whom She Will and *The Nature of Passion* also reveal Jhabvala's awareness of a post-Independence society in transition. She focuses in these novels on such matters as the clash between the modern and traditional worlds, the clash between generations, and the growth toward maturity of her young protagonists (particularly Amrita in *To Whom She Will* and Nimmi in *The Nature of Passion*), and also, in a wider, postcolonial sense, of a young nation still fettered by the legacy of its recent colonial history.

In 1957 Jhabvala published her first story, "The Interview," in *The New Yorker* magazine, and for the next twenty-five years she contributed regularly to that magazine and others including the *Yale Review, The Kenyon Review, Cornhill Magazine, The New Statesman, Encounter,* and *The London Magazine*. Most of the fifty stories she first published in journals were later included in her six collections of stories: *Like Birds, Like Fishes and Other Stories; A Stronger Climate: Nine Stories* (1968); *An Experience of India* (1971); *How I Became a Holy Mother, and Other Stories* (1976); *Out of India: Selected Stories* (1986); and *East into Upper East*.

In *Esmond in India* (1958), Jhabvala's domestic comedy takes a darker turn with the introduction of a mixed marriage between the eponymous central character—the first of Jhabvala's detailed studies of displaced Europeans in India that characterizes her later Indian fiction—and the passive Gulab. She also brings the politics of the period into greater relief by focusing on a family that has been actively involved in the freedom movement. The main focus of this novel, however, is Jhabvala's portraits of three women: Uma, Gulab's widowed mother; Gulab; and Shakuntala, who falls for Esmond. The accord that characterized the endings of her previous novels is not repeated here. The novel closes with Gulab leaving Esmond, who in turn abandons Shakuntala in order to return home with his English mistress, Betty.

The Householder (1960)—which marks a shift away from the style of Jane Austen toward that of R. K. Narayan—is at once Jhabvala's most comic and most sensitive portrait of an Indian marriage. In this delightful domestic comedy Jhabvala shows the insecure Prem, a lower-middle-class Hindi teacher, and his wife, Indu, struggling to get to know each other as they contend with Prem's low wages, their high rent, and the arrival of Prem's widowed mother. The novel also introduces the first—and probably most positive—of the many guru or swami figures to appear in Jhabvala's fiction.

Jhabvala's first four novels can be characterized as domestic comedies that reflect her early, untrammeled love for India, a country that, as she told Caroline Moorehead in an interview conducted for *The Times* (20 November 1975), she initially saw as a "paradise on earth." In "Disinheritance" she recalls savoring "The smells and sights and sounds of India—the mangoes and jasmine on hot nights—the rich spiced food—the vast sky—the sight of dawn and dusk—the birds flying about—the ruins—the music."

Her first trip back to England, in 1960, shattered Jhabvala's rose-tinted view of India, as she explained in an interview published in *The New York Times* (17 July 1973): "I saw people eating in London, everyone had clothes, and everything in me began to curdle about India." After that visit Jhabvala felt "strapped to a wheel" that took her through a series of stages she believes all Europeans who visit India experience. She explains those stages in the important essay "Myself in India," included as an introduction to *An Experience of India:* "There is a cycle that Europeans—by Europeans I mean all Westerners, including Americans—tend to pass through. It goes like this: first stage, tremendous enthusiasm—everything Indian is marvellous; second stage, everything Indian not so marvellous; third stage, everything Indian abominable. For some people it ends there, for others the cycle renews itself and goes on. I have been through it so many times that now I think of myself as strapped to a wheel that goes round and round and sometimes I'm up and sometimes I'm down."

The changed attitude to India this essay enunciates is evident in *Get Ready for Battle* (1962)—the first novel after her epiphanic trip back to Britain—

Dust jacket for Jhabvala's 1976 collection of stories. The title story is one of several the author wrote on the subject of Indian ashrams and their Western devotees (Richland County Public Library).

and in all her later fiction. In *Get Ready for Battle,* the last of Jhabvala's novels to deal predominantly with Indian characters, her growing discontent with India is evident. In this novel she moves away from domestic comedies of manners to a much darker fictional representation of the mammoth social problems in India. The title, again part of an epigraph from the *Bhagavad Gita,* urges the path of action rather than renunciation, and much of that action centers around Sarla Devi's battle to save Bundi Busti. Her actions pit naive aesthetic beliefs against the rapacious business world of postindependence India represented by her husband, Gulzari Lal. As Yasmine Gooneratne explains in her *Silence, Exile and Cunning: The Fiction of Ruth Prawer Jhabvala* (1991), the novel contrasts "the luxurious world inhabited by a wealthy businessman with that other world of sickness and destitution which his wife Sarla Devi, a woman of conscience, struggles to alleviate."

If her trip back to England in 1960 had a profound effect on the future direction of her fiction, another pivotal moment in her career occurred in 1961 when James Ivory and Ismail Merchant asked her to write a screenplay based on her novel *The Householder;* the movie was released in 1963, the same year *Like Birds, Like Fishes and Other Stories* was published. She went on to write several original screenplays with Indian themes, including *Shakespeare Wallah* (cowritten with Ivory, 1965), a motion picture inspired by the lives of the Kendal family and their experiences as traveling players in India, which is now widely regarded as a classic; *The Guru* (1969); *Bombay Talkie* (1970); *Autobiography of a Princess* (1975); and *Hullabaloo over Georgie and Bonnie's Pictures* (1978), as well as an adaptation of her own novel *Heat and Dust,* released in 1983. Much of her later fiction, particularly *Heat and Dust,* has been greatly influenced by the techniques Jhabvala learned writing for the screen as part of the Merchant-Ivory-Jhabvala triumvirate, as she outlined in an interview with Anna Rutherford and Kirsten Holst Petersen for *World Literature Written in English* in 1976, shortly after the publication of *Heat and Dust.*

Jhabvala's next three novels and two collections of stories in many ways represent a discrete phase in her career. In these works she moves away from the interest in India that marked her earlier work to examine the way India acts on westerners who live or travel there, particularly women. As she stated in her revealing essay "Myself in India": "I am no longer interested in India. What I am interested in now is myself in India."

This increasing interest in Europeans in India is signaled in the title of her sixth novel, *A Backward Place* (1965), which, as Paul Sharrad convincingly argues in his "Passing Moments: Irony, Ambivalence and Time in *A Backward Place*" (1991), refers to the expatriate enclave in India rather than to India itself. Like her earlier novel *Esmond in India, A Backward Place* features a mixed marriage. In this novel, however—as in her earlier story "The Aliens," first published in the *Yale Review* in 1963 and included in *Like Birds, Like Fishes and Other Stories,* and the later story "The Young Couple," published in the *London Magazine* in 1967 and included in *A Stronger Climate* the following year—Jhabvala reverses the usual colonizer-colonized dynamic in the relationship between Bal and his English wife, Judy. Instead of looking at the effects of colonialism and the frequently damaging presence of the West on Indian culture (represented by an English male figure such as Esmond), which has been something of a commonplace in postcolonial literatures, in *A Backward Place* Jhabvala locates India in the dominant or male position and considers the effects that country has on the three main

female, European characters in the novel—Clarissa, Judy, and Etta, who each represent one of the stages (enthusiasm, lack of enthusiasm, and hatred) through which she suggests all Europeans living in India pass.

Jhabvala's increasing interest in the effects of India on Westerners dominates the rest of her Indian fiction. In *A Stronger Climate* all nine stories are concerned with Europeans in India, which is also the focus of many of her later stories, as well as her next two novels, *A New Dominion* (1972) and the Booker Prize–winning *Heat and Dust.* These two novels, which are far more complex than any of Jhabvala's earlier fictions, also reveal her intertextual interest in Forster's seminal Anglo-Indian novel, *A Passage to India* (1924), and both novels move out of Delhi, the location of all her earlier novels.

This shift away from the domestic milieu of her earlier fiction is evident in the opening description of the landscape in *A New Dominion,* which is immediately reminiscent of the opening of Forster's novel. The major characters in this novel are all questers, though what they are looking for is rarely clear, even to themselves. The principal quester in *A New Dominion* is the young woman Lee, and each of the three parts of the novel—located in Delhi, the holy city of Benaras, and the ashram at Maupur—focus on a particular stage of her quest "to find herself," a quest that attempts to find spiritual enlightenment through sexual experience. The third section, which presents a particularly negative picture of an ashram and its fraudulent and dangerous guru, Swamiji, shares much in common with earlier stories such as "An Experience of India" and "A Spiritual Call." The later story "How I Became a Holy Mother," in contrast, presents a far more positive portrait of the relationship between a guru and his disciples.

Although Jhabvala has never lived the life of a memsahib, she has admitted to "a certain nostalgia" for the British Raj, which she explores in her screenplay for *Autobiography of a Princess* and then two years later in *Heat and Dust.* In her best-known novel, parallel stories are skillfully interwoven to contrast two time periods fifty years apart: the first, Olivia's story, is set in 1923, the year Fielding returns to India in Forster's *A Passage to India,* and the second, which follows the journey of the unnamed narrator in the 1970s, updates Olivia's story and reveals Jhabvala's interest in the effect of history and text on life.

The narrator's claim that "this is not my story, it is Olivia's as far as I can follow it," highlights both her desire to find out all she can of Olivia's life and to experience, as far as she is able, what Olivia, her grandfather's first wife, experienced two generations earlier. She makes a conscious attempt to merge with India, a gesture that links her to the many female seekers that populate Jhabvala's earlier fictions. The skillful use of mirror characters (such as Olivia and the narrator, and the Nawab and Inder Lal) and events (the two seduction scenes, for example) closely connects the two stories, which are, in turn, intertextually linked to *A Passage to India* and *A New Dominion*. This interweaving of the two stories is aided by Jhabvala's frequent use of time shifts, a technique she has borrowed from her writing for the cinema, notably *Autobiography of a Princess,* which, like *Heat and Dust,* interweaves two time periods: London in the 1970s and princely India in the 1920s.

Heat and Dust, which draws on the whole tradition of Anglo-Indian (Raj) fiction in its exploration of the effects of India on those Europeans—1920s administrators and 1970s seekers alike—is perhaps Jhabvala's most ambitious Indian novel. It is possibly also, as Gooneratne suggests in *Silence, Exile and Cunning: The Fiction of Ruth Prawer Jhabvala,* a novel in which "Ruth Jhabvala is externalising and probing through fiction certain aspects, painful, exhilarating, puzzling and comic, of her own experience of India."

While writing *Heat and Dust,* Jhabvala became ill with jaundice. This was the first endemic disease she had contracted in twenty-five years in India, and that, along with a terrible homesickness for Europe—which, according to Sadie in "The Englishwoman," published in the *London Magazine* in 1973 and in the American edition of *How I Became a Holy Mother,* "becomes worse and worse till in the end life becomes almost unbearable"—caused her to move to New York, the only place she knew that reminded her of the Europe of her childhood, and to complete the passage her parents had been unable to realize forty years earlier. Since 1975 Jhabvala has divided her time between India and the United States, and in 1986 she became an American citizen.

During her twenty-five years in India, Jhabvala produced eight novels and four collections of short stories as well as several screenplays, all with Indian settings, that have earned her a reputation as a major writer of India. Her geographical shift to the United States also prompted a move toward that country in both her writing for the screen and in her fiction.

This shift is evident in the first screenplay she wrote after moving to New York. *Roseland* (1977), an original screenplay with three connecting stories set in the popular New York dance palace, is the first Merchant Ivory movie to have a contemporary American setting. New York is also the setting of her television play *Jane Austen in Manhattan* (1980).

Jhabvala continued her move away from India with her adaptation of Henry James's 1878 novel *The Europeans* (1979). This screenplay was the first of a series of screen adaptations of other people's novels Jhabvala

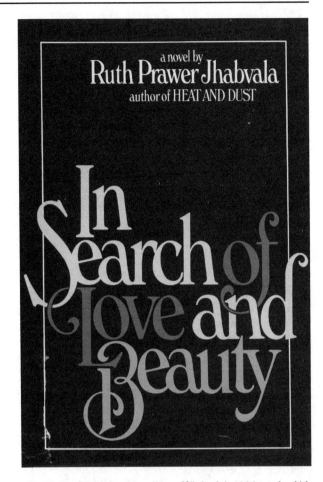

Dust jacket for the American edition of Jhabvala's 1983 novel, which chronicles three generations of German-Jewish immigrants in New York City who are held in thrall by the charismatic guru Leo Kellerman (Richland County Public Library)

has written, all, with the exception of her and John Schlesinger's adaptation of Bernice Rubens's 1962 novel, *Madame Sousatzka* (1988), for the Merchant Ivory Production team. She also adapted James's *The Bostonians* (1886) in 1984; Forster's 1908 novel, *A Room with a View,* in 1985; *Mr. and Mrs. Bridge* (1990), based on Evan S. Connell Jr.'s two novels *Mrs. Bridge* (1959) and *Mr. Bridge* (1969); Forster's *Howards End* (1910) in 1992; Kazuo Ishiguro's *The Remains of the Day* (1989) in 1993; *Surviving Picasso,* from Arianna Stassinopoulos Huffington's book *Picasso: Creator and Destroyer* (1988), in 1996; Kaylie Jones's *A Soldier's Daughter Never Cries* (1998) in 1998; and James's *The Golden Bowl* (1904) in 2000. During this time she also wrote the original screenplay for *Jefferson in Paris* (1995), about the years Thomas Jefferson spent as the American ambassador to France.

Jhabvala's next four novels—all set predominantly in the United States—focus on such postcolonial issues as the search for identity and explore in detail the sense of dislocation that Jhabvala herself, like so many of her European characters, has experienced. *In Search of Love and Beauty* (1983) marks an important new phase in Jhabvala's writing, previously signaled in the story "Commensurate Happiness" (*Encounter,* 1980), and confirms the shift away from India as the exclusive subject and setting of her fiction, already seen in her work for the cinema.

In Search of Love and Beauty, which looks at a group of German and Austrian refugees in New York, is a cathartic book in which Jhabvala explores her European Jewish heritage as well as draws on contemporary American settings and revisits many of the themes that characterize her Indian fiction. The novel examines the ties that bind three generations of a single family–Louise and Bruno Sonnenblick; their daughter, Marietta; and her children, Mark and Natasha–and the family's relationship with a charismatic guru figure, the psycho-spiritual therapist and likely charlatan Leo Kellerman. It also explores the search for love and beauty in which each of the main characters in this novel–like all Jhabvala's protagonists–is engaged.

Three years later, the success of the Merchant Ivory adaptation of *A Room with a View* and the release of *Out of India: Selected Stories* launched Jhabvala to celebrity writer status, as Laurie Sucher outlines in her monograph, *The Fiction of Ruth Prawer Jhabvala: The Politics of Passion* (1989), and guaranteed her next novel considerable publicity. Jhabvala failed to ride the wave of success: her tenth novel, *Three Continents* (1987), which, as the title suggests, is set in Europe, the United States, and India, is her weakest and bleakest novel. In this novel Jhabvala examines once more the effects of India on the lives of westerners, but without any of the fresh insights with which earlier novels have treated the subject. Here, the American twins Michael and Harriet Wishwell fall prey to the charms of the Rawul of Dhoka and his corrupt Fourth World Movement. At the heart of the novel is the idea of the family under siege from within and without, bluntly symbolized by the mock family of the Rawul: his "wife," Renée; and their "son," Crishi. This book has much in common with *A New Dominion*–both structurally and in the figures of the predatory Crishi, whose menace matches that of the Swami of the earlier novel, and Harriet, who recalls earlier questers such as Lee–but it lacks the humor and delicacy of Jhabvala's earlier work.

Jhabvala's next two novels, *Poet and Dancer* (1993) and *Shards of Memory* (1995), continue the shift away from India as a location. Indeed, India is all but absent from *Poet and Dancer,* which focuses on the destructive relationship between two cousins, Angel and Lara. Their relationship, with its clear lesbian undertones and its exploration of the split between good and evil,

Dust jacket for the American edition of Jhabvala's 1998 collection of stories set in the two cities she calls home, New York and New Delhi (Richland County Public Library)

proves fatal for Angel–who is pushed into committing suicide by her diabolical cousin–in much the same way that similar relationships with fraudulent gurus had been harmful to the naive seekers found in *A New Dominion* and many of the stories.

In *Shards of Memory,* Jhabvala returns to peak form. The main settings are again New York (Manhattan) and London (Hampstead), though India, like continental Europe, is an important landscape in the memories of a some of the characters. In this four-generation family saga of the Kopf and Keller families and their involvement with "the Master," the latest of Jhabvala's long line of dubious spiritual leaders, the focus is less on whether or not the Master is a fraud and more on the importance of family ties–the propinquity explored in all her four American novels.

Two clear locations characterize Jhabvala's fiction: East and West, India and the United States, Delhi and New York. These specific locations are deliberately juxtaposed in *East into Upper East,* a collection of stories written over two decades. Again there is a focus on the dislocation and cross-cultural themes that have characterized all her fiction to date.

My Nine Lives is potentially the most autobiographical of Jhabvala's works. In the nine chapters, as she calls them, Jhabvala deliberately blurs the boundary between autobiography and fiction, offering nine alternative life stories, all of which she claims she could have lived, though none is quite the story of her own life. As she explains in the short "Apologia" that opens the book, "even when something didn't actually happen to me, it might have done so. Every situation was one I could have been in myself, and sometimes, to some extent, was." Moving freely between Britain, the United States, and India and focusing on European refugees who have escaped Nazi Germany as well as spiritual questers in India, this novel offers something of a retrospective of Jhabvala's career as a writer of fiction.

Jhabvala has received many awards for her writing. In 1975 she was awarded the prestigious Booker Prize for *Heat and Dust.* She has also received a Guggenheim Fellowship, the Neil Gunn International Fellowship, a MacArthur Foundation Award, the Literary Lion Award of the New York Public Library, and an Award in Literature from the American Academy of Arts and Letters. Jhabvala's work as a screenwriter for Merchant Ivory Productions has earned her two Academy Awards—for *A Room with a View* and *Howards End*—as well as a British Academy of Film and Television Arts Award for *Heat and Dust,* a New York Film Critics Award for *Mr. and Mrs. Bridge,* and the Writers Guild of America's Screen Laurel Award. In 1983 London University made her an honorary doctor of letters, and in 1998 she was made a Companion of the British Empire.

Ruth Prawer Jhabvala has been described by Agarwal as an "outsider with unusual insight." The phrase is an apt one to describe a writer whose own sense of dislocation has informed all her fiction. Her characters are frequently expatriates, refugees, travelers, or people marginalized in some other way. There are, as the chapters of *My Nine Lives* affirm and as Jhabvala herself commented in a 1977 *Newsweek* interview with Patricia W. Mooney, "aspects of myself in everyone that I write about."

Interviews:

"A Novelist of India Reflects 2 Worlds," *New York Times,* 17 July 1973, p. 31;

Ramlal G. Agarwal, "An Interview with Ruth Prawer Jhabvala," *Quest,* 91 (1974): 33–36;

Yolanta May, "Ruth Prawer Jhabvala in Conversation with Yolanta May," *New Review,* 2, no. 21 (1975): 53–57;

Alex Hamilton, "The Book of Ruth," *Guardian,* 20 November 1975, p. 12;

Caroline Moorehead, "A Solitary Writer's Window on the Heat and Dust of India," *Times* (London), 20 November 1975, p. 16;

Anna Rutherford and Kirsten Holst Petersen, "*Heat and Dust:* Ruth Prawer Jhabvala's Experience of India," *World Literature Written in English,* 15 (1976): 373–377;

Patricia W. Mooney, "Another Dimension of Living," *Newsweek* (31 October 1977): 52;

Lyn Owen, "A Passage from India to America," *Observer,* 9 April 1978, p. 30;

Bernard Weinraub, "The Artistry of Ruth Prawer Jhabvala," *New York Times Magazine,* 11 September 1983, pp. 64, 106, 110, 112, 114.

Bibliography:

Ralph J. Crane, "Ruth Prawer Jhabvala: A Checklist of Primary and Secondary Sources," *Journal of Commonwealth Literature,* 20, no. 1 (1985): 171–203.

References:

Ramlal G. Agarwal, *Ruth Prawer Jhabvala: A Study of Her Fiction* (New Delhi: Sterling, 1990);

Ralph J. Crane, *Ruth Prawer Jhabvala* (New York: Twayne, 1992);

Yasmine Gooneratne, *Silence, Exile and Cunning: The Fiction of Ruth Prawer Jhabvala,* second edition (New Delhi: Orient Longman, 1991);

Vasant A. Shahane, *Ruth Prawer Jhabvala* (New Delhi: Arnold-Heinemann, 1976);

Paul Sharrad, "Passing Moments: Irony, Ambivalence and Time in *A Backward Place,*" in *Passages to Ruth Prawer Jhabvala,* edited by Crane (New Delhi: Sterling, 1991), pp. 37–49;

Laurie Sucher, *The Fiction of Ruth Prawer Jhabvala: The Politics of Passion* (London: Macmillan, 1989);

Haydn Moore Williams, *The Fiction of Ruth Prawer Jhabvala* (Calcutta: Writers Workshop, 1973);

Renée Winegarten, "Ruth Prawer Jhabvala: A Jewish Passage to India," *Midstream* (March 1974): 72–79.

Girish Karnad

(19 May 1938 –)

Sridhar Rajeswaran

BOOKS IN ENGLISH: *Tughlaq,* translated from Kannada by Karnad (Delhi & Oxford: Oxford University Press, 1972);

Hayavadana, translated from Kannada by Karnad (Calcutta & Oxford: Oxford University Press, 1975);

Naga-Mandala: Play with a Cobra, translated from Kannada by Karnad (Delhi & Oxford: Oxford University Press, 1990);

Tale-Danda, translated from Kannada by Karnad (Delhi: Ravi Dayal, 1993);

Three Plays (Delhi & Oxford: Oxford University Press, 1994)—comprises *Naga-Mandala, Hayavadana,* and *Tughlaq;*

The Fire and the Rain, translated from Kannada by Karnad (Delhi & Oxford: Oxford University Press, 1998);

The Dreams of Tipu Sultan; Bali: The Sacrifice (New Delhi: Oxford University Press, 2004).

Collection: *Collected Plays,* 2 volumes (Delhi & Oxford: Oxford University Press, 2005)—volume 1 comprises *Tughlaq, Hayavadana, Bali: The Sacrifice,* and *Naga-Mandala;* volume 2 comprises *Taledanda, The Fire and the Rain, The Dreams of Tipu Sultan,* and *Macaulay's Children.*

PLAY PRODUCTIONS: *Tughlaq,* Bombay, Indian National Theatre, December 1965; translation, Bombay, Bhulabhai Auditorium, August 1970;

Yayati, Bombay, Indian National Theatre, August 1967;

Hayavadana, New Delhi, AIFACS Theatre, May 1972; translation, Madras, Museum Theatre, December 1972;

Naga-Mandala: Play with a Cobra, Minneapolis, Guthrie Theatre, 1992;

Tale-Danda, Srirangapatna, Karnataka Nataka Rangayana, February 1994;

Agni Mattu Male (The Fire and the Rain), Minneapolis, Guthrie Theatre, 1995;

The Dreams of Tipu Sultan, Srirangapatna, Karnataka Nataka Rangayana, 1997; Madras Players, Madras, 2000;

Girish Karnad (photograph by Mahesh Bhat; www.maheshbhat.com)

The Fire and the Rain, Bangalore, Arjun Sajnani, 1999;

Bali: The Sacrifice, Leicester, U.K., Haymarket Theatre, 31 May 2002;

Odakalu Bimba/A Heap of Broken Images, Bangalore, Ranga Shankara, 2005.

PRODUCED SCRIPTS: *Samskara* (Funeral Rites), motion picture, Ramamanohara Chitra, 1970;

Kaadu (Forest), motion picture, L.N. Combines, 1973;

Godhuli (The Dust *[dhuli]* Kicked up by the Cows *[go]* Returning Home at Twilight), motion picture, Maharaja Movies, 1977;

Kondura, motion picture, Raviraj International, 1978;

Ondanondu Kaladalli (Once upon a Time), motion picture, L.N. Combines, 1978;

Kanooru Heggadithi, motion picture, based on the novel *The Mistress of the House of Kanooru,* Aniketana Chitra, 1999.

TRANSLATION: Badal Sircar, *Evam Indrajit* (Calcutta & London: Oxford University Press, 1974).

Girish Karnad is an Indian dramatist who writes in Kannada and then translates his plays into English; he has earned international recognition as a playwright and translator. Multifaceted, he has also carved a niche for himself as a scriptwriter, actor, and director in the world of Indian cinema. Karnad has served as director of prestigious Indian institutions. His work has been recognized in the form of several state- and national-level awards in India.

Girish Raghunath Karnad was born in Matheran, a small hill resort near Mumbai, 19 May 1938, the son of Raghunath (a doctor) and Krishnabai (Mankikar) Karnad. Little else is known about Karnad's early life, given his reluctance to discuss private matters. However, what is known is that he received a bachelor of arts degree from Karnataka University, Dharwar, in 1958, where he was ranked first in the university. He then went to Magdalen College, Oxford, on a Rhodes scholarship and was conferred a master's degree in philosophy, politics, and economics in 1963. At Oxford he was the president of the Magdelen Junior Common Room in 1962–1963 and president of the Oxford Union Society in 1963. In 1964 he returned to India and joined the Oxford University Press, where he worked as assistant manager from 1963 to 1969 and manager from 1969 to 1970. Karnad lives in Bangalore with his wife, Saraswathy Ganapathy, whom he married in 1980, and has a daughter, Shalmali Radha (1981), and a son, Raghu Amay (1983).

Initially, Karnad had wanted to win fame as a poet and had written poetry in English as a teenager. However, his first journey to England led him to write a play in 1961, *Yayati* (performed, 1967; published in Kannada, 1971; never published in English). For Karnad the play redefined his dreams, for he knew now that he would not be a poet but a dramatist, writing not for himself or an elite but for his home audience.

Yayati is based on a story borrowed from the *Adiparva* (the first canto) of the *Mahabharata* (A.D. 400). A carefully constructed play in four acts and a prologue in the Aristotelian vein, *Yayati* has a balanced beginning, middle, and end; follows the unities; has a lofty theme and an exalted hero; and achieves a catharsis of sublimated emotions. The dramatic action consists of the interaction among eight protagonists—four male and four female. The male protagonists include Yayati and Puru, while the female characters are Devayani, Sharmishtha, Swarnalata, and Chitralekha. Chitralekha is Puru's wife; Devyani, Yayati's wife (Sharmishta is her "other"); and Swarnalata exists as a foil. Of the two other male protagonists, Sukracharya, Devyani's father, does not actually appear on stage, though he is integral to the action; his celestial counterpart, Brihaspati, is his absent "other."

The play begins with a prologue that employs the metaphor of a wayfarer lost in a huge, dark cavern. A tangential reference to the wayfarer's blindness is that he gropes for an old forgotten bag, rummaging through the clutter of his past life. The play of four acts occurs by virtue of what one may assume he has retrieved from his past. The four acts consist of an interplay between youth and its dreams, and old age and its wisdom. The central action concerns questions of responsibilities and is engendered through the conflict and tension between a son and a father. The women protagonists, though, are an integral part of the action, as their actions are what lead to the curse on Yayati, the basis of the plot. At the end of the play Yayati realizes the futility of pursuing sensuous pleasures and power.

To achieve his dramatic ends, Karnad resorts to the techniques of the multicultural dramatist who traverses both the Western world of scholarship and that of his own cultural heritage. His Western inspirations are Jean Anouilh and Jean-Paul Sartre in particular and the entire existential and absurdist schools in general. Though he was also impressed by the naturalistic plays of George Bernard Shaw and Henrik Ibsen, Karnad looked to them only for methods of depiction. Native sources include the *Natyasastra* (the ancient Indian treatise on dramaturgy), which decreed that the utterance be punctuated by action that is dance-like in movement and ritualistic. At the level of performance and stage, the folk theater of Yakshagana and Bayalata, the local, traditional/folk drama of Karnad's Karnataka, is another influence (Yakshagana, celestial drama, with the word *gana* privileging music; Bayalata is a generic term for movement, as also game). A dramatic device that predominates at this early stage in Karnad's career is the use of masks.

When the prologue and four acts are taken together, the mystical chamber becomes the nation symbolically, and the entire play, a transcendent drama of life defined by a search for a knowledge that would enable the negotiation of spaces—public, private, and, more importantly, national. The "O God in heaven! What does all this mean?" that epitomizes the ending of this play can be linked to the cry of anguish in *Tughlaq*—"God, What's this country coming to!" *Yayati* won the Mysore State Award in 1962.

Cover for Karnad's play (1972) about the fourteenth-century sultan Muhammad bin Tughlaq, who moved his capital from Delhi to Daulatabad (Thomas Cooper Library, University of South Carolina)

Karnad's second play, *Tughlaq,* was written in 1964, translated into English by Karnad, and published in English in 1972. The bafflement that marks the ending of *Yayati* reappears at the beginning of this play and continues throughout it. *Tughlaq* ends with a shrieking head that has not been able to understand the "madness of God." The source of this play, however, is not myth but history: the play is based on historical texts.

Sultan Muhammad bin Tughlaq of fourteenth-century India was a complex man. He could dream and also act. He appeared to be a godless man but was actually quite devout. He was a good man who could at times be cruel. The action in Karnad's play ensues from these contradictions in the protagonist's personality and the position of power he held. They seem to have offered Karnad apt correlates with the action in the play and the disenchanting contemporaneity of Nehruvian India. Toward the end of his life, in the 1960s, Nehru

was apparently, like Tughlaq, seen by contemporary historians as a failed dreamer.

Tughlaq is a play in thirteen scenes marked by a progressive degeneration of the public/political order. Karnad has located this process of degeneration in five significant years of the approximately fourteen-year tenure of Tughlaq's reign. In this period the major changes that rocked his kingdom took place.

Tughlaq's decision to move his capital from Delhi in the north to Daulatabad in central India was extremely unpopular with his court and his subjects. Historically, Delhi had been the capital of all the great empires that had ruled India. However, Tughlaq's move to Daulatabad, which was located at the center of his kingdom, was immensely practical, as most kings ruling from Delhi had found controlling their southern Indian provinces difficult. The major logistical planning required and the political and social will to be generated to effect this shift finally led to Tughlaq's downfall. Court intrigues also contributed to his being labeled insane for even having suggested such a move, not only in terms of the geographical distance from Delhi, but also in the context of the different culture, language, and climate of Daulatabad.

At the end of *Tughlaq,* the audience is left with some unanswered questions regarding national spaces as well as the need for redefining them. These questions were in the context of India in the 1960s, which, though independent from 1947 on, was still struggling to define itself as a modern nation. Nehru's vision of a modern India was at this time being challenged by counter-political forces that saw it as too idealistic and impractical.

Between 1971 and 1988 Karnad's career took off impressively, although he actually wrote only two plays during this period. His success at this time came from the many motion pictures in which he participated as director, scriptwriter, or actor, or in all these capacities. His first involvement in movies was in U. R. Ananthamurthy's *Samskara* (1970), in which he acted and for which he wrote the script. The other movies with which he was associated at this time were *Vamsa Vriksha* (1971), *Kaadu* (1973), *Godhuli* (1977), *Ondanondu Kaladalli* (1978), and *Utsav* (1986).

The strain of bafflement with God's purposes continued in Karnad's next play, *Hayavadana* (English translation, 1975; production in Hindi, 1972). The Bhagavata/narrator begins the action in this play by saying, " . . . the completeness of God is something no poor mortal can comprehend." The Bhagavata guides the audience through two definitive acts and a prologue, which, though not titled thus, is inscribed into the play. The Bhagavata has a counterpart in an orthodox Greek chorus, but the edges blur progressively when the three principal protagonists, toward the end of act 1, perform the strophe/antistrophe.

Included within the pages of this text are two stories that, though apparently independent, in actuality are linked. The stories are told in the form of plays, as Karnad uses the play-within-the-play format. Another technique he employs is to make the audience within the first story become the actors of the second story. Thus, the audience of the play is made to become proactive and complicitous, instead of remaining mere spectators.

The source of this play is Thomas Mann's *The Transposed Heads* (1941), which is itself based on the sixth story in Vidyasagar Jivanand's *Vetala Parichavimashati* (1873), based in turn on part of Somdeva Bhatta's *Kathasaritsagara* and Kshemendra's *Brihatkatha Manjari*. Karnad was inspired at this stage, too, by Brecht, Sudraka, and Federico García Lorca; their influence led him to create a complex array of types/archetypes and characters with the help of masks and puppets within a Brechtian format.

Just as the Bhagavata is about to narrate the first story, that of the transposed heads, a man with a horse's head, the titular Hayavadana (horse-headed, in Sanskrit), rushes on stage, and his story becomes linked with that of Devadatta and Kapila, the two men with transposed heads. Hayavadana was born to a Karnataka princess and was sired by an Arabian horse—trope for land and lady. An implication is of a curse that accrues on the progeny by virtue of the actions of the parents, a thought that links this play to *Yayati*. Hayavadana must find a solution to his predicament. Since God does not enable him to overcome it, he rushes on stage to the Bhagavata. The dramatist brings the case to the court of the audience for judgment. At this point the playwright actively involves the audience in the play. While onstage, Hayavadana keeps slapping himself on the forehead and saying, "What a forehead! What a forehead!" Karnad is alluding to the Hindu belief that when one is born, his future is already written on his forehead, originating in one's actions in his past life, just as future rebirths in their turn are dependent on one's present actions. Hayavadana is unable to circumvent fate in spite of his deep sense of civic duty, which makes him traverse the length and breadth of the country for a solution to the question of which is superior, the mind or the body, not just for himself but for society at large.

After Hayavadana leaves the stage to continue his quest for a human head to complete his human body, the Bhagavata once again initiates the action to stage the play of the transposed heads, and the actors begin enacting the story of Devadatta and Kapila, who have independent bodies but are twinned together by their heads. This twinning is echoed in the two-headed bird perched in the doorway of the house of the central female protagonist, Padmini.

Padmini plays a significant role in this play. She is the wife of one of the male protagonists, Devadatta, and is loved by the second man in the play, Kapila. When she begins to be attracted to him also, the two men, who are friends, behead themselves over this issue. Padmini prays to the goddess Kali, who instructs her to put the heads back onto the bodies to restore them to life. Padmini in her excitement puts the wrong heads on the wrong bodies. So Devadatta, the intellectual, gets the athletic body of Kapila and vice versa. However, the bodies soon start overriding the minds, and Devadatta ceases intellectual pursuits; this change upsets Padmini, although she is happy with his new body. Kapila is equally unhappy with his friend's body. Padmini now can no longer control the situation she initiated by transposing their heads. The story ends with a duel in which both men die, and Padmini commits the ritual suicide act of suttee (former Indian practice in which the widow cremated herself on her husband's funeral pyre).

The subtext of the horse man, Hayavadana, underlines the absurdity of trying to play god and change naturally endowed characteristics, as in the case of Kapila and Devadatta. Hayavadana at the end of the play finds that his search for completeness ends with his body becoming a horse's to match his horse's head.

The two stories—that of the horse and that of Padmini—overlap. The horse is at one level happy with its head, since it has beaten the human body to its required shape, that of a horse, instead of the other way around. At another level, the victory of matter over mind, in the case of Devadatta and Kapila, causes the death of the two men and Padmini. Mann had used the original Sanskrit story of transposed heads to mock religion and philosophy, which considered the head to be superior to the body. According to Mann, intellect—that is, the head, cannot override the limitations of nature, meaning the body. Karnad in this play has also brought in the issue of identity or human personality and the difficulty in assigning it to either the mind or the body. An additional twist to Karnad's play is the inclusion of Hayavadana, whose horse's head tames his human body in an exactly opposite reaction to what had happened in the case of Kapila and Devadatta.

This phase in Karnad's career won him many awards. The President's Gold Medal for the Best Indian Film for *Samskara* in 1970 was followed by the Sangeet Natak Akademi Award (National Academy of the Performing Arts) for playwriting in 1972, the Kamaladevi Award of the Bharatiya Natya Sangh for the Best Indian Play of the year for *Hayavadana* for 1972, the Padma Shri Award in 1974, and many more

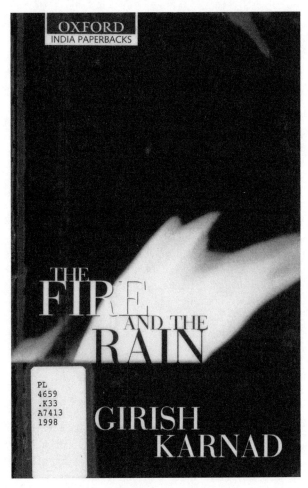

Cover for Karnad's play (performed in 1995 and published in English in 1998) that depicts a sacrificial ritual enacted to bring rain to a drought-stricken kingdom amid political maneuvering and betrayals (Newton Gresham Library, Sam Houston State University)

awards for directing and acting in movies. During this period he received the Homi Bhabha Fellowship for Creative Work in Folk Theatre (1970–1972), followed by the directorship of the Film and Television Institute, Pune (1974–1975). Then he was chosen the president of the Karnataka Nataka Academy (1976–1978), Indian co-chairman for the Joint Media Committee of the Indo–U.S. Sub-commission on Education and Culture (1984–1993), and Visiting Professor and Fulbright Scholar in Residence at the University of Chicago (1987–1988).

Naga-Mandala: Play with a Cobra (English translation, 1990) has a prologue and two acts and was written during the time Karnad spent at the University of Chicago. It was presented in 1992 at the Guthrie Theatre of Minneapolis as part of its thirtieth anniversary season. The play tells a story that is personified as a woman clad in a sari, accompanied by a song and

escorted by flames. The *Naga* of the title refers to a cobra, while *Mandala* refers to the circle in which it exerts its power—that is, a circle into which humans step and become enchanted. The action takes place in the sanctum sanctorum of a ruined temple, defiled by a broken idol, within the partial darkness of a cracked roof and wall, where flames exchange notes. These flames come from different sources and different homes—for instance, a kerosene lamp flame and a *Kusbi* lamp flame. They all carry images of the lives and homes from which they come. A new flame has just joined the other flames. All of them try to save a dying man—a man shocked by the floating images. He is saved, and the flames and the story tell him that he has to pass on the story in order to continue living. The man honors this promise by presenting the story told him in the form of the play that follows.

The main story is of the "innocent" Rani married to Appanna (Anyman), who keeps her incarcerated. A blind relative, Kurudavva, helps her win back her husband from the "other" one, who is conspicuously faceless and nameless. The behavior of the husband is completely different during the day from his behavior at night. Kurudavva gives Rani a couple of roots from an original bunch of three so that she can make a magic potion to entice her husband back. The plan backfires when a frightened Rani empties the potion into an anthill where a king cobra resides. Allured, the cobra takes the guise of the husband and discharges "his" duties with such zeal that she has a child by him. Appanna, a nonbeliever in the stork story, slighted by the malicious denial of his patriarchal rights, literally screams for justice. Helped by the otherworldly knowledge of the cobra, Rani alters the conditions of her trial, succeeds, and wins for herself respect, credibility, and the status of goddess—all because of the test she devises: holding the cobra in her hand, she swears to the truth as instructed. The dramatic resolution involves her taking an oath that she has held no one in her arms other than the cobra and her own husband.

The story is multilayered and has two endings—one that makes it a "play pleasant" and another a "play unpleasant." It has subplot through the blind relative, Kurudavva, and her vehicle—the spectral son who carries her on his back. Like her son, her knowledge is otherworldly but becomes suspect when Rani, instead of regaining her husband, has a liaison with the cobra and has a child by him. The conflict that existed in the earlier plays may be said now to extend to doubles and spectral doubles. The cobra is at one level a husband impersonator and at another level from another world, one distinct from the human one.

In 1988 Karnad became the chairman of the Sangeet Natak Akademi, a post he held until 1993. He wrote *Tale-Danda* in 1989 (English translation, 1993) against the backdrop of the Mandir and Mandal movements in India. *Tale-Danda* literally means punishment for the head, but the title suggests beheading. The source of the play is historical, and the focus is on ideological conflicts of caste/class and religion that threaten to destroy the secular fabric of India. In his preface to the play, Karnad says that when he wrote *Tale-Danda* he had in mind the social havoc caused in India by the Mandir and Mandal issues. The Mandal Commission in the 1980s had created major social problems when it sought to widen the scope of the extant policy in India of positive action concerning the lower castes by including more castes and subcastes in the original list of castes that would benefit from positive discrimination. The resistance to Mandal's report was from the higher castes, who felt that the action further empowered the lower castes and eroded their own power base. The Mandir issue refers to the conflict between the Hindus and the Muslims over a mosque in Ayodhya, which the Hindus contended was the birthplace of their Lord Ram. They wanted the Muslims to hand over the site to them for the construction of a *mandir,* a temple. The Muslims resisted, and militant Hindu hordes ultimately tore down the temple in December 1992, thereby causing Hindu-Muslim riots. According to Karnad, this act made the issues of caste politics portrayed in *Tale-Danda* relevant for modern-day India.

In this play Karnad goes back to the year 1168 and the city of Kalyan to focus on Basavanna of the Veerashaiva movement, a movement dedicated to Lord Shiva, the powerful Destroyer of the Hindu Trinity of Bhrahma (the Creator), Vishnu (the Preserver), and Shiva. Shiva is important since out of destruction is born construction: the old order must be destroyed before a new one can emerge. Another concern of the play is the institution of caste and the importance of dismantling the barriers that perpetuate it.

Three strains interlock to make three important statements in *Tale-Danda*. One concerns a class group seeking reform; another concerns a class group that rules; and a third concerns a class group that maintains its superior position by clinging to the privileges that had first made possible their reaching a position of power. While certain correspondences are possible between the first two groups, none is possible with the third. The reformist group, with Basavanna at its head, ignores the elitist, upper-caste language of Sanskrit and talks of God in the language of the common people, condemning idol worship and superstition. They not only preach caste equality but also put it into practice. The caste system among the Hindus in India has four categories—the Brahmans (the priests), the Kshatriyas (the warriors), the Vaisyas (the traders), and the Shu-

dras (the menials). The Shudras belong to the lower caste, and even their shadow can supposedly pollute the upper castes. The upper castes jealously preserve their power matrix and do not like the lower castes to claim equality with them. The Reformist Group headed by Basavanna therefore faces tremendous opposition from the upper castes. The second group, the ruling group, has a thinking and conscientious king in Bijjala, but because of certain compulsions rooted in caste loyalties, he does not support Basavanna in his attempts at ridding the state of caste inequalities and other related injustice. The third group consists of people from the upper castes who, governed by self-interest and self-preservation, forsake their traditional intellectual status and become reactionary. They are masters at the art of intrigues, through which they try to usher in unpalatable changes.

Basavanna and his group fail to effect social reforms, as they are blocked by the group that seeks to maintain a status quo in order to protect its own superior social position. The saintly Basavanna is martyred, and the reformists lose the battle for social change. The king who was a friend of the common man and wanted to rid society of inequalities, but not at the cost of caste affiliations, also pays with his life. The people of the kingdom end up worse off than ever before.

Even as the power group crowns a dubious prince and propitiates him, behind the propitiation are hidden cords, strings with which the puppet king may be jerked and maneuvered. Beyond the "urn" of a thousand holes that jets water into a thousand streams is the fire; the symbols fire and water, one raging, one anointing, point at the title of Karnad's next play, *The Fire and The Rain* (English translation, 1998).

The awards continued accumulating in this phase of Karnad's career. The Writer of the Year Award from Granthaloka Journal of the Book Trade went to *Tale-Danda* in 1990. *Tale-Danda* also received the Karnataka Sahitya Academy Award for Best Play and the Booksellers and Publishers Association of South India Award in 1992. In the same year *Tale-Danda* won the B. H. Sridhar Award. The Karnataka Sahitya Academy Award for the Most Creative Work went to *Naga-Mandala* in 1992. Karnad also received the Padma Bhushan, one of India's highest national-level awards for distinctive services in 1992. His movies also earned many awards.

The Fire and the Rain was the result of a commission from the Guthrie Theatre, Minneapolis, in 1993 to write a play. In 1994 Karnad fine-tuned the play for the stage in a workshop in Minneapolis, working with American actors. The play opens on a land laid waste by a long drought. A *yajna* (a ritual of sacrifice, typically the pouring of food offerings or oblations into Agni, the

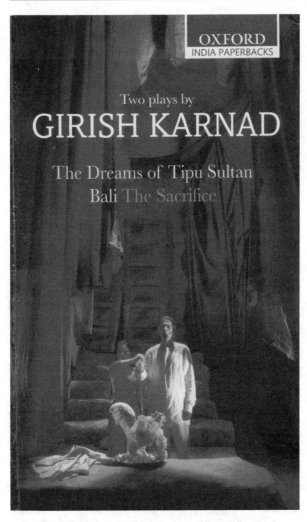

*Cover for Karnad's 2004 collection, comprising a 1997 play about
the inner life of a famed eighteenth-century sultan of Mysore and
a 2002 retelling of a tenth-century myth in which a king is
compelled to violate the tenets of the Jain faith by
making a sacrifice (University of
Georgia Library)*

sacrificial fire) is offered by the king to propitiate Indra, the king of the gods and also the rainmaker. It is being conducted by the chief priest, Paravasu. The play has as its source the *Vanaparva* (the forest canto) of the *Mahabharata*. The plot is complex, as are the characters. According to Karnad, the play had germinated in his mind for thirty-seven years. The format again includes a play-within-the-play. The action is set in and around the forest homes of the sages Raibhya and Bharadwaja and the courtyard of the king's palace, the location of the *yajna*.

The action of the prologue may be read as a foil to the epilogue, and the active participants of one become the passive observers of the other and vice versa. The audience, too, is built into the play by virtue of the actors who enact one part of it and witness the other.

The story of Paravasu's *yajna* to propitiate Indra and bring rain to the parched kingdom is interwoven with stories of sexual desire, betrayals, and power seeking. His wife, Vishakha's, sexuality is exploited by Paravasu and his cousin Yavakri for their own selfish ends. This exploitation is countered by the innocent passion of Paravasu's brother, Arvasu, and his beloved Nittilai. Paravasu's betrayal of Arvasu is at two levels—the personal and the political. In an attempt to seek political position, he lets Arvasu take the blame for the death of their father but then betrays him by not telling the truth about this death. The betrayal also results in Arvasu's separation from his beloved Nittilai, as he could not meet her father at the appointed time to claim her hand in marriage.

These complex relationships embody the indivisible presence of good and evil. In Karnad's world, evil is something that is ever present and cannot be destroyed, though it may be kept under control. Not surprisingly, then, the ending of the play finds tears mingling with the rain. Retribution and liberation, absolution and the spectacle of people dancing with joy and rolling in the mud, alternate with one another. One sees Paravasu walking into the *yajna* as the fire is desecrated by first the presence of the spirit—the Brahma Rakshasa—and then by the starving common people, who cease being the passive audience to the play-within-the-play being enacted by Arvasu and rush into the *yajna* enclosure, where they help themselves to the choice food kept there for the gods. This action is retribution against Paravasu for his exploitation of his wife and betrayal of his brother. The Brahma Rakshasa is liberated and his soul allowed eternal peace by the boon given by the god Indra, who appears on the scene. One also sees Arvasu receiving absolution from his pain and sorrow.

At this stage of his career, too, the awards kept coming for Karnad. He received the Gubbi Veeranna Award for 1996–1997 and the highest Indian literary prize, the Jnanapith Award, in 1999. He received the appointment to the prestigious position of Director of the Nehru Centre, the Cultural Wing of the High Commission of India, London, from 2002 to 2004. While he was in Britain, the Leceister Haymarket Theatre commissioned him to write *Bali: The Sacrifice* (English translation, 2004), his eighth play, which was first performed in May 2002.

Although Karnad has received so many awards and also been decorated by the Indian Government with a Padma Shri and a Padma Bhushan, his reception in the world of Kannada theater has been rather ambivalent. As noted by C. N. Ramachandran, Kannada critics feel he is an outsider and not deeply rooted in their culture. This judgment has occurred because although he writes in Kannada, he quickly translates his plays into English, and they are then staged in Europe and the United States. This pattern makes him more a pan-Indian dramatist than a Kannada dramatist. In spite of this critique, considerable critical work is available on him in English in India, and his plays have become the subject of research dissertations at many Indian universities.

Girish Karnad occupies a distinctive niche in the world of Indian theater. No other dramatist is writing in an Indian language or in English with his kind of hybrid mix–concerns of class, caste, and gender presented within such dramatic skills. Anyone who studies representations of India and Indian history through the theater will need to come to terms with Karnad's works, whether she/he encounters them in Kannada or in English, in the theater or in print.

Interviews:

Allen J. Mendonca, "Breaking into the Big League," *Indian Express* (Bombay), 22 August 1993;

Madhuri Valegar, "In Conversation, with Girish Karnad," *Sunday Observer* (Bombay), 4 September 1994.

References:

Brian Crow and Chris Banfield, *An Introduction to Post-Colonial Theatre* (Cambridge: Cambridge Studies in Modern Theatre, 1996);

Jaydipsinh Dodiya, ed., *Plays of Girish Karnad, Critical Perspectives* (Delhi: Prestige Books, 1999; London: Sangam, 1999);

Thomas Mann, *The Transposed Heads,* translated by Helen T. Iowa-Porter (London: Vintage, 1972);

Tutan Mukherjee, ed., *Girish Karnad's Plays* (Delhi: Pencraft International, 2006);

Bharata Muni, *Natyasastra,* translated by Adya Rangachary (Bangalore: India Book House Prakashana, 1986; revised, New Delhi: Munshivan Manoharlal, 1996);

M. K. Naik, *A History of Indian English Literature* (Delhi: Sahitya Akademi, 1997);

Naik and S. Mokashi-Punekar, eds., *Perspectives on Indian Drama in English* (Madras: Oxford University Press, 1977);

Sudhakar Pandey and Freya Barua, eds., *New Directions in Indian Drama,* with special reference to the plays of Vijay Tendulkar, Badal Sircar, and Karnad (New Delhi: Prestige Books, 1994);

C. Rajagopalachari, *The Mahabharata* (Bombay: Bharatiya Vidya Bhavan, 1971);

C. N. Ramachandran, "Girish Karnad: The Playwright in Search of Metaphors," in *Journal of Indian Writing in English,* 27 (July 1999): 21–34;

Vibha Saxena, "Did the Andhaka See Too Much?: Redefining Girish Karnad in a Postcolonial Perspective," thesis, University of Mumbai, 2000;

Vatsayana, Preface and Introduction, *The Kamasutra: Love Precepts of the Brahman* (Paris: Libraire "Astra," n.d.).

Adib Khan

(29 January 1949 –   )

Rebecca Sultana
McMaster University

BOOKS: *Seasonal Adjustments* (St. Leonards, N.S.W.: Allen & Unwin, 1994);

Solitude of Illusions (St. Leonards, N.S.W.: Allen & Unwin, 1996);

The Storyteller (Pymble, N.S.W.: Flamingo, 2000);

Homecoming (Pymble, N.S.W.: Flamingo, 2003).

SELECTED PERIODICAL PUBLICATIONS–UNCOLLECTED: "It's about Your Family," *Australian Author,* 26, no. 4 (1995): 16–17;

"Writing Homeland," *Australian Book Review,* 170 (May 1995): 24–25;

"In Janus' Footsteps," *Australian Humanities Review,* 22 (June 2001): 26–28.

The Bangladeshi immigrant Adib Khan is gradually transforming himself from a best-selling Australian novelist into one who is critically acclaimed in Anglophone literature generally. He has also written essays on issues faced by immigrants from the Third World to the West such as multiculturalism and race relations. Among subcontinental writers who have attained fame in English literature, Khan especially credits Salman Rushdie for the sudden interest in writing from the region: "He made us realize we could reinvent the language which shook the West," he told interviewer Matt Condon in 2000.

An only child, Khan was born in Dhaka, East Pakistan (today Bangladesh), on 29 January 1949 to Atiquz Zaman Khan, a journalist, and Zebun Nessa Qasem. He attended Holy Cross School and St. Joseph's High School in Dhaka. He took his GCE "O"-level (General Certificate of Education Ordinary-level) examination in 1965 and completed his higher secondary certificate in 1967 at Notre Dame College in Dhaka. His first attempt at writing was a short story, "A Cloud without a Lining," which he wrote at nineteen; it was broadcast on the BBC World Service but was never published. In 1972 he received first-class honors in English literature at Dhaka University and married Sharukh Haq. He went to Australia in 1973 for post-

Adib Khan (from the cover for Seasonal Adjustments, *1994; James Branch Cabell Library, Virginia Commonwealth University)*

graduate studies at Monash University, where he wrote his master's thesis on Robert Browning's poetry in 1975. He completed his diploma in education at Monash the same year, and in 1976 he began teaching English, English literature, and history at Damascus College in Ballarat. He became a permanent resident of Australia in 1977 and a citizen in 1978. The Khans have two daughters: Aneeqa, born in 1980, and Afsana, born in 1984.

Khan revealed in a 2000 interview with Ziaul Karim in Dhaka's *Star Weekend Magazine* that he started writing his first novel, *Seasonal Adjustments* (1994), "out of a sense of midlife crisis" as he confronted his sense of displacement as an immigrant and pondered his academic future. He wrote the novel as therapy, but a bookseller friend suggested that he send the typescript to a publisher. Khan submitted the work to the first name in an alphabetical list of Australian publishers, Allen and Unwin, who accepted it. Khan told Jane Sullivan in 2000, "Had I known then what I know about the publishing world now I wouldn't have had the courage. I went into it in a state of total naivety."

Seasonal Adjustments is characterized by a profound sense of emotional and physical dislocation that also permeates Khan's later works. Dismayed and disillusioned by the barbarity of the war for independence from Pakistan, Iqbal Chaudhary abandons the life of wealth and social standing he enjoys as a member of the Bengali landowning class and immigrates to Australia. Eighteen years later he returns to Dhaka but fails to revive the ties he severed. He discovers that an unbridgeable gulf exists between himself and his family as cultural and social norms that he has not encountered for eighteen years now seem antiquated. His relatives are indignant when he reveals to them his daughter's lack of religious conformity, his own agnosticism and inability to pray, and his skepticism about his mother's blind devotion to a holy man. He finally decides that "You get sick of wearing masks to hide your confused aloneness. You can never call anything your own." He returns to Australia, the illusion of "home" that he had carried within him back to Bangladesh lost forever. He realizes that there is no place he can call home: he is homeless, in between, neither here nor there. The third space in which he dwells is not an interval between fixed points of departure and arrival but a mode of being of perpetual migration. Philosophical and bitter at the same time, he sums up his position: "Do you know what it means to be a migrant? A lost soul forever adrift in search of a tarnished dream?" *Seasonal Adjustments* sets the tone for Khan's lonely, troubled heroes. In 1994 it won the Christina Stead Award for Fiction and the Australian Book of the Year Prize and was short-listed for *The Age* Book of the Year Award. In 1995 it won the Commonwealth Prize for Best First Book.

In 1995 Khan began teaching creative writing part-time at the Technical and Further Education (TAFE) branch of Ballarat University. That same year he published the essay "Writing Homeland," in which he emphasizes the need for a place that one can call home: "It fills those gigantic gaps in the past and makes the present more bearable because it diminishes that sense of loss." The place, however, need not be one's actual birthplace: "That creation is essentially an illusion, and deep inside one knows that the purpose will not be fulfilled because illusions are transient."

Khan's second novel, *Solitude of Illusions* (1996), deals with memory, family, home, love, and death. Khalid Sharif, a successful Calcutta businessman stricken with a terminal illness, reassesses his life while visiting his son in Melbourne. He recalls his youth in the 1940s when he fell in love with a beautiful courtesan, Nazli. His separation from her, forced by his indignant family, left him overwhelmed with guilt and self-reproach and has haunted him for the rest of his life. Khan's words in "Writing Homeland" aptly describe Sharif's view of his past: "It is an amalgamation of remembrances, half-truths, fragmented images, gaunt shadows, snatches of conversations and yearnings structured into a shimmering mirage by an imagination that feeds itself uneasily on an awareness of the discrepancy between the way it was and the way it possibly is." On the *Liquid Reviews* website (<http://members.tripod.com/liquid_review/books.htm>) Mike Somerset characterized Sharif's as "a life that has corroded with regrets of missed opportunities" and said that *Solitude of Illusuions* "is a book that inspires us to re-assess our way of life and may give us courage to make the decisions that will give our lives meaning." The novel won the Tilly Ashton Award for Best Braille Book of the Year and was short-listed for the 1997 Christina Stead Award and New South Wales Ethnic Commission Award.

Vamana, the title character of Khan's third novel, *The Storyteller* (2000), is an ugly dwarf who tells stories in the streets of New Delhi and reinvents himself into a heroic figure through his fictional characters. Khan draws a hideous picture of a deformed human being with a humpback, scarred face, scaly lips, huge head, jagged teeth, and floppy ears; his description of Vamana is replete with animal metaphors. Vamana realizes that his appearance is at once repulsive and fascinating to others. By surrounding the protagonist with characters such as eunuchs, transvestites, prostitutes, and corrupt police officers, the novel illuminates issues of intolerance and prejudice, the price of progress, and inequities in wealth and power. Vamana gets into trouble when he loses the ability to distinguish between reality and the illusions that he creates; he ends up in prison, facing execution. Annie Greet observed in *The Age* (9 September 2000) that "Vamana is a metaphor, a reminder of our creative natures and an indictment of how we have crippled and distorted ourselves, failing our potential as human beings." Calling Khan "brilliant," she found *The Storyteller* "confident of winning gold in an impressive number of areas." One of his greatest achievements in the book, in her opinion, is

Cover for Khan's 1994 novel, about an immigrant who returns to Bangladesh after eighteen years in Australia and finds that he does not feel at home in either society (James Branch Cabell Library, Virginia Commonwealth University)

that "in his focus on extreme ugliness and perversion, the antitheses of our fancied 'norm' for the human condition, Khan pinpoints the sad, twisted nature of the species as a whole."

Because his first three novels are set, in part or in whole, on the Indian subcontinent, Khan was criticized by some Australian critics for being too "exotic." Sullivan compared him with the Indian writers Rohinton Mistry and Vikram Chandra because of his "unashamedly 'exotic' writing" in *The Storyteller*. In his otherwise favorable review of *Solitude of Illusions* in the *Sydney Morning Herald* (16 November 1996), Andrew Riemer expressed the hope "that there will be nothing about the Indian subcontinent in his next novel: he is far too good a writer to remain predictably 'exotic.'"

Khan seems to respond to such criticism in his fourth novel, which he wrote with the aid of a $50,000 grant from the Australian Council for the Arts. Work-

ing with one of Australia's foremost fiction editors, Judith Lukin-Amundsen, he produced *Homecoming* (2003). The protagonist, Martin Godwin, is a middle-aged Australian male of European descent. A Vietnam veteran coping with posttraumatic stress disorder, he is impotent; a gambling addict; divorced from his wife, Moira; has an uneasy relationship with his son, Frank; and is the caregiver for Nora, who was paralyzed by a stroke shortly after they became lovers. He is haunted by the fear that his exposure to Agent Orange has caused Frank's depression and also by the events of one sweltering afternoon when, during a raid on a village, he turned away as four members of his platoon raped a Vietnamese girl. He is living an isolated life in Melbourne when another veteran, Ken Davis, who is embarking on a political career, visits to ask for his silence about the rape. The novel winds the strands of Martin's life as father, comrade, lover, unwilling conspirator, and reluctant spiritual seeker into a framework in which the reader is given a snapshot of contemporary Australia groping toward meaning in a rapidly changing world. Greet noted in *The Age* (1 November 2003) that Khan provides Australian icons and images "almost to the point of cliche, involving vignettes of road rage, psychotherapists and patients, bank managers and corporate manipulation, pub culture, football mania, gambling, moments with Buddhism, copping the lot from feminists, recent migrants in the community, sexual exploitation—everyday events which contribute to the impression of the pulsating social web to which the veterans return." In the *Sydney Morning Herald* (15 November 2003) Riemer praised Khan's skill in "constructing a layered narrative, swinging back and forth through time, from a sequence of short, at times almost impressionistic section," but he was critical of Khan for endowing this "low-key novel with a measure of philosophical weight." The novel was a finalist for the Best Book Award of the Commonwealth Writers Prize for South East Asia and the South Pacific Region.

In an unpublished interview Khan revealed that his novel "Spiral Road," scheduled to be published in late 2006, concerns the Alams, a proud and aristocratic Bengali family that implodes after discovering that one of its younger members is involved with a terrorist group in the Chittagong Hill Tracts. This hilly region in southeastern Bangladesh is inhabited by indigenous tribes involved in armed conflict with the Bangladesh military; the situation has its roots in the forced settling of Bengalis after independence from British colonial rule in 1947. The political issues remain in the background in the novel, with most of the action taking place in Dhaka and the Alams' ancestral village. Major plot threads include a secret love affair, an "honor killing," and the emotionally stunted life of the main protagonist, who returns to Dhaka from Australia to visit his family. Khan commented, "I chose to write about the corrosive effects of terrorism on a family instead of focusing on the violence perpetrated by terrorists."

In addition to teaching creative writing part-time at Ballarat University, Adib Khan also teaches a course for gifted year-ten students at Ballarat Grammar School. He has served as an examiner for Ph.D. dissertations at Adelaide University and is preparing a teaching project on creative writing for the Australian National University, where he will teach for three months in 2006 as part of a writing fellowship.

South Asian writers in English have opened windows into a myriad of cultures for a wider Anglophone audience. Khan's *Seasonal Adjustments,* for example, deals with the aftereffects of Bangladesh's brutal civil war for independence from Pakistan, while *Solitude of Illusions* emphasizes the heavy emotional price one has to pay for maintaining honor and family pride. Like many South Asian writers, Khan takes a secular humanist perspective that emphasizes tolerance and is suspicious of veneration of the past.

Khan falls within the category of South Asian diaspora writers for whom the act of writing is a way to reclaim their homelands. Memory figures prominently in such narratives, and it plays an important role in all of Khan's novels as the protagonists try to reconstruct and reconfigure their identities. In Khan's first three novels conventional ideas of home and belonging that depend on clearly defined, static notions of being "in place," firmly rooted in a community or a particular geographical location, no longer seem suited to a world in which the experience of migration has altered the ways in which individuals think of their relation to place. But instead of considering the dual identity of the migrant as a handicap, Khan points out in his essay "In Janus' Footsteps" (2001), one might regard it as a double enrichment. He describes the contributions of the dual cultures of East and West in his own formation: "On the one side there were Homer, Virgil, Dante, Shakespeare and Milton. On the other there were the influences of *The Ramayana, Mahabharata,* the Moghul poets, Iqbal and Tagore. The two sides met, not in combat, but in a synthesis of ideas out of which I emerged considerably enriched in thought and feeling but without any clearly defined sense of belonging to a mono-

cultural society. I would not have it any other way." On the other hand, he warns of the danger of a rise in nationalism in Western states as they experience increased immigration from the East:

> Discourse on gender, ethnic and class identity appears to have subsided for the moment and we are caught in a mesh of aggressive nationalism that encourages a somewhat naïve and illusory view of a heroic identity. Guilt and alienation are frequently evoked to lash individuals into an acceptance of an advanced tribal mentality, and these are often achieved by clearly defined characteristics of unacceptable non-conformity. Probably this is a communal reaction to fear, a backlash against globalisation that is perceived to be a threat to national identity.

Although it is a frequently discussed issue among Third World writers, racism does not interest Khan as a topic. He told Sullivan: "It's a peculiar thing here. If you can speak the idiomatic language, you're pretty right. If you know the language of abuse and sweating, unfortunately it works." His immigrant characters rarely face bigotry, and when they do, it is presented as a consequence of ignorance rather than of hatred.

Discussing his writing technique in the *Star Weekend Magazine* interview, Adib Khan said that he weaves words like "candy floss" and that "Character for me is of fundamental importance, far more important than the story or the plot." He does not dictate the movement of the story but lets the characters take over. The characters who appear in Khan's fiction, subcontinental or otherwise, are mostly eccentric creations rather than representative middle-class figures.

Interviews:

Rosemary Sorensen, *Australian Book Review,* 160 (May 1994): 14–15;

Ziaul Karim, "Bangladeshi Story-teller in World Fiction," *Star Weekend Magazine* (Dhaka), 28 April 2000, pp. 4–10;

Jane Sullivan, "Outside Edge," *Age Extra* (Melbourne), 2 September 2000, pp. 7–8;

Matt Condon, "An Encounter with a Charismatic Street Performer Inspired Adib Khan's *The Storyteller,*" *Sun-Herald* (Sydney), 15 October 2000, pp. 1–2.

Arun Kolatkar
(1 November 1932 – 25 September 2004)

Mala Pandurang
Dr. B. M. N. College

BOOKS IN ENGLISH: *Jejuri* (Bombay: Clearing House, 1976; London: Peppercorn, 1978; New York: New York Review Books, 2005);
The Kala Ghoda Poems (Mumbai: Pras Prakashan, 2004);
Sarpa Satra (Mumbai: Pras Prakashan, 2004).

OTHER: "Three Cups of Tea" and "Irani Restaurant in Bombay," in *Contemporary Indian Poetry in English,* edited by Saleem Peeradina (Bombay: Macmillan of India, 1972), pp. 42–44;
"Woman" and "Suicide of Rama," *Twelve Modern Indian Poets,* edited by Arvind Krishna Mehrotra (Oxford & Delhi: Oxford University Press, 1992).

TRANSLATION: Tukaram, *Nine Translations of Tukaram's Poems* (Bombay: Poetry India, 1966).

SELECTED PERIODICAL PUBLICATIONS–
UNCOLLECTED: "The Renunciation Dog," *Quest,* 1 (1955): 40;
"Boatride," *Damn You* (1968).

Arun Kolatkar is one of the foremost postindependence Indian poets writing in English. While Kolatkar's poems appeared in magazines and anthologies beginning in 1955, his reputation rests largely on *Jejuri* (1976), a lengthy sequence of thirty-one poems about a small town, visited by Hindu pilgrims in Western Maharashtra. In 1977 Kolatkar won the Commonwealth Poetry Prize for *Jejuri* and gained international acclaim. The collection has subsequently been republished three times–in 1976, 1978, and 1982. Kolatkar's collection of Marathi poems, *Arun Kolatkarchi Kavita* (1976), was published in the same year as *Jejuri.* The thematic complexity of *Jejuri* generated a series of intense critical debates over the next two decades, not only on Kolatkar's work but also on the metropolitan/urban mind-set of the Indian poet writing in English. Kolatkar lived for the larger part of his life in the city of Mumbai (formerly known as Bombay) and remained extremely elusive about his private life until his death.

Arun Kolatkar (photograph by Gowri Ramnarayan © 2004, The Hindu)

He refused to own a telephone, television, or even a wristwatch. On rare occasions he offered autobiographical details of his childhood and upbringing in a middle-class Hindu Brahmin family. In July 2004, twenty-eight years after the publication of *Jejuri,* Kolatkar released two new volumes of poetry in English–*Sarpa Satra* (a transcreation from Marathi) and *The Kala Ghoda Poems.*

Arun Balkrishna Kolatkar was born 1 November 1932 in Kolaphur, situated in the Western Indian state of Maharashtra. A city known for its art, culture, and

198

music, Kolaphur is often referred to as Dakshin Kashi, or the Varansi of the South. Kolatkar spent his early youth in what was mostly a Marathi-speaking culture. He was thus exposed to Marathi folklore, Bhakti poetry, and other forms of religious literature. Kolatkar attended the Rajaram Marathi medium school in Kolaphur, where English was only one of the many subjects that he studied. He developed an affinity for the language through a passion for comic books and American movies. He graduated from the University of Bombay in 1949.

As a student, Kolatkar was more interested in art and painting than in academic subjects. His father's collection of black-and-white picture-postcards showing the architectural marvels of Greece and sculptures from museums of Italy and France may have sparked this interest. Through them he was introduced at an early age to the schools of Baroque and Renaissance art, and the works of Gian Lorenzo Bernini and Michelangelo. Kolatkar attended art schools in Kolaphur and Pune, and then joined the renowned J. J. School of Art in Bombay in 1949. Although he dropped out after a year or so, according to C. P. Surendran, Kolatkar maintained a long-distance association with the school and finally obtained a diploma in painting in 1957. In the course of his formal training in art, Kolatkar came into contact with Western aesthetic movements of Surrealism, Imagism, and symbolism, all of which are characteristic products of modernity. These schools of expression had an important influence on his poetry.

Kolatkar subsequently decided that he had nothing to contribute to art and instead opted for a career as a freelance graphic designer and a visualizer for advertising agencies in Mumbai. He wrote between jobs. Nissim Ezekiel, another Indian poet in English, was working at an advertising agency (Shilpi) in Mumbai. Ezekiel had been asked to edit a new magazine and was looking out for new poets. Art critic Dyaneshwar Nadkarni showed him some of Kolatkar's poetry, and Ezekiel was particularly impressed with "The Renunciation Dog," which became Kolatkar's first published poem; according to Arvind Krishna Mehrotra, it appeared in the inaugural issue of *The QUEST* (Bombay) in 1955.

In 1954 Kolatkar met Dilip Chitre, a prolific poet in Marathi, who also wrote in English. Chitre was instrumental in organizing a group of young Mumbai poets who began to publish a series of *laghu aniyatakaike* (little magazines) of experimental poetry. The most important of this series was *Sabda* (Word), which appeared in 1961, co-edited by Kolatkar. This group of poets explored ordinary, though disaffected, experiences through the use of surreal techniques. The little magazines published Kolatkar's seminal *Kalya Kavita* (Black Poems), which reflected the influence of radical

poetry from European dadaists, futurists, and Surrealists to the Beat poets of the United States. (Beat poet Allen Ginsberg is believed to have enjoyed Kolatkar's hospitality during his visit to India in the 1960s.) Although the experimental poetry of Marathi modernists of the 1940s—such as B. S. Mardhekar, P. S. Rege, and Vinda Karandikar—had a strong formative influence on Kolatkar, his own work became representative of the next literary generation of modernists, who wrote more obscure and esoteric poetry. By the mid 1960s, Kolatkar and other regional writers—such as Ayappan Panicker (Malayalam), Raghuvir Sahay (Hindi) and Chitre (Marathi)—had ushered in a new era of modernism in Indian poetry.

Although Kolatkar's bilingual background has enabled him to write poetry in both Marathi and English, critics vary in their response to his bilingual ability. Mehrotra regards Kolatkar's poetry in English and in Marathi as "two distinct, independent and very different bodies of work." On the other hand, R. Parthasarthy argues that Kolatkar does not use English and Marathi for different purposes. Chitre refers to Kolatkar as "an Anglo-Marathi poet." Vilas Sarang argues that Kolatkar's work in English shows much greater regard for logic and reason than does his work in Marathi: Kolatkar's poems in English "are more the product of the conscious mind, while the Marathi poems draw more deeply upon the resources of the unconscious." Bhalacandra Nemade is critical of Kolatkar's English masterpiece *Jejuri* but accepts his work in Marathi as important in its own right.

Kolatkar himself, in an interview with Eunice De Souza, refers to the kind of Marathi he uses as "rootless." Some of Kolatkar's early poems are transcreations from his Marathi verse into English and vice versa. Poems such as "Three Cups of Tea" (originally written in Bombay Hindi) and "Irani Restaurant in Bombay" first appeared in *An Anthology of Marathi Poetry* (1967) and were later collected in Saleem Peeradina's anthology *Contemporary Indian Poetry in English* (1972). Only a fraction of Kolatkar's work in Marathi has been translated into English, and consequently, it remains largely inaccessible to the non-Marathi reader.

Kolatkar's skill as a competent visualizer (he won several awards of the Commercial Artists Guild in India in the course of his involvement in the visual arts until the 1990s) is reflected in the unfolding of visual images in minute details in "The Boatride," first published in 1968 in *Damn You,* a stenciled little magazine edited by Mehrotra. Kolatkar re-creates the experience of a boat ride from Bombay harbor, at the Gateway of India, into the Arabian Sea. The first verse of the poem offers a graphic description as the boat ride gets under way:

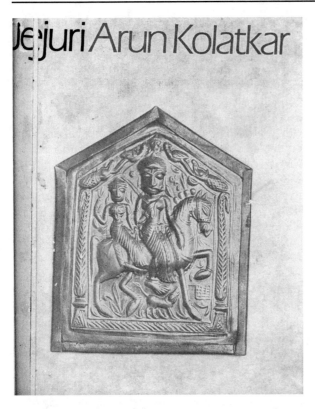

Cover for the 1978 edition of Arun Kolatkar's 1976 sequence of poems about a small town in western Maharashtra that is a destination for Hindu pilgrims (University of Georgia Library)

The long hooked poles
know the nooks and crannies
find flaws in stonework
or grappling with granite
ignite a flutter
of unexpected pigeons
and the boat is jockeyed away from
the landing

This long narrative poem in eleven sections is composed in lowercase letters and without punctuation marks in order to capture everything on the sea and in life as a ceaseless flux. Kolatkar's treatment of his subject matter is similar to that of American poet William Carlos Williams. The surrealistic snapshots of the journey on the sea can be interpreted in terms of a man's journey through life.

Kolatkar's masterpiece, *Jejuri,* first appeared in a little magazine, *Opinion Literary Quarterly,* in 1974. It was revised and published by Clearing House in 1976 and later by Pras Prakashan in 1977. It won the Commonwealth Poetry Prize for 1977. In fall 2005 *Jejuri* was republished, with an introduction by Amit Chaudhuri, as a New York Review Classic.

All the poems in *Jejuri* concern an important pilgrimage site about forty-eight kilometers from the city of Pune in the western part of the state of Maharashtra. The narrator undertakes a journey to the pilgrim town. He is conscious that he does not travel with the faith felt by the thousands of pilgrims who throng to Jejuri to pay homage to Khandoba, the god of the nomadic and pastoral tribe, also considered an incarnation of Lord Siva. Instead, the narrator is an alienated observer, "handicapped" by his modern, urban skepticism. Kolatkar's tone in *Jejuri* is ironic.

A common argument among postcolonial critics, according to G. K. Bansiramani, is that any Indian poet who writes in English is bound to be distanced from his natal culture and will inevitably "fall back on his self as a substitute for a linguistic or literary culture." This argument has led to multilevel readings of Kolatkar's *Jejuri* as the quest of an urban young man who attempts to connect with his roots. In an early review of the novel, Homi Bhabha states, "with *Jejuri,* Indo-Anglian Poetry has finally established itself [and ceased] to commune solely with its strange, unrepresentative urban existence." R. S. Kimbahune raises two crucial questions about Kolatkar's reasons for writing *Jejuri:* "Why does the narrator go to Jejuri in the first place?" and "Why does he tell about the journey in English?" Kolatkar, for his part, asserts in his interview with De Souza: "I have never felt the need to use the word *alienation.* What use does it serve? I am not sure since it can be used in so many different ways. It's not a disease of some kind. It may come in different shapes and sizes. Who is not alienated in some way? . . . Indianness is no abstract model to which anyone can conceivably try to conform."

Unlike several of his contemporaries writing in English—for example, Parthasarthy and A. K. Ramanujan—Kolatkar never ventured abroad either for academic or professional purposes. In fact, his first visit to the United Kingdom occurred when he won the Commonwealth Prize for Poetry in 1977. He visited the United States for the first time in 1986 during the Festival of India, at the invitation of Ginsberg. Kolatkar therefore was not preoccupied with issues linked to migration to the West. Themes of geographical dislocation and exile from the "homeland" are not central to his work.

Jejuri has a descriptive narrative format and can be divided into sections. First, the journey to and arrival at the temple town (poems 1–2); then the visit through the temple complex (poems 3–13); the walk down to the old temple complex (poems 14–23); the visit to the new temple complex (poems 24–28); the visit to the temple town at the foot of the hill (poems 29–30); finally, the journey back to the railway station (poem 31); and the world of the railway station (poems 31–36).

The collection begins with "Bus Ride." The protagonist, Manohar (through whom impressions of Jejuri are conveyed), boards a bus. He makes the trip with his friend Makarand (his alter ego). He is going by bus and will return by train. His younger brother and his friend accompany the narrator to Jejuri. He finds himself seated opposite an old man wearing spectacles. He can see his reflection but cannot probe the old man's mind and therefore cannot enter into the man's consciousness:

> At the end of the bumpy ride
> With your own face on either side
> when you get off the bus
> You don't step inside
> the old man's head.

Jejuri was first published in *Dionysius* (volume one) in the 1960s. Bruce King of the *Indian Literary Review* points out that although Kolatkar revised the manuscript of *Jejuri,* the change in the text between the *Dionysius* version and a later version in *Opinion Literary Quarterly* (1974) is minor, and Kolatkar's style had not altered much in a decade.

This collection of poems is the literary outcome of a single visit by Kolatkar to Jejuri; he had once read a book on the temples and legends of Maharashtra in which there was a chapter on this temple town. Some critics, such as Shubhangi Raykar, argue that Kolatkar, partly because of his Brahmanic background, is not sufficiently informed about the Khandoba culture, and the information in any case has no significance for him. Nemade reads the collection as a reflection of Kolatkar's bicultural values and cynical agnosticism, as is evident in "A Scratch":

> What is god
> And what is stone
> The dividing line
> it exists
> Is very thin
> At Jejuri
> And every other stone
> Is god or his cousin.

Nemade writes, "Kolatkar comes and goes like a weekend tourist from Bombay." Asked by King if he believed in God, Kolatkar replied, "I leave the question alone. I don't think I have to take a position about God one way or the other." His position is made clear in "The Butterfly," a short poem of four three-line stanzas and a single line. It is a celebration of "isness"–that is, of all things living in the present. According to S. K. Desai in Raykar's *Arun Kolatkar's* Jejuri: *A Commentary and Critical Perspectives,* the sheer existence of the butterfly is in contrast to the sterile hills. It exists for what it

is, requiring neither a legend nor a myth to justify its existence.

In contrast to the general tone of skepticism that pervades the collection are the three Chaitanya poems that occupy the core of the text. The Vaishnavaite Saint Chaitanya Mahaprabhu visited the temples in the sixteenth century intent on correcting the superstitious ways of the people:

> Sweet as grapes are the stories of Jejuri
> Said Chaitanya
> He popped a stone
> In his mouth
> And spat out gods.

Kolatkar was always keenly interested in the Bhakti tradition and translated the work of the seventeenth-century Bhakta poet Tukaram in *Nine Translations of Tukaram's Poems* (1966). Tukaram's poetry, written in colloquial Marathi, is in the form of dialogues with his family deity, Vitthal. Irreverence is an attitude found in nonconformist traditions such as the Bhakti cult, with the saint constantly questioning his/her deity. The cult of Vithal is synonymous with Marathi poetry. Devotees of Vithal make regular visits to Pandharpur and sing songs to Vithal. Kolatkar visited Pandharpur and describes Chaitanya as a Bhakti character. In the third Chaitanya poem, Kolatkar expresses regret at the continuation of old superstitions and describes the commercialization of the temple town.

Almost three decades after *Jejuri* was first published, critics still debate about Kolatkar's perspective in writing about his visit to the temple town. On the one hand, *Jejuri* is read by certain critics as a debunking of Indian religious practices and beliefs. Other critics, such as M. K. Naik, however, opine that the poems were written "out of serious fascination bordering on love" and believe that the poet is able to strike a balance between skepticism and acceptance.

The publication of *Arun Kolatkarchi Kavita* brought together Marathi poems written by Kolatkar over two decades. The international recognition accorded to *Jejuri* also initiated a reevaluation of Kolatkar's work in Marathi, according to Mehrotra, bringing it from the fringes into the mainstream. This collection includes poems that were written in English and translated into Marathi by the poet himself. Two such poems are "Biography" and "Crabs." In "Biography" the poet offers a satirical sketch of incidents in the narrator's life, which starts from the deep-rooted Indian desire to have a male child, then to the humiliation of the narrator at the hands of his peer group, at work and after marriage. "Crabs" is written in seventeen stanzas of four lines each. The poet uses the visual image of the crab as a symbol for the id and superego. In a conversational mode, the narrator scares his companion about a possible attack of "big fat crabs" on his eyes, an inlet to the physical world:

> All you have to do is give the word.
> And once they've eaten your eyes,
> their job is done.
> You'll never see them again.

In 2003 Kolatkar published *Chirimiri* in Marathi; this publication was followed by *Droan* and *Bhijki Vahi* (Soaked Notebook) in 2004. In *Chirimiri,* a group of whores are traveling to the pilgrimage site of Pandharpur. During the journey, they turn into "gopis," companions and playmates of Lord Krishna. According to Gowri Ramnarayan, *Bhijki Vahi* hints at Saint Tukaram's trial, when his verses were flung into the waters, only to be returned by the river, unscathed. This collection of 450 poems presents images of "weeping women" forgotten by history, from ancient Alexandria to contemporary Vietnam.

In the last three decades of his life, Kolatkar remained reticent about his work. He steadfastly refused to talk about his poetry. He remained a regular figure, however, at meetings of poets, publishers, and editors every Thursday at the Wayside Inn at the Kala Ghoda circle in South Mumbai, until the restaurant made way for a more elitist establishment in its place. He then shifted location to the Military Café and Beer Bar, an Iranian restaurant off the Flora Fountain. *The Kala Ghoda Poems* (2004) is a collection of poems written during the 1980s and 1990s. The poems in this collection describe ordinary, day-to-day scenes of life around Kala Ghoda (an important art and business center in Mumbai city) and other parts of South Mumbai. As with *Jejuri,* the poems in this collection can be read separately and also in sequence. Surendran compares the structure of the poem to a geodesic dome. Kolatkar captures the sights, sounds, and tastes of street life in Mumbai with his characteristic combination of wry humor and compassion, and his poems bring to life what would otherwise be considered ordinary and commonplace. The poems give space to the denizens of the underbelly of the city: "The little vamp, the grandma, the blind man, / the ogress, / the rat-poison man, / the pinwheel boy, / the hipster queen of the crossroads, / the Demosthenes of Kala Ghoda, / the pregnant queen of tarts, / the laughing Buddha, / the knucklebones champ." They also include the pirate in a bandanna, the shoeshine boy, the paralytic, the hunchback,

the leper, a spine-broken rat, and a delegation of crows with "all their beaks / like magnetic needles / pointing in one direction." In "Lice," Kolatkar sketches the figure of the street girl-woman with sensitivity:

> She hasn't been a woman for very long
> that girl who looks
> like a stick of cinnamon.
> Yes, the one in the mustard colored sari
> and red glass bangles,
> sitting on that upright concrete block
> as if it were a throne,
> though it's hardly broad enough
> for a kitten to curl up on.
> The slender wooden pillar
> of the Wayside Inn porch
> rises behind her
> like some kind of exotic backrest
> —how well it seems to fit
> the space between her shoulder blades.

"Breakfast Time at Kala Ghoda" is the central and longest poem in the collection. A clock across the road tells the poet the time in different places around the world. Those having breakfast at Kala Ghoda are placed in a universal community of "breakfasters" across the world—in Tokyo breakfast is "sliced raw fish! sushi balls and tofu with soy sauce," while at a restaurant in Seoul "a dog is slowly being strangled before it's thrown into a cooking pot," and in Alaska "freshly butchered reindeer meat" is being prepared. According to Shanta Gokhale, "The lady with . . . wirewool hair" and a "motherly smile" who brings "a jumbo aluminum box full of idlis" to Kala Ghoda becomes a metaphor for the poet, inviting the world to feast at the table of poetry. The all-knowing "Pi-dog" of the city celebrates its syncretic identity, claiming descent on his mother's side from "the only bitch to survive the 30 foxhounds imported from England" and on his father's side from "the dog that followed / Yudhisthira / on his last journey" and "became the only dog / to have made it to heaven / in recorded history." "The Boomtown Lepers' Band" includes another subtle reference to the poet in "the noseless singer" who belts out "a tuneless song / for a city without soul."

In *Sarpa Satra,* Kolatkar uses a story from the Mahabharat region (an area that encloses the valleys of Kathmandu and Pokhara) to develop a passionate commentary on the "festival of hatred" and the vicious cycle of genocide and retribution of contemporary times. The poem comprises three sections that are interdependent and form a continuous narrative—"Janamejaya," "Jaratkaru Speaks to Her Son Aastika," and "The Ritual Bath."

Arjuna of the Mahabharatha decides, without any rational justification, to burn down the Khandava forest, "Just for kicks, maybe." Kolatkar describes the ensuing inferno wherein everything in the forest is destroyed. The primeval forest contained ". . . five thousand / different kinds of butterflies alone / and a golden squirrel found nowhere else. / Some of the trees in that place / were, oh / hundreds and hundreds of years old, easily; / and it contained a wealth / of medicinal plants / that were not found anywhere else." Not just the wild life was eliminated but also the original inhabitants of the forest—"Not just the trees, birds, insects and animals / herds upon herds / of elephants, gazelles, antelopes / but people. . . . simple folk, children of the forest."

The cycle of violence is endless, as one act of violence leads to another. Takshak, a *naga* (Sanskrit for snake), loses his snake-wife in the burning forest, and to avenge her death, he kills Arjuna's grandson, Parikshit. Parikshit's son, Janameyaja, then vows to annihilate the entire species of snakes from the world. He holds the *Sarpa Satra* (or the fire sacrifice) to which snakes are drawn by a spell, only to be burned to death. The mass killing of snakes has resonance in the terrible genocide of the communal riots of Gujarat of 2002. Takshak's younger sister (Jaratkaru) instructs her son, Aastika, to stop Janmejaya from fulfilling his terrible vow.

> Go, Aastika;
> and my prayers go with you.
> Go, my son,
> and all our hopes
> go with you.
> My heart tells me
> you'll find a way
> to put a stop
> to that festival of hatred.

While Aastika is able to stop the sacrifice in the Mahabharata, in *Sarpa Satra* the reader is left with disturbing images of smoldering flames blackening the air and the stench of burning flesh. Although Kolatkar released *Sarpa Satra* and *The Kala Ghoda Poems* simultaneously, these two collections are not complementary texts. Kolatkar's bemused wryness in *The Kala Ghoda Poems* suggests a serious concern with hatred within the hearts of modern-day human beings.

Kolatkar has been associated mainly with *Jejuri*. The recent release of his latest two collections of poetry, however, will invite a new series of critical responses to Kolatkar's work. His verse remains marked by irony, intensity, and a characteristic blend of detachment and immediacy. Although responses to the thematic issues of his poetry are varied, critics are in consensus that Kolatkar's talent lies in his versatility and daring experimentation with techniques. As is characteristic of his other work, Kolatkar has not prefaced these two works

Cover for Kolatkar's 2004 narrative poem ("Fire Sacrifice") based on a legend about a cycle of retributive violence in what is now Nepal (Brandeis University Library)

with an introduction or commentary of any sort. He thanks his lifelong friends Adil Jussawalla and Mehrotra, thereby acknowledging the role played by these two poets in his own recognition as a poet.

In an interview published in *Ruca* (1977), Sunil Karnik asked Kolatkar to name his favorite poets and writers. The poet gave a long and varied catalogue in reply:

Manmohan, Eliot, Pound, Auden, Hart Crane, Dylan Thomas, Kafka, Baudelaire, Heine, Catullus, Villon, Dnyaneshwar, Namdev, Janabai, Eknath, Tukaram, Wang Wei, Tu Fu, Han Shan, Ramjoshi, Honaji, Mandelshtam, Dostoevsky, Gogol, Isaac Bashevis Singer,

Babel, Apollinaire, Breton, Brecht, Neruda, Ginsberg, Barth, Duras, Joseph Heller . . . Günter Grass, Norman Mailer, Henry Miller, Nabokov, Namdev Dhasal, Patthe Bapurav, Rabelais, Apuleius, Rex Stout, Agatha Christie, Robert Shakley, Harlan Ellison, Bhalchandra Nemade, Durrenmatt, Aarp, Cummings, Lewis Carroll, John Lennon, Bob Dylan, Sylvia Plath, Ted Hughes, Godse Bhatji, Morgenstern, Chakradhar, Gerard Manley Hopkins, Balwantbuva, Kierkegaard, Lenny Bruce, Bahinabai Chaudhari, Kabir, Robert Johnson, Muddy Waters, Leadbelly, Howling Wolf, Jon Lee Hooker, Leiber and Stoller, Larry Williams, Lightning Hopkins, Andre Vajda, Kurosawa, Eisenstein, Truffaut, Woody Guthrie, Laurel and Hardy.

As Karnik points out, the list offers an overview of the amazing extent of influences on Kolatkar. This multiplicity of influences across cultures, nationalities, and even genres is what characterizes Kolatkar's work.

On 25 September 2004, Arun Kolatkar died at the age of seventy-two after suffering from intestinal cancer. According to Ranjit Hoskote, the shock of discovering that he was suffering from cancer stirred his fellow poets and friends–such as Arvind Shahane, Mehrotra, and Jussawalla–into bringing out as many of Kolatkar's uncollected writings as they could. In his obituary for Kolatkar, Hoskote summarized Kolatkar's ability thus: "Mr. Kolatkar treated literature, not as a language art, but as a plastic art; he sculpted poetry out of language with the chisels of surprise and epiphany."

Interview:

Eunice De Souza, *Talking Poems: Conversations with Poets* (New Delhi: Oxford University Press, 1999), pp. 15–28.

References:

G. K. Bansiramani, *An Assessment of Modern Indian English Poets and Poetry* (Mumbai: Vipual Prakashan, 1998);

Homi Bhabha, "Indo-Anglian Attitudes," *TLS* (3 February 1978): 136;

Dilip Chitre, "Introduction," in *An Anthology of Marathi Poetry (1945–1965)* (Bombay: Nirmala Sadananda, 1967), pp. 1–26;

Eunice De Souza and Arun Kolatkar, "Four Indian English Poets," *Bombay Review,* 1 (1989): 71–84;

A. N. Dwivedi, *Papers on Indian Writing in English* (Delhi: Amar Prakashan, 1991);

Shanta Gokhale, "Of Laughter and Hatred," *Mid-Day* (20 July 2004) <http://web.mid-day.com/columns/shanta_gokhale/2004/July/88174.htm>;

Ranjit Hoskote, "Poetry Loses a Major Presence" (27 September 2004) <http://www.thehindu.com/2004/09/27/stories/2004092702971000.htm> [accessed 20 December 2005];

Sunil Karnik and Arun Kolatkar, "Prasana Uttare," *Ruca,* 2 (1977): 92–96;

R. S. Kimbahune, *New Quest,* 19 (January–February 1980): 27–30;

Bruce King, *Indian Poetry in English* (New Delhi: Oxford University Press, 1988);

Paranjape Makarand, *Indian Poetry in English* (Madras: Macmillan, 1993);

Arvind Krishna Mehrotra, "The Unseen Genius" (28 August 2004) <http://www.tehelka.com/story_main5.asp?filename=hub082804the_unseen.asp&id=2> (Available to subscribers only);

M. K. Naik, "*Jejuri:* A Thematic Study," *Perspectives on Indian Poetry in English* (New Delhi: Abhinav, 1984), pp. 169–179;

Bhalacandra Nemade, "Against Writing in English: An Indian Point of View," *New Quest,* no. 49 (January–February 1985): 31–36;

R. Parthasarthy, *Ten Twentieth Century Indian Poets* (Delhi: Oxford University Press, 1976), pp. 1–11;

Gowri Ramnarayan, "The Bhakti Poet of Our Times" <http://www.thehindu.com/thehindu/lr/2004/09/05/stories/2004090500230300.htm> [accessed 20 December 2005];

Ramnarayan and Arun Kolatkar, "No Easy Answers" <http://thehindu.com/lr/2004/09/05/stories/2004090500110100.htm.>;

Shubhangi Raykar, *Arun Kolatkar's Jejuri: A Commentary and Critical Perspectives* (Pune: Prachet, 1995);

Vilas Sarang, *Indian English Poetry Since 1950: An Anthology* (Delhi: Disha Books, 1990), pp. 1–38;

C. P. Surendran, "The Outsider," <http://216.198.217.19/story_main.asp?filename=hu013004outsider.asp> (available to subscribers only) [accessed 20 December 2005].

Jhumpa Lahiri
(11 July 1967 –)

Rezaul Karim
Humber College

BOOKS: *Interpreter of Maladies: Stories* (Boston: Houghton Mifflin, 1999; London: Flamingo, 1999);
The Namesake (Boston: Houghton Mifflin, 2003; London: Flamingo, 2004).

OTHER: Xavier Zimbardo, *India Holy Song,* foreword by Lahiri (New York: Rizzoli, 2000).

Jhumpa Lahiri belongs to a new generation of East Indian writers of fiction that includes Arundhati Roy, Raj Kamal Jha, and Pankaj Mishra, who, as Mervyn Rothstein suggests in an article for *The New York Times* (3 July 2000), have "broken away" from Salman Rushdie's magic realism and embraced reality. It is, however, more useful to compare Lahiri and Bharati Mukherjee as chroniclers of the East Indian experience in American fiction. Daughters of Calcuttans, the two authors delineate the Indian Americans' relationships to their homeland, as well as their responses to immigration and assimilation. The differences between the writers, however, indicate what Lahiri's special contribution to American fiction has been. Mukherjee examines immigration broadly from the perspectives of immigrants of various nationalities, while Lahiri concentrates on Indians. Three of Lahiri's stories are set in India and employ the narrative voices and indigenous experiences of Indians living in India. Also, as Fakrul Alam argued in an unpublished paper presented to the Nepal Association of American Studies on 22 September 2001, while Mukherjee "tailor[s] her fiction to illustrate specific arguments about immigration," about its "conflicts" and "exuberance," Lahiri is not bent on illustrating any such thesis. Instead, she focuses on people "meeting each other, or separating," or on their "subtle tensions and quiet moments of happiness or pain." Lahiri portrays Indians abroad who face displacement, adhere to their native culture, attempt to integrate themselves into their adopted homeland, and suffer tensions over moral and emotional issues. Their Indianness plays a subsidiary role in Lahiri's fiction, however, since she emphasizes—through their interactions with

Jhumpa Lahiri (photograph © Marion Ettlinger; from the dust jacket for The Namesake, *2003; Richland County Public Library)*

Indians and other Americans—such perennial themes as love, marital difficulties, adultery, guilt, alienation, communication, personal relationships, and self-discovery.

Nilanjana Sudeshna Lahiri was born in London on 11 July 1967 and grew up in South Kingstown, Rhode Island. Her father, Amar K. Lahiri, is professor librarian at the University of Rhode Island, and her mother, Tapati Lahiri, who holds an M.A. in Bengali, is a schoolteacher; her younger sister, Jhelum, has a Ph.D. in history. As a child Jhumpa (her nickname was given to her by an elementary-school teacher) used to write extended fictional works in notebooks and composed stories jointly with friends during recess at her elementary school. Lahiri also published stories in her high-school newspaper but discontinued writing when she entered college. She attended Barnard College in New York City, obtained a B.A. in English literature, and decided to pursue graduate studies in English.

Lahiri unsuccessfully applied to several universities. Postponing graduate studies, she began working as a research assistant with a nongovernment organization in Cambridge, Massachusetts. While at the job she committed herself to the craft of fiction writing, eventually applying to the creative-writing program at Boston University. There she earned four graduate degrees: an M.A. in English, an M.A. in creative writing, a third M.A. in comparative literature and arts, and a Ph.D. in Renaissance studies. She decided, however, that her true avocation was not scholarship but fiction, which she continued to publish while at graduate school. Having completed her dissertation, she held a two-year fellowship at Fine Arts Work Center in Provincetown, which allowed her more freedom to write stories. Written over a seven-year period, her stories appeared in *The New Yorker,* the *Louisville Review, AGNI,* the *Harvard Review, Salamander, Epoch,* and *Story Quarterly,* and she received many literary awards. At the age of thirty-two, Lahiri incorporated the stories into her debut collection, *Interpreter of Maladies: Stories* (1999). Two years later, on 15 January 2001, she married Alberto Vourvoulias-Bush, deputy editor of the Latin American edition of *Time.*

The material of Lahiri's fiction and her worldview derive considerably from her own experiences. Her parents obeyed Indian traditions and sought to raise their children as Indian. In *The Week* (14 May 2000), Tapash Ganguly mentions that in her childhood Lahiri visited Calcutta with her parents once every two years; there she observed traffic from the window of her aunt's apartment, wore Indian dresses, enjoyed Indian dishes, and conversed in Bengali. Not surprisingly, then, Lahiri's stories frequently use Indian names, include Bengali words and descriptions of Indian customs, food, and dress, and use Calcutta as setting and Bengalis as protagonists. The importance of the city in her life and work cannot be overemphasized. It is noteworthy thus that she celebrated her marriage by having a traditional Bengali marriage ceremony in Singhi Palace in Calcutta.

The first story in *Interpreter of Maladies,* "A Temporary Matter," concerns a marital relationship; though she was not married when she wrote the story, she told Vibhuti Patel in an interview for the Pacific edition of *Newsweek* (20 September 1999) that "being involved in serious relationships enabled me to fill in the blanks." The story examines the marriage of Shoba and Shukumar, second-generation East Indian Americans, who deal with the effects of a miscarriage. The narrative perspective of the husband, the imagery, and ironic details of the couple's daily routine in their Boston home emphasize the wife's alienation, as do the authorial comments. A series of power outages over the span of a few days allows the couple to confess and, apparently, to overcome their distance, but their intimacy proves fleeting. In the end, as the husband reveals that he had held the baby before his cremation, the couple "wept together, for the things they now knew," an act that implies that, perhaps, marital difficulties can be overcome if there is love.

The next story in the collection, "When Mr. Pirzada Came to Dine," includes spare but engaging details and images and employs the perspective of a young girl, Lilia. Lahiri told Patel that the story draws upon her memory of a man who came to their home when she was four years old and whose photographs she had seen in a family album. In the story, Lilia observes her parents hosting Pirzada in their Boston home. Her parents appreciate the opportunity they have of raising their daughter in the United States. They also live as Indians, however, thus embracing two worlds. Pirzada also follows Indian customs and has the same tastes as Lilia's parents. Moreover, he is displaced, as suggested by his pocket watch, which gives the local time in Dhaka. Watching television images of the destruction of the city during the movement for independence in Bangladesh in 1971, the perceptive child-narrator sympathizes with Pirzada, who is separated from the wife and children he has left behind in his war-torn country. Lilia admires the bond between herself and the visitor, suggested by her prayer for the safety of his family and his affection and concern for her safety during Halloween. After Pirzada's departure, she feels empathy for the guest as she is now in the same situation as he had been while away from loved ones: "what it meant to miss someone who was so many miles away." The characters' closeness during the war in Bangladesh suggests that the main focus of the story is on people's need to connect with one another during moments of crisis in their lives.

"Interpreter of Maladies," the third story in the collection, originated in Lahiri's chance meeting with an acquaintance in 1991. Lahiri conceived the titular phrase after learning that the acquaintance had a job acting as an interpreter for a doctor whose patients could only speak Russian. In the story, Kapasi, a middle-aged Indian tour guide and interpreter of patients' complaints, takes sightseeing second-generation Indian Americans Raj and Mina Das and their children, who are visiting India. Written in the third person and in a style marked by occasional overwriting, excessive symbolism, unnatural dialogue, an ironic tone, and some editorializing, the story portrays the Das family's attitude to India as one of snobbish distance and their interest in India as tourists' interest. The story not only exposes the weaknesses of the self-centered couple but also those of their guide, who misunderstands the wife's curiosity about his job as interest in him, when she only hopes to receive from him a remedy for her guilt caused by her adultery. As she confesses to committing adultery, he is rid of his delusions and concludes that she "loved neither her husband nor her children." The couple's loveless marriage, as well as the distance between Kapasi and his wife, is a reminder of similar themes in "A Temporary Matter."

In an interview with Gaiutra Bahadur for *Citypaper.net* (16 September 1999), Lahiri related that the next story in *Interpreter of Maladies*, "A Real Durwan," was based on her "observations of people" when she was in Calcutta. Ganguly corroborates that the story is about a refugee woman whom Lahiri met at her aunt's Calcutta apartment. Written primarily in the descriptive mode—frequently using similes and metaphors—the story delineates unremarkable residents of a rundown building who own nothing valuable. The narrative perspective is that of Boori Ma, a slender sixty-four-year-old woman who sleeps below the stairwell. She rants about her prosperous life prior to the partition of India and Pakistan but now sweeps the stairwells and guards the building. She is, however, ejected from the building when at a time of renovations the stairwell basin is stolen, and she is held responsible. Her rejection by ungrateful tenants, recipients of years of her service, confirms her marginalized existence.

The moral inquiry into the characters' lives continues in "Sexy," the next story in the collection, which is set in Boston and reworks the theme of adultery introduced in "Interpreter of Maladies." Narrated in unobtrusive prose, the story concerns two extramarital affairs: the first between Dev, a married Indian, and Miranda, the white protagonist, and the second between an Indian married to the cousin of Miranda's colleague Laxmi and another white woman. The story is told from the perspective of Miranda, who shows considerable interest in Indian foods, Bengali language, and culture, caused by her affair with Dev, a Bengali; but the focus of the story is on the two affairs. Frequently, the treatment of one affair is followed up with the account of the other, or one affair is presented with reference to the other. The juxtaposition of the two affairs, together with the illuminating remarks by a

Front cover for Lahiri's 1999 collection of stories mostly about Indians and Indian Americans attempting to bridge the gap between Eastern and Western culture (Richland County Public Library)

child who resembles Lilia, develops the theme of the story. Laxmi's cousin—who is facing a divorce—makes a stopover in Boston en route to California. Laxmi tries to cheer her up by taking her to different places, while Miranda baby-sits the woman's precocious son, Rohin. Rohin characterizes his father's affair as falling for someone "sexy" or "loving someone you don't know," inadvertently implying that the affair between Miranda and Dev, a virtual stranger who has betrayed his own wife, has been nothing other than loveless sexuality and adultery. Consequently, she breaks up with Dev.

Lahiri revealed to Patel that the protagonist of the next story in *Interpreter of Maladies*, "Mrs. Sen's," is based on her own mother, who baby-sat in their home. The third-person point of view—alternately stressing the perspectives of Mrs. Sen and Eliot, her young charge—and the plain style employed result in a memorable depiction of what Lahiri has described as "the challenges of exile." To Sen, "Everything is there"—meaning India; she finds the silence in the United States oppressive, the Americans "too much in their world," and driving in Boston traffic terrifying. To cope with her displacement, she chops vegetables in the Indian way, applies crushed vermilion to her hair, and reads letters from home, trying to connect with India, just as Lahiri's own parents, she explained to Bahadur, refer to India as home even after thirty years in the United States. Despite her dislocation, she tries to assimilate by taking driving lessons. The story, however, emphasizes the bond between the characters and the boy's maturation. Separated from his mother during the day, Eliot observes, with fascination, Sen's performance of daily chores and listens to her nostalgic stories sympathetically, while she fights her loneliness by caring for Eliot like a mother looking after her own child. Their relationship helps develop Eliot's moral outlook so he disapproves of his mother's distrust of Sen.

In the next story in the collection, "This Blessed House," Lahiri returns to the subject of marriage of second-generation Indo-Americans. Twinkle and Sanjeev, who are well educated and westernized but who are also Indian in their arranged marriage as well as in their taste in food, have just moved into their new house in Connecticut, where they keep finding hidden Christian bric-a-brac. Told from the husband's perspective in a playful tone, the story describes the responses of the couple to these paraphernalia. Twinkle is excited each time she finds a new object, including a silver bust of Christ, and wants to keep it in the house, which irritates Sanjeev. Such responses—given as leitmotivs—suggest that he does not know her, and the husband and wife cannot communicate or abandon self-centered desires.

In the penultimate story of *Interpreter of Maladies,* "The Treatment of Bibi Haldar," Bibi, who lives in a tiny storage room of a Calcutta apartment building, is as marginalized as Boori Ma of "A Real Durwan." In an interview with Arun Aguiar for the on-line magazine *Pif* (28 July 1999), Lahiri said that the narrative voice of "a group of women" in her story was inspired by the point of view of an entire town in William Faulkner's "A Rose for Emily" (1931). The perspective in Lahiri's story is, however, more sympathetic than that in Faulkner's story. Lahiri's story describes in prolix prose the helpless young Bibi's delirium, her desire to marry and have a family, and the efforts of the town to help her achieve her goals and find a cure for her ailments. She becomes cured when, after a sexual encounter with an unknown man, she gives birth to a child. Lahiri told Aguiar that she came to know such a young woman while visiting Calcutta: "I knew she wanted to be married. She lived in the same building as my aunt and uncle, and we struck up a friendship. . . . she had some epileptic-like disease." In the story, when Bibi faints because of convulsions, she needs to smell leather to recover. Lahiri clarified this particular detail for Aguiar: "I had a brief conversation with my aunt. . . . she said, 'If you hold up something close to her that's made of leather, it helps her.' It sort of stuck in my head."

"The Third and Final Continent," the final story in the collection, is "based on my father's past," Lahiri stated in the interview with Bahadur. Like her father, the protagonist is a Bengali, a librarian at an American college who has lived in the United States for thirty years. The first-person narration by the librarian and the restrained language of the story render a moving account of his emigration from Calcutta to London to Boston—the route taken by Lahiri's father—and the way he makes the United States home. The details about milk and cereal (his first American meal), about reading newspapers, and about getting his wife used to life in the United States, as well as the expression of his fear that his son may not eat with his hands after he and his wife die, illustrate the process of integration and the accompanying loss of culture. There are gains also, as he reflects in gratitude and amazement on his ownership of a house and his success in raising a son who goes to Harvard. Such achievements mean a great deal to him, although they may seem "ordinary" when compared to the planting of the American flag on the moon by the astronauts, who are "heroes forever." He, too, however, has been an adventurer, having been "in this new world" for decades whereas the astronauts "spent mere hours on the moon." To him, his performance of simple tasks such as eating a meal and sleeping in a room are "bewildering" and "beyond my imagination," just as the astronauts' landing on the moon is to Mrs. Croft, his 103-year-old landlady. Glorification of immigration notwithstanding, the story emphasizes more the recurrent theme of relationships in the collection, thus unifying and fittingly concluding the volume. The protagonist's relationship with Mrs. Croft shows how human beings from different cultures can connect in isolation and admire one another. As well, the knowledge of his wife's helplessness in a new land, which resembles his own challenges upon his arrival in the United States, helps him form a relationship with her that has been a sustaining force in their lives.

Critical reception of *Interpreter of Maladies* has been largely favorable. In its "The Future of American Fiction" issue (21–28 June 1999), *The New Yorker* described Lahiri as one of "the twenty best young fiction writers in America." The collection also won the 2000 Pulitzer Prize in fiction. David Kirpen, in the *San Francisco Chronicle* (24 June 1999), praised her ability to write "about the Indian American experience from all angles," her "meaningful but never portentous detail," and her "humane, attentive style"; Caleb Crain, in *The New York Times Book Review* (11 July 1999), admired her capacity to "breathe unpredictable life into the page," so "the reader finishes each story reseduced, wishing he could spend a whole novel with its characters." Occasionally, however, reviews have been less than approving. Nisid Hajari, writing in *Time* (13 September 1999), praised the author's "rare eye for the details of displacement" but argued that some of the stories "read like journal entries, or schematics to the collapse of a relationship." Lahiri's book, nevertheless, has continued to fascinate readers as well as attract scholarly attention. It has also had much commercial success globally.

After the success of *Interpreter of Maladies,* Lahiri made the transition from short-story writer to novelist with *The Namesake* (2003). *The Namesake,* however, is not a technically ambitious work. Except for two extended flashbacks in the early chapters and a few brief ones employed later in the novel, it applies a predictable linear narrative with shifts in time and avoids convoluted narrative structuring that allows for much thematic and artistic complexity and varied characterization. Instead, Lahiri relies on her often acclaimed descriptive powers to reexplore the themes of her previous work—immigration, displacement, assimilation, self-knowledge—and to offer an extended examination of the quest for identity of second-generation Indo-Americans.

The novel opens with Ashima Ganguly, a Bengali wife in her apartment in Cambridge, Massachusetts, in 1968, making an Indian snack. She resembles Mrs. Sen of the *Interpreter of Maladies* in her sense of displacement. She feels alienated from other American would-be mothers in a hospital delivery room and is terrified "to raise a child in a country where she is related to no one." She compares her situation to "a sort of lifelong pregnancy—a perpetual wait," but while she maintains her cultural heritage she also learns to adapt in the United States, where she succeeds materially, enjoys freedom of work and movement, and makes friends with Americans. After her husband's death, she decides to "spend six months in India, six months in the States." Ashoke, her husband, was nearly killed in a train wreck in India at the age of twenty-two but was saved when rescuers spotted him after noticing a book by Nikolai Gogol that he had been reading when the train derailed. Ashoke earns a doctorate from MIT, finds a university teaching job, and observes Indian customs but at the same time becomes increasingly fond of American life. Because a letter from Ashima's grandmother providing a name for the couple's newborn son does not arrive, Ashoke names the child Gogol after the Russian writer whose work, he believes, saved his life.

Soon the perspectives of the couple give way to that of Gogol in the narrative. His name becomes a source of his unhappiness and a means of plot and character development, as the novel describes his repeated

Dust jacket for Lahiri's 2003 novel, in which a young, second-generation Indian American, named for Russian writer Nikolai Gogol, grows increasingly infatuated with American culture but is led to reconcile with his family's heritage after his father's death (Richland County Public Library)

rebellions against his family and his search for identity. He hates his name, does not enjoy attending Bengali classes, and dislikes the family trips to Calcutta. He acquires American habits and enjoys television and junk food. He smokes pot and, at a party, drinks beer and kisses a girl, to whom he introduces himself as Nikhil, which he adopts as his name when he is eighteen, before his first year at Yale. At Yale he registers for drawing classes. Later, at Columbia he studies architecture, to the dismay of his parents. In a series of encounters with women, Gogol's desire to become an American is also evident. At Yale, his relationship with another student, Ruth, causes him to pity "his parents . . . for having no experience of being young and in love." When he is twenty-six, Gogol wanders into another relationship, with Maxine Ratliff in New York. When he encounters her parents, he discovers that the Ratliffs are, unlike his parents, easygoing, charming, and sophisticated. Lydia and Gerald Ratliff's affection for each other and their vacationing lifestyle appear superior to his parents' Indian ways. Gogol's increasing desire to craft an American identity by immersing himself in the lives of the New York upper class, however, is jolted when one of the Ratliffs' guests at their lake house thinks he is "Indian."

In other words, try as he may, Gogol cannot erase his Indian background. His father's death accelerates the process of his reconciliation with his family, which Lahiri describes vividly in her portrayal of him grazing "his father's mustache, an eye brow, a bit of hair on his head" with his index finger at a hospital in Cleveland. Together with Sonia, his sister, he helps Ashima come to terms with the loss of her husband. He grieves over the sight of his mother's bare wrists, a symbol of her widowhood, and ultimately breaks up with Maxine, who is unable to appreciate his attachment to his family. The final phase of Gogol's journey involves his marriage to Moushumi, a Bengali woman. Gogol turns into a cuckold and feels like a misfit in the company of Moushumi's intellectual friends; Moushumi, given to promiscuity, has an affair—reminiscent of the marital infidelities in *Interpreter of Maladies*—which results in the dissolution of their marriage. In the end Gogol is at Pemberton Road, playing host to his family's Bengali friends, and he begins to read the work of his namesake, a gift from his father. It appears as if he has learned to conform to his parental expectations, since he realizes that "for most of his adult life . . . there was nothing, apart from his family, to draw him home," even though, now an architect in New York, he will continue to be an American professional and will continue to use the name he adopted because it sounded American to him. In short, he will continue to be both Indian and American.

Lahiri's novel has garnered mixed reviews. According to Michiko Kakutani in *The New York Times* (2 September 2003), *The Namesake* "more than fulfills the promise of Ms. Lahiri's debut collection of stories," as it shows her ability to recast the "themes of exile and identity" of *Interpreter of Maladies* "to create a symphonic work . . . as assured and eloquent as the work of a longtime master of the craft." Andrew Reimer in *The Sydney Morning Herald* (25 October 2003) described *The Namesake* as the work of "a highly accomplished novelist" that has "a pleasing coherence" and a "supple, elegant, economical, simultaneously ironic and compassionate" style. C. J. Gillen, reviewing the work for the South Asian Women's NETwork Internet site (October 2003), observed that Lahiri's "quiet language" and "eye for details" create "tactile experience of her settings,"

which enables readers to appreciate the characters' "longings . . . their struggles to find their own individual spaces and identities across a double continental divide." Julia Hanna's review in the *Boston Phoenix* (12 September 2003), on the other hand, called "Lahiri's extensive use of descriptive detail . . . more decorative than effective" and noted her "cool intellectual distance," which "poses a barrier to feeling the pain of [Gogol's] quandary." Sam Munson's review in *Commentary* (November 2003) was critical of Lahiri's narrative structure, which is "linear to the point of monotony," as well as of her portrayal of Gogol's women, who "pass in and out of his life with an unchanging absence of any incident worth remarking upon."

With her fiction, Jhumpa Lahiri has brought variety and complexity to the literature of East Indian experience: her characters long for India but value the United States; go about their daily routines as Americans, revealing their frailties and dealing with their problems; interact with people of different backgrounds, form relationships, and discover their complex, hyphenated identity; and live ordinary lives in India. She shows a remarkable ability to transcend the topical, since her characters represent universal concerns. Her narrative and stylistic devices—understated prose, descriptive and dramatic modes, curious events and human perceptivity as means of plot and character development, and perspectives of males and females of varying ages and backgrounds—are the hallmarks of a gifted artist. She seems certain to be one of the leading Asian American writers of her generation in the years to come.

Interviews:

Arun Aguiar, "Interview with Jhumpa Lahiri," *Pif* (28 July 1999) <www.pifmagazine.com/vol28/i_agui.shtml>;

Gaiutra Bahadur, "Jhumpa Lahiri," *Citypaper.net* (16 September 1999) <www.citypaper.net/articles/091699/feat.20q.shtml>;

Vibhuti Patel, "The Maladies of Belonging," *Newsweek*, Pacific edition (20 September 1999): 60.

References:

Suman Bala, ed., *Jhumpa Lahiri, the Master Storyteller: A Critical Response to* Interpreter of Maladies (New Delhi: Khosla, 2002);

Mervyn Rothstein, "India's Post-Rushdie Generation," *New York Times*, 3 July 2000, p. E1.

Jayanta Mahapatra

(22 October 1928 –   )

Sukhbir Singh
Osmania University

BOOKS: *Close the Sky, Ten by Ten* (Calcutta: Dialogue, 1971);

Svayamvara and Other Poems (Calcutta: Writers Workshop, 1971);

A Father's Hours (Calcutta: United Writers, 1976);

A Rain of Rites (Athens: University of Georgia Press, 1976);

Waiting (New Delhi: Samkaleen, 1979);

The False Start (Bombay: Clearing House, 1980);

Relationship (Greenfield Center, N.Y.: Greenfield Review Press, 1980);

Life Signs (Delhi & Oxford: Oxford University Press, 1983);

Dispossessed Nests: The 1984 Poems, edited by Yuyutsu Ram Dass Sharma and Ramanand Rathi (Jaipur: Nirala, 1986);

Burden of Waves and Fruit (Washington, D.C.: Three Continents, 1988);

Temple (Sydney: Dangaroo Press, 1989);

A Whiteness of Bone (New Delhi & New York: Viking, 1992);

The Green Gardener and Other Stories (Hyderabad: Disha, 1997);

Shadow Space (Kottayam, Kerala: D.C. Books, 1997);

Bare Face (Kottayam, Kerala: D.C. Books, 2000);

Random Descent (Bhubaneswar, Orissa: Third Eye, 2005).

Collections: *Selected Poems* (Delhi & Oxford: Oxford University Press, 1987);

The Best of Jayanta Mahapatra, edited by P. P. Raveendran (Kozhikode, Kerala: Bodhi, 1995).

OTHER: Fakir Mohan Senapati, *Tales from Fakir Mohan,* adapted by Mahapatra (Cuttack, Orissa: Cuttack Students' Store, 1969);

True Tales of Travel and Adventure, adapted by Mahapatra (Cuttack, Orissa: Cuttack Students' Store, 1969);

"Recent Commonwealth Fiction: Writing from Three Different Cultures," in *Commonwealth Literature: Problems of Response,* edited by C. D. Narsimhaiah (Madras: Macmillan India, 1981), pp. 30–37;

Orissa, text by Mahapatra (New Delhi: Lustre Press, 1988);

Jayanta Mahapatra, 1988 (photograph by Jan Kemp; from Contemporary Authors Autobiography Series, *vol. 9, 1989; Bruccoli Clark Layman Archives)*

"Jayanta Mahapatra," in *Contemporary Authors Autobiography Series,* volume 9 (Detroit: Gale, 1989), pp. 137–150.

TRANSLATIONS: Saubhagya Kumara Misra, *Countermeasures* (Calcutta: Dialogue, 1973);

Jadunath Das Mohapatra, *Wings of the Past* (Calcutta: Rajasree, 1976);

Sitakant Mahapatra, *The Song of Khubja and Other Poems* (New Delhi: Samkaleen, 1980);

Sitakant Mahapatra, *Selected Poems,* translated by Jayanta Mahapatra, Sitakant Mahapatra, and Bikram K. Das (New Delhi: Prachi, 1986);

Sitakant Mahapatra, *Death of Krishna and Other Poems,* translated by Jayanta Mahapatra, Sitakant Mahapatra, and Das (Calcutta: Rupa, 1992);

Sakti Chattopadhyay, *I Can, but Why Should I Go* (New Delhi: Sahitya Akademi, 1994);

Sachi Raut-Roy, *Verticals of Life: Selected Poems of Sachi Raut-Roy,* edited by Jayanta Mahapatra, translated by Jayanta Mahapatra and others (New Delhi: Sahitya Akademi, 1996);

Gangadhar Meher, *Tapaswini,* translated by Jayanta Mahapatra and Madhusudan Pati (Bhubaneswar: Orissa Sahitya Akademi, 1998);

Ranjita Nayak, *Discovery & Other Poems* (Calcutta: Writers Workshop, 2001);

Pratibha Satpathy, *A Time of Rising* (New Delhi: Har-Anand, 2003).

SELECTED PERIODICAL PUBLICATIONS–
UNCOLLECTED: "Enduring Silence," *Indian Literature,* 23, nos. 1–2 (1980): 177–180;

"The Inaudible Resonance in English Poetry in India," *Literary Criterion,* 15, no. 1 (1980): 27–36;

"Face to Face with the Contemporary Poem," *Journal of Literary Studies,* 6, nos. 1–2 (1983): 9–17;

"The Stranger Within: Coming to Terms through Poetry," *Dalhousie Review,* 63, no. 3 (1983): 434;

"The Voice in the Ink," *Illustrated Weekly of India,* 111 (1 April 1990): 28–30;

"Slow Swim in Dim Light: Quest for Modernity in Poetry," *Indian Horizons,* 40, nos. 3–4 (1991): 35–41;

"Through the Looking Glass," *Times of India,* 28 March 1992, p. 2;

"Excusing Myself Everyday," *Journal of Indian Writing in English,* 21, no. 1 (1993): 14.

Jayanta Mahapatra writes largely about the people and places of Orissa, an eastern Indian state. His sensibility is deeply submerged in the local landscape—a vast panorama of temples, rivers, mountains, marketplaces, cafés, whorehouses, and forests—and the rites, rituals, ceremonies, and seasons of the place. In *Orissa* (1988) he writes, "Orissa is a land of repose, of faith and dream, basking in the tropical sun, caressed by the wind and the rain, its precious tranquility contained in its songs and its stones, and pervading its social and cultural fabric. Each season unfolds the earth to its way of peace, and the earth reveals it again and again. Never and nowhere does Orissa make one feel alone." Mahapatra discerns in these images reflections of the spirit and civilization of ancient India. The broken temples, deserted villages, drought-stricken countrysides, and suffering souls appear to him to be crying for salvation. He notes in "Through the Looking Glass" (1992) that contemporary Orissa is struck with "sickness and hunger, the suffering of people from malnutrition and diseases—a terrible form of disorder of the universe that made me question myself the goodness of God we had been taught to believe in." He senses in all this disintegration and death a silent enactment of the Hindu myth of the dance of Shiva, sym-

bolizing the perpetual decay of every living thing in the material world. The cultural rites of his native land manifest the mythical message of Shiva's dance. Mahapatra's poetry embodies an attempt to invert the myth of mortality on behalf of the eternal. These rites, according to Devinder Mohan in *Jayant[a] Mahapatra* (1987), generate a sense of the belief that "human life is a complex maze of *Maya,* a play of illusions towards a spiritual growth of mind, an orchestration of labor of love for God suffering through fleshly existence, in suffering through the resistance of the material prison making of [the] terrestrial rooted-ness of human life."

In his poetry Mahapatra transforms the profane into the sacred in order to retrieve the continuity of construction and destruction in the cultural life of his people. Many of his poems therefore acquire a sermonic aura. They act as a medium of redemption for the poet by retracing his relationship with his country folk. He makes the barren fragments of the Konark temple stand for the poet's severed relationship with the temporal world and with the timeless spirit of Hinduism and Christianity. The Konark ruins fill him with a mysterious darkness that rises in the form of a dragon to be subdued for rejuvenation and reaffirmation. Mahapatra confronts this debilitating darkness with a view to expiating it. As Mohan observes, "His self-exploratory journey leads him to the point of heightened self-awareness, then to self-actualization and of course ultimately towards self-realization, which has forever remained the highest goal of every *sadhaka* (devout practitioner) of all arts." Like T. S. Eliot, Mahapatra creates order out of disorder and cohesion out of chaos by way of performing his duty as a poet.

Born on 22 October 1928 in Cuttack, Orissa, Mahapatra was the first child of Lemuel Mahapatra, an inspector of primary schools, and Sudnasubala Rout Mahapatra, a housewife of simple habits and no education. Jayanta's paternal grandfather, Chintamani, was a poor farmer who married Rupabati, a woman from a different caste of the same state. He met her in a mercy camp run by Christian missionaries, where he had staggered after almost dying of destitution and hunger. In the camp Chintamani embraced Christianity at the urging of the Baptists. Mahapatra recalls this incident from the remote past with much pain and anguish in "Jayanta Mahapatra," a 1989 autobiographical essay published in *Contemporary Authors Autobiography Series.*

Mahapatra was brought up in a lower-middle-class Christian family, according to Christian rules and in strict separation from the surrounding Hindu way of life. The tension slowly began to tell upon his personality, and he began to have differences with his mother in ways that constrained him from relating with others outside the house. Mahapatra thus developed a permanent aversion to his mother (although he was fond of his father) and grew up as a reclusive and dreamy boy in perpetual need of communicating with others. His family situation and dreamworld made for complex emotions that found their way into his poetry. As he explains in "Jayanta Mahapatra," "There is invariably a lot of pain in childhood. I remember mine and all of it seems so long ago; and yet the pain, or whatever I choose to call it today, paces quietly behind the breastbone."

Mahapatra's father was always a source of consolation, education, and inspiration for him. The two enjoyed a pleasant and gratifying relationship. Lemuel Mahapatra fostered in his son a love for narrative art and stimulated his creative imagination early in life. Jayanta Mahapatra earned a B.S. degree with honors from Ravenshaw College, Cuttack, in 1946 and an M.S. from Science College, Patna, in 1949. He married Jyotsna "Runu" Rani Das in 1951, and their son, Mohan, was born in 1955. After receiving his master's degree, Mahapatra began to work as a lecturer in physics at Ravenshaw College in 1949. Subsequently, he taught at other colleges in Orissa: Gangadhar Meher College, Sambalpur (1958–1961); Regional Engineering College, Rourkela (1961–1962); Buxi Jagabandhu Bidyadhar College, Bhubaneswar (1965–1969); and Fakir Mohan College, Balasore (1969–1970). He returned to Ravenshaw College in 1970. Mahapatra wrote poems while working as a teacher but had a late start as a professional writer, for he was in his early forties before he started to publish his works. Successive volumes of his verse brought him recognition not only in India but also in other countries. In 1975 Mahapatra became the first Indian to receive the coveted Jacob Glatstein Memorial Prize, given by *Poetry* magazine.

Perhaps because Mahapatra started publishing poetry only in his early forties, he was not initially taken as seriously by reviewers and researchers as other Indo-Anglian poets such as A. K. Ramanujan, Nissim Ezekiel, and P. Lal. It therefore took some time for him to make his presence felt on the Indian literary scene. Like the works of his favorite poet, John Keats, Mahapatra's early poems met with a hostile reception from many critics and commentators. He recalls their criticism in "Jayanta Mahapatra": "The reviews of my early books depressed me. Some of them were scathing indeed, and dealt with the obscurity encountered in the poems. But I held on to the published books in my room, hurt and saddened." Slowly, however, Mahapatra gained ground in Indian criticism and eventually came to be recognized as one of the significant poets of his generation.

Mahapatra's early verse was collected in *Close the Sky, Ten by Ten* (1971), *Svayamvara and Other Poems* (1971), and *A Father's Hours* (1976). The theme in these early poems is a stark sense of alienation, mainly caused by his estrangement from his mother. They reveal someone caged at home and craving relationships. For this reason Mahapatra's early poetic endeavors met with a hostile response from critics, further aggravating his sense of separation from his surroundings. His strained relationship with his mother created in him what the psychiatrist R. D. Laing calls "ontological insecurity" in *The Divided Self* (1960) and made him feel alone in the world. Mahapatra was a pris-

JAYANTA MAHAPATRA

A Rain of Rites

Front cover for Mahapatra's 1976 poetry collection published shortly before he traveled to the United States to join the International Writing Program at the University of Iowa (Thomas Cooper Library, University of South Carolina)

oner of a past stretching far behind him. As he writes in "Jayanta Mahapatra," "the picture of my mother, swathed in a sari, holding on to the oil lamp in the shadows, . . . seemed to establish itself firmly in my mind. . . . It was only later, much later, when I started to write poetry myself, that I found myself abandoned in this past. . . ." He failed to relate to his relatives, friends, and the common folk of Orissa. His situation was the "loneliness of a winner / turned loser, traitor and beggar / in a centrifuge of possessions." In this period of poetic creativity Mahapatra felt the need to retrieve his long-lost contacts with the world. What he had lost in life was replaced in his poetry by relationships between man and woman, mother and son, husband and wife, self and others, nature and society, morality and religion, and the temporal and the transcendental.

The inherent urge to relate to himself seems to have impelled Mahapatra to write the poems in *Close the Sky, Ten by Ten* and *Svayamvara and Other Poems*. While writing these early poems, he made an arduous effort at bridging this gap between his outer and inner self at the level of his themes. Each poem, he observes in "Jayanta Mahapatra," was "a painful struggle, each poem . . . an exploration, of an idea or a subject, which I thought would hopefully shine with coherence and truth when I was writing the poem."

Mahapatra's struggle in his early poetry was compounded by his efforts to synchronize his Indian experience with the English language. For this reason, in his early verse, "earth, life, and language become exterior blinking spaces, isolated yet longing for a sense of simultaneity, a sense of possibility of segmental intermingling." Mahapatra carried out this crusade of experimentation and exploration both in themes and language for the projection of the reality of his experience. Yet, he was unable to achieve in his early poems the desired coherence of vision, ideas, and language. His writing failed to reflect the truth of his dark perceptions.

Mahapatra's endeavor to fuse form with content continued in his third collection, *A Father's Hours,* which epitomizes his effort at transcending time. To overcome the darkness of the world he tries to latch onto his cultural past for support. In his view, the treatment of the past as useless has generated the prevalent chaos in contemporary society: "Like a café's chairs turned over with their legs in the air / perhaps our past lives are raised in surrender to the sky." To remedy the situation, Mahapatra believes that the past must be integrated into the present to achieve relatedness, coherence, and order in a fragmented world: "There is a past which moves over / the magic slopes and hamlets of the mind, / whose breath measures the purpose of our lives." Like his first two books, *A Father's Hours* did not receive an enthusiastic response from critics.

From 1976 to 1977 Mahapatra was a visiting writer in the International Writing Program at the University of Iowa; he traveled to Australia and Japan in 1978 and 1980. In "Poetry in the Enemy's Tongue: On Two Indian Poets Writing in English" (1979), Dilip Chitre writes that "Mahapatra is what the Indian poet writing in English is generally expected to be: an interpreter of a unique, complex and exotic culture through its landscape and people. This is the kind of role that Satyajit Ray's films have played internationally." During this phase Mahapatra published his next four poetry volumes, *A Rain of Rites* (1976), *Waiting* (1979), *The False Start* (1980), and *Relationship* (1980). In these books he is preoccupied with the mundane and metaphysical themes of time, religion, arts, woman, and man's origin and place in the universe. Silence, skepticism, and sarcasm toward people in public life, politics, poverty, cultural abstractions, and social conventions mark his poetry of this period. Here, Mahapatra appears to be more sensitive and reactive than before to the superfluities of the world around him. The change in his outlook came from a deepening and broadening of his worldview and from more experience of life. In the years when these collections were published, he was invited abroad and met many foreign writers, from whom he was able to gather new themes,

poetic techniques, and linguistic innovations. Mahapatra's travels abroad also introduced him to exciting and exuberant landscapes, which gave more color to his thoughts. As a result, his imaginative forays stretched beyond the boundaries of his native Orissa and encompassed new terrains, imaginative as well as real. His excursions gave more significance to his poetry, taking him beyond himself and enabling him to compare his view of poetry with that of poets from the United States and other countries. As he recalls in "Jayanta Mahapatra," in Iowa City he "had opportunities for the first time to meet with renowned writers from different countries. Paul Engle and his wife, Hualing, the Chinese novelist, were warm in their welcome and soon saw me to my apartment at the Mayflower. I was to share it for the period of my stay with the Greek writer Thanassis Valtinos." Although Mahapatra remained aloof from others for a while because of his habit of keeping to himself and his inability to make friends easily, he was eventually able to overcome his shyness. Occasional visits to the area around Iowa City acquainted him with a folk culture different from that of Orissa.

A Rain of Rites was published a few days before his departure to the United States in 1976. In "To the Wall" (1977) Dick Allen observes that "Mahapatra, in contrast to most American poets, is most at home with poems which touch the beyond. The poetry of *A Rain of Rites* is that of a man taking up a stance against or within mysteries, sensitive to the moods of days and years." The collection is largely devoted to women and their position in Indian society: "an Indian woman, piled up to her silences, / waiting for what the world will let her do." Mahapatra's subject is mainly the maltreatment of women in India and their passive submission to fate for reasons such as hunger and poverty. His preoccupation with women in these poems reflects his experiences with his mother in the past and his relationship with his wife in the present. Reviewing *A Rain of Rites* in *The Hudson Review* (Winter 1976–1977), Vernon Young wrote, "The manner of apprehension in [Mahapatra's] wonderful, sensate poems inevitably brings to the tongue the word 'sophistication.' . . . Evident in every cadence is the long over-ripening of a sardonic wisdom, the tired consciousness of too many beginnings." In *Waiting* and *The False Start,* Mahapatra once again attempts to express his sense of belonging to his culture and to relate himself to history. In these collections he does not glorify the past but highlights its immortal and transient aspects. For Mahapatra, change destroys all glorious human acts. Fragmentation of matter and the follies of men go hand in hand. In a review of *The False Start* (*The Hudson Review,* Autumn 1982), Finn Cotter observed, "In his reflective, melancholy sixth book of poems he gropes for direction, listening and watching, but he finds new signs to enlighten his way."

Mahapatra's growing creative abilities are evident in the long poem *Relationship,* a personal work that was different from his earlier compositions. As he describes it in "Jayanta Mahapatra," "I had tried here to build up a long contemplation on the meanings of symbols on the stones of a crumbling, once-glorious Orissan temple. In twelve sections, the poem, fugue-like in construction, dealt with the mystery of suffering, with triumph and disaster. It was, in many ways, my romance with my own land and my innermost self." One aspect of this romance with his own self arose from a loss of warmth between Mahapatra and his wife owing to his excessive preoccupation with poetry and the departure of their son, Mohan, for higher studies. For that reason, "Of that love, of that mile / walked together in the rain, / only a weariness remains." He also felt that his friends had deserted him, envious over his poetic achievements although he was such a late starter. He writes that "friendship is like a pool of water / where shadows move about and dance, / and winds of doubt cloud some of the drifting faces, / the sun of envy sucks the others away."

In the next stage of his literary career Mahapatra was honored with several awards. He was given the prestigious Sahitya Akademi Poetry Prize in 1981 for *Relationship*. In 1985 he traveled to the Soviet Union for the Indo-Soviet Cultural Exchange Program and participated in the Asian Poets' Conference. In 1986 he attended the Bellagio Study and Conference Center of the Rockefeller Foundation in Bellagio, Italy, and in 1988 he took part in the Singapore Festival of Arts as a visiting writer. His subsequent international assignments took him to the New Literatures in English Conference in Giessen, West Germany, and the Association for Commonwealth Language and Literature Studies Silver Jubilee Conference in Canterbury, both in 1989.

Mahapatra's next books were *Life Signs* (1983), *Dispossessed Nests: The 1984 Poems* (1986), *Burden of Waves and Fruit* (1988), *Temple* (1989), and *A Whiteness of Bone* (1992). His poetry of this phase is characterized by reconciliation, release, and a sense of rejoicing coming from the attainment of age and experience. As he writes in "Jayanta Mahapatra," "I don't have much to do today, but only those things I want to do. . . . I have turned down lucrative offers of employment; among them the directorship of the All India Poetry Centre at Bhopal in Central India. Perhaps in my freedom I have found ample reward." As a result, Mahapatra's themes in the poems of this period are more visionary and mystical. He appears more reconciled to the vagaries of life and the vanity of human wishes. In *Life Signs* he apprehends the symptoms of an imminent death in every small and large act of creation. This apprehension brings him closer to the acceptance of the natural cycle of life and death and instills in him the feeling that there is no escape: "In the end / I come back to the day and the rain." In an essay in *Perspectives on Indian Poetry in English* (1984), edited by M. K. Naik, Vasant Shahane praises Mahapatra for his steady journey into maturity to become "a major Indo-English poet." Similarly, Ayyappa Paniker in *Indian Literature in English* (1989) hails him as an icon of Indian-English poetry: "It is time for someone, I believe, to declare

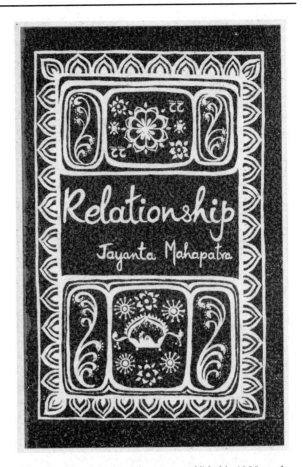

Front cover for Mahapatra's long poem, published in 1980, on the meanings of symbols found in the ruins of a temple in his native Indian state of Orissa (Thomas Cooper Library, University of South Carolina)

on the basis of objective evidence now available that Indian poetry in English has come of age. And nowhere does it seem to reveal this maturity more emphatically than in the works of Jayanta Mahapatra."

Dispossessed Nests shows Mahapatra writing in a vein completely different from that of his earlier verse. It deals with terrorism in the Punjab and human misery in Bhopal following the accidental release of deadly gas from the plant of a Union Carbide subsidiary in December 1984. *Burden of Waves and Fruit* portrays pain and death as perennial conditions of human life and bears a stark sense of acceptance of the realities of life and an Albert Camus–like optimism. As Mohan observes, "The poem becomes an emblem of the poetic presence of death. Death's terror and fear in life, in earth and language, are integrated to the signifiers of the general condition of the human loss."

The Poetry of Jayanta Mahapatra: A Critical Study, a useful collection of essays edited by Madhusudan Prasad, was published in 1986. The essays touch on various aspects of Mahapatra's poetry by leading students of English verse. John Oliver Perry hails Mahapatra as a cultural icon of

Mahapatra reading at the 1985 World Poetry Festival, New Delhi (photograph by A. K. Mital; from Contemporary Authors Autobiography Series, *vol. 9, 1989; Bruccoli Clark Layman Archives)*

Orissa; Pushpinder Sayal highlights the beauty and terseness in his verse. Prasad praises Mahapatra's realistic portrayal of Indian women, and John Stachniewsky compliments his dexterous handling of syntax. Mohan's *Jayant[a] Mahapatra,* published the following year, is a short but important scholarly study of Mahapatra's verse. Mohan finds Mahapatra "the most intense of the Indian poets writing in English and perhaps at par with those European poets who are obsessed with modernistic impulse of man's finitude: his psychology, economics and culture. His poetic focus transforms what is regional in culture, myth and thought to a universal human predicament."

In *Temple,* Mahapatra returns to his earlier theme of the lot of Indian women. As he states in "Jayanta Mahapatra," "Woman . . . represents *sakti* in Hindu mythology—both creator and destroyer." He depicts three different stages in the lives of an Indian woman: the exuberance of youth, the indulgence of middle age, and the "redemptive ripeness" of womanhood in old age. In *Modern Indian Poet Writing in English: Jayanta Mahapatra* (2000) Laxminarayana Bhat writes that while traversing these successive phases, Mahapatra "captures, with rare insight, the burden of tradition on women at all stages of their lives in the predominantly patriarchal system of [Indian] society." Bhat's book is a biographical and sociological study treating in detail such aspects of Mahapatra's verse as culture, heritage, society, relationships, myths, rites, and rituals. In Bhat's opinion, Mahapatra's poetry is "a journey into the self and becomes truly a rewarding, redemptive encounter for the poet in particular and the reader in general."

Mahapatra is known for his distinctively discursive poetic style. The absence of sympathy with suffering humanity in much Indo-Anglian poetry troubles him. For that reason, he emphasizes key contemporary social issues in his verse, thereby generating critical debate among readers and scholars. His subjects include poverty, hunger, prostitution,

death, suicide, crime, war, violence, religious bigotry, and the exploitation of women and children. These problems afflict the entire Indian nation, and he feels them even more acutely in his native state of Orissa. Mahapatra has formulated a poetic idiom of his own; he does not concern himself with coherence in metrical arrangements and grammar in syntactical constructions in capturing the human soul. At times randomly scattered words converge into fine specimens of poetry: "You purse / Your lips / as though / in prayer / Cows / leave off the grass." He occasionally resorts to peculiar poetic coinages to suggest the condition of Indian people in intolerable cultural and economic conditions: "What thin air your face is now, / now that I touch it? Out here, / the stupid code of the crickets, / the wind's low whine; who knows / what's dying underneath / a growing blade of grass." Mahapatra uses symbols and images either from his immediate surroundings or from elsewhere in nature for an easy evocation of the native sensibility. His allusions to a variety of subjects make his poetry richer in meaning and resonant with deep erudition. As Ujjal Dutta notes, "Mahapatra is fond of juxtaposition of images in a sequence of disorder. . . . For him, the external reality is not something out there, but something that yields to the pressure of the consciousness and is sieved through it."

Jayanta Mahapatra has become a favorite with scholars and readers in India and abroad. Reviewers have responded warmly and favorably to his poetry. He has by now acquired the status of a leading Indian-English poet and is currently one of the most active Indian cultural ambassadors to the rest of the world. Mahapatra continues to live in Cuttack. At present he seems to be troubled, like the older William Butler Yeats and Ezra Pound, with life in an age of wars, ethnic violence, national rivalries, religious fundamentalism, and international terrorism. The channels of his creativity have flowed to form poems on Bosnia, South Africa, Chechnya, Kashmir, and Indonesia. As Bhat observes, "Taken as a whole, Jayanta Mahapatra's broad spectrum of poetry demonstrates the gradual evolution of the poet from the stages of his unsteady groping in the dark to the level of finding a personal voice. What need to be appreciated are Mahapatra's persistent efforts to explore the dark recesses of the human soul which act as a constraint for self-actualization." Certainly, his rich perception of life and experimentation with the English language have made him a major and mature presence in contemporary Indian poetry in English.

Interviews:

N. Raghvan, "Inner View," *Tenor,* 1 (June 1978): 61–62;

Deepak Sammantrai, "Poets Are Ordinary People: An Interview with Jayanta Mahapatra," *Sunday Observer* (Bombay), 27 May – 2 June 1984;

Jan Kemp, "Poet to Poet," *Kunapipi,* 11, no. 3 (1989): 45–49;

Arun Ludra, "An Interview with Jayanta Mahapatra," *Indian Literary Review,* 7, nos. 1–3 (1991): 53;

R. Raj Rao, "An Interview with Jayanta Mahapatra," in his *Ten Indian Writers in Interview* (Calcutta: Writers Workshop, 1991), pp. 13–26;

Abraham, "Jayanta Mahapatra: In Conversation with Abraham," *Indian Literature,* 40, no. 4 (1997): 149–157.

References:

Meena Alexander, "Jayanta Mahapatra: A Poetry of Decreation," *Journal of Commonwealth Literature,* 18, no. 1 (1983): 42–47;

Dick Allen, "To the Wall," *Poetry,* 130 (September 1977): 342–352;

Frank Allen, "Crisis of Belief," *Parnassus,* 9, no. 1 (1981): 332–341;

Laxminarayana Bhat, *Modern Indian Poet Writing in English: Jayanta Mahapatra* (Jaipur: Mangal Deep, 2000);

Dilip Chitre, "Poetry in the Enemy's Tongue: On Two Indian Poets Writing in English," *New Quest,* 14 (March–April 1979): 77–82;

Chirantan Kulshrestha, ed., *Contemporary Indian English Verse: An Evaluation* (New Delhi: Arnold-Heinemann, 1980);

Devinder Mohan, *Jayant Mahapatra* (New Delhi: Arnold-Heinemann, 1987);

Niranjan Mohanty, "Recollection as Redemption: The Poetry of Jayanta Mahapatra," *Poetry* (1985): 24–40;

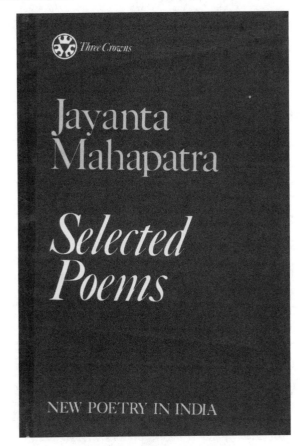

Front cover for Mahapatra's 1987 collection, which includes poems from A Rain of Rites, Waiting *(1979),* The False Start *(1980),* and Life Signs *(1983), as well as five sections from the long poem* Relationship *(Thomas Cooper Library, University of South Carolina)*

Ayyappa Paniker, *Indian Literature in English* (Madras: Anu Chithra, 1989), pp. 42–57;

D. R. Pattanaik, "Silence as a Mode of Transcendence in the Poetry of Jayanta Mahapatra," *Journal of Commonwealth Literature,* 26, no. 1 (1991): 117–126;

John Oliver Perry, "Neither Alien nor Postmodern: Jayanta Mahapatra's Poetry from India," *Kenyon Review,* 8, no. 4 (1986): 55–66;

Madhusudan Prasad, ed., *The Poetry of Jayanta Mahapatra: A Critical Study* (New Delhi: Sterling, 1986);

Krishna Rayan, "The Tendril and the Root: A Study of Jayanta Mahapatra's *Relationship,*" *Literary Criterion,* 26, no. 1 (1991): 61–70;

John Stachniewsky, "Life Signs in the Poetry of Jayanta Mahapatra," *Indian Literary Review,* 6 (2 April 1986): 79–84.

Kamala Markandaya

(1924 – 16 May 2004)

Premila Paul
American College, Madurai

BOOKS: *Nectar in a Sieve* (London: Putnam, 1954; New York: John Day, 1954; Bombay: Jaico, 1956);

Some Inner Fury (London: Putnam, 1955; New York: John Day, 1956);

A Silence of Desire (London: Putnam, 1960; New York: John Day, 1960);

Possession (London: Putnam, 1963; New York: John Day, 1963; Bombay: Jaico, 1967);

A Handful of Rice (Delhi: Hind Pocket Books, 1966; London: Hamilton, 1966; New York: John Day, 1966);

The Coffer Dams (Delhi: Hind Pocket Books, 1969; London: Hamilton, 1969; New York: John Day, 1969);

The Nowhere Man (New York: John Day, 1972; London: Allen Lane, 1973; New Delhi: Orient Longman, 1975);

Two Virgins (New York: John Day, 1973; London: Chatto & Windus, 1974);

The Golden Honeycomb (London: Chatto & Windus, 1977; New York: Crowell, 1977);

Pleasure City (London: Chatto & Windus, 1982); republished as *Shalimar* (New York: Harper & Row, 1982).

Kamala Markandaya (from the cover for the American edition of The Golden Honeycomb, *1977; Richland County Public Library)*

Kamala Markandaya's novels use East-West ties as contexts to focus on interpersonal relationships between Indian and British characters. Such ties often lead to a clash of cultures but also at times to a meaningful exchange and fusion of goals. The cultural interaction is usually presented from a woman's point of view. In spite of traumatic experiences, the central women characters emerge strong and resilient.

Markandaya preferred to be a private person; little biographical information is available, and she gave few interviews. Kamala Purnaiya Markandaya was born in 1924 to a South Indian upper-middle-class Brahmin family in what was once Mysore and is now known as the state of Karnataka. Her father (to whose memory her 1963 novel, *Possession,* was dedicated) was a high-level railway officer. Because of his job, the fam-

ily had to move often, which meant the young Kamala had to study in different schools. Frequent travel and adjusting to new environments became a part of her early life, but she began to enjoy the experience immensely. She enrolled herself in a degree course in history at the University of Madras in 1940, but the family's relocations disrupted her academic pursuits. However, her exciting experiences and keen observation of a variety of places and people eventually directed her to creative writing. She took up journalism between 1940 and 1947 and also tried her hand at clerical and liaison work for the army during World War II. She also worked in a solicitor's office for a while in London. Markandaya married Bertrand Taylor, an English journalist, in 1948 and had a daughter, Kim Oliver, to whom her novel *The Golden Honeycomb* (1977) is dedicated. She lived in England from 1948 onward, though she returned to India for visits.

Markandaya's debut novel, *Nectar in a Sieve* (1954), is probably her best known. It evoked enthusiastic responses from many different countries. Apart from becoming a Book-of-the-Month Club main selection in the United States, it was translated into seventeen languages and was named a Notable Book of 1955 by the American Library Association. It is still used in the colleges and universities in the West that offer courses on India. The novel depicts the plight of villagers affected by the onslaught of industrialism. They find it difficult to deal with the new lifestyle forced on them by rich businessmen. The tannery established by the British in the village stands for the evils of capitalism and imperialism. There is a medical missionary, Dr. Kennington, whose commitment to the poor puts him on the other side of the establishment, but he too furthers Western interest in India. He longs for acceptance from the villagers but is merely respected as a giver and benefactor. He is unable to get rid of his status as an outsider.

Protagonist Rukmani and her husband, Nathan, are uprooted from their peasant existence. Nathan is forced off the land he has farmed for thirty years and out of the hut he has built with his own hands. The family's predicament becomes worse when they move to the city to make a living. Iravadi, their daughter, is rejected by her husband after being accused of barrenness and has to resort to prostitution to feed her dying brother Kuti. Later, an albino son is born to her and is seen as a punishment for her sins. Rukmani also undertakes the responsibility of caring for Puli, a leper boy.

In spite of these pictures of degradation, the novel is affirmative in tone. Rukmani is an admirable picture of stoicism and resilience. Dr. Kennington's hospital gets built, and Puli is healed. Sharing is a way of life for the poor. However, "Dr. Kenny" will never be accepted by the Indian villagers as one of their own. His efforts to free the villagers from fatalism prove futile. Rukmani's statement to him, "Our ways are not yours," seems to emphasize that total interracial understanding is impossible, despite the respect the villagers have for him.

Markandaya's next novel, *Some Inner Fury* (1955), explores the strength of interracial relationships. Ultimately, characters emerge as Indians or Britons, nationalists or loyalists of the establishment. Intimate relationships between Indians and the English remain a distant dream. The Independence Movement itself fails in its professed nonviolence: sporadic violence erupts, betraying deep-rooted resentments. Moreover, political tension invariably continues to affect personal relationships.

The spirit of Premala, the central character in the novel, is stifled in the Westernized household of her husband, Kitasamy (Kit). But she relates easily to the British missionary Hichey and enjoys working with him on a village resettlement scheme. Divided loyalties at the national level are reflected in Kit's house. The Western-educated Kit leads a modern lifestyle, but his brother Govind's parochial nationalism drives him to militancy. Kit's parents maintain two guest rooms, one for Indian and the other for English guests, showing how Indian and English identities remain distinct even in the consciousness of liberal Indians. The interracial couple Richard and Mira are also forced to acknowledge the ethnic disparity between them and declare their narrow allegiances. Thus, this novel reiterates the impossibility of equality between Indians and the English as long as they continue to play the roles of colonizers and the colonized. The ability to absorb the good in both cultures and work it to one's advantage is represented by the successful journalist Roshan; but her self-sufficiency is established only after her separation from her husband. On the whole, *Some Inner Fury* depicts failed relationships in the context of political allegiance.

A Silence of Desire (1960) deals with the age-old dichotomy of head and heart, reason and emotion. The importance given to reason over emotion is seen to be the result of Western influence. In this novel the divide takes the form of the domestic conflict between Dandekar and his wife, Sarojini. Dandekar tries to wean Sarojini away from superstitions and rituals, whereas she wants him to put aside Western notions and see "what lies beyond reason." She seeks medical attention from a faith healer, a swami; Dandekar regards her faith trips as futile. The tumor in Sarojini's womb is a challenge to her faith cure. The conflict between Dandekar and Sarojini eventually subsides into silence and total noncommunication. Even a team sent to investigate the swami is divided in its understanding of his relevance for people. Only after this man leaves the village can Dandekar sense the solace he offered villagers. The swami's absence is felt acutely by the sick and the needy. Markandaya's stance on him, however, remains ambiguous at the end of the novel.

Possession raises powerful issues relating to ownership. The novel is set in both India and England, and its characters move between the two countries. The continual shift of setting helps the novelist deal with the

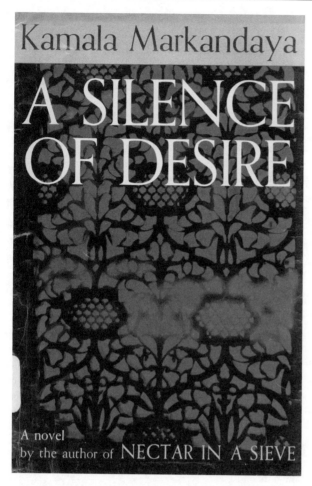

*Dust jacket for the American edition of Markandaya's 1960 novel,
in which a Western-influenced husband tries to dissuade his
tumor-stricken wife from her superstitious belief in the power
of a faith healer (Richland County Public Library)*

novels published. Caroline is callous enough to assume that Valmiki could be productive and salable only as her possession. Her treatment of him as a rare oriental commodity contrasts with the humane sustenance and inspiration that the swami provided.

At one level the novel is about the psychological aspects of possessiveness in human relations. At another level, Caroline Bell's dominance is suggestive of the imperial will. Valmiki's struggle is that of India trying to free itself from colonial clutches. In Anusuya one can see the postcolonial attempt to strike an egalitarian partnership with the West.

In *A Handful of Rice* (1966), Markandaya returns to the concern with hunger and social justice that had originally impelled her to turn to creative writing. The rural poor mistakenly see urban life as a way out of their penury. In Madras, the son of the central character, Ravi Shankar, dies of meningitis, and all Ravi's attempts to survive in the city prove to be demoralizing. His educational qualifications are a hindrance to his employability. Underworld criminals tempt him with easy prosperity, but in vain. Ravi ends up joining an angry mob of rioters, but he is too principled to hurt anyone with his raised hand or to grab a handful of rice illicitly.

In *The Coffer Dams* (1969), Indians and the British come in close contact to build a dam across the turbulent river in Malnad. Though a few Britons are eager to relate to Indians, the master-servant relationship continues, and the exploitation is blatant. Indians, however, are no longer apathetic: they show more resistance and demand their rights. Tension between native pride and imperial arrogance mounts as the dam goes up. Clinton, the head of the British firm that helps to build the dam, pretends to want to benefit the local tribals by employing them for the construction work. But the tribals are uprooted from their familiar habitat for the housing facilities built for the British engineers. Clinton is a picture of indomitable will and is bent on completing the task at all costs. He is more interested in machines and progress than in human beings. Totally devoid of ethical values, he is unmindful of the welfare and safety of the Indians. The tribals become victims of several accidents, including a premature bomb blast that kills about forty of them. Clinton suspends work in honor of Bailey and Wilkins, two British victims of the accident, and arranges a Christian burial for them; but he finds no reason to rescue the corpses of the Indians, which could end up as part of the foundation.

Clinton's wife, Helen, on the other hand, is ashamed of the insensitiveness of the British toward Indians. She suspects foul play when her people urge Bashiam, a tribal, to operate a faulty crane that Smith, a British engineer, had declined using. She realizes the

psychological implications of possession in the colonial context.

In the story, a swami encourages a shepherd boy, Valmiki, to realize his potential as a painter. The boy enjoys painting Hindu gods and goddesses on rocks. Caroline Bell, an Englishwoman, takes him to her country as if he is an exotic discovery. His name becomes "Val," and the money and the fame earned overnight in the new surroundings intoxicate him. This situation leads to a conflict of values in the boy. He does not even visit his dying mother in India, because Caroline is unwilling, even temporarily, to let go of her oriental "find." She adopts devious ways to spoil his relationship with Ellie, a younger woman, in order to retain her prized possession. But the native in Valmiki eventually wins, and he returns to the caves to be able to paint what he wants to again. He achieves his release and moral victory with the help of another woman, Anusuya, who visits England in an attempt to get her

futility of progress in the absence of human values. Her fascination for the enigmatic jungle and the exotic ways of the tribals, and her guilt at being part of the British establishment, drive her to an extramarital relationship with Bashiam.

The Coffer Dams also deals with the lives of the English who had stayed on in postindependence India. Their sense of belonging is upset when their privileged position as the rulers of the land is lost. The novel presents not only Englishmen who continue to uphold imperial stereotypes but also younger Britons eager to make amends for the mistakes of their colonizing ancestors. Some of the Indians admire the strength, determination, and work ethic of the British. But they also resent the high-handedness of some of the expatriates. Despite their scientific orientation and knowledge, the Britons are in the end forced to depend on tribals, who have a better understanding of the vagaries of nature.

The Nowhere Man (1972) is the only work by Markandaya set entirely in London, and it is the most pessimistic of all her novels. Here acculturation is presented as a mere myth and an ideal that can never be realized. Srinivas is an Indian who lives in London with his family. His efforts toward integration with the Londoners prove futile. His wife, Vasantha, has no inclination to adapt and has to live and die like an alien. Srinivas's life in London is a story of loss and disillusionment. His son Seshu dies for the country that refuses to accept him: he is an ambulance driver killed by a German bomb during World War II. The younger son, Lakshman, becomes thoroughly Anglicized and marries a British girl. He rejects his Indian heritage and his parents. He denies them the right to visit him at the birth of his child, under the pretext of not having a spare bedroom for them. When Vasantha dies of tuberculosis, Srinivas loses his most important support system. The help provided by his neighbors does not amount to a lasting form of support. His status as an outsider is confirmed when he contracts leprosy, considered an oriental disease. The marginalized Indian is thus ostracized as a "nowhere man" even after decades of living in England.

The Nowhere Man offers little hope regarding race relations. Srinivas looks down on Christianity and the meat-eating English. The resident Indians wish to immerse the ashes of their dead in the Thames River, but the British police regard this practice as tantamount to polluting the river. The younger generation of Britons resent the Asian presence in England as a threat to their position. Asians are perceived as competitors for jobs, and that attitude does not improve the prospect of better race relations.

Two Virgins (1973) contrasts rural with urban life but maintains a deliberate vagueness of location. Only

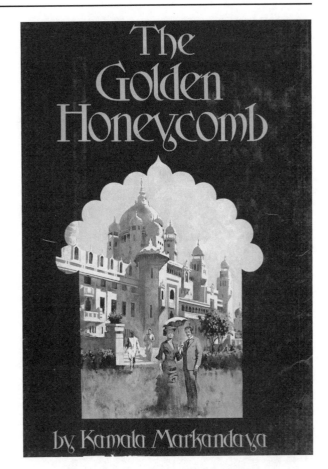

Dust jacket for the American edition of Markandaya's 1977 novel, in which Rabi, an Indian prince, supports the cause of the working class, while other Indian royals guard their privileged positions but are beneath the British rulers (Richland County Public Library)

the names indicate that the background is South India. The novel makes several generalizations that do not in any way add to the understanding of race relations. Two Virgins does not offer any fresh insight into the rural-urban divide, a recurrent theme in Markandaya's fiction. The only significant addition to her earlier writing is the thematic strand of initiation into adult awareness and the resultant reaction against parental restrictions. The West is squarely blamed for the erosion of human values and for whatever has upset the tranquility of Indian life.

The basic difference in outlook between Lalitha and Saroja, the two adolescent sisters in this novel, and their responses to life form the structuring principle of Two Virgins. Lalitha's introduction to two Western-educated friends, Mr. Gupta and Miss Mendoza, leads to her moral degeneration. Lalitha goes to an unspecified city to appear in a documentary movie produced by Gupta. The premarital abortion she has to

Dust jacket for the American edition of Markandaya's 1982 novel (first published as Pleasure City*), about the friendship between a young Indian man and the British director of a holiday resort (Richland County Public Library)*

particularly his mother and grandmother. He relates to the working class with ease and mingles freely with the servants' children. He even gets involved in a demonstration in support of the laborers. Some of the other Indian royals are eager to protect their superior position but are mere lackeys before the British. The British viceroy upholds the rule of the state by an illegitimate prince, an ascension bound to be a fragile "golden honeycomb." Sophie, the daughter of Sir Arthur Copeland, involves herself initially with the cause of the working class and motivates Rabi to do so. But her inherited race-consciousness soon reveals itself, and she withdraws from the cause. Rabi realizes that he could work better with Usha, a fellow Indian, for a common cause, without having to worry about interference arising out of racial disparity. The novel depicts events set in different locations without making specific reference to these places. This fact contributes to its episodic nature.

Markandaya's tenth novel, *Pleasure City* (1982), was published as *Shalimar* in the United States. The main action in the novel is the construction of a holiday resort near a fishing village. The resort is named Shalimar after Emperor Jehangir's pleasure garden. British and Indians come together in a working relationship in this project, undertaken by the Atlas International Development Corporation. But the racial hierarchy remains. The chairman and the director are British, whereas the construction workers are all Indians. The urbanization initiated by the British in India is seen here as a cause for the gradual erosion of traditional values. But the brighter aspects of urbanization are not entirely overlooked. There is no downright condemnation of the influence of the West on India either. Markandaya glorifies the possibilities of genuine race relations, as seen in the two friends Rikki and Tully.

Though Rikki is an orphan, he is lucky to receive genuine love and become the object of concern of his foster parents and of an English couple, Mr. and Mrs. Bride, who are in charge of a school. He communicates well in English because of his early associations with this couple. This relationship also brings him close to Tully, the director at Shalimar, who employs Rikki as a tea-boy. Rikki learns to make a boat, and Tully's wife, Corinna, teaches him surfing. His instinctive knowledge of the sea saves her from drowning in one of the more dramatic moments in the novel.

The Tully family develops close ties with Rikki: "They shared a language that went beyond English, and was outside the scope of mere words." But some of the British characters in the novel blame the Tullys for dishonoring race boundaries and race proprieties in their friendship with Rikki. Despite his skill and closeness with some influential Britons, Rikki's Indian identity gets in the way of his participation in a surfing

undergo in no way destroys her fascination for city life. The village-bound Saroja does not give into temptation, as sexuality is more safely dealt with in fantasy than in reality. She is sure of what she wants in life. She is mature enough to understand that sexual needs can be different for different people. She can even accept homosexual men as they are. She recognizes that rural problems are different from urban ones and that there are problems everywhere that one must be mentally prepared to handle.

The Golden Honeycomb deals with the attitudes of three generations of Indians toward their colonial rulers. The Indian characters belong to the privileged class: Markandaya contrasts the position and mentality of the colonial rulers with that of princely Indians. The curious relationship between the two is presented through the consciousness of Rabi, a prince. His nationalistic spirit is encouraged by the women in his family,

competition. Many of the Britons have a condescending attitude toward the Indians and feel a compulsive need to "civilize" them. Compared to Markandaya's earlier novels, however, *Pleasure City* has a positive outlook and an optimistic tone. Some of the Indians and the English in the novel show mutual respect and love and recognize the good that emerges out of their close interaction.

Markandaya died at home in London on 16 May 2004 at the age of eighty. At first her death went largely unnoticed by the press. Yet, there are hundreds of published articles on Markandaya, and most of them focus on the East-West relationship depicted in her work. There are also several full-length studies of her fiction. Of these, Pravati Misra's 2001 book confines itself to class consciousness, whereas Lakshmi Kumari Sharma's 2001 book deals with the position of women in Markandaya's novels.

The books by Rochelle Almeida (2000) and Uma Parameswaran (2000) also analyze in detail different aspects of Markandaya's novels. The strength of Almeida's book is the close textual analysis. Almeida also identifies elements of Indianness in the novels and discusses the impact of the West on indigenous modes of writing. The inferences that she makes with regard to the influences on Markandaya could be attributed to the many conversations that she had with the novelist. Parameswaran, a reputed Indo-Canadian writer who celebrates diasporic consciousness in her own creative work, calls her approach to the novelist "revisiting Kamala Markandaya." Parameswaran takes into account the fact that critical perspectives have changed completely since Markandaya's last novel was published, because of the evolution of feminist and postcolonial thinking.

A reading of the existing critical material shows that the novels of Kamala Markandaya evoke two entirely different critical positions. While some critics credit her novels with acute perception and sensitive portrayal of East-West relationships, others feel that her fiction fails to grapple with the complexities of racial interaction. Some critics even feel that because of her long stay in England she was out of touch with Indian reality, and therefore her understanding of India was superficial; but all of her novels abound in closely observed sociological details. This detail, however, has led some of her critics to contend that she attempted to package India for a Western audience. However, the least that should be said in her defense is that in the three decades of Markandaya's active writing career, India remained an unfailingly rich source for her work and kept stimulating her creatively despite her immigrant status. Living away from India enabled her, in her fiction, to have a complex and rich perspective on what was once her home.

References:

John F. Adkins, "Kamala Markandaya: Indo-Anglian Conflict as Unity," *Journal of South Asian Literature,* 10, no. 1 (1974): 89–102;

S. K. Aithal, "Indo-British Encounter in Kamala Markandaya's Novels," *Journal of South Asian Literature,* 22, no. 2 (1987): 49–59;

Rochelle Almeida, *Originality and Imitation: Indianness in the Novels of Kamala Markandaya* (Jaipur: Rawat, 2000);

Barry Argyle, "Kamala Markandaya's *Nectar in a Sieve,*" *Ariel,* 4, no. 1 (1973): 35–45;

Ramesh Chadha, *Cross-Cultural Interaction in Indian-English Fiction: An Analysis of the Novels of Ruth Prawer Jhabvala and Kamala Markandaya* (New Delhi: National Book Organization, 1988);

Chadha, "Cross-Cultural Interaction in Markandaya's *Pleasure City,*" in *The New Indian Novel in English: A Study of the 1980s,* edited by Viney Kirpal (New Delhi: Allied Publishers, 1990), pp. 57–64;

P. S. Chauhan, "Kamala Markandaya: Sense and Sensibility," *Literary Criterion,* 12, no. 2–3 (1976): 134–147;

Alice Drum, "Kamala Markandaya's Modern Quest Tale," *World Literature Written in English,* 20, no. 2 (1983): 323–332;

Yasmine Gooneratne, "Traditional Elements in the Fiction of Kamala Markandaya, R. K. Narayan and Ruth Prawer Jhabvala," *World Literature Written in English,* 15, no. 1 (1976): 121–134;

S. C. Harrex, "A Sense of Identity: The Early Novels of Kamala Markandaya," in his *The Fire and the Offering: The English Language Novel of India 1937–70,* 2 volumes (Calcutta: Writers Workshop, 1977), I: 245–260;

C. T. Indra, "The True Voice of Endurance: A Study of Rukmani in Markandaya's *Nectar in a Sieve,*" in *Feminism and Recent Fiction in English,* edited by Sushila Singh (New Delhi: Prestige, 1991), pp. 64–71;

Jasbir Jain, "The Novels of Kamala Markandaya," *Indian Literature,* 18, no. 2 (1975): 31–35;

Jain, "Strangers in Enemy Territory: Expatriates and Exiles," *Littcrit,* 4, no. 2 (1978): 36–43;

Rekha Jha, *The Novels of Kamala Markandaya and Ruth Prawer Jhabvala* (New Delhi: Prestige, 1990);

Margaret P. Joseph, *Kamala Markandaya* (New Delhi: Arnold-Heinemann, 1980);

Feroza F. Jussawalla, "The Twice Born Versus Those Who Have Crossed the Seven Seas: Thematic Concerns of Alienation and Expatriation," in her *Family Quarrels: Towards a Criticism of Indian Writing in English* (New York: Peter Lang, 1985), pp. 133–156;

Prem Kumar, "Conflict and Resolution in the Novels of Kamala Markandaya," *World Literature Today,* 60, no. 1 (1986): 22–27;

Shiv K. Kumar, "Tradition and Change in the Novels of Kamala Markandaya," *Osmania Journal of English Studies,* 7, no. 1 (1969): 1–9;

Pravati Misra, *Class Consciousness in the Novels of Kamala Markandaya* (New Delhi: Atlantic, 2001);

Meenakshi Mukherjee, "Inside the Outsider," in *The Awakened Conscience,* edited by C. D. Narasimhaiah (New Delhi: Sterling, 1978), pp. 86–91;

Mukherjee, "The Theme of Displacement in Anita Desai and Kamala Markandaya," *World Literature Written in English,* 17 (1978): 225–253;

Emmanuel S. Nelson, "Kamala Markandaya, Bharati Mukherjee, and the Indian Immigrant Experience," *Toronto South Asian Review,* 9, no. 2 (1991): 1–9;

Uma Parameswaran, "India for the Western Reader: A Study of Kamala Markandaya's Novels," *Texas Quarterly,* 11, no. 2 (1968): 29–35;

Parameswaran, *Kamala Markandaya* (Jaipur: Rawat, 2000);

Parameswaran, "Native-Aliens and Expatriates—Kamala Markandaya and Balachandra Rajan," in her *A Study of Representative Indo-English Novelists* (New Delhi: Vikas, 1976), pp. 85–140;

Premila Paul, "Kamala Markandaya," in *Writers of the Indian Diaspora: A Bio-Bibliographical Critical Sourcebook,* edited by Emmanuel S. Nelson (Westport, Conn.: Greenwood Press, 1993), pp. 181–197;

Madhusudan Prasad, ed., *Perspectives on Kamala Markandaya* (Ghaziabad: Vimal Prakashan, 1984);

David Rubin, "Kamala Markandaya and the Novel of Reconciliation," in his *After the Raj: British Novels of India Since 1947* (Hanover, N.H.: University Press of New England, 1986), pp. 157–171;

Lakshmi Kumari Sharma, *The Position of Woman in Kamala Markandaya's Novels* (New Delhi: Prestige, 2001);

Dorothy Blair Shimer, "Sociological Imagery in the Novels of Kamala Markandaya," *World Literature Written in English,* 14, no. 2 (1975): 257–270;

Edwin Thumboo, "Kamala Markandaya's *A Silence of Desire,*" *Journal of Indian Writing in English,* 8, nos. 1–2 (1980): 108–136;

K. Venkatachari, "Sense of Life in Kamala Markandaya's *Nectar in a Sieve,*" *Osmania Journal of English Studies,* 9, no. 1 (1972): 55–59;

Ann Lowry Weir, "Worlds Apart: Feminine Consciousness in Markandaya's *Nectar in a Sieve* and *The Coffer Dams,*" *CIEFL Bulletin,* 13, no. 2 (1977): 71–85;

H. M. Williams, "Some Characters in Markandaya's Novels," in his *Galaxy of Indian Writings in English* (Delhi: Akshat, 1987), pp. 111–121.

Ved Mehta
(21 March 1934 –   )

Felicity Hand
Universitat Autònoma de Barcelona

BOOKS: *Face to Face: An Autobiography* (Boston: Little, Brown, 1957; London: Collins, 1958; Bombay: Jaico, 1963);

Walking the Indian Streets (Boston: Little, Brown, 1960; London: Faber & Faber, 1961; revised edition, London: Weidenfeld & Nicolson, 1971; Delhi: Vikas, 1972);

Fly and the Fly-bottle: Encounters with British Intellectuals (Boston: Little, Brown, 1962; London: Weidenfeld & Nicolson, 1963);

The New Theologian (New York: Harper & Row, 1965; London: Weidenfeld & Nicolson, 1966);

Delinquent Chacha (New York: Harper & Row, 1966; London: Collins, 1967);

Portrait of India (New York: Farrar, Straus & Giroux, 1970; London: Weidenfeld & Nicolson, 1970; Delhi: Vikas, 1971);

John Is Easy to Please: Encounters with the Written and the Spoken Word (New York: Farrar, Straus & Giroux, 1971; London: Secker & Warburg, 1972);

Daddyji, Continents of Exile, volume 1 (New York: Farrar, Straus & Giroux, 1972; London: Secker & Warburg, 1972);

Mahatma Gandhi and His Apostles (New York: Viking, 1977; London: Deutsch, 1977);

The New India (New York: Penguin, 1977; Harmondsworth, U.K.: Penguin, 1978);

Mamaji, Continents of Exile, volume 2 (New York & Oxford: Oxford University Press, 1979);

The Photographs of Chachaji: The Making of a Documentary Film (New York & Oxford: Oxford University Press, 1980);

A Family Affair: India under Three Prime Ministers (New York & London: Oxford University Press, 1982; Madras: Sangam, 1982);

Vedi, Continents of Exile, volume 3 (New York: Oxford University Press, 1982; Oxford: Oxford University Press, 1983);

The Ledge between the Streams, Continents of Exile, volume 4 (New York: Norton, 1984; London: Harvill, 1984);

Ved Mehta (photograph by Clayton Evans; from the dust jacket for Face to Face: An Autobiography, *1957; Richland County Public Library)*

Sound-Shadows of the New World, Continents of Exile, volume 5 (New York: Norton, 1985; London: Pan, 1985);

Three Stories of the Raj (Berkeley, Cal.: Scolar, 1986; London: Scolar, 1986);

The Stolen Light, Continents of Exile, volume 6 (New York: Norton, 1989; London: Collins, 1989);

Up at Oxford, Continents of Exile, volume 7 (New York: Norton, 1993; London: Murray, 1993);

Rajiv Gandhi and Rama's Kingdom (New Haven: Yale University Press, 1994; New Delhi: Penguin, 1995; London: Yale University Press, 1996);

Remembering Mr. Shawn's New Yorker: *The Invisible Art of Editing,* Continents of Exile, volume 8 (Woodstock, N.Y.: Overlook Press, 1998; London: Sinclair-Stevenson, 2005);

A Ved Mehta Reader: The Craft of the Essay (New Haven & London: Yale University Press, 1998; New Delhi: Penguin, 1999);

All for Love, Continents of Exile, volume 9 (New York: Thunder's Mouth Press/Nation Books, 2001; London: Granta, 2001);

Dark Harbor: Building House and Home on an Enchanted Island, Continents of Exile, volume 10 (New York: Thunder's Mouth Press/Nation Books, 2003; London: Sinclair-Stevenson, 2003);

The Red Letters: My Father's Enchanted Period, Continents of Exile, volume 11 (New York: Nation Books, 2004; London: Sinclair-Stevenson, 2005).

PRODUCED SCRIPT: *Chachaji, My Poor Relation,* television, *World,* WGBH Boston, 17 June 1978.

Indian prose writing in English in the colonial era tended to deal either with religious and philosophical themes or with political and social issues. The writings and speeches of Swami Vivekananda, Dadabhai Naoroji, and Sri Aurobindo, which emphasized the superiority of Indian spirituality to European materialism, established a high standard for such writing. Political figures such as Mohandas Karamchand Gandhi and Jawaharlal Nehru wrote extensively on India's role in the turbulent years leading up to independence. The work of Ved Mehta both adds to and diverges from those of these earlier writers: it has the same polished, precise command of the language as his predecessors, but his vision is much more cosmopolitan. With the exception of one novel and several short stories, Mehta does not write fiction but has devoted his career to factual accounts of contemporary India, modern philosophy, current affairs, and his own life. His prose style is elegant, straightforward, and clear, and his use of lavish visual imagery is striking in a man blind since age three: Mehta writes as though he could see. His early work, in particular, is impregnated with colors and visual details in an attempt to compensate for his own loss of sight. Indeed, loss features as a recurrent theme in all his works, from his physical loss of vision, to the loss of his home in Lahore after the partition of the subcontinent, and the loss of his homeland, India. Most of his twenty-five books first appeared in serial form in *The New Yorker* magazine, where he worked for more than thirty-three years. The series Continents of Exile, which comprises eleven of his works, was written over a period of thirty years, in between his books on Indian and Western history and ideas.

Ved Parkash Mehta was born in Lahore on 21 March 1934 to Amolak Ram Mehta and Shanti Devi Mehra. He has three older sisters—Promila, born in 1926; Nirmila, born in 1928; and Urmila, born in 1929—and an older brother, Om, born in 1931. His younger sister, Usha, was born in 1937. An attack of cerebrospinal meningitis shortly before his fourth birthday left Mehta blind. His mother refused to accept her son's disability and constantly tried to prove, more to herself than to him, that he could see. To reassure his mother that he could perceive his surroundings, he acquired a knack that he calls "facial vision": a sense of the appearance of objects that are in close proximity to him. Mehta's brothers Anand and Ashok were born in 1939 and 1944, respectively; Anand died in his first year.

Mehta was educated for three years at the Dadar American Mission School for the Blind in Bombay (known since 1997 as Mumbai). His stay at the school damaged his health, and he remained at home until he was accepted at the Arkansas School for the Blind in the United States when he was fifteen. In 1952 he enrolled at Pomona College in California, where he was elected Phi Beta Kappa in 1955 and graduated in 1956. That year he became a Hazen Fellow at Balliol College of the University of Oxford. During the summer vacation of 1957 he visited his hometown in India.

In his first book, *Face to Face: An Autobiography* (1957), Mehta describes the difficulties he had to surmount as an Indian and a handicapped child in the United States. He contrasts the cultured atmosphere to which he was accustomed in Lahore with the rough surroundings and tough companions he found in the American South. John Slatin says that in *Face to Face* Mehta tries to accomplish two contradictory objectives: to show that his blindness makes him interesting enough to justify his writing an autobiography at the age of twenty and to make the reader perceive him as a normal human being whose blindness makes no difference.

Mehta obtained a second bachelor's degree from the Honours School of Modern History at Oxford in 1959 and enrolled at Harvard University, where he was a Harvard Prize Fellow in 1959–1960 and a resident fellow of Eliot House from 1959 to 1961. In 1960 he published his second book, *Walking the Indian Streets,* in which he recounts his 1957 visit to India. Whereas *Face to Face* analyzed the culture shock of a blind adolescent boy in the United States, *Walking the Indian Streets* recounts a young adult's attempt to reinsert himself into the society of his family and his childhood friends after ten years of study in America and Britain. Although Mehta employs a lighthearted tone, the work includes serious reflections and deep feelings about the country of his birth. Thus, along with such trivialities as "All of a sudden, Delhi begins to smile. The heat is no longer like kilns but like animals. We drink beer in mugs; after each fill we say 'Cheers,' and we talk of Michelangelo and Yehudi Menuhin and Oxford. It seems we are smoking the fag end of an Oxford cigarette," one finds passages that reveal Mehta's attitude toward India following independence: "Everyone must belong, yet those of us who were born in the twilight of the British raj were wounded for life"; "We were condemned to live with a permanent hangover"; "to critical eyes we appear shoddy imitations of our various masters"; "We can, but we should not, load on a British scapegoat our divisions and our shortcomings." In the final chapter, "Between the Two Worlds," he juxtaposes conversations with his family's tailor and with Prime Minister Nehru. The tailor defends the hierarchy of classes and castes and rejects the "young sahib's" egalitarian views, while Nehru, torn in his loyalties between the autochthonous and the imported British way of life, embodies both the traditional and the new India. Mehta comes away from the meeting filled with admiration for Nehru and optimistic about the future of the country.

Mehta obtained a master's degree from Harvard in 1961 and was hired by William Shawn, editor in chief of *The New Yorker,* as a staff writer for the magazine. His next two books, like many of the others he published during the next thirty years, were collections of his articles from the magazine. *Fly and the Fly-bottle: Encounters with British Intellectuals* (1962) consists of interviews with philosophers, including A. J. Ayer, Gilbert Ryle, Ernest Gellner, Bertrand Russell, and Iris Murdoch, and historians, including Arnold Toynbee, A. J. P. Taylor, Herbert Butterfield, and E. H. Carr. Mehta was criticized by some of the interviewees or their colleagues, who, while acknowledging his skill in presenting complex ideas in a straightforward way, objected to what they considered the parodistic tone of his commentaries. Reviewing the book in *The Guardian* (27 September 1963), Anne Duchene said that Mehta writes in "*The New Yorker*'s special kind of sophisticated vulgarization for those whose ignorance is not innocent. . . . In one sense the book is a very high-toned gossip column: a vignette of each scholar, and a long interview, usually ending with tea served by a faceless wife." William Barrett wrote in *The Atlantic Monthly* (November 1963) that Mehta "eavesdrops shamelessly upon some squabbles now going on among philosophers and historians. He also preserves a sense of proportion and takes their problems very seriously. Beneath the gaiety of its surface, Mr. Mehta's book is an illuminating report on two sectors of British intellectual life." *The New Theologian* (1965) is a collection of interviews with Protestant thinkers, including Rudolf Bultmann, Paul

Dust jacket for the U.S. edition of Mehta's first book (1957), written when he was twenty years old (Richland County Public Library)

Tillich, John Robinson, Karl Barth, and Reinhold Niebuhr. In 1965 Mehta spent six months traveling in India.

Mehta's only novel to date, *Delinquent Chacha* (1966), was originally serialized in *The New Yorker.* It was inspired by "the long and successful career" of Mehta's father's cousin. Chacha is torn between nostalgia for the British raj and England as an ideal, on the one hand, and a more forward-looking approach to modern India, on the other hand. An amiable fraud, Chacha travels to London in search of adventure and ends up as commissionaire of the All India Taj Mahal Curry, Chutney and Soup Restaurant. Mehta's portrayal of his relative is poignant and farcical and tragic and comic. Charles Poore in *The New York Times* (6 April 1967) called the novel "an enjoyable escapade. In a solemn time, when various cares make the whole world a 'be-in' of trouble, I recommend Ved Mehta's gift of laughter."

Mehta's 1965 travels in India resulted in *Portrait of India* (1970), comprising more than forty essays that

*Dust jacket for the U.S. edition of Mehta's second book (1960),
in which he describes his visit to India in 1957
(Richland County Public Library)*

were first published in *The New Yorker*. Descriptions of mountains, rivers, and people are intermingled with analyses of famine, birth control, and the fate of frontier tribes. Life in India's major cities–New Delhi, Bombay, and Calcutta (known since 2001 as Kolkata)–is vividly depicted. *Portrait of India* was praised for its honesty and absence of sensationalism or bias. In *The New York Times* (25 April 1970) Thomas Lask wrote:

> If you can get past the first 75 pages of Ved Mehta's documentary you will find yourself in a first-class book. It is unusually informative and full of pertinent details that Mr. Mehta has expertly manipulated and arranged to fill out and color the larger picture. . . . By quiet and reiterative references to the variety of beliefs, sects and languages, Mr. Mehta conjures up the complexities and the distinctions that divide this great Asian nation.

> These qualities, though, are not immediately apparent. The opening chapters, devoted to a guided tour, a

session on birth-control indoctrination, the tantrums of a Bombay jazz band, emphasize the quaint and the odd. They are the kind of pieces that any American travel writer with a generous expense account and a 10-day stay in a foreign country can turn out by the yard. The pieces sounded essentially frivolous, and a tone of faint amusement that suffuses the writing does not help.

In the *Saturday Review* (25 April 1970) Linda Hess said that

> I have been in many of the places he describes, and not once in more than 400 pages was I jarred by a flagrant oversimplification or a stagey exaggeration. I began half expecting a spotty overview, sophisticated no doubt (Mehta has been a staff writer for *The New Yorker* since 1961), but perhaps alienated from the Indian scene, perhaps condescending. It soon became clear, however, that the author respected the magnitude of his task. Again and again I stopped to admire his thoroughness, his willingness to linger, to participate in the daily activities and concerns of his subjects.

Interviews figure largely in the essay collection *John Is Easy to Please: Encounters with the Written and the Spoken Word* (1971), but they are not reproduced word for word; instead, Mehta provides impressionistic accounts of his subjects and their thoughts. The title piece deals with the revolution in linguistics inaugurated by Noam Chomsky of the Massachusetts Institute of Technology. Mehta's profile of the Indian writer R. K. Narayan, "The Train Had Just Arrived at Malgudi Station," provides an example of Mehta's "facial vision": he describes Narayan's eyes as "impish and mischievous, peering out from behind thick, black-rimmed glasses" or "twinkling" and notes that Narayan laughs "flashing his teeth."

Mehta received a two-year Guggenheim Fellowship and a five-year Ford Foundation Travel and Study Grant in 1971. After a prolonged psychoanalysis he began to examine his life in detail in what became the eleven volumes of Continents of Exile. In these deeply personal autobiographical works he uses a detached, almost documentary style. The reader is struck by the enormous wealth of visual imagery and by Mehta's ability to infer details about his characters and their surroundings.

In the first book in the series, *Daddyji* (1972)–the title means "Beloved Father"–Mehta traces his family history on his father's side from the nineteenth century to the onset of his own blindness. His father studied medicine and public health in Britain and the United States and was appointed junior public-health officer for the Punjab in the late 1920s. He became a major figure in the Red Cross Society and toured the British provinces and the princely states in charge of the society's antituberculosis campaign. After India attained independence from British rule in 1947, he became deputy director general of the Indian health services. The attitudes and aspirations of upper-middle-class north Indians in the last decades of the raj are convincingly conveyed in Mehta's elegantly concise style.

Wanting to be judged solely for his writing, Mehta had long discouraged any blurbs that alluded to his blindness; he also refused to use a white cane or a guide dog. While he mentioned the condition in *Face to Face, Daddyji* is the first work in which he deals with it at length. Thus, the publication of the work led some readers to doubt that he had written the previous ones, which are filled with vivid images and colors.

Mehta became an American citizen in 1975. In 1977 he received another two-year Guggenheim Fellowship and published two books. *Mahatma Gandhi and His Apostles* uses newspaper clippings, recordings, Gandhi's writings and speeches, and interviews with people who knew Gandhi to probe into the "subtler and more lasting shapes" that the Indian leader has assumed since his death. *The New India* deals with the Emergency Rule of Prime Minister Indira Gandhi, Nehru's daughter; during this period, which lasted from June 1975 to March 1977, civil liberties were suspended, and the press was censored. Mehta received the Association of Indians in America Award in 1978 and became a member of the Council on Foreign Relations in 1979.

A Ford Foundation Public Policy Grant from 1979 to 1982 enabled Mehta to carry on the Continents of Exile series. *Mamaji* (1979) begins with the story of the author's maternal great-grandfather, Bulaki Ram, in the mid nineteenth century and contrasts the lifestyles and aspirations of the Mehtas, who "had retained the easygoing but proud natures and rustic values" of the *paindus* (villagers), with those of the Mehras, who had the "brooding nature and shifting values" of the *shehris* (city dwellers). Mehta's mother, a traditionally brought-up woman, was educated only as much as a conventional Indian wife needed to be: she was taken out of school at fourteen. When she married Mehta's father in an arranged union in 1925–as was customary, they did not meet until the wedding ceremony–she could not speak English, even though her parents had assured him that she could. They had also told him that she could sing and was socially accomplished, neither of which was true. In spite of that inauspicious beginning and the fact that she retained all of her life the Hindu beliefs that her scientifically minded husband considered superstitions, the marriage was a happy one. Like *Daddyji*, this book ends with the onset of the author's blindness.

The Photographs of Chachaji (1980) is the story of the making of the 1978 television movie *Chachaji, My Poor Relation*. Mehta tells how he wrote and narrated the documentary about the curious lifestyle of his father's rascally elderly cousin, Chachaji (Beloved Uncle). Chachaji survives partly by working at two low-paying jobs–although he was fired from one of them during the filming–but mainly by sponging on his wealthier relatives. The documentary received the Dupont Columbia Award for Excellence in Broadcast Journalism.

A Family Affair: India under Three Prime Ministers (1982) analyzes the brief interregnum in independent India's history when it appeared that the country might have an alternative to the Nehru dynasty. The book begins with the defeat of Indira Gandhi in 1977; recounts the administrations of her successors, Morarji Desai and Charan Singh; and ends with her return to power in 1980.

The third volume of the Continents of Exile series, *Vedi* (1982), relates Mehta's three years at the "orphanage-cum-asylum" of the Dadar American Mission School for the Blind. He was sent there because his father did not want him to live the life of dependency and uselessness that was typical for blind Indians at the time. The student body consisted of forty blind and partially sighted boys and girls; all except Mehta were poor. Often ill and far from the warmth and support of his family, the boy had to learn to fend for himself; he also had to learn to make himself understood in Marathi, which he did not speak. The headmaster, Ras Mohun, was not accustomed to blind pupils with normal-looking eyes and cheerful expressions. In one passage Mehta recalls:

> Some of us who were totally blind had been sighted once, but we could no longer remember what that was like. We thought of sighted people as awesome and powerful, always able to take a discarded shoe to one who wasn't sighted. For when we thought of being sighted we could think of ourselves only as the Sighted Master.... we would dream of growing up and becoming the Sighted Master–living in the boys' dormitory, snoring away, catching boys doing naughty things, beating them with a discarded shoe–even as we would automatically straighten ourselves at the very mention of the Sighted Master.

Unlike most of Mehta's works, this book is devoid of visual descriptions. Their absence provides the reader with an approximation to the experience of blindness.

In 1982 Mehta received a five-year John D. and Catherine T. MacArthur Foundation Fellowship and became a member of the Usage Panel of the American Heritage Dictionary. The following year he was awarded the Signet Medal by Harvard University. In 1983 he married Linn Cary, who teaches English at

Dust jacket for the U.S. edition of Mehta's 1970 collection of essays, in which he recounts his travels around his homeland five years earlier (Richland County Public Library)

Barnard College and is the great-great-great-granddaughter of the author James Fenimore Cooper. They have two children: Alexandra Sage, born in 1984, and Natasha Cary, born in 1987.

The fourth volume of Continents of Exile, *The Ledge between the Streams* (1984), describes the horrors of the partition of the subcontinent into India and Pakistan in 1947. Mehta's family, like thousands of other Hindus living on the "wrong" side of the border, were obliged to flee from the newly created Muslim state of Pakistan into India. In *Sound-Shadows of the New World* (1985), the fifth volume in the series, Mehta tells of his move to the United States after being accepted at the Arkansas School for the Blind in Little Rock in 1949. He spoke relatively little English when he arrived but managed to squeeze twelve years' schooling into three. In Arkansas his extraordinary verbal gifts were discovered; he developed his senses of touch and hearing to a high degree of sensitivity; and he was trained to stretch his memory to an outstanding level of acuteness.

Three Stories of the Raj (1986) comprises semifictional tales of Mehta's boyhood under British rule. "Four Hundred and Twenty" and "Music Master" were previously published in *The New Yorker,* and "Sunset" originally appeared in *The Atlantic Monthly.* The sto-

ries are poignantly drawn pictures of village families during the twilight of the raj. In 1986 Mehta received the Distinguished Service Award of the Asian/Pacific American Library Association and the New York City Mayor's Liberty Medal. The following year Pomona College conferred on him the Centenary Barrows Award.

While a visiting fellow at Balliol College in 1988–1989 Mehta wrote *The Stolen Light* (1989), the sixth volume of Continents of Exile. It relates his years at Pomona College, where he was the first Indian student. He tells how he was inspired by overwhelming loneliness to write *Face to Face* but also describes the playful atmosphere of an American campus of the 1950s.

From 1990 to 1993 Mehta held the Rosenkranz Chair in Writing at Yale University. In 1990 he received the New York Public Library Literary Lion Medal and in 1991 the New York State Asian-American Heritage Month Award. *Up at Oxford* (1993), the seventh volume of Continents of Exile, is a memoir of his Oxford years; departing from his usual *New Yorker* style, he includes lengthy digressions in the Indian storytelling fashion. The text conveys the feelings of an outsider who has no place in the rigid hierarchy of Oxford society but dearly wants to belong.

In 1994 Mehta left the staff of *The New Yorker* and began a two-year term as visiting professor of English and history at Vassar College. In his book of essays on India since 1982, *Rajiv Gandhi and Rama's Kingdom* (1994), he deals with the complexities of Indian politics. He says that the new rich act like a "super race" and are obsessed with Western consumerism and globalization and notes with chagrin that the ideals of egalitarianism, austerity, and avoidance of religious conflicts have yielded to a corrupt and unmanageable chaos. Nevertheless, he argues that despite their many ills, including poverty, famine, and illiteracy, Indians are optimistic about the future. The book includes a variety of events, from domestic squabbles in Indira Gandhi's household to the rise of Hindu nationalism and the destruction by Hindu extremists of the Babri Masjid mosque in Ayodhya in 1992. In *Rajiv Gandhi and Rama's Kingdom* the conflict between the democratic political system and the perpetuation of a rigid social hierarchy still rages. In a review in *The Independent* (London) for 22 January 1994 Sunil Khilnani wrote that

> Mehta has an admirable ability to unpack and simplify the byzantine opacity of Indian politics, and especially the to-doings of New Delhi–still an imperial city, with its courts and courtiers. The studiously cultivated poise of Mehta's prose, even when he recounts absurdities that beggar belief, lends a low comedy to his descriptions of the activities of political leaders, of their relatives and in-laws, and of what he has termed "sundry other collaterals."

In 1996 Mehta received the New York Public Library Literary Lion Centennial Medal. During the academic year 1996–1997 he was a senior fellow at Columbia University, and in 1997–1998 he was a fellow at Stanford University.

The eighth volume of Continents of Exile, *Remembering Mr. Shawn's* New Yorker: *The Invisible Art of Editing* (1998), is Mehta's tribute to the man who was editor in chief of *The New Yorker* from 1952 to 1987. The subtitle reflects Mehta's portrait of Shawn as an intensely private person who shunned publicity and was meticulous in his editing, examining every word in an article to ensure that the precise desired effect was obtained. Shawn was so careful in his reading and so generous with his time that Mehta developed a respect for him that verged on filial affection:

> I am aware that I sound as if I had fallen in love with Mr. Shawn. . . . his kindness and generosity, his lack of preconceptions and of condescension, and his publication of my writing as if I were a typical writer rather than a blind or an Indian writer made me believe that I was not losing myself to him but, rather, discovering my true self–that, for once, I was, as it were, speaking

not in an Indian-American voice or an English voice but in my own. That was, in a sense, an illusion, though, since under Mr. Shawn's influence I was developing a writing style–a new voice–that was a fusion of my various selves.

A Ved Mehta Reader: The Craft of the Essay (1998) comprises selections from Mehta's previously published books, with one exception: the essay "Naturalized Citizen No. 984-5165," which appeared in *The New Yorker* in 1977, appears here in book form for the first time. It relates the long process Mehta underwent to become a citizen of the United States. Much of the essay is based on interviews with American authorities, which show the intricate and often humorous procedures to which foreigners are subjected before being admitted as citizens. Mehta characterizes his decision to commit himself to his adopted country as a rational one, based on the affluence, egalitarianism, and political freedom of the United States. But he is honest enough to include a comment by a friend: "Of course, you may consciously think that you are becoming an American citizen because Nixon resigned . . . or because of your expectations of America, but, unconsciously, you are trying to reject part of your childhood."

All for Love (2001), the ninth volume of Continents of Exile, is Mehta at his most confessional as he reveals the anguish of loneliness he suffered in his desperate quest for love. According to traditional Indian thinking, blindness was a divine punishment; Mehta's mother, therefore, refused to accept that her son was blind, which contributed to his delusion that he could see–a delusion that served him well in his professional life but played havoc with his personal life. The belief among Indian families that a blind boy could never marry increased Mehta's obsession with sex and marriage, which he thought would make him whole. With an almost ruthless sincerity he tells the stories of four women with whom he fell in love, all of whom ended up leaving him. His account of these relationships runs parallel to his description of his thirty-year fantasy that he could see. Mehta's statement in the foreword that the women gave permission for their letters to be published adds to the poignancy of the stories, as the reader knows that nothing has been invented. Stephen Amidon wrote in *The Atlantic Monthly* (February 2002):

> This would make for gloomy reading if it weren't for Mehta's wonderfully self-lacerating style and his gentlemanly refusal to blame these troubled women for his heartaches. . . . Rather than taking revenge, the author turns his focus inward, admitting that what these women shared was not sadism but the illusory belief that Mehta's blindness would allow him to look

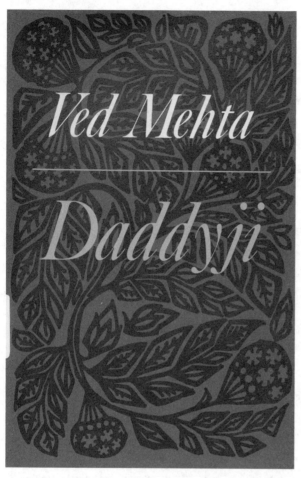

Dust jacket for the U.S. edition (1972) of Mehta's paternal family history, the first volume of his autobiographical series, Continents of Exile *(Richland County Public Library)*

beneath their skin and see some better selves within them.

Anne Chisholm wrote in the London *Sunday Telegraph* (29 August 2001):

> Like all Ved Mehta's work, this book is written with a calm lucidity. For those who have never read him it would be a good place to start; this is more than the story of the sentimental education of an exceptionally brave and gifted blind man. It is a subtle examination of the relationship between thought and feeling, the crucial links between the ability to love and ability to work.

In *Dark Harbor: Building House and Home on an Enchanted Island* (2003), the tenth volume in the Continents of Exile series, Mehta describes the difficulties he faced in building a house on the remote thirteen-mile-long island of Islesboro off the coast of Maine. In bus-

tling Manhattan, the other island where he owns a home, what Mehta calls the "sound-shadows" allow him to live as if he were not blind, whereas the challenge of living on an unspoiled island forces him to come to terms with his disability. The book relates his struggles as he deals with architects, contractors, landscapers, and handymen as he tries to build a house that will blend in with the natural environment of Islesboro. In his review in the *Boston Globe* (27 July 2003) Edgar Allen Beem described Mehta's home, which was completed in 1985:

> Designed by architect Edward Larrabee Barnes, the Mehta house is a fusion of modernism and regionalism, a tall, shingled structure that resembles a boathouse marooned high and dry on the wooded shore. . . . The house does not reflect Ved Mehta's life or personality at all, nor, in its precipitous site and frequent level changes, does it make any concessions to his blindness. And that is the way Mehta wanted it.

In 2004 Mehta published *The Red Letters: My Father's Enchanted Period*. It is the eleventh and, he has announced, the final volume of the Continents of Exile series. It describes his discovery of his father's two-year affair in the 1930s with a married socialite; a friend of the Mehta family, she was known to the children as "Auntie Rasil." Mehta interviews his mother, who tells him that she knew of and resented the affair, but, as a traditional submissive Indian wife, chose to ignore it. Mehta's father gave him Rasil's love letters—the red letters of the title—in which she addresses her lover in phrases such as "God, good fortune of women, master of forsaken ones." Another revelation in the book is Mehta's father's tearful confession that he may have caused his son's blindness by waiting for a day before taking the boy to a hospital. This book is a deeply personal work that is more about Mehta himself than about his father. It reveals how the discovery of his father's affair forced him to rethink his own relationship with his parents. In a sense, *The Red Letters* brings the autobiographical series full circle: it ends where it had begun, with Mehta's parents' differing reactions to their four-year-old son's blindness.

Apart from book reviews, few critical analyses of Mehta's writing have appeared. Mehta regretted the scarcity of literary criticism not only of his own work but also in general in a 2002 interview with Sheela Reddy: "We are living in an age where hype has taken the place of good criticism. Even the review space you get is determined by how much a publisher has paid for the book."

Ved Mehta is the contemporary voice of a long tradition of Indian prose writing in English that started in the late eighteenth century with Ram Mohan Roy.

He combines the autobiographical mode of inquiry into the complexities of the Indian family with the balanced, detached analysis of his *New Yorker* articles and essays. His style stands out for its simplicity. Reviewing *Face to Face* in *The Illustrated Weekly of India* (5 December 1982), Sudhansu Mohanti praised Mehta's art:

> He is completely blind, yet he excels in the minutest description of places, persons, faces, grimaces. His literary qualities are his own. Where there were no forms to accommodate what he wanted to say, he created new forms; and his prose style–airy, elegant, marvellously clear–is his signature. He writes about various matters without solemnity, about scholarly matters without pedantry, about abstruse matters without obscurity.

Mehta has successfully resisted the efforts of reviewers to pigeonhole him as a "blind" or "Indian" or "expatriate" author. His works provide insights that reach far beyond the Indian context and, as he says in *All for Love,* explore "the boundaries of time and memory, the clash of culture and self, and the meaning of place and exile–as I have experienced them."

Interview:

Sheela Reddy, "It's the Age of McDonald's Booksellers," *Outlook India.com* (11 March 2002) <http://www.outlookindia.com/fullprint.asp?choice=1&fodname=20020311&fname=Ved+Mehta+%28F%29&sid=1> [accessed 20 December 2005].

References:

David Scott Philip, *Perceiving India through the Works of N. C. Chaudhuri, R. K. Narayan and Ved Mehta* (New Delhi: Sterling, 1986);

D. A. Shankar, "Suspended Judgement as a Literary Device: A Note on Ved Mehta," *Cygnus,* 2, no. 1 (1980): 41–47;

John Slatin, "Blindness and Self-Perception: The Autobiographies of Ved Mehta," *Mosaic,* 19 (Fall 1986): 173–193;

Frederick Sontag, "The Self-Centred Author," *Quest,* 76 (July–August 1989): 229–233;

Craig Tapping, "South Asia/North America: New Dwellings and the Past," in *Reworlding: The Literature of the Indian Diaspora,* edited by Emmanuel S. Nelson (New York: Greenwood Press, 1992), pp. 35–49;

William Walsh, "Prose: Sages and Autobiographers," in his *Indian Literature in English* (London & New York: Longman, 1990), pp. 31–61.

Website:

Ved Mehta <http://www.vedmehta.com/index.html> [accessed 20 December 2005].

Dom Moraes

(19 July 1938 – 2 June 2004)

Kaiser Haq
University of Dhaka

BOOKS: *Green Is the Grass* (Bombay & Calcutta: Asia Publishing House, 1951);

A Beginning (London: Parton, 1957; revised, 1958);

Poems (London: Eyre & Spottiswoode, 1960);

Gone Away: An Indian Journal (London: Heinemann, 1960; Boston: Little, Brown, 1960);

Penguin Modern Poets 2, by Moraes, Kingsley Amis, and Peter Porter (Harmondsworth, U.K.: Penguin, 1962);

John Nobody (London: Eyre & Spottiswoode, 1964);

Beldam Etcetera (London: Turret Books, 1966);

Poems, 1955–1965 (New York: Macmillan, 1966);

My Son's Father: An Autobiography (London: Secker & Warburg, 1968); republished as *My Son's Father: A Poet's Autobiography* (New York: Macmillan, 1969);

The Tempest Within: An Account of East Pakistan (Delhi: Vikas, 1971; New York: Barnes & Noble, 1971);

From East to West: A Collection of Essays (Delhi: Vikas, 1971);

A Matter of People (London: Deutsch, 1974; New York: Praeger, 1974);

A Family in Goa: Vasantrao Dempo Sixtieth Birthday Commemorative Volume, with drawings by Mario Miranda (Goa: Damodar Narcinva Naik for the Dempo Group of Companies, 1976);

The Open Eyes: A Journey through Karnataka, with illustrations by Miranda (Bangalore: Director of Information and Publicity, Government of Karnataka, 1976);

Bombay, with photographs by Bruno Barbey (Amsterdam: Time-Life, 1979);

Mrs. Gandhi (London: Cape, 1980); republished as *Indira Gandhi* (Boston: Little, Brown, 1980);

Answered by Flutes: Reflections from Madhya Pradesh (Bombay: Asia Publishers, 1983);

Absences (N.p.: Privately published, 1983);

Collected Poems, 1957–1987 (New Delhi: Penguin / New York: Viking Penguin, 1987);

Trishna (Bombay: Perennial, 1987);

Sunil Gavaskar: An Illustrated Biography (Madras: Macmillan India, 1987);

Dom Moraes (photograph by Jerry Bauer; from the cover of My Son's Father: A Poet's Autobiography, *1969; Richland County Public Library)*

Rajasthan, Splendour in the Wilderness, with photographs by Gopi Gajwani (New Delhi: Himalayan Books, 1988);

Serendip: Poems (New Delhi & New York: Viking, 1990);

Never at Home (New Delhi: Viking, 1992);

In Cinnamon Shade: New and Selected Poems (Manchester, U.K.: Carcanet, 2001);

Out of God's Oven: Travels in a Fractured Land, by Moraes and Sarayu Srivatsa (New Delhi: Penguin, 2002);

Typed with One Finger (New Delhi: Penguin, 2003);

The Long Strider: How Thomas Coryate Walked from England to India in the Year 1613, by Moraes and Srivatsa (New Delhi: Penguin, 2003);

Collected Poems: 1955–2003 (New Delhi: Viking Penguin, 2004).

Collection: *A Variety of Absences: Collected Memories* (New Delhi: Penguin, 2003).

OTHER: T. Carmi, *The Brass Serpent: Poems,* translated by Moraes (London: Deutsch, 1964);

Voices for Life: Reflections on the Human Condition, edited by Moraes (New York: Praeger, 1975);

Jeet Thayil and Vijay Nambisan, *Gemini,* volume 1, foreword by Moraes (New Delhi & New York: Viking, 1992);

The Penguin Book of Indian Journals, edited by Moraes (New Delhi: Penguin, 2001).

In 1957, at the age of nineteen, Dom Moraes became the youngest and the first non-English writer to win the Hawthornden Prize. Moraes's winning book, *A Beginning* (1957), was his first and, with only twenty-three pages of text, was the slimmest book ever to have won the prize.

Though Moraes did not win any other international prize after the early success of *A Beginning,* in *Poems* (1960), a Poetry Book Society Choice; *John Nobody* (1964); and the American collection *Poems, 1955–1965* (1966), he demonstrates literary development, albeit of an unsensational variety. Several years later Moraes privately printed a collection of eleven poems, titled *Absences* (1983). Slowly, Moraes's creative vitality returned: *Collected Poems, 1957–1987* (1987) includes enough new poems to make a slim collection on their own; *Serendip: Poems* (1990) is a sizable volume; and *In Cinnamon Shade: New and Selected Poems* (2001) again includes enough new work to make a separate volume. This book was given a Poetry Book Society Special Commendation. It also won the Sahitya Akademi Award, the highest literary accolade in India.

Dominic Francis Moraes was born on 19 July 1938, the only child of a well-known journalist, Frank Moraes, and Beryl Moraes, a pathologist. Theirs was an illustrious upper-middle-class family with impressive connections.

Moraes's two volumes of autobiography, *My Son's Father* (1968) and *Never at Home* (1992), give a vivid account of his life and times. Both his parents were Roman Catholic, but from different communities. Influenced by the Hindu caste system, the communities had become endogamous, so that Moraes's parents had to defy their families in order to get married.

On Moraes's father's side the family was Goan. His grandfather had been an engineer. His father trained as a barrister but had literary interests and became literary editor of *The Times of India.* His mother's parents were both doctors; his maternal grandmother had the distinction of being the first Indian woman doctor. His mother followed in her parents' footsteps and became a medical practitioner, eventually specializing as a pathologist.

Moraes recalls in *My Son's Father* that his "parents were one of the bright young couples of Bombay. They gave and attended expensive cocktail parties. . . . both drank and smoked." They had a serious side as well, "and, unusual in Indian Christians, held nationalist views. They supported Mohandas K. Gandhi and Jawaharlal Nehru." They also played an active role in the independence struggle: "the flat was always full of unshaven and furtive young nationalists who had either just emerged from prison or were hiding from the police."

As World War II broke out, "a sequence of young English officers on their way to the Burma front" called on Frank Moraes; among them was the poet Alun Lewis, who died in Burma. Moraes soon became the first Indian war correspondent, posted to the Burma front. During his absence his wife began to show the first signs of the mental illness that eventually led to her institutionalization.

Beryl Moraes was still functioning as a doctor, though, and was called to minister to Gandhi during one of his hunger strikes. One day she took her son along to the Mahatma's camp and was shown around by Sarojini Naidu, "who in her youth had lived in England and written quantities of verse which was praised by Yeats and Gosse" but now "was about sixty, a large, grey-haired, talkative lady, who had long since abandoned verse to become a heroine of the revolution." She addressed Gandhi as "my Mickey Mouse" and introduced Moraes, who was adjured by him to learn Hindi, of which he knew only a few words.

Frank Moraes's return from the front prompted a whirlwind of parties, but the jollity was undermined by his wife's rapidly aggravating mental illness. When a change of scene was recommended, Moraes accepted the offer of the editorship of the *Times of Ceylon.* The move did not help the patient, who was now advised by doctors to return home, which she did so that she could undergo the recommended insulin treatment, not available then in Ceylon. Moraes and his father stayed on for some time and found an opportunity to see a bit of the country, its people as well as its ancient ruins; the experience later found its way into Moraes's poetry.

In Ceylon, Moraes began writing verse, initially inspired by the poetry in his father's collection. In par-

A BEGINNING

DOM MORAES

THE PARTON PRESS

MCMLVII

Title page for the revised edition of Moraes's 1957 collection of verse, which was awarded the British Hawthornden Prize for poetry. At age nineteen, Moraes was the youngest person, and the first non-English writer, to receive the prize (Perkins Library, Duke University).

ticular, A. C. Swinburne's "thunderous rocking-horse lines intoxicated" him. He was also influenced by the early William Butler Yeats and anthologies such as *The Golden Treasury* (1861) and *Poems of Today* (first series published in 1915).

The Ceylonese sojourn ended soon after the assassination of Gandhi, when Frank Moraes was offered the editorship of his old paper, *The Times of India.* Dom Moraes discovered the anthology *Traveller's Library* (1933), edited by W. Somerset Maugham, which included the work of modernist poets such as T. S. Eliot, W. H. Auden, and Stephen Spender. "It excited me immensely," notes Moraes in *My Son's Father.* "I seemed to see for the first time how to write verse." His new work varied in style between the verse of these three poets. "An adolescent reaction to Eliot filled my own poems with a cosmic despair: from the early work

of Auden and Spender I took a crude Marxism. I struck these attitudes in three different styles, one day pouring out imitation Waste Lands, on the next curt, mysterious sonnets full of spies and frontiers, and the day after invoking young men and young comrades in the early Spender manner. I wrote all day, and produced not only half a dozen poems a day, but also short stories rather like Saroyan, and a book about my travels." Eventually, he had a short story published in a local newspaper.

Publication brought him to the attention of his father's writer friends Mulk Raj Anand and G. V. Desani, the latter just back from London, where his novel *All about Mr. Hatterr* (1948) had been praised by Eliot. With adolescent naiveté Moraes thought one had "to look like them if one was to be a writer." As he puts it in *My Son's Father,* "I brushed my hair upward a dozen times a day in an attempt to broaden my brow, and constantly pulled at my fingers, to make them longer." To Moraes the chief distinction of these senior writers was that they had hobnobbed "with writers who were myths" to him. Two of these living myths soon traveled to a writer's conference in Bombay, much to Moraes's delight, since he had the opportunity to see them there:

. . . there they actually were, physically present: Auden with a lined, expressive face, grave and heavy: Spender tall and stooped, with a white cloud of hair and large, intent blue eyes. I had thought of them as very young men, and was surprised: then a new idea of the poet came to me, the poet dedicated, apart, carrying his work on through a lifetime, wrapped in a vatic cloak. Afterwards my father introduced me to Spender. I was too awestruck to speak, and stood gaping raptly up at him while he stared at me in a kind, rather puzzled way. At last I blurted out the words, "I want to be a poet." Spender began to laugh, then stopped and said gently, "Perhaps you are one." This innocent remark intoxicated me: in it I saw a recognition of one poet by another, transcending all barriers, and under this gratifying illusion doubled my output of verse.

Moraes's first book, however, was not a collection of verse but a volume of essays on cricket, the only game to spark his interest. A "publisher friend of the family's" thought the essays were marketable and produced the book, which Moraes looked back on with embarrassment and did not mention in the list of his works on the flyleaf of any of his later books.

Spender eventually became Moraes's mentor, but meanwhile he benefited greatly from the tutelage of Nissim Ezekiel. Ezekiel had just returned after a long sojourn in London, where the Fortune Press had published his first collection, *A Time to Change* (1952), and joined the *Illustrated Weekly of India* as an assistant editor, whose brief included looking after the literary pages of the magazine. Ezekiel impressed on the teenage poet the importance of craftsmanship and self-criticism, both of which required painstaking work. Moraes met Ezekiel once a week, as he recalled in *My Son's Father:* "A coffee in a seafront café, when I showed him my new work, tutorial followed, in course of which the master would scissor it softly to pieces: then, into my dismay he would drop the two words of hope: 'work harder.'"

Ezekiel introduced Moraes to the work of Arthur Rimbaud, and soon the latter was deciphering the original French of the poet as well as of Paul Verlaine and Guillaume Apollinaire with the help of a dictionary. The involvement with French took a new turn when Moraes began taking private lessons from the beautiful wife of the director of the Local Alliance Française, with whom he promptly fell in love. The one-sided amour resulted in "French Lesson," a poem Moraes realized was different from his usual efforts: "whereas normally before my poems rose from other poems I had recently read, in this one I tried to express my own emotions with precision." Ezekiel responded with enthusiasm: "Congratulations. . . . This is a good poem. It's the first poem you've ever written." The poem is included in Moraes's second collection, *Poems.*

Precocious and mature beyond his years, Moraes was a misfit in his Jesuit-run school. He looked forward to Oxford and in fact had already decided that he would make England his home. Spender, who paid another visit to Bombay, liked the poems Moraes showed him. He gladly recommended Moraes to Nevill Coghill at Oxford. Admission, however, entailed success in examinations in English and Latin, and Moraes sailed to England in 1955 to attend a private school that prepared candidates for the examinations. There was a distressing leave-taking from his mother, immured in a mental asylum in Bangalore, and some sightseeing, in the course of which, as he recalls in *My Son's Father,* Moraes developed what he had not had before: "a strange detached love for the country of my birth."

Moraes took to London immediately, especially to its literary and bohemian side. His autobiographies provide a vivid account of his encounters with a wide range of personalities, from establishment figures like Spender, E. M. Forster, and Cyril Connolly to the bohemian habitués of Soho. He also fit in a continental tour before the term began at Jesus College, Oxford, in October 1956.

Moraes's three years at Oxford were chaotically divided between poetry and romantic involvements, with studies receiving little attention. More than once the college authorities considered expelling him. That they did not do so had much to do with the sensational success of his first collection, *A Beginning,* published by David Archer from the Parton Press, an adventurous

small house that had published Dylan Thomas, George Barker, David Gascoyne, and W. S. Graham and at this time operated out of Archer's bookshop in Soho.

The characteristic poetic traits of *A Beginning* can be readily gauged from the poem "Autobiography":

> I have grown up, I think, to live alone
> To keep my old illusions, sometimes dream,
> Glumly, that I am unloved and forlorn,
> Run away from strangers, often seem
> Unreal to myself in the pulpy warmth of a sunbeam.
> I have grown up, hand on the primal bone,
> Making the poem, taking the word from the stream,
> Fighting the sand for speech, fighting the stone.

The Romantic stance, the rapid progression of images, and the smooth polish of the verse became characteristics of Moraes's poetry.

As a Hawthornden laureate Moraes was in a different class from his fellow undergraduates. Despite his cavalier attitude toward studies, he was allowed to stay the full course and obtained a degree. *My Son's Father* gives a vivid account of his bohemianism as well as literary activities and encounters but is misleading when it comes to his love life. Henrietta Moraes, Moraes's first wife, is the dedicatee of *A Beginning. My Son's Father* not only does not mention her but also devotes numerous pages to an affair with someone represented by the initial *K.* Like Henrietta, K worked in Archer's bookstore when Moraes met her, was somewhat wild, and was Moraes's significant other when the Hawthornden Prize was awarded. As he recounts it in his autobiography, however, the affair with K was over before Moraes graduated from Oxford, which was not the case with Henrietta.

Henrietta was born Audrey Wendy Abbott in Simla, India, to an Indian Air Force officer who deserted her English mother. She grew up in England and was befriended and loved by writers and artists, including Francis Bacon, Lucian Freud, and Maggi Hambling. One of Freud's portraits of her embellishes the cover of her memoir, *Henrietta* (1994), in which she recounts her relationship with Moraes, whom she married in 1961 after a five-year affair. Not long after, misunderstandings arose. In her memoir she recalls, "I became disoriented. I could not understand Dom's need to tell lies, or at best to evade the truth." One day he disappeared and was discovered in a tenement in Pimlico: "he was in a frightful condition. Shaking, trembling, he looked ill and in need of care and attention." The final break came abruptly. Moraes told Henrietta that he was going out to buy cigarettes, and he never returned.

Even amid his literary bohemian life, Moraes was not untouched by political events. When India annexed

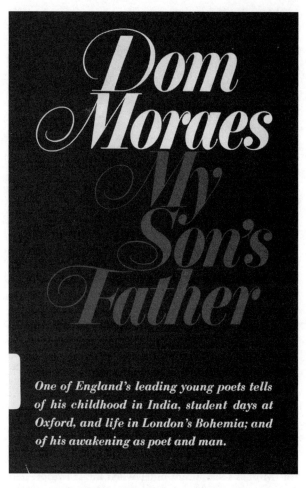

Dust jacket for the U.S. edition of Moraes's 1968 autobiography, in which he recounts how his parents' social connections led to his youthful acquaintances with Mohandas Karamchand Gandhi and poets W. H. Auden and Stephen Spender (Richland County Public Library)

the Portuguese colony of Goa, where his family was from, he gave up his Indian citizenship in protest and adopted British citizenship. The decision formalized for Moraes his awareness that he belonged in Britain rather than the country of his birth.

My Son's Father ends with Moraes meeting and promptly marrying Judith in 1963 and two years later fathering Francis, the son referred to in the title of the book. Before these events, however, Moraes visited India in 1959, and he and Ved Mehta, who had been at Oxford with him, traveled across India and into Sikkim and Nepal. Both writers published accounts of their travels, Moraes's being *Gone Away: An Indian Journal* (1960). An outcome of the India tour was a sense of reconciliation with his mother. As Moraes puts it in *My Son's Father,* "I left India at peace with myself. Something very important to me had happened. I had explained myself to my mother, there was love between us, the

closed window that had darkened my mind for years had been opened, and I was free in a way I had never been before."

For a means of earning his livelihood, Moraes chose a journalistic career, which he memorializes in *Never at Home,* his second memoir. He worked as a war correspondent; as the editor of magazines in different countries; for the United Nations; and on documentary motion pictures as scriptwriter and sometimes as director as well. Assignments took him to every continent except Antarctica. In 1961 Moraes went to Israel, where he covered the trial of Adolf Eichmann and translated the Hebrew poet T. Carmi. The translations were published in the volume *The Brass Serpent: Poems* (1964). In 1962 the second volume in the series *Penguin Modern Poets* included Moraes alongside Kingsley Amis and Peter Porter; that year he traveled to Algeria to cover the war for independence and to India and Cuba as a television journalist. As features editor of *Nova,* a British magazine, from 1963 until 1967, he traveled to the United States, where he interviewed Marshall McLuhan and Lyndon B. Johnson, and to Mexico, Guatemala, and Russia.

Though it was journalism that took Moraes away from London and its literary hub, he had already begun to experience an existential crisis that created a distance between Moraes and England, the land he had felt was his true home. In *Never at Home* he recounts an incident that made him realize that he was an alien in England. He was convalescing after an illness and went out to buy cigarettes. He happened to be unshaven and shabbily dressed and was accosted by a policeman on the beat, who demanded to see his papers. When Moraes protested vigorously, his Oxford accent made the policeman realize that he was dealing with an educated person, a gentleman. At once the policeman apologized and withdrew. After the episode, Moraes recalls, "I felt even more furious. England was my home. Was I to be treated like an immigrant? Then it occurred to me that I *was* an immigrant and that I knew very little about how other immigrants lived. I felt suddenly very guilty about this."

Soon after, Moraes worked on a BBC production on immigrants; on another assignment he had an encounter with the racist National Front. Meanwhile, his marriage to Judith broke up after a visit to India in 1968. While making a movie in India in 1969 Moraes met a childhood friend, Leela Naidu, an actress who was once listed among the ten most beautiful women in the world, and they married soon after. In 1970 Moraes covered East Pakistan (now Bangladesh) for *The New York Times* and wrote a perceptive account of the country, *The Tempest Within: An Account of East Pakistan* (1971). He then became associate editor of *Asia Magazine,* which was published from Hong Kong. From 1972 to 1977 he worked for the United Nations as a researcher and writer on population problems. His travels through Africa, Asia, and South America in connection with his work resulted in *A Matter of People* (1974), a memoir focusing on his personal experience of the population explosion. In 1975 his anthology *Voices for Life: Reflections on the Human Condition* appeared, with contributions by such diverse personalities as Indira Gandhi, Günter Grass, Eugène Ionesco, and Arnold Toynbee.

In 1974 Moraes and Leela settled in Delhi, where he worked as a movie consultant. His return to India as a resident gave him the opportunity to write books about the land and its people. *The Open Eyes: A Journey through Karnataka* (1976) was commissioned by the government of Karnataka; *Bombay* (1979) was written for inclusion in the Great Cities series published by Time-Life. *Answered by Flutes: Reflections from Madhya Pradesh* (1983) shows a hidden side of rural India. Moraes wrote a biography of Indira Gandhi after her fall from power in 1977, which was published in 1980. In 1979 he moved to Bombay (now Mumbai), which remained his home until his death in 2004. He was associated with newspapers such as the *Indian Express* and magazines such as *Keynote* and had the reputation of being the best-paid freelance journalist in India. In 1987 he published a biography of the cricketer Sunil Gavaskar.

For years Moraes wrote little poetry. Critics casually suggest reasons for this silence, though not with much confidence. Thus, Bruce King, who remarks in his *Three Indian Poets: Ezekiel, Moraes, and Ramanujan* (2005) that Moraes had been transformed from a promising poet "to a talented writer of superior coffee table books," ventures this explanation: "An off-and-on problem with drinking did not help. Although the 'Interludes' and other poems were written during 1965–78, the Muse, probably feeling neglected, no longer came with any regularity and seemed unfaithful." Moraes was still not free of his drinking problem, however, and was still a full-time journalist when he had his second major burst of creativity. Moraes records the change that came over him in *Never at Home:* "A peculiar shiver ran down my spine, and at first I thought I must be ill. Then I recognized my own symptoms. I had not felt like this for seventeen years." The poem that he wrote was "Absences," which inaugurated the later phase of his poetic career. "Absences" has a plangent ending that provides an insight into the poet's emotional world:

No longer any foreshore

Nor any abyss, this

World only held together

By its variety of absences.

Moraes not only wrote more poetry but also began to play the role of mentor to young Indian poets, two of whom, Jeet Thayil and Vijay Nambisan, he introduced in a volume published by Viking Press titled *Gemini* (1992).

The death of Moraes's mother in 1989 marked a watershed in his emotional life, as he recalls in *Never at Home:* "As we took the corpse out of the morgue and to the crematorium, the undertaker's men holding handkerchiefs to their noses, it struck me that all this might represent for me the shedding of an obsession, and some kind of belated rebirth." A transition of another kind followed the publication of *Never at Home* in 1992: Moraes's marriage with Leela ended.

Moraes found a new companion in the writer Sarayu Srivatsa, with whom he collaborated on two books, the first being *Out of God's Oven: Travels in a Fractured Land* (2002), the result of six years of travel and ratiocination within India. The other is *The Long Strider: How Thomas Coryate Walked from England to India in the Year 1613* (2003), the life of a curious adventurer interspersed with Moraes's own impressions of the cities Coryate traversed. Also in 2003 he published *Typed with One Finger,* a volume of new and selected poems, and *A Variety of Absences,* an omnibus volume including the memoirs *Gone Away, My Son's Father,* and *Never at Home.*

By this time Moraes was a sick man, struggling against cancer. A malignant tumor was removed, but he refused to follow up the surgery with the radiation therapy prescribed by his physicians. He kept on trying to write until the end, which came suddenly with a heart attack on 2 June 2004.

Looking back over Moraes's poetic output over nearly a half century, one identifies a Romantic stance that remains virtually unchanged, though there is a gradual move toward a sparer diction and a more relaxed form. The Romanticism goes back to Byronic roots but also incorporates the languor of *les poètes maudits* (the cursed poets), a group of which Rimbaud and Verlaine were a part, and establishes a kinship with the poets of the 1940s with whom Moraes had both literary and personal links, notably Barker and Gascoyne. As for the main line of development in modern English poetry, from Yeats through Eliot to Auden, its significance to Moraes should not be downplayed, but his Romantic sensibility remains his most conspicuous trait.

His Romanticism was highlighted by Geoffrey Thurley in his book *The Ironic Harvest: English Poetry in the Twentieth Century* (1974). Thurley, who was one of the promising young critics of his generation, argued that the ironic tradition in modern poetry had been played out and that a revaluation would raise more Romantic kinds of poetry in critical esteem. At one

NEVER AT HOME

Dom Moraes

VIKING

Title page for Moraes's 1992 account of his journalistic career, during which he traveled around the world covering wars, producing documentaries, and interviewing heads of state (Perkins Library, Duke University)

point he tries to elevate Moraes into an exemplar for contemporary poetry. No other English critic has made such a large claim for Moraes. Few, however, will take Thurley's claims seriously. In relation to the main line of development in contemporary English poetry, from Philip Larkin and the other poets of "The Movement" through Ted Hughes and the poets of "The Group," to Seamus Heaney and beyond, Moraes is a recherché figure.

Ian Hamilton's brief review of *John Nobody* in *London Magazine* (October 1965) is representative of the dominant critical opinion of Moraes in the 1960s and 1970s. Hamilton finds Moraes "a slave to the regular iambic line . . . melodramatising a parody version of the alienated, fierily Bohemian romantic artist." His poetry suffers from "the tepid adjective, the unrelenting rhyme-

scheme, the over-all tendency of his language to seek out a level of polished anonymity and rest there."

In India, Moraes's English prosodic finesse and tone is generally regarded as foreign, a view expressed even by his early mentor Ezekiel in a 1988 *Indian Post* review of his *Collected Poems, 1957–1987* (quoted in Raja Rao's *Nissim Ezekiel: The Authorized Biography*, 2000). Ezekiel concedes that it is an "impressive collection" from which "much may be learnt . . . about the art," but then comes the telling counterpoint: "It may argued that Dom has nothing special to offer those Indians who use English for creative purposes. He writes like an English poet, and does not reflect any significant aspect of Indian life. There are allusions to his life in India but they are personal, with no social and cultural implications."

It is best to approach Moraes as an individual talent who, despite his intertextual connections with various poets, should not be seen in the context of any group or national tradition. He is a loner who defies fashionable labels such as *postcolonial* or *postmodern*.

In Moraes's poetic career a breakthrough occurs in "Letter to My Mother," first collected in *Poems, 1955–1965* and placed at the head of the section "Later Poems." While the earlier poems are all in regular meters (all but a few are in iambic pentameters) and use rhyme, this one is in short lines of two or three stresses, with only a few scattered and inconspicuous rhymes. There is no attempt to mythologize or hide behind a mask; the tone is frankly confessional, the subject is the primal hurt in the poet's psyche, caused by his mother's ailment:

> I address you only,
> My lonely mother.
> . . . .
> You do not understand me.
> I am tidying my life
> In this cold, tidy country.
> I am filling a small shelf
> With my books. If you should find me crying
> As often when I was a child
> You will know I have reason to.
> I am ashamed of myself
> Since I was ashamed of you.

The second section of the poem extends the view to take in the entire subcontinent. The speaker does not deny his umbilical connection with the land, even though he has exiled himself from it:

> Your eyes are like mine.
> When I last looked in them
> I saw my whole country.
> A defeated dream
> Hiding itself in prayers,

A population of corpses,
Of burnt bodies that cluttered
The slow, deep rivers, of
Bodies stowed into earth
Quickly before they stank
Or cooked by the sun for vultures
On a marble tower.

Here, Moraes's work has larger cultural resonance. In it and increasingly in his later poems, Moraes avoids formal conventionality. These poems alternate between mythopoeisis and forthright personal statement, often intimate and erotically charged.

Dom Moraes eventually found his niche in literary history in the context of the Indian subcontinent. His position in the canon of Indian poetry in English is secure, alongside Ezekiel, A. K. Ramanujan, Arun Kolatkar, R. Parthasarathy, Kamala Das (Surayya), Arvind Krishna Mehrotra, Vikram Seth, and Agha Shahid Ali. Whatever caveats one might have, whether about his un-Indian/English traits or his lack of a sense of belonging vis-à-vis India, the fact remains that the bulk of his readership is Indian. More importantly, as an influence on promising young poets, he rivals figures such as Ezekiel and Jayanta Mahapatra.

References:

Kaiser Haq, ed., *Contemporary Indian Poetry* (Columbus: Ohio State University Press, 1990), pp. xxii–xxiii;

Bruce King, *Modern Indian Poetry in English,* revised edition (Delhi & New York: Oxford University Press, 2001), pp. 74–75, 108–111, 296–297;

King, *Three Indian Poets: Ezekiel, Moraes, and Ramanujan,* second edition (New Delhi & New York: Oxford University Press, 2005);

Chitantan Kulshreshtha, ed., *Contemporary Indian English Verse: An Evaluation* (New Delhi: Arnold-Heinemann, 1980);

E. N. Lall, *The Poetry of Encounter: Three Indo-Anglian Poets, Dom Moraes, A. K. Ramanujan, and Nissim Ezekiel* (New Delhi: Sterling, 1983);

Henrietta Moraes, *Henrietta* (London: Hamilton, 1994);

Raja Rao, *Nissim Ezekiel: The Authorized Biography* (New Delhi: Viking, 2000);

Vasant A. Shahane and M. Sivaramakrishna, eds., *Indian Poetry in English: A Critical Assessment* (Delhi: Macmillan, 1980);

Geoffrey Thurley, *The Ironic Harvest: English Poetry in the Twentieth Century* (London: Arnold, 1974).

Bharati Mukherjee

(27 July 1940 –   )

Radha Chakravarty
Gargi College, University of Delhi

See also the Mukherjee entries in *DLB 60: Canadian Writers Since 1960, Second Series* and *DLB 218: American Short-Story Writers Since World War II*.

BOOKS: *The Tiger's Daughter* (Boston: Houghton Mifflin, 1972; London: Chatto & Windus, 1973);

Wife (Boston: Houghton Mifflin, 1975);

Kautilya's Concept of Diplomacy: A New Interpretation (Columbia, Mo.: South Asia Books, 1976; Calcutta: Minerva, 1976);

Days and Nights in Calcutta, by Mukherjee and Clark Blaise (Garden City, N.Y.: Doubleday, 1977; revised and enlarged edition, Markham, Ont. & Harmondsworth, U.K.: Penguin, 1986);

Darkness (Markham, Ont. & New York: Penguin, 1985; Harmondsworth, U.K.: Penguin, 1985); selections republished as *Wanting America: Selected Stories* (Stuttgart: Reclam, 1995);

The Sorrow and the Terror: The Haunting Legacy of the Air India Tragedy, by Mukherjee and Blaise (Markham, Ont. & New York: Viking, 1987);

The Middleman and Other Stories (Markham, Ont.: Viking, 1988; New York: Grove, 1988; London: Virago, 1988);

Jasmine (New York: Grove Weidenfeld, 1989; London: Virago, 1990);

Political Culture and Leadership in India: A Study of West Bengal (New Delhi: Mittal, 1991);

Regionalism in the Indian Perspective (Calcutta: K. P. Bagchi, 1992);

The Holder of the World (Toronto: HarperCollins, 1993; London: Chatto & Windus, 1993; New York: Knopf, 1993);

Leave it to Me (London: Chatto & Windus, 1996; New York: Knopf, 1997);

Desirable Daughters (New York: Theia, 2002);

The Tree Bride (New York: Theia, 2004).

OTHER: "A Four-Hundred-Year-Old Woman," in *The Writer and her Work,* volume 2, edited by Janet Sternburg (New York: Norton, 1991), pp. 33–38.

Bharati Mukherjee (photograph © Tom Victor; from the dust jacket for the U.S. edition of The Middleman and Other Stories, *1988; Richland County Public Library)*

SELECTED PERIODICAL PUBLICATIONS–UNCOLLECTED: "An Invisible Woman," *Saturday Night,* 96 (March 1981): 36–40;

"Immigrant Writing: Give Us Your Maximalists!" *New York Times Book Review,* 28 August 1988, pp. 1, 28–29;

"After the Fatwa: The Satanic Verse Controversy," by Mukherjee and Clark Blaise, *Mother Jones,* 15 (April–May 1990): 61–65.

"I really do hear a voice when things are going well," Bharati Mukherjee told interviewers for *The Iowa Review* in 1990. "I am like a medium. I am both inside and outside the character. I'm hearing this voice that's writing itself." Finding a voice to express a complex, cross-cultural sensibility is the literary mission of Mukherjee, one of the major writers of the Indian diaspora in the United States. Dislocation, cultural alienation, survival, and adaptability remain persistent themes in the fiction of this courageous and versatile author, whose own biographical trajectory spans India, Canada, and the United States. Through an array of vibrant, larger-than-life characters and their often extraordinary experiences, Mukherjee charts the lives of immigrants in North America: their trials and tribulations as well as their zest for survival, desire for visibility, and ingenuous modes of self-refashioning. As a writer who straddles multiple cultures, combining history, myth, and philosophy with stringent social critique, Mukherjee has carved a niche for herself in the burgeoning field of Indian writing in English.

Mukherjee was born in Calcutta (since 2001 Kolkata) India, on 27 July 1940. She was the second of three daughters. Her father, Sudhir Lal Mukherjee, was a respected chemist who had done advanced research in Germany and earned a doctorate from the University of London. A Bengali Brahmin, his ancestral home was in Faridpur, East Bengal (now Bangladesh). Bharati's mother, Bina (Bannerjee) Mukherjee, was from Dhaka. (Both Faridpur and Dhaka became part of East Pakistan when the region was partitioned in 1947, at the time of India's independence.) During the years preceding the Partition, their families moved to Calcutta, where Bharati Mukherjee spent her early years. About forty members of their joint family lived together in their home on Rash Behari Avenue in Calcutta.

Growing up in what she called an "extraordinarily close-knit family" in *Days and Nights in Calcutta* (a 1977 memoir she wrote with her husband, Clark Blaise), Mukherjee was accustomed to having aunts, uncles, cousins, and other members of the extended family all around her, but the major influence on her life at this stage was her father. A vibrant, impressive personality, he was "an extraordinary man," Mukherjee told interviewer Geoff Hancock, "very much the benevolent patriarch." He encouraged his daughters to study and actively promoted Mukherjee's interest in creative writing. Her mother, like many Bengali women of her time, was not highly educated. Though outwardly quiet, Bina Mukherjee nursed a lifelong craving for the education that had been denied her and did not want her daughters to be similarly deprived. She also wanted to protect her daughters from the constraints endured by many middle-class Indian women trapped in conventional arranged marriages. She was determined, as Mukherjee recalled in *Days and Nights in Calcutta,* to make sure that her daughters were well educated so that no one could "make them suffer."

At the age of three, Mukherjee was sent to a school run by Protestant missionaries. Though the instruction was bilingual, the school laid greater emphasis on fluency in English than did other similar institutions in Calcutta. This early exposure to an Anglicized education bred in Mukherjee a degree of detachment from Calcutta culture. Her early upbringing was thus riven with contradictions, many of which became defining features of her creative work. Though orthodox and traditional in their approach to religion, her parents encouraged their daughters to pursue education, independent careers, and self-fulfillment. All three sisters rejected arranged marriages and chose instead to marry for love; all left home in pursuit of work and education. Bharati Mukherjee, however, did not become an apostate. When she left India to settle abroad, Mukherjee carried with her deep ties to her native land and an abiding faith in the Hinduism she had learned from her parents. In her life, as in her fiction, she never resolved the dualities that her childhood had bred in her psyche.

After a successful start to his pharmaceuticals company in Calcutta, Sudhir Lal Mukherjee's business floundered when he and his partner developed differences. In 1947 he moved with his wife and daughters to England, where he engaged in chemical research. His business partner pursued him to England to seek reconciliation and persuaded him to represent the company's interests by continuing his research. The scientific work of Mukherjee's father later took the family to Basel, Switzerland. Part of Mukherjee's childhood was thus spent in London, where she attended a small private school and became proficient in English, and Basel, where she went to a German school. She and her sisters were successful, prizewinning students.

When the family returned to Calcutta in 1951, Sudhir Lal Mukherjee's business was flourishing because of his having developed new drugs for the market. Instead of returning to reside in the joint family home, he moved his wife and daughters into a luxury mansion within his factory compound. The house had all the comforts that money could buy—a lake, a swimming pool, and many servants—but the girls were now isolated from the world of middle-class Kolkata and no longer felt a sense of belonging to the city of their childhood.

Mukherjee's school experience in Calcutta distanced her even further from everyday life in the city and her indigenous cultural ties. She and her sisters were taken to the Loreto Convent School in a chauffer-driven car, accompanied by a bodyguard and sometimes by an escort vehicle to protect them from the violence that was becoming a regular part of life in Calcutta as a result of clashes between labor unions and the privileged classes. Unlike her previous school in

Calcutta, Loreto Convent was not bilingual. The Irish nuns who ran the convent regarded their institution as an extension of England. Like others in her class, Mukherjee took lessons in English elocution and participated in Gilbert and Sullivan operettas.

Mukherjee attended the University of Calcutta, receiving her B.A. degree with honors in English in 1959. She continued her studies at the University of Baroda in western India, earning an M.A. degree in English and ancient Indian culture in 1961. Her education at Baroda gave her a thorough grounding in Indian tradition and heritage, counterbalancing the influence of her earlier Anglicized education, and also enhanced her understanding of the Hindu religious beliefs she had received from her parents.

Mukherjee had displayed an interest in writing from an early age. While in London, she had begun writing a novel about English children. As a student at Loreto Convent, she published short stories based on European history in the school magazine, *Palm Leaves*. In college she decided to become a writer, a decision her father encouraged. After consulting with a visiting American scholar, he wrote to the poet Paul Engle, who at that time was associated with the Creative Writing Program at the University of Iowa. In September 1961, Bharati Mukherjee was admitted to the Writers' Workshop at the university. The following year she received a P.E.O. International Peace Scholarship. In 1963 Mukherjee was awarded an M.F.A. Her thesis, a collection of short fiction, earned her admission to the doctoral program in English.

At the Writers' Workshop, Mukherjee met Clark Blaise, a Canadian American and fellow student, and the couple married during a lunch hour one day in September 1963. Mukherjee has described their relationship as "an intensely literary marriage." Not only do both have distinguished independent careers as writers and academics but also each has influenced the other's work and together they have collaborated on more than one literary venture. Over the years, though sometimes forced to live separately for professional reasons, they have spent most of their time together, raising their two sons and simultaneously pursuing their literary vocation.

In 1964 and 1965 Mukherjee taught English at Marquette University in Milwaukee and at the University of Wisconsin in Madison. In 1966 she moved with her husband to Montreal and took a position as a lecturer at McGill University. She taught while continuing work on her dissertation thesis and earned her Ph.D. in English and comparative literature from the University of Iowa in 1969. Mukherjee remained at McGill until 1980, becoming a full professor by 1978. During her years at McGill, she served as chairwoman of the writ-

ing program and as director of graduate studies in English.

In Mukherjee's first novel, *The Tiger's Daughter* (1972), the central character, Tara, is a Vassar-educated expatriate who returns to India after several years abroad to find a different world from the one she has preserved in her memory. Instead of being comforted by middle-class Brahmin traditions, she is now struck by overwhelming impressions of poverty, hunger, and political turmoil. Much in the novel is clearly autobiographical, as Tara's trajectory, as expatriate revisiting her native country, matches that of her creator and the character known as Tiger is modeled on Mukherjee's own father. Tara's awareness of change and of sharp cultural difference between East and West also parallels Mukherjee's own perceptions about contemporary India. Mukherjee's early fiction shows the influence of English literature, and the writer's appreciation of the work of Jane Austen is apparent in her use of irony and the omniscient point of view in *The Tiger's Daughter*. At the same time, the novel reveals a sense of self that is non-Western, especially in Tara's belief in rebirth and reincarnation.

The Tiger's Daughter drew praise from reviewers for its descriptive qualities and Mukherjee's sharp ear for dialogue. The reviewer for the 29 June 1973 issue of *TLS: The Times Literary Supplement,* though calling it an "elegant first novel," faults its characterization, arguing that because Mukherjee "controls her emotions with such a skilled balance of irony and colourful nostalgia her novel is charming and intelligent—and curiously unmoving." The main problem for the reviewer is Tara, who he asserts "remains so ineffectual a focus" that "it is hard to care whether or not she will be able to return."

In 1973 Mukherjee went on a sabbatical with her husband, spending a year in India, where she began work on *Wife,* her next novel. She received a grant from the Canada Arts Council to support her project. Published in 1975, *Wife* is the story of Dimple Basu, a traditional young woman trained in passivity who submits to an arranged marriage and immigrates to the United States with her husband, an engineer. They reside in New York City, where she lives an idle life, sleeping, watching television, and reading housekeeping journals. Timid and shy, she feels herself threatened by the violence she senses all around her and is afraid to go out alone. Emotionally unhinged, she begins to think of suicide and murder. Eventually, she kills her husband, expressing the rage that has been suppressed within her.

Wife received a mixed reception from reviewers and critics, both in the United States and India. In her review in *Ms.* (October 1975), Rosalind Klass was criti-

Dust jackets for the U.S. edition of Mukherjee's first novel (1972) and her second novel (1975), both of which feature a young Indian woman caught between Indian and Western cultures (Richland County Public Library)

cal of the message of the novel, which she takes as suggesting that stabbing one's husband can solve the problems of an Indian immigrant woman in New York. In her 1985 essay "Foreignness of Spirit: The World of Bharati Mukherjee's Novels" in *Journal of Indian Writing in English,* Indian critic Jasbir Jain argues that what she reads as the indictment in the novel of patriarchy in the Indian social system is undermined because Dimple's mental instability makes her an unreliable point of reference. Others, however, praised Mukherjee's novel for its representation of the plight of Indian expatriates in North America. In his essay on the author for *International Literature in English: Essays on the Modern Writers* (1991) Liew-Geok Leong approved her exploration of "the psychology and geography of displacement." In his 1996 book *Bharati Mukherjee,* Fakrul Alam praised her skillful use of parody in evoking the language of advice columns, advertisements, and talk shows. *Wife* was short-listed for the Governor General's Award in Canada.

The year Mukherjee and Blaise spent in India also yielded a collaborative semi-autobiographical work. *Days and Nights in Calcutta,* written with her husband, was published in 1977. Mukherjee and Blaise created separate records of their responses to India during this visit. The two parts of the book thus recreate their individual experiences in the unusual format of a double journal. For Blaise the journey to India was a voyage of discovery. Initially overwhelmed by visions of squalor, he soon found enchantment in the blend of myth and reality in Indian culture. Mukherjee, however, was bitterly disappointed to find that her memories had misled her. In the traditions she had cherished, she now detected a hidden desire to oppress women; in the upper-class women of her circle, she saw images of what she would have become had she remained in India. Love and sympathy combine with anger and resentment to make her journal a record of an intense struggle with her own dual identity. By the end of her trip, Bharati realized that she thought of herself "more as an immigrant than an exile," because in spite of all the difficulties she faced there, Canada remained the new world where she wanted to live.

Through its formal structure and dual authorship *Days and Nights in Calcutta* conveys the intersection of cultures that is its major theme. In "Bharati Mukherjee as Autobiographer," an essay Emmanuel S. Nelson included in *Bharati Mukherjee: Critical Perspectives* (1993), Pramila Venkateswaran described the complexity of the approach: "Unlike the confessional mode of traditional autobiography, *Days and Nights* occupies the indeterminate area between self-portraiture and journalistic reportage, between autobiography and ethnography, between self-writing and cultural anamnesis." The book combines cultural commentary with personal angst: Mukherjee records, with compelling honesty, a quarrel with her husband during which she charges him with "forcing expatriation" on her. Blaise answers the charge in his section of the narrative, arguing that it would have been impossible for him to live and work in Calcutta, suggesting that for her, at least, life in Canada is feasible.

Though best known as a writer of fiction, Mukherjee has also published several works of nonfiction. *Kautilya's Concept of Diplomacy,* the first of three books she has written on politics in India, appeared in 1976. The following year she was awarded another Canada Arts Council grant and in 1978–1979 a Guggenheim Foundation Award.

Despite her professional success, Mukherjee was increasingly unhappy with her life in Canada. At first, as a newcomer, she had felt like an exile in Canada, tormented by nostalgia for the world she had left behind. She attributed such feelings to an expatriate sensibility, an emotional state in which she felt a sense of superiority to those whom she described as immigrants, who had disowned their former home country without assimilating fully into their new world. After her yearlong visit to India in 1973, Mukherjee's view changed, and she recognized that the new world was where she wanted to be. Her growing unease with racism in Canada, however, made it difficult for her to continue there. In the 1970s the economy of Canada had been affected by rising unemployment and an influx of immigrants from Asia. A wave of resentment against blacks, Indians, and Chinese immigrants swept cities such as Toronto, Montreal, and Vancouver. Despite her professional standing, Mukherjee felt the humiliating effects of racism. For a while she became a civil rights activist, but it soon became clear to her that she would not feel at home in Canada until the government altered its policies on immigration and multiculturalism.

In 1980 Mukherjee and Blaise gave up their tenured positions at McGill, leaving Canada to move to New York. The following year she published the essay "An Invisible Woman" (*Saturday Night,* March 1981), in which she attacked the Canadian policy of multicultur-

alism and described the racism encountered by immigrants in Canada. She describes her own experience of racial discrimination—how she became "a housebound, fearful, aggrieved, obsessive, and unforgiving queen of bitterness"—placing it in the context of the overall situation of Asians in Toronto. "An Invisible Woman" received the second prize at the National Magazine Awards.

Deciding to settle in the United States, Mukherjee became a freelance teacher, taking assignments at several institutions in the area surrounding New York City. She taught at Skidmore College, Mountain State College, Queen's College of the City University of New York, and Columbia University. From 1984 to 1987 she was associate professor at Mountain State College in New Jersey. In 1984 she was also writer-in-residence at Emory University, where she wrote many of the stories included in her first book of short stories.

A collection of twelve short stories, *Darkness* (1985) explores the experience of immigrants and their attempts to come to terms with their memories of their former lives as they negotiate the demands of the present. In the introduction to the collection, Mukherjee describes the stories as a celebration of her own transformation, from the "aloofness of expatriation" to the "exuberance of immigration." In her interview with Hancock, Mukherjee claimed that her literary model for these stories was Bernard Malamud, with his optimistic narratives of minority groups who adapt themselves to the dominant American culture. In a 1988 interview with Alison B. Carb in the *Massachusetts Review,* she rejected V. S. Naipaul's bleak vision of the immigrant experience.

Despite Mukherjee's claim of a positive tone to the collection, *Darkness* includes several stories haunted by the anxiety of expatriation as characters struggle to understand the norms and social codes of an unfamiliar world. The trauma of displacement, coupled with the racism they frequently encounter, generates alienation and despair that sometimes results in confrontations. "Angela" presents the narrative of a Bangladeshi girl adopted by a family in Iowa after she is orphaned during the struggle for her country's independence. In "The World According to Hsu," Ratna Clayton, a Canadian journalist of mixed parentage, tries to communicate her anxieties to her white Canadian husband while they are vacationing on an island off the African coast. "Tamurlane" describes a violent encounter between South Asians working in a Toronto restaurant and a team of Canadian Mounties tracking down illegal immigrants. In "Nostalgia," Dr. Manny Patel, living in New York City with his white American wife and a son, longs for an affair with a girl embodying classical Indian femininity, only to discover that the woman he desires is a prostitute in the pay of a blackmailer. In "A Father," Mr. Bhowmick, a successful metallurgist in Detroit, finds his traditional Indian beliefs and values challenged by his daughter, who becomes impregnated through a sperm bank. "Courtly Vision" offers, through its exposition of a Mughal painting up for auction, an indirect statement of Mukherjee's own artistic credo: for what Emperor Akbar expects of his court painter is nothing less than "*total vision*," "*infinite vistas*," the unsparing truth-telling that Mukherjee sought to achieve in her fiction. In "Isolated Incidents," Mukherjee uses the perspective of Anne Vane, a white Canadian Human Rights Officer, to underscore the cultural misunderstandings that mar even the most well-meaning of interventions by persons belonging to mainstream Canadian society when they seek to solve the problems faced by immigrants. "Isolated Incidents" was awarded the first prize by the Periodical Distributors' Association.

After completing *Darkness,* Mukherjee began working on another collection of short stories, also dealing primarily with Asian immigrants in North America. Aided by a grant from the National Endowment for the Arts, and with a semester off from teaching, she wrote several stories over a period of eight months. Before she could complete the projected volume, however, other events intervened. On 23 June 1985 an Air India jet crashed over Ireland, killing 329 persons, most of whom were South Asian immigrants to Canada. The disaster was attributed to Sikh extremists campaigning for the creation of a new state for themselves in India, but Mukherjee strongly suspected that Canadian immigration policy was an important factor underlying the despicable act. Together with her husband she undertook an investigation into the circumstances surrounding the plane disaster. Beginning in January 1986, Mukherjee and Blaise made weekend trips to Toronto to interview the families of crash victims, police officers, and others involved in the disaster. They also traveled to Montreal, Ottawa, Detroit, and Vancouver to gain a better understanding of the political background to the crash. They studied Canadian government files, media reports and transcripts, and attended the trials for compensation that took place in New York and Toronto. They were present at a ceremony in Ireland, where Irish, Canadian, and Indian officials jointly dedicated a memorial to victims of the airline disaster.

In *The Sorrow and the Terror: The Haunting Legacy of the Air India Tragedy* (1987), Mukherjee and Blaise write that the plane crash was "fundamentally an immigration tragedy with terrorist overtones." The authors take a long view of the factors leading up to the disaster, locating its chief cause in "Canadian immigration and

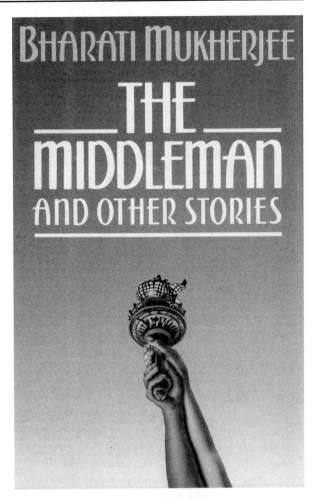

Dust jacket for the U.S. edition of Mukherjee's second collection of stories (1988), her first book published after she became an American citizen (Richland County Public Library)

racial policies reaching back over eighty years." Describing the Canadian policy of multiculturalism "not as an ideal but as an expedient," Mukherjee and Blaise see it as a strategy for excluding nonwhite Canadians from the mainstream. They point out that for the Canadian government, the airline disaster was an Indian, not a Canadian, problem, although most of the victims held Canadian passports.

Though caught up in her memories of Canada, Mukherjee continued with her academic and creative work in the United States. In 1987 she became professor at the City University of New York. Her story "The Tenant" was selected for inclusion in *Best American Short Stories of 1987.* Told from an omniscient perspective, the narrative describes the situation of a Bengali woman seeking stability in the United States.

Mukherjee included "The Tenant" in her next major publication, *The Middleman and Other Stories,* which appeared in April 1988, two months after she had become an American citizen. Written in two intensely creative spells, one immediately after the completion of *Darkness* and the other following the completion of *The Sorrow and the Terror,* these stories focus on changes in American society brought about by the influx of immigrants, especially those from Asia. Mukherjee is particularly interested in the effect of immigration on the American family. In her 1988 interview with Carb, she maintained that "the American family has become very different, not just because of social influences and new sexual standards, but because of the interaction between mainstream Americans and new immigrants."

In contrast to the collection *Darkness,* the tone of *The Middleman and Other Stories* is confident and optimistic, and its settings and characters demonstrate a much greater range. The title story, "The Middleman," presents the first-person narrative of Alfie Judah, a gunman who hails from Iraq. "A Wife's Story" is about the impending rebellion of an Indian wife in America. "Loose Ends" depicts the impact of war on the psyche of Vietnam veteran Jeb Marshall. In "Orbiting" the protagonist is a woman of Italian Spanish parentage who is involved with an Afghan man. Griff, the central character of "Fighting for the Rebound," faces pressure to commit himself to his Filipino girlfriend. "Fathering" presents the perspective of a Vietnam veteran torn between the conflicting demands of his common-law wife in America and his half Vietnamese daughter. "Jasmine" presents American culture viewed through the eyes of a Trinidadian Indian teenager. In "Danny's Girls" an Indian teenager develops an infatuation for a Nepalese mail-order bride. "Buried Lives" is about a man from Sri Lanka who is determined to migrate to Canada. Mrs. Bhave, the Indo-Canadian protagonist of "The Management of Grief," struggles to come to terms with the loss of her family in a plane crash.

The Middleman and Other Stories, which won the National Book Critics Circle Award for Fiction in 1988, was recognized as the work of an artist who was developing her craft and enlarging her vision. In "Love and the Indian Immigrant in Bharati Mukherjee's Short Fiction," an essay included in Nelson's collection of criticism, Mitali R. Pati draws attention to her use of eroticism in her construction of the immigrant psyche: "Desire, both for material advancement and for sexual fulfillment, becomes the central motif in the South Asian immigrants' self-fashioning in the New World." In his essay "Migration and Settlement in North America in Bharati Mukherjee's Fiction," Alam notes that in this collection she "has widened her coverage of the South Asian in the United States to include illegal as well as legal immigrants who have come into the country to remake themselves."

After she became an American citizen, Mukherjee published the essay "Immigrant Writing: Give Us Your Maximalists!" in the 28 August 1988 issue of *The New York Times Book Review.* The essay opens on a note of eager anticipation, referring to the ceremony at a federal district courthouse where she was declared an American citizen. Claiming the right to address older-generation Americans on behalf of "the new Americans from nontraditional immigrant countries," she asserts that persons like herself have altered the definition of what constitutes America. Impatient to establish themselves and rejecting self-effacement, these new immigrants, she maintains, are reshaping American culture.

In 1989, the year she took a position as a distinguished professor at the University of California at Berkeley, Mukherjee published her third novel, *Jasmine,* which was acclaimed by reviewers for its representation of cultural diversity in America. The protagonist of *Jasmine* is reminiscent of her namesake and fictional predecessor, the Trinidadian girl in the eponymous story in the *Middleman* volume. In the novel, however, Jasmine is of Indian origin, and her original name is Jyoti Vijh. Born in rural Punjab in India, she is widowed when her husband is killed by a terrorist bomb. Traveling to New York on forged papers, she adapts to the life of an illegal immigrant. The narrative portrays the stages of her "Americanization," each transition marked by a change of name. The motif of reincarnation recurs in the novel, as Jyoti becomes at different moments in her life, Jasmine, Jase, and, eventually, Jane.

Violence haunts Jasmine's life, transforming her from docile Indian wife to tough-minded American survivor. After she is raped by Half-face, the man who had offered to take care of her during her illegal journey to the United States, she kills him in a blood-spattered ritual that casts her in the role of Kali, the Indian goddess of vengeance and destruction. After a brief spell in an American professor's household where she acts as caregiver, Jasmine becomes Jane, the live-in companion of a crippled bank officer in the Midwest. Together, they adopt a Vietnamese refugee boy. Jasmine, however, continues to harbor romantic dreams of being rescued from her life in the Midwest by "Professorji," her one-time mentor. At the end of the novel, her dream comes true; big with child and full of reckless hope, she abandons her life of duty and sacrifice, running away with Taylor to create a new future. No longer "caught between the promise of America and old world dutifulness," she feels a sense of relief rather than guilt and she brims with optimism: "Adventure, risk, transformation: the frontier is pushing indoors through uncaulked windows. Watch me reposition the stars."

While *Jasmine* was well received by reviewers in the West, Indian critics were more ready to find fault.

In "'In the Presence of History': The Representations of Past and Present Indias in Bharati Mukherjee's Fiction," an essay included in Nelson's *Bharati Mukherjee: Critical Perspectives,* Debjani Banerjee points out that Mukherjee does not provide the necessary context for her reader to understand the separatist movement in the Punjab, instead presenting Sikh activism as mere terrorism. In another essay from the same collection, "Born Again American: The Immigrant Consciousness in *Jasmine,*" Gurleen Grewal appreciates Mukherjee's adaptation of the American pioneer model to the narrative of her female immigrant protagonist but complains that the novel remains based on the false premise that anyone can reinvent himself or herself in America, irrespective of race, gender, or class. In *The Law of the Threshold: Women Writers in Indian English* (1995), Malashri Lal suggests that Mukherjee has created a protagonist who is appealing without being credible: "In the case of Jasmine, the adaptations are unrealistically rapid and clearly superficial . . . Mukherjee has made up a formula which apparently works—Indian characters in search of American citizenship retain sufficient Indianness to be exotic but float gleefully into American materialism."

Mukherjee returned to nonfiction in the early 1990s. In their essay "After the Fatwa: The Satanic Verse Controversy" (*Mother Jones,* April–May 1990), Mukherjee and her husband catalogue a new generation of writers, including Salman Rushdie, Hanif Kureshi, Ben Okri, and Kazuo Ishiguro, who they say question established attitudes toward immigrants. She endorses Fay Weldon's praise of the American "melting pot" theory, which she claims does not produce the fragmented identities generated by Canadian multiculturalism. In "A Four-Hundred-Year-Old Woman," an essay published in *The Writer and her Work* (1991), Mukherjee describes herself as "a four-hundred-year-old woman, born in the captivity of a colonial, pre-industrial oral culture, and living now as a contemporary New Yorker." She finds the American context suitable for the fashioning of hybrid identities, because immigrants there, according to her, are initiated into a fluid reality with great liberating potential. Her position, she says, gives her "a sense of the interpenetration of all things." At the same time, she asserts her aim as a writer is to be accepted as an "American writer, in the American mainstream," seeking to "redefine the nature of *American* and what makes an American." Mukherjee, however, did not forsake writing about India, as her next two books dealt with political issues in her native land: *Political Culture and Leadership in India* (1991) and *Regionalism in the Indian Perspective* (1992).

Mukherjee's next book, *The Holder of the World* (1993), is a novel that combines history and fantasy to

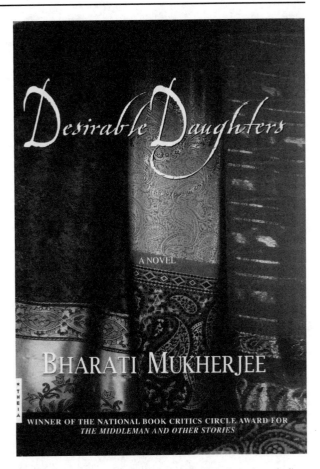

Dust jacket for Mukherjee's 2002 novel, in which she explores the lives of three Calcutta-born sisters who separately leave India, but remain tied to their native culture (Richland County Public Library)

explore the cultures of New England at its founding and South Asia. The novel has two female protagonists: Beigh Masters, a woman of Indian descent in present-day America who specializes in tracking down elusive antiques for collectors; and Hannah Easton, a seventeenth-century inhabitant of the Massachusetts Bay Colony who escapes her Puritan environment to marry an Irish adventurer and eventually becomes the mistress of an Indian raja in the days of Mughal emperor Aurangzeb. Mukherjee contrives to connect these women through Beigh's search for a missing jewel called the Emperor's Tear, which leads her to trace the life story of Salem Bibi, a blonde woman who is shown in the emperor's court in a Mughal miniature painting. Bibi turns out to be none other than Hannah Easton, with whom Beigh develops a strange sense of affinity. Beigh is able to more fully explore her feelings with the help of her lover Venn Iyer, another American of Indian descent, who is a computer scientist involved in a project that uses virtual reality to permit time travel. Apart from sharing biographical parallels such as their New

England background and their respective Indian lovers, Hannah and Beigh turn out to be distantly related. More important, they share a spirit of romance, adventure, passion, and curiosity that draws them away from familiar settings to seek out unknown worlds. In the course of her discovery of Hannah Easton's life, Beigh learns more about her own inner motives and compulsions. The most significant lesson that she learns concerns the connectedness of all people.

In his review of *The Holder of the World* in the 10 October 1993 issue of *The New York Times Book Review*, K. Anthony Appiah says that the novel "reminds us of the interconnections among cultures that have made our modern world." Mukherjee is able to place debates over immigration in the context of a long history of cross-cultural migrations. There are overt literary echoes, most notably of Nathaniel Hawthorne's *The Scarlet Letter* (1850), in Mukherjee's evocation of New England Puritanism. (Hannah Easton's child by her Indian lover is named Pearl, the name of Hester Prynne's daughter in Hawthorne's novel.) The narrative fuses these Western influences with Indian myth, particularly in the transformation of identities and names in ways that suggest rebirth and reincarnation.

Metamorphosis is also the dominant theme in *Leave it to Me* (1996), a novel about the search for identity of a child abandoned by her Indian father and an American hippie mother. Left in a Catholic orphanage in Asia, she is adopted and grows up as Debby DiMartino in a middle-class, Italian American family in Schenectady, New York, "a tall girl in a small school, a beautiful girl in a plain family, an exotic girl in a very American town." Driven by a desire to recover her past and identity, she leaves her adopted parents and sets out to find her biological parents. The quest leads her to San Francisco, where she takes the name Devi Dee and discovers the residue of life in the 1960s in the local counterculture.

Through Debby/Devi's adventures Mukherjee captures the mood of an era when civil disobedience often became an excuse for decadent self-indulgence and the Vietnam War left its mark on an entire generation of Americans. In particular, Mukherjee's narrative focuses on the psychological damage suffered by children who inherited the legacy of the 1960s. The novel is full of violence, merging personal self-discovery with sweeping social critique. She renders authentic American speech rhythms, even as she uses Indian myth to vitalize the dual sensibility of Debby/Devi, a figure straddling two cultures.

Desirable Daughters (2002), a first-person narrative, describes the anguish of Tara, an Indian woman in San Francisco who feels suddenly threatened by the disclosure that her family's past conceals some dark secrets.

After her arranged marriage to an Indian ends in divorce, Tara carves out a life of her own, with her lover, Andy, and her son, Rabi. Her relatively peaceful life is disrupted by the arrival of Chris Dey, a young man who claims to be the unacknowledged illegitimate child of Tara's sister Padma. In an atmosphere of growing danger, Tara delves into the past, trying to seek out the truth about the long-forgotten past that she had shared in India with her two sisters, Padma and Parvati, as daughters of a wealthy tea merchant. The narrative leads back into the days of British rule in rural East Bengal, where Tara's ancestress had become something of a cult figure. The search for connections also revives Tara's memories of life in India with her sisters before each went her separate way. The exploration of Tara's Indian past contrasts with a vibrant rendering of life in contemporary America: the lavish lifestyle of the ultrarich in Silicon Valley, the social scene in suburban New Jersey, and the criminal underbelly of American society that threatens to engulf Tara and her family. The novel ends in a dramatic denouement that leaves Tara reunited with her former husband, but on radically altered terms.

In spite of Mukherjee's avowed affiliation with America, *Desirable Daughters* shows her continued preoccupation with Indian society and traditions. The novel provides a clear autobiographical parallel, as Tara and her sisters, brought up in a privileged but conventional Bengali home, recall Mukherjee's own upbringing in Kolkata. The impulse to immigrate and the ensuing crisis of identity are familiar themes in Mukherjee's fiction. As the mystery unfolds, Tara learns more about herself and her own past, but objective truth remains elusive. The novel presents in both India and the United States highly stratified societies that are threatened by those they seek to ignore or exclude. Padma's escapade with Ronald Dey (the alleged father of Chris) is as unacceptable to her orthodox Hindu family in India as Tara's relationship with Andy is to her millionaire former husband Bish. Both relationships destabilize accepted hierarchies and pose a threat to the precariously sustained social order of a particular time and place.

Reviewers found strengths as well as weaknesses in *Desirable Daughters*. In her review in *India Today* (17 March 2003), Geeta Doctor noted Mukherjee's deliberate exoticization of Indian culture: "It's as if Mukherjee is asked to join an American quilting bee where each woman may contribute a small square in which she is permitted to embroider her own story within the fixed colors of the main design. Their skill is in stitching in pieces of folk wisdom and sequined fragments of exotic scenery that they have kept hidden in the treasure chest of their past life." Ken Forster in the 28 April 2002 *San*

Francisco Chronicle chided Mukherjee for choosing melodrama when "her prose is strong enough to carry subtler shades of storytelling," but he still found the novel compelling: "Readers are certain to pick upon the seismic, rumbling machinations of the plot, but even the most reluctant of them will find it hard to deny the result is compulsively entertaining." Lee Siegel in his review in the *Washington Post* (28 April 2002) detects a pattern in Mukherjee's cultural observations: "The 'desirable daughters' of this novel represent three ways of relating, as South Asian women, to modernity and the West, three ways of understanding the manifold meanings of culture itself."

The immigrant's experience of the clash of cultures and the question of identity the immigrant must face continue to be Mukherjee's major preoccupations. She draws upon multiple cultural traditions, combining ancient Indian philosophy with the modern mythology of the American Dream and the oral folktales of India with the speech rhythms and cultural iconography of contemporary California. She uses violence, a frequent feature of her fiction, as a metaphor for cultural conflict. Her immigrant protagonists undergo changes of identity, metamorphosing according to the demands of the unfamiliar environments in which they find themselves. Fluid identities, name changes, altered personalities—through insistent repetition, these motifs in Mukherjee's fiction come to represent not only modes of personal survival for Asian immigrants but also their ways of altering the American reality of which they seek to become a part.

"Finding the right voice," as she told the *Iowa Review* interviewers, remains the prime feature of Mukherjee's aesthetic: "The sense of voice being the way one controls fiction. Voice can be the sum total of every artistic trick in your bag. It's how to use texture, how to use metaphor, how to choose the right point of view, character, and therefore the idioms, the language." Although she deals with the lives of women who resist imposed destinies, Mukherjee does not think of herself as a feminist: "For some non-white, Asian women, our ways of negotiating power are different. There is no reason why we should have to appropriate—wholesale and intact—the white, middle-class women's tools and rhetoric." Mukherjee rejects the minimalist trend in American art, complaining that American novels concentrate only on personal relationships. Instead, she seeks to locate her characters in the context of social and political realities to create a fuller representation of the immigrant experience.

Although Bharati Mukherjee is not the first author to address the issue of immigration and dual identities, her importance as a writer of the Indian diaspora in the United States is enduring. Her courage and success have helped to inspire a generation of younger authors of South Asian origin, including Jhumpa Lahiri, Shauna Singh Baldwin, and Anita Rau Badami, who write today with confidence about the immigrant experience. As Nelson notes in *Bharati Mukherjee: Critical Perspectives,* "there are many immigrant women writers of colour who share Mukherjee's predicament. What is fascinating, however, is Mukherjee's determined rejection of the emotional paralysis of exile and her enthusiastic affirmation of the immigrant condition; her remarkable success in forging a coherent vision out of the chaos of her multiple displacements; and her ability to articulate that vision in a voice that is as subtle as it is insistent, as graceful as it is provocative."

Interviews:

Geoff Hancock, "An Interview with Bharati Mukherjee," *Canadian Fiction Magazine,* 59 (May 1987): 30–44;

Alison B. Carb, "An Interview with Bharati Mukherjee," *Massachusetts Review,* 29, no. 4 (1988): 645–654;

Michael Connell, Jessie Grierson, and Tom Grimes, "An Interview with Bharati Mukherjee," *Iowa Review,* 20 (Spring 1990): 7–32.

References:

Fakrul Alam, *Bharati Mukherjee* (New York: Twayne, 1996);

Alam, "Migration and Settlement in North America in Bharati Mukherjee's Fiction," *Dhaka University Studies,* 53–54 (December 1996, June 1997) 1–20;

Jasbir Jain, "Foreignness of Spirit: The World of Bharati Mukherjee's Novels," *Journal of Indian Writing in English,* 13 (July 1985): 12–19;

Malashri Lal, *The Law of the Threshold: Women Writers in Indian English* (Shimla: Indian Institute of Advanced Study, 1995);

Liew-Geok Leong, "Bharati Mukherjee," in *International Literature in English: Essays on the Modern Writers,* edited by Robert L. Ross (New York: St. James, 1991), pp. 487–500;

Emmanuel S. Nelson, ed., *Bharati Mukherjee: Critical Perspectives* (New York: Garland, 1993).

R. K. Narayan

(10 October 1906 – 13 May 2001)

Fakrul Alam
University of Dhaka

BOOKS: *Swami and Friends: A Novel of Malgudi* (London: Hamilton, 1935; East Lansing: Michigan State College Press, 1954);

The Bachelor of Arts (London & New York: Thomas Nelson, 1937; East Lansing: Michigan State College Press, 1954);

The Dark Room (London: Macmillan, 1938);

Mysore (Mysore: Government Branch Press, 1939);

Malgudi Days (Mysore: Indian Thought Publications, 1943; expanded edition, New York: Viking, 1982; London: Heinemann, 1982);

The English Teacher (London: Eyre & Spottiswoode, 1945); republished as *Grateful to Life and Death* (East Lansing: Michigan State College Press, 1953);

An Astrologer's Day and Other Stories (London: Eyre & Spottiswoode, 1947);

Mr. Sampath (London: Eyre & Spottiswoode, 1949); republished as *The Printer of Malgudi* (East Lansing: Michigan State University Press, 1957);

The Financial Expert (London: Methuen, 1952; East Lansing: Michigan State College Press, 1953);

Waiting for the Mahatma (London: Methuen, 1955; East Lansing: Michigan State University Press, 1955);

Lawley Road and Other Stories (Mysore: Indian Thought Publications, 1956);

Next Sunday: Sketches and Essays (Mysore: Indian Thought Publications, 1956);

The Guide (London: Methuen, 1958; New York: Viking, 1958; Mysore: Indian Thought Publications, 1958);

My Dateless Diary: An American Journey (Mysore: Indian Thought Publications, 1960);

The Man-Eater of Malgudi (New York: Viking, 1961; London: Heinemann, 1962 [i.e., 1961]; Mysore: Indian Thought Publications, 1968);

Gods, Demons, and Others (New York: Viking, 1964; London: Heinemann, 1965; Mysore: Indian Thought Publications, 1967);

R. K. Narayan (photograph by Joyce Ravid; from the cover for the 1982 American edition of Malgudi Days *[1943]; Richland County Public Library)*

The Vendor of Sweets (New York: Viking, 1967); republished as *The Sweet-Vendor* (London: Bodley Head, 1967);

A Horse and Two Goats (New York: Viking, 1970; London: Bodley Head, 1970; Mysore: Indian Thought Publications, 1970);

The Ramayana: A Shortened Modern Prose Version of the Indian Epic (New York: Viking, 1972; Delhi: Hind Pocket Books, 1972; London: Chatto & Windus, 1973);

My Days: A Memoir (New York: Viking, 1974; London: Chatto & Windus, 1975; Mysore: Indian Thought Publications, 1975);

Reluctant Guru (Delhi: Hind Pocket Books, 1974);

The Painter of Signs (New York: Viking, 1976; London: Heinemann, 1976; Mysore: Indian Thought Publications, 1977);

The Emerald Route (Bangalore: Director of Information and Publicity, Government of Karnataka, 1977);

The Mahabharata: A Shortened Modern Prose Version of the Indian Epic (New York: Viking, 1978; London: Heinemann, 1978; Delhi: Hind Pocket Books, 1978);

A Tiger for Malgudi (New York: Viking, 1983; London: Heinemann, 1983; New Delhi: Allied, 1983);

Under the Banyan Tree and Other Stories (New York: Viking, 1985; London: Heinemann, 1985);

Talkative Man (London: Heinemann, 1986; Mysore: Indian Thought Publications, 1986; New York: Viking, 1987);

A Writer's Nightmare: Selected Essays 1958–1988 (Harmondsworth, U.K., New York & New Delhi: Penguin, 1988);

A Story-Teller's World (New York & New Delhi: Penguin, 1989 [i.e., 1990]);

The World of Nagaraj (Mysore: Indian Thought Publications, 1990; London: Heinemann, 1990; New York: Viking, 1990);

Grandmother's Tale (Madras: Indian Thought Publications, 1992); enlarged as *The Grandmother's Tale: Three Novellas* (London: Heinemann, 1993); enlarged as *The Grandmother's Tale and Selected Stories* (New York: Viking, 1994);

Salt & Sawdust: Stories and Table Talk (New York & New Delhi: Penguin, 1993);

A Malgudi Omnibus (London: Minerva, 1994)—comprises *Swami and Friends, The Bachelor of Arts,* and *The English Teacher;*

The Indian Epics Retold: The Ramayana, the Mahabharata, Gods, Demons, and Others (New York & New Delhi: Penguin, 1995);

More Tales from Malgudi (London: Minerva, 1997)—comprises *Mr. Sampath: The Printer of Malgudi, The Financial Expert, Waiting for the Mahatma,* and *The World of Nagaraj;*

A Town Called Malgudi: The Finest Fiction of R. K. Narayan, edited by S. Krishnan (New York, London & New Delhi: Viking, 1999);

The Magic of Malgudi, edited by Krishnan (New York, London & New Delhi: Viking, 2000)—comprises *Swami and Friends, The Bachelor of Arts,* and *The Vendor of Sweets;*

Memories of Malgudi, edited by Krishnan (New York, London & New Delhi: Viking, 2000)—comprises *The Dark Room, The English Teacher, Waiting for the Mahatma, The Guide,* and *The World of Nagaraj;*

The World of Malgudi, edited by Krishnan (New York & New Delhi: Viking, 2000)—comprises *Mr. Sampath, The Financial Expert, The Painter of Signs,* and *A Tiger for Malgudi;*

The Writerly Life: Selected Non-fiction, edited by Krishnan (New York, London & New Delhi: Viking, 2001).

Editions: *The Guide* (New York: Penguin, 1980);

The Man-Eater of Malgudi (Harmondsworth, U.K.: Penguin, 1983).

OTHER: *Indian Thought: A Miscellany,* edited by Narayan (New York & New Delhi: Penguin, 1997).

When R. K. Narayan died on 13 May 2001 at the age of ninety-four, he left behind a body of work that will continue to impress generations of readers. Surveying Narayan's work, one is struck by the breadth and depth of his achievement. His first novel, *Swami and Friends: A Novel of Malgudi,* was published in 1935, and at the time of his death almost sixty-six years later, Narayan was still writing. In between, he had published novels, short stories, travel books, essays, and retellings of Indian epics, not to mention the articles he had produced as a journalist in his early years. From the 1930s to the early 1990s, when old age finally slowed him down, he managed to write at least three books every decade.

Chronologically, Narayan's fiction takes up the major events of Indian history, including British rule, World War II, the independence movement and the last days of the Raj, Gandhism as a phenomenon, the anxieties and traumas of nation-building, cross-cultural encounters after independence, and ideological debates between tradition and modernity. His characters include schoolboys, college students, teachers, housewives, small tradesmen, lawyers, rogues turned sadhus, taxidermists, dancers, feminists, foreigners in India, and even a tiger who has his own story to tell. Thematically, Narayan deals with such topics as the rites of passage, the education of a young man, a woman's place, death and life, sainthood, destiny and free will, and passivity versus activism. Stylistically, his technique ranges from simple, almost naive, realism to subtle irony. Not averse to using traditional myths and weaving fables into his stories of ordinary people, he is also able to write full-length allegories

*Dust jacket for the 1982 expanded American edition of Narayan's
1943 collection of stories about the fictional town that
provides the setting for most of his work
(Richland County Public Library)*

that manage to be realistic as well and that rely on experiments with narrative perspectives.

Rasipuram Krishnaswami Narayan was born on 10 October 1906 in his grandfather's home in Madras, the son of R. V. Krishnaswami Iyer and Gnana Iyer. His father was a schoolteacher in Mysore. Narayan spent the early years of his life in Madras in the care of his grandmother and a maternal uncle, joining his parents mainly during vacations. In *My Days: A Memoir* (1974), the novelist notes that his grandmother was a major influence on his life and storytelling. The maternal uncle, who published a literary journal in Tamil, also played a part in the growth of the novelist's mind in these years.

Narayan first went to school in Madras. In 1922 he was shifted to the school in Mysore where his father was the headmaster. *My Days* indicates that Narayan was an indifferent student but an avid reader

in his childhood. He failed the school entrance examination twice and also was unable to get through college easily. Eventually he graduated from Maharaja College of Mysore with a B.A. degree in 1930.

Narayan began to write seriously in the 1920s. In *R. K. Narayan: The Early Years: 1906–1945* (1996), his biographers Susan Ram and N. Ram describe his intense desire to see his name in print and the hard work he did, not only reading major English writers and periodicals but also going through books on how to sell one's manuscripts. He soon got accustomed to receiving rejection slips from publishers and newspaper editors; however, Narayan continued to harbor hopes of making a living as a writer, until his father persuaded him to take up a teaching position in a school. The experience proved distasteful to him, and he soon resumed corresponding with English publishers for his manuscripts. He eventually succeeded in getting an article on the Indian cinema published in the *Madras Mail* in July 1930.

In his memoir, Narayan recalls that he was wandering the streets of Mysore one day at this time of his life when Malgudi, the setting of most of his fiction, just seemed to "hurl" into his mind while he was thinking of a name for a railway station for one of his works. Along with the station, he had a vision then of a character called Swaminathan. He thus began his first novel, *Swami and Friends,* completing it two years later. Meanwhile, he managed to get a short story titled "A Night in a Rest House" published in *The Indian Review* (August 1932). What was even more satisfying was seeing a short satirical piece that he wrote called "How to Write an Indian Novel" appear in *Punch* on 27 September 1933.

That year he also fell in love with a fifteen-year-old girl named Rajam Iyer, whom he spotted as she was waiting to fill water in a brass vessel from a street tap. Too shy to approach her, he persuaded his father to send a proposal of marriage to her father. However, their horoscopes did not match as required by religious custom. Not deterred by this obstacle, Narayan had his father find a way around it. He married Rajam on 1 July 1934. Around this time, he also became the Mysore reporter of a newspaper called *The Justice.*

When Narayan had finished *Swami and Friends* in 1932, the odds against an Indian publishing English fiction in England were still high. Conscious that his book would not find a publisher in his country and failing to get a positive response from the English publishers to whom he had sent the manuscript, sometime in 1934 Narayan contacted his friend Krishna Raghavendra Putra, who was then studying at Oxford. When Putra at first had no luck getting publishers to respond, Narayan told his friend to throw the manuscript into the Thames. Instead, Putra persuaded the famous English novelist Graham Greene, who was already attempting to get some of Narayan's short stories published in English magazines, to take a look at *Swami and Friends*. Greene was so impressed that he recommended the book to the publisher Hamish Hamilton. After suggesting a few changes, including the title (originally "Swami, the Tate"), Hamilton agreed to publish the novel. It appeared in October 1935, and Malgudi was launched as a fictional place to be mentioned almost in the same breath as Thomas Hardy's Wessex, William Faulkner's Yoknapatawpha County, or Gabriel García Márquez's Macondo.

Swami and Friends is a fictional account of Narayan's childhood. Although modeled on Mysore, Malgudi could be any midsize provincial town in the Indian subcontinent progressing through the twentieth century. Swaminathan, the titular character, grows up against the backdrop of colonial rule and the resistance movement that had already gained momentum throughout the subcontinent. His relationships with schoolmates and family members are rendered with great charm and humor in the novel. The deftness with which Narayan presents the mind of a young boy moving toward adolescence and the skill with which the novelist introduces readers to life in a provincial town make the novel noteworthy.

Typical of the few reviews that greeted the novel in England is the comment of the reviewer of the *Morning Post* (3 December 1935) that *Swami and Friends* is "a portrait of childhood pure and simple." The review in the *Daily Mail* (7 November 1935) was in the same vein: the work was "an entirely delightful story about life in an Indian school with equally vivid glimpses of life in Indian homes." But Narayan's biographers point out that although the reviews of the book were almost all favorable, the book was a failure if judged on the basis of its sales and the fact that Hamish Hamilton declined to be Narayan's publisher in the future.

Nevertheless, Narayan was buoyed by the fact that he had published a book in England and by the laudatory reviews. He began work on his second novel, *The Bachelor of Arts* (1937), as soon as the first one had been accepted for publication. While he was working on it, his wife gave birth to the couple's only child, a girl called Hema, in February 1936. The novel was completed by March of that year. Narayan sent the manuscript to Greene along with a collection of short stories. Greene was once again enthusiastic and found a literary agent for Narayan in the London firm of Pearn, Hollinger, and Higham. The novel was chosen for publication by Thomas Nelson and Sons and came out in March 1937.

The Bachelor of Arts is a fictional rendering of another phase of the writer's life. The protagonist, Chandran, is an undergraduate student in a missionary college. The resistance movement against the British presence seems to have intensified in the novel, and there is a lot of talk about political reforms, much anticolonial rhetoric, and ideas about the future course of Indian history aired by a few of the characters. However, the main focus of the novel is again on the protagonist's emotional growth, this time from adolescence to manhood. In the first part of the novel Chandran's relationships with friends and family members as well as his teachers are presented endearingly. In the middle part of the book Narayan depicts Chandran in love with a girl called Malathi. He feels intensely for her even though he has only seen her from a distance, but he becomes obsessive about her to the point that he clashes with his parents, who initially will not allow him to marry the girl because of her father's social standing. Even after they relent, he comes across another obstacle that he fails to overcome: the horoscopes of Chandran and Malathi do not match, and so the marriage cannot take place. In the final part of the novel, the frustrated Chandran leaves Malgudi and becomes for some time a mendicant, opting for the life of a holy man to assuage his grief. But he eventually realizes that he has made the wrong decision by deserting his family and has been guilty of self-deception in thinking that he could be a holy man. The chastened Chandran returns to his parents and is finally ready to settle down and marry a girl of their choosing.

The Bachelor of Arts was more widely reviewed than *Swami and Friends,* and the critics were as appreciative of the book as the reviewers of the first novel had been. The novel came with an enthusiastic introduction by Greene, who compared the Indian writer to Anton Chekhov. The combination of favorable reviews and Greene's endorsement meant that the novel did somewhat better in terms of sales than the previous one, but it still fell far short of being a success in the literary marketplace.

Narayan began work on his third novel, *The Dark Room* (1938), soon after the second was in print. He was able to send the typescript to Greene by October 1937. Greene was once more positive in his response to the book. Because the publishing house of Nelson declined to publish the new work, Narayan's agent had to locate a new publisher for him and found one in Macmillan in 1938.

The Dark Room shows Narayan moving away from autobiographical fiction. It is also unusual in Narayan's canon because it has a female protagonist. The novel has an almost tragic quality as it portrays

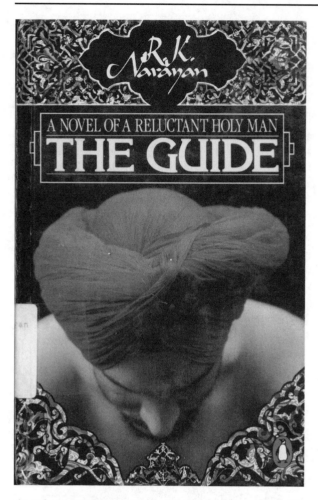

Cover for a 1980 American edition of Narayan's 1958 novel, one of his best-known works, about a rogue who is taken for a holy man and spiritual leader despite his attempts to dissuade the villagers by telling the story of his shady past (Richland County Public Library)

the unfulfilled life of Savitri, a woman married to an uncaring but rich husband. In *My Days,* Narayan explains the frame of mind that led him to write *The Dark Room:*

> I was somehow obsessed with a philosophy of woman as opposed to man, her constant oppressor. This must have been an early testament of the "Woman's Lib" movement. Man assigned her a secondary place and kept her there with such subtlety and cunning that she herself began to lose all notion of her independence, her individuality, stature, and strength. A wife in an orthodox milieu of Indian society was an ideal victim of such circumstances. My novel dealt with her, with this philosophy broadly in the background.

Deeply unhappy after fifteen years of married life, and because she finds out that her husband was having an affair with an employee in his office, Savitri decides to

drown herself in the river. But a locksmith-thief who takes her to his home prevents her from taking her life. She then finds employment in the village temple, but the priest is a disagreeable character, and she feels totally depressed about staying without her children. In the end, therefore, she returns to her home and to the dark room that Fate seems to have set aside for her so that she could resume the role of Savitri—the Hindu archetype of the long-suffering, all-sacrificing wife.

Like the previous novels, *The Dark Room* was a success with the English critics when it was published. Typical of the laudatory reviews was John Brophy's comment in the *Daily Telegraph* (4 November 1938) that it was "a short, poignant, delicately shaped and finished novel . . . entirely convincing and charming in its reticent sympathy." In India, too, most critics praised the novel, as they had his first two books. The critic K. R. Srinivasa Iyengar, for example, found it to be a carefully and sensitively done portrait of middle-class South Indian society and compared Savitri to the heroine of Henrik Ibsen's *A Doll's House* (1879), though he concluded Narayan's presentation of Savitri is not a match for the Norwegian dramatist's portrait of Nora. Some Indian reviewers, however, were critical of Narayan's depiction of an Indian marriage, perhaps because, as his biographers indicate, the theme of the mistreated wife was bold for its period.

This novel did as poorly in terms of sales as the first two. Narayan was thus happy to find a regular outlet for his short fiction in the Madras daily, *The Hindu.* He also received a commission from the Mysore government to write a book on the state, and he researched extensively to write *Mysore* (1939), a travel narrative interspersed with historical events. Even though he received little money for this project, it allowed him to know Mysore even more intimately.

In June 1939 Narayan entered the darkest period of his life: five years into his marriage, his wife died after a short illness of what was probably typhoid. Overwhelmed with grief, he stopped writing for a while and withdrew into himself. He finally managed to get out of his depression, partly because he had to look after his daughter, but also because he felt that he had succeeded in renewing contact with Rajam through séance sessions. But although he slowly resumed normal activities, the outbreak of World War II impeded literary activity. Also, because Greene became inaccessible then, owing to his involvement in the war effort, Narayan found paths to publishing doubly difficult.

Narayan managed to sustain himself in this difficult period through his journalism and by giving talks on Madras radio. In 1941 he found a further outlet for his work and another vocation when he became the editor of a journal called *Indian Thought*. Although the periodical proved to be short-lived, the move was important for Narayan's career because it led him ultimately to publish his works in India through his own imprint, Indian Thought Publications. In the first half of the 1940s, three collections of his short stories as well as *Swami and Friends* and the travelogue *Mysore* came out in low-priced editions under this imprint. In the process, Narayan became one of the pioneers in publishing South Asian writing in English.

By 1944 Narayan had finished writing his fourth and most autobiographical novel, *The English Teacher* (1945). This novel is about Krishna, who teaches English in the missionary college that Chandran had graduated from and who vacillates between writing in English and Tamil. It is also a tale about Krishna's family life and bereavement after the death of his wife. Despite their different protagonists, *Swami and Friends*, *The Bachelor of Arts*, and *The English Teacher* can be read together to present the story of the novelist as a boy, a young man, and an adult. The autobiographical connections can be easily made by anyone who has read Narayan's memoir, *My Days*, even though Narayan inevitably fictionalized his experiences throughout the novels.

The English Teacher can be divided into two parts. The first half of the novel depicts Krishna's delight in his personal life and the satisfaction he derives from his marriage to Susila and the birth of his daughter. The second half presents his initial sense of shock and overwhelming grief at the sudden death of his wife and his efforts to reconcile himself to her loss by attempting spiritual communion with her. The movement of the novel is from bliss to grief to an affirmation of love that can transcend death. Near the end, the protagonist offers a bleakly cyclical vision of life:

> Wife, children, brothers, parents, friends. . . . We come together only to go apart again. It is one continuous movement. They move away from us as we move away from them. The law of life can't be avoided. The law comes into operation the moment we detach ourselves from our mother's womb. All struggle and misery in life is due to our attempt to arrest the law or get away from it or in allowing ourselves to be hurt by it. The fact must be recognized. A profound unmitigated loneliness is the only truth of life.

However, the novel concludes with Krishna feeling that he had united with Susila in a mystic moment.

Of Narayan's early novels, *The English Teacher* was easily the most popular. It was widely praised and sold well in England. Writing in the Glasgow *Evening News* (29 October 1945), Compton Mackenzie declared it to be "an exquisite experience." A review

in *The Spectator* (12 October 1945) found the novel to be "quite out of the ordinary run." It was the first Narayan novel to be published in the United States: Michigan State College Press brought it out as *Grateful to Life and Death* in 1953. After the success of this work, Narayan found it much easier to get publishers for his works, and his reputation in the West as well as in India began to grow steadily.

The English Teacher closed one phase of Narayan's career, since it is the last of his novels that depended mostly on the writer's life as the chief source of the narrative. In the next phase of his work as a novelist, he broadened his vision to depict individuals from all parts of society and convey the comic aspects of life as well as its tragic, heartrending moments. Having come to terms with the death of his wife and having achieved a measure of financial stability, he settled into a routine of writing, parenting, and taking the occasional trip out of Mysore. He built his own house in 1948 and saw his daughter get married in 1956. That year he was in the United States for an extended period of time and records his travels there in *My Dateless Diary: An American Journey* (1960). The critic William Walsh quotes Narayan as saying in 1974 that by then his life "had fallen firmly into a professional pattern: books, agents, contracts, and plenty of letter writing" in addition to visiting his daughter and grandchildren, who lived a hundred miles away.

After *The English Teacher*, Narayan began to draw on his contacts with people in the outside world for his novels. He also attempted to enrich his presentation of individuals, as he had done before with Savitri in *The Dark Room*, by searching for character archetypes in the Hindu holy books. As he observes in his essay "English in India," reprinted in *A Story-Teller's World* (1989), it was necessary to look "at the gods, demons, sages, and kings of our mythology and epics, not as some remote concoctions but as types and symbols, possessing psychological validity even when seen against the contemporary background." Narayan was ready to embark on a major fictional phase of his career, in which he went beyond autobiography and combined his experience of people and places with the founding myths of his nation as well as his thoughts about an India coping with the dawning of independence.

Mr. Sampath (1949), the first novel that Narayan wrote after India's independence, combines his knowledge of the motion-picture world (derived from a stint as a scriptwriter in the late 1940s) with his newfound interest in Indian myths. The novel is an ambitious attempt to represent Malgudi in the final years of British rule and to connect it with a mythical period of Indian history, arriving at a complex perspective on

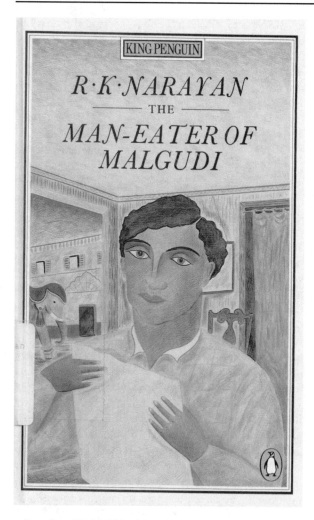

Cover for a 1983 British edition of Narayan's 1961 comic novel, in which a mild-mannered printer is perplexed by his tenant, a demonic taxidermist (Richland County Public Library)

successive waves of colonization. The protagonist, Srinivas, is a rather confused but likable journalist who turns to scriptwriting for a movie on the god Shiva, the god's love for Parvithi, and his encounter with Kama, the god of love. But Srinivas's bid to come up with a script that would do justice to the mythical tale fails, apparently because the ancient tales cannot be presented in the contemporary world except in an adulterated form. The quotidian, too, constantly diverts Srinivas from the mythical past. In a vision, Srinivas learns the essential lesson about the perspective to be taken on what was happening in the country: "Dynasties rose and fell. Palaces and mansions appeared and disappeared. The entire country went down under the fire and sword of the invader.... But it always had its rebirth and growth." In other words, Indian history existed in a state of flux, and change

was inevitable, as was the resilience of India and Indians.

The titular character is an egotistical, domineering, and amoral printer with whom Srinivas has to work to bring out his journal. Sampath is the one who leads Srinivas away from journalism to the movie industry. But Sampath's energy and egotism as well as lack of scruples create a mess that is further complicated by the unstable studio artist Ravi's passion for the actress Shanti, who has an affair with Sampath. In his vitality as well as selfishness, Sampath becomes a forerunner of other Narayan characters who disrupt social life because of their egotism and indifference to others or the norms of society. He thus stands in contrast with Srinivas, who, as the critic A. Hariprasana observes, "realizes that he cannot achieve self-identity in isolation" and learns to value the importance of becoming involved "in the web of human relationships" and of restraint and self-knowledge as precursors to the coming of wisdom.

The Financial Expert (1952), Narayan's next novel, uses Hindu myths creatively. The book is a realistic novel of Malgudi in the 1930s and early 1940s as well as an effective fable. Margayya, its protagonist, has acquired a fortune by publishing a quasi-pornographic book whose rights he had purchased for a paltry sum from the eccentric Dr. Pal, and he continues to raise money through questionable means. But he forgets the injunction of a priest who had cautioned him that one cannot appease Saraswati, the goddess of knowledge, and Lakshmi, the goddess of wealth, at the same time. Margayya tries to buy his son, Balu, an education by making himself the head of the school board and by neutralizing the fiercest teacher of the school. The result, however, is that Balu ends up a totally spoiled individual, indifferent to education, work, or the wife Margayya chooses for him.

Margayya discovers thus that all his wealth does not bring happiness either to him or to his wife and only corrupts his son. Narayan's point in the novel is a simple but profound one: true riches can never accrue when one makes money into a god or pursues dubious paths to wealth. At the conclusion of the novel, Margayya has lost all the wealth he had acquired from his financial shenanigans, but in the process he has learned that money is not everything. When he had wealth, he lacked enlightenment; when he loses everything he has acquired illicitly, he comes closer to self-knowledge. The novel ends as it begins, with Margayya ready to resume his old profession of adviser to peasants seeking help; but he appears to have learned his lesson and seems ready to start again in life.

The Financial Expert shows Narayan the novelist at his best in the way he handles the central theme of the vanity of human wishes, in his deft manipulation of events and structuring of the events in Margayya's life, and in the portrait of the central character, who is deeply flawed but also all too human and thus capable of retaining the reader's sympathy. The novel is memorable too for the portraits of Dr. Pal, the archetypal confidence man; Meenakshi, Margayya's long-suffering wife; and Balu, his prodigal son. Margayya's rise and fall take place against a backdrop of a world full of poverty, corruption, red tape, and the opportunism displayed by cynical businessmen and officials in wartime India. Narayan manages to be serious and comic throughout the novel; he also alternates details of everyday life in Malgudi with moments when readers get to view the workings of Margayya's mind. The critic William Walsh writes that the novel "has an intricate and silken organization, a scheme of composition holding everything together in a vibrant and balanced union."

Narayan followed *The Financial Expert* with his most political novel: *Waiting for the Mahatma* (1955). Written eight years after India's independence and the death of Mohandas Karamchand Gandhi, this work portrays in considerable detail the years leading to the partition of India. It is something of a postmortem on the roles played by Gandhi and his followers in the independence struggle and the way in which India had become vulnerable afterward because many Indians had not taken Gandhi's message of nonviolence and communal harmony to heart. Sriram, the central character, joins the freedom movement not because of his devotion to Gandhi but because of his passion for the Gandhian activist Bharati. Nevertheless, he becomes involved in almost all the major events leading to Indian independence and even goes to jail for taking part in a terrorist movement aimed at driving the British from India.

Narayan suggests through this novel that the bloodshed and divisiveness that accompanied the partition of India was inevitable, because people driven by personal passions and self-interest had cast the great leader's message aside. In the novel, except for Bharati, no one appears to be in the freedom struggle for love of India or seems inclined to follow Gandhi's teachings faithfully. The consequence is that post-independence India is, if anything, in worse condition than it was when the British had left it, for it has become a land full of religious riots, hunger, and unscrupulous politicians like the unprincipled Jagadish, a former terrorist who is now thriving financially. The novel concludes with Gandhi's assassination, although the great man blesses Sriram's marriage to Bharati before he is shot, suggesting that perhaps the couple will be able to keep Gandhi's spirit alive despite the many who have deviated from his philosophy and idealism.

Perhaps Narayan's most famous novel is his subsequent one, *The Guide* (1958), a work he wrote while he was in Berkeley, California, during his visit to America in 1958. It is the story of Raju, a scamp who ends up being perceived as a savior by many people. When the novel begins, he has just been released from jail. He wanders into a small town, where he finds Velan, a villager who is soon convinced that he has confronted a holy man and makes himself Raju's disciple. Soon after the meeting, Raju tries to dissuade Velan from hero worship by telling him the story of his life. While Raju relates to Velan his progress—from a wide-eyed child to the owner of a railway stall, a tourist guide, the lover and impresario of the classical dancer Rosie, and finally a jailbird—the narrator punctuates Raju's story by showing his dealings with Velan and the villagers who embrace him as a spiritual guide capable of leading the village out of a drought through a penitential fast. Raju's purpose in telling his story to Velan is to demystify his spiritual powers and to emphasize his shady past. Velan, however, is unmoved by the story and continues to see Raju as a guru. After Raju concludes his narrative, the omniscient narrator takes sole charge of the narration duties. The conclusion shows a Raju who may or may not be at the point of achieving transcendence.

Characteristically, Narayan interlaces the story of Raju with frequent references to Hindu theology. *The Guide* sets out to compare Raju's progress to that of Devaka, a man from India's legendary past, whose story Raju's mother used to tell him before the child used to doze off, so that he never could come to learn the ending, and so that as an adult, he could only remember that Devaka was "a hero, saint, or something of the kind." Also, Raju's excessive lust for sex and wealth and his taste for a life of luxury are precisely the sins Hindu metaphysical tradition cautions against, because giving in to such desires means forgetting that the world is *maya* (an illusion) and losing sight of the belief that a man must transcend this world by showing *bhakti* (true devotion).

The Guide is Narayan's most popular book, partly because of its witty presentation of Raju's character and partly because of its intricate narrative technique of the first-person account of Raju alternating with the omniscient narrator's presentation of the lovable rogue who becomes unwittingly a hero. The novel is also memorable because of its presentation of Rosie, who grows in stature throughout the work: she begins as a bored housewife who enters into an adul-

Dust jacket for the American edition of Narayan's 1967 novel, about the conflict between a traditional businessman and his son, who has married a Korean American woman and wants to market new ideas (Richland County Public Library)

terous relationship with Raju, but by the time the novel ends, she has become a classical dancer of repute.

Typical of the praise heaped on the novel and its writer is the comment made by Anthony West in *The New Yorker* (19 April 1958): "*The Guide* is the latest, and the best, of R. K. Narayan's enchanting novels about the South Indian town of Malgudi and its people. . . . It is a profound statement of Indian realities." *The Guide* won India's highest literary prize, the Sahitya Akademi Award, in 1960. The novel was also made into a highly popular movie in 1965 that made Narayan even more famous in India. However, he disapproved of the script and distanced himself from it because he felt it had vulgarized his work.

Narayan followed *The Guide* with another triumph: *The Man-Eater of Malgudi* (1961). It is the story of Nataraj, an amiable and docile printer of Malgudi, who encounters Vasu, a taxidermist from outside the

town who takes over Nataraj's attic to use it as a base for his grisly profession. Vasu is brisk, powerfully built, egotistical, and totally indifferent to the community's values. Narayan implies in his narrative that Vasu is a *rakshasha,* the type of demon who challenged the gods themselves. Nataraj's assistant Sastri, well-versed in Indian myths, even views Vasu as Bhasmasura, the demon of Indian myth who blights everything he touches, defies the heavens, and puts humanity into peril. But Bhasmasura is also an overreacher whose pride results in self-annihilation. In the novel, too, Vasu self-destructs when he inadvertently kills himself while squashing a mosquito that had landed on his forehead.

But *The Man-Eater of Malgudi* is also the story of its narrator, Nataraj, who is initially a passive character. He prefers to spend his time in the first part of the novel by chatting with his friends but is transformed by his contact with Vasu and the latter's intimidating ways into taking the offensive to contain "the man-eater of Malgudi." Thus, in the concluding parts of the novel Nataraj finds himself acting more like Vasu. He even wonders if in a fit of aggression he had been instrumental in cornering the taxidermist, perhaps thereby forcing himself to self-destruct.

Narayan presents the Vasu-Nataraj relationship against the backdrop of everyday life in Malgudi and a cast of idiosyncratic minor characters. His skill in depicting life in a midsize provincial town of India is evident. *The Man-Eater of Malgudi* is also a funny novel and reveals Narayan's delight in the human comedy. Narayan's technique in the work is an unobtrusive one as he takes readers from the tranquil opening to the frenzied climax of the story. Like *The Guide,* this book was received enthusiastically on publication. Donald Barr commented in *The New York Times Book Review* (12 February 1961): "it is classical art, profound and delicate art, profound in feeling and delicate in control."

Narayan's next novel, *The Vendor of Sweets* (1967), once again appears to set up tradition against disruptive Western influences. V. S. Naipaul sees the novel as characteristic of Narayan's work because of its theme: "there is a venture into the world of doing, and at the end there is a withdrawal." Tradition and the unchanging Indian world is here represented by Jagan, the vendor of sweets, and modernity by his son Mali, who has come back from America with Grace, a Korean American woman, and innovative business schemes. The novel is set in the 1960s, but Jagan keeps thinking about India's Gandhian past and his role in it as an activist inspired by the Mahatma. Jagan, a traditionalist by instinct, also treasures, paradoxically, mementos of the Raj as well as Indian greats, valuing the works of William Shakespeare as well as those of Rabindranath Tagore.

As Ashok Berry has stressed, Narayan is setting up an opposition between tradition and modernity in a way that will invert "the dominant hierarchy." Thus, the novel concludes with Jagan retreating from the world of Mali and Grace, but he does not forget to take his checkbook with him. Jagan also approves of Grace and is only upset because his son had backed off from his promise to marry her. While Naipaul says that the novel concludes with Jagan's withdrawal from modernity, Berry emphasizes Narayan's complex perspective on the novel when he says that it is "precisely about accommodating imperfection and hybridity. By destabilizing ideas of purity, it paves the way for different conceptions of identity."

Although not as successful as either *The Guide* or *The Man-Eater of Malgudi*, *The Vendor of Sweets* reveals Narayan's gift for characterization, as Jagan is a complex creation: comic, shrewd, and vain but also an idealist and a caring father whose loneliness attracts the reader's compassion. The portrait of Mali and his scheme of marketing a storytelling machine is Narayan's way of satirizing harebrained business ideas and uncritical acceptance of Western values, but Grace is portrayed with sympathy and understanding. The novel, typically, reveals the changing world of Malgudi, where cross-cultural exchanges take place even as the traditional values of the *Bhagavad Gita*, the Hindu sacred text that is Jagan's constant companion, continue to be a guide for people of his generation.

Narayan's subsequent novel, *The Painter of Signs* (1976), is one of his most impressive longer works of fiction. It echoes many of Narayan's earlier novels in its themes as well as its structure. The plot—about an obsessive young man, Raman, who pursues Daisy, a woman dedicated to easing overpopulation, the national issue of the 1970s—echoes *Waiting for the Mahatma*, which was about Sriram's single-minded pursuit of the zealous Gandhian, Bharati. Throughout the novel Raman broods on philosophical as well as topical issues, as did Srinivas of *Mr. Sampath*. Like Rosie of *The Guide*, Daisy is a modern woman, not afraid of transgressing conventional notions of morality in pursuit of her vocation. However, Daisy is even more independent minded than Rosie, for in the end she makes a clean break from Raman, something Narayan's earlier women seemed unable or unwilling to do. As Sadhana Allison Puranik points out, such a "radical overturning of convention" indicates that there is a subversive element in Narayan even though it coexists with "his love of traditional elements of Indian life and art." Puranik also stresses the political dimension of the novel and its contemporaneity: con-

necting Daisy's fanaticism about family planning with Indira Gandhi's excesses in enforcing it in India, Puranik thinks that "Narayan implicitly criticizes the attitude of cultural extremism apparent in the government's domestic policies."

As if to mark the change in Indian mores, the novel is much more explicit about sexuality than Narayan's other longer works of fiction. Also, Narayan seems more reform minded in this novel than in his earlier works. Daisy appears to have no inclination to be like Savitri from *The Dark Room*, and Narayan shows her leaving conventional notions of womanhood behind altogether. While it is too much to say that Narayan endorses Daisy's independence totally or upholds the ideology of the single woman or family planning unambiguously, the novel accepts her modernity to a great extent and shows her ideas gaining acceptance among quite a few women even when they conflict with other upholders of tradition.

Narayan's twelfth novel, *A Tiger for Malgudi* (1983), is distinctive in having a protagonist who is a tiger. He is called Raja, and he narrates the story of the spiritual changes he undergoes. In the introduction to the novel, Narayan writes that the idea of adopting such an unusual point of view came to him when he saw a tiger accompanying a sadhu in the Hindu Kumbh Mela, a major Hindu festival. What struck him in particular was that the tiger was not on a leash, and that the holy man accounted for the tiger's freedom by saying "they were brothers in previous lives." This encounter led Narayan to think about the tiger's perspective on life—which, he would have readers believe, evolved not unlike that of human beings. The book presents details of Raja's life as a cub, his brashness as he arrives at his physical peak, his capture and conversion into the star attraction of a circus, his "elevation" into a celebrity after being cast in movie roles, his escape from captivity, and his adoption by an ascetic. This sagacious man's views give Raja insight into life and death, making him appreciate that "separation is the law of life right from the mother's womb" and thus has to be accepted as part of God's plans for all animals. He also accepts the notion that one should free oneself from worldly attachments. Raja ends up in a zoo but appears to have achieved enlightenment and a mature acceptance of life. Because the protagonist is a tiger, the novel often strikes a comic note.

A Tiger for Malgudi was the last of Narayan's novels to receive wide critical attention. But it got mixed reviews, and a few critics recorded their disappointment with it. Writing in *The New York Times Book Review* (4 September 1983), for example, Noel Perrin noted that the book is "distinctly not drenched with humanity" and that "most of the flavor of Malgudi is

Dust jacket for a 1994 collection, in which the title novella (first published in 1992) is Narayan's recounting of his great-grandmother's determined and successful search for her missing husband (Richland County Public Library)

missing." Similarly, Carlo Coppola observed in a review in *World Literature Today* (Spring 1984) that although there are good things in the book, "in the last analysis . . . the novel falls short of Narayan's best achievements (viz., *The Financial Expert, The Guide, The Man-Eater of Malgudi*) because the author fails to convince us of the final phase of Raja's quest."

Narayan was eighty years old when he published his next novel, *Talkative Man,* in 1986. This story is another take on a theme that fascinated him throughout his career as a novelist: the fate of the long-suffering Indian wife. Although Malgudi has changed, the wife of this tale, Sarasa, continues to suffer because of her indifferent and philandering husband, the confidence man Rann, who claims to be working for the United Nations. She is financially independent, but she cannot part from him despite his obtuseness and tendency to abandon her. In her determination to stick to him, she is, in some ways, like

Savitri of *The Dark Room*. The novel is of interest because of the titular character, the talkative man, a persona Narayan has used in many of his short fictions to reveal his delight in raconteurs and their garrulousness, which at times makes them sound comically gullible.

Narayan published his last novel, *The World of Nagaraj* (1990), four years after *Talkative Man*. The title character follows a holy man who has renounced the world and is bent on leaving it behind, freeing himself from the world of the senses so that he can concentrate fully on God. Nagaraj, too, appears to be preparing himself for forsaking earthly attachments and welcoming death. Nevertheless, Nagaraj continues to be dragged back into the quotidian because of his spoiled nephew Tim, who has a nose for trouble and involves Nagaraj in his problems. This entanglement makes him unable to renounce the world effectively, putting him in contrast with the mythical sage Narada, who has given up all earthly desires for the benefit of humanity at large.

The last long work of fiction that Narayan published in his lifetime is *Grandmother's Tale* (1992). It is essentially a novella, but the author himself points out in an explanatory note that it is a work located in "the borderline between fact and fiction, between biography and tale," and between family history and quest narrative. In it Narayan retells his great-grandmother's search for her husband, who had disappeared after telling her "laconically" one day, "I am going away." Re-creating the world of nineteenth-century India, where women were forced to lead much more confined lives than characters such as Sarasa of *Talkative Man,* this novel shows the triumph of Narayan's great-grandmother's love and the indomitable spirit that led her to her husband and allowed her to end her life happily.

Among Narayan's strengths as a novelist are the economy of his storytelling and the skill with which he manipulates his plot so that events that complicate the lives of his central characters are resolved within a couple hundred pages. Narayan is also a master of shorter forms of fiction, and he brought out five collections of short stories, most of them published first in the Madras newspaper *The Hindu.* They cover the same territory as the novels; indeed, the first collection was called *Malgudi Days* (1943). The stories of the early collections are slight pieces and usually reportorial in style, lacking the plotted quality of the novels. Some are anecdotal or no more than character sketches. The stories of the later collections are longer and more intricately built. Usually they show people as fallible, eccentric, or merely amusing. Some are about animals, and some present children and deal with the theme of growing up. Most often Narayan uses the short story to depict ordinary people in everyday situations with a light touch but also in a manner that reminds readers that his mission is to be the chronicler of Indian life. He registers the poverty of Malgudians and occasionally ventures into social criticism. A few of the stories are satirical in tone, and there is even a touch of the absurd in one or two of them. As in the novels, the dominant mood is of mild irony; but the best of them can be funny, as is the case with "A Horse and Two Goats," a hilarious account of cultural misunderstanding.

Narayan's collections of short tales include the volume *Gods, Demons, and Others* (1964). These stories are, as the title indicates, attempts to re-create Indian myths. They show Narayan adopting the role of the traditional storyteller who regales his audience with tales about a supernatural world that is of interest to mortals and that combines instruction with enjoyment. Narayan evidently enjoyed this role and found that modern audiences delighted in his versions; he thus went on to create his own versions of India's great epics, the *Ramayana* and the *Mahabharata*. These volumes, published in 1972 and 1978 respectively, complement the world of Malgudi portrayed in the novels and the short fiction, in which his situations and characters often allude to the Hindu holy books and legends. Patrick Swinden has noted that what Narayan's narrator says about the sage Narada in *The World of Nagaraj* could also be applied to the author: he "floats with ease from one world to another . . . carrying news and gossip, often causing clashes between gods and demons, demons and demons, and gods and gods, and between the creatures of the earth."

Any survey of Narayan's career should also take note of his miscellaneous writings and essays on literature, for as a practicing journalist as well as an author often invited to present his thoughts on writing and art, he published several collections of nonfictional prose. Essays such as his "Introduction to *The Financial Expert*," collected in *A Story-Teller's World*, and "Misguided Guide," reprinted in *A Writer's Nightmare* (1988), give readers the contexts of his novels. Essays such as "Mysore City" (in *A Story-Teller's World*) furnish them with details that are helpful in understanding the Malgudi setting. They also remind readers how close his novels are to the South Indian world he knew so intimately. Other essays provide information about his views on storytelling, the problems facing the Indian writer, the status of English in India, East-West encounters, and his delight in everyday life and simple events as well as his eye for the oddities of people. His two extended works of nonfiction are his memoir, *My Days*, and *My Dateless Diary*, in which he

describes his travels in America and encounters with Americans during a nine-month visit sponsored by the Rockefeller Foundation.

Narayan received some major awards for his work. In addition to the Sahitya Akademi Award for *The Guide*, the Indian government conferred on him the Padma Bhushan, one of India's leading awards, in 1964 for his overall achievement. He was also decorated with the Royal Society's Benson Medal in 1980 and was made a Fellow of the Royal Society of Literature that year. He was a visiting professor at Michigan State University and Columbia University in the United States. Major Indian universities and the University of Leeds conferred honorary degrees on him.

Narayan died on 13 May 2001. Viewing Narayan's achievement in perspective at the beginning of the twenty-first century, one can see that he has been one of the leading Indian writers in English of the previous century. The first wave of Indians writing in English, comprising men and women such as Bankim Chandra Chatterjee, Raja Rammohon Roy, Michael Modhusudhan Dutt, and Toru Dutt, had little or no impact on English literature. Many of these writers failed in using a language that was not their own and soon switched to their mother tongues. The second generation were the true pioneers: writers such as Nirad C. Chaudhuri, Narayan, Mulk Raj Anand, and Kamala Markandaya managed to attract a limited but devoted following not only in India but also all over the world. A few of them, Chaudhuri and Narayan for instance, even managed to win major literary awards overseas. Significantly, of these writers, Narayan was the only one ever considered for the Nobel Prize in literature. His fame continued to increase decade by decade, and his work continued to be published both in India and the West throughout the twentieth century.

The arrival of the third wave of Indian writers in English with Salman Rushdie's *Midnight's Children* (1981), a wave that swept forward writers such as Amitav Ghosh, Vikram Seth, Anita Desai, and Arundhati Roy, did not distract attention from Narayan but rather showed the solidity of his achievement. His peers as well as successors have been quick to acknowledge Narayan's contribution to Indian writing in English. In an essay written at Narayan's death, the distinguished Indian poet Dom Moraes called Narayan "by far the best writer of English fiction that his country has ever produced." Pankaj Mishra, one of the Indian writers in English now making their mark globally, declared in another eulogy that Narayan was "a precursor I could look up to and learn from, and I can't overestimate the importance of this to a young writer working in a tradition that doesn't seem very coherent."

With only Greene's help, but without the flamboyance of Rushdie or the benefit of postcolonial theory, R. K. Narayan carved a niche for himself nationally and internationally. For more than half a century he produced quality work despite writing in a language not his own while staying in India almost all the time. Mishra's *New York Review of Books* obituary survey can be invoked again to sum up Narayan's achievement: his "unmediated fidelity" to his world and "instinctive understanding of it" make him "a more accurate guide to modern India than the intellectually more ambitious writers of recent years."

Biography:

Susan Ram and N. Ram, *R. K. Narayan: The Early Years: 1906–1945* (New Delhi: Viking, 1996).

References:

Ashok Berry, "Purity, Hybridity and Identity: R. K. Narayan's *The Vendor of Sweets,*" *WLWE,* 35 (1996): 51–62;

A. Hariprasana, *The World of Malgudi: A Study of R. K. Narayan's Novels* (New Delhi: Prestige Books, 1994);

Pankaj Mishra, "The Great Narayan," *New York Review of Books,* 22 February 2001: 44–47;

Dom Moraes, "A Gentle Enchantment," www.tehleka.com;

V. S. Naipaul, *India: A Wounded Civilization* (New York: Vintage, 1976);

Sadhana Allison Puranik, "*The Painter of Signs:* Breaking the Frontier," in *R. K. Narayan: Contemporary Critical Perspectives,* edited by Geoffrey Kain (East Lansing: Michigan State University Press, 1993), pp. 125–140;

Patrick Swinden, "Gods, Demons and Others in the Novels of R. K. Narayan," in *R. K. Narayan: An Anthology of Recent Criticism,* edited by C. N. Srinath (Delhi: Pencraft International, 2000), pp. 36–49;

William Walsh, *R. K. Narayan: A Critical Appreciation* (Chicago: University of Chicago Press, 1982).

Papers:

R. K. Narayan's papers are in Mugar Memorial Library, Boston University, and the Harry Ransom Humanities Research Center, University of Texas at Austin. His correspondence with Graham Greene is in the John J. Burns Library, Boston College.

Pandit Jawaharlal Nehru

(14 November 1889 – 27 May 1964)

Christel R. Devadawson
University of Delhi

BOOKS: *Soviet Russia: Some Random Sketches and Impressions* (Allahabad, India: Allahabad Law Journal Press, 1928);

Letters from a Father to His Daughter: Being a Brief Account of the Early Days of the World Written for Children (Allahabad, India: Allahabad Law Journal Press, 1929; Calcutta: Oxford University Press, Indian Branch, 1945);

Glimpses of World History (N.p., 1934); republished as *Glimpses of World History: Being Further Letters to His Daughter, Written in Prison, and Containing a Rambling Account of History for Young People,* 3 volumes (Allahabad, India, 1934–1935; London: Lindsay Drummond, 1939; New York: John Day, 1942; centenary edition, Delhi & London: Oxford University Press, 1989);

India and the World (London: Allen & Unwin, 1936; New Delhi: Allied, 1962);

Jawaharlal Nehru: An Autobiography (London: John Lane The Bodley Head, 1936; augmented, 1942); republished as *Toward Freedom: The Autobiography of Jawaharlal Nehru* (New York: John Day, 1941); republished as *Jawaharlal Nehru: An Autobiography* (New Delhi: Jawaharlal Nehru Memorial Fund, 1980; centenary edition, Delhi & Oxford: Oxford University Press, 1989);

Provincial Autonomy (under the Government of India Act, 1935), by Nehru and K. T. Shah (Bombay: Vora, 1937);

Recent Essays and Writings on the Future of Indian Communalism, Labour and Other Subjects (Allahabad, India: Kitabistan, 1937);

Eighteen Months in India, 1936–1937 (Allahabad, India & London: Kitabistan, 1938);

China, Spain, and the War: Essays and Writings (Allahabad, India: Kitabistan, 1940);

The Parting of the Ways and the Viceroy-Gandhi Correspondence (London: Lindsay Drummond, 1940);

The Discovery of India (London: Meridian, 1945; Calcutta: Signet, 1945; New York: John Day, 1946);

Pandit Jawaharlal Nehru (AFP/Getty Images)

India on the March. Statements and Selected Quotations from the Writings of Jawaharlal Nehru, Relevant to the Subject Only, Covering Three Decades of His Political Career, from 1916 to 1946, edited by Jagat S. Bright (Lahore: Indian Printing Works, 1946);

Nehru on Gandhi (New York: John Day, 1948);

Mahatma Gandhi (Calcutta: Signet, 1949);

Inside America: A Voyage of Discovery (New Delhi: National Book Stall, 1950);

Visit to America (New York: John Day, 1950);

Talks with Nehru: India's Prime Minister Speaks Out on the Issues of Our Time (New York: John Day, 1951);

India Today and Tomorrow (New Delhi: Indian Council for Cultural Relations, 1959);

India's Freedom (London: Allen & Unwin / New York: Barnes & Noble, 1962);

Nehru, the First Sixty Years; Presenting in His Own Words the Development of the Political Thought of Jawaharlal Nehru and the Background Against Which It Evolved, edited by Dorothy Norman (New York: John Day, 1965; London: Bodley Head, 1965; Bombay: Asia, 1965);

Jawaharlal Nehru: An Anthology, edited by Sarvepalli Gopal (Delhi & Oxford: Oxford University Press, 1980).

Collections: *The Unity of India: Collected Writings, 1937–1940,* edited by V. K. Krishna Menon (London: Lindsay Drummond, 1941);

Important Speeches: Being a Collection of Most Significant Speeches Delivered from 1922 to 1945, edited by Jagat S. Bright (Lahore: Indian Printing Works, 1945);

Independence and After: A Collection of the More Important Speeches of Jawaharlal Nehru from September 1946 to May 1949 (Delhi: Ministry of Information and Broadcasting, 1949; New York: John Day, 1950);

Speeches, 1949–1953 (Delhi: Ministry of Information and Broadcasting, Government of India, 1954);

Planning and Development: Speeches of Jawaharlal Nehru, 1952–1956 (Delhi: Ministry of Information and Broadcasting, 1956);

Speeches in Parliament, November 16–December 7, 1956 (Delhi: Information Service of India, 1957).

The most prolific writer of South Asian history in English during the first fifty years of the twentieth century was Jawaharlal Nehru. He was the first person in the twentieth century to attempt to write India into history. These histories became a kind of life writing as well: he documents not merely his part in the ongoing freedom struggle but also his own nature as he explores his country and the world. All his books on the evolution of civilization, on India, and on himself were written in jail; the rest of his writing deals with politics and his political duties.

Nehru, the first prime minister of India, was born on 14 November 1889 in Allahabad, in what was then the United Provinces and is now the state of Uttar Pradesh. His father was Motilal Nehru, a lawyer who practiced first in the district courts of Kanpur and was subsequently one of four admitted to the Roll of Advocates at the Allahabad High Court in 1896. Motilal Nehru's area of specialization, Hindu land inheritance,

formed the groundwork for a lucrative practice that sustained the family into the days of the freedom struggle. Jawaharlal's mother, Swarup Rani, was the second wife of Motilal Nehru, a widower. His was a Kashmiri Brahmin family. Nehru later drew attention to this point in *Jawaharlal Nehru: An Autobiography* (1936) to explain a particular kind of freedom that he believed went with this background:

> Kashmiris have had one advantage over many others in India, especially in the north. They have never had any *purdah,* or seclusion of women, among themselves. Finding this custom prevailing in the Indian plains, when they came down, they adopted it, but only partly and in so far as their relations with others and non-Kashmiris were concerned. That was considered then in northern India . . . an inevitable sign of social status. But among themselves they stuck to the free social life of men and women, and every Kashmiri had the free *entrée* into any Kashmiri house.

The family acquired a new home, Anand Bhavan (abode of joy), in 1900. Initially, it was the epitome of westernized luxury. Subsequently, it became a coordinating center for nationalist activity. Finally, it was renamed Swaraj Bhavan (abode of freedom) and, on the advice of Mohandas Karamchand Gandhi, turned over to the nation.

Apart from a brief stint at the local St. Mary's Convent School, Nehru studied at home for the first fifteen years of his life with a range of teachers. These included British governesses, a Pandit who came in to teach him Hindi and Sanskrit (with little success), and resident tutors. In the last category was Ferdinand T. Brooks, who interested him in general reading, science, and theosophy. Annie Besant, founder of the Theosophical Society, initiated Nehru into the society when he was thirteen. At fifteen he joined Harrow, an institution about which he remarked ruefully much later in *Jawaharlal Nehru: An Autobiography,* "I was never an exact fit." He went to Cambridge to read for the Natural Sciences Tripos in 1907. What followed, according to his autobiography, were "three quiet years with little of disturbance in them, moving slowly on like the sluggish Cam." Nehru spent the next two years in London, reading law with no more than a tepid interest in the subject. In 1912 he was called to the bar, after which he returned to what he felt was a politically quiescent India. In March 1916, the year of the Lucknow pact that brought about a brief rapprochement on the Hindu-Muslim question in Indian National Congress politics, Nehru married Kamala Kaul. Their daughter Indira Priyadarshini was born 19 November 1917.

During World War I, the Home Rule movement gained momentum in India. Nehru joined it in 1917 and became secretary of the Home Rule League in the following year. At the start of 1919 in India, general disappointment resulted from the limited installment of self-government offered by the Montague-Chelmsford reforms. Outrage succeeded mere disappointment with the introduction of the draconian Rowlatt bills, which sought to suspend civil liberties. The army's massacre of peaceful protesters at Jallianwala Bagh in Amritsar prompted the total involvement of both Motilal Nehru (president of the Congress for that year) and his son in the freedom struggle. Gandhi's call for the inauguration of the noncooperation movement against the British government in India in 1920 further strengthened their resolve. From this year Nehru dated his involvement with agrarian reform and the peasant movement in rural India.

Between 1920 and 1947 Nehru served ten terms of imprisonment for his role in national politics. He introduced the "Independence Resolution" at the Madras session of the Congress in 1926. In 1928 the British government set up the Simon constitution (the Simon Commission, headed by Sir John Simon, had no Indian members) to suggest constitutional reforms. The Congress's response was to set up a committee headed by Motilal Nehru to draft a constitution for the India of the future. Father and son debated the relative merits of dominion status and independence. Meanwhile, the rest of the family (including Indira) went up to Mussoorie for the summer. Nehru wrote regularly to Indira at this time. A year later he published his share of the correspondence as *Letters from a Father to His Daughter: Being a Brief Account of the Early Days of the World Written for Children* (1929).

The text of the book comprises thirty letters. The first twenty-seven deal with the formation of the earth, the origins of humankind, the beginnings of race, tribe, language, religion, trade and class, and the development of early civilizations. Those discussed include Egypt, Crete, China, and India. The last three letters (as Nehru acknowledges) are different. They deal specifically with prehistoric India: the Aryans and the writing of the *Ramayana* (circa 300 B.C.) and the *Mahabharata* (circa A.D. 400). Nehru's foreword to the first edition outlines the context and objective of the collection:

These letters were written to my daughter Indira in the summer of 1928 when she was in the Himalayas at Mussoorie and I was in the plains below. They were personal letters addressed to a little girl, ten years of age. But friends, whose advice I value, have seen some virtue in them, and have suggested that I might place them before a wider audience. I do not know if other boys and girls will appreciate them. But I hope that such of them as read these letters may gradually begin

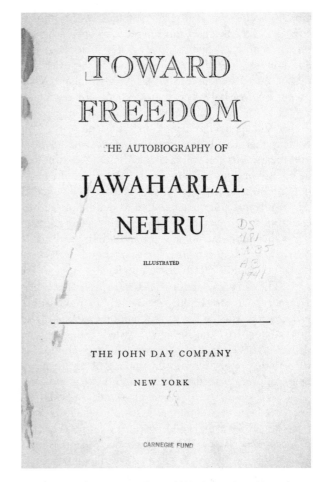

Title page for the 1941 edition of Nehru's 1936 autobiography, which, like many of his books, he wrote while jailed for his political activism (Thomas Cooper Library, University of South Carolina)

to think of this world of ours as a large family of nations.

At the beginning of the first letter, Nehru reminds his readers that no history or geography that is limited to the study of one nation—whether the nation is India or Britain—can ever be complete. He recommends internationalism even for children. He drives the point home again in a subsequent letter that warns gently against jingoism: "As Indians we have to live in India and work for India. But we must not forget that we belong to the larger family of the world and the people living in other countries are after all our cousins." On a personal level, the letters are also intended to supplement an earlier holiday, shared by Indira and her parents in Europe, which Nehru had intended as a learning experience. In the fourth letter he alludes to their meeting botanist Jagdish Chandra Bose in Geneva and their visit to the natural history museum at South Kensington in London. In the eleventh letter he recalls their first sight of amputees in Paris, as a grim reminder of the human cost of war. Nehru uses this reference to open a debate on the nature of civilization. "So if you look at this question in this way you will say that the countries that fought and killed in the Great War–England, Germany, France, Italy, and many others–are not at all civilised. And yet you know that there are many fine things and many fine people in these countries. You will say that it is not easy to understand what civilisation means and you will be right." The discussion that he opens but does not close is interestingly on the question of India. Having pointed out that in languages derived from Latin the term used to denote one's own country is translatable as "fatherland," Nehru introduces this question: "In Sanskrit and Hindi we think of our country as the mother or motherland–*matribhumi* [the motherland]. Which do you prefer?"

The first edition of *Letters from a Father to His Daughter* sold out within a year of its publication. Nehru's foreword to the second edition explains: "The first edition has long been exhausted and even the author of the 'Letters' has no copy left." He reminds his readers that public life and the making of history have held him in their thrall. Although he has another project in mind, yet another jail sentence would be needed to give him time and leisure in which to complete it. This yet unnamed project became *Glimpses of World History* (1934), Nehru's next book-length study. Meanwhile, as he put it, "Domestic affliction and the whirlpool of public affairs caught me in their swirl and cast me hither and thither. And I await again the peace and quiet of the prison cell to continue this task."

The combination of public and private concerns at this time was taxing. Nehru presided over both the All-India Trade Union Congress and the Lahore session of the Indian National Congress. These two meetings were significant because they marked a phase of informed cooperation between the labor movement and the national movement. He introduced the "Purna Swaraj" resolution (for complete independence as opposed to Dominion Status) at the Lahore session of 1930. The three Round Table conferences between Indian and British leaders held in London brought about the adoption, temporary abandonment, and resumption of the civil disobedience movement by Gandhi and the Congress. Between 1930 and 1938, Nehru sustained personal losses: the deaths of his father (1931), his wife (1936), and his mother (1938).

During this period, however, Nehru wrote his most exhaustive survey of civilization, *Glimpses of World History*. This study, developed–except for a short interlude–during a series of jail terms over nearly three years (October 1930 to August 1933), comprises 196 letters addressed to Indira, as with *Letters from a Father to*

His Daughter. The dedication stresses this continuity: "Being further letters to his daughter, written in prison, and containing a rambling account of history for young people." Yet, these letters never got beyond the walls of the jail until they were collected in book form and published two years after the last was written. The second edition includes a postscript, written at the publisher's suggestion and intended to bring the reader up to the moment of its publication (1938).

Nehru sets out the objectives and the difficulties of such a collection in his preface to the original edition:

> The idea of continuing them [the letters to his daughter] hovered in my mind, but a busy life full of political activity prevented it from taking shape. Prison gave me the chance I needed, and I seized it. Prison-life has its advantages; it brings both leisure and a measure of detachment. But the disadvantages are obvious. There are no libraries or reference books at the command of the prisoner, and, under these conditions, to write on any subject, and especially history, is a foolhardy undertaking. . . . The letters are personal and there are many intimate touches in them which were meant for my daughter alone. I do not know what to do about them, for it is not easy to take them out without considerable effort. I am therefore leaving them untouched. Physical inactivity leads to introspection and varying moods. I am afraid these changing moods are very apparent in the course of these letters. . . .

The collection begins with a detailed cross-chronological table. This table allows the reader to compare a range of civilizations and historical periods with each other. The ancient civilizations cited are those of Greece, Carthage, Rome, Byzantium, Chaldea, Palestine, Persia, India, China, Korea, and Japan. Western Europe and the Americas enter with the shift from B.C. to A.D. The time chart ends at 1933, with the world attempting to recover from the Great Depression in the economic sphere and with the Japanese aggression in China in the military sphere.

Nehru uses the first letter of the collection to offer Indira his birthday wishes: ". . . what present can I send you from Naini Prison? My presents cannot be very material or solid. They can only be of the air and of the mind and spirit, such as a good fairy might have bestowed on you–things that even the high walls of prison cannot stop." He reminds Indira of the ever-present slogan of the freedom struggle, "Inquilab zindabad" (Long live revolution), and goes on to interleave the study of one civilization with another. For example, a survey of the village republics of ancient India succeeds that of the Greek city-states. An account of the early tribal invasions and settlements in early China follows. Nehru's intention is to give his reader as broadbased an understanding of the past as possible, without focusing on one culture at the expense of the other. He emphasizes that control of the past is essential if one wishes to control the future. He reminds the reader of this aim toward the end of the collection. "If the past has given us some part of the truth, the future also hides many aspects of the truth, and invites us to search for them. But often the past is jealous of the future and holds us in a terrible grip, and we have to struggle with it to get free to face and advance towards the future." Nehru believes that the impulse to shape the future motivates him to examine the past. A subsidiary impulse is his desire to write history that is centered in Asia rather than in Europe. In that sense he alters the paradigm of history on which H. G. Wells (his near-contemporary) relies.

Nehru also acknowledges a more personal aim. Occasionally, when he addresses Indira directly in the letters, he speaks of the personal release and enrichment the exercise brings him. In a sense, the exercise continues without her, for the letters accumulate with him and are to be read by her only after the collection is complete and he is free. As he says in Letter 120: "And now perhaps you will understand what these letters to you have meant to me. They may be dull reading to you and tedious and prolix. But they have filled up my gaol life and given me an occupation which has brought me a great deal of joy.... When the mood to write captured me and I sat down with pen and paper, I moved in a different world, and you were my darling companion, and gaol with all its works was forgotten. These letters thus came to represent for me my escapes from gaol." The personal note is never absent from this collection. In the postscript, Nehru writes of the convergence of minds between himself and Indira, his "companion in thought" despite the divergence of their ways: "And so we parted, and you went to the sheltered paths of study, and I to the din and tumult of the struggle." He also reminds his daughter of their shared loss of Kamala and of his more personal narrative, which follows this study.

As with *Glimpses of World History,* Nehru wrote his autobiography in jail (from 1934 to 1935) with the exception of the postscript and some minor changes. He sets out to trace his own development and warns therefore that this "autobiographical narrative" remains a sketchy, personal, and incomplete account of the past, verging on the present but cautiously avoiding contact with it. Nehru tries to evaluate the critical significance of individuals in his life against the background of their developing significance to the nation. For example, he attempts a comparison between his own father and Gandhi while explaining the complicated relationship between the Swaraj Party and the Congress at the level of provincial government. He begins by referring to his

father's quotation of A. C. Swinburne's lines to describe Gandhi: "Have we not men with us royal / Men the masters of things?" He then goes on to point out that despite their differences, Motilal Nehru and Gandhi share "strength of personality and a measure of kingliness" that accounts for their equally real closeness.

Nehru also analyzes the critical significance of India as an icon. He looks at both the enchanting and the disenchanting consequences of iconization, which he places at the heart of the freedom struggle:

> It is curious how one cannot resist the tendency to give an anthropomorphic form to a country. Such is the force of habit and early associations. India becomes *Bharat Mata,* Mother India, a beautiful lady, very old but ever youthful in appearance, sad-eyed and forlorn, cruelly treated by aliens and outsiders, and calling upon her children to protect her. Some such picture rouses the emotions of hundreds of thousands and drives them to action and sacrifice. And yet India is in the main the peasant and the worker, not beautiful to look at, for poverty is not beautiful. . . . We seek to cover truth by the creatures of our imaginations and endeavor to escape from reality to a world of dreams.

Apart from analyzing the way in which the image of the nation is constructed, Nehru examines the way in which he has developed. He tries to think through the way in which his mental and emotional reflexes remain inherently British even while he strenuously opposes British government in India: "Personally, I owe too much to England in my mental make-up ever to feel wholly alien to her. And, do what I will, I cannot get rid of the habits of mind, and the standards and ways of judging other countries as well as life generally, which I acquired at school and college in England. All my predilections (apart from the political plane) are in favour of England and the English people, and if I have become what is called an uncompromising opponent of British rule in India, it is almost in spite of myself."

Nehru concludes with an attempt to trace his complicated relationship with Kamala against the background of her gradual decline. He writes of the way they began to care for each other after her involvement in the freedom movement. The movement seemed to draw them emotionally closer when it kept them physically apart. Yet, when they "had just begun to know and understand each other really . . . [and their] joint life was only . . . properly beginning," she died. Nehru dedicates the book to her memory.

Nehru is continually aware of the unresolved tensions within himself. In a sketch, "The Rashtrapati," written (under a pseudonym) for the *Modern Review* in 1937, he explores the twin impulses toward apparent democracy and actual dictatorship concealed in his

GLIMPSES OF
WORLD HISTORY

BEING FURTHER LETTERS TO HIS DAUGHTER
WRITTEN IN PRISON, AND CONTAINING
A RAMBLING ACCOUNT OF HISTORY
FOR YOUNG PEOPLE

JAWAHARLAL NEHRU

With 50 maps by
J. F. HORRABIN

THE JOHN DAY COMPANY
NEW YORK

Title page for the 1942 edition of Nehru's 1934 survey of civilization written in the form of letters to his daughter, Indira (Thomas Cooper Library, University of South Carolina)

book to his "colleagues and co-prisoners in the Ahmadnagar Fort Prison Camp from 9 August 1942 to 28 March 1945."

In *The Discovery of India,* Nehru wryly acknowledges the high standard of erudition that obtained in jail: "My eleven companions in Ahmadnagar Fort were an interesting cross-section of India and represented in their several ways not only politics but Indian scholarship, old and new, and various aspects of present-day India. Nearly all the principal languages, as well as the classical languages which have powerfully influenced India in the past and present, were represented and the standard was often that of high scholarship." Among his colleagues Nehru names Maulana Abul Kalam Azad, Govind Ballabh Pant, Narendra Deva, and Maulana Abul Asaf Ali.

The Discovery of India begins with a condemnation of the prevailing political scene. The brutal apathy and ineptitude with which the British government in India had handled the recent Bengal famine and the inability of Europe to handle the challenges of fascism and Nazism are condemned. Nehru goes on to chart his response to his personal and intellectual legacy. He then introduces what he sees as the major reality with which that legacy has to contend: India. He traces the cultural, political, and economic evolution of India from the Indus Valley civilization to the present, at which point India is poised on the threshold of partition. He concludes with a postscript written after his release and reminds his readers that although World War II has ended, and India is about to begin general elections, without freedom in India or the world, no enduring peace can exist.

The text of *Discovery of India* seeks to open up a range of areas of inquiry. For instance, Nehru analyzes the tragic irony that intellectual advance in Britain coincides with repression in India:

> Which of these two Englands came to India? The England of Shakespeare and Milton, of noble speech and writing and brave deeds, of political revolution and the struggle for freedom, of science and technical progress, or the England of the savage penal code and brutal behaviour, of entrenched feudalism and reaction? For there were two Englands, just as in every country there are these two aspects of national character and civilisation. . . . It was inevitable that the wrong England should play . . . [the wrong] role in India and should come in contact with and encourage the wrong India in the process.

This sense of fracture feeds into the way in which people such as Nehru feel both about India and about Britain. It provides him with one motive for his journey through the past and present of India. Nehru tries to

nature. Tongue in cheek, he discusses his anxieties for the Congress, for his political ideology, and for his own human goodness: "In spite of his brave talk, Jawaharlal is obviously tired and stale and he will progressively deteriorate if he continues as president. He cannot rest, for he who rides a tiger cannot dismount. But we can at least prevent him from going astray. . . . His conceit is already formidable. It must be checked. We want no Caesars" (collected in *Jawaharlal Nehru: An Anthology* [1980]).

Meanwhile, political tension continued to mount. Nehru held talks with the Cabinet Mission, led by Sir Stafford Cripps, in 1942. Later in the same year, he introduced the Quit India resolution on 8 August. The government arrested Nehru almost immediately, along with all the other members of the Congress Working Committee. While serving his longest prison sentence, he wrote *The Discovery of India* (1945) over a period of five months (April–September 1944) and dedicated the

understand how someone such as himself can simultaneously appreciate the inheritance of democracy he associates with British philosophy and literature and condemn the way in which Britain bars a country such as India from sharing this inheritance. He also tries to understand how he can appreciate the inheritance of India that seems to journey ceaselessly–both strengthened and weakened by its unchanging nature. He works toward this answer in a way that allows him to outline the India of the past and also the India of the present, which tries to prepare itself for the challenge of partition. Nehru restates his opening premise. India, characterized by both diversity and unity, is indivisible:

> The discovery of India–what have I discovered? It was presumptuous of me to imagine that I could unveil her and find out what she is today and what she was in the long past. Today she is four hundred million separate individual men and women, each differing from the other, each living in a private universe of thought and feeling. . . . Yet something has bound them together and binds them still. India is a geographical and economic entity, a cultural unity amidst diversity, a bundle of contradictions held together by strong but invisible threads.

This apparent indivisibility cannot keep the reality of partition away. The book closes with the recognition that even while freedom must prevail, India has to meet the challenge of communalism if this freedom is to be genuine. Nehru published this book in 1946 when signs of communal tension were visible everywhere.

Nehru's speech that marks Indian independence in 1947 ("A Tryst with Destiny," presented to the Constituent Assembly, 14 August 1947; collected in *Jawaharlal Nehru: An Anthology*) is one of his most frequently anthologized pieces and shares with *The Discovery of India* the notion of India's endless journey: "At the dawn of history India started on her unending quest, and trackless centuries are filled with her striving and the grandeur of her success and her failures. Through good and ill fortune alike, she has never lost sight of that quest or forgotten the ideals which gave her strength." He does not mention communalism as one of the realities that had interposed between the earlier commitment to total freedom and the present fulfillment of it. He is less circumspect in his response to the assassination of Gandhi. "The Light Has Gone Out" (originally a broadcast to the nation following the assassination of Gandhi, 30 January 1948; collected in *Jawaharlal Nehru: An Anthology*), too, is often anthologized. He speaks openly of the cause of the assassination as being the "poison spread in this country during the past years and months . . . [that] has had an effect on people's minds."

Between 1947 and his death in 1964 Nehru contested three General Elections successfully, presided over the reorganization of states, and campaigned for socialism and cooperative farming. Surveying the Bhakra-Nangal Dam over the river Sutlej (the outcome of such a project), Nehru is quoted by Sarvepalli Gopal in *Jawaharlal Nehru: A Biography* (1984) as having said, ". . . these are the new temples of India where I worship." As an architect of nonalignment, Nehru formulated *Panchsheel,* or the listing of five principles for the regulation of international relations. The Chinese aggression of 1962 was the most serious threat he faced as head of government. He died on 27 May 1964 in New Delhi.

Yet, when he drew up his will–which is both anthologized and featured independently today ("Will and Testament," 21 June 1954; collected in *Jawaharlal Nehru: An Anthology*)–Nehru weighed the balance between past and present poetically rather than politically:

> My desire to have a handful of my ashes thrown into the Ganga at Allahabad has no religious significance. . . . I have been attached to the Ganga and the Jamuna rivers in Allahabad ever since my childhood and, as I have grown older, this attachment has also grown. I have watched their varying moods as the seasons changed, and have often thought of the history and myth and tradition and song and story that have become attached to them through the long ages and become part of their flowing waters.

Indeed, his literary distinction may be seen in the way in which he uses one kind of history to think his way into another. The three book-length studies seem to represent different exercises in the writing of history. *Glimpses of World History* is the grand civilizational sweep; *An Autobiography* is the personal chronicle; and *The Discovery of India* is an analysis of nation building. Each text is actually a palimpsest that at any one point allows one line of narrative to be read as and for another. Nehru works through the history of a personal commitment against the background of national redefinition and the larger background of international relations.

Nehru's passionate championship of the cause of a national language for India led him to quote Milton in "The Question of Language" (*The Bombay Chronicle,* 11–13 August 1937; collected in *Jawaharlal Nehru: An Anthology*) on the controversy of the relative merits of Hindi and Urdu: " . . . let the words of a country be in part unhandsome and offensive in themselves, in part debased by wear and wrongly uttered, and what do they declare but . . . that the inhabitants of that country are an indolent, idly yawning race, with minds already long prepared for any amount of servility?" Yet, the language in which he debates their merits is English.

THE

DISCOVERY

OF INDIA

JAWAHARLAL

NEHRU

THE JOHN DAY COMPANY

NEW YORK

Title page for the 1946 edition of Nehru's 1945 assessment of India's condition under British rule (Thomas Cooper Library, University of South Carolina)

English makes the discovery of Asia, of India, and indeed of himself possible. Through English he conveyed "the call of India [while] . . . spiritually (he) often felt a stranger in (his) own country" ("The Call of India," a letter to Bharati Sarabhai, 21 November 1935; collected in *Jawaharlal Nehru: An Anthology*). The defining quality of Nehru's achievement is that in India, as elsewhere, the domestic becomes the exotic, and the exotic, the domestic.

Letters:

Freedom's Daughter: Letters between Indira Gandhi and Jawaharlal Nehru 1922–1939, edited by Sonia Gandhi (London: Hodder & Stoughton, 1988);

Two Alone, Two Together: Letters between Indira Gandhi and Jawaharlal Nehru, 1940–1964, edited by Sonia Gandhi (London: Hodder & Stoughton, 1992);

Before Freedom: Nehru's Letters to His Sister, edited by Nayantara Sahgal (New Delhi: HarperCollins, 2000).

References:

Jad Adams and Philip Whitehead, *The Dynasty: The Nehru-Gandhi Story* (Harmondsworth, U.K.: Penguin, 1997);

M. J. Akbar, *Nehru: The Making of Modern India* (Harmondsworth, U.K.: Penguin, 1984);

Tariq Ali, *The Nehrus and the Gandhis: An Indian Dynasty* (London: Pan, 1995);

Michael Brecher, *Nehru: A Political Biography* (London: Oxford University Press, 1959);

Judith Brown, "The Architect and His Designs," *TLS* (8 August 1997): 7–8;

Walter Crocker, *Nehru: A Contemporary's Estimate* (London: Allen & Unwin, 1962);

The Dynasty: The Nehru-Gandhi Story, BBC-WGBH, 4 videotapes, Brook Associates, 1997;

Katherine Frank, *Indira: The Life of Indira Nehru Gandhi* (London: HarperCollins, 2001);

Sarvepalli Gopal, *Jawaharlal Nehru: A Biography,* 3 volumes (Bombay: Oxford University Press, 1975–1984);

Krishna Hutheesing, *We Nehrus* (New York: Holt, 1967);

Beatrice Lamb, *The Nehrus of India: Three Generations of Leadership* (New York: Macmillan, 1967);

Frank Moraes, *Jawaharlal Nehru: A Biography* (New York: Macmillan, 1956);

B. R. Nanda, *Jawaharlal Nehru: Rebel and Statesman* (Delhi & Oxford: Oxford University Press, 1995);

Nanda, *The Nehrus: Motilal and Jawaharlal* (London: Allen & Unwin, 1962);

Marie Seton, *Panditji: A Portrait of Jawaharlal Nehru* (London: Dobson, 1967);

Stanley Wolpert, *Nehru: A Tryst with Destiny* (New York: Oxford University Press, 1996).

Papers:

Pandit Jawaharlal Nehru's papers are in the Nehru Memorial Museum and Library, New Delhi.

Michael Ondaatje

(12 September 1943 –   )

Anthony R. Guneratne
Florida Atlantic University

See also the Ondaatje entry in *DLB 60: Canadian Writers Since 1960, Second Series.*

BOOKS: *The Dainty Monsters* (Toronto: Coach House Press, 1967);

the man with seven toes (Toronto: Coach House Press, 1969);

Leonard Cohen (Toronto: McClelland & Stewart, 1970);

The Collected Works of Billy the Kid: Left-Handed Poems (Toronto: Anansi, 1970; New York: Norton, 1970);

Rat Jelly (Toronto: Coach House Press, 1973);

Coming through Slaughter (New York: Norton, 1976; Toronto: Anansi, 1976);

Elimination Dance (Ilderton, Ont.: Nairn, 1978; revised edition, Ilderton, Ont.: Brick Books, 1980);

There's a Trick with a Knife I'm Learning to Do: Poems 1963–1978 (New York: Norton, 1979; Toronto: McClelland & Stewart, 1979);

Tin Roof (Lantzville, B.C.: Island, 1982);

Running in the Family (New York: Norton, 1982; Toronto: McClelland & Stewart, 1982);

Secular Love (Toronto: Coach House Press, 1984);

In the Skin of a Lion (New York: Knopf, 1987; Toronto: McClelland & Stewart, 1987);

The Cinnamon Peeler: Selected Poems (London: Pan, 1989);

The English Patient (New York: Knopf, 1992; Toronto: McClelland & Stewart, 1992; London: Bloomsbury, 1992);

Handwriting (Toronto: McClelland & Stewart, 1998);

Anil's Ghost (New York: Knopf, 2000; Toronto: McClelland & Stewart, 2000; London: Bloomsbury, 2000);

The Conversations: Walter Murch and the Art of Editing Film (New York: Random House, 2002).

PLAY PRODUCTIONS: *The Man with Seven Toes*, dramatic reading, Vancouver, Gallimaufry Repertory Theatre, 1968;

Michael Ondaatje (photograph by Adam Elder; from the cover for the U.S. edition of Anil's Ghost, *2000; Richland County Public Library)*

The Collected Works of Billy the Kid, dramatic reading, Toronto, St. Lawrence Centre, 23 April 1971; revised, Toronto, Toronto Free Theatre, 22 October 1974;

Coming through Slaughter, Toronto, dramatic reading, Theatre Passe Muraille, January 1980.

PRODUCED SCRIPTS: *Sons of Captain Poetry*, Mongrel Films/Canadian Film-Makers Distribution Centre, 1970;

Carry on Crime and Punishment, Mongrel Films/Canadian Film-Makers Distribution Centre, 1972;

The Clinton Special, Mongrel Films/Canadian Film-Makers Distribution Centre, 1972.

OTHER: *The Broken Ark: A Book of Beasts*, edited by Ondaatje (Ottawa: Oberon Press, 1971);

Personal Fictions: Stories by Munro, Wiebe, Thomas, and Blaise, edited by Ondaatje (Toronto: Oxford University Press, 1977);

The Long Poem Anthology, edited by Ondaatje (Toronto: Coach House Press, 1979);

From Ink Lake: Canadian Stories, edited by Ondaatje (New York: Viking, 1990; Toronto: Lester and Orpen Dennys, 1990; London: Faber & Faber, 1990).

For most of his career Michael Ondaatje revealed few traces of his origins in his writing. The winner of Canada's most prestigious awards for his poetry and for other works of various genres, and the recipient of Britain's most renowned literary prize, the Booker, he has long been acclaimed as his adopted country's most versatile writer. He was, however, rebuked by some critics for his refusal to write about his "postcolonial" past. His guarded attitude to self-revelation stems principally from his position as a New Critic that his oeuvre has a life separate from his own: "Nothing is as irritating as finding one's work translated by one's life," he wrote in *Leonard Cohen* (1970), his only formal work of literary scholarship to date.

Philip Michael Ondaatje was born on 12 September 1943 to Philip Mervyn and Enid Doris Gratiaen Ondaatje in Kegalle, Ceylon (now Sri Lanka), about fifty miles east of the capital, Colombo, near his paternal grandfather's tea plantation; the plantation is described in *The Man-Eater of Punani: A Journey of Discovery to the Jungles of Old Ceylon* (1992), by Ondaatje's older brother, Christopher. His father's alcoholism provoked Ondaatje's mother to move to London with his brother and his sister, Gillian, in 1948. Ondaatje remained behind and attended St. Thomas College in Colombo. By 1952 his mother had saved enough money to have him join her and to send him to Dulwich College, a boarding school. In 1962 he immigrated to Canada to join Christopher, who was living in Montreal. He attended Bishop's University in Lennoxville, Quebec, from 1962 to 1964. In June 1964 he married the artist Betty Jane Kimbark "Kim" Jones; she was the former wife of one of his professors, the poet and critic D. G. Jones, who agreed to be godfather when their son, Quintin, was born less than a month after the wedding. Ondaatje received a B.A. from the University of Toronto in 1965; that same year he became a Canadian citizen. In 1967 he earned an M.A. at Queen's University in Kingston, Ontario, and was hired as an instructor at the University of Western Ontario in London. The Ondaatjes' second child, Griffin, was born that same year, shortly after the appearance of Michael Ondaatje's first book, the poetry collection *The Dainty Monsters.*

Douglas Barbour describes *The Dainty Monsters* as "more complex and mature than is usual for a young poet" and says that its fragile, ill-fated birds and animals are icons of Surrealist and symbolist irony that have the power to shock readers into emotional involvement. He cites the incongruous image of "orgasm" for the blood oozing from the mouth of an acquaintance of Ondaatje's who died in a fall at a construction site and the association of the religious symbol of the cross with the rape of Tara in the poem "Peter." In this extended narrative poem Ondaatje also introduces a technique that he builds into a formidable device in his later fiction: an early foreshadowing of the climactic event. At the beginning of the poem Peter appears to defile the corpse of a stolen cow, which leads to his capture and maiming and "the poured loathing of fifteen years" that he eventually visits on Tara.

Ondaatje's next collection, *the man with seven toes* (1969), is a series of vignettes inspired by an exhibition of Sidney Nolan's paintings commemorating Australia's first mythic femme fatale, Eliza Fraser. Not as daring a formal experiment as his next reworking of a national myth, that of Billy the Kid, *the man with seven toes* initiates Ondaatje's long engagement with spatiotemporal fragmentation and multiplication of points of view and flirts with the genre that became his trademark, biographical fiction. Barbour claims that the germ of his transformation from modernist to postmodernist can be found in this move from the "programmatic" school of Wallace Stevens to the "collagistic" one of Ezra Pound. Ondaatje's skeptical reimaginings of historical sources, unorthodox use of intertextuality, and refusal to be hemmed in by the boundaries of genre have also led critics such as Dennis Cooley (in a 1985 critical anthology on Ondaatje edited by Sam Solecki), Maria Rosa Giordani, Michael Greenstein, Linda Hutcheon, Leslie Mundwiler, and Tom Penner to label him a postmodernist.

Ondaatje's national recognition dates from the 1970 Canadian Governor General's Award for *The Collected Works of Billy the Kid: Left-Handed Poems* (1970), although he suggests that the recognition stemmed less from the award itself than from an unprecedented press conference called by former Prime Minister John Diefenbaker to denounce the selection of a work about an American hero "in a coonskin hat." The most significant stylistic influence on the work seems to be that of the English novelist, art critic, and socialist philosopher John Berger. Ondaatje uses poetry, invented journalism, and simulated period photographs to challenge conventional notions of history and the historical status of national myths. In "Two Authors in Search of a Character" (1972) Stephen Scobie sees Ondaatje's Billy the Kid as a transgressive, self-mythologizing artist in the mold of his creator.

Around this time Ondaatje revived a dream he had had in his youth by producing, directing, and writing three movies. *Sons of Captain Poetry* (1970) traces the career of the poet bpNichol (Barrie Phillip Nichol), with whom Ondaatje shared the 1970 Governor General's Award; in *Carry on Crime and Punishment* (1972) he goes in search of his lost dog; and in *The Clinton Special* (1972) he records the interactions of a theatrical troupe with some farmworkers.

Ondaatje had been dismissed from the University of Western Ontario in 1971 because he refused to pursue a Ph.D., but he had quickly been hired as an assistant professor of English at Glendon College of York University in Toronto. His second biographical fiction, *Coming through Slaughter* (1976), was inspired by a figure who is as poorly documented as Billy the Kid: the New Orleans jazz cornetist Buddy Bolden, who became a legend when, according to a newspaper article quoted by Ondaatje, he "went berserk in a parade" in 1907. Months of research uncovered a few other items in newspapers and a single photograph of the subject. At times factual reportage, at others pure invention, and throughout a philosophical meditation on the nature of lost histories, *Coming through Slaughter* attempts to re-create Bolden's life through a collage of competing narratives. Instead of documentary images, Ondaatje supplies "snapshots" in the form of poems that annotate the prose. The solitary, tantalizing photograph is explained midway through the book in a concrete poem-like schematic in which Ondaatje informs the reader that it has endured fire and water. Once explained, the authenticity of the lone image begins to erode; thus, even as Bolden's story gains substance, its historical underpinnings disintegrate. *Coming through Slaughter* received the 1976 Books in Canada Award for a best first novel by a Canadian writer. Ondaatje has said that *The Collected Works of Billy the Kid* is the Sergio Leone–style Western he could not make and that *Coming through Slaughter* is a preliminary draft of a screenplay he has never had the time to complete. He adapted them as dramatic readings in 1971 and 1980, respectively.

In 1979 Ondaatje published *There's a Trick with a Knife I'm Learning to Do: Poems 1963–1978* (1979), which includes poems from *Dainty Monsters* and another collection, *Rat Jelly* (1973); the third section, "Pig Glass," comprises previously uncollected pieces. The volume pares Ondaatje's poetry down to a core of immediate experience and sensation, free of cerebration or sentimental artifice. Henceforth, his more elaborately allusive flights of intertextuality are concentrated in his prose, and his poetry attains an ever-deeper intimacy and introspection. A poem from *Rat Jelly*, "Letters &

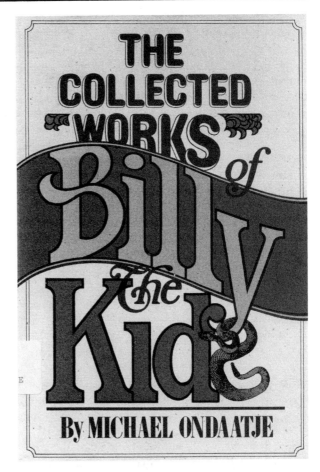

Dust jacket for the U.S. edition of Ondaatje's 1970 book of poems, invented journalism, and simulated period photographs about the American outlaw (Richland County Public Library)

Other Worlds," is widely recognized as one of his greatest achievements; according to Barbour, it is his "first attempt to place and placate his father's ghost." The volume won the 1979 Governor General's Award.

By the late 1970s Ondaatje was receiving regular invitations as a speaker and visiting professor, and his wife was equally in demand as a photographer. In 1979, while she was photographing churches in Alaska, he was attending a conference in Hawaii. There he met Linda Spalding, a social worker who later became a novelist. Ondaatje and his wife separated in 1980, and Ondaatje began living with Spalding.

Ondaatje apologizes for the "fictional air" of his celebrated mock autobiography, *Running in the Family* (1982), with the explanation that in Sri Lanka "a well-told lie is worth a thousand facts." In 1978 he and his wife and children had gone to Sri Lanka for a five-month stay. There he had rediscovered his family history with the help of his sister, who had moved back to the island, and his Aunt Phyllis, whom he describes as a minotaur leading him on a long journey back through a labyrinth of stories. His third and most iconoclastic biographical fiction, with himself as the principal subject, *Running in the Family* is in part a travel narrative, in which he playfully updates Robert Knox's *An Historical Relation of Ceylon* (1681), which influenced Daniel Defoe's *Life and Strange and Surprising Adventures of Robinson Crusoe* (1719); in part a parody of oral history; and in part a fanciful autobiography. Ondaatje's "memoir" is a gesture of forgiveness and benediction to the ghosts of his past, in which he transforms his alcoholic father into an engaging rogue and imagines his grandmother Lalla, an inveterate flower thief, perishing in the branches of a blossoming jacaranda tree when it was swept away in a great flood. Hutcheon (in the Solecki anthology) points to the affinities of the work to Gabriel García Márquez's magic realism. *Running in the Family* is a spoof of a narrative form that, since St. Augustine, has relied on at least a pretense of truthful confession. Despite near-universal critical acclaim, the work received no major awards.

An almost religious sense of doubt, insecurity, and guilt color most of the poems Ondaatje wrote during the breakup of his marriage and that survived into his next major verse collection, *Secular Love* (1984). In "Tin Roof" a series of allusions to wounded self-abandonment include a cattle-scarred John Wayne and a limping Burt Lancaster. But neither they, nor the unlikely duo of the poet Rainer Maria Rilke and Rick Blaine in "Bogart in Casablanca"–Blaine is too drunk after his second abandonment by Ilsa to notice that he has slipped into the role of the actor who played him in the 1942 movie–can offer much solace.

In 1985 Ondaatje and Spalding took over the editorship of *Brick: A Journal of Reviews,* which had been founded in 1977 by Stan Dragland and Jean McKay. The publication, which is now known as *Brick: A Literary Journal,* has attained international stature.

As he grappled with the perennial "postcolonial" problem of finding a "place" for himself, Ondaatje became fascinated with the history of his adopted city. The result was a novel, *In the Skin of a Lion* (1987), the title of which is taken from the Sumerian *Gilgamesh* epic: "The joyful will stoop with sorrow, and when you have gone to the earth I will let my hair grow long for your sake, I will wander through the wilderness in the skin of a lion." Ondaatje's brother, Christopher, had become a well-known financier, while Ondaatje's literary friends tended to be socialists. Ondaatje biographer Ed Jewinsky speculates that this contradiction drew him to a study of the ruthless theater impresario Ambrose Small, who dominated the city until his mysterious disappearance in 1919; Christopher told Jewinsky that Ondaatje thoroughly disliked Small, whose

role grew smaller with each draft of the novel. In the published work he is all but hidden in a subplot; the main protagonist is Patrick Lewis, a migrant from rural Canada who, like the teeming immigrants from Macedonia and other disturbed parts of the Old World, is a newcomer to Toronto. The novel signals a decisive movement on Ondaatje's part from Surrealism to realism. Critics such as Katherine Acheson, Gordon Gamlin, Michael Greenstein, Fotios Sarris, and Susan Spearey consider it a dazzling virtuoso treatment of issues of social class, ethnicity, and the immigrant experience that never rigidifies into a political treatise. The many prizes it won include the Toronto Book Award, the Toronto Art Award, and the Trillium Book Award. Ondaatje followed *In the Skin of a Lion* with *The Cinnamon Peeler: Selected Poems* (1989).

Although Ondaatje's next novel, *The English Patient* (1992), unfolds with an Aristotelian unity of time, place, and action in the ruins of a Tuscan convent in the closing months of World War II, it employs an intricate flashback structure that allows the characters gradually to reveal their histories. Hana, the adopted daughter of Patrick Lewis from *In the Skin of a Lion,* is a twenty-year-old nurse who, for reasons that are revealed only in the closing pages, is devoting herself to the care of a mysterious, badly burned patient who seems to cling to life only to tell her his story. The misidentified "English" patient is actually the Hungarian count Ladislaus de Almásy, a desert explorer. Another character from *In the Skin of a Lion,* David Caravaggio, a Toronto thief who was trained as a British spy and is now a maimed victim of the war, tracks Hana down when he hears of her stubborn refusal to abandon her immolated "saint." Caravaggio appears to be unaware, until Almásy reveals it to him, that his first name refers not to the eternally youthful and self-confident Renaissance statue by Michelangelo but to the Baroque painter Michelangelo Merisi da Caravaggio's *David with the Head of Goliath* (1609–1610), in which the two faces are, according to legend, self-portraits of the artist in handsome youth and haggard middle age. Almásy is Hana's sole preoccupation until an idealistic Sikh bomb-defusing expert, Kirpal "Kip" Singh, bivouacs in their garden, and she falls in love with him. As the love story of the present develops, that of the English patient gradually takes form. In what is perhaps the most nuanced of Ondaatje's foreshadowings, while Hana reads aloud from the works of Stendhal and Rudyard Kipling and the Romantic novels of the nineteenth century, the English patient recounts the story from Herodotus of Candaules and Gyges that was read to him one day by Katharine Clifton, the wife of a fellow desert explorer, with whom he fell in love. In the elegiac conclusion Hana writes to complete the story of

Patrick Lewis, and Ondaatje then carries her and Kip fourteen years into their future–only to leave them there and confess that he can say no more about them. References in *The English Patient* to Herodotus, the Bible, Giuseppe Verdi, Tacitus, Simonetta Vespucci, Girolamo Savonarola, Piero della Fancesca, James Fenimore Cooper's *The Last of the Mohicans* (1826), Leo Tolstoy's *Anna Karenina* (1875–1877), the Sistine Chapel ceiling, Richard Rogers and Lorenz Hart, Django Reinhardt and Stéphane Grapelli, and, of course, the painter Caravaggio attracted an immense outpouring of academic criticism and exegesis. The novel was the first work by a Canadian to win the Booker Prize, sharing it with Barry Unsworth's *Sacred Hunger*.

Ondaatje's next book, *Handwriting* (1998), consists of a condensed, aphoristic group of poems of lingering loss and of the power of words to keep things alive. "The last Sinhala word I lost was vatura," he says as he remembers Rosalin, who took care of him after his mother moved to England and whom he last saw when he was eleven; a fourteenth-century Chinese poet immortalizes a dead friend with a single brush stroke; and in the fourth part of "Buried 2" the line "what we have lost" introduces a list of forgotten and abandoned knowledge and traditions of Sri Lanka, to which the poems keep returning.

The seeds of Ondaatje's next novel, the detective story *Anil's Ghost* (2000), had long lain dormant. In 1971 he had criticized Roloff Benny's lavish photographic anthologies of the ruins of the ancient Sri Lankan capitals of Anuradhapura and Polonnaruwa for their obliviousness to the twentieth-century ethnic conflicts that had transpired amid the monuments. But twenty-nine years elapsed before he confronted this violent past in his own work. The eponymous hero is a once-famous athlete turned forensic pathologist who returns to her native island to examine the remains of victims of possible war crimes. The array of interesting characters in the novel includes the blind forger-epigrapher Palipana and the craftsman and eye-painter Ananda. The mode of narration is remarkably straightforward for Ondaatje: it is a combination of a search for a missing political victim, as in a Costa-Gavras movie, and an Alfred Hitchcock thriller. Ondaatje has hinted at a possible reason for the shift in style: previously, he allowed his characters the license to suggest scenes, which he then winnowed and threshed into a novel; but, seized by a sudden inspiration, he composed *Anil's Ghost* straight through from beginning to end. According to Anthony R. Guneratne's article "Michael Ondaatje" (2003), Ondaatje's engagement with the island's recent past "suggests a need to speak to his own history" and is "obviously a work of courage, open in its condemnation of political slaughter and state-sponsored terror."

Dust jacket for the Canadian edition of Ondaatje's 1987 historical novel about the development of Toronto in the early twentieth century (Richland County Public Library)

Some critics have taken exception to his disregard for historical accuracy; yet, as in *The English Patient,* much of the real action unfolds in an imaginary "virtual space." Thus, it is best read with one of Ondaatje's observations about the nature of his craft in mind: "with fiction the events in the story also become a metaphor for other events." The majority of critical opinion on the novel has been favorable, and it has won several international awards. Feminist critics, such as Susan Ellis, Sangeeta Ray, and Eleanor Ty, who expressed concern about Ondaatje's harsh treatment of female characters in his earlier works, have had little to say about the resourceful protagonist of this novel and her unwavering refusal to consign the victims of violence to oblivion.

At a presentation in Miami in 2002 Ondaatje responded to a question about the extent to which movies had influenced his writing by suggesting that his "visual focus" might as well have been "picked up from

Dust jacket for the U.S. edition of Ondaatje's 1992 novel, about a nurse who cares for a burn victim in
a ruined convent in Italy during World War II (Richland County Public Library)

[Joseph] Conrad as much as movies" but added that "film editing is far more sophisticated than a lot of written texts." While helping the director Anthony Minghella adapt *The English Patient* into the 1996 motion picture, Ondaatje conducted a series of discussions with the erudite and articulate editor of the movie that he published as *The Conversations: Walter Murch and the Art of Editing Film* (2002). The book opens with Ondaatje attempting to understand the alchemy through which the detailed verbal descriptions of sensory impulses in his novel could be translated into sight and sound, and there are revelations about the shifts in balance between the relationships of the characters as scenes are excised, condensed, or amplified according to the needs of the medium. The title is based on Francis Ford Coppola's *The Conversation* (1974), a movie that in terms of sound montage is rivaled only by a few of Coppola's later pictures and by George Lucas's *THX 1138* (1970), all of which were edited by Murch; but, surprisingly, the only formative influence on Murch's conception of sound appears to have been Orson Welles: some of the most illuminating pages of the book are devoted to discussions of sound in *Citizen Kane* (1941) and Murch's re-editing, incorporating all of Welles's suggested changes, of the studio-mangled *Touch of Evil* (1958) for

its 1998 rerelease. While Murch had already discussed his craft in his own book, *In the Blink of an Eye* (2001), his conversations with Ondaatje probe more deeply into what lies behind the creative process. For both men even the seemingly most casual decision regarding arrangement, abridgment, inclusion, or exclusion has been informed by intuitions based on knowledge and experience. Discussions of the actual craft of editing and incidental methodological insights tend to be concentrated in the introduction—Murch's method of "banking" the sounds from scenes to create mystery and his use of silence—or in the midst of treating larger issues brought up by individual movies, such as the importance of ambiguous sounds or why the audience can still see Ondaatje's improvised drawing of a dovecote or hear Murch's impromptu imitation of a dog barking in *The English Patient*. The collaboration with Murch is another experiment in genre and—as with construction work in *In the Skin of a Lion*, bomb disposal and mapmaking in *The English Patient*, and forensic pathology and traditional art in *Anil's Ghost*—the celebration of a self-effacing craft. In the *Los Angeles Times* (22 September 2002) the director John Boorman wrote that the book should be "required reading for anyone working in film" and added that Murch fails only "to acknowledge that the underlying power of movies is that they so closely approximate the condition of dreaming." Ondaatje has claimed in an unpublished conversation that his discussions with Murch have inspired him to reedit his *Sons of Captain Poetry* and *The Clinton Special.*

Michael Ondaatje remains on the faculty of Glendon College and is a frequent visiting professor on campuses as far afield as Italy. Regarded as a major Canadian writer from a relatively early stage in his career, Ondaatje has, by returning to his Sri Lankan heritage in his later work, followed a trajectory that is the reverse of those of the majority of diasporic authors: V. S. Naipaul's novels had Caribbean settings in the beginning, Anita Desai's have gradually expanded out of India, Salman Rushdie's have never quite left South Asia, and Bharati Mukherjee's initially concentrated on the immigrant experience. Even an abbreviated list of the writers for whom Ondaatje professes admiration–Charles Baudelaire, W. H. Auden, William Butler Yeats, T. S. Eliot, Robert Browning, Edwin Muir, Phyllis Weeks, J. M. Coetzee, Italo Calvino, and Yasunari Kawabata–suggests the immigrant, British-Canadian education he received after the age of eleven. Despite the compulsive irreverence he attributes to his Ceylonese origins, his preoccupation with space and time, his meditations on the phenomenology of being, his rejection of Cartesian mind-body duality, and his modification of Friedrich Nietzsche's self-willed Superman into the accidental agent of history have led to such philosophical readings of his works as Nicoletta Scarpa's 1999 book on his supposedly Heideggerian leanings. The universality of the themes he explores in his later novels are traceable to his fascination with *Gilgamesh,* which he regards as the first work of fiction. A trademark of his writing is a preoccupation with the fragility of human lives and the bodies that contain them. His dissatisfaction with "official" history, sometimes meditative, sometimes taking the form of ribald satire, derives less from a rebellion against the conventions of genre than from an objection to the anonymity that history demands of its victims. Thus, his characters are not engaged in the pursuit of a great cause or grand design, as are those of Stendhal, Kipling, or Conrad, but are ordinary people plunged into extraordinary situations. It should come as no surprise, then, that Nick Temelkoff in *In the Skin of a Lion* and Kirpal Singh are among the names of actual individuals Ondaatje has grafted onto his characters. Discussing his methods in an unpublished letter, he said, "I do not consciously prepare for the book, or consider my preoccupations; they emerge as I write. So I don't know where I am heading in my work. . . . Now, ten years later, I can just about work out what was going on in *The English Patient.* Don't think I can say much more."

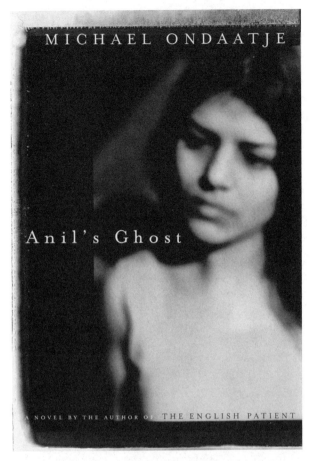

Dust jacket for the U.S. edition of Ondaatje's 2000 detective novel, about a forensic pathologist who returns to her native Sri Lanka to search for evidence of war crimes (Richland County Public Library)

Biography:
Ed Jewinski, *Michael Ondaatje: Express Yourself Beautifully* (Toronto: ECW Press, 1994).

References:
Katherine Acheson, "Anne Wilkinson in Michael Ondaatje's *In the Skin of a Lion:* Writing and Reading Class," *Canadian Literature,* 145 (Summer 1995): 107–119;

Douglas Barbour, *Michael Ondaatje* (New York: Twayne, 1993);

Christian Bök, "Destructive Creation: The Politicization of Violence in the Works of Michael Ondaatje," *Canadian Literature,* 132 (Spring 1992): 109–124;

Rufus Cook, "Being and Representation in Michael Ondaatje's *The English Patient,*" *Ariel,* 30 (October 1999): 35–49;

Cook, "Imploding Time and Geography: Narrative Compressions in Michael Ondaatje's *The English*

Patient," *Journal of Commonwealth Literature,* 33, no. 2 (1998): 109–125;

Susan Ellis, "Trade and Power, Money and War: Rethinking Masculinity in Michael Ondaatje's *The English Patient,*" *Studies in Canadian Literature,* 21, no. 2 (1996): 22–36;

Gordon Gamlin, "Michael Ondaatje's *In the Skin of a Lion* and Oral Narrative," *Canadian Literature,* 135 (1992): 68–77;

Maria Rosa Giordani, *Il romanzo postmoderno canadese: Polifonie e dissonanze* (Bologna: CLUEB, 1998), pp. 37–92;

Michael Greenstein, "Ondaatje's Metamorphoses: *In the Skin of a Lion,*" *Canadian Literature,* 126 (Autumn 1990): 116–130;

Anthony R. Guneratne, "The Chronotopes of Mongrel Literatures: Rushdie, Ondaatje, Naipaul and the Problems of Postcoloniality," *World Literature Written in English,* 37, nos. 1–2 (1999): 5–23;

Guneratne, "Michael Ondaatje," in *South Asian Novelists in English: An A-to-Z Guide,* edited by Jaina Sanga (Westport, Conn.: Greenwood Press, 2003), pp. 201–206;

Steven Heighton, "Approaching That 'Perfect Edge': Kinetic Techniques in the Poetry and Fiction of Michael Ondaatje," *Studies in Canadian Literature,* 13, no. 2 (1988): 223–243;

Anne Hilliger, "And this is the world of nomads in any case: *The Odyssey* as Intertext in Michael Ondaatje's *The English Patient,*" *Journal of Commonwealth Literature,* 33, no. 1 (1998): 23–33;

Linda Hutcheon, "Ex-centric," *Canadian Literature,* 117 (1988): 132–135;

Manina Jones, "*The Collected Works of Billy the Kid:* Scripting the Docudrama," *Canadian Literature,* 122–123 (1989): 26–38;

Marilyn Jones, "Review of Essays on Canadian Writing: Michael Ondaatje," *Canadian Review of Contemporary Literature* (March 1995): 155–169;

Chelva Kanaganayakam, "A Trick with a Glass: Michael Ondaatje's South Asian Connection," *Canadian Literature,* 132 (Spring 1992): 33–41;

Tanya Lewis, "Myth-manipulation through Dismemberment in Michael Ondaatje's *the man with seven toes,*" *Studies in Canadian Literature,* 24, no. 2 (1999): 100–113;

Leigh Matthews, "The Bright Bone of a Dream: Drama, Performativity, Ritual, and Community in *Running in the Family,*" *Biography,* 23 (Spring 2000): 352–371;

Arun Mukherjee, "The Poetry of Michael Ondaatje and Cyril Dabydem: Two Responses to Other-

ness," *Journal of Commonwealth Literature,* 20, no. 1 (1985): 49–67;

Leslie Mundwiler, *Michael Ondaatje: Word, Image, Imagination* (Vancouver, B.C.: Talon, 1984);

Tom Penner, "Four Characters in Search of an Author-Function: Foucault, Ondaatje, and the Eternally Dying Author in *The English Patient,*" *Canadian Literature,* 165 (Summer 2000): 78–93;

Sangeeta Ray, "Memory, Identity, Patriarchy: Projecting a Past in the Memoirs of Sara Suleri and Michael Ondaatje," *Modern Fiction Studies,* 39 (Winter 1993): 37–58;

David Rokborough, "The Gospel of Almásy: Christian Mythology in Michael Ondaatje's *The English Patient,*" *Essays on Canadian Writing,* 67 (Spring 1999): 236–254;

Fotios Sarris, *In the Skin of a Lion:* Michael Ondaatje's Tenebristic Narrative," *Essays on Canadian Writing,* 44 (Fall 1991): 183–201;

Nicoletta Scarpa, *Il transito heideggeriano nell'opera di Michael Ondaatje* (Pasian di Prato: Campanotto, 1999);

Stephen Scobie, *Coming through Slaughter:* Fictional Magnets and Spider's Webs," *Essays on Canadian Writing,* 12 (Fall 1978): 5–23;

Scobie, "Two Authors in Search of a Character," *Canadian Literature,* 54 (Autumn 1972): 37–55;

Sam Solecki, "Making and Destroying: Michael Ondaatje's *Coming through Slaughter* and Extremist Art," *Essays on Canadian Writing,* 12 (Fall 1978): 24–47;

Solecki, ed., *Spider Blues: Essays on Michael Ondaatje* (Montreal: Véhicule Press, 1985);

Susan Spearey, "Mapping and Masking: The Migrant Experience in Michael Ondaatje's *In the Skin of a Lion,*" *Journal of Commonwealth Literature,* 29, no. 2 (1994): 45–60;

Eleanor Ty, "The Other Questioned: Exoticism and Displacement in Michael Ondaatje's *The English Patient,*" *International Fiction Review,* 27 (2000): 10–19;

W. M. Verhoeven, "How Hyphenated Can You Get? A Critique of Pure Ethnicity," *Mosaic,* 29 (September 1996): 97–106;

David Williams, "The Politics of Cyborg Communications: Harold Innis, Marshall McLuhan and *The English Patient,*" *Canadian Literature,* 156 (Spring 1998): 30–55;

Raymond A. Younis, "Nationhood and Decolonization in *The English Patient,*" *Literature/Film Quarterly,* 26, no. 1 (1998): 2.

Taufiq Rafat

(25 October 1927 – 2 August 1998)

Tariq Rahman
Quaid-i-Azam University

BOOKS: *Arrival of the Monsoon: Collected Poems 1947–78* (Lahore: Vanguard, 1985);

A Selection, edited, with an introduction, by Athar Tahir (Karachi & New York: Oxford University Press, 1997).

OTHER: Bulleh Shah, *Bulleh Shah: A Selection,* translated by Rafat (Lahore: Vanguard, 1982);

Qadir Yar, *Puran Bhagat,* translated by Rafat, introduction by Athar Tahir (Lahore: Vanguard, 1983);

Next Moon: Five Pakistani Poets, edited by Tahir (Lahore: Quaid-i-Azam Library, 1984), pp. 14–22;

A Dragonfly in the Sun: An Anthology of Pakistani Writing in English, edited by Muneeza Shamsie (Karachi & New York: Oxford University Press, 1997; Oxford: Oxford University Press, 1997), pp. 53–64.

SELECTED PERIODICAL PUBLICATIONS–UNCOLLECTED: "Towards a Pakistani Idiom," *Venture,* 6 (1969): 60–73;

"English Poetry in Pakistan," *Pakistan Quarterly,* 17, no. 2 (1970): 51–64;

"Contemporary English Verse in Pakistan," *Ravi,* 70 (December 1980): 6–14.

Taufiq Rafat is widely acknowledged to be among the best English-language poets of Pakistan. The critic Jamal Rasheed, in his 1984 essay "English Verse Writing and the Political Plight of Pakistan's Impoverished Poets," calls him "Pakistan's doyen of English poetry," and he can be seen as having pioneered verse in English in Pakistan along with Ahmed Ali and Shahid Suhrawardy. As Muneeza Shamsie puts it, "he is a towering presence in Pakistani English poetry, pivotal to its short history."

Rafat was born in Sialkot on 25 October 1927, the fourth of eight children of Khwaja Ghulam Muhammad Hazir, a businessman who made a living as a supply contractor to the British Indian Army and who lived for a time in Dehra Dun, and Mehr Fatima. Rafat studied in Dehra Dun and Aligarh but graduated from Halley School of Commerce in Lahore. He then became a business executive and in 1956 married Rehana Rafat, a social worker and a women's-rights activist, and settled in Lahore, where he spent the rest of his life. The couple had six children.

Not much information is available about Rafat's life and career as a poet, although he appears to have started to write poetry when he was about to enter his teens. It can be surmised that he published poetry occasionally in newspapers and periodicals from 1947 onward. He eventually began to publish in trendsetting Pakistani literary magazines of the 1960s and 1970s such as *Perspectives, Vision,* and *Pakistan Quarterly,* which came out from Karachi, and *Pakistan Review,* which was published in Lahore. He also published in *Ravi,* the magazine of the Government College in Lahore. *Ravi* proved to be a nursery for later generations of Pakistani English writers. Rafat's work was regarded highly by them, and many of them became his disciples.

Rafat's first significant appearance as a poet was in the 1965 book *First Voices: Six Poets from Pakistan,* a groundbreaking anthology for Pakistani English poetry, in which he appeared along with Shahid Suhrawardy, Ahmed Ali, Shahid Hossain, Zulfikar Ghose, and Kaleem Omar. By this time he had also succeeded in publishing a few poems in overseas periodicals. A play that remains unpublished, *The Foothold,* was written in the 1960s and performed at Government College Dramatic Club, Lahore. Shamsie comments that the play was "apparently inspired by T. S. Eliot's *The Cocktail Party*" and that "it remains one of the very few, original English plays to have been written in Pakistan." In the 1970s Oxford University Press published two other anthologies of English-language Pakistani poetry–*Pieces of Eight: Eight Poets from Pakistan* (1971) and *Wordfall: Three Pakistani Poets* (1975)–in which Rafat is prominently featured.

By the 1970s, apparently, Rafat had consolidated his position as the leading Pakistani poet writing in English. The painter Mian Ijaz ul Hassan, who was friendly with Rafat, reminisced in the Lahore *Daily Times* (14 May 2003) that he was a poor reader of his own verse

arrival of
the monsoon

COLLECTED

POEMS
1947-78

TAUFIQ RAFAT

*Cover of Rafat's first collection of poetry, published in 1985 after the
author had established himself as one of the premier Pakistani poets
writing in English (University of Virginia Library)*

but also that his enthusiasm for poetry was unlimited and
was infectious. Hassan revealed that Rafat would write
poetry "while commuting between Sialkot and Lahore or
in the company of carpenters who worked in the wood-
work factory established by his father at the turn of the
last century." From Hassan's reminiscences it is also clear
that Rafat was treated affectionately by others and eventually became a source of inspiration for younger poets,
some of whom were quite devoted to him. Indeed, by the
1970s Rafat became a mentor to aspiring poets, who
would visit him in his office. Among those who fre-
quented such meetings were Khaled Ahmed, Tariq
Yazdani Malik, Kaleem Omar, Shuja Nawaz, Alamgir
Hashmi, and Athar Tahir, all destined to be well-known
names among Pakistani poets writing in English. Tahir,
who mentions these meetings in his introduction to *A
Selection* (1997), claims that all these poets were influenced
by Rafat's ideal of using a distinctively Pakistani idiom for

writing English-language poetry in the country. Thus, for
many decades, Rafat dominated the English literary
world of Pakistan. Rafat's office itself became one of the
centers for workshops, readings, and discussions of Pakistani English poetry. Shahid Hosain, a fellow poet who
had become director general of Radio Pakistan, invited
him to do readings, and he was thus able to reach listen-
ers all across the country. His work represented Pakistani
poetry in English in anthologies published abroad. Shamsie notes in her entry on Rafat for the Internet site *The Literary Encyclopedia* that "he was the one Pakistani poet to
appear in all three major anthologies of Pakistani poetry
between 1965–1975." She includes a generous selection of
his verse in her own anthology, *A Dragonfly in the Sun: An
Anthology of Pakistani Writing in English* (1997).

In the 1980s Rafat distinguished himself further,
this time as a translator of Punjabi verse, through two collections that were published in successive years. In 1982
he published a book of translations of the poet Bulleh
Shah. A year later he published *Puran Bhagat,* a translation
of the Punjabi epic poem by Qadir Yar. Shah was an
eighteenth-century mystic poet whose iconoclastic verse
is admired much among Pakistani liberals. Yar's work is
the epic tale of the eponymous much-wronged outcast,
who finally attains redemption because of his humanity
and fortitude. Rafat's translations are free renditions into
English verse that dispense with fidelity to the original but
retain their power and beauty. The translations are
important and pioneering, since there has been little translation of note of Punjabi verse into English.

Rafat was in his late fifties when he published his
first collection of poems, *Arrival of the Monsoon: Collected
Poems 1947–78* (1985). In her introductory headnote to
her selections of Rafat's verse in *A Dragonfly in the Sun,*
Shamsie declares that the publication of *Arrival of the Monsoon* was "greeted as a momentous event for Pakistani literature in English." The collection consists of 116 poems
and is divided into four parts: "Arrival of the Monsoon"
(poems written from 1947 to 1969), "Going after Geese"
(1970 to 1973), "Wedding in the Flood" (1974 to 1976),
and "A Rumour of Change" (1977 to 1978).

After the success of his translations and *Arrival of the
Monsoon,* Rafat began work on another collection of
poems that he titled "Half Moon." He fell ill while the
work was in progress, however, and was unable to complete the volume. A few of these poems were later collected in *A Dragonfly in the Sun,* which was published to
coincide with the fiftieth anniversary of the founding of
Pakistan. Rafat's *A Selection* and other individual volumes
of the verse of some importance were likewise published
by the Oxford University Press in the same year. *A Selection* was edited and introduced by Tahir, one of Rafat's
disciples. The forty-five poems in the collection include

verse from Ragat's whole lifetime of work as poet. Rafat died on 2 August 1998 of a heart attack.

Seen in retrospect, Rafat's achievement as a poet was to incorporate into his poetry Pakistani landscapes and situations and to adapt the English language to express a distinctive Pakistani sensibility. Like many other South Asian poets writing in English, Rafat came to the conclusion that the English language was a fit vehicle to render the way of life of his people. Rejecting the notion that one could only express oneself in a South Asian language and not in English, he declared in his essay "Towards a Pakistani Idiom" (published in *Venture* in 1969) that "it is not by the use of Hindi or Urdu words that you can create Indian or Pakistani English. . . . the roots of an idiom lie much deeper" and can be reflected by the English-language poet sensitive to the heritage and culture of his country as well as by the poet using a language such as Urdu or Punjabi.

Many of Rafat's poems are testimony to the rootedness of his vision. In "Kitchens," first published in a 1970 volume edited by Syed Ali Ashraf called *The New Harmony: An Anthology of Pakistani Poetry,* Rafat contrasts modern kitchens with those where people of his generation grew up in the small towns of Pakistan. Those kitchens were full of life, and people sat in them discussing important events such as births, marriages, and deaths. They were spaces filled with the warmth of a mother's care and love. He finds the modern kitchen, however, to be as clean as a hospital and as cold and unnatural, smelling of "Chromium and Formica," which have replaced "the textured / homeliness of plaster, teak." In short, the urban Pakistani lifestyle is remote from the supportive lives of rural communities. "A Positive Region" depicts the beauty of the foothills and mountains as fresh and inspiring. The men of the mountainous regions of his country are strong and the women beautiful. The world of business and management force the narrator down into the plains, however, where the tall pines have dwindled to shrubs. By implication, human relations too seem to take on the tenuous quality of shrubs in this region, although in the other world, the one closer to nature, they had the sturdiness of tall pines.

Nature provides the dominant imagery in most of the early poems by Rafat. Besides the flowers and the grass images, these poems feature all sorts of animals. They range from the wild snow leopards and snakes to domesticated animals such as goats, horses, and dogs. According to Shamsie in her *Literary Encyclopedia* entry, poem after poem "reveals Rafat's love for the outdoors and his wonderful observations of wildlife, particularly birds," and his preoccupation with "the hunter and the hunted, the insidious predator and the innocent prey." A typical poem is "Kingfisher," from *Arrival of the Monsoon,* which begins with his homage to a bird that is

also a hovercraft, a creature that he addresses as something that "flash[es] / rainbows, as you plunge to kill."

Rafat's use of natural imagery reinforces the theme of the healing powers of nature while stressing that alienation from it is the beginning of disquiet. These themes inspire some of the poet's best work. Thus, the poem "Arrival of the Monsoon" depicts birds struggling to retain their balance against the gusting monsoon winds but leaves no doubt about the regenerative power of the monsoons: "A welcome darkness descends. Harsh contours / dissolve, lose their prosaic condition / All the sounds we have loved are restored."

Two of Rafat's recurring themes are loneliness and the trauma and reality of death. In the series of eleven powerful poems, "Poems for a Younger Brother 1930–1979," Rafat narrates how a younger brother faces the impending death of an older one who is going to London for an operation for cancer. The younger brother, who is the narrator, attempts to control his tears, but the emotion breaks through. At the end, he is conscious of loss and loneliness.

Rafat is a poet of love as well as of nature. One of his most memorable poems is "The Time to Love," which first appeared in *First Voices*. The poem begins defiantly with the declaration that "The time to love / is when the heart says so. / Who cares / if it is muddy / August / or tepid April?" and concludes confidently with the statement that "Love is a country / with its own climate." Another poem, "When We Kiss," from *A Selection*, reflects an intensity of desire that is remarkable in the English poetry of the subcontinent though a well-known feature of the amorous *ghazal* poetry of Urdu as well as other erotic genres in that language, such as *vasokht* and *masnavi*.

Rafat's work is steeped in liberal humanist values. Such values are expressed in his sympathy for human and animal suffering and for the everyday life of ordinary people in Pakistan. One of his poems, "Sacrifice," first published in *Pieces of Eight*, movingly portrays the slaughter of a goat as part of the ritual sacrifice often observed to bless the construction of a house. For the poet the bloodletting is the beginning of a history of insensitivity toward suffering and pain. A society that permits such practices is in danger of deteriorating into fascism and organized savagery. The poem ends on these haunting lines: "We are not laying the foundations of a house / but another Dachau." The ultimate import of such poems is to impress upon readers how such rituals move human beings toward inhuman practices. Poems such as "Sacrifice" and "A Kicked Dog" also show his sympathy for animals and the unwitting cruelty of people. On the other hand, the early poem "Circumcision" evokes through the perspective of a six-year-old boy the way the painful ritual prepares people for the disappointments life has in store.

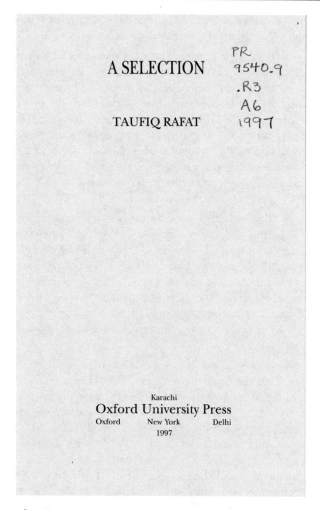

A SELECTION

PR
9540.9
.R3
A6
1997

TAUFIQ RAFAT

Karachi
Oxford University Press
Oxford   New York   Delhi
1997

Title page for the collection of Rafat's poetry published as part of a series commemorating the fiftieth anniversary of the creation of Pakistan (Thomas Cooper Library, University of South Carolina)

poetry and for tackling frontally the issue of the language of poetry appropriate for Pakistani poets. He has also taken a stand on the debate between tradition and modernity, urging his contemporaries to avoid lapsing into stale romanticism, to resist atavistic tendencies in the name of nationalism, and to confront and come up with an idiom suitable for a world that is evolving. Rafat felt that instead of falling back on the diction of English Romantic poetry, as most young poets did in Pakistan in the 1950s, or borrowing themes from Urdu poetry, it was better to forge an idiom that could be indigenous while reflecting contemporary and universal themes.

In short, Taufiq Rafat's contribution to English poetry in Pakistan is immense. In the words of Tahir in his introduction to *A Selection,* he was "the foremost poet of English in Pakistan," someone who for five decades "had been bending words from a foreign domain to the purpose of his province" and who had in the process carried the English language in his country to "a new creative and imaginative terrain." Rafat's significance goes beyond his own achievement as a poet, however, because, besides being a major practitioner himself, he had consistently and for a long time been an inspiration for younger poets and an active promoter of their work. Moreover, he had initiated a debate about the kind of poetic idiom suitable for Pakistani poets writing in English through essays of lasting significance for Pakistani English literature. Further, he introduced the English-speaking public to Punjabi classical poetry through his skillful translations, thereby giving some gems of that tradition to people who have no access to the language.

References:

Carlo Coppola, "Recent English-Language Poetry from Pakistan," *Ariel: A Review of International English Literature,* 29 (January 1998): 203–220;

Mian Ijaz ul Hassan, "The Way It Was: Rendering Verse," *Daily Times* (Lahore), 14 May 2003;

Tariq Rahman, *A History of Pakistani Literature in English* (Lahore: Vanguard, 1991), pp. 161–163;

Rahman, "Pakistani English Poetry: A Survey," *Journal of Indian Writing in English,* 16 (July 1988): 27–44;

Jamal Rasheed, "English Verse Writing and the Political Plight of Pakistan's Impoverished Poets," *Far Eastern Economic Review* (2 August 1984): 32–34;

Muneeza Shamsie, "Taufiq Rafat (1927–1998)" (16 July 2002), *The Literary Encyclopedia* <http://www.litencyc.com/php/speople.php?rec=true&UID=5132>.

Papers:

Taufiq Rafat's papers are in the possession of his eldest son, Sirat Hazir, in Lahore.

At his best, Rafat succeeds in using imagery that is precise, vivid, and original. As Tahir notes in his introduction to *A Selection,* Rafat has found for Pakistani poetry "a new, exciting, more modern way of seeing and saying." He also manages to present situations directly and concretely. There is an economy of words, and the narrative creates a moving effect in poems such as "Wedding in the Flood," which depicts a rural wedding amid steady rain and a rising river. Some poems, such as "Mr Nachimota," create a haunting sense of the inexpressible. Starting innocuously as if it were an ordinary anecdote of a man who promises to give away whatever he possesses, this poem turns into another version of the archetypal story of the man who gives away his son to Death. The casual conversational tone Rafat adopts for the poem becomes intensely haunting as the poem develops.

Rafat has written some critical essays that have been important in forging a poetics for Pakistani English

A. K. Ramanujan

(16 March 1929 – 13 July 1993)

Sukhbir Singh
Osmania University

BOOKS IN ENGLISH: *The Striders* (London: Oxford University Press, 1966);

Relations (London & New York: Oxford University Press, 1971);

The Literatures of India: An Introduction, by Ramanujan, Edward C. Dimock Jr., and others (Chicago: University of Chicago Press, 1974);

Selected Poems (Delhi & New York: Oxford University Press, 1976);

Second Sight (Delhi & New York: Oxford University Press, 1986);

Who Needs Folklore? The Relevance of Oral Traditions to South Asian Studies (Honolulu: Center for South Asian Studies, School of Hawaiian, Asian, and Pacific Studies, University of Hawaii at Manoa, 1990);

The Collected Essays of A. K. Ramanujan, edited by Vinay Dharwadker (New Delhi & New York: Oxford University Press, 1994);

The Collected Poems of A. K. Ramanujan, preface by Krittika Ramanujan, introduction by Dharwadker (Delhi: Oxford University Press, 1995);

A Flowering Tree and Other Oral Tales from India, edited by Stuart Blackburn and Alan Dundes (Berkeley & London: University of California Press, 1997);

The Black Hen, edited by Dharwadker and Molly Daniels-Ramanujan (New Delhi: Oxford University Press, 2000);

Uncollected Poems and Prose, edited by Daniels-Ramanujan and Keith Harrison (Delhi, Oxford & New York: Oxford University Press, 2001).

Collection: *The Oxford India Ramanujan,* edited by Molly Daniels-Ramanujan (New Delhi: Oxford University Press, 2004).

OTHER: *A Newspaper Reader: Excerpts from Tamil Dailies, Weeklies, and a Monthly, with Special Vocabulary and Glossary,* compiled by Ramanujan (Chicago: University of Chicago, 1963);

"Sociolinguistic Variation and Language Change," by Ramanujan and W. Wright, in *Sociolinguistics:*

A. K. Ramanujan (© K. L. Kamat/Kamat's Potpourri)

Selected Readings, edited by J. B. Pride and J. Holmes (London: Penguin, 1964);

Fifteen Poems from a Classical Tamil Anthology, translated by Ramanujan (Calcutta: Writers Workshop, 1965);

The Interior Landscape: Love Poems from a Classical Tamil Anthology, translated by Ramanujan (Bloomington: Indiana University Press, 1967);

Some Kannada Poems, translated by Ramanujan and M. G. Krishnamurthi (Calcutta: Writers Workshop, 1967);

Speaking of Siva, translated, with an introduction, by Ramanujan (Harmondsworth, U.K. & Baltimore: Penguin, 1973);

U. R. Anantha Murthy, *Samskara: A Rite for a Dead Man,* translated by Ramanujan (Delhi: Oxford University Press, 1976);

Nammalvar, *Hymns for the Drowning: Poems for Visnu,* translated by Ramanujan (Princeton, N.J.: Princeton University Press, 1981);

"The Indian Oedipus," in *Oedipus: A Folklore Casebook,* edited by Alan Dundes and Lowell Edmunds (New York: Garland, 1983), pp. 234–261;

"On Folk Puranas," paper presented at the Conference on Puranas, University of Wisconsin, Madison, August 1985;

Poems of Love and War: From the Eight Anthologies and the Ten Long Poems of Classical Tamil, selected and translated by Ramanujan (New York: Columbia University Press, 1985);

"Two Realms of Kannada Folklore," in *Another Harmony: New Essays on the Folklore of India,* edited by Ramanujan and Stuart H. Blackburn (Berkeley: University of California Press, 1986), pp. 41–75;

Brenda E. F. Beck, ed., *Folktales of India,* foreword by Ramanujan (Chicago: University of Chicago Press, 1987);

"The Relevance of South Asian Folklore," in *Indian Folklore,* edited by Peter J. Claus, J. Handoo, and D. P. Pattanayak (Mysore: Central Institute of Indian Languages, 1987), pp. 79–156;

"Classics Lost and Found," in *Contemporary India: Essays on the Uses of Tradition,* edited by Carla M. Borden (New Delhi: Oxford University Press, 1989);

"Is There an Indian Way of Thinking?" in *India through Hindu Categories,* edited by McKim Marriott (New Delhi & Newbury Park, Cal.: Sage, 1990);

"Three Hundred Ramayanas," in *Many Ramayanas: The Diversity of a Narrative Tradition in South Asia,* edited by Paula Richman (Berkeley: University of California Press, 1991);

Folktales from India: A Selection of Oral Tales from Twenty-Two Languages, selected and edited by Ramanujan (New Delhi: Pantheon, 1991);

"Toward a Counter-System: Women's Tales," in *Gender, Genre, and Power in South Asian Expressive Traditions,* edited by Arjun Appadurai, Frank J. Korom, and Margaret Ann Mills (Philadelphia: University of Pennsylvania Press, 1991);

"On Folk Mythologies and Folk Puranas," in *Purana Perennis: Reciprocity and Transformation in Hindu and*

Jaina Texts, edited by Wendy Doniger (Albany: State University of New York Press, 1993);

The Oxford Anthology of Modern Indian Poetry, edited by Ramanujan and Vinay Dharwadker (Delhi & New York: Oxford University Press, 1994);

When God Is a Customer: Telugu Courtesan Songs by Ksetrayya and Others, edited by Ramanujan, Velcheru Narayana Rao, and David Shulman (Berkeley: University of California Press, 1994).

SELECTED PERIODICAL PUBLICATIONS–UNCOLLECTED: "Where Mirrors Are Windows: Toward an Anthology of Reflections," *History of Religions,* 28, no. 3 (1989): 187–216;

"A Story in Search of an Audience," *Parabola,* 17, no. 3 (1992): 79–82;

"Some Thoughts on 'Non-Western' Classics, with Indian Examples," *World Literature Today* (1994): 68.

A. K. Ramanujan started writing poetry in his mother tongue, Kannada, at the early age of fifteen or sixteen. He later became a trilingual Anglophile writer who wrote poetry, fiction, and prose in Kannada, Tamil, and English. His poetry and fiction are deeply rooted in Indian culture, and his subjects are widely spread over the Indian social landscape. He believed throughout his artistic career that "creativity does not come from cosmopolitanism. Creativity comes out of sustained attention to one's own experience, one's own landscape," as he told Rama Jha in the January–June 1981 issue of *Humanities Review.* He therefore portrayed in his poems a realistic picture of Indian society in a variety of aspects–sometimes sacred, sometimes sunny, and sometimes somber. His work offers an elaborate collage of everyday Indian life, reflecting the emotional ups and downs experienced by the people because of prevalent social contradictions and persistent cultural compulsions in Indian society. As a poet, Ramanujan highlighted the existing hypocrisies of Indian society–especially in such key areas as religious taboos, marital relations, cultural conventions, family ties, and caste consciousness. In his poetry he treated many of these issues with mild sarcasm, because most Indian social institutions depend on conventional beliefs that often prove detrimental to the natural growth of one's body, mind, and soul. In satirizing some of these beliefs, Ramanujan operated out of the rationalist and reformist convictions of an artist. As he put it in conversation with A. L. Becker and Keith Taylor, included in *Uncollected Poems and Prose* (2001), "And, of course, I had the notion that only a kind of modern rationalism was the answer to all the problems that we had: the caste system, the problems of a hierarchy by birth. It seemed to me then, it still does, as unfair. That's true of many modern Indians." His avowed aim was to diversify the notions of Indian civilization, since he considered the Brahminical view of Hindu upper-class society as a hierarchical one.

Attipat Krishnaswami Ramanujan was born on 16 March 1929 in Mysore, India, to Attipat Asuri and Seshamal Krishnaswami. His father was a professor of mathematics who fostered in him a rationalistic bent of mind and fired his imagination with creative zeal. His mother was a housewife who induced in him a taste for culture, literature, mythology, and folklore. Tales in south India are not bedtime stories but food-time tales. And the local folks taught him native wisdom and turned him to native literature in Kannada. Hence, some of his poetic concerns characterizing his ironic view of Indian society reflect certain early influences on him of classical Kannada and Tamil literature and the life of people in the state of Karnataka. To attack the oppressive conventions of conservative Indian society, Ramanujan makes use of the native myths, legends, folklore, and folktales in his poetry. In his talk with Becker and Taylor, Ramanujan affirmed: "My interest has always been in the mother tongues . . . because I have always felt that mother tongues represent a democratic, anti-hierarchic, from-the-ground-up view of India. And my interest in folklore has also been shaped by that. I see in these counter-systems, anti-structures, a protest against official systems."

Ramanujan obtained his B.A. (Honors) degree in 1949 and an M.A. in English in 1950 from the University of Mysore, and he earned graduate diplomas in Dravidian linguistics from Deccan College, Poona, in 1958 and 1959. Following the completion of his master's degree, Ramanujan worked as a lecturer in different colleges in India from 1950 until 1957 and at the University of Baroda in 1957–1958. He then went to the United States in 1959, having received a Smith-Mundt Fellowship that enabled him to work for his Ph.D. in linguistics from Indiana University in Bloomington, which he received in 1963. While in the United States, he married Molly Daniels, a Syrian Christian from India, in 1962. Daniels-Ramanujan did her Ph.D. on Saul Bellow with Bellow himself and later became a journalist and a writer of fiction. Her novel *The Salt Doll* (1978) was given the Illinois Arts Council Award for fiction. Ramanujan and Daniels-Ramanujan were married and divorced twice in their long life together.

Despite the many years he spent in the United States, his interest in the native languages and the people of his native land never diminished. As a nonresident Indian in the United States, Ramanujan refused to see himself as an exile or an expatriate. In his opinion, a writer who is forced like Aleksandr Solzhenitsyn to live

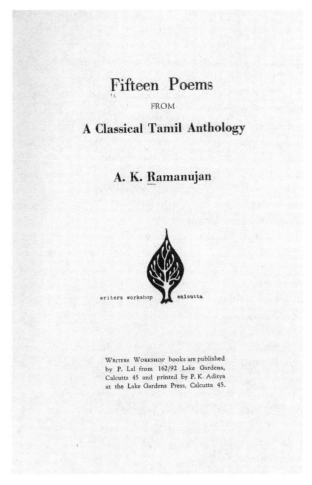

Fifteen Poems
FROM
A Classical Tamil Anthology

A. K. Ramanujan

WRITERS WORKSHOP books are published by P. Lal from 162/92 Lake Gardens, Calcutta 45 and printed by P. K. Aditya at the Lake Gardens Press, Calcutta 45.

Title page for Ramanujan's first book, published in 1965, a collection of his translations of love poems from the eight anthologies of classical Tamil verse, written between 100 B.C. and 250 A.D. (Perkins Library, Duke University)

in another country may be an exile or an expatriate, but he denied that someone like Bharati Mukherjee can consider herself to be so since she had willingly chosen to live abroad. He said in conversation with Jha, "I think it's sentimental to call oneself an exile because this is voluntary and one is fulfilling oneself in various ways by living in this country. So to sentimentalize it and say that oh I am an expatriate, I am an exile . . . these are words which I would not use about myself." With his easy sense of settlement to the nonnative environment, Ramanujan shows even in his poetry how a poet can adapt the English language for the expression of a native Indian sensibility. He imbues his English prosody with his native spirit and exploits his knowledge of Kannada poetics to enhance the sonority of the English verse. "My knowledge of English has been deeply affected by my knowledge of Indian literature and poetics," he told Jha. "If English cuts us from our culture it won't get us very far. . . . Indian English when it is good, does get its nourishment . . . from each individual's knowledge of Indian culture and Indian languages. It certainly does for me. That is what binds us back to our childhood and early years."

Because he supplemented his English verse with the knowledge of his mother tongue and its poetics, Ramanujan avoided the common predicament of most Indo-Anglian poets who invariably feel divided because they have to express a native sensibility in an alien dialect. He negotiates this schism between his Indian sensibility and English idiom by artistically synchronizing the "inner" form of his thought with the "outer" form of the English language. As R. Parthasarathy quotes Ramanujan, "English and my disciplines (linguistics, anthropology) . . . give me my 'outer' forms–linguistic, metrical, logical and other such ways of shaping experience: and my first thirty years in India, my frequent visits and field trips, my personal and professional preoccupations with Kannada, Tamil, the classics and folklore give me my substance, my 'inner' forms, images and symbols. They are continuous with each other, and I can no longer tell what comes from where." Ramanujan thus formulates an artistically viable idiom to synchronize freely his experiences, beliefs, social issues, and cultural diversity with his poetry.

With his belief in cultural plurality, Ramanujan used his work to address certain fundamental cultural, social, and religious issues that he encountered in both India and the United States. These issues appeared to him appropriate for the language he chose for them. To him a poem comes in a language suitable to the idea it expresses. As he told Jha, "You cannot choose the language. I don't think there is a choice. If there is a choice, it is not a poem. I would even define the poem as that where the line between language and thought is not there, or between form and content, which is what the etymology of the Sanskrit word *sahitya* implies." He wrote in whichever language the poem came to him spontaneously–Kannada, Tamil, or English. If he chose any one of these languages for his verse, his expression was enriched by his knowledge of the other two. As he told Becker and Taylor, "In the three languages I know well, whichever one I am working in, the other two are present. I am not a *tabula rasa*. I always think of my languages as certain kinds of musical instruments. If you pluck one string there are other strings that resonate. Like the Indian sitar, there are strings that the musician never touches. They are resonating strings. It is like that for all of us. Everything we know is resonating with what we talk about in the foreground." The creative path he pursued was also part of his efforts at advancing multiculturalism in the world, for he did so by writing in two native languages and one international language. His poetry and translations acquainted people in the East and the West with what they did not know about the Indian culture.

While completing his doctorate, Ramanujan worked with the University of Chicago as a research associate in 1961 and thereafter as an assistant professor of linguistics, specializing in Tamil and Dravidian languages, until 1965. During this period, in 1963, he received the American Institute of Indian Studies and the Indian School of Letters Fellowship. He also translated poems from classical Tamil literature and published them as his first collection, *Fifteen Poems from a Classical Tamil Anthology* (1965). The collection includes translations of love poems from the earliest of the eight anthologies of classical Tamil. These poems are in the form of dramatic monologues of the lover or the beloved in a figurative language. They evoke a vast panorama of picturesque landscapes before the eyes of the reader. In an interview with Chirantan Kulshrestha, republished in *Uncollected Poems and Prose,* he recalled that "These classical Tamil poems attracted me by their attitude to experience, to human passion, and to the external world; their trust in the bareness, the lean line with no need to jazz it up or ornament it. They seemed to me Classical, anti-Romantic, using the words loosely as we know them in European literature." Ramanujan's promotion as associate professor at the University of Chicago in 1966 coincided with the publication of *The Striders,* his first collection of original poetry, which clearly evidences in themes, techniques, and symbolism the impact of classical Tamil poetry on his sensibility. The themes in *The Striders* are connected to his native place and the people with whom he interacted in early life. His subjects include family members, local festivals, ceremonies, rituals, forests, birds, beasts, rivers, and reptiles. As he affirms, "I have tried [in *The Striders*] to keep the human scene central. . . . The more I pay attention to the human world, for me the line between the poem and the novel, the lyric and the story, begins to blur; and anyway in Indian poetry there's never been a clear line. Any single poem implies a persona, a voice, and a specific scene, a whole dramatic situation." For that reason, in these poems the personal emotions dominate over technical concerns.

Ramanujan simultaneously worked on his next volume of translations, *The Interior Landscape: Love Poems from a Classical Tamil Anthology,* which he published a year later, in 1967. Under the influence of the classical Tamil poetry included in *The Interior Landscape,* Ramanujan reveals in *The Striders* a nostalgia for landscapes of places he had visited in early life. His love of the landscape frequently surfaces in the images of moonlit and starlit nights, noontime sun, evenings, lakes, flowers, marketplaces, birds, and beautiful women. He perceives in them the primal energy that propels humans through life. In "I Could Have Rested," Ramanujan measures the motion of time and the movement of life in terms of nesting birds: "I would have sold / and fled my treeless island youth / and told her several birds ago / before they nested / in the south / of my burning foolish mouth." In "On a Delhi Sundial," he astutely mingles the temporal and the transcendental: "Only they / sleep with us in the dark and wake into time / with the light of the moon like antiquity's / lovers." In this context, Vinay Dharwadker observes that "the clock that clicks inside the natural mechanism of any living body is also the clock ticking away in the natural world outside, and it is the nature of this universal clock to tick inexorably towards the terminal irony of death."

Ramanujan worked as professor of Dravidian studies and linguistics at the University of Chicago from 1968 until 1972. He also lectured as guest faculty at the University of California, Berkeley, in 1968 and the University of Wisconsin, Madison, in 1971. By now he was an established translator and was given the Tamil Writers' Association Award in 1969. With respect to his own poetry, he attained considerable technical and thematic maturity with his second collection, *Relations* (1971), which is written in the classical Tamil and medieval style of *bhakti* poetry. In this collection Ramanujan depicts human bondage through family affiliations that deny freedom. Such social trappings create disharmonies at different levels of life. In his opinion, the social network of relationships is a necessity as well as a snare. As he says in "It Does Not Follow, but When in the Street," "I walk on water, can even bear / to walk on earth for my wife / and I will someday somehow share / a language, a fire, a clean first floor / with a hill in the window; and eat / on an ancient sandalwood door." After he divorced Daniels-Ramanujan the first time, he wrote a poem titled "Love Poem for a Wife, 1." The poem reveals how the unshared past before marriage with the wife becomes a source of agony and estrangement: "Really what keeps us apart / at the end of years is unshared / childhood."

In these poems, the nostalgia of *The Striders* volume for homeland is replaced by an objective assessment of the past. This detachment is amply evident from the ironic humor ingrained in his projections of family members such as his parents, aunts, wife, and father-in-law. He achieves such objectivity after a long stay in the United States, where his engagement with an alien culture led him to look at people and places from his early life more dispassionately. Treating humorously his parents and other relatives helps him overcome his earlier absorption in his childhood and attachment to his people. In "Small-Scale Reflections on

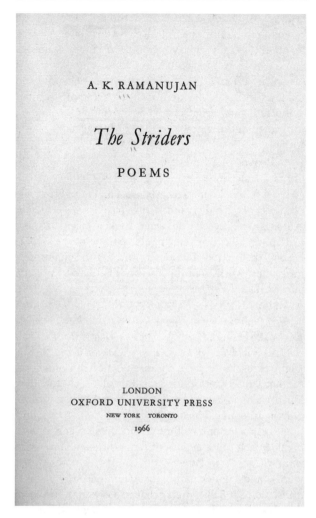

A. K. RAMANUJAN

The Striders

POEMS

LONDON
OXFORD UNIVERSITY PRESS
NEW YORK   TORONTO
1966

Title page for Ramanujan's first collection of original poetry, which combines his interest in the themes and techniques of classical Indian poetry with his recollections of his youth in southern India (Ekstrom Library, University of Louisville)

a Great House," Ramanujan portrays an ironic picture of his childhood home, saying that nothing that comes into this house goes out: "Nothing stays out: daughters / get married to short-lived idiots; sons who run away come back." Similarly, in "Obituary," his reaction to the death of his father verges on cynicism: "Father, when he passed on, / left dust / on a table full of papers, / left debts and daughters, / a bedwetting grandson / named by the toss / of a coin after him." In "Love Poem for a Wife, 2," he pacifies himself after undergoing the agony of his remarriage with Molly through the poetic description of a dream: "I dreamed one day / that face my own yet hers, / with my own nowhere / to be found; lost; cut / loose like my dragnet past."

With his dispassion, Ramanujan even looks mockingly at Hinduism and Indian history. Some aspects of Hindu culture and Indian history have become remote for him. He declares that he was "anti-hierarchic"—that is to say, against the Hindu caste system—right from his youth. He therefore makes use of the ancient Tamil and Kannada myths, legends, and folktales in his poetry because they are more secular, democratic, and egalitarian. They give due recognition to women and the downtrodden of Indian hierarchical society.

Between 1971 and 1986, Ramanujan did not publish any collection of poetry. From 1972 he was associated with the Committee on Social Thought at the University of Chicago and lectured as visiting professor at the University of California, Berkeley, in 1973 and Carleton College in Northfield, Minnesota, in 1978. During this period Ramanujan did a good amount of translation work from the ancient Tamil and Kannada into English; he translated *Speaking of Siva* (1973), U. R. Anantha Murthy's *Samskara: A Rite for a Dead Man* (1976), Nammalvar's *Hymns for the Drowning: Poems for Visnu* (1981), and *Poems of Love and War: From the Eight Anthologies and the Ten Long Poems of Classical Tamil* (1985). These translations project a rare poetic achievement of the Dravidian culture in the south of India, and they portray a complete picture of the ancient Indian civilization in the subcontinent. Taken together, they show how the poetry and culture complemented and supplemented each other in ancient India. Ramanujan always supplied his translations with prefaces, notes, afterwords, and commentaries to offer models of genuine translations. It helped him produce a coherent theory of translation from Indian languages into English. For him the art of translation is immensely useful but never original and perfect. It involves merely turning one language into another for the convenience of a target audience. A work in translation never carries the full fragrance and absolute originality of the actual text, since the author never wrote his work for translation into another language. He was catering precisely to a particular group of people at a certain time. So the time, people, and place are extremely important in the life of a text. As Ramanujan told Becker and Taylor, "Literatures are so deeply grounded in their cultures and in the cultures they carry. . . . To cross from one language to another—which is, after all, what translation means—is a very imperfect business. And there is much damage in translating. But there it has to be pointed to [as notes], and in pointing itself some of the damage is undone. In showing what can be done, the reader can make the leaps that are necessary." Ramanujan turned the ideas of Walter Benjamin and Jacques Derrida about translation to his own favor, and his skills as a translator exceeded those of many established translators in the subcontinent. In Ramanujan's view, the translator cannot escape the shadow of the original, and his task is to develop a relevant supplement. How well the text can be translated does not depend upon the inherent treasure in the poem but on certain crucial outside factors. With the efforts of the translator the text is reborn.

In Ramanujan's later years he published *Second Sight* (1986), *Another Harmony: New Essays on the Folklore of India* (1986), which he coedited with Stuart Blackburn, and *Folktales from India: A Selection of Oral Tales from Twenty-Two Languages* (1991). This period climaxes his creative life in terms of aesthetic assessment and acceptance of certain earlier ideas and issues. His perceptions, preferences, and projections of the two societies he had lived in and their social dichotomies are now presented far more coherently and convincingly than earlier. His preoccupation with the mysteries of life evidences an acceptance of change over fixed specificity. Also, in this collection he reveals a more complex understanding of Indian myths, legends, history, rituals, customs, and conventions. A. N. Dwivedi observes that "taken together, these poems tend to reinforce the thought that the poet is heavily inclined towards all that is India, including his Indian associations and Hindu gods and goddesses." This propensity intensified in him as a result of his translations from the classical Kannada and Tamil literatures and his continued contact with India over the years. He visited India regularly and collected new materials, met old friends, delivered lectures, and read from his latest poems to poetry lovers.

In this phase, Ramanujan frequently entertains the thoughts of birth and death in his poems. His references to fire, water, darkness, and death in many poems point to a subliminal awareness of the approaching end of his life. "Fire," "Birthdays," "Shadows," "One More on a Deathless Theme," "Elegy," "Death and the Good Citizen," and "Death in Search of a Comfortable Metaphor" are some examples of poems in which he displays his apprehension of death. Images of death and ruin, the passing of time, and darkness point to his reconcilement to the idea of the transience of life and the temporariness of the world. This mood further results in a transcendence of earthly bonds and boundaries. Many poems in *Second Sight* reflect his penchant for meditation and philosophy, and, in Dharwadker's opinion, these preoccupations appear "interspersed with passages reflecting on certain 'epiphanic' moments in his life."

Ramanujan's death anxiety in *Second Sight* could as well be a part of his increasing age and the maturing influence of the modernist British and American writers on him. This influence is evident from his poems, which are concrete embodiments of his ideas. He synchronizes his technique of writing poetry with his experience, education, erudition, and vision of life. His language is simple, his rhythms musical, and his imagery suggestive. In "Snakes," one of his more popular poems, the poet uses the language of daily conversation to articulate his childhood apprehensions. His choice of words, however, their placement in a rhythmical pattern, and the play of sounds and colors bring the picture alive with relevant suggestions and sensations. Similarly, in another short but suggestive poem, "Still Life," Ramanujan conveys his response to a woman who has left him feeling like a half-eaten salami sandwich. The half-eaten sandwich "carrying the shape / of her bite" offers a visually comic image of incompleteness and disconnection, simultaneously evoking a picture of the woman as a biting animal.

Like the modernists to European culture, Ramanujan's attitude to Indian culture in some of his poems can often be satirical. His satire tended to be mild, however. For instance, in "The Last of the Princes" he gently mocks the poor financial condition of the erstwhile rulers of India: "Two girls, Honey and Bunny, go to school / on half fees. Wife, heirloom pearl in her nose-ring, / pregnant again. / His first son, trainee / in telegraphy, / has telegraphed thrice already for money." Similarly, in "History" he makes fun of greedy relatives: "her two / daughters, one dark one fair, / unknown each to the other / alternately picked their mother's body clean / before it was cold / or the eyes were shut, / of diamond ear-rings, / bangles, anklets, the pin / in her hair." A few poems even verge on being caricatures. In "At Forty," he mimics Jatti, the gym teacher, "Eggs and meat for breakfast, messages / of iguana fat, / till he glows in the dark, a lit medallion / figure." In "Pleasure," he lampoons a Jain monk craving the female body after a long spell of celibacy: "his several mouths / thirsting for breast, / buttock, smells of finger, / long hair, short hair, / the wet of places never dry."

As a Hindu Brahmin living in Chicago from the early 1960s, Ramanujan at times resorts to a jocular style to overcome his nostalgia for the world he left behind, as in "Conventions of Despair": "I must seek and will find / my particular held only in my Hindu mind." Withdrawal into his Hindu mind brings him equanimity and enables him to have an objective and detached view of a mundane world. Ramanujan's grandmother, parents, wife, aunts, and their children surface frequently in his poetry. They inhabit his poetic world as living entities and impart an autobiographical hue to his art, as in "Love Poem for a Wife, 2": "in the morning, in the waking / my wife's face still fast / asleep, blessed as by / butterfly, snake, ship-rope, / and grandmother's other / children, / by my only love's only / insatiable envy." They all inspire his imagination

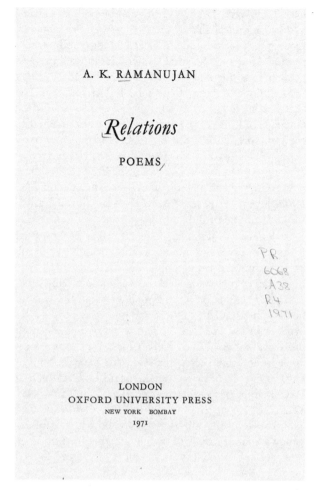

A. K. RAMANUJAN

Relations

POEMS

LONDON
OXFORD UNIVERSITY PRESS
NEW YORK   BOMBAY
1971

Title page for Ramanujan's collection of original poems about the limiting effects of familial relationships, written in the style of medieval Indian bhakti *poetry (Thomas Cooper Library, University of South Carolina)*

and ignite the creative spark in him. At the thought of his family members and other acquaintances Ramanujan plunges into a world of odds and oddities, fun and frivolities, and greed and grief. His relatives acquire symbolic forms, and they quite often appear as the embodiments of abstract ideas in his poetry: "Sons-in-law who quite forget / their mothers, stay to check / accounts or teach arithmetic to nieces."

Ramanujan also makes abundant use of figures, images, and symbols to convey his poetic thoughts in a distinctive manner. His study of anthropology, William Butler Yeats, Ezra Pound, T. S. Eliot, Wallace Stevens, William Carlos Williams, Sanskrit poetics, and haiku poetry of Japan had given him a figurative and symbolic bent of mind. From the French symbolists he had learned to concretize the delicate nuances of his deep emotions and observations. Because of his mathematician father, he also made frequent use of Euclidian figures that were familiar from childhood–geometrical and astronomical shapes such as lines, circles, squares, rectangles, triangles, quadrangles, oblongs, and parabolas. In "Anxiety," the speaker identifies himself as "Not geometric as the parabolas / of hope, it has loose ends / with a knot at the top / that's me." In "Astronomer," he sketches his father as a "fat man full of proverbs, / the language of lean years, / living in square after / almanac square / prefiguring the day / of windfall and land slide." Because of Ramanujan's geometric perfection and figurative delineation, Nissim Ezekiel, a fellow poet, remarked in the 18 June 1972 issue of the *Illustrated Weekly of India* that "A. K. Ramanujan is the precision instrument of Indian English poetry."

Similarly, Ramanujan employs trees, flowers, fruits, and leaves as symbols of unity, beauty, and fertility in his poems. For example, he would prefer to "rise in the sap of trees" and "feel the weight / of honey-hives in my branching / and the burlap-weave of the weaver birds / in my hair." In "Birthdays," the poet subtly brings out the oneness of nature with humans both dead and alive: "Even universities, / art museums, apple trees, / that recycle the seasons, / have their birthdays / like St. Francis, Shakespeare, / Gandhi and Washington / marked on calendars." In "The Day Went Dark," he combines the colors of flowers and leaves to infuse erotic energy into the patterns of his newly acquired carpet: "I bought a carpet / with orange flowers / and green leaves / but all my furniture looked bilious yellow / in its gorgeous light."

Allusions also play a significant role in Ramanujan's poetry. He alludes to ancient myths, stories, legends, literary figures, folklore, artists, scientists, and gods and goddesses of several countries and cultures. These allusions broaden the horizons of his thoughts and themes; they often give his poetry a universal dimension. Weaving together the folk with the canonical, the mythical with the mundane, and the national with the international, Ramanujan uses the technique of allusion to ballast his poetry with humanist values. The poet was not sure whether this aspect of his creativity was something his readers were aware of, however. He told Becker and Taylor, "I actually put in quotes. Very few people have noticed those quotes. But that's part of my expressive means. I've read Pound, and I've read Indian things. I think with them. Why shouldn't I use what I have?" Thus, in "The Opposable Thumb," Ramanujan identifies three types of hands to show the importance of the thumb by obliquely alluding to Swami Vivekananda's description of the Purusha, who "no bigger than a thumb stands in man's central self and is lord of what was and what shall be." In "Love Poem for a Wife, 2," the "half-woman half- / man contained in a common / body, / androgynous as a god /

balancing stillness in the middle / of a duel to make it dance," alludes to the Hindu god Shiva and goddess Shakti–together in one form as *ardhanareshwar* (half-man and half-woman). Similarly, in "Entries for a Catalogue of Fears," the poet evokes William Shakespeare's *Hamlet* (circa 1600–1601) in the lines "see karma / in the fall of a tubercular sparrow," or John Keats's *Ode to a Nightingale* (1819) in "To cease upon midnight with no pain." Ramanujan's allusions to sources past and present often juxtapose antiquity and modernity, thereby making both European and Indian traditions relevant to the contemporary Indian poet writing in English.

Ramanujan died suddenly of a heart attack on 13 July 1993 in Chicago at the age of sixty-four. He was survived by a daughter, Krittika, and a son, Krishnaswami, and left behind a substantial body of unpublished poetry, essays, and translations. At the time of his death he did not enjoy good relations with his former wife, Daniels-Ramanujan; they were divorced a few years earlier. Writing in the *Times of India* on 25 July 1993, Ramanujan's colleagues and friends of old standing, Susanne and Lloyd Rudolph, paid him a rich tribute: "Raman's distinguishing characteristics were his humanity and modesty. He spoke softly but deftly. He picked friendships, not fights. . . . He preferred irony and humor to scoring points. A polymath; a demanding scholar with demanding standards; a teller of tales." Much of the material Ramanujan left behind has been published posthumously by Daniels-Ramanujan, Krittika Ramanujan, and Ramanujan's friend Dharwadker. Volumes they have published include *When God Is a Customer: Telugu Courtesan Songs by Ksetrayya and Others* (1994); which Ramanujan had compiled with Velcheru Narayana Rao and David Shulman; *The Collected Essays of A. K. Ramanujan* (1994); *The Collected Poems of A. K. Ramanujan* (1995); *A Flowering Tree and Other Oral Tales from India* (1997), and *Uncollected Poems and Prose.* One therefore does not find a note of finality in his poetic career, unlike in the cases of his literary gurus such as Yeats, Pound, and Eliot. As one moves from the earlier poems in *The Striders* to the later pieces in *The Black Hen* (2000), however, it becomes evident that Ramanujan was moving toward a more conclusive and concrete phase. His early poems are more personal–they speak about the poet's youthful anger, anxiety, anguish, and apathy toward social, cultural, and religious anomalies around him. In them he derides the inhuman and the unjust and chides the guilty vociferously. In *Relations* and *Second Sight,* he seems to have come out of the early phase of excitement and experimentation. In those collections the poet exhibits more clarity of thought and better control over his language. As Bruce King observes, "*Relations* is somewhat different from the earlier book in that the style is less imagistic, the movement of lines more supple, the narrator more present as speaker. There is intelligence and personality. The poetry is more discursive, more conversational as well as more reflective. There is less flatness of tone, more humor, wit, irony, comedy." In *Second Sight,* Ramanujan further improves his control over his subject matter and speaks more freely about personal, spiritual, and sexual matters.

In *The Black Hen,* Ramanujan establishes himself among the well-known Indian poets writing in English because of his mature vision, variety of themes, felicity of expression, and metaphysical subtlety. The titles of the poems in *The Striders* ("The Striders," "Self-Portrait," "Sometimes," "Conventions of Despair," "Anxiety," "Images," and "The Fall"), compared to the poems in *The Black Hen* ("Shadows," "Fire," "Fog," "Fizzle," "Difficulty," "Elegy," "Pain," and "Fear No Fall"), testify to his range of movement and mature preoccupations in this phase. In Krittika Ramanujan's assessment, the poems in this posthumous collection are "in some ways different from their predecessors. At first reading, they seem light, easy, some almost like exercises. After a few readings, a complete reversal takes place. When the poems are read in sequence, they seem entirely different. The ear begins to hear the voice as full, rhythmic, passionate, complex, changeable, and in variety of voices, styles and forms." The poems in the early collections are replete with details and documentation. In contrast, the later volumes are characterized by precision and coherence and aimed at the evocation of the spiritual. For instance, in "The Fall," the falling man fears he is "a mere body, a surrender, / a will-less plunge into the downward / below his blindness, cannot find the word / for a curse, nor an eye for a hook." In "Fear No Fall," the fallen man does not fear as he hears a spiritual calling from both within and without: "Fall, fall, / you'll never fear a fall again, / fall now!"

Critics have, on the whole, received Ramanujan's work favorably. In "How It Strikes a Contemporary: The Poetry of A. K. Ramanujan" (1976), an appreciation written for the *Literary Criterion,* R. Parthasarathy, a fellow poet, declares: "What sets Ramanujan apart from other poets is his unique tone of voice, a feature that accounts for the characteristic style of his poetry." In "The Self in A. K. Ramanujan's Poetry," an essay included in *Contemporary Indian Verse in English: An Evaluation* (1980), Kulshrestha praises Ramanujan for making unconventional use of the English language. He believes that for Ramanujan "the cultivation and enrichment of a unique personal idiom is not a process that takes place in a vacuum, but is symptomatic of a poet's active concern with the dynamics of his sensibility, the precious tones, movements, and distinctions of

Front cover for Ramanujan's 1986 collection of poems, his first original work in fifteen years, in which he reflects on his life and expresses anxiety over his approaching mortality (Z. Smith Reynolds Library, Wake Forest University)

his own being as an individual and artist." G. N. Devy, in "Alienation as a Means of Self-Exploration: A Study of A. K. Ramanujan's Poetry" (*Chandrabhaga,* Winter 1981), observes that the sense of alienation implicit in some of Ramanujan's significant poems "seems to be the inevitable outcome of the nature of his life-pattern—an Indian Brahmin married to a Syrian Christian, living in Chicago, teaching Dravidian languages and linguistics, twice removed from his natural linguistic context, first from Tamil to Kannada and then from Kannada to English."

S. G. Jainapur, in the chapter on Ramanujan for his book *Poetry, Culture, and Language: Indo-Anglian Poets from Karnataka* (1987), hails him as "a distinguished poet, with an individual voice of his own, both in English and Kannada" and highlights such distinct qualities of his poetry as "nostalgia and memory, family relationships, self-search as a Hindu, and love."

Dust jacket for the 1991 anthology edited by Ramanujan,
the last of the poet's books published in his lifetime
(Richland County Public Library)

commends him for having "cultivated and enriched a unique personal idiom, that shows the poet's concern with the dynamics of his sensibility in terms of concrete images." King, in his *Three Indian Poets: Nissim Ezekiel, A. K. Ramanujan, Dom Moraes* (1991), admires Ramanujan's erudition, which is reflected in his poems in the variety of his allusions and range of his references, from Sigmund Freud to the Upanishads.

Longer studies of Ramanujan's poetry are equally appreciative of his poetic art and liberal humanism. S. N. Pandey, in "Feminist Concerns in Ramanujan's Poetry" (1998), applauds the poet for supporting the cause of women in his poetry: "Ramanujan strives to express his solidarity with women's cause whatever be the genre, poetry or folktales." Among full-length studies of Ramanujan's poetry, Dwivedi's *A. K. Ramanujan and His Poetry* (1983) focuses on the Indian themes, and his *The Poetic Art of A. K. Ramanujan* (1995) notes gratifyingly that Ramanujan "has not naturalized the Western themes and traditions so much as the Indian ones, and that he has stood his ground and proved his mettle, without shifting his allegiance."

Ramanujan steadily achieved ripeness by evolving an idiom well suited to deeper explorations of the innermost areas of his poetic psyche. According to Jainapur, "There are very few poets in the Indo-Anglian milieu today who equal him." He lived a life of diverse experiences that lent variety, richness, and depth to his poetry. There is hardly any aspect of life, whether sacred or profane, material or spiritual, that he has left untouched in his poems. As an Indian he found his culture and religion full of possibilities for poetic treatment; as a resident of the United States he informed Indian people about the need to review some of their traditions in the wake of Western ideas of progress; and as a humanist he stressed the need for social equality and universal peace. The publication of his uncollected poems posthumously has allowed readers to view the extent of his achievement even more readily.

Interviews:

Rama Jha, "A Conversation with A. K. Ramanujan," *Humanities Review,* 3 (January–June 1981): 5–13;

Chirantan Kulshrestha, "Interview One," in *Uncollected Poems and Prose,* edited by Molly Daniels-Ramanujan and Keith Harrison (Delhi, Oxford & New York: Oxford University Press, 2001), pp. 41–51;

A. L. Becker and Keith Taylor, "Interview Two," in *Uncollected Poems and Prose,* pp. 52–79.

References:

S. K. Desai, "Mixing Memory and Desire: Small-Scale Reflections on the Poetry of A. K. Ramanujan," in *Perspectives on Indian Poetry in English,* edited by

Emmanuel Narendra Lall, in an essay about Ramanujan for his 1983 book *The Poetry of Encounter: Three Indo-Anglian Poets, Dom Moraes, A. K. Ramanujan, and Nissim Ezekiel* (1983), praises the poet for his deft use of irony, images, control over language, and the synthesis of the Eastern and Western traditions in his poetry: "His poems take their origin in a mind that is simultaneously Indian and Western; therefore they succeed in opening more passages to India." S. K. Desai, in an essay for the 1984 collection *Perspectives on Indian Poetry in English,* compares Ramanujan with Eliot and Pound in terms of prosody and expatriate sensibility: "For Ramanujan, memories, which are perceptions that live through time, are a means to explore the nature of Time. Through memories he is not seeking his roots in the area of darkness, nor is he exploring the wounded or healthy Hindu civilization. He is using them simply to explore the existential problems of time and what it does to life." P. K. J. Kurup, in a chapter on the poet for the anthology *Contemporary Indian Poetry in English* (1991),

M. K. Naik (New Delhi: Abhinav, 1984), pp. 107–123;

G. N. Devy, "Alienation as a Means of Self-Exploration: A Study of A. K. Ramanujan's Poetry," *Chandrabhaga,* 6 (Winter 1981): 5–20;

Vinay Dharwadker, "A. K. Ramanujan: Author, Translator, Scholar," *World Literature Today,* 64 (1994): 279–280;

Dharwadker, "A. K. Ramanujan's Theory and Practice of Translation," in *Post-colonial Translation: Theory and Practice,* edited by Susan Bassnett and Harish Trivedi (London & New York: Routledge, 1999), pp. 114–140;

A. N. Dwivedi, *A. K. Ramanujan and His Poetry* (Delhi: Doaba House, 1983);

Dwivedi, "A. K. Ramanujan as Poet of Love," *Journal of Indian Writing in English,* 12 (January 1984): 1–6;

Dwivedi, *The Poetic Art of A. K. Ramanujan* (New Delhi: B. R. Publishing, 1995);

Dwivedi, "The Poetry of A. K. Ramanujan," *Journal of South Asian Literature,* 1 (Summer 1982): 241–248;

Nissim Ezekiel, "The Poets: A. K. Ramanujan and Keki N. Daruwalla," *Illustrated Weekly of India,* 93 (18 June 1972): 43, 45;

S. G. Jainapur, "A. K. Ramanujan," in his *Poetry, Culture, and Language: Indo-Anglian Poets from Karnataka* (Calcutta: Writers Workshop, 1987), pp. 108–140;

Bruce King, "A. K. Ramanujan," in his *Three Indian Poets: Nissim Ezekiel, A. K. Ramanujan, Dom Moraes* (Madras & New York: Oxford University Press, 1991), pp. 60–80;

King, *Modern Indian Poetry in English* (Delhi & New York: Oxford University Press, 1987);

Chirantan Kulshrestha, "The Self in A. K. Ramanujan's Poetry," in *Contemporary Indian English Verse: An Evaluation,* edited by Kulshrestha (New Delhi: Arnold-Heinemann, 1980), pp. 175–186;

P. K. J. Kurup, "A. K. Ramanujan," in his *Contemporary Indian Poetry in English* (New Delhi: Atlantic, 1991), pp. 150–202;

Emmanuel Narendra Lall, "A. K. Ramanujan: Beyond Poetry as Family History," in his *The Poetry of Encounter: Three Indo-Anglian Poets, Dom Moraes, A. K. Ramanujan, and Nissim Ezekiel* (New Delhi: Sterling, 1983), pp. 42–64;

Rabi S. Mishra, "A. K. Ramanujan: A Point of View," *Chandrabhaga,* 1 (Summer 1979): 60–66;

S. Nagarajan, "A. K. Ramanujan," *Quest* (Delhi), 74 (January–February 1972): 18–37;

M. K. Naik, "A. K. Ramanujan and the Search for Roots," *Humanities Review,* 3 (January–June 1981): 14–19;

S. N. Pandey, "Feminist Concerns in Ramanujan's Poetry," in *Studies in Contemporary Poets* (New Delhi: Atlantic, 1998), pp. 91–101;

R. Parthasarathy, "How It Strikes a Contemporary: The Poetry of A. K. Ramanujan," *Literary Criterion,* 12 (1976): 187–197;

Parthasarathy, ed., *Ten Twentieth-Century Indian Poets* (Delhi & New York: Oxford University Press, 1976), pp. 95–96;

Susanne Rudolph and Lloyd Rudolph, "Remembering Raman," *Times of India,* 25 July 1993, p. 8;

Vasant A. Shahane and M. Sivaramkrishna, eds., *Indian Poetry in English: A Critical Assessment* (Delhi: Macmillan, 1980);

K. R. Srinivasa Iyengar, *Indian Writing in English,* second edition (London: Asia Publishing House, 1973);

K. N. Vaish, "A. K. Ramanujan: Essayist?" *Thought* (21 June 1969): 14–15;

H. M. Williams, *Indo-Anglian Literature, 1880–1970: A Survey* (Madras: Orient Longman, 1976).

Raja Rao

(8 November 1908 –   )

Shyamala A. Narayan
Jamia Millia Islamia University

BOOKS: *Kanthapura* (London: Allen & Unwin, 1938; Bombay: Oxford University Press, 1947; New York: New Directions, 1963);

The Cow of the Barricades and Other Stories (Madras: Oxford University Press, 1947; London & New York: Oxford University Press, 1947)—comprises "Javni," "The Little Gram Shop," and "The True Story of Kanakapala, Protector of Gold"; "Akkayya," "Narsiga," "A Client," "In Khandesh," "Companions," and "The Cow of the Barricades";

The Serpent and the Rope (London: John Murray, 1960; New York: Pantheon, 1963; Delhi: Hind Pocket Books, 1968).

The Cat and Shakespeare: A Tale of India (New York: Macmillan, 1965; New Delhi: Orient Paperbacks, 1969);

Comrade Kirillov (New Delhi: Vision, 1976);

The Policeman and the Rose: Stories (New York: Oxford University Press, 1978; Delhi & Oxford: Oxford University Press, 1978)—comprises "The True Story of Kanakapala, Protector of Gold," "In Khandesh," "Companions," "The Cow of the Barricades," "Akkayya," "The Little Gram Shop," "Javni," "Nimka," "India: A Fable," and "The Policeman and the Rose";

The Chessmaster and His Moves (New Delhi: Vision, 1988);

On the Ganga Ghat (New Delhi: Vision, 1989);

The Meaning of India (New Delhi: Vision, 1996);

The Best of Raja Rao, edited by Makarand Paranjape (New Delhi: Katha, 1998);

The Great Indian Way: A Life of Mahatma Gandhi (New Delhi: Vision, 1998).

Edition: *Kanthapura* (Delhi: Orient, 1971).

OTHER: *Changing India: An Anthology,* edited by Rao and Iqbal Singh (London: Allen & Unwin, 1939);

Whither India? edited by Rao and Singh (Bombay: Padma, 1948);

Raja Rao (from <www.onr.com/user/digleha/rijarao>)

Jawaharlal Nehru, Soviet Russia: Some Random Sketches and Impressions (first published 1929), introduction by Rao (Bombay: Chetana, 1949);

"The Case of English," in *Awakened Conscience: Studies in Commonwealth Literature,* edited by C. D. Narasimhaiah (Delhi: Sterling, 1978), pp. 420–422;

"The Cave and the Conch," in *The Eye of the Beholder: Indian Writing in English,* edited by Maggie Butcher (London: Commonwealth Institute, 1983), pp. 44–45.

SELECTED PERIODICAL PUBLICATIONS–
UNCOLLECTED:

POETRY

"Expiation of a Heretic," *Jaya Karnataka* (Dharwar), 10,
    no. 1 (1931): 27–33.

FICTION

"The Moon in Lucknow," *Illustrated Weekly of India,* 5
    November 1961, pp. 13, 15, 17; 12 November
    1961, pp. 21, 23;

"A Nest of Singing Birds," *Illustrated Weekly of India,* 10
    December 1961, pp. 27, 29;

"Fables for the Feeble," *Illustrated Weekly of India,* 9
    December 1962, pp. 46–47;

"Diwali Comes for Ramu," *Illustrated Weekly of India,* 17
    November 1963, pp. 15, 16, 17, 19.

NONFICTION

"Pilgrimage to Europe," *Jaya Karnataka,* 10, no. 3
    (1931): 27–33;

"Europe and Ourselves," *Jaya Karnataka,* 10, no. 3
    (1931): 204–207;

"Romain Rolland, the Great Sage," *Jaya Karnataka,* 11,
    no. 1 (1933);

"Pandit Taranath," *Asia* (New York) (January 1935):
    10–15;

"The Premier of Sakuntala," *Asia* (New York) (June
    1943): 365–368;

"Jupiter and Mars," *Pacific Spectator,* 8 (1954): 369–373;

"Aurobindo Ghose: An Anniversary Meeting Address,"
    *Arts and Letters: Journal of the Royal India and Pakistan
    Society,* 31, no. 2 (1957): 4–6;

"Varanasi: Cities of India," *Illustrated Weekly of India,* 3
    September 1961, pp. 12–15;

"Trivandrum: Cities of India," *Illustrated Weekly of India,*
    25 February 1962, pp. 12–16;

"The Indian Destiny," *Illustrated Weekly of India,* 27 Janu-
    ary 1963, p. 39;

"Irish Interlude," *Saturday Review* (New York), 49, no.
    26 (25 June 1966); also in *Illustrated Weekly of India,*
    9 April 1967, p. 21;

"Autobiography: Entering the Literary World," *Journal
    of Commonwealth Literature* (London), 13, no. 3
    (April 1979): 28–32.

The first full-length Indian novel in English, *Rajmohan's Wife,* by Bankimchandra Chatterjee, was published in 1864; but the novel came of age in India in the
1930s with the emergence of three major writers: Mulk
Raj Anand, R. K. Narayan, and Raja Rao. Their first
novels were published in a span of four years: Anand's
Untouchable and Narayan's *Swami and Friends* in 1935,
and Rao's *Kanthapura* in 1938. These three writers,
though, are quite unlike each other. Anand is a novelist
of ideological commitment, and each of his novels
focuses on a specific evil of Indian society–untouchabil-

ity, child labor, the exploitation of workers, whether in
a tea plantation or in industry, or the ill treatment
meted out to women. Narayan is distinguished by his
ironic vision–he has created the small town of Malgudi
and its middle-class characters. Rao, a philosophical
novelist, is the most complex of the three. His three
major novels–*Kanthapura, The Serpent and the Rope*
(1960), and *The Cat and Shakespeare: A Tale of India*
(1965)–are quite different from each other. *Kanthapura,*
dealing with the impact of Gandhian ideology on a
remote village in south India, is primarily a novel of
social realism. *The Serpent and the Rope* takes its title from
the Advaita Vedanta of Shankaracharya, in which the
serpent and the rope are symbols of ultimate reality and
cosmic illusion. *The Cat and Shakespeare* is a "metaphysical comedy" (Rao's words) dominated by the worldview of Ramanujacharya's Visistadvaita school of
Indian philosophy.

    Rao's fiction is distinguished by experimentation
in form and language. His foreword to *Kanthapura*
expresses the problems of the Indian writer succinctly:
"One has to convey in a language that is not one's own
the spirit that is one's own." He molds the language to
suit the narrator. *Kanthapura* expresses the sensibility of
a village grandmother and employs a simple vocabulary and sentence structure. Later novels such as *The
Serpent and the Rope* and *The Chessmaster and His Moves*
(1988) are written in a dense, convoluted style, reflecting the intellectual concerns of the narrator. Rao's
greatest achievement is to Indianize the novel by adopting traditional Indian modes of storytelling, based on
the *Puranas.* He is also a distinguished short-story
writer; though not many (only about a dozen stories),
they are varied in theme and treatment.

    Rao was born on 8 November 1908 in the small
town of Hassan in southern India into a family of Brah-
mins who had been advisers to kings for generations.
He was born at the precise moment when his father
was receiving the Maharaja of Mysore, Krishna Raja
Wodeyar, at their ancestral home, so the child was
named Raja (King) instead of Ramakrishna after his
grandfather. Rao was only four years old when his
mother died; his father remarried, and although his
work includes references to a kind and loving stepmother, the theme of being an orphan finds a dominant
place in the two novels that have an autobiographical
strain: *The Serpent and the Rope* and *The Chessmaster and
His Moves.* Rao was the eldest of two brothers and seven
sisters. His father taught at Nizam's College, Hyderabad, and so Rao was educated there, the only Hindu in
the Madrasa-e-Aliya, a school meant for the children of
Muslim noblemen. Annual vacations were spent in
Hassan and Malnad, the hilly region of Mysore state,
with his grandfather, who greatly influenced him: his

Frontispiece and title page for the 1971 edition of Rao's 1938 novel, about the impact of Gandhian ideology on a remote village in southern India (University of South Carolina Upstate Library)

grandfather taught him to love Sanskrit and kindled his interest in Indian philosophy. As a child, Rao often suffered from lung trouble, so he was encouraged to spend time in his "home mountains" and later sent to Aligarh in northern India. He took his B.A. degree in 1929 from Nizam's College, specializing in English and history. As he records in the preface to his collection of stories *The Policeman and the Rose* (1978): "My *karma* had certainly something to do with my Muslim connections," for Rao, a quintessential Brahmin, whose vision of India is essentially Hindu, lived in predominantly Muslim towns and studied in Muslim institutions. At the Aligarh Muslim University he studied French for the first time. He received the Asiatic Scholarship awarded by the government of Hyderabad for study abroad and went to France, since Sir Patrick Geddes had invited him to study at the international college he had established at Montpellier. Rao studied at the Sorbonne for three years, working Indian influence on

Irish literature under the supervision of Louis Cazamian. But he gave up formal academic pursuits to return to India in 1933 to live in Pandit Taranath's ashram in Tungabhadra in southern India. Rao's spiritual quest took him to various ashrams: he met Sri Aurobindo at Pondicherry, Ramana Maharshi at Tiruvannamalai (in Tamil Nadu), and Mohandas Karamchand Gandhi in Sevagram. In 1943 Rao succeeded in finding his guru, Sri Atmananda Guru, in Trivandrum: the epigraphs of Rao's novels *The Serpent and the Rope* and *The Cat and Shakespeare* are taken from Atmananda Guru's works on Vedanta.

The most important influence on Rao's early work was his first wife, Camille Mouly, a professor of French at Montpellier; she had translated the *Bhagavad Gita* and Aurobindo's commentaries into French and was interested in India. She encouraged Rao to develop a style of his own. As he writes in his article "Entering the Literary World": "She did not think my Tagore-

Yeats English (with some Macaulay added to it) was at all literary." He started writing in Kannada almost immediately after getting married in 1929. He wrote in French, too, and was influenced by such contemporary writers as Franz Kafka, who had "broken the fable of realism"; André Gide; André Malraux; James Joyce; and other Irish writers such as Frank O'Connor and Sean O'Faolain. Just four examples of Rao's Kannada work remain; these appeared in *Jaya Karnataka*, a journal published from the small town of Dharwar in Karnataka State. Rao's characteristic preoccupation with the meaning of India is found in the articles "Pilgrimage to Europe" (1931) and "Europe and Ourselves" (1931). "Romain Rolland, the Great Sage" (1932) comprises a personal interview and a brief introduction to Rolland and his work. "The Expiation of a Heretic" (1933), an autobiographical poem expressing the feeling of an Indian expatriate, is Rao's only excursion into Kannada verse. Both G. S. Amur (in his article "Raja Rao: The Kannada Phase") and M. K. Naik feel that these Kannada writings have no great intrinsic worth. Their value lies in enabling Rao to "find the richness of the English language." Rao says that he "emerged out of this holy dip a new man, with a more vigorous and maybe a more authentic style."

Most of the short stories in *The Cow of the Barricades and Other Stories* (1947) were written in the 1930s. "Javni," a story that appeared in *Asia* (New York) in 1933, was his first publication in English. The French version of "Akkayya," a short story, also appeared in the same year. Two other stories in *The Cow of the Barricades and Other Stories* first appeared in French: "A Client" (1934) and "The Little Gram Shop" (1937). "A Client" is the only story based on a Kannada original. But all the stories use English in an original manner.

Rao's short fictions fall into two broad categories. The stories written during the 1930s and early 1940s are generally in the mode of social realism, while the stories written in the 1950s and 1960s, and first published in book form in *The Policeman and the Rose*, tend to be metaphysical, with metaphorical and symbolical overtones. The stories in *The Cow of the Barricades and Other Stories* offer amazing variety. "Akkayya," "Javni," and "The Little Gram Shop" have memorable women characters and expose the cruel treatment of women, especially widows, by Indian society. The social concern of the writer is evident; the poverty of the low-caste Javni is made clear through small details, such as Javni considering an anna (a sixteenth of a rupee) a great deal of money: "It is what I earn in two days," she says. "In Khandesh," revealing the poor villagers' unquestioning love for their king, is expressionistic in technique and filled with the ominous throbbing of the drums. "The True Story of Kanakapala, Protector of Gold" is

entirely different. Rangappa, a pious villager, sets out on a pilgrimage to Kashi; on the way he has a vision of the divine couple Shiva and Parvati and builds a shrine at that spot. His greedy descendants wish to appropriate the holy pot containing Rangappa's savings dedicated to the holy couple. A cobra, Kanakapala, protects the gold day and night but does not bite the thieves because they are of Rangappa's line. Realizing that his treasure has been robbed, the snake commits suicide. The narration has all the vigor of a folktale and captures a facet of Indian life that has seldom been presented in English.

"Companions" shows that Indian culture includes both Hindu and Muslim elements. Pandit Srinath Sastri, a devout but greedy Brahmin, is born as a serpent because of a curse and can get redemption only when Moti Khan, a Muslim basket maker, sees God. The Muslim travels north to Sheikh Chisti's tomb in Fatehpur Sikri and has a mystic experience there. "Narsiga" and "The Cow of Barricades" offer vignettes of India's struggle for freedom, the central theme of Rao's first novel, *Kanthapura*.

In his foreword to *Kanthapura*, Rao writes, "There is no village in India, however mean, that has not a rich *sthala-purana*, or legendary history, of its own. . . . One such story from the contemporary annals of my village I have tried to tell." The novel describes the impact of Gandhi and the struggle for freedom on a small village in southern India. Through his narrator, a garrulous grandmother, and his range of characters, Rao re-creates village life and reveals human nature in its rich diversity. Two stock elements of the village, the temple and the greedy moneylender, are present, but in *Kanthapura* the baseness of Bhatta, the village priest who grows rich by lending money, is a study of the degeneration of the Brahmin. Rao also gives a graphic account of the exploitation of the coolies in the nearby Skeffington coffee estate. The novel was a pioneering effort; Meenakshi Mukherjee refers to *Kanthapura* as "a remarkably radical text, in which he [Rao] experimented with language and used a collective feminine perspective, fusing myth and history in an innovative narrative mode." The narrative structure of *Kanthapura* exhibits many features of the *Puranas*, such as the *upakatha* ("subsidiary narrative"), which allows the narrator to digress freely. Like the *harikatha*, an oral performance of the *Purana* by a single speaker, the idiom of *Kanthapura* is colloquial, and the narrator uses songs to enliven the story. Rao never presents Mahatma Gandhi as a flesh-and-blood character in his novels; he shows Gandhi's impact through the influence of Moorthy, an educated young villager who has a mystic vision of the Mahatma. *Kanthapura* is a work of social realism, but it is not confined to that plane alone;

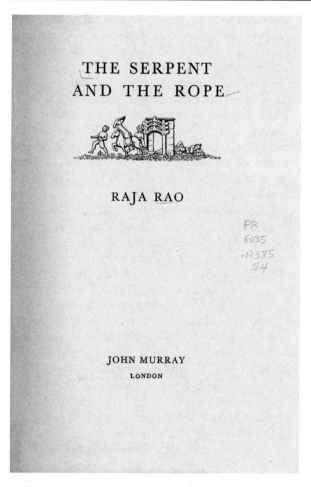

THE SERPENT
AND THE ROPE

RAJA RAO

JOHN MURRAY
LONDON

Title page for Rao's 1960 novel, about the troubled marriage of an Indian scholar and his European wife (Thomas Cooper Library, University of South Carolina)

as critic H. M. Williams has observed, "*Kanthapura,* which looks in many ways like a realistic epic of the freedom struggle, turns out on introspection to be the first of Raja Rao's explorations of the nature of India."

Rao's second novel, *The Serpent and the Rope,* has a much wider scope than *Kanthapura;* it moves to Benares, France, and England from the protagonist Ramaswamy's ancestral village of Hariharapura. It ends with the narrator finding his guru at Trivandrum; this novel includes a strong autobiographical element that describes the failure of the marriage between a south Indian Brahmin and a French girl (Rao's marriage was dissolved in 1949). Many novelists have explored the encounter between India and the West. But in Rao's novel, the West is not merely Madeleine, whom Ramaswamy marries, but a multitude of characters: her cousin Catherine; her uncle Charles Rousselin and aunt Zoubeida; Lezo, the exile from Spain; the religious Russian, Georges Khuschbertieff; the French taxi driver, Henri; the porter at Girton College, Cambridge;

and the patron at the café at Aix. The novel is not only about contemporary Europe, but also its cultural history through the centuries: Tristan and Isolde, Jacques-Bénigne Bossuet, Karl Marx, Friedrich Nietzsche, Adolf Hitler, Joseph Stalin, the troubadours of Provençe, the cathedrals of France, the operas of Richard Wagner, and *The Brothers Karamazov* (1879–1880) by Fyodor Dostoevsky. It is a *soutenance de theses* at the Sorbonne and the coronation of Queen Elizabeth in London.

The Serpent and the Rope is narrated by Ramaswamy, who goes to Europe in 1946 to study; three years later he marries Madeleine, whom he meets at the University of Caen. The novel begins with Rama's visit to India at the age of twenty-two, when his father falls ill and dies. Rama's meeting with Savithri, the unwilling fiancée of his friend Pratap, highlights what he misses in Madeleine. The death of both their children, one at seven months, another at birth, proves too much for Madeleine. Rama's second visit to India, for the marriage of his sister Saroja, increases the rift between Madeleine and Rama. Madeleine turns to Buddhism, withdrawing from the world; she mistakenly thinks that all Rama needs to be happy is an Indian wife nearer his age (she is five years older than he) and so completes the divorce proceedings when he returns to France. All these experiences breed *vairagya* (a sense of detachment) in Rama, and he realizes that only a guru can show him the way out of this *samsara* (career or the soul); at the end of the novel he is at peace, having found his guru. The novel deals with the themes of love, death, and marriage; the repeated allusions lend rhythm to the narrative. An important organizational principle is that of cyclic repetition. Rao explores the theme of marriage through parallel instance: Tristan and Isolde, Abelard and Heloise, the Upanishadic story of sage Yajnyavalkya and Maitreyi, Satyavan and Savithri, Rama and Sita, and Krishna and Radha. Many other repeated motifs relate to Buddha's great renunciation, Paul Valéry's "Le Cimetière Marin," and the Cathars. The scene shifts back and forth in time and space with frequent flashbacks.

Rao has said that the novel is an attempt at "a Pauranic recreation of Indian storytelling: that is to say, the story as a story is conveyed through a thin thread to which are attached (or which passes through) many other stories, fables and philosophical disquisitions, like a *mala* [beads used to count mantras or prayers]." Many stories are attached to the main narrative, like beads in a necklace. Some, such as the story of Satyavrata (a king of the *Puranas,* who has to choose between giving up the deer that had sought refuge or breaking his vow of silence), or the parable about the man who tried to cover the whole world with leather instead of buying himself some footwear, are a part of Ramaswamy's consciousness. The folktale about Prince Satyakama and the princess who comes out of a pumpkin provides a parallel to the life of Ramaswamy and Savithri. The novel includes many philosophical discussions between Ramaswamy and his friends abroad. This inclusion is contextually appropriate, because the protagonist is an intellectual, researching a complex concept, trying to establish the link between the Druzes, the Manicheans, the Cathars, the Albigensian heresy, and Buddhism. Rao attempts to infuse something of the rhythms of Sanskrit into his English prose. Some Sanskrit literary texts mix prose and verse *(champu-kavya)*. Rao incorporates poetry (French and German), Sanskrit hymns and chants, the *bhajans* of Mirabai, Provençal songs, snatches of opera (with musical notations), diary entries, legends, and folktales to give his prose a distinctive texture.

The Serpent and the Rope won the Sahitya Akademi Award in 1964, and the government of India honored Rao with the Padma Bhushan in 1969. In 1965 Rao accepted an invitation from the University of Texas, Austin, to teach philosophy, and in the same year he married Katherine Jones, a young American actress. They have a son. His third novel, *The Cat and Shakespeare,* was published in 1965. It is also philosophical, but in the comic mode, and presents an authentic picture of life in India in the 1940s. It is a kind of sequel to *The Serpent and the Rope,* which posited *mukti* (salvation) through *jnana* (knowledge). The symbol of the cat is from the philosophy of Ramanujacharya, which lays emphasis on Divine Grace, and salvation through *bhakti* (devotion). Just as the kitten allows itself to be carried by the mother cat, so humanity can attain salvation by complete surrender to the Divine. An earlier version called "The Cat" was published in *The Chelsea Review* in 1959, but in terms of composition, the novel came earlier. According to Naik, "*The Cat and Shakespeare* was actually written about two years after *The Serpent and the Rope* was completed in 1955–1956."

Ramakrishna Pai, the narrator, and Govindan Nair are clerks in a government rationing office in Trivandrum in the 1950s. Pai's wife, Saroja, is so busy managing the ancestral property that she has no inclination to travel to Trivandrum to look after her husband. Nair, Pai's neighbor, helps him at every step; through his grace, Pai is vouchsafed a mystic vision. The novel includes bizarre incidents such as a scene of cat worship in the ration office and a trial in which the cat is a witness. While *The Serpent and the Rope* shows the hero struggling for enlightenment and looking for a guru, *The Cat and Shakespeare* shows the grace of the guru in operation. Holy men are stock characters in Indian fiction. The majority of novelists—for example, Anand, Khushwant Singh, Narayan (in *The Guide* [1958]), and

Manohar Malgonkar—present them as frauds who exploit the faith of gullible people. Rao's Govindan Nair is far from the popular image of the holy man; that this guru is credible is a measure not only of Rao's talent as a novelist but also of his deep understanding of the Indian spiritual tradition and the concept of the *jivanmukta,* a person who has attained salvation while continuing with worldly life. The language of *The Cat and Shakespeare* is simple; yet, Nair can express complex truths because he works through parables similar to those in the Upanishads (commentaries on the Vedas [earliest Hindu sacred writings]).

Comrade Kirillov (1976), written a few years before *The Serpent and the Rope,* is a sketch of an Indian communist whose real name is Padmanabha Iyer. It was first published in a French version by Georges Fradier in 1965. The epigraph of the novel is from Dostoevsky's *The Possessed* (1872), and Rao's characters are as obsessed with India as Dostoevsky's Shatov is with Mother Russia. The style is involved, featuring long words and sentences. Critics such as Naik, D. S. Maini, and Narsingh Srivastava feel that this novella lacks form and seems to be merely a rehash of material left undeveloped in Rao's earlier work. P. K. Rajan admires the book for its satire, though he feels that the novel is "divested of literary form" and is "deficient in what precisely is Raja Rao's superb achievement in *Kanthapura,* a sublime artistic cohesion." But other critics—such as Esha Dey, V. V. Badve, and Vineypal Kaur Kirpal—praise its form; Kirpal, in fact, believes that the novel has "perfect structural unity."

The narrator, "R," a friend of Padmanabha Iyer (Kirillov), resembles the novelist himself. Kirillov marries a Czech girl, Irene, and they have a son, Kamal. When Irene dies in childbirth a few years later, Kamal is sent to his grandfather in south India. The novel is lyrically intense in its description of "R" taking the child to the temple of the Virgin Goddess at Kanya Kumari and thus providing a kind of vicarious homecoming for the Moscow-bound Kirillov and Irene, who loved India. The narrative is interspersed with a twenty-six-page excerpt from Irene's diaries covering the period 1939–1945, which provides a different perspective on events. The book includes interminable discussions of communism and allied matters. Rao appears to be saying that an Indian communist is a contradiction in terms, that an Indian can only be a Gandhian.

Rao's second collection of short stories, *The Policeman and the Rose,* has an informative preface by Rao about his writing practice. He had published several sketches and short stories in a popular magazine, *The Illustrated Weekly of India,* in the 1960s. Three of these stories are included in *The Policeman and the Rose,* which reprints seven earlier stories (with only slight revisions).

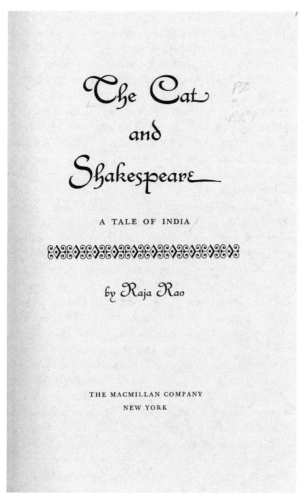

The Cat

and

Shakespeare

A TALE OF INDIA

by Raja Rao

THE MACMILLAN COMPANY
NEW YORK

*Title page for Rao's 1965 novel, about a government clerk
in Trivandrum who finds a guru of sorts in a
fellow clerk (Thomas Cooper Library,
University of South Carolina)*

"The Cow of the Barricades," the title story of the earlier collection, has an allegorical dimension. In this story about India's struggle for independence (the theme of *Kanthapura*), the cow is a real creature as well as a symbol of Mother India, and the "Master" parallels Mahatma Gandhi. In "India: A Fable," too, the subjects are valid both as symbols and at the realistic level. Critics have praised this story, which mixes fact and fancy, but the uninitiated reader may find the philosophy obtrusive. "The Policeman and the Rose" presents reality through the parable of a nameless narrator who is "arrested when born." Rao makes no attempt at realism, and the action takes place at an unspecified time. The policeman and the rose have multiple meanings— such as the fetters of the ego, the sensual life, and karma—ably explicated by Naik and C. D. Narasimhaiah. "Nimka" is the story of a young white Russian living in self-exile in Paris with her mother. The girl is attracted to the young Indian narrator (who appears to be a clone of Ramaswamy, the narrator of *The Serpent and the Rope*) and loves nineteen-year-old Michel, a student of Sanskrit. She marries an old Russian count, but he soon deserts her and their son.

Rao taught at Texas from 1966 to 1980. In 1972 he was named a Fellow of the Woodrow Wilson International Center, Washington, D.C. He was elected an Honorary Fellow of the Modern Language Association of America in 1984. After his divorce from Katherine, he married for a third time in 1986. In 1988 he won the Neustadt International Prize in literature, sponsored by the University of Oklahoma. The essays in the special issue of *World Literature Today* published on the occasion speak highly of his work, especially his fifth novel, *The Chessmaster and His Moves,* the first volume of a projected trilogy. The concept of life as *lila* ("play of the Divine") is present in *The Cat and Shakespeare;* in *The Chessmaster and His Moves* worldly existence is likened to a game of chess. The hero, Sivarama Sastri, is a brilliant mathematician working in Paris. Like Moorthy, Ramaswamy, Ramakrishna Pai, and "R" of the earlier novels, he is a south Indian Brahmin. He has many women in his life: Suzanne, an actress who lives with him and hopes to marry him; Jayalakshmi, the Indian princess married to Surrendar Singh; and Mireille, married to a close friend of Sastri. The hero's sister Uma is portrayed vividly; the way she almost worships her brother recalls Saroja in *The Serpent and the Rope.* The 729-page *The Chessmaster and His Moves* includes many philosophical discussions, with Sastri meeting his match in the "rabbi," Michel, a survivor of the concentration camps. As in his other novels, Rao is preoccupied with India and the real meaning of being a Brahmin.

Critical opinion is sharply divided on the merits of *The Chessmaster and His Moves.* Edwin Thumboo calls it "the most international novel we have" and "Rao's greatest achievement." R. Parthasarathy considers it "a metaphysical novel without equal in our time." Prema Nandakumar, however, is forthright in condemning it in her book review published in *The Hindu:* "The tedium is often unbearable . . . Raja Rao goes on and on mesmerized by his own voice." Naik feels that *The Chessmaster and His Moves* is little more than a reworking of material already presented. As he says in *Indian English Literature 1980–2000: A Critical Survey:* "The chief difficulty with *The Chessmaster and His Moves* is that at every step, it fills one with an uncomfortable sense of *déjà vu;* the narrative reads almost like a more prolix and rather confused retelling of Raja Rao's acknowledged masterpiece, *The Serpent and the Rope.*"

On the Ganga Ghat (1989) is a series of stories delineating a variety of characters, including birds and animals, in the holy city of Benares. Rao's claim that the eleven chapters are part of a linked narrative "so structured that the whole book should be read as a single novel" is difficult to justify. The last chapter includes musings on life in general and on Benares in particular.

Rao was elected a Fellow of the Sahitya Akademi (New Delhi) in 1997. *The Meaning of India* (1996) brings together his nonfiction work published earlier in journals as varied as *The Texas Quarterly, Encounter,* and *The Literary Criterion* (Mysore). *The Meaning of India* also includes articles as well as speeches (such as his acceptance speech of the Neustadt International Prize in 1988) and prefaces to anthologies of essays (such as the memorial volume to Indira Gandhi). Just one piece, "The Silence of Mahatma Gandhi," was written especially for this collection. Rao has written about the significance of Mahatma Gandhi in novels (especially *Kanthapura* [1938], and *Comrade Kirillov* [1976]) and short stories. He has now published a biography, *The Great Indian Way: A Life of Mahatma Gandhi* (1998), which employs the convoluted, philosophical prose of his later novels.

Raja Rao has dealt extensively with the meaning of India, whether the village (*Kanthapura*), the small town (*The Cat and Shakespeare*), or the young intellectual abroad (*The Serpent and the Rope*). These three novels have attained the status of classics. Critics differ in their valuation of *The Chessmaster and His Moves;* but they all agree that Rao is one of the most important Indian-English novelists of the twentieth century, because he Indianized the novel in form, language, and theme.

Front cover for the Indian edition of Rao's 1978 short-story collection, which includes "The Cow of the Barricades," an allegory of India's struggle for independence that was also the title story of Rao's first collection, published in 1947 (Thomas Cooper Library, University of South Carolina)

Interviews:

S.V.V., "Raja Rao: Face to Face," *Illustrated Weekly of India,* 5 January 1964, pp. 44–45;

A. S. Raman, "A Meeting with Raja Rao Recalled," *Illustrated Weekly of India,* 25 September 1966, p. 13; 25 October 1966, p. 63;

A. P. O'Brien, "Meeting Raja Rao," *Prajna* (Benares), Golden Jubilee Number (1966): 16–17;

Som P. Ranchan, "A Meeting with Raja Rao," *Thought,* 20, no. 28 (1968): 14–16; 20, no. 28 (1968): 14–16; 20, no. 29 (1968): 14–16; 20, no. 30 (1968): 14–16; 20, 31 (1968): 14–16;

R. Parthasarathy, "An Interview with Raja Rao," *Span* (September 1977): 29–30;

Shobhana Bhattacharya, "Interview with Raja Rao," *Book Review* (New Delhi) (September–October 1982): 63–67;

Asha Kaushik, "Meeting Raja Rao: An Interview," in *Literary Criterion,* 18, no. 3 (1983): 33–38.

Bibliographies:

S. R. Jamkhandi, "Raja Rao: A Select Checklist of Primary and Secondary Material," *Journal of Commonwealth Literature,* 16, no. 1 (1981): 132–141;

R. Parthasarathy, "Raja Rao: Selected Bibliography 1931–1988," *World Literature Today,* 62, no. 4 (1988): 556–560.

References:

Ahmed Ali, "Illusion and Reality: The Art and Philosophy of Raja Rao," *Journal of Commonwealth Literature,* 5 (1968): 16–28;

G. S. Amur, "Raja Rao: The Kannada Phase," *Journal of the Karnatak University,* 10 (1966): 40–62;

Mulk Raj Anand, "Roots and Flower: Content and Form in *Untouchable* and *Kanthapura,*" *Littcrit,* 8, no. 1 (1982): 47–60;

V. V. Badve, "Comrade Kirillov," *New Quest,* 14 (1979): 121–128;

P. C. Bhattacharya, *Indo-Anglian Literature and the Works of Raja Rao* (Delhi: Atma Ram, 1983);

P. Dayal, *Raja Rao: A Study of His Novels* (New Delhi: Atlantic, 1991);

Esha Dey, *The Novels of Raja Rao: The Theme of Quest* (New Delhi: Prestige, 1992);

Janet Powers Gemmill, "Narrative Technique in the Novels of Raja Rao," *DAI* (University of Wisconsin at Madison), 33 (1972): 6309A–6310A;

Robert L. Hardgrave Jr., ed., *Word as Mantra: The Art of Raja Rao* (New Delhi: Katha in association with the University of Texas at Austin, 1998);

V. Y. Kantak, "The Language of Indian Fiction in English," in *Critical Essays on Indian Writing in English,* edited by M. K. Naik and others (Dharwar: Karnataka University, 1968), pp. 147–159;

Vineypal Kaur Kirpal, "Comrade Kirillov," *Journal of Indian Writing in English,* 5, no. 2 (1977): 46–49;

Winfred P. Lehmann, "Literature and Linguistics: Text Linguistics," *Literary Criterion,* 17, no. 1 (1982): 18–29–includes a study of "The Cow of the Barricades";

David McCutchion, "The Novel as Sastra," review of *The Serpent and the Rope, Writers Workshop Miscellany,* 8 (1961): 91–99; reprinted in *Essays on Indian Writing in English* (Calcutta: Writers Workshop, 1968);

Meenakshi Mukherjee, "Raja Rao's Shorter Fiction," *Indian Literature,* 10, no. 3 (1967): 66–76;

Mukherjee, *The Twice Born Fiction: Themes and Techniques of the Indian Novel in English* (New Delhi: Arnold-Heinemann, 1971);

S. Nagarajan, "A Note on Myth and Ritual in *The Serpent and the Rope,*" *Journal of Commonwealth Literature,* 7, no. 1 (1971): 45–48;

M. J. Naik, *Raja Rao,* revised edition (Madras: Blackie, 1982);

Naik and Shyamala A. Narayan, *Indian English Literature 1980–2000: A Critical Survey* (New Delhi: Pencraft International, 2001);

Naik, ed., *Perspectives on Indian Fiction in English* (New Delhi: Abhinav, 1985), pp. 58–92;

Prema Nandakumar, "Polite Passion of the Bourgeois Drawing Room," *Hindu* (Madras) (23 August 1988): 22;

C. D. Narasimhaiah, *Raja Rao,* Indian Writers Series (New Delhi: Arnold-Heinemann, 1973);

Narayan, *Raja Rao: Man and His Works* (New Delhi: Sterling, 1988);

Reza Ahmad Nasimi, *The Language of Mulk Raj Anand, Raja Rao and R. K. Narayan* (New Delhi: Capital, 1989);

Shiva Niranjan, *Raja Rao, Novelist as Sadhaka* (Ghaziabad: Vimal Prakashan, 1985);

Alastair Niven, *Truth within Fiction: A Study of Raja Rao's The Serpent and the Rope* (Calcutta: Writers Workshop, 1987);

Rajesh K. Pallan, *Myths and Symbols in Raja Rao and R. K. Narayan: A Select Study* (Jalandhar: ABS, 1994);

Chandrashekar B. Patil, "The Kannada Element in Raja Rao's Prose: A Linguistic Study of *Kanthapura,*" *Journal of Karanatak University,* 13 (1969): 143–167;

P. K. Rajan, "Introducing *Comrade Kirillov,*" *Littcrit,* 3, no. 1 (1977): 51–54;

Ragini Ramachandra, ed., *Raja Rao: An Anthology of Recent Criticism* (New Delhi: Pencraft, 2000);

K. R. Rao, *The Fiction of Raja Rao* (Aurangabad: Parimal Prakashan, 1980);

K. K. Sharma, ed., *Perspectives on Raja Rao,* Indo-English Writers Series (Ghaziabad: Vimal Prakashan, 1980);

Paul Sharrad, *Raja Rao and Cultural Tradition* (New Delhi: Sterling, 1987);

R. Shepherd, "Raja Rao: Symbolism in *The Cat and Shakespeare,*" *World Literature Written in English,* 14, no. 2 (1975): 347–356;

Narsingh Srivastava, *The Mind and Art of Raja Rao* (Bareilly: Prakash Book Depot, 1981);

H. M. Williams, *Indo-Anglian Literature 1800–1970: A Survey* (New Delhi: Orient Longman, 1976);

World Literature Today (University of Oklahoma), special Raja Rao issue, 62, no. 3 (1988).

Arundhati Roy

(24 November 1961 –   )

E. Nageswara Rao
Osmania University

BOOKS: *The Soviet Intervention in Afghanistan: Causes, Consequences and India's Response* (New Delhi: Associated Public House, 1987);

The God of Small Things (London: HarperCollins, 1997; New York: Random House, 1997; New Delhi: IndiaInk, 1997);

The End of Imagination (Kottayam: D. C. Books, 1998);

The Greater Common Good (Bombay: India Book Distributor, 1999);

The Cost of Living (New York: Modern Library, 1999)– comprises *The End of Imagination* and *The Greater Common Good;*

Power Politics (Kottayam: D. C. Books, 2001; expanded edition, Cambridge, Mass.: South End Press, 2001)–expanded edition comprises "The Ladies Have Feelings, So . . . ," *Power Politics,* "On Citizens' Right to Express Dissent," "The Algebra of Infinite Justice," and "War Is Peace";

The Algebra of Infinite Justice (New Delhi & London: Viking, 2001; expanded edition, London: Flamingo, 2002)–expanded edition comprises *The End of Imagination, The Greater Common Good, Power Politics,* "The Ladies Have Feelings, So . . . ," "The Algebra of Infinite Justice," "War Is Peace," "Democracy," and "War Talk";

War Talk (Cambridge, Mass.: South End Press, 2003)–comprises "War Talk," "Ahimsa," "Democracy," "Come September," "The Loneliness of Noam Chomsky," and "Confronting Empire";

In Which Annie Gives It Those Ones (New Delhi & New York: Penguin, 2003);

The Ordinary Person's Guide to Empire (Cambridge, Mass.: South End Press, 2004; London: Flamingo, 2004)–comprises "Peace Is War," "Instant Mix: Imperial Democracy," "When the Saints Go Marching Out," "In Memory of Shankar Guha Niyogi," "Do Turkeys Enjoy Thanksgiving?" and "How Deep Shall We Dig?";

Public Power in the Age of Empire (New York: Seven Stories Press, 2004).

Arundhati Roy (photograph © Pradip Krishen; from the dust jacket for the U.S. edition of The God of Small Things, *1997; Richland County Public Library)*

PRODUCED SCRIPTS: *In Which Annie Gives It Those Ones,* television, Grapevine Media, 1989;

Electric Moon, television, Channel 4, 1992;

DAM/AGE: A Film with Arundhati Roy, television, BBC Films, 2002.

SELECTED PERIODICAL PUBLICATIONS– UNCOLLECTED: "Democracy and Religious Fascism," *CounterPunch,* 3 May 2002 <http://www.counterpunch.org/roy0503.html>;

"The Day of the Jackals," *CounterPunch,* 2 June 2003 <http://www.counterpunch.org/roy06022003.html>.

Arundhati Roy achieved international fame in 1997 with her debut novel, *The God of Small Things,* which not only garnered large advances from publishers but also earned her the prestigious Booker Prize. She has also been an architect, a scriptwriter, an actress, and a journalist and is now well known as an essayist, a forceful speaker, a social activist, and a feminist. Her writings are published worldwide, and her speeches at international forums on important issues such as the war in Afghanistan and in Iraq, the environment, big dams, religious fanaticism, and nuclear weapons have made her an influential spokesperson for the world outside Europe and America. In the foreword to her 1989 screenplay, *In Which Annie Gives It Those Ones* (published in 2003), however, she explains that she has not "leap-frogged" from one profession to another: "Everything that I have done so far has been a process of refining a way of thinking, of seeing the world." Her clear and impassioned articulation of her vision is perhaps one of the reasons *People Magazine* named her in 1998 as one of the fifty most beautiful people in the world.

Roy was born on 24 November 1961 at Shillong, Meghalaya, India. She was christened Susanna Arundhati Roy, but she ultimately dropped her first name. Her mother, Mary Roy, is a Syrian Christian from Kerala who later became a social activist. Her father is a Bengali Hindu and was a tea planter who worked in the northeast of India. Mary Roy divorced her husband after having two children, Arundhati and her brother, Lalith. About her father, Roy has told *Sunday Plus:* "I don't know him. I've only seen him a couple of times, that's it." After the divorce, Mary Roy returned to her native village, Ayamanam, near Kottayam, Kerala, with her children. She fought and won a legal battle in the Indian Supreme Court that delivered a landmark judgment giving Christian women in Kerala the right to their parents' property.

Roy was educated at an informal school, Corpus Christi, set up by her mother. Later she spent a few years in a boarding school in Kerala. She moved to Delhi at sixteen and started leading a bohemian life. She lived in a hut in a slum in Ferozshah Kotla for some time and made a living by selling empty beer bottles and by teaching aerobics. She studied architecture in the Delhi School of Architecture but did not complete a degree. In her foreword to *In Which Annie Gives It Those Ones,* she writes that as a student of architecture, she saw that "there was a design behind the apparent chaos in the society in which we live." She realized that "in India we have citizens and 'non-citizens,' those who matter and those who don't." Her sojourn in the school of architecture made her "understand the endless conflict between power and powerlessness—the conflict that is the central preoccupation of much of my work now." The study of architecture made her observe the structure, design, and minute details of things other than buildings. Although she rates her teachers as "medio-

cre," her training in architecture was "invaluable," because she could apply the principles of her discipline to novels, screenplays, and essays.

While she was in the school of architecture she married a fellow student, Gerard De Cunha. Their marriage was not official, however, as it was not registered: there was a long queue in the registrar's office, and they did not have the time and patience to wait for their turn. They went to Goa to be flower children, and they made and sold cakes on the beach for seven months. But she eventually got tired of the tourists and of selling cakes. She left De Cunha after four years and returned to Delhi almost penniless; however, she soon got a job at the National Institute of Urban Affairs. Her dress and demeanor were distinctive: she wore shells on her ankles, smoked cigarettes by placing them vertically in a holder, and rode a rented red bicycle to work.

In 1984 the movie director Pradip Krishen spotted Roy and offered her a small role in his motion picture *Massey Sahib* (1985). The offer was conveyed through Krishen's then-wife, who worked in the same office as Roy. After a good deal of persuasion by her colleagues, Roy agreed to appear as Saila, whom she called (in a 1997 interview with Vir Sanghvi) "a tribal bimbo." Eventually, Roy and Krishen got married. She won a scholarship to go to Italy for eight months to study the restoration of monuments. During her stay in Italy she realized that she would like to be a writer. Between 1985 and 1987 Roy and her husband worked on a twenty-six-episode television epic titled "Bargad" (The Banyan Tree). It was set in Allahabad between 1921 and 1950. The aim of this serial was to depict India's freedom movement from the perspectives of five different characters from various professions who were all graduates of Muir Central College. The story line was written in opposition to the idea of India as depicted in either the sentiments of the Jewel-in-the-Crown school of absurd colonial nostalgia or the emotions associated with homegrown varieties of chest-thumping nationalism. Much to the disappointment of Roy and her colleagues, however, this ambitious project was given up after a few episodes as the production company, ITV, faced financial difficulties.

In 1987 Roy wrote *The Soviet Intervention in Afghanistan: Causes, Consequences and India's Response.* It signaled Roy's deepening interest in politics, current affairs, and journalism. Her next venture was the story and screenplay of *In Which Annie Gives It Those Ones,* written in 1988. The genesis of this work is interesting. At an informal gathering of friends at which Bhaskar Ghose, the director-general of Door Darshan (the Indian broadcasting service), was present, Roy wondered why moviemakers in India turned the cameras away from themselves and their milieu. This resistance to introspection and reluctance to focus on "fractured hybrid selves" puzzled her. Ghose encouraged her to write on such a theme and promised funds. The result was *In Which Annie Gives It Those Ones,* which Krishen directed. Although it was shown only once on national television, in a late-night slot, it became popular among the English-speaking urban Indian youth.

The setting is a school of architecture in 1974. The movie depicts the lives of dope-smoking, bell-bottom-wearing, vaguely idealistic final-year students who are about to submit their architectural theses. The main character is Anand Grover (or Annie), who is repeating his fifth-year examinations for the fourth time. He attributes his failure to his feud with the dean, Dr. Y. D. Billimoria, whose initials are said by students to stand for Yam Doot (messenger of the god of death). Annie's friends decide to lure the dean away with a fake phone call when Annie's turn to be examined comes. Also, they conspire to see that Annie's oral examination comes at the end of the day when all the examiners are tired and hungry. The students thus get the better of their dean and help Annie pass the examination.

In the movie, Roy plays the role of Radha, "a bright, brash and not so sweet thing." However, the main attraction of Roy's debut movie is the dialogue: she gives the language the status of a character. She attempts to reproduce English as students in Delhi University spoke it in the early 1970s. In her foreword, written in 2003, she describes this language as "an alloy melted down and then refashioned, soldered together with Hindi (occasionally even a little Punjabi) to suit our communication requirements." One reason for the success of the movie is its phonographic fidelity to the speech of contemporary Delhi youths. An example may be found in the coy young student Lekha's appeal to the dean: "Hai sir, I'm so confused pata nahi, kuch samajh mei nahi aa raha what to do?"

Looking at *In Which Annie Gives It Those Ones* in retrospect, Roy described it in her foreword as "lunatic fringe cinema." The script prefigures Roy's activism and is an early indication of her commitment to the underprivileged. In defending her architectural thesis, Radha tells the jury:

> Every Indian city consists of a "City" and a "Non-City." And they are at war with one another. The city consists of a number of institutions, houses, officers, shops, roads, and sewage systems. . . . These institutions are designed by the architect-engineer. The noncitizen has no institutions. He lives and works in the gaps between institutions, he shits on top of the sewage system. So in this way he designs these institutions . . . these symbols, the architect-engineer is telling the noncitizen, "keep out," "stay out of here," "this does not belong to you". . . . It's a way of establishing territory.

Dust jacket for the American edition of Roy's 1997 Booker Prize–winning novel, told mainly from the perspective of a girl twin who witnesses the decline of her family, a cousin's death, and her mother's affair with an employee from a lower caste (Richland County Public Library)

In Roy's view, the architect stakes his or her territory by manipulating the built environment.

In Which Annie Gives It Those Ones won two awards given by the government of India. One of these was for the best screenplay, while the second one was for the best movie in languages other than those specified in Schedule VIII of the Indian Constitution. The latter award was presented at the National Film Festival in 1989. Roy's unconventional attire at the awards ceremony provoked the cabinet minister to say that he would prescribe a dress code for such functions thereafter.

Roy wrote the screenplay for Krishen's movie *Electric Moon* in 1992. It was telecast on Britain's Channel 4 but was not a success. She admitted later to Sanghvi that when she wrote it she did not know enough about motion pictures and was thus unable to introduce "a more anarchic quality" to it. This script is no longer available.

In 1994 Roy ventured into movie criticism by writing a scathing review of Shekhar Kapur's much-hyped movie *Bandit Queen,* released that year. The review, "The Great Indian Rape Trick I and II," appeared in *Sunday* (22 August and 3 September 1994). Kapur claimed that his movie was based on Mala Sen's book *India's Bandit Queen: The Story of Phoolan Devi* (1991), a biography of a famous gang leader and modern Robin Hood figure imprisoned in 1983. In her review, Roy charges Kapur with exploiting Devi and misrepresenting both her life and the cause she stood for. Roy points out that Kapur did not care to meet or talk to Devi and had not bothered to show his movie to her. Roy felt that Kapur was not fair to either Devi or Sen's book. Kapur's movie, Roy declares, "seriously jeopardized Phoolan Devi's life," because it shows her as a murderer, a charge that she had denied. Since the court had not yet given its verdict on her case, Roy argues, the movie should not have passed a judgment on it either. (Devi was released in 1994; she was elected to Parliament in 1996 and was assassinated in 2001.) This controversial review in which Roy defended Devi and pilloried the icons of the Hindi motion-picture industry drew a good deal of media attention. The review also involved her in court cases.

Roy then returned to writing a novel she had started some years earlier that was eventually titled *The God of Small Things.* She finished it in May 1996 and showed it to Pankaj Mishra, an author and editor at HarperCollins in India; he was so impressed that he sent it to British publishers for consideration, and within days Roy was receiving unprecedented offers for publication rights. She eventually chose HarperCollins in Britain and Random House in the United States. After the novel appeared, Roy went on a promotional tour that took her to seventy cities. The novel was translated into twenty-seven languages in the same period. The book sold half a million copies within a few months and was on the best-seller lists all over the world for a long time.

The God of Small Things is based on Roy's childhood experiences in Kerala, where major religions such as Christianity, Hinduism, Islam, and Judaism coexist with ideologies such as Marxism. The inspiration for the novel was an image that came to her and that became the central scene of the novel: "the image of this sky blue Plymouth stuck at the railroad crossing with the twins [Rahel and Estha] inside and this Marxist procession raging around it."

The novel is set in the 1960s in the fictitious village of Ayemenem, near Kottayam in the southern state of Kerala. It deals with the decline of the Ipe family through three generations. The world of the Ipes, a Syrian Christian family, is a microcosm of the tensions, interfamily jealousies, conspiracies, and politics that are rife in Indian homes where a joint family system still prevails. Almost everyone in this novel has an unhappy married life and/or an unfulfilled love affair. Pappachi (Bennan Ipe) is an imperial entomologist in Delhi. He suffers from a sense of deprivation since he feels that his discovery of a moth was not given due recognition. He is a habitual wife beater. His wife, Mammachi (Soshamma), suffers silently but continues to respect him. Pappachi's sister, Baby Kochamma (Navomi Ipe), has been jilted in love. She lives in the same house but adopts the position of an old spinster who lays down the moral code for the family. At eighty-three, she "lives her life backwards." Pappachi and Mammachi have a son, Chacko, and a daughter, Ammu. Chacko goes to Cambridge, does not do well in his studies, and marries a British woman, Margaret. They have a daughter, Sophie Mol, but are soon divorced. Chacko returns home and takes charge of his mother's pickle business. Margaret marries a second time, but when her second husband dies, she visits Chacko with Sophie Mol. Denied the opportunity for higher education, Ammu goes to Calcutta, marries a tea planter in Assam against the wishes of her parents, and gives birth to twins, Estha (a boy) and Rahel (a girl).

Ammu then divorces her irresponsible husband and returns to her parental home. She falls in love with Velutha, an "untouchable" employee (with whom contact is forbidden because he is of a lower caste). They carry on their affair secretly for thirteen nights in an ancient house on a riverbank. Velutha has several skills that attract the twins to him. He also helps them out in many ways. He repairs an old boat in which the twins and their cousin, Sophie Mol, go for rides on the river; but on one of these rides, Sophie Mol is drowned. Just before that, the Ammu-Velutha liaison is discovered. Ammu is locked up at home, while Velutha is dismissed. The Communist Party, of which he is a member, stands on high moral ground and refuses to help him. Baby Kochamma twists facts to make it appear that Velutha had kidnapped the children as an act of revenge for his dismissal and was responsible for Sophie Mol's death. The twins are silenced and separated. The boy is sent back to his father in Calcutta, later returning to the village when his father migrates to Australia. Rahel studies architecture in Delhi, marries an American, migrates to the United States, divorces, and then returns to her ancestral village after sixteen years. Ammu is not allowed to make a statement before the police; Chacko expels her from the house at the instigation of Baby Kochamma, and she dies at the age of thirty-one as a destitute in a lodge. Thus the lives of almost all the characters are wrecked. The twins have incestuous relations; they also feel guilty for their role in allowing the innocent and good-natured Velutha to be beaten to death by the police.

While narrating the story of the fall of the house of the Ipes through Rahel, Roy also attacks the lack of humanity, understanding, and sympathy within the family. The other pillars of society such as the Church, the elected Communist government, the trade union, and the police establishment also come in for satiric comments. Lack of harmony at home and an unjust society are striking features of the events depicted in the novel.

The novel has definite autobiographical undertones. As Roy put it in a press interview at the British Council in New Delhi on 5 April 1997 (reported by Claire Scobie), "all fiction does spring from your experience, but it is also a melding of the imagination and your experience. It is the emotional texture of the book and the feelings which are real." She explained that writing a book is like designing an intricately balanced structure. There were no drafts, no rewriting of sentences, because "my thought and my writing are one thing." She said that although she titled her novel casually, she finds it to be appropriate since it conveys "how in these small events and in these small lives the world intrudes. And because of this, because of people being unprotected . . . the world and the social machine intrudes into the smallest, deepest core of their being and changes their life."

Her novel resembles the fiction of William Faulkner in its narrative technique of flashbacks and fast-forwards and its disregard for linear chronology. In its play on words and with language, it reminds one also of James Joyce's work, as she uses palindromes, alliteration, rhymes, coinages, split syllables, re-formed words, and unconventional capitalization. Her description of the lovemaking between Ammu and Velutha reminds one of passages in the work of D. H. Lawrence. (In fact, a lawsuit charging obscenity was filed in June 1997, primarily because the book depicted sex between members of different castes.) She has acknowledged her indebtedness to Salman Rushdie and his magic realism.

The novel received laudatory reviews. Writing in *The New Yorker* (23 and 30 June 1997), John Updike commented, "like a devotionally built temple, 'The God of Small Things' builds a massive interlocking structure of fine, intensely felt details. A rosary is held up to the light: 'Each greedy bead grabbed its share of sun.'" However, the Indian academic C. D. Narasimhaiah, in an editorial in *The Literary Criterion* (1997), faulted her because "the words don't mediate experience as she is busy peddling them." The Communists in Kerala expressed their disapproval of Roy's criticism of their party and her caricature of their leader, E. M. S. Nam-

boodiripad. The picture of India as it emerges in Roy's novel is "a vast, violent, circling, driving, ridiculous, insane, unfeasible, public turmoil of a nation."

The God of Small Things received the Booker Prize on 14 October 1997. This prize was instituted in 1968 to reward literary merit and raise the status of the writer in society. That year there were eighty-eight entries for the prize, although the jury reviewed an additional eighteen books. However, Roy's novel was a unanimous choice. That Roy got the Booker Prize is significant for South Asian writing in English in several ways. She was not educated abroad and had not lived overseas, unlike the previous winners from the region. She herself also pointed out that she was not a well-educated person. Indeed, she was the first Indian woman and the first nonexpatriate Indian to receive the Booker Prize. The chairperson of the jury, Gillian Beer, said of Roy's achievement: "With extraordinary linguistic inventiveness, Roy funnels the history of South India through the eyes of a seven-year-old twin. The story is fundamental as it is local: it is about love and death and yet tells the tale quite clearly."

After *The God of Small Things,* Roy shifted her attention to issues of public concern and has been writing well-researched, closely argued, and persuasive articles and essays that have been published in many Indian and European newspapers, including *The Guardian, Le Monde,* and *El Mundo.* The first of these, *The End of Imagination,* was originally published in *Outlook* on 3 August 1998 and is based on a speech she gave at a seminar on Hiroshima Day in New Delhi. She attacks the conducting of nuclear tests and takes the Indian government to task for its enthusiastic support. She has basic objections to nuclear testing anywhere: "To me, it signifies dreadful things. The end of imagination. The end of freedom actually, because, after all, that's what freedom is. Choice." She warns that in the event of a nuclear war, "The very elements–the sky, the air, the land, the wind and water will turn against us. Their wrath will be terrible." She also taunts the right-wing Indian government that dreams of Hindu revival: "Coke is Western Culture, but the nuclear bomb is an old Indian tradition? There's no such thing as an Authentic India or a Real Indian. . . . There are, and can only be, visions of India, various ways of seeing it." Roy declares that the nuclear bomb is the "final act of betrayal of the Indian people," because it is far easier to make a bomb than to educate four hundred million illiterate Indians. She adds, "The nuclear bomb is the most anti-democratic, anti-national, anti-human, outright evil thing that man has ever made." In the euphoria generated in her country by India's joining an exclusive nuclear club, dissenting voices such as Roy's were

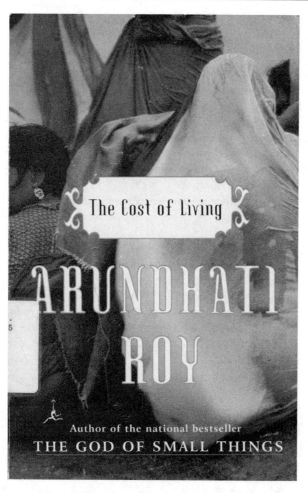

Paperback cover for the 1999 republication of two of Roy's essays: The End of Imagination *(1998), in which she criticizes nuclear proliferation, and* The Greater Common Good *(1999), in which she examines the negative consequences of large-scale dam construction in India (Richland County Public Library)*

In *The Greater Common Good,* an essay published in 1999, she takes the Indian government, the World Bank, bureaucrats, and politicians to task for their insensitivity to the misery of millions of tribal people in the Narmada valley. She points out the enormous loss in terms of human suffering and the long-term adverse consequences of large dams. She broadens the issue of building dams to raise basic questions such as "Who owns the land? Who owns its rivers? Its forests? Its fish?" She regrets the fact that the large dams are touted as symbols of modern development and that their construction is justified on the grounds of the greater common good. She stresses that tribal people gather everything they need, such as food, fuel, fodder, rope, gum, tobacco, tooth powder, medicinal herbs, and housing materials, from the forest but are being driven away from rivers and forests by such projects. She points out that they now have become wage earners, getting a pittance for the work they do and having to use a hand pump instead of a river. Roy concludes: "Big dams are to a Nation's 'Development' what Nuclear Bombs are to its Military Arsenal. They're both weapons of mass destruction. Both Twentieth-Century emblems that mark a point in time when human intelligence has outstripped its own instinct for survival." Roy participated in protests along with thousands of other antidam activists and was arrested at Salgaon in March 1999. *The End of Imagination* and *The Greater Common Good* were republished together in October 1999 as *The Cost of Living.*

In *Power Politics* (2001) Roy focuses her attention on a huge power project in the state of Maharashtra constructed by Enron, a Houston-based energy company. She exposes the dangers of privatization of productive public assets such as power. Enron's deal with the Maharashtra government was highly profitable to itself, and the cost of power for consumers was consequently exorbitant. When the issue was raised, the U.S. government backed Enron, and the Maharashtra government continued to incur heavy losses on the project. (Enron itself eventually became bankrupt in the United States.) One interesting point that Roy makes while examining the complex political, commercial, and economic issues surrounding the Enron deal is the way language is "ritualistically slaughtered" at international forums by interested parties. She cites the example of an American panelist (at the World Water Forum in Holland in March 2000) who said: "God gave us the rivers, but he didn't put in the delivery systems. That's why we need private enterprise!" Roy believes that in such cases language is used "to mask intent" rather than to clarify goals. She states her case against privatization of such projects forcefully: "To snatch these [natural resources such as water] away and sell them away as

hardly audible, and if they were heard, they had little influence on policy makers.

The next issue of public importance that Roy focused on was the building of huge dams in her country. India is the world's third largest dam builder. The pace of building dams accelerated greatly after India gained its independence in 1947, but Roy felt that projects were commissioned without considering the impact of the dams on the environment or people. She took the Sardar Sarovar Projects across the Narmada River in India as a case study. She spoke at the Hague in January 1999 at the World Water Forum. She also delivered the Nehru Memorial Lecture in 1999 at Cambridge University on big dams. In the same year she participated in the mass protest organized at Salgaon on the banks of the Narmada.

stock to private companies is a process of barbaric dispossession on a scale that has no parallel in history."

Roy delivered the third annual Eqbal Ahmad Lecture at Hampshire College in Amherst, Massachusetts, in February 2001. Her lecture, "The Ladies Have Feelings, So . . . ," discusses the roles of writers and artists in society. These people are expected "to worry the edges of the human imagination, to conjure beauty from the unexpected things"; yet, the prevailing notions of morality and values circumscribe their freedom. Roy argues that art, in whatever form it is practiced, imposes its own discipline on the artist. A writer cannot remain a mute witness to the social and political upheavals of the contemporary world. As a person she or he has to take a position on issues of grave importance and write about them. Roy pleads for keeping the "experts" away from public debates on matters that vitally affect the lives of common people.

In October 2001 Roy found a new topic in the U.S.-led invasion of Afghanistan in the search for terrorist mastermind Osama bin Laden and members of his network, al-Qaeda. In *The Algebra of Infinite Justice* she expresses her opinion that the U.S. government's proclaimed intention of stamping out terrorism does not carry conviction, because the same government had been supporting "military and economic terrorism, insurgency, military dictatorship, religious bigotry, and unimaginable genocide *outside* America." She identifies terrorism as a symptom rather than a disease. She believes that terrorism is not confined to any single country but is global in scope. She blames the "marauding multinationals" of the United States as the source of all evil in the world. The title of the essay alludes to the code name "Operation Infinite Justice," which the U.S. military used to launch their mission in Afghanistan.

Roy also voiced her opposition to the U.S.-led war on Afghanistan in the essay "War Is Peace," first published in *Outlook* (29 October 2001). In language reminiscent of George Orwell's prose, Roy underscores the absurdity of President George W. Bush's declaration "We are a peaceful nation" even as he was announcing the air strikes in Afghanistan. As she sees it, the issue in the Afghan war is not about "Good or Evil or Islam or Christianity as much as it is about *space*. About how to accommodate diversity, how to contain the impulse towards hegemony—every kind of hegemony, economic, military, linguistic, religious and cultural." She feels sorry for the American people whom, in her opinion, the American establishment, including the mass media, has drugged and who are kept in the dark about the real state of the world and the "meddlesomeness" of their own government.

When six essays on public issues were published in a single volume with the title *The Algebra of Infinite Justice,* Roy was honored by the Asian Human Rights Commission for her courage in speaking out. A few months later, in March 2002, she was jailed for a day and fined two thousand rupees for contempt of court. During a long, drawn-out court case on the construction of the Sardar Sarovar Project, Roy had criticized the government on this issue. Roy stated in her affidavit to the Supreme Court in this case that it is "disquieting on the part of the court to silence criticism and muzzle dissent, to harass and intimidate those who disagree with it." The court felt these remarks were "scandalizing [the court] and lowering its dignity." In sentencing her to jail for one day, the court said that it was "showing the magnanimity of law, by keeping in mind [that] the respondent is a woman." Roy came out of jail on 6 March 2002 and was unrepentant for her past comments on the court. She complained in a statement to the press on 7 March that the Supreme Court was endangering freedom of speech: "If even this right is denied, it would expose the country to the dangers of judicial tyranny."

On 3 May 2002 Roy published the article "Democracy and Religious Fascism" in *CounterPunch.* The immediate context was the March 2002 riots in Gujarat after the right-wing Bharatiya Janata Party government allegedly encouraged its Hindu supporters to take revenge on the Muslims who were believed to have set fire to a train carrying Hindus at Godhra. Like most liberal-minded Indians, Roy criticized the fanatic elements in the ruling party for the riots in Gujarat.

The Lannan Foundation in Santa Fe, New Mexico, invited Roy to speak on the first anniversary of the 11 September 2001 terrorist attacks on the United States. In an address titled "Come September," she once again focuses on what she feels are the hypocrisy and contradictions of U.S. government policies. In her view, the American government indulged in the "cynical manipulation of people's grief" at the immense loss of 11 September in order to start the war on Iraq. She details the ignoble role of the United States in many South American countries and in Palestine. She examines the effects of U.S.-led corporate globalization, which she sees as one of the main causes for conflict and disharmony in the twenty-first century. She prophesies: "A world run by a handful of greedy bankers and CEOs who nobody elected can't possibly last." The Lannan Foundation awarded Roy its fourth annual Prize for Cultural Freedom, worth $350,000. She promptly donated the entire amount, splitting it among some fifty groups, institutions, movements, and individuals in India. The citation noted that the prize was given for "her precise and powerful writing highlighting her commitment to social, economic, and environmental justice."

Paperback cover for Roy's 2003 collection of political essays, including "Come September," in which she accuses the American government of manipulating people's grief over the 11 September 2001 terrorist attacks in order to justify declaring war on Iraq (Richland County Public Library)

Roy was the star speaker at the World Social Forum (WSF) at Porto Alegre, Brazil, on 25 January 2003. This organization, an important platform for alternative ideas and practices in the contemporary world, brings together groups upholding civil society from all over the world. This first meeting of the WSF was held to coincide with the World Economic Forum that was held in Davos, Switzerland. Roy spoke on the subject of "Confronting Empire." She declared that corporate globalization is the modern name for imperialism. The so-called free market undermines democracy; in a "globalized" world there is neither free speech nor free press. She stressed what she thinks to be the lies on which the war on Iraq is based. She declared, however, that one can confront the empire by laying siege to it. People can refuse to buy the ideas, history, weapons, and wars peddled by the multinationals. She ended the

speech on an optimistic note: "Another world is not only possible, she is on her way. On a quiet day, I can hear her breathing."

On 13 May 2003 Roy spoke in New York City on "Instant Mix: Imperial Democracy." The Centre for Economic and Social Rights and the Lannan Foundation sponsored the event. On 31 May 2003 she gave a talk on "The Day of the Jackals" at the national antiwar teach-in in Washington, D.C. The thesis of these speeches is the indefensibility of the U.S. war on Iraq and the vise-like grip of American corporations on U.S. government policies. She also focused on the misery of war-ravaged Iraqis. She bemoaned the deliberate destruction of an ancient civilization by invoking the fate of Mesopotamia and Babylon.

Roy's next major engagement was a speech she delivered at the World Social Forum held in Mumbai (Bombay) in January 2004. In this speech, "Do Turkeys Enjoy Thanksgiving?" she dwelt on the entire range of her favorite themes: development projects displacing and dispossessing millions of people; religious bigotry; state-sponsored terrorism; U.S. hegemony; and corporate greed. At the end of her speech she made a stirring call for nonviolent resistance, in the manner of Mahatma Gandhi, to the U.S. occupation of Iraq. She suggested an action plan for such resistance. She concluded by saying, "We must consider ourselves at war."

In recognition of her championing of the rights of the deprived and the underprivileged, the Sydney Peace Foundation announced the award of the Sydney Peace Prize for 2004 to her. The jury's citation read: "Arundhati Roy has been recognized for her courage in campaigns for human rights and for her advocacy of non-violence, as expressed in her demands for justice for the poor, for the victims of communal violence, for the millions displaced by the Narmada dam projects and for her opposition to nuclear weapons." This citation epitomizes Roy's major concerns and methods as a social activist and notes her primary activities after she won the Booker Prize. In 2005 she was given the Sahitya Akademi Award for her 2001 essay collection, *The Algebra of Infinite Justice*.

Arundhati Roy believes that there is no essential difference between fiction and nonfiction. As far as she is concerned, they are two ways of telling stories; but she believes that writing nonfiction is more demanding. For her fiction as well as her nonfictional writings she has attracted many admirers across the world while continuing to be criticized by some people for her beliefs. Without a doubt Roy's only novel created a lot of critical interest, partly because of the hype associated with the Booker Prize. But its originality and the skills and passion with which it was written were appreciated by readers and critics all over the world. It can also be said that Roy has attained celebrity status as a champion of many issues of public importance. The thoroughness of her research, the clarity of her expression, the precision of her language, the conviction with which she articulates her views, and above all, the courage of her convictions, are remarkable. Nevertheless, the view of Ramachandra Guha, writing in *The Hindu* (26 November 2000), is representative of those who are critical of her stance: "Her essays are vain, shrill, unoriginal, oversimplified, hyperbolic and lacking any voices but her own." There can be little doubt, however, that she is supplementing the work of Noam Chomsky, Edward Said, and other dissenting intellectuals and that in *The God of Small Things* she has written one of the more original and captivating novels in English to come out of the Indian subcontinent.

Interviews:

Vir Sanghvi, interview with Roy, *Rediff Special* (1997) <http://www.rediff.com/news/apr/05roy.htm>;

Claire Scobie, "The God of Small Things: Arundhati Roy," *INDIA50* (1997) <http://www.india50.com/arundhatI.html>;

Reena Jana, "Winds, Rivers & Rain," *Salon* (30 September 1997) <http://www.salon.com/sept97/00roy.html>;

David Barsamian, *The Checkbook and the Cruise Missile: Conversations with Arundhati Roy* (Cambridge, Mass.: South End Press, 2004).

References:

Indira Bhatt and Indira Nityanandam, eds., *Explorations: Arundhati Roy's* The God of Small Things, Creative New Literatures Series, 27 (New Delhi: Creative Books, 1999);

R. K. Dhawan, ed., *Arundhati Roy: The Novelist Extraordinary* (New Delhi: Prestige, 1999);

Jaydipsinh Dodiya and Joya Chakravarty, eds., *The Critical Studies of Arundhati Roy's* The God of Small Things (New Delhi: Atlantic, 1999);

R. S. Pathak, ed., *The Fictional World of Arundhati Roy,* Creative New Literatures Series, 48 (New Delhi: Creative Books, 2001);

R. S. Sharma and Shashi Bala Talwar, *Arundhati Roy's* The God of Small Things: *Critique and Commentary,* Creative New Literatures Series, 25 (New Delhi: Creative Books, 1998).

Salman Rushdie

(19 June 1947 –   )

Farhad B. Idris
Frostburg State University

See also the Rushdie entry in *DLB 194: British Novelists Since 1960, Second Series.*

BOOKS: *Grimus* (London: Gollancz, 1975; Woodstock, N.Y.: Overlook, 1979);

Midnight's Children (London: Cape, 1981; New York: Knopf, 1981);

Shame (London: Cape, 1983; New York: Knopf, 1983);

The Jaguar Smile: A Nicaraguan Journey (London: Pan/Cape, 1987; New York: Viking, 1987);

The Satanic Verses (London: Viking, 1988; New York: Viking, 1989);

Two Stories (London: Sixth Chamber Press, 1989);

Is Nothing Sacred? The Herbert Read Memorial Lecture, 6 February 1990 (London & New York: Granta, 1990);

In Good Faith (London & New York: Granta, 1990);

Haroun and the Sea of Stories (New York: Granta/Viking, 1990; London: Granta/Penguin, 1991);

Imaginary Homelands: Essays and Criticism, 1981–1991 (London: Granta / New York: Viking, 1991);

The Wizard of Oz (London: British Film Institute Publications, 1992);

East, West: Stories (London: Cape, 1994; New York: Pantheon, 1994);

The Moor's Last Sigh (London: Cape, 1995; New York: Pantheon, 1995);

The Ground beneath Her Feet (London: Cape, 1999; New York: Holt, 1999);

The Screenplay of Midnight's Children (London: Vintage, 1999);

Fury (London: Cape, 2001; New York: Random House, 2001);

Step across This Line: Collected Nonfiction, 1992–2002 (London: Cape, 2002; New York: Random House, 2002);

Shalimar the Clown (London: Cape, 2005; New York: Random House, 2005).

Edition: *Midnight's Children,* with an introduction by Anita Desai, Everyman's Library (New York: Knopf, 1995).

Salman Rushdie (photograph © Annie Leibovitz; from the dust jacket for the U.S. edition of Fury, *2001; Richland County Public Library)*

PLAY PRODUCTIONS: *Haroun and the Sea of Stories,* by Rushdie, David Tushingham, and Tim Supple, London, National Theater, 10 October 1998;

Midnight's Children, by Rushdie, Supple, and Simon Reade, London, Barbican Theater, 18 January 2003.

PRODUCED SCRIPTS: "The Painter and the Pest," BBC Channel 4, 2 June 1985;

"The Riddle of Midnight: India, August 1987," BBC Channel 4, 27 March 1988.

OTHER: "The Indian Writer in English," in *Eye of the Beholder: Indian Writing in English,* edited by Maggie

Butcher (London: Commonwealth Institute, 1983), pp. 75–83;

Derek Bishton and John Reardon, *Home Front,* introduction by Rushdie (London: Cape, 1984);

Günter Grass, *On Writing and Politics, 1967–1983,* translated by Ralph Manheim, introduction by Rushdie (San Diego: Harcourt Brace Jovanovich, 1985);

Angela Carter, *Burning Your Boats: Stories,* introduction by Rushdie (London: Chatto & Windus, 1995);

The Vintage Book of Indian Writing, 1947–1997, edited by Rushdie and Elizabeth West (London: Vintage, 1997); republished as *Mirrorwork: 50 Years of Indian Writing, 1947–1997* (New York: Holt, 1997).

SELECTED PERIODICAL PUBLICATIONS–
UNCOLLECTED:
POETRY
"6 March 1989," *Granta,* no. 28 (August 1989).
NONFICTION
"The Empire Writes Back with a Vengeance," *Times* (London), 3 July 1982, p. 8;

"Marquez the Magician," *Sunday Times,* 24 October 1982, p. 41;

"After Indira, an Awakening of the Whirlwind?" *Times* (London), 1 November 1984, p. 16;

"Goodness: The American Neurosis," *Nation* (22 March 1986): 344–346;

"A Platform of Closed Minds," *Guardian Unlimited* (28 September 2002) <books.guardian.co.uk/review/story/0,12084,799748,00.html>.

Because of the controversy surrounding *The Satanic Verses* (1988), Salman Rushdie became known all over the world in the late 1980s and early 1990s. In those days he was often the lead story on television news broadcasts and in newspapers. Rushdie, however, was already well known among English-language writers since the publication of *Midnight's Children* (1981) and *Shame* (1983). He has continued to add other significant works to his oeuvre since *The Satanic Verses* and has emerged as a major presence in the contemporary literary scene.

Born on 19 June 1947 in Bombay–now Mumbai–in India, to wealthy Muslim parents, Ahmed Salman Rushdie grew up in affluence. Rushdie's father, Anis Rushdie, had been to Cambridge, was a barrister, and had a taste for owning books. He possessed the gift for telling stories and loved to do so for his children. A greater paternal influence on the Rushdie family, however, was Rushdie's maternal grandfather, Ataullah Butt. A medical doctor, he held enlightened views. He did not enforce *purdah* laws–laws requiring Muslim

women to put on headdress–on his daughters. He accepted the wedding of Rushdie's parents even though when Rushdie's mother, Negin Butt, met Anis Rushdie she was a married woman; Anis himself was divorced from his former wife. Their wedding occurred at a time when romantic nuptials in India were rare, let alone marriage between two divorced persons. It should be pointed out that Rushdie's family saga finds a parallel in the Sinai family in *Midnight's Children.*

Rushdie received an elite education, first in Bombay and then in Rugby, England. At Rugby, at the age of thirteen, he expended considerable effort in conforming to the typical image of an English public-school student. As a result, he graduated with high honors, with the Queen's Medal for History, the highest award in the subject. Rushdie's family immigrated to Pakistan at about this time. Rushdie was not pleased at the move, but after graduation he went to Pakistan to live with his family. He did not adjust well to Pakistan's political and intellectual climate, however. Soon he returned to England to study history at King's College, Cambridge.

Rushdie did not do as well in college as he had done in school, perhaps because he had become involved in theater production by this time and had set acting as his career goal. After graduating from Cambridge without distinction, he went home to Pakistan but refused to take charge of his father's towel factory. Instead, he returned to England to pursue an acting career. Secretly, though, Rushdie wanted to be a writer. His father did not think much of this pursuit. When Rushdie appeared during the Michigan residency of the dramatization of *Midnight's Children* by the Royal Shakespearean Company, he recalled his father's reaction to his decision to opt for the theater: "What will I tell my friends?" What is more, as an actor Rushdie did not do well. When the stage seemed to offer him an uncertain future, he tried his luck as a copywriter for successive advertising agencies. During this period he worked also on a novel, "The Book of the Pir." Completed in 1971, this work is about a Muslim spiritual leader who is appointed the ceremonial president of a country by a corrupt military regime to legitimize its misdeeds. The work was rejected by several publishers.

Rushdie was more fortunate with his next literary venture, *Grimus* (1975), which tells the story of Flapping Eagle, an American Indian, who seeks out his sister Bird-Dog, a captive of Grimus, a European magician, on a Mediterranean island. Though no significant acclaim followed the publication of *Grimus*–it received serious critical attention only after Rushdie's later works had made him famous–it is a rich combination of science fiction and folklore. *Grimus* includes technical elements Rushdie developed more effectively in his later fiction. The fantasy in *Grimus* bears a resemblance

Dust jacket for the U.S. edition of Rushdie's 1981 novel, winner of
the Booker Prize, in which the children born during the first hour of
Indian independence are linked by telepathy and by the fact
that each of them possesses supernatural abilities
(Richland County Public Library)

to the "magical realism" Rushdie used with great success later in *Midnight's Children*. Magical realism is a mode of narrative in which fantastic phenomena occur in a realistic, matter-of-fact setting. Deftly used by South American authors such as Miguel Angel Asturias, Alejo Carpentier, and Gabriel García Márquez, this method allows the author a great deal of subversive potential, a potential Rushdie exploits fully in *Midnight's Children* and *Shame*.

Rushdie, meanwhile, was living with Clarissa Luard, later his first wife, who came from an upper-middle-class background. After *Grimus* was accepted for publication, they went on a trip to India and Pakistan. Apparently, the idea for a novel about India came to Rushdie on this trip, and he felt that he could write with great confidence if he chose his native home and its history as his subject. Rushdie called his new novel "Madame Rama" after its central character, who resembles Indira Gandhi. The work was rejected. Although

disappointed, he was intent on doing a better job. He felt that changing the narration from third to first person would give him a better handle on the experience and events he wanted to tell in this novel.

Rushdie completed the manuscript of *Midnight's Children* in 1979. Meanwhile, he and Clarissa had gotten married in 1976. Their first child, Zafar, was born in 1979, soon after Rushdie completed *Midnight's Children*. This work, Rushdie's first major novel, considered by some his best and acknowledged by many a masterpiece of world literature, brought him worldwide recognition. A sprawling work of more than 550 pages, *Midnight's Children* narrates the story of three generations of an Indian Muslim family that migrates to Pakistan after the independence of the Indian subcontinent and its partition into two countries along religious lines in 1947. Saleem Sinai, the narrator/protagonist, recounts his family's experience of events spanning from 1915 to the late 1970s in the region. Personal history merges with political history in the novel, which is set against a mythic backdrop gathered from Indian and Middle Eastern sources. The mythic dimension allows Rushdie to do justice to the ambitious purpose he set for himself in the novel. The tale told in *Midnight's Children,* which spreads out over more than six decades and includes personal as well as major political events, indicates the scope of his ambitions.

Saleem uses flashbacks and flash-forwards, which are continuously juxtaposed. The narrative strategy creates indeterminacy, compelling the reader to question the narrator's reliability. Saleem's confession in the last chapter confirms the suspicion that his representation of events has been less than authentic. He reminds his readers that "since the past exists only in one's memories and the words which strive to encapsulate them, it is possible to create past events simply by saying they occurred." Such doubts cast uncertainty on the narrative; nevertheless, it has a coherent, linear plotline. Aadam Aziz, Saleem's maternal grandfather, is a German-trained medical doctor in Kashmir. Reminiscent of Dr. Aziz in E. M. Forster's *A Passage to India* (1924) and named in Arabic after Adam, the arch father, Aadam Aziz suffers a psychic wound from his encounter with the West, "a hole . . . a vacancy in a vital inner chamber," which continuously baffles his attempt to define and redefine his place in the universe. Saleem's father, Ahmed Sinai, marries Aadam's daughter, and the family moves to Bombay, where Saleem is born at the exact moment of Indian independence, a feat he accomplishes ahead of several other children who are born slightly later than midnight. For being so fortunate, he receives a letter from Jawaharlal Nehru, the first prime minister of independent India, who pronounces that Saleem's future will be "a mirror" to the nation. Saleem is not, however, the biological son of his presumed parents, because he was swapped at birth in the nursing home by one of the nurses. Though he does not resemble his father closely, he shares one impressive trait with his maternal grandfather: an oversized nose, considered by many the mark of blue blood. Yet, Saleem's nose has a non-Indian origin: an Englishman departing from India in the wake of independence fathered him when he seduced Vanita, the wife of a poor street performer. The Englishman's nose was not entirely English, either; it was, in fact, "the legacy of a patrician French grandmother–from Bergerac." Rushdie's reasons for giving Saleem such murky roots are several. First, it demystifies the notion of origin based on physiognomy; second, it stresses his hybridity and status as a mongrel; last, it suggests the multiple religious and ethnic ancestries of India–Muslim and Arab, Hindu and Aryan, Christian and European–since Saleem, allegorically, represents the modern nation of India.

Saleem is aware that he is "mysteriously handcuffed to history." While he grows up in affluence and is treasured by not only the neighborhood but also the country, the true son of Sinai, Shiva, struggles with poverty. When Saleem is a little older, he discovers that he has the power of telepathy, derived apparently from his auspicious birth. It turns out that all children born in the hour of Indian independence have supernatural powers and that Saleem is able to communicate with all of them. He forms an organization for them, which he calls Midnight Children's Conference, or MCC (a well-known acronym in cricket-loving countries for Marleyburn Manchester Cricket Club). Saleem himself presides over this association, thereby symbolically assuming the role of the consciousness of postindependence India and embodying its promise and potential.

Faced with hostility from the government, from the rise of Hindu fundamentalism, and from regional separatist movements, the Sinai family moves to Pakistan in the late 1950s. Saleem witnesses all the major events that follow in the next two decades in Pakistan as well as in India. He plays a behind-the-scenes role in the military coup in Pakistan in 1958, records the Indo-Chinese war of 1962, becomes wounded and develops amnesia in the Indo-Pakistani war of 1965, serves as a field agent of the occupying Pakistani army in Bangladesh in 1971, and finally, loses his telepathic power during the state of emergency declared by the Indian prime minister Indira Gandhi in 1975.

Regarded as a key postcolonial text, *Midnight's Children* has generated and continues to generate substantial critical attention. The work rewards the scholar who wants to study Rushdie's intertextual strategies or his allegorization of the history of the subcontinent. The author's ability to tell an Indian tale so effortlessly

in English has led some scholars to look for sources for the innovations in the text. Many attempts have been made to place the work in the Indian/Middle Eastern tradition of storytelling as well as the British/Western tradition of nonlinear narrative such as that of Laurence Sterne's *Tristram Shandy* (1760–1767). Clement Hawes points out that both works include the motif of a prominent nose and that both condemn the quest for origin, thus parodying the discourse of physiognomy. Rushdie himself acknowledged, in a 1982 interview with Jean Ross for *Contemporary Authors* (reprinted in *Conversations with Salman Rushdie,* 2000), that when writing *Midnight's Children,* he was aware of the intertextual link between Saleem's nose and Shandy's. He indicates, however, that the nose is the most prominent feature also of the Hindu deity Ganesh, who is supposed to have been endowed with an elephant's trunk. In the same interview Rushdie claims that he conflated the two traditions to create "dual reverberations." Saleem likens himself to Scheherazade, the teller of stories in *The Arabian Nights* who is only one bad story away from execution. Like Scheherazade, who tells her stories to her husband, the king, Saleem tells his to a live audience, Padma, an illiterate coworker in the pickle factory where he has found employment after his long ordeal.

To enhance the comic potential of Saleem's nose, Rushdie at one point in *Midnight's Children* compares it to the Deccan Peninsula, a prominent landmark on the Indian map. This passage suggests to many scholars the allegorical implications of the text, and allegory in *Midnight's Children* has engendered a growing body of criticism dwelling on the way the text treats nationalism, politics, and history. Neil Ten Kortenaar, in his essay "*Midnight's Children* and the Allegory of History" (1995), demonstrates how through its use of dead metaphors, Rushdie's allegory in *Midnight's Children* offers an alternative to official Indian history. A good example of such a metaphor would be the bruise that Aziz suffers in the Amritsar massacre, because it exhibits "a literalization of the metaphor, so common as to be dead, of the wound that never heals." Similarly, Nadir Khan, who lives in a cellar in Aziz's house to hide from Muslim fanatics seeking his blood, illustrates to Kortenaar that "the memory of those Muslims who supported a secular state characterized by religious tolerance has been rudely shoved 'under the carpet.'"

A major thrust in criticism of *Midnight's Children* is to examine Rushdie's ability to mingle English with words and idioms from different Indian languages. Rushdie's borrowings are primarily from Urdu, the preferred language of Indian Muslims–a derivative of Hindi, Arabic, and Persian–though echoes of other languages can be detected in *Midnight's Children* as well. The special flavor of his prose, on the other hand, does

Dust jacket for the U.S. edition of Rushdie's 1983 novel, which follows the fortunes of an unscrupulous doctor and the woman he attempts to cure of her "plague of shame," against the backdrop of a corrupt and fanatical Pakistani society (Richland County Public Library)

folk, the learned and the popular, the parochial and the universal." While the "great" tradition—to which belongs Sanskrit, the language of the Brahmin or the pedant—often claims to be the official, the "little" tradition is composed of local dialects and customs. The two feed each other, and Rushdie "tapped into . . . [the] unquenchable vitality and fecundity created by just such fluidity and interconnectedness." Indeed, English in Rushdie's hand became a "'chutney' made up of English, Hindi, Urdu, Konkani, Marathi, Gujrati and various dialects thereof." Desai rightly observes that Rushdie's style is "eclectic," that it does not care for the "purity of race or tongue," and that his many borrowings from Indian and Western popular culture, combined with his "Babble," "form a cacophony, a Bakhtinian 'heteroglossia.'" Similarly to Desai, Michael Gorra examines Rushdie's handling of English in *Midnight's Children* in his *After Empire: Scott, Naipaul, Rushdie* (1997) and shows that with his telepathic ability Saleem himself is the "site" where innumerable voices vie for expression. Hence, Rushdie's narration, according to Gorra, has strong subversive potential. Thus, Rushdie, "in whose sentences Bombay street slang continuously flirts with Oxbridge English," ensures that truth is not absolute; instead it is "multiple, overlapping, conflicting." At the same time, the liberties that Rushdie takes with the English language, in Gorra's view, also suggest "a challenge to the idea of proper English, the King's English, and therefore to British colonialism."

Midnight's Children made Rushdie a world-famous writer. Translated into more than a dozen languages, the novel won the prestigious British Booker Prize in 1981 and in 1993, the "Booker of Bookers" Prize, the special prize given on the occasion of the silver anniversary of the Booker to the best of the twenty-five previous prizewinners. Showing its continuing appeal, a drama adaptation based on the novel has been produced by the Royal Shakespearean Company.

After *Midnight's Children,* Rushdie published several short stories and essays in literary magazines. Among them, the article "The Empire Writes Back with a Vengeance," published in *The Times* (3 July 1982), expounded an ideological base of his fiction. Rushdie argued that a new form of writing in English about non-English societies and by authors from non-English backgrounds was emerging in Britain, that it was new because it had rid itself of its former imperial and oppressive baggage, and that it would create a fresh cultural identity for Britain as well as for its former colonies.

Rushdie's next novel, *Shame,* appeared in 1983. Set in Pakistan, *Shame* can be seen as a counterpart to *Midnight's Children,* which uses the entire South Asian subcontinent as its canvas but focuses mainly on India

not derive only from the Indian words he uses but also from the way he handles the language to convey non-English, Indianized idioms. Michael Harris, in his *Outsiders & Insiders: Perspective of Third-World Culture in British and Post-Colonial Fiction* (1992), observes that the technique is consistent with Rushdie's narrative strategy in *Midnight's Children,* which struggles to lend coherence to a ruptured reality: "[All] such syntactic efforts to hold things together also imply, by their very presence and nature, the centrifugal force of the diversity that makes them necessary, as do the equally frequent foreshadowings and recapitulations." On the other hand, Anita Desai, who in her introduction to the 1995 Everyman's Library edition of *Midnight's Children* calls the novel "a modern epic," sees both "the 'great' and 'little' traditions of India" in the language of the text. She notes that the two traditions represent "the classical and the

in the 1970s. *Shame* takes up the political history of Pakistan until the early 1980s and presents a marginal hero, Omar Khayyam Shakil, who never occupies the center of action but hovers on its boundary. His name, like many other names in Rushdie's novels, reminds readers of the renowned twelfth-century Persian poet and astrologer Omar Khayyam. Intended as a caricature of the towering historical figure well known in Islamic societies, Shakil resembles the famous person only in name and not in gift or vision. Like Saleem, he is the bastard child of an Englishman, but unlike Saleem, whose maternity is never in doubt, Shakil has three mothers who are sisters. They never tell him who his true mother is, so the dishonor of giving birth out of wedlock can be borne equally by all of them. The mothers give Shakil an excellent survival mechanism in a society where having an *Angrez* or English father, known or unknown, is worse than having none—no sense of shame. Hence, he never experiences the emotion and does well in his career as a doctor. Like Saleem, Shakil too is an allegorical figure. If Saleem with his power to consume many consciousnesses represents the psyche of postindependence India, Shakil is narcissistic, completely lacking in a sense of honor as well as a conscience. Pakistan is no dream of Shakil, or it is his flawed dream at best, because the country is rife with religious fanaticism, political corruption, and military despotism. As the *Shame* narrator puts it, "Pakistan, the peeling, fragmenting palimpsest, increasingly at war with itself, may be described as a failure of the dreaming mind."

Shame shows how deep a sense of shame exists in Pakistan. The narrator goes on to explain that the English word *shame* lacks the "encyclopaedias of nuances" that its Urdu counterpart, *sharam,* possesses; he uses it for lack of a better equivalent. In the novel, shame operates on many levels in Pakistani society. It obliges the rulers of Pakistan to pretend that everything is in order though corruption of their own making is eating up its innards—reaching a proportion that resembles Shakil's shamelessness. Shame also leads the ruling elite to suppress women. Rushdie shows the extent of the misogyny of Pakistani society on many occasions in his book. For example, in the "Sind Club in Karachi . . . there is still a sign reading 'Women and Dogs Not Allowed Beyond This Point.'"

One of the two rulers of Pakistan, Raza Hyder—modeled after a military dictator who ruled Pakistan in the 1970s and 1980s—becomes a national hero by capturing from the enemy (unnamed, but it can be only India) Aansu Ki Wadi, "a mountain valley so high and inaccessible that even goats had difficulty in breathing up there." Though some claim that there was actually no battle because the enemy did not bother to defend

this useless terrain "where your spit froze before it hit the ground," Hyder receives high renown for adding to the honor of the country. His glory turns to shame, however, when his wife fails to deliver a male child. Despite Hyder's attempt to prove otherwise in the military clinic, the doctor tells him the baby's protruding genitalia has the "not uncommon postnatal swelling of the female"; Hyder accepts the fact with undisguised chagrin. His deep shame causes Sufiya Zinobia to blush right after her birth, a habit that does not go away even when brain fever affects the growth of her mind, rendering her a child for life.

Sufiya, too, represents Pakistan, a country created from the collective shame of the Muslims at being a minority in a land of Hindus. Though Sufiya and Shakil are polar opposites, they are married despite their huge difference in age. The occasion that brings them together is interesting to explore. Sufiya is put in the hospital during a life-threatening illness under Shakil's care. The disease is of immunological origin, manifesting in "a hot flush spread from scalp to the soles of her feet," possibly brought by Sufiya upon herself as a "plague of shame." Shakil seems the right consultant to treat her not only because he is an immunologist, but also because he is one with no shame—the best curer of shame being the shameless.

As a political satire, *Shame,* in its critique of the society it treats, goes beyond *Midnight's Children*. Rushdie's unflattering portrait of Pakistani politicians promptly led to the banning of *Shame* in Pakistan. *Shame* was acknowledged as another masterpiece everywhere else and consolidated Rushdie's reputation as a major contemporary novelist. It too was short-listed for the Booker Prize, although the prize eventually went that year to J. M. Coetzee for his *The Life and Times of Michael K.* Nevertheless, *Shame* demonstrates Rushdie's further maturing as a writer. Its unnamed narrator—clearly Rushdie himself—controls the narrative with remarkable self-assuredness. Even his unreliability is never in doubt, as when early in the novel he insists that he is not writing about Pakistan, "not quite," because he finds a certain "off-centering to be necessary." The narrator in *Shame,* on the other hand, is angrier than Saleem of *Midnight's Children*; consequently, as James Harrison notes in *Salman Rushdie* (1992), *Shame* is the "darker" book. Harrison also notes that while fragmentation in *Midnight's Children* "become[s] a feature of the creative process . . . in *Shame* fragmentation is given an immediate narcissistic role . . . [whose] implications are neither ontological, nor psychological, nor even stylistic, but strictly satiric." Aijaz Ahmad, a Marxist literary scholar of Indian/Pakistan origin—much like Rushdie himself—has, however, taken Rushdie to task for his representation of women in *Shame*. According to

Dust jacket for the U.S. edition (1989) of Rushdie's controversial 1988 novel. His treatment of the prophet Muhammad and the Qu'ran led to accusations of blasphemy in the Muslim world and a fatwa by Ayatollah Khomeini calling for the author's murder (Richland County Public Library).

Ahmad, they appear in a "sexually overdetermined" light, the prime example of such characterization being Sufiya Zinobia. Despite her blushes and her retarded childish mind, she is capable of inflicting unimaginable horror on her prey when the incubus rules her in her nightly prowls. Though Rushdie's overt intention in *Shame* is to expose misogynous tendencies in Pakistani culture, Ahmad finds the book derogatory of women, who are associated with violence and destruction.

In the years following the publication of *Shame*, Rushdie traveled extensively. In Australia he met Robyn Davidson and experienced, according to Ian Hamilton in his profile of Rushdie for *The New Yorker* (25 December 1995 – 1 January 1996), "love at first sight." His relationship with Davidson was stormy. Some critics think that she appears as the character of Alleluia Cone in *The Satanic Verses*—which, however, is not a negative portrait. The affair continued for the next two years; Rushdie had separated from Clarissa, meanwhile, and divorced her in 1987. That same year

Rushdie met the American author Marianne Wiggins, and they married in 1988.

In 1986 Rushdie went to Nicaragua as a guest of the Sandinista government. The three-week trip yielded a travelogue, *The Jaguar Smile: A Nicaraguan Journey*, published in 1987. Rushdie's account of his Central American trip treats his communist hosts in a favorable light–though Rushdie does provide a mild warning to them about censorship. By this time he had begun working on *The Satanic Verses*. Word of the project spread, and Rushdie changed his publisher when Viking Penguin paid him $850,000 for his new book, causing a sensation among writers and publishers. When the novel finally appeared in 1988, it amazed readers. Robert Irwin commented in *TLS: The Times Literary Supplement* (9 September 1988) that if readers thought that Rushdie's storytelling power would diminish after *Midnight's Children* and *Shame,* they were in for a surprise because actually there had been "an alarming increase."

The Satanic Verses begins with its two airborne heroes defying the law of gravity. Saladin Chamcha and Gibreel Farishta, who were on a scheduled commercial flight until their plane was blown up by terrorists, are falling, or rather gently wafting, down on Sussex, England. A remarkable process sets in as they drop: Saladin develops hooves and horns and Gibreel a halo, thus metamorphosing into the devil and the angel Gabriel, respectively. Like other events of major concern in a typical Rushdie novel, the midair explosion of an aircraft is based upon an actual crash of an Air India plane caused by Sikh terrorists in the mid 1980s, when the Sikh separatist movement was at its peak in India. Figuratively, on the other hand, Saladin and Gibreel's flight symbolizes the condition of migrancy Rushdie treats in this book.

While *The Satanic Verses* is a novel about South Asian immigrants in England, other narratives are to be found in Gibreel's dream sequences in the book. One takes place in seventh-century Arabia, describing the birth of Islam, and the other in modern India, recounting the journey of a group of devout Muslims led by a woman prophet who believes the Arabian Sea will part to make their passage to Makkah. Other tales, such as one about Ayatollah Khomeini, the Iranian spiritual leader in exile, are woven into the main story. Though apparently unrelated, they bring into focus issues related to women, censorship, exile, police brutality on immigrants, popular art, and movies, giving the novel its distinctive texture.

Because of the blasphemy controversy, other features of *The Satanic Verses,* such as Rushdie's distinctive humor, are often ignored. For example, his portrait of the Sufyan family suggests mirth without satire.

Muhammad Sufyan, proprietor of the Shaandaar ("Glamorous") Café, has just returned from Makkah with the distinct marks of a hajji. He is the "seen-it-all type, least doctrinaire of *hajis* and most unashamed of VCR addicts, ex-schoolteacher, self-taught in classical texts of many cultures." He had to flee from his home in Dhaka, former East Pakistan—that is, present-day Bangladesh—because he angered certain generals in the Pakistani regime by becoming a member of the Communist Party. His wife, Hind, disliked leaving home because of the cultural and religious differences they were having to negotiate, but Sufyan has no problem in adjusting. Weaker in some ways and stronger in others than his wife, he is a full two inches shorter than she, and she attributes her failure to have sons to his lack of sexual prowess, though her own attitude toward sex is that of a puritan. An intelligent man who has cultivated the mind at the expense of the body all his life, Sufyan is passive by nature. Indeed, passivity characterizes everything he does—including sex: "Sufyan appeared to get through it all with an absolute minimum of action, she took it . . . that the two of them were of the same mind on this matter, viz., that it was dirty business, not to be discussed before or after. . . . that . . . [the children] both turned out to be girls she refused to blame on Allah, preferring, instead, to blame the weakling seed implanted in her by her unmanly spouse."

About the alleged blasphemy in the text, the list of Rushdie's offenses against Islam varies according to the detractors' points of view. The chapters on Muhammad—whom Rushdie calls Mahound, a disparaging label applied by Christians when Islam first began to spread—develop as Gibreel's dream sequence, thus insinuating the fictive origin of Muhammad's life. Two issues that Rushdie raises in these chapters form the crux of the accusation against him. One is his insinuation that the revelation that Muhammad received was not of divine origin, and the other is his treatment of the Prophet's polygamy. The former gives the book its title. Rushdie uses an apocryphal source to show that some verses of the Qur'an were deleted later because Satan, in the guise of Gabriel, had inspired them. If such deception had resulted in the creation of some of the chapters of the holy book, Rushdie implies, could not the authenticity of the entire text be doubted? Rushdie's other offense, the one dealing with Prophet Muhammad's polygamy, is highly insulting to Muslims since he depicts a brothel where prostitutes take up the names of the Prophet's wives.

Some critics, on the other hand, have noted that Rushdie's critique of Islam in *The Satanic Verses* in fact comes from a distinctive sense of belief and that what he depicts as fiction should not be seen as his view of history. Sara Suleri's comment in her 1992 essay "Sal-

man Rushdie: Embodiments of Blasphemy, Censorships of Shame" can be examined to illustrate the point. Observing that "Rushdie has written a deeply Islamic book," she goes on to show that "blasphemy can be articulated only within the compass of belief." Suleri discusses some of the Indian influences on Rushdie's style in *The Satanic Verses,* such as Urdu *ghazal* poetry and Sufism, and explains that both traditions allow remarkable freedom in the expression of resentment against doctrinaire preaching of religion. Such readings of *The Satanic Verses,* though, are possible only by sophisticated literary analyses, acts many Muslim readers of Rushdie's works are unable or unwilling to perform.

The violent consequences following the publication of *The Satanic Verses* helped reconfirm the stereotypes about non-Western cultures that Rushdie attempted to dismantle in the novel. After its publication, the book raised a storm in many Muslim countries. At least six people were killed in India and Pakistan in street agitations that often turned violent and led to clashes with the police. The Japanese translator of the book was murdered, the Norwegian and Italian translators were seriously wounded, and Muslim intellectuals who came to Rushdie's defense faced threats from terrorists. In 1989 the Ayatollah Khomeini, who figures in the book as a nutty but dangerous spiritual leader, proclaimed a fatwa sentencing Rushdie to death. Rushdie immediately went into hiding. For several years he lived in thirty to forty safe houses protected by the British police. Initially, the Iranian government offered a bounty of $1 million to Rushdie's assassin; the amount was raised to $5 million subsequently. Although after the death of Khomeini in 1989, the Iranian government tried to distance itself from the promise of a reward to Rushdie's murderer, other fanatic Islamist groups underwrote the bounty with private donations.

Not surprisingly, Rushdie's next literary venture deals with the issue of censorship. Published in 1990, *Haroun and the Sea of Stories,* a children's novel, tells the story of a father and his son and of two cities: Gup (Chatter) and Chup (Hush). The motif also appears in *East, West: Stories,* which he published in 1994. Rushdie's most significant work in these years, however, was *Imaginary Homelands: Essays and Criticism, 1981–1991,* published in 1991. In it Rushdie selected more than seventy essays he had previously published. The topics are varied and range from politics and literature in the South Asian subcontinent to comments on contemporary authors. A few deal with Rushdie's response to the debacle following *The Satanic Verses.* "In Good Faith" explains that his intention in writing the novel was neither to insult Muhammad nor denigrate Muslims;

Dust jacket for the U.S. edition of Rushdie's 1990 children's book, about two cities called Gup (Chatter) and Chup (Hush) (Richland County Public Library)

rather, he had sought to portray the plight of immigrants in Britain. In a telling metaphor in "One Thousand Days in a Balloon," Rushdie compares his self-imposed confinement to escape assassination with living in a "hot-air balloon [that] drifts slowly over a bottomless chasm."

In spite of the constraints that the fatwa placed him under in the early 1990s, Rushdie was able to write a major novel, *The Moor's Last Sigh* (1995), which also prompted a backlash, albeit on a much smaller scale. Since *The Moor's Last Sigh* parodies a fundamentalist Hindu political leader of Bombay, it was unofficially banned in that city. Bal Thackeray, the leader of the Shiv Sena Party, an extremist political organization for fanatic Hindus, appears as Raman Fielding, a caricature in which he resembles a frog or a "mainduck." Thackeray soon responded by forbidding local bookstores to carry the novel.

The Moor's Last Sigh tells the story of Moraes Zogoiby, whose lineage derives from several non-

Indian religions and cultures. His mother, Aurora da Gama, the last in her line, comes from a family of prosperous spice traders of Portuguese origin, with links to the explorer Vasco da Gama himself. Da Gama, who discovered the sea route to India via the Cape of Good Hope and reached India in the late fifteenth century, was followed by other European adventurers. They began as traders but became rulers of India as well as several other Asian countries.

Moraes's paternity is a reminder of the Middle Eastern influence on India, since the Zogoibies were members of a little-known Jewish community in south India who fled from Spain when the last Moorish king, Sultan Boabdil, fell to Christian powers. Boabdil acquired a Jewish mistress in exile after the loss of his kingdom. She stole his crown and headed toward India on a ship, carrying his child in her belly, when the conquering Christians deported the Jews from Spain. Named Abraham after his birth, Moraes's father learns the secret of his mother's family in a serendipitous find. He takes up the name Zogoiby–meaning *unlucky*–the same name his Moorish ancestor assumed after he lost his kingdom.

Abraham marries Aurora, moves to Bombay–the center of the Indian economy–rises phenomenally in business, and also becomes the undisputed ruler of the underworld. In a curious confluence, Abraham and his son, Moraes, represent the three major Western influences on India–those of Judaism, Christianity, and Islam. Like other Rushdie characters, Moraes, the narrator, has strong allegorical resonances. Though he is not a player in the events, he witnesses the major upheavals that rocked India in the 1980s and early 1990s. Crucial in his experience is the rise of Hindu fundamentalism, leading to the demolition of the Babri Mosque in Ayoddha and the terrorist bomb attacks on Bombay that came as its backlash. Moraes is unnaturally big and suffers from a disease that ages him at twice the normal rate, which hints at the hollow economic growth of a decolonized country. Political leaders in decolonized third-world countries impress themselves with tall buildings and large cities; certainly, the sprawling city of Bombay illustrates the phenomenon. Bombay is enormous but lacks the civic amenities to serve its huge populace. Nor does it have an equitable political system to settle differences between its multiple ethnicities. It is no coincidence that Abraham, through kickbacks and influence peddling, bags lucrative construction deals in postindependence Bombay. A good part of the narrative describes how he and his Hindu counterpart, Raman Fielding, stir up religious sentiments to assume control of the city.

At the end of the tale, Moraes, the last in the Zogoiby clan, leaves a burning Bombay and returns to his family's point of origin, Spain. Bombay is burning because religious extremists have used explosives to eliminate each other and wipe out public places. Moraes's journey to Spain is to retrieve the priceless paintings done by his mother but stolen by Vasco Miranda, her former lover and a rival painter. Vasco puts Moraes in a prison tower; often called the "Moor" in this chapter, Moraes spends long days and nights accompanied by a Japanese woman, a fellow prisoner, who specializes in restoring palimpsests to their original state. Vasco needs her to reconstruct Aurora's paintings, because she has hidden her true work under layers of lesser ones. Under these circumstances, Moraes writes his tale. Reviewers of *The Moor's Last Sigh* saw biographical echoes in the work; Moraes's anguish was taken to be Rushdie's own because he wrote *The Moor's Last Sigh* during the darkest days of the fatwa. Rushdie revealed later, however, in a 1996 interview with Charlie Rose (collected in *Conversations with Salman Rushdie*) that Aurora represents him more than Moraes does because she is an "encyclopedic painter" and that "the kind of painter she is is a little bit the kind of writer I would like to be."

Recognized as another masterpiece, *The Moor's Last Sigh* raises complex issues of imperialism, nationalism, migration, and hybridity. But while Saleem in *Midnight's Children,* despite all the shifts in his narrative, is able to sustain a coherent vision of his nation through the end, Moraes's India is torn apart from within. "While Saleem is a crumbling figure of national allegory," Laura Moss argues in her 1998 essay "'Forget Those Damnfool Realists!' Salman Rushdie's Self-Parody in *The Moor's Last Sigh*" that "Moraes is forced into a migrant position beyond the nation." Moraes's last words in the narrative do not fully wipe out the possibility of a better future, however, because he "hope[s] to awaken, renewed and joyful, into a better time." Such a reawakening, according to Stephen Baker in his "'You Must Remember This': Salman Rushdie's *The Moor's Last Sigh*" (2000), "remains as [a] reminder to us too that we need not surrender the imagination to models of historical inevitability or resign ourselves to the fact that there is no alternative."

While *Midnight's Children* treats imperialism obviously as exploitation, *The Moor's Last Sigh* depicts it with a great deal of ambivalence. While the spice trade was instrumental in drawing the Portuguese to India, many in the Portuguese community felt that they possessed as much nationalistic fervor as did other Indians. It is in fact Aurora who grows critical of her da Gama ancestors when she recalls why they came to the Indian "subcondiment": "'They came for the hot stuff, just like any man calling on a tart." Her paintings in palimpsests are a rich metaphor suggesting the many imprints left on

India by peoples of disparate origins. These influences bear the promise of a vibrant multicultural society, which India seemed to be becoming before the chaos of sectarian strife. Such a society also existed in the Spain ruled by the Moors, who too were its former invaders. The expulsion of the Moors after the Christian conquest of Spain led to a monolithic society. Imperialism, thus, can be liberating as well as limiting; in *The Moor's Last Sigh,* Rushdie does not treat it as evil per se. Paul Cantor's remark on the issue in his 1997 essay "Tales of the Alhambra: Rushdie's Use of Spanish History in *The Moor's Last Sigh*" well explains Rushdie's position. Cantor notes that in *The Moor's Last Sigh,* "Rushdie views religious conflict as marking the inevitable limit to the success of cultural hybridity"; but Rushdie, Cantor states, also realizes that religious differences cannot be eliminated by mere "aestheticizing" because they are "the fundamental beliefs that give meaning to life."

Perhaps on some intellectual level, Rushdie understands the ire of the Muslims he enraged with *The Satanic Verses,* but his emotional response to a life of confinement they placed him under has been angry desperation. In 1990 he made a public announcement that he had "embraced" Islam, but the fatwa was not lifted, and Rushdie's gesture of appeasement went unheeded by the zealots out for his blood. His marriage with Wiggins broke up in 1993; she found it difficult to adjust to a life filled with terror.

Rushdie met Elizabeth West, an editor, in 1994; they married in 1997, and a son, Milan, was born to them the same year. Rushdie and West coedited a selection of Indian prose, *The Vintage Book of Indian Writing, 1947–1997,* which came out also in 1997. Some statements Rushdie made in the introduction to the anthology—he wrote it himself and had published it in *The New Yorker* earlier (23 June 1997)—provoked many Indian authors and academics to denounce him and question his credentials to pass judgments on Indian literature. They were deeply disturbed by Rushdie's claim that in India, literature written in English is far superior to those in the local languages. Rushdie's response to their anger was dismissive. He explained to Dave Weich of *Powells.com* that his statements had provoked Indian authors because he had been "politically incorrect" and that he had become a victim of their "envy aimed at writers in English because they make more money, they get published around the world."

Rushdie increased his public appearances in the mid 1990s, embarking on book tours, granting interviews, and moving somewhat more freely. During the years immediately after the fatwa, airlines, even British Airways, had refused to carry him. In 1993 Rushdie became an honorary professor of humanities at the Massachusetts Institute of Technology. His meeting

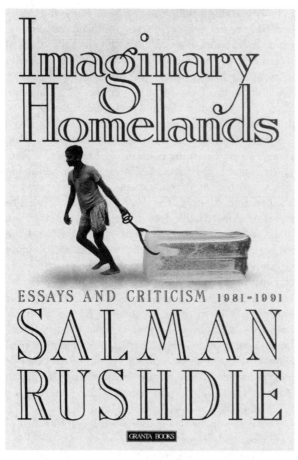

Dust jacket for Rushdie's 1991 collection of more than seventy essays, including some about his experience living underground following the threats on his life because of The Satanic Verses *(Richland County Public Library)*

with President Bill Clinton the same year paved the way to greater recognition of his plight from other world leaders. Pressure from the European Union, in particular Britain, forced the government of Iran to relent and rescind the execution order in 1998. The Iranian foreign minister categorically stated that his government would not reward Rushdie's assassin with the millions it had promised. The nature of a fatwa is such, however, that only the religious authority that issued it has the power to revoke it. Since Khomeini has died, no authority is competent enough to cancel his fatwa. Still, the withdrawal of a government-backed bounty for his head has lessened the threat to his life.

In 1999 Rushdie published a major novel, *The Ground beneath Her Feet.* Nearly six hundred pages long, the work is markedly different from his previous fiction in that it does not dwell on political issues but focuses, instead, on love and music. Ormus Cama, a rock star from India, makes it big in the West, especially the

United States. His lover, Vina Apsara, is equally gifted as a singer. Rai Merchant, the narrator, on the other hand, is a professional photographer. Not gifted musically, he is Vina's other lover and also Ormus's friend. Rushdie utilizes the age-old motif of a lovers' triangle in *The Ground beneath Her Feet.* The motif of music in the novel, on the other hand, derives from the Orpheus myth—overlaying which is the Kama-Rati myth, pertaining to the Indian divinities of love and desire. True to the spirit of this synthesis is the multireligious interaction in the book. Ormus is a Zoroastrian; Vina has a mixed Hindu-Christian background; and Rai is a Muslim. All of them grew up in Bombay—a city Rushdie found distinctive in its tolerance of many faiths when he was growing up there in the 1950s and 1960s.

An odd twist in *The Ground beneath Her Feet* is that it exists in a parallel reality. In this alternate universe, John F. Kennedy survives the assassination attempt in Dallas, but both he and Robert Kennedy are killed in a dual assassination in Los Angeles; and there are novels such as *Catch 18* and *The Watergate Affair.* Such mingling of fact and fiction suggests the possibilities of other realities. While *The Ground beneath Her Feet* does not build on the political ramifications of these possibilities, it creates uncertainty by hinting at them. The fluid reality is made even more unstable by the earthquakes that occur frequently in the alternate realm of the novel. Vina disappears in the first chapter when a mammoth earthquake swallows her in Mexico. As Rai tells her story in flashback, the lives of all three main characters unfold. Rushdie adds to this vision of alternate dimensions and earthquakes by utilizing the motif of twins. Both Ormus and Vina had twins who died at birth and who haunt them in the twin world in which they dwell. In a 1999 interview with Peter Kadzis for the *Boston Phoenix,* Rushdie himself summed it up best: "[I]n this novel, the character has a shadow self running through the corridors of his mind. . . . I may have pushed it to the limit with two sets of twins and, indeed, a twin world, a parallel world as well as the real world." The fact that Ormus survived while his twin died at birth links him to singer Elvis Presley; Rushdie also compares him to Bob Dylan and John Lennon, while Vina is a mix of both Madonna and Princess Diana. Ormus's dead twin, presumably from the real world, communicates rock classics to him through telepathy: "Yesterday," for example, and "I Got You, Babe." Lyrics written by Rushdie himself also turn up in *The Ground beneath Her Feet,* including some that were adopted by the band U2.

The Ground beneath Her Feet nevertheless disappointed many Rushdie readers. Writing for *The Sunday Times* (5 April 1999), Peter Kemp noted that the book marked "a steep literary downturn" in Rushdie's career. Pankaj Mishra, in the *New Statesman* (4 September 1999), rated *The Ground beneath Her Feet* poorly and even worried that it was the portent of "an alarming new kind of anti-literature." Many critics agreed that the chapters in which Rushdie describes the young Ormus, Vina, and Rai in Bombay are well written—in contrast to those set in New York, where Cama and Vina are adult celebrities, addicted to drugs and prisoners of their own fame.

Rushdie wrote the New York chapters of *The Ground beneath Her Feet* in England, based on notes he had taken during his trips to the city. His interest in the United States, particularly New York, grew in the 1990s. A possible reason could be he felt more secure making public appearances in the United States than in Britain. Several of his books came out in the 1990s, which made travel necessary for book tours. Another reason was his increasing dislike of British politics and its social and cultural establishments. The news media in Britain had often expressed concerns over the government money spent on protecting the controversial author and had even insinuated that he contributed to his misfortune himself. In an interview with D. T. Max of *The New York Times* (17 September 2000), Rushdie praised New York because it had "less of the 'backbiting and incestuous' literary culture of London." Rushdie's observation caused a huge uproar in Britain. He had, meanwhile, moved to New York and had been living with Padma Lakshmi, an Indian model and cookbook author, whom he had met at a party. (The couple was married on 19 April 2004). According to Max, at the time, Rushdie's marriage with West was still continuing, and Rushdie frequently returned to England to visit her, their son, and his other son—it is likely that he had separated from West by this time but was not legally divorced. News of Rushdie's lifestyle raised eyebrows in Britain. Baroness Uddin, a female Muslim labor M.P. (member of Parliament), declared that Rushdie had discredited Muslims and had not been grateful enough of the protection he had received from the British government. She was joined by another Muslim labor M.P., Lord Ahmed—both of whom are from South Asia—in urging the government to withdraw Rushdie's security and spend the money (£1,000,000 per year) elsewhere. In a strong rejoinder, Rushdie clarified that he had never discredited Muslims, that his lifestyle in New York had been grossly exaggerated, that the amount spent on his security was not what it had been alleged to be, and that whatever money the British government had spent on his security had been amply repaid by him through his income tax.

Rushdie was drawn to New York also because of the history of migrants that distinguishes the city; the teeming ethnicities reminded him of his childhood Bombay. In the interview with Max, he, in fact, described New York as "a western rewrite of Bombay." While only a part of the action in *The Ground beneath Her Feet* happens in New York, Rushdie's next novel, *Fury*, is set almost entirely in New York; it appeared in 2001. Malik Solanka—no other Rushdie protagonist is closer to the author than this one—was born in Bombay, lived in London, and now resides in New York. In Bombay, he grew up in the Methwold Estate, the same neighborhood where several well-known Rushdie characters, such as Saleem Sinai, Saladin Chamchawalla, and Moraes Zogoigby, spent their childhoods. A professor at King's College, Cambridge, Solanka was living with his second wife and a four-year-old son—until his departure to Manhattan. Derided by his colleagues for his interest in doll making, Solanka struck it rich when one of his dolls became immensely popular. Known as Little Brain, it earned him huge fame from television appearances in a variety of manifestations: first a doll, then a puppet, then an animated cartoon character, and finally an actress and talk-show host. Solanka got rich from the royalties he earned from these creations, but he was pursued by demons or furies. When one possessed him, he found himself holding a knife at his sleeping wife and baby boy—hence his parting from his family.

Solanka's Manhattan apartment hideout, although costing him $8,000 a month, does not protect him from the furies. There is a psychopath at large, known as the concrete killer, who bludgeons his victims to death with a lump of concrete, and Solanka wonders if he commits those crimes himself during alcoholic blackouts. Assailed by blackouts and explosive bouts of rage, Solanka muses on his reconstructed life and how it fits in his new environment. Though he thinks he is done with women, a beautiful Serbian woman, Mila Milo, dressed as his Little Brain, befriends him and educates him on computer culture. Solanka, however, dumps Mila in favor of a ravishing Indian beauty, Neela, a television producer, whose appearance in Central Park literally stops men in their tracks. Neela's political activism leads her to Lilliput-Blefuscu, a country in the South Pacific experiencing a civil war, and Solanka follows her. In the end he is back in London, making his presence felt to his son by shouting at the top of his voice at the sky. It is unclear if this gesture brings them closer to a reunion.

Fury is overloaded with references to American national events and notable figures at the turn of the century, including the "Gush-Bore" presidential election; Elian Gonzalez; the 2000 Puerto Rican Day incident in which gangs of boys and men sexually assaulted fifty women in Central Park; Monica Lewinsky; Meg Ryan; Dennis Quaid—the list runs long. The technique

Dust jacket for the U.S. edition of Rushdie's 1995 novel in which the narrator, imprisoned in a dungeon in Spain by his mother's former lover, tells the story of his father's rise to power in the Bombay underworld (Richland County Public Library)

strates that Rushdie blurs the boundary between New York and the United States in essays he has written since the 1990s. Michiko Kakutani, who had admiringly reviewed Rushdie's other works (except *The Ground beneath Her Feet*), wrote in *The New York Times* (13 September 2002) that "when it comes to discussing specific aspects of America . . . Mr. Rushdie can sound decidedly naïve or glib." Kakutani points out the solution Rushdie proposed during the 2000 presidential election impasse: a coalition of both George Bush and Al Gore, the two men being president and vice president and switching roles midterm. This piece appears as "December 2000: A Grand Coalition" in *Step across This Line* and ends with a footnote that Rushdie attached on hindsight. In it he expresses dissatisfaction at the Bush administration for being "a hard-line, ideological, right-wing regime" and laments his "columnist's fate to be rendered absurd by events." Curiously, Rushdie seems unaware of the absurdity of his election fix.

Rushdie appears critical of the Bush administration for its conservative propensities in the above statement, but its policy toward the Islamic world in the wake of 11 September 2001 receives his full endorsement; he, in fact, recommends a harsher approach in dealing with Muslims, making no attempt to distinguish between the fanatics on the fringe and the moderates in the majority. His leftist orientation, which dates back to the 1960s when he participated in peace marches to protest the Vietnam War, goes through a drastic shift. In "November 2001: Not about Islam?" Rushdie unequivocally expresses his loathing of Islam and justifies it with a sampling of rabid Muslim opinions on the attack on the World Trade Center. In essays such as "October 2001: The Attacks on America" and "February 2001: Anti-Americanism," he strikes at the Western intellectual establishment that, after 11 September, sought to examine the sociopolitical causes of anti-American feelings in the Islamic world and to determine if U.S. foreign policy had unwittingly contributed to such a virulent brand of Islam. In the introduction to a special issue of *Twentieth Century Literature* (Spring 2001), which is appropriately titled "Reading Rushdie after September 11, 2001," Sabina Sawhney and Simona Sawhney postulate that perhaps on 11 September, Rushdie experienced an echo of the fatwa and that this reminder accounts for his reaction to the catastrophe. They recall Rushdie's earlier views on Palestine and Kashmir, indicate his changed perspectives on these issues since 2001, and describe Rushdie as "not the first writer to present us with a set of political writings incongruent with the general trajectory of his work." Both critics, however, feel that Rushdie's fiction still preempts any accusation that the excitement of writing about the United States has thoroughly blinded him to its ills.

enables Rushdie to write what unmistakably is an "American novel," though he risks dating the novel for later generations of readers. The Americanness of *Fury* is indelibly stamped also on Rushdie's English, which now conforms to American usage, both in spelling and idiom. Like Solanka, Rushdie tries hard to fit.

If Solanka succeeds somewhat in adapting himself as a New Yorker, however, Rushdie has not necessarily been able to convince others that he can grasp American culture and politics. In the late 1990s and early 2000s, he wrote several journalistic articles in *The New York Times* and *The Guardian* that expressed, somewhat superficially, his optimism and assumptions about the United States. *Step across This Line: Collected Nonfiction, 1992–2002,* which he published in 2002, reprints many of these articles. Though Rushdie admits in an interview with Weich that "I don't feel American, but I *do* feel like a New Yorker," *Step across This Line* demon-

They point out "the caustic description of American imperialism in *Fury*," the work immediately preceding *Step across This Line*.

Indeed, articles on literature and authors in *Step across This Line* present a Rushdie who is eccentric as well as perceptive. The essay on J. M. Coetzee, for example, is quite unusual. About the South African author's novel *Disgrace* (1999), Rushdie writes: "The book unquestionably fulfills the first requirement of a great novel: it powerfully creates a dystopia that adds to the sum total of the imagined worlds at our disposal and by doing so, increases what is possible for us to think." In addition to such indeterminate pronouncements, Rushdie calls Coetzee's language in *Disgrace* "bone-hard" and opines that the novel is "coherent enough–coherent in its privileging of incoherence, striving to make of its blindness a sort of metaphoric insight." Hermione Lee of *The Guardian* (14 December 2002) suggests that this "occasional mean streak" in *Step across This Line*, Rushdie's "grudging reaction to Coetzee's *Disgrace*," occurs because it "beat Rushdie to the Commonwealth prize."

Nevertheless, *Step across This Line* balances such want of critical breadth by offering fine essays on the motion-picture version of *The Wizard of Oz* (1939) and on authors such as Angela Carter, Arthur Miller, and Edward W. Said. Equally beautifully written are Rushdie's reflections in the section "Messages from the Plague Years," where he recounts his days under the fatwa. Rushdie is an avid proponent of freedom of expression in the third world and is always willing to lend his support to a persecuted author. He has come to the defense of other controversial writers and activists–for example, Michel Houellebecq of France, Taslima Nasrin of Bangladesh, and Ken Sarawiwi of Nigeria–and has written to champion their right to dissent. The letter he wrote to espouse the cause of Nasrin is republished in *Step across This Line*. "A Dream of Glorious Return" describes his trip back to India in 2000 after the fatwa–the title, Rushdie does not forget to remind his readers, echoes words from *The Satanic Verses*. The trip was an emotional one to Rushdie because he went back to India after thirteen years; it was memorable also because his son Zafar accompanied him.

Step across This Line ends with a two-part essay, Rushdie's Tanner lecture at Yale University in 2002; it is the piece that gives the book its title. In this essay–musing on boundaries, examining the compulsion of border crossings, contemplating what seems to be a postnationalist future, and meandering on many topics–Rushdie finally dwells on the plight of the immigrants in the United States and advocates globalization. Rushdie's fiction since *Shame* has been moving toward such a prospect. In *Shame* he introduces the idea that

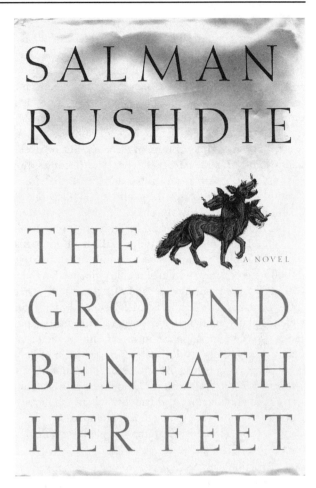

Dust jacket for the U.S. edition of Rushdie's 1999 novel, about a love triangle between two rock musicians and a photographer, set in an alternate reality in which President John F. Kennedy survives the attempt to assassinate him in Dallas (Richland County Public Library)

mohajirs or immigrants "come unstuck from their native land," that they "fly" and "flee" in search of freedom, that their "anti-gravity" is "anti-belonging." *The Satanic Verses*, which demonstrates Rushdie's powerful treatment of migrancy, depicts London as a city experiencing clashes of ethnicities and "offers," in Peter Kalliney's words in "Globalization, Postcoloniality, and the Problem of Literary Studies in *The Satanic Verses*" (2002), "a narrative of globalization as a cure for the ills of postcolonialism." Indeed, *The Moor's Last Sigh*, *The Ground beneath Her Feet*, and *Fury*, works Rushdie wrote since *The Satanic Verses*, deal with diasporic characters and issues of global migration. Not many would agree, however, that globalization in the form of mass migration of the third-world underprivileged into Western countries, such as Britain and the United States, can solve the ills of postcolonialism.

Rushdie shows an awareness of the complexity surrounding migrancy in *Shalimar the Clown* (2005). Spanning three continents–North America, Europe, and Asia–the novel treats the themes of globalization and terrorism. The title character grows up in Kashmir in a community of gastronomes and actors who, when their service is called upon, provide both food and fun for rich patrons. Shalimar marries his childhood sweetheart, Boonyi, a Hindu Brahmin teenager, but he eventually joins Muslim terrorists when she becomes the mistress of the American ambassador in India, Max Ophuls, in order to escape the confines and boredom of Kashmir. Shalimar ends up in Los Angeles years later, having murdered his wife, and he finds employment as the retired Ophuls's valet and chauffeur. Biding his time for a while, Shalimar slits his employer's throat at the doorstep of India Ophuls, the illegitimate daughter Ophuls fathered with Boonyi and raised himself. What spurs Shalimar into action is a television talk show in which Ophuls fulminates raw hatred at Kashmiri separatists receiving support from Islamic jihadists. Ophuls's rage falls on deaf ears because the interview takes place years before the attacks of 11 September, at a time when the American public did not view Islamic terror as a credible threat to national security. The violence in Kashmir received even less attention. Ophuls's claim that pre-separatist Kashmir was paradise inflames the taciturn Shalimar.

Reactions to *Shalimar the Clown* were mixed at best. Reviewers pointed out many flaws in the novel. Their major concern was Rushdie's style, which takes the reader on frequent digressions. Kakutani complained in *The New York Times* (6 September 2005) of "Rushdie's determination to graft huge political and cultural issues onto a flimsy soap opera plot." Kakutani deemed the book as disappointing as Rushdie's two preceding novels *The Ground beneath Her Feet* and *Fury*. Also writing in *The New York Times* (23 October 2005), Laura Miller observed that "Cascading clauses are a Rushdie trademark; they can be taken as a manifestation of abundant imagination or as a symptom of poor writerly discipline," implying that the latter is the case with Rushdie. John Updike's review in *The New Yorker* (5 September 2005), Marco Roth's in *TLS: The Times Literary Supplement* (25 September 2005), and Mishra's in *The New York Review of Books* (5 October 2005) expressed strikingly similar opinions on Rushdie's writing. Not only did these reviewers object to the overabundance of words in *Shalimar the Clown,* they also deplored the implausible characters that inhabit the tale. Indeed, both Max and India Ophuls are so outstanding in their accomplishments that they cease to be credible. Roth sarcastically noted that Rushdie's characters "[n]o longer . . . have personalities, they have resumes."

According to some reviewers, the locales in *Shalimar the Clown,* both Los Angeles and a Kashmir village, also appear improbable. Mishra wondered if the idealized villagers could ever have existed in any part of the real Kashmir before the separatist movement. He astutely questioned the religious harmony in the community and took Rushdie to task for making the Muslims more accommodating of Hindu customs and beliefs than vice versa. Mishra also attacked Rushdie for vastly oversimplifying the troubled politics behind the political divide, pointing out that the "anti-India insurgency" was owing in large measure to "the thwarted Kashmiri desire to embrace 'the modern' . . . and was not dominated by jihadi Islamists until the mid-1990s."

Updike explained that some of the problems in *Shalimar the Clown* arose from the fact that Rushdie is both "a cause célèbre and a free-speech martyr" and that the years he spent in hiding honed his interest in two topics: "celebrity and human cruelty." Less kind than Updike, Roth attributed the weaknesses of the novel to Rushdie's "pursuit of that elusive beast, the great global novel." It should be clarified, however, that, although a "global" novel, *Shalimar the Clown,* in contrast to the views expressed in *Step across This Line,* does not champion migrancy, nor does Rushdie paint terrorism with a broad brush. Shalimar's vengeful trek from his native Kashmir to Los Angeles is beset with violence and comes to a gory conclusion when an arrow shot by India, who happens to be a competent archer, hits him. Since his embrace of terrorism is to avenge a great personal loss, Shalimar can hardly be called a holy warrior with an ideological motive. Those who become terrorists, Rushdie seems to suggest, are often motivated by nonideological reasons; they accept a militant doctrine because of political instability in their native lands. Another aspect of *Shalimar the Clown* is its potential for allegorical interpretation. Ophuls's dalliance with Boonyi, who is also called "Bhoomi" or "the earth" and whose restive temperament leads her to the American ambassador of German Jewish origin, offers fertile interpretive ground and will occupy scholars for years to come.

Salman Rushdie remains an immense figure in postcolonial and postmodern studies. Regardless of the controversies he raises, he is an acknowledged master of storytelling, one who boldly experiments with new techniques, questions long-held beliefs, and opposes dogmatism in his fiction. The strongest evidence of Rushdie's prominence in the contemporary literary scene is the overwhelming scholarly attention he has received. Book-length studies of Rushdie alone number about twenty, while reviews of his books, critical essays on his work, and interviews of him in magazines, scholarly journals, and books are plentiful. Doctoral dissertations and master's theses that treat Rushdie or view him in relation to other authors number nearly eighty titles. Any researcher of Rushdie has to grapple with nearly two thousand items, which also include a daunting quantity of sociological and ethnic studies written in the wake of the controversy over *The Satanic Verses.* Such critical attention to an author is indicative of his canonical status. Especially in South Asian English writing, he is an awesome presence–so much that a whole new generation of Indian writers has been labeled as "Rushdie's Children" by *Time* magazine (16 December 1991) and as "India's Post-Rushdie Generation" by *The New York Times* (3 July 2000).

Interviews:

"When Life Becomes a Bad Novel," *Salon.com* (25 January 1996) <www.salon.com/06/features/interview.html>;

David Scheff, "Playboy Interview: Salman Rushdie," *Playboy* (April 1996): 49–62, 165;

Peter Kadzis, "Salman Speaks," *Boston Phoenix,* 7 May 1999, pp. 28–31;

Michael Reder, ed., *Conversations with Salman Rushdie,* Literary Conversation Series (Jackson: University Press of Mississippi, 2000);

D. T. Max, "The Concrete beneath His Feet," *New York Times,* 17 September 2000, VI: 68;

Pradyumna S. Chauhan, ed., *Salman Rushdie Interviews: A Sourcebook of His Ideas* (Westport, Conn.: Greenwood Press, 2001);

Dave Weich, "Salman Rushdie, Out and About," *Powells.com* (25 September 2002) <www.powellsbooks.com/authors/rushdie.html>.

Bibliography:

Joel Kuortti, *The Salman Rushdie Bibliography: A Bibliography of Salman Rushdie's Work and Rushdie Criticism* (Frankfurt am Main & New York: Peter Lang, 1997).

Biographies:

Anuradha Dingwaney, "Salman Rushdie," in *Writers of the Indian Diaspora: A Bio-Bibliographical Critical Sourcebook,* edited by Emmanuel S. Nelson (Westport, Conn.: Greenwood Press, 1993), pp. 363–383;

Ian Hamilton, "The First Life of Salman Rushdie," *New Yorker* (25 December 1995 – 1 January 1996): 90–113.

References:

Anouar Abdallah and others, *Pour Rushdie: Cent intellectuels arabes et musulmans pour la liberté d'expression* (Paris: La Découverte/Carrefour des littératures/ Colibri, 1993); translated as *For Rushdie: Essays by Arab and Muslim Writers in Defense of Free Speech* (New York: Braziller, 1994);

Chinua Achebe, "Today, A Balance of Stories," in his *Home and Exile* (Oxford & New York: Oxford University Press, 2000), pp. 73–105;

Aijaz Ahmad, "Salman Rushdie's *Shame:* Postmodern Migrancy and the Representation of Women," in his *In Theory: Classes, Nations, Literatures* (London & New York: Verso, 1992), pp. 123–158;

Robert Alter, "The Novel and the Sense of the Past," *Salmagundi,* 68–69 (1985–1986): 91–106;

Lisa Appignanesi and Sara Maitland, eds., *The Rushdie File* (Syracuse, N.Y.: Syracuse University Press, 1990);

Stephen Baker, "'You Must Remember This': Salman Rushdie's *The Moor's Last Sigh,*" *Journal of Commonwealth Literature,* 35, no. 1 (2000): 43–54;

John Clement Ball, *Satire and the Postcolonial Novel: V. S. Naipaul, Chinua Achebe, and Salman Rushdie* (New York: Routledge, 2003);

M. Keith Booker, ed., *Critical Essays on Salman Rushdie* (New York: G. K. Hall, 1999);

Timothy Brennan, *Salman Rushdie and the Third World: Myths of the Nation* (New York: St. Martin's Press, 1989);

Paul Cantor, "Tales of the Alhambra: Rushdie's Use of Spanish History in *The Moor's Last Sigh,*" *Studies in the Novel,* 29 (Fall 1997): 321–341;

Roger Y. Clark, *Stranger Gods: Salman Rushdie's Other Worlds* (Montreal & Ithaca, N.Y.: McGill-Queen's University Press, 2001);

Catherine Cundy, *Salman Rushdie* (Manchester: Manchester University Press / New York: St. Martin's Press, 1996);

M. D. Fletcher, ed., *Reading Rushdie: Perspectives on the Fiction of Salman Rushdie* (Amsterdam & Atlanta: Rodopi, 1994);

Michael Gorra, *After Empire: Scott, Naipaul, Rushdie* (Chicago: Chicago University Press, 1997);

Michael Harris, *Outsiders & Insiders: Perspective of Third-World Culture in British and Post-Colonial Fiction* (New York: Peter Lang, 1992);

James Harrison, *Salman Rushdie* (New York: Twayne, 1992);

Sabrina Hassumani, *Salman Rushdie: A Postmodern Reading of His Major Works* (Madison, N.J.: Fairleigh Dickinson University Press, 2002);

Clement Hawes, "Leading History by the Nose: The Turn to the Eighteenth Century in *Midnight's Children,*" *Modern Fiction Studies,* 39 (Winter 1993): 147–168;

Peter Kalliney, "Globalization, Postcoloniality, and the Problem of Literary Studies in *The Satanic Verses,*" *Modern Fiction Studies,* 48 (Spring 2002): 50–82;

Steve MacDonough and others, eds., *The Rushdie Letters: Freedom to Speak, Freedom to Write* (Lincoln: University of Nebraska Press, 1993);

Harveen Sachdeva Mann, "'Being Borne Across': Translation and Salman Rushdie's *The Satanic Verses,*" *Criticism,* 37 (Spring 1995): 281–308;

Vijay Mishra, "Postcolonial Differend: Diasporic Narrative of Salman Rushdie," *Ariel: A Review of International English Literature,* 26 (July 1995): 7–45;

Laura Moss, "'Forget Those Damnfool Realists!' Salman Rushdie's Self-Parody in *The Moor's Last Sigh,*" *Ariel: A Review of International English Literature,* 29 (October 1998): 121–139;

Daniel Pipes, *The Rushdie Affair: The Novel, the Ayatollah, and the West,* second edition (New Brunswick, N.J.: Transaction, 2003);

David Price, "Salman Rushdie's 'Use and Abuse of History' in *Midnight's Children,*" *Ariel: A Review of International English Literature,* 25 (April 1994): 91–107;

Jaina Sanga, *Salman Rushdie's Postcolonial Metaphors: Migration, Translation, Hybridity, Blasphemy, and Globalization* (Westport, Conn.: Greenwood Press, 2001);

Sabina Sawhney and Simona Sawhney, "Reading Rushdie after September 11, 2001," *Twentieth Century Literature,* 47 (Spring 2001): 431–443;

Alexander W. Schultheis, "Postcolonial Lack and Aesthetic Promise in *The Moor's Last Sigh,*" *Twentieth Century Literature,* 47 (Spring 2001): 569–595;

Sara Suleri, "Salman Rushdie: Embodiments of Blasphemy, Censorships of Shame," in her *The Rhetoric of English India* (Chicago: University of Chicago Press, 1992), pp. 174–206;

Neil Ten Kortenaar, "*Midnight's Children* and the Allegory of History," *Ariel: A Review of International English Literature,* 26 (April 1995): 41–62;

Keith Wilson, "*Midnight's Children* and Reader Responsibility," *Critical Quarterly,* 26, no. 3 (1984): 23–27.

Nayantara Sahgal

(10 May 1927 –   )

Satish C. Aikant
H.N.B. Garhwal University

BOOKS: *Prison and Chocolate Cake* (New York: Knopf, 1954; London: Gollancz, 1954; Bombay: Jaico, 1964);

A Time to Be Happy (New York: Knopf, 1958; London: Gollancz, 1958; Bombay: Jaico, 1963);

From Fear Set Free (London: Gollancz, 1962; Delhi: Hind Pocket Books, 1962; New York: Norton, 1963);

This Time of Morning (London: Gollancz, 1965; New York: Norton, 1965; New Delhi: Kali for Women, 2000);

Storm in Chandigarh (New York: Norton, 1969; London: Chatto & Windus, 1969; Delhi: Hind Pocket Books, 1970);

Freedom Movement in India (New Delhi: National Council of Educational Research and Training, 1970);

The Day in Shadow (New York: Norton, 1971; Delhi: Vikas, 1971; London: London Magazine Editions, 1975);

A Situation in New Delhi (London: London Magazine Editions, 1977; New Delhi & New York: Penguin, 1988);

A Voice for Freedom (Delhi: Hind Pocket Books, 1977);

Indira Gandhi's Emergence and Style (Durham, N.C.: Carolina Academic Press, 1978; New Delhi: Vikas, 1978); revised as *Indira Gandhi: Her Road to Power* (New York: Ungar, 1982; London: Macdonald, 1983);

Rich Like Us (London: Heinemann, 1985; New York: Norton, 1986; New Delhi: HarperCollins, 1999);

Plans for Departure (New York: Norton, 1985; London: Heinemann, 1986; New Delhi: HarperCollins/ India Today Group, 2003);

Mistaken Identity (New York: New Directions, 1988; London: Heinemann, 1988);

Point of View: A Personal Response to Life, Literature, and Politics (New Delhi: Prestige, 1997);

Lesser Breeds (New Delhi & London: HarperCollins, 2003).

OTHER: *Sunlight Surround You: A Birthday Bouquet from Chandralekha Mehta, Nayantara Sahgal, Rita Dar,*

Nayantara Sahgal (photograph by Avinash Pasricha; from the dust jacket for the American edition of Rich Like Us, *1986; Richland County Public Library)*

edited by Sahgal, Chandralekha Mehta, and Rita Dar (New Delhi: Nayantara Saghal, 1970);

Ruskin Bond, *Beautiful Garhwal: Heaven in Himalayas,* introduction by Sahgal (Dehra Dun, Uttaranchal: EBD Educational, 1988);

Before Freedom: Nehru's Letters to His Sister, edited by Sahgal (New Delhi: HarperCollins, 2000).

Nayantara Sahgal is a preeminent Indian English author. Writing in a style noted for its "Flaubert like obsession with paring language to the minimum," as the critic Jasbir Jain observes, Sahgal has written novels, memoirs, and other nonfictional works, imbuing the texture of her narratives with a wide range of interconnected political, social, and cultural issues. Rejecting the currently fashionable terms *colonial* and *postcolonial* to categorize her works and the Indian experience, she is reported to have stated, at an Association for Commonwealth Language and Literature Studies conference at the University of Kent in 1989, "I have wondered when postcolonial is supposed to end . . . the British came, and stayed, and left. And now they're gone, and their residue is simply one more layer added to the layer upon layer of Indian consciousness. Just one more" ("The Schizophrenic Imagination," in *Point of View: A Personal Response to Life, Literature, and Politics,* 1997). To put it somewhat differently, in Sahgal's work one finds a sense of continuity, of recognizing the past and building on it, rather than breaking away from it entirely. Dismissing the postcolonial label for its imprecision and lack of historical particularity, she instead focuses on ordinary lives as they cut across the grand narratives of history. For Sahgal, national identity is a source of selfhood. Her clearly defined nationalist ideology is her legacy from the cosmopolitan dynasty of the Nehru family and from Gandhian principles. The gradual erosion of the values espoused by Jawaharlal Nehru and Mohandas Karamchand Gandhi is a refrain in her novels, in which the historical and political landscape is invariably India, before and after Independence. Two crucial events, the Partition of India in 1947 and the state of emergency declared by Prime Minister Indira Gandhi in 1975 following a court ruling setting aside her reelection to parliament, left a deep impression on the Indian psyche and figure prominently in Sahgal's writings.

Sahgal was born Nayantara Pandit on 10 May 1927 in Allahabad. Her family was in the forefront of the Indian freedom movement and, later, in the governance of free India. Her father, Ranjit Sitaram Pandit, besides being a leading lawyer and freedom fighter, was a Sanskrit scholar who had translated into English several Sanskrit classics, including a twelfth-century history of Kashmir, *Rajatarangini* (River of Kings). Her mother was Vijaya Lakshmi Pandit, sister of Nehru, the first prime minister of independent India and the political heir of Mohandas Gandhi. Vijaya herself had a distinguished career, serving as the world's first female cabinet minister and, later, as the Indian ambassador to the Soviet Union, the United States, and England. She also became the first woman president of the United Nations General Assembly.

Sahgal, the second of three sisters, did not have a normal upbringing since her parents were in and out of prison for long spells during the struggle for independence. The atmosphere of Anand Bhawan, her family home in Allahabad, was charged with intense nationalism. Responding to the call of Mohandas Gandhi to boycott British goods, Nehru's father, Motilal Nehru, made

a bonfire of his family's foreign goods, and Sahgal's father gave up his profession to work full-time for the Indian National Congress, led by Mohandas Gandhi. In "The Schizophrenic Imagination," published in *Point of View,* Sahgal writes,

> At home, I was nourished on revolt. My elders were committed to rooting out foreign rule and had made a personal beginning by giving up their scholarship and their careers at the Bar to devote their lives and all their resources to the struggle for freedom. They were so enthralled with organizing for it, and being imprisoned for it, that I thought going to jail was a career.

The chief influence on Sahgal was Jawaharlal Nehru, her uncle. In a 1942 letter to her from Ahmadnagar Fort, where he was imprisoned, he wrote, "Merely to exist and carry on is of course not good enough; anybody can do that. We have to be thoroughly alive and vital, awake in mind and body, and eager to play our part in the great dramas that surround us" (*Before Freedom: Nehru's Letters to His Sister,* 2000).

For her early education Sahgal was sent to Woodstock, an American mission school in Mussoorie, in northern India, at a time when British institutions were being boycotted by the Indian National Congress. She later attended Wellesley College in Massachusetts because, as a member of a rebel family, she would not have been permitted to attend a university in India without pledging not to take part in anti-British political activity. Her parents, who were then in prison, did not accept such curbs on self-respect; yet, they were keen to ensure a university education for their daughters. On receiving the message "Wellesley is proud to welcome your daughters," in a cable from the college president, Sahgal and her elder sister, Chandralekha, were sent off to America.

Finding herself in America was a liberating experience that widened Sahgal's intellectual horizons, but India never left her consciousness: "I took it all with me, the loves, the loyalties, the way of life I had known. I found they grew and blossomed and found new ways of expressing themselves in what was, for the first time in my experience, a free country." She met famous Americans, such as Paul Robeson and Helen Keller, and she spent a summer vacation at Pearl S. Buck's country home in Pennsylvania. At Wellesley, Sahgal studied Russian with Vladimir Nabokov, an experience that was a happy prologue to her foray into the world of letters.

At Wellesley, Sahgal received a glimpse of the world outside India and a taste of free society that she describes in her first book, the autobiographical *Prison and Chocolate Cake* (1954). A war was being fought to liberate European countries from Nazi occupation, but Sahgal learned to her dismay that the countries occupied by the British Empire were not considered fit for liberation.

In "Illusion and Reality," published in *Point of View,* she writes that they were considered "lesser breeds," in Rudyard Kipling's colorful phrase.

The death of her father in 1944 as a result of his latest imprisonment was a traumatic experience for Sahgal. She returned to India after earning a B.A. at Wellesley in 1947, the year the country gained independence. With her father dead and her mother away in the Soviet Union serving as the Indian ambassador, she found solace under the protective wings of Jawaharlal Nehru, who was assuring the Indian nation of its "tryst with destiny." The horror of the Partition that year was an enormous dislocation that played an important role in the constitution of collective identity and thinking in India. In 1949 she married Gautam Sahgal, who was employed with a British firm. The couple had three children, Nonika, Ranjit, and Gita, but the marriage did not turn out to be a meeting of minds. She underscores her apprehensions in her second autobiographical volume, *From Fear Set Free* (1962). In "Turning Point," published in *Point of View,* Sahgal reflects that she was "uneasy and restless adjusting to the demands of a personality and an environment whose goals and texture were different from anything I had known or been comfortable with."

All of Sahgal's work is characterized by a sense of history. Her first novel, *A Time to Be Happy* (1958), is set in the transitional era of the Indian quest for freedom. Politics is integral to her narratives; as she states in "The Schizophrenic Imagination," "Politics for me was an environment in which every issue was a political issue, and personal and political fates were inextricably bound." This situation gave her the opportunity to investigate the momentous era of the dawn of freedom and its aftermath in a country emerging from two hundred years of British occupation. British colonialism, as Ashis Nandy has observed, was made possible by the psychological structures and cultural forces of a comprador class, and these "support systems of colonialism" have not altogether disappeared. Indeed, the colonial state owed its continuing existence to the cooperation of its subjects. The uneven terrain of Indian colonial history is marked by an alliance between nationalism and colonialism, which in a sense secured Indian modernity in the early twentieth century, an era dominated by Gandhian politics. The nationalist intelligentsia could not remain unaffected by Gandhian ideology. Some people vacillated between loyalty to the British and allegiance to the mother country. In *A Time to Be Happy,* the character Sanad swings between these opposite pulls. His redemption comes about after he meets Kusum, through whom he reconnects with his past and cultural roots.

In the early 1960s Sahgal met E. N. Mangat Rai of the Indian Civil Service, who was chief secretary of the Punjab and later of Jammu and Kashmir; he also went

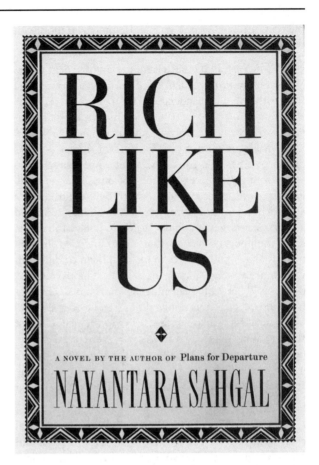

Dust jacket for the 1986 American edition of Sahgal's 1985 novel about a female government worker who opposes the authoritarian crackdown on civil liberties during the 1975–1977 state of emergency in India (Richland County Public Library)

on to serve as secretary to the Ministry of Petroleum and Chemicals in Delhi. She decided to make a life with him after her divorce from Gautam Sahgal in 1967. Her relationship with Mangat Rai is revealed through their extensive correspondence, some of which was published as *Relationship: Extracts from a Correspondence* (1994).

In 1965 Sahgal published *This Time of Morning,* a novel focusing on the Indian search for identity as the nation emerged from British domination. The critical question of governance engaged the attention of the new class of rulers and leaders. The British had provided what was known as a "steel frame" in the form of the Indian Civil Service, which in free India had to be directed to the needs and aspirations of the people. Mohandas Gandhi's popularity and his dominance on the national scene suggested an indigenous mode of governance, which he envisioned in his *Hind Swaraj* (1909, Indian Home Rule). Jawaharlal Nehru understood his mentor's ethical imperatives, but he was also influenced by the socialist model and favored partial state control of the economy; he tried to harmonize modernization with the Gandhian principles of a welfare state.

This Time of Morning tells of the involvement of the Vrind family in the Indian freedom movement and the aftermath of Independence. The period covered is roughly the 1930s to the 1960s. Within a setting of political corruption and decaying idealism, Sahgal inscribes the crucial question of gender. Rashmi, Kailas Vrind's daughter, seeks solace in a love affair while struggling to adjust to a marriage that is not working. The narrative follows a dialectical pattern, with two contradictory approaches to time and history. Kalyan Sinha is a man in a hurry who believes in quick action to relieve the miseries of the poor, no matter what means are used. In contrast, Kailas Vrind adheres to the Gandhian tradition, in which means are as important as ends. The narrative is thus poised between the conflicting viewpoints. This dialectic, however, is not resolved in a synthesis; the views of the idealistic Kailas are favored over the realpolitik of Kalyan. Sahgal witnessed from close quarters this transitional era and the gradual dissolution of political morality engineered by machinations of power and the reversal of priorities, especially after the era of Jawaharlal Nehru's leadership.

Storm in Chandigarh (1969) centers on the political crisis following the reorganization of states in India and the subsequent divisive tendencies it bred. Religion and language were freely used as instruments of coercive state power, undermining the grand vision of a unified Indian nation in which different communities would coexist in peace and harmony. The events in the novel are based on the actual division of the state of Punjab into Punjab and Hariyana; the chief ministers of the two states symbolize a conflict of interest as well as of ethics. On a deeper level the division is overshadowed by the trauma of the Partition of 1947; as Harpal Singh, a character in the novel, observes, "there was something sinister at the root of the Partition mentality and those who upheld it. Mankind's journey was towards integration, not the breaking up of what already existed." In *Storm in Chandigarh,* Sahgal interweaves personal history and political incidents, so that the social and marital problems faced by the Mehra and Sahni families are influenced by the course of political events. Vishal Dubey, an upright civil servant, is deputed by the central government to sort out some problems between the two states of Punjab and Hariyana, where he comes into close contact with two young couples, Inder and Saroj Mehra and Jit and Mara Sahni. Inder uses a "premarital lapse" on the part of Saroj to humiliate her and proclaim his domination over her. Vishal's company gives Saroj reassurance about her own individuality, but Inder frustrates her every move for equal partnership. This situation is in fact a continuing dilemma for women in modern India, and Saroj is seen as a voice of personal freedom.

In *Storm in Chandigarh,* Sahgal underlines the need to devise coherent norms, values, and commitments to bring Indians together under modern conditions and define a public sphere for all. As she reconstructs public history through personal history, the imbrication of the various pasts and presents of India acquires validity through temporal, spiritual, and material coordinates. The negative consequences of Independence included a rise in violence, ethnic conflict, and abdication of Gandhian ideology, highlighting the need for another movement to consolidate the gains of freedom and cleanse public life. For Sahgal, a return to the Gandhian way of life alone can reinstate the confidence of the people in the institutions of democracy and governance. In the novel Vishal regrets the passing of the Gandhian world: "Gandhian politics had also meant open action. No stealth . . . and therefore no shame. Every act proudly performed in the sunlight."

In her next novel, *The Day in Shadow* (1971), Sahgal touches on the theme of gender relations in the changing Indian social and political climate. Fulfillment in marriage more often than not eludes women. Simrit, a sensitive woman, desirous of comradeship and understanding with Som, her husband, is disappointed when she finds in his world nothing but ruthless ambition and an inordinate craving for money. Som wants to see his wife in a stereotypical way, as a subdued housewife who makes no demands on him and does not question his motives. She is expected to reconcile herself to an unequal relationship of power, which virtually denies every freedom to a woman, particularly a married one. Sahgal, however, does not suggest that marriage, as a social institution, has failed. As Jennifer Livett observes in "When Less Is More: Nayantara Sahgal's *The Day in Shadow,*" published in *Nayantara Sahgal's India: Passion, Politics, and History* (1998),

> in *The Day in Shadow*, every aspect of the personal is political, public and private are inseparable, creating an extensive and subtle analysis of India's difficulties in dealing with a changing world. Sahgal demonstrates that the passive subject position constructed for the female in the discourse of Hinduism is dangerously close to the position it sets up for itself in relation to the dominant discourses in the modern world, especially those of Western business and world politics.

In the novel Simrit's subjective consciousness is emphasized in order to call attention to the marginalization of women in Indian society. Unable to reconcile herself to Som's way of life, she walks out of her marriage, setting off a new wave of revenge in Som. He uses the instrument of divorce to disenfranchise Simrit of her material sustenance, which aggravates her emotional deprivation. The "Consent Terms" that he draws up are so unjust that Simrit is trapped financially, but she is left with no option because she has signed the document. Som has no pity for her and gains custody of their son, Brij, while he takes no further interest in their several daughters, unnumbered in the novel.

Simrit finds some solace in the company of Raj, a Christian member of parliament. He tries to inspire her with confidence in herself. Although she does find emotional and sexual satisfaction in communion with Raj, who is genuinely concerned for her well-being, life has not equipped her to find her own voice. Simrit thus remains fragmented and disoriented. In her experience the dominant discourse has always silenced her, but she begins to find herself in her association with Raj. *The Day in Shadow* brings to the fore the idea of the personal as political and highlights the issues of women in Hindu society. Joya Uraizee argues that "*The Day in Shadow* uses a narrative pattern of constant displacement to depict the oppression and silencing of marginalized voices in Indian society."

A Situation in New Delhi (1977) is more specifically concerned with power politics, as the title suggests, New Delhi being the center of political power in India. The story, a saga of free India, is set in the mid 1960s. The narrative concerns the new rulers and their style of functioning. The characters are modeled on well-known political figures. The late Shivraj, based on Jawaharlal Nehru, is shown in the novel to have been a charismatic figure who is fondly remembered by Devi, his sister. She bemoans the loss of the politicians of Shivraj's generation, who were committed to high ideals. The present political generation in the novel, however, has lost sight of that idealism, and Devi finds no sense of direction among her cabinet colleagues. Her friend Usman, an educational theorist, advocates enlightened humanist values in education but finds himself at odds with members of the new ruling class, who subvert his every attempt at educational reform. Rishad, Devi's radical nineteen-year-old son, a communist who advocates militant violence and is impatient with slow social change, represents the young generation. For such a generation neither Mohandas Gandhi nor Jawaharlal Nehru is an example. Usman believes that concentration of political power is inimical to liberal education. For Sahgal, only characters such as Usman can carry forward the legacy of Jawaharlal Nehru. Sahgal received much critical acclaim for *A Situation in New Delhi,* which makes telling use of the trope of violence running through the history of India.

While Sahgal was mostly preoccupied with her writing in the 1970s and 1980s, she also visited several academic institutions the world over, interacted with writers and scholars, and aired her political concerns on several public platforms. She served as writer in residence at

Dust jacket for the U.S. edition of Sahgal's 1985 novel about a Danish woman who visits India in 1913 and is sympathetic to the cause of Indian nationalists (Richland County Public Library)

Southern Methodist University in Dallas in 1973 and 1977, and she was a research scholar at the Radcliffe Institute for Independent Study (now the Mary Ingraham Bunting Institute of Radcliffe College) in Cambridge, Massachusetts, in 1976. In 1978 she was member of the Indian delegation to the United Nations General Assembly, and she served from 1978 to 1979 on the Committee on Autonomy for Radio and Television established by the Indian government. Sahgal married Mangat Rai in 1979. She was a fellow of the Woodrow Wilson International Center for Scholars in Washington, D.C., from 1981 to 1982 and of the National Humanities Center in Research Triangle Park, North Carolina, from 1983 to 1984. In the 1980s she was also vice president of the People's Union for Civil Liberties in India.

Sahgal closely watched the national scene in India. Her next novel, *Rich Like Us* (1985), is set against the backdrop of the 1975–1977 state of emergency, when Indira Gandhi assumed authoritarian powers and brought about constitutional changes that resulted in a new political and bureaucratic culture, undermining general civil society. Sahgal felt strongly about the curtailment of individual liberties during the state of emergency and resigned from the advisory board of the Sahitya Akademi (National Academy of Letters). The emergency period dislocated a democratic order and shocked the people of India, who had expected democratization to take further roots. In the novel Sonali, a career bureaucrat trapped within the new power structure, is a courageous woman who experiences the pervasive oppression within and outside her workplace and decides to take a stand against authoritarianism. She has to pay the price for her uprightness, which she conceived as a sine qua non for working for the prestigious Indian Civil Service. Sonali was brought up on idealism and belief in the rule of law, but in the political climate she faces, the authority of law has eroded and the ground rules have changed. She receives a rude shock when she learns that she is expected to accept unquestioningly the line of her political masters, who often put aside the demands of the welfare state. She wonders why no one questions the culpability of those who exercise state authority only to perpetuate violence. In contrast, Sonali's colleague in the civil service, Ravi Kachru, has mastered the art of survival in the changing political climate. Their conflicting principles get in the way of their personal relationship.

In *Rich Like Us,* Sahgal investigates the notion of tradition and modernity within the matrix of social and personal relationships. Ram, a businessman running a private enterprise, is married to Mona, a traditional Indian woman from a Hindu family. In London he meets Rose, a British cockney who falls in love with him, much to the disappointment of her parents. With a quiet defiance Rose overcomes their resistance and goes to India with Ram to be his wife, although she knows he is already married. To her disappointment, Rose finds that her private space is drastically circumscribed, and she feels constricted in an incomprehensible way. She and Mona live in Ram's house "on different floors," but the spatial difference also extends to their inhabiting different worlds. The Western mores, values, and cultural practices that Rose knew do not serve her in a society that denies them. In politically decolonized India she is not a privileged subject but rather an intruder into a closed cultural system. Her friendship with Sonali is perhaps the only satisfactory relationship she is able to establish in India. Although a member of traditional Hindu society, Sonali has rejected many of its patriarchal tenets, and because of her idealism she finds herself sidelined in the civil service. Thus, both Sonali and Rose live on the fringes.

Sonali heralds the arrival of the new Indian woman, whose emergence is an assertion that gender-specific roles cannot define a person. These roles are largely cultural constructions and ought to be redefined in keeping with the demands of a progressive society. Sahgal does not, however, advocate complete disruption from a tradition that has ensured the continuity and stability of the social order. She makes it clear that Rose's difficulties are not the result of cultural antipathies: if she has problems, they are of a different and more personal nature. Sahgal places Sonali at a crucial point in Indian history for exploring tensions between tradition and modernity. The novel is dedicated "To the Indo-British Experience and what its sharers have learned from each other." For *Rich Like Us,* Sahgal was awarded the 1985 Sinclair Prize in fiction and the 1986 Sahitya Akademi Prize.

Cultural encounter is again emphasized in *Plans for Departure* (1985). The central character in the novel is Anna Hansen, a Danish woman visiting India in 1913 for a year before her marriage to an English diplomat. She comes to India as an outsider, both to the Indian and the British cultures, but she wants to make sufficient inroads into Indian culture to challenge even the natives' views of themselves. Appointed to assist an Indian scientist, Sir Nitin Basu, she is considered an ideal assistant by Didi, Basu's sister, for her "European efficiency" as well as for her interest in Hindu scriptures. Anna is a seeker of sorts, but she is not a protégé of any one Indian. As a Dane, she sees herself as a champion of egalitarian social order, having been born "nine centuries after Denmark gave up raiding, colonizing, and lusting after worlds to conquer." She is fascinated with the life of Bal Gangadhar Tilak, the leading Indian patriot of the period in which the novel is set, who demanded independence from England. Basu, an enlightened scientist, is baffled by Anna's unquestioning acceptance of myth in her exploration of the past of India. He tells her that she is confusing history with myth. For Anna, however, it is difficult to decide "where myth ended and history began," as myths and legends constitute part of reality and cannot therefore be dismissed. Anna's journey to India is in the nature of a quest to define herself. She scrutinizes the Indian freedom movement to disabuse herself of the legitimizing forces of Western hegemonic powers, especially that of British imperialism. The journey also answers her need to grow inwardly and not to remain content with her matrimonial prospects. Sahgal does not make Anna a symbol of Western power; rather, her unique Danish powerlessness coupled with her strong feminist stance lead her to identify with Indians fighting for independence. In the process she demolishes several orientalist myths. *Plans for Departure* brought Sahgal the 1987 Commonwealth Writer's Prize (Eurasia region).

In *Mistaken Identity* (1988), Bhushan Singh is an antihero and a playboy who finds himself jailed in 1929, ostensibly for conspiring against the British authorities, along with communists and followers of Mohandas Gandhi. In an era dominated by violent and nonviolent revolutionary ideas inspired by Vladimir Lenin and Gandhi, the British presence in India was understandably precarious. Fearing conspiracies real and imagined, the government made arrests all over the country and jailed anyone suspected of not sympathizing with British aims. Bhushan is finally released from jail as no charges can be proved against him, but he does not remain unaffected by the absurdity of his sham trial. He reflects that not only are the British the common enemy of Hindus and Muslims, but also unity between the two communities is under threat. Such disunity affected women most. Bhushan is in love with a Muslim girl, Razia, but his interest in her sparks a Hindu-Muslim riot. To keep him away from her, his wealthy landlord father packs him off to America, where he meets Willie Mae Goldburger, makes love to her, and learns from her the fashionable ballroom dances of the 1920s. Back in Bombay, Bhushan has a long-standing relationship with a Parsi beauty called Sylla, but all along, his quest is for Razia, and his search continues until the narrative reaches a surprising end.

Bhushan's quest is for the wholeness of the composite Hindu-Muslim culture that blossomed over the centuries and was fed by mystics such as Kabir but is now under threat from fundamentalists on both sides. His point of view is that of Sahgal herself; in "India's Identity in *Mistaken Identity*," published in *Point of View*, she writes of the "collective selfhood" that is "not a mythical identity we were born into, but the fruit of our conscious labour and striving, built by our conscious endeavour." In "Female Autonomy: Linking the Public and Private Worlds in *Plans for Departure* and *Mistaken Identity*," an essay in *Nayantara Sahgal's India*, Julie Scott writes that "the irony inherent in the title of *Mistaken Identity* challenges many assumptions based on gender, race and culture which categorise identity."

In the 1990s Sahgal continued to appear at literary conferences across the world. She was elected an honorary member of the American Academy of Arts and Sciences in 1990, and she was the chairwoman of the jury for the Commonwealth Writers' Prize in 1990 and 1991. The University of Leeds conferred an honorary doctorate of letters on her in 1997.

The central concern in *Lesser Breeds* (2003) is the relevance of nonviolence in the contemporary world. The novel centers on Nurullah, a young English teacher who typifies a general skepticism about the concept of ahimsa (nonviolence): "Good old fashioned war was waged against ahimsa and ahimsa did not escape war's legacies and tragedies, war's prisoners, its wounded and its killed. The war on ahimsa wreaked havoc. It left orphans and widows like any other war. No lethal weapon-wielder stood back and said this man before me is unarmed so I will not strike." Nurullah comes to live in the fictional city of Akbarabad in 1932, a time when Indians were engaged in the freedom movement against the British. He lives

Dust jacket for the U.S. edition of Sahgal's 1988 novel, about an Indian man who is wrongly jailed by the British colonial authorities in 1929 on charges of sedition (Richland County Public Library)

with the family of a charismatic leader, Nikhil, or Bhai, as his friends and supporters call him. The family residence is a huge mansion that has become every nationalist Indian's mecca. While teaching at the university, Nurullah undergoes his political apprenticeship with Nikhil. Yet, through the years of his intellectual and political growth, he has nagging doubts: "Is ahimsa going to change anything? What use is non-violence?" To these doubts Nikhil answers, "What else have unarmed people got?" He adds that this "great human experience" has already "changed *us.* . . . Other changes will come."

In the second half of *Lesser Breeds* the action shifts to "An Island Called America." Sahgal underlines the message that Mohandas Gandhi's ideology of nonviolence and noncooperation affected not only Indians but also many others the world over. As far as India was concerned, nonviolence was an essential instrument in the fight for swaraj (self-rule) against the might of an unjust empire. The title of the novel comes from Kipling's poem "Recessional" (1897), in which native Indians under their colonial masters are called "lesser breeds." Although Kipling was referring to the days of empire, when the world was divided into rulers and the ruled, Sahgal sees more ramifications to the term: it not only denotes Indians under British rule but also highlights the discriminations still practiced in modern India, where the Hindu-Muslim divide, as well differences of caste and community, have vitiated social harmony. The name of the fictional city, Akbarabad, suggests the Mogul emperor Akbar the Great, who tried to bring about syncretism among the people of India. Sahgal believes that the pluralistic ethos of the country promoted by the nonviolent and secular vision of Mohandas Gandhi and Jawaharlal Nehru is coming under increasing strain.

Sahgal lives in Dehra Dun, a city in the foothills of the Himalayas. Her second husband, Mangat Rai, died in 2003. The previous year, Wellesley, her alma mater, gave her the Alumnae Achievement Award. The citation reads,

Through your novels, essays and articles you reveal the complex socio-political fabric of India and educate the world about the many challenges faced by postcolonial societies as they struggle to forge a new identity. Bravely confronting authority in defense of the world's largest democracy, you challenge India's political leaders to uphold civil and human rights and to prove themselves worthy of the public confidence with which they are entrusted. Your critical and courageous examination of gender, class and race reaches far beyond India and resonates throughout the world. As an ardent and eloquent writer whose bravery and passion have inspired all of us as we seek freedom through just democratic government, Wellesley honors you.

An astute and dedicated observer, Nayantara Sahgal has commented extensively on the Indian social and political scene and on the wider relationship of India with the rest of the world in the "age of globalization," of which, she believes, one needs to take a qualified view. In her journalism, which complements her fiction, as well as in her addresses at various forums, she advocates a cosmopolitan spirit deeply rooted in one's native culture. She says, "My continuing character is India and my books have been about contemporary hopes and fears, set in political situations, and the implications of political events on people's lives." Her implicit point is that political struggles must be waged in tandem with the larger struggle for social regeneration and that a sense of humanity consists in recognizing the indivisibility of human dignity. Sahgal raises original and radical questions that break through traditional categories of thought to open up new possibilities for social conduct. Her vision, therefore, never degenerates into a sentimental and politically naive humanism.

Letters:

Sahgal and E. N. Mangat Rai, *Relationship: Extracts from a Correspondence* (New Delhi: Kali for Women, 1994).

References:

Satish C. Aikant, "Woman in National Discourse: A Reading of Nayantara Sahgal's *Rich Like Us*," *Language Forum*, 24, nos. 1–2 (1998): 121–130;

Ralph J. Crane, ed., *Nayantara Sahgal's India: Passion, Politics, and History* (New Delhi: Sterling, 1998);

Anna Guttman, Secularism as Syncretism in Nayantara Sahgal's *Lesser Breeds*," *Journal of Commonwealth Literature*, 40, no. 3 (2005): 47–62;

Jasbir Jain, *Nayantara Sahgal*, revised and enlarged edition (Jaipur: Printwell, 1994);

Feroza Jussawalla, "Of Cabbages and Kings: *This Time of Morning* and *Storm in Chandigarh* by Nayantara Sahgal," *Journal of Indian Writing in English*, 5, no. 1 (1977): 43–50;

Asha Kaushik, *Politics, Aesthetics, and Culture: A Study of Indo-Anglian Political Novel [sic]* (New Delhi: Manohar, 1988), pp. 44–81;

Viney Kirpal, ed., *The New Indian Novel in English: A Study of the 1980s* (New Delhi: Allied, 1990);

Ashis Nandy, *The Intimate Enemy: Loss and Recovery of Self Under Colonialism* (Delhi: Oxford University Press, 1983);

Vijaya Lakshmi Pandit, *The Scope of Happiness: A Personal Memoir* (New York: Crown, 1979);

Makarand Paranjape, "The Crisis of Contemporary India and Nayantara Sahgal's Fiction," *World Literature Today*, 68, no. 2 (1994): 291–298;

Anna Rutherford, ed., *From Commonwealth to Post-Colonial* (Sydney & Coventry: Dangaroo Press, 1992);

Kumkum Sangari and Sudesh Vaid, eds., *Recasting Women: Essays in Indian Colonial History* (New Brunswick, N.J.: Rutgers University Press, 1990);

K. R. Srinivasa Iyengar, *Indian Writing in English*, fifth edition (New Delhi: Sterling, 1985);

Joya Uraizee, *This Is No Place for a Woman: Nadine Gordimer, Buchi Emecheta, Nayantara Saghal [sic], and the Politics of Gender* (Trenton, N.J.: Africa World Press, 2000);

Dennis Walder, *Post-Colonial Literatures in English: History, Language, Theory* (Oxford & Malden, Mass.: Blackwell, 1998), pp. 87–115.

Papers:

Nayantara Sahgal's papers are in the Howard Gotlieb Archival Research Center, Boston University.

Shyam Selvadurai
(1965 –)

Ruvani Ranasinha
Brunel University

BOOKS: *Funny Boy* (London: Cape, 1994; Toronto: McClelland & Stewart, 1994; New Delhi: Penguin, 1994; New York: Morrow, 1996);

Cinnamon Gardens (Toronto: McClelland & Stewart, 1998; New Delhi: Penguin, 1998; London: Anchor, 1999; New York: Hyperion, 1999);

Swimming in the Monsoon Sea (Toronto & New York: Tundra, 2005).

PRODUCED SCRIPT: "What's in a Name?" *Many Voices,* TV Ontario, 1991.

OTHER: "The Influence of Canada in *Funny Boy*," *Across Cultures: Issues of Identity in Contemporary British and Sri Lankan Writing,* edited by Neluka Silva and Rajiva Wijesinghe (Colombo: British Council, 2001), pp. 4–10;

Story-Wallah: Short Fiction from South Asian Writers, edited by Selvadurai (Toronto: Thomas Allen, 2004; New York: Houghton Mifflin, 2005).

Shyam Selvadurai (photograph by Lilly Dong; from the dust jacket for the U.S. edition of Funny Boy, *1996; Richland County Public Library)*

Sri Lankan-born Shyam Selvadurai, who has spent the past two decades in Canada, became an internationally acclaimed writer after the publication of his debut novel, *Funny Boy,* in 1994. One of a handful of renowned Sri Lankan-born writers living in the West, Selvadurai constantly draws on his Sri Lankan background in his fiction. However, Selvadurai eludes classification. *Funny Boy* and *Cinnamon Gardens* (1998) do not foreground the thematics of migrancy and exile in the manner of Romesh Gunesekera and Michael Ondaatje. On the contrary, Selvadurai is a celebrated gay writer in Canada whose explorations of sexuality in his first two novels are located in the tradition-bound society of his Sri Lankan homeland.

Selvadurai was born in Sri Lanka in 1965 to a Sinhalese mother and Tamil father, Christine and David Selvadurai. A product of an unconventional marriage, Selvadurai's Sinhala-Tamil heritage may partly explain his engagement with issues of identity in relation to ethnicity and gender that are at the heart of the

questions of nationhood contested in the private and public spaces in Sri Lanka. Not only has he powerfully re-created the complexity of growing up gay in Sri Lanka in his first novel, but also his work destabilizes nationalist, sexist, as well as heterosexual identity.

Born into an affluent, anglicized family, he grew up in Colombo. Precociously talented, Selvadurai directed a large-scale production of *The Wizard of Oz* (1939) at the age of thirteen. He attended the Royal College in Colombo until he was nineteen, when the anti-Tamil riots of July 1983 led the family to seek asylum and settle in Toronto the following year. His childhood interest in theater developed into a B.F.A. in theater studies at York University in Toronto. After graduating, he taught English for a year at York Univer-

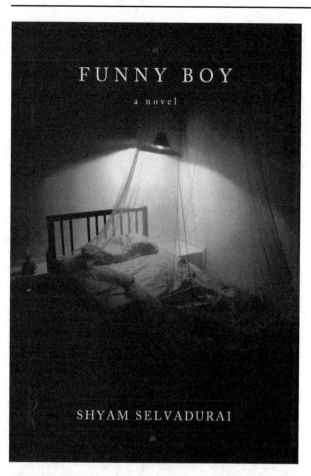

Dust jacket for the U.S. edition (1996) of Selvadurai's 1994 novel about a gay Tamil boy growing up amid ethnic and political conflicts in 1970s Sri Lanka (Richland County Public Library)

sity. He then studied creative writing and journalism. Encouraged by his tutor and the success of emerging writers such as Rohinton Mistry and Moiz Vassanji, he began to think of writing as a full-time career; he then worked as a waiter and in bookstores in order to support himself as a writer. His family encouraged his choice of career, just as they had accepted his homosexuality.

In interviews, Selvadurai has cited a range of literary influences, including Naguib Mahfouz, Alice Munro, Satyajit Ray, and most specifically, the structure and tone of Anita Desai. A versatile writer, Selvadurai has experimented with different genres. In the early 1990s he wrote a short movie for children, "What's in a Name?" for the *Many Voices* series on TV Ontario, dramatizations portraying some of the different ways in which ethnic minority children cope with forms of racial and ethnic stereotyping. Selvadurai's story concerns Premila, who changes her name to Pamela to avoid being teased by two boys. The story relates the

consequences of her act. This story suggests the role Selvadurai was beginning to play in redefining Canadian multiculturalism. In "The Influence of Canada on *Funny Boy,*" Selvadurai describes how he gravitated toward proactive minority organizations that focused on showcasing art that "dealt with the current dilemmas and events of their communities that had a present day contribution to make to the mosaic of Canadian culture."

Experimenting with different prose styles, Selvadurai found his own voice in "Pigs Can't Fly," a writing exercise that became a short story about a young boy watching his mother put on a sari. The story attracted the attention of Alberto Manguel, who included it in an influential anthology of gay writing that he was editing. This story paved the way to the publication of Selvadurai's first novel, *Funny Boy* (the product of four years' work), in October 1994, with "Pigs Can't Fly," one of the six self-contained but interlinking stories that formed the novel. Set in the shifting contexts of Sri Lanka in the 1970s, this poignant bildungsroman sensitively portrays the young and gay Tamil narrator Arjie's bewildering sexual awakening, alongside his increasing awareness of family conflicts, political realities, and ethnic polarization and tensions between the Sinhalese and Tamils. These events erupt in the horrific anti-Tamil violence of 1983, in which Arjie's grandparents are killed, and he and his family go into hiding before migrating. Delineating a network of forbidden zones and covert, transgressive relationships–the short-lived love affair between Radha Aunty and the Sinhalese Anil, Arji's mother Nalini's suppressed love for the Burgher journalist Daryl Uncle, and Arjie's own doubly forbidden love for his Sinhalese boyfriend Shehan Soysa–*Funny Boy* masterfully unifies its twin themes: its critique of sexual norms and its powerful portrayal of the brutalizing effects of the ethnic conflict and the violence of displacement. (Selvadurai has noted in "The Influence of Canada on *Funny Boy*" that his determination to foreground sexual as well as ethnic marginalization was in part inspired by the gay South Asian activists he met in Canada in the course of his work with the radical protest group Desh Pardesh.) Politics gradually encroaches on Arjie's seemingly idyllic, privileged childhood of "spend the days," evocatively re-created in the early part of the novel: Radha Aunty is attacked by a Sinhalese mob on a train; Daryl Uncle is abducted and murdered; and Jegan, the young man employed by Arjie's father, is victimized by Sinhalese coworkers. The youthful outlook of the naive, first-person narrator necessarily limits the historical and political context of the complex ethnic conflict at the center of the novel. At the same time, Arjie's confused innocence underscores the absurdity of the intolerance

that surrounds him—when, for instance, his grandmother objects to Radha's "illicit relations" with Anil on
the grounds of race:

> The intensity of Ammachi's reaction had shaken me. I
> wondered why Anil's being Sinhala upset her so? I was
> in a Sinhala class at school and my friends were Sin-
> halese. My parents' best friends were, too. Even our
> servant was Sinhalese, and, in fact, we spoke with her
> only in Sinhalese. So what did it matter whether Anil
> was Sinhalese or not?

Witnessing the internal and external policing of desire
across communal boundaries, Arjie is told that "People
usually marry their own kind." Ultimately, all the transgressive pairings across ethnic divides do not survive.
In contrast to the subversive thrust of the novel, these
failures serve to reinforce rather than disrupt the fixity
of ethnic difference. Arjie is more successful in contesting the gender roles demarcated territorially at the outset of the novel:

> Territorially, the area around my grandparents'
> house was divided into two. The front garden, the road
> and the field that lay in front of the house belonged to
> the boys, although included in their group was my
> cousin Meena. . . . The second territory was called "the
> girls'," included in which, however, was myself, a boy.
> It was to this territory of "the girls," confined to the
> back garden and the kitchen porch, that I seemed to
> have gravitated naturally. . . .

For Arjie "the primary attraction of the girls' territory
was the potential for the free play of fantasy." Experimenting with women's clothes and makeup allows him
"to leave the constraints of [himself] and ascend into
another, more brilliant, more beautiful self." After Arjie
is caught dressed in a sari while playing "bride-bride"
with his female cousins, he is forced to play cricket with
his male cousins. His mother's sympathetic yet resigned
response exposes the illogic of the heterosexual norms
to which Arjie is asked to adhere: "Life is full of stupid
things and sometimes we just have to do them."

This normative heterosexual code is further scru-
tinized in the penultimate novella. Arjie's homophobic
father sends him to "The Best School of all" in the hope
that it will make him more "manly." Arjie's experiences
provide a searing critique of the oppressive codes of
masculinity that young men experience in leading
schools in contemporary Sri Lanka, a tradition established and perpetuated since such schools were founded
in colonial times. In a parodic echo of British public
school ethos, Arjie's brother Diggy advises him to
endure any physical abuse in silence: "Never complain.
. . . Once you come to The Queen Victoria Academy

Dust jacket for the U.S. edition (1999) of Selvadurai's 1998 novel
about the hypocrisy of upper-class Tamil families in 1920s colonial
Ceylon (Richland County Public Library)

you are a man. Either you take it like a man or the
other boys will look down on you."

In the final story of this coming-of-age narrative,
Arjie's homosexual relationship with Shehan marks the
complete emergence of marginalized sexual identity,
alongside Arjie's self-separation from his family: "What
had happened between Shehan and me . . . changed my
relationship with [Amma] forever. I was no longer a
part of my family in the same way. I now inhabited a
world they didn't understand and into which they
couldn't follow me." However, Arjie and Shehan's clandestine liaison is overshadowed by the climactic conclusion—the final explosion of anti-Tamil violence in
Colombo. While some members of Arjie's family find
refuge with their Sinhalese neighbors, his grandparents
are burned to death when their car is set afire, and the
family home is violated. Upheavals in the personal and
domestic sphere merge with the wider disruption of the
postcolonial nation in crisis: family, home, and nation
have become uninhabitable.

*Dust jacket for Selvadurai's 2005 young-adult novel about a
Ceylonese teen who becomes aware of his sexual identity
when he falls in love with a male cousin visiting from
Canada (Richland County Public Library)*

The clarity, tenderness, and crisp humor of *Funny Boy* brought Selvadurai mainstream success, winning him the W. H. Smith Books/Books in Canada First Novel Award, along with the Lambda Literary Award for Best Gay Men's Fiction in the United States. Nominated for Canada's prestigious Miller Prize and named a Notable Book by the American Library Association, *Funny Boy* was reviewed to great acclaim in *The New York Times Book Review*.

Selvadurai spent the next four years writing and researching his second novel, *Cinnamon Gardens*. Set in 1920s colonial Sri Lanka (then Ceylon), this historical novel encompasses the social concerns of caste oppression; women's emancipation, particularly the Women's Franchise Union's campaign for universal suffrage, won in 1931; the growth of the labor movement; and the economic exploitation of the colonial era during the early twentieth century. It required considerable cul-

tural and historical research. In 1996 Selvadurai and his partner, Andrew Champion, spent several months in Sri Lanka so that Selvadurai could examine Sri Lanka's national archives.

Where *Funny Boy* exposed the racism, sexism, and class tensions of the middle class in contemporary Sri Lanka, the second novel takes up the theme of the morality and hypocrisy of Sri Lanka's wealthy, upper-class Tamil families at the turn of the century. At the center of the novel is the subversion of social conventions, played out in the intergenerational conflicts of two related, anglicized, Christian upper class/caste Tamil families living in Colombo's residential area, Cinnamon Gardens. Like Arjie, the central characters, Annalukshmi and Balendran, transgress sexual norms, albeit in different ways. Annalukshmi—an unconventional, well-educated, independent, and determined young schoolteacher—refuses to marry and compromise her freedom, despite the best efforts of her mother, Louisa, and her aunt, Philomena. Evading not only the restrictions imposed on her as a woman, through her work and engagement with a broader cross-section of society, Annalushmi transcends the limited horizons of her insular, repressive social milieu. Her story is counterpointed with that of her uncle Balendran's conflict with his father, Mudaliyar Navaratnam. The wealthy, autocratic patriarch stifles his closeted son's homosexual passion for his English lover, Richard Howland, when he is studying in England.

The domineering Mudaliyar uses his wealth as a tool of parental control. Conforming to his father's wishes and societal expectations, Balendran ends his relationship with Richard, returns to Sri Lanka, enters into a nominal, unfulfilling marriage to his cousin Sonia, and receives his inheritance. By contrast, his elder brother Arul lives in poverty in Bombay, disinherited for marrying Pakkiam, a servant girl. Later, Mudaliyar's double standards and false morality emerge when his own lust for Pakkiam and formerly for her mother is exposed.

Set in a single year, the novel charts both protagonists' moves toward greater freedom and empowerment, albeit to differing degrees. For Balendran, this process is precipitated by Howland's unexpected visit to Sri Lanka. Toward the close of the novel Balendran confronts his father and fully recognizes the extent to which he has lived so much without asking for what he wanted. Writing to Richard, Balendran acknowledges his continuing love for him, and asks for his friendship in the context of his commitment to his wife and son. In this way, although Balendran comes across as weak, the success of the novel lies in its sympathetic engagement with a range of characters, who "struggle to bridge the space between who [they were] and who [they] felt they should be." The epigraph of the novel, a citation from George Eliot's *Middlemarch* (1871–1872), provides a context within which to assess Selvadurai's protagonists' actions: ". . . for the growing good of the world is partly dependent on unhistoric acts; and that things are not so ill with you and me as they might have been, is half owing to the number who lived faithfully a hidden life, and rest in unvisited tombs." Selvadurai's text suggests such small "unhistoric" acts of courage initiate wider societal change.

Interweaving a varied cast of characters' personal dilemmas with the shifting sociopolitical contexts and concerns of preindependence Sri Lanka, the novel provides a complex, wide-ranging portrait of a society in transition. Richard Howland arrives in Colombo as a member of the Donoughmore Commission from England. Its purpose was to prepare for the transfer of power by creating a new constitution that would reflect the complex multicultural population of the city. In this way the novel is set against the backdrop of an emerging nation. The struggle over political representation is dramatized in the widening rifts between the majority Sinhalese and minority Tamil politicians. They debate the relative merits of territorial and communal representation: the majority Sinhalese lobby to consolidate their power in a centralized system, while non-Sinhala minorities opt for a federal one, fearing a "Sinhala Raj" will replace a British one.

In different ways the text disrupts dominant Sinhala narratives, particularly the conflation of Sinhala Buddhist ethnoreligious identities with the nation. For instance, Balendran's Sinhalese best friend and Congress member, F. C. Wijewardena, bemoans that "Divisions are appearing where I didn't even know there were any. Up-country Sinhalese versus low-country Sinhalese, Karava caste verses Goyigama caste, Moors, Malays, Christian Tamils, Hindu Tamils, Buddhists and so on. . . . And not a bloody bugger is thinking nationally, except us in the Congress." Balendran's understated rejoinder punctures his friend's complacent conception of the nation, suggesting "Perhaps the Congress needs to redefine what 'national' is." Revisiting this formative era, the novel speaks powerfully to the contemporary political crisis of Sri Lanka, to a society riven by years of bitter, protracted ethnic war, fueled to a large extent by the right-wing exclusionary logic and model of nationalism depicted in this novel.

At the same time, the text does not simplify the conflict in terms of a Sinhala-Tamil binary. Instead, it signals the competing cultural, class, caste, and religious interests that complicate these broad groupings. The pompous Mudaliyar's resistance to the demands for universal suffrage unlinked to property and educational qualification appear as a transparent bid to maintain his position of privilege as a member of the indigenous elite; the text underscores the class ties that override ethnic difference:

> Gentlemen, whatever our differences, we are agreed on one thing. Universal suffrage would be the ruin of our nation. People like Dr. Shiels do not understand what it would mean to an Oriental society like ours. It would put the vote in the hands of the servants in our kitchen, the beggar on the street. Illiterate beings to whom the sophistication of politics is as incomprehensible as advanced mathematics is to a child. It would lead to mob rule.

While *Funny Boy* earned Selvadurai swift acclaim, the reception of *Cinnamon Gardens* was more mixed: some critics found the pervasive irony somewhat heavy-handed and suggested the characters lacked psychological depth, functioning as mouthpieces for the issues of the era. Feminist critics in Sri Lanka (*Island* newspaper [3 March 1999] and Salon.com [16 July 1999]) argue that while some of the unsympathetic characters border on the farcical, Selvadurai's protagonists elude caricature, and these critics welcome his subtle critique of societal norms.

Selvadurai has become a valuable voice in the literary landscape of Canada, regularly participating in creative writing workshops in Canada and the United States and attending international literary festivals. He is at the same time perceived as one of Sri Lanka's most distinctive and talented new voices. He visits Sri Lanka every couple of years, where his work is extremely popular among the English-speaking middle class, particularly for his frank treatment of homosexuality, still largely considered a taboo subject. *Funny Boy* provoked a national debate on the laws against homosexuality. Its moving portrayal of the traumas and victimization endured by Sri Lanka's minority Tamils is required reading for degrees in literature in several Sri Lankan universities. The novel has been translated into Sinhala (although not yet into Tamil), an act that is sure to broaden Selvadurai's readership beyond the English-speaking minority. What is striking about Selvadurai's work is that while it is shaped by his metropolitan location, it shows a commitment to speak to a Sri Lankan readership and to explore Sri Lanka's past in order to understand, rather than simply rehearse, its conflicted present.

Interviews:

Afdhel Aziz, "Growing up Gay in Lanka," *Sunday Times,* 29 January 1995, p. 17;

Jim Marks, "The Personal Is Political: An Interview with Shyam Selvadurai," *A Review of Contemporary Gay and Lesbian Literature,* 5, no. 2 (August 1996): 1, 6–7;

Wathsala Mendis, "In His World," *Sunday Times,* 2 April 2000.

References:

Manique Gunesekera, " Review of Funny Boy," *Nethra,* 1, no. 1 (1996): 70–77;

Chelva Kanaganayakam, "Remembering Ceylon: A Reading of *Funny Boy*," *Navasilu,* 15–16 (1998): 1–7;

R. Raj Rao, "Because Most People Marry Their Own Kind: A Reading of Shyam Selvadurai's Funny Boy," *ARIEL,* 28 (January 1997): 117–128.

Vikram Seth

(20 June 1952 –)

Frank Day
Clemson University

See also the Seth entries in *DLB 120: American Poets Since World War II, Third Series; DLB 271: British and Irish Novelists Since 1960;* and *DLB 282: New Formalist Poets.*

BOOKS: *Mappings* (Saratoga, Cal.: Vikram Seth, 1980; Calcutta: Writers Workshop, 1981; New Delhi & London: Viking, 1994);

From Heaven Lake: Travels through Sinkiang and Tibet (London: Chatto & Windus, 1983; New York: Vintage, 1987);

The Humble Administrator's Garden (Manchester, U.K.: Carcanet, 1985; New Delhi: Viking, 1994);

The Golden Gate: A Novel in Verse (New York: Random House, 1986; London & Boston: Faber & Faber, 1986; New Delhi: Penguin, 1993);

All You Who Sleep Tonight (New York: Knopf, 1990; London: Faber & Faber, 1990);

Beastly Tales from Here and There (New Delhi & New York: Viking, 1992; London: Phoenix House, 1992);

A Suitable Boy (1 volume, New Delhi: Viking, 1993; London: Phoenix House, 1993; New York: HarperCollins, 1993; 3 volumes, London: Phoenix House, 1995);

Arion and the Dolphin: A Libretto (London: Phoenix House, 1994; New Delhi & New York: Penguin, 1994);

Arion and the Dolphin (London: Orion Children's Books, 1994; New York: Dutton Children's Books, 1995);

An Equal Music (New Delhi: Viking, 1999; New York: Broadway Books, 1999; London: Phoenix House, 1999);

Two Lives (New York: HarperCollins, 2005; London: Little, Brown, 2005).

Edition and Collection: *A Suitable Boy* (New York: HarperPerrenial, 1994);

The Poems, 1981–1994 (New Delhi & New York: Penguin, 1995).

TRANSLATION: *Three Chinese Poets: Translations of Poems by Wang Wei, Li Bai, and Du Fu* (London & Boston: Faber & Faber, 1992).

Vikram Seth (photograph © Mr. Kitty Hazuria; from the dust jacket for the U.S. edition of The Golden Gate: A Novel in Verse, *1986; Richland County Public Library)*

Most American readers probably first became aware of Vikram Seth when his *The Golden Gate: A Novel in Verse,* captured the attention of readers and critics in 1986. Seven years later *A Suitable Boy* appeared, at around 1,500 pages the longest one-volume novel ever published in English. These novels were not just distinctive achievements in form, for they were judged by most readers as excellent creative accomplishments in substance as well as style. *A Suitable Boy* depicts postindependence life in India in satisfyingly realistic detail with credible and mostly likable characters. Besides these two major achievements in fiction, Seth published in 1983 an account of his hitchhiking adventure in central Asia, *From Heaven Lake: Travels through Sinkiang and Tibet,* and in 1992 *Three Chinese Poets: Translations of Poems by Wang Wei, Li Bai, and Du Fu.* Along the way he wrote the verse that was collected as *The Poems, 1981–1994* in 1995. By the time he published *An Equal Music* in 1999, Seth had established himself as a writer of consequence and been paired off by some critics as the natural competitor of Salman Rushdie.

Vikram Seth was born in Calcutta on 20 June 1952. His father, Prem Seth, was a shoe-company executive, a fact that explains a good deal that is central to the plot of *A Suitable Boy,* and his mother, Laila Seth, was a judge. He has a younger brother and a younger sister. Seth's education was prestigious. He attended the Doon School in Dehra Dun, India, and Tonbridge School in Kent, England, before receiving a B.A. from Corpus Christi College of Oxford University in 1975 and an M.A. from Stanford University in 1979. He began study toward a Ph.D. in economics at Stanford, but his success in writing overwhelmed his interest in economic demography. He was a Wallace Stegner Fellow in Creative Writing at Stanford (1978–1979) before leaving to do doctoral research in China.

In Seth's first collection of poems, *Mappings* (1980), the title poem scans the "mappings" of his earlier selves, and the descriptiveness reveals the talent for depicting nature that graces his later works. The volume includes translations from Heinrich Heine ("Sleep and Death"), the Urdu poet Faiz Ahmed Faiz ("Last Night"), and the Chinese poet Du Fu ("Thoughts While Travelling at Night"). It indulges in literary allusions, such as the Shakespearean lines in "Switching Off"–"There are no fears of undiscovered countries / Or bournes from which no traveler returns / To one who knows this life is all there is"–and the dunking of a Proustian "pseudo-madeleine" in "To a Fellow-Traveller."

Seth's next poetry collection, *The Humble Administrator's Garden* (1985), is divided into three sections: "Wutong," comprising poems related to his experiences in China; "Neem," in which the poems are on Indian themes; and "Live-Oak," comprising poems about northern California. The dedication, "To my family, pictured within," anticipates the witty family vignette depicted in "The Comfortable Classes at Work and Play." The second son has no independent mind:

His girlfriend is feminist, and he is feminist.
When his girlfriend was anarchist, he was anarchist.

He has begun of late to talk in psychobabble
And his elder brother does not improve energy interflows
By cynical imitation of his style of speech
Or cynical puncturing of his current ism.

The daughter of the house remains "immersed in sociology," planning to study "The much-examined customs of the Todas / (Who have learned how to exploit their data-pickers)." Their mother, all this time, sits on the verandah and "wrestles with a judgement / Of Justice Krishna Iyer of the Supreme Court" before asking for "another cup of ginger tea." During this same interlude "The father sits in bed reading the *Indian Express,* / Inveighing against politicians and corruption." *The Humble Administrator's Garden* won the Commonwealth Poetry Prize for Asia in 1985.

Seth studied at Nanjing University, compiling material for a doctorate in economics at Stanford, and in the summer of 1981 he traveled with a group of foreign students to western China. On an impulse he went to the General Police Station in Turfan, got his travel pass stamped for Lhasa, and began a hitchhiking trip through Lhasa and Kathmandu from Liuyuan–the journey he describes in *From Heaven Lake.* In Liuyuan he caught the first of several rides with truckers, in a cab crowded with the driver's fifteen-year-old nephew and a tall Tibetan named Gyanseng.

At their first stop, Dunhuan, flooding of the River Dang slowed their departure for three days, but on 13 August they crossed into the rich pastureland of northern Tibet and stopped at the village of Naqu, which delighted Seth with its colorful street life. When on 15 August, 150 kilometers from Lhasa, the travelers' Isuzu sank into mud, Seth grabbed his gear and managed a ride with a trucker who took him to Lhasa, where he witnessed a dramatic funeral ceremony near the Sera monastery. He arrived at the mountain site about 5:45 A.M. and watched men stripping and hacking up human corpses on a rock. At 8:10 the mincing and bone crushing was well under way, and after the meat was mashed and mixed with barley meal, the cloth-covered skulls were pulverized with large rocks, and a monk blessed the meal on the rock, the waiting eagles settled in to glut themselves.

Seth's journey ended with a bus ticket to Kathmandu, prompting a coda in *From Heaven Lake* inspired by the flute player he listened to there: "Yet to hear any flute is, it seems to me, to be drawn into the commonalty of mankind, to be moved by music closest in its phrases and sentences to the human voice. Its motive force too is living breath: it too needs to pause and breathe before it can go on." The appeal of Seth's travelogue derives in great part from the manner in which he allows himself to be drawn into this commonalty of mankind with the many strangers whose kindnesses he is open to. Seth's account of his hazardous but exciting passage across the top of the world won him the Thomas Cook Travel Book Award for 1983.

Seth's facile versifying served him well in his next work, *The Golden Gate,* a novel arranged in thirteen books, or chapters, totaling 590 intricately constructed sonnets modeled after the Charles Johnston translation of Aleksandr Pushkin's *Eugene Onegin* (1823–1831). The lines are iambic tetrameter with an added unstressed syllable attached to the first and third, the fifth and sixth, and the ninth and twelfth lines, creating double, feminine rhymes (for example, "movement" and "improvement," "reason" and "treason," and "mother" and "other" in stanza 3.23). The rhyme scheme is *abab-ccddefefgg.* Within this structure Seth can be not only quite agile with sound effects but also witty and surprising. The framework is from Pushkin, but the tone is often from George Gordon, Lord Byron. John Bayley analyzed this stanza form and its "endless permutations of tone, stress and flow" in his introduction to the 1979 edition of Johnston's translation, pointing out that Pushkin "seems to have hit on the stanza form of *Eugene Onegin* by regularizing a more or less chance arrangement that occurs in the *contes* of La Fontaine." Seth justifies composing his novel in verse on the grounds of the pleasure it gives him, saying of Johnston's "luminous translation" in stanza 5.5 of *The Golden Gate* that "like champagne / Its effervescence stirs my brain."

Appreciation of Seth's diction constitutes one of the major pleasures of *The Golden Gate.* Byron's spirit emerges in rhymes such as "volition / Titian," "a poster / the most a," and "iguana / Nirvana," and Seth can put a noun into action with convincing ease: "That Saturday the coaxing weather / Confetties the blue sky with sails" (12.13). Striking epithets abound, as in "putrefied orangutan" and "indulgent fermentation of one-night stands" (11.30), and obscure terms such as "fianchetto" (a chess move) in stanza 5.14, "morendo" (a musical notation) in stanza 6.3, and "grame" (an archaic word for wrath or sorrow) in stanza 6.34 add a sophisticated note. Another consciously literary quality of *The Golden Gate* is its allusiveness. References to Thomas Mann and the Venerable Bede appear in stanza 1.3, and other stanzas refer to popular music, Horatian odes, Friedrich von Schiller, sculptors Henry Moore and Alexander Calder, Wang Wei, Pushkin's story "The Queen of Spades," John Donne, Buster Keaton, Francisco de Goya, Peter Paul Rubens, Thomas Hardy, Giacomo Leopardi, Robert Louis Stevenson, Hannah Arendt, William Shakespeare, Theodore Roethke, Andrew Marvell, and John Milton. The most elaborate textual interplay, though, comes in stanzas 9.24–9.26, which reference Bianca Castafiore, Haddock, and Gorgonzola

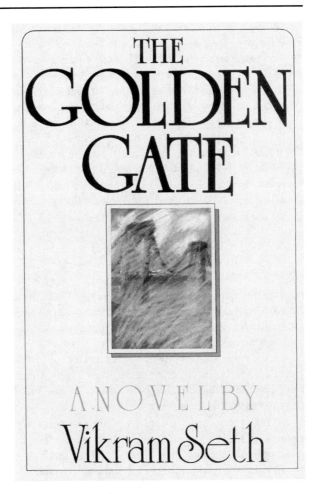

Dust jacket for the U.S. edition of Seth's 1986 novel in verse, inspired by Aleksandr Pushkin's Eugene Onegin, *about romance and misfortune among a group of young adults in northern California (Richland County Public Library)*

among other characters in the comic strip *Tintin* by Hergé (Georges Rémi). In all of this elaborate tissue of cultural reference in *The Golden Gate,* readers are left to make sense of the allusions on their own.

The Golden Gate tells the stories of five characters with interlocking fates. John Brown, a computer engineer, in 1980 is twenty-six, acerbic, and lonely. On an impulse he phones the sculptor Janet Hayakawa, his lover from years past and the drummer for the band Liquid Sheep. She tells John he needs a good woman and submits to the *Bay Guardian* a notice of a "Well-rounded and well-meaning square / Lusting for love" (2.3). The ad yields a harvest of several grating rendezvous before Liz Dorati, a former Stanford law student, responds with the caution "If you flout / My charms, you are a tasteless lout" (2.27). Their romance speeds to its inevitable "amorous mist" (3.1).

Despite the sexual pleasure that Liz and John enjoy, their life together remains edgy because of John's blunt, rigid personality and the mutual animosity he endures with Liz's cat, Charlemagne. Section 10 brings several issues to a climax. It is Thanksgiving Day at the Doratis', a close family whose everyday lives focus on their vineyards, and the family scene presents Mr. and Mrs. Dorati settled comfortably in the evening, reading their novels: "Thus together / They pool their prose, and intertwine / Their lives along a common vine" (10.24). Mrs. Dorati has been not so subtly hinting to Liz and her sister, Sue, that she would like to see them married soon. Sue has won a scholarship to study for a year in Paris, however, and Liz thinks, "There's more to life than love. / I've got to think this out" (10.27). Neither sister knows yet that their mother, stricken by cancer, has only a short time to live. The events that conclude section 10 occur too fast to be convincing. John finds an unopened letter to Liz, and when he recognizes the handwriting of an old Berkeley buddy, Phil, he with no justification thinks that Phil is Liz's secret lover. Liz has just learned the truth about her mother, and compounding the improbability of the scene, she enters the room on her way to visit Mrs. Dorati only to have John lash out at her over the letter. John storms out of the weeping Liz's life permanently as she holds her mother tightly.

The dénouement speeds by in the last three sections, with section 11 catching the reader by surprise by opening with Liz and Phil's wedding. Seth apologizes for having to insert a flashback ("I should grovel / At this cheap stratagem") and admits to a "Drainage of brain" (11.14). The epithalamia leave John sulking until Jan undertakes his salvation and they enjoy an idyllic spring of renewed love, deflated somewhat by the crushing reviews of Jan's exhibition of her sculptures. Bracing up, Jan converts her celebration party to a wake and invites all her friends, including Liz and Phil, whom she hopes to reunite in friendship with John. Things go wrong. Jan has to hitch a ride home with Phil's old neighbors, Matt and Joan Lamont, and their son, Chuck. As everyone awaits her, a telephone call informs the guests that Jan has died with Matt and Joan in a car wreck. Seth develops an elegiac feeling in the final section, with his genius for the right word and the telling image displayed at its best.

The Golden Gate was generally received well. The first printing of twenty-five thousand copies was ultimately increased to one hundred thousand. Among the Indian reviewers of *The Golden Gate,* Dilip Bobb and Vincent Digirolamo, in *India Today* (15 June 1986), had high praise for Seth's technical accomplishments as a poet, and Rukmani Bhaya Nair, in her essay "Gender, Genre, and Generative Grammar: Deconstructing the Matrimonial Column" (1992), looked for East-West cultural differences in ads from *The Times of India,* the

Hindustan Times, The New York Review of Books, and *The New Statesman and Society.* Gore Vidal called *The Golden Gate* "the great Californian novel," a judgment generally shared in India and the United States. Rowena Hill, however, in the *Literary Criterion* (1986), criticized what she interpreted as Seth's "gloating" over being a fully assimilated citizen of a culture that she sees as arrogant. Feroza Jussawalla, in his essay "Chiffon Saris: The Plight of Asian Immigrants in the New World" (1988), similarly complains that Seth ignores the conflicts in the ethnic community he represents, a position that Seth rejects.

After his debut in fiction, Seth published three volumes of poetry. In *All You Who Sleep Tonight* (1990), a collection in various genres, the poem "Sit" expresses his attitude at the time, that of a young man enjoying his powers:

Sit, drink your coffee here; your work can wait awhile.
You're twenty-six and still have some life ahead.
No need for wit; just talk vacuities, and I'll
Reciprocate in kind, or laugh at you instead.

Beastly Tales from Here and There (1992) collects ten fables for children, each featuring a pair of animals in some kind of contest. In "The Hare and the Tortoise" it is the hare who uncharacteristically becomes the media star: "And thus the hare was pampered rotten / And the tortoise was forgotten." The volume is enriched by Ravi Shankar's whimsical illustrations. In *Three Chinese Poets,* Seth's polished collection of translations of poems by Wang Wei, Li Bai, and Du Fu, eighth-century poets of the T'ang dynasty, his informative introduction reflects his study at Nanjing. The commentary on Wang Wei's "Living in the Hills: Impromptu Verses" is especially interesting for its straightforward explanation of his theory: "the translator's task is not to improvise cadenzas in the spirit of the piece but to stick, as tellingly as he can, to the score." For that reason, "The famous translations of Ezra Pound, compounded as they are of ignorance of Chinese and valiant self-indulgence, have remained before me as a warning of what to shun." Not many readers would value Seth's poems as highly as his novels, but they often achieve a graceful expression of delicate feeling. Mala Pandurang, in her *Vikram Seth: Multiple Locations, Multiple Affiliations* (2001), provides an excellent discussion of Seth's poetry, commenting on its themes, its treatment of an Indian identity, and the "emerging cosmopolitan identity" that is revealed.

A Suitable Boy, massive and distinctive in size and range, is set in the fictional city of Brahmpur, with excursions to Calcutta and a rural village in the imagined state of Purva Pradesh in the early 1950s. The plots and subplots follow the swirl of events around four families.

The Mehras, led by the widowed Rupa Mehra, include her oldest son, Arun, married to Meenakshi (née Chatterji), and their daughter, Aparna, all of Calcutta. Rupa's daughter Savita is the wife of Pran Kapoor; her younger son, Varun, is bullied by Arun but enjoys life with his feckless friends at the racetrack. Lata, Rupa's younger daughter, finds herself the subject of her mother's search for "a suitable boy." Rupa's irascible but lugubriously sentimental father, Dr. Kishen Chand Seth, and his second, much younger, wife, Parvati, complete the clan.

The Kapoors live in Brahmpur. Mahesh Kapoor is minister of revenue for Purva Pradesh, and he and his good-hearted but somewhat long-suffering wife have four children. Veena is married to a businessman in the shoe trade, Kedarnath Tandon, whose mother still shudders in recalling their escape from Lahore during the partition slaughters in 1947, and they have a young son, Bhaskar, who at nine is a prodigy in mathematics like the twelfth-century Indian mathematician Bhaskara II. (Seth also sneaks in a minor character named Abdus Salaam, Kapoor's parliamentary secretary, recalling the Pakistani Nobel Prize winner in physics for 1979, Abdul Salam.) Pran Kapoor, Savita's husband, is a university lecturer in English, and his brother, Maan, likable but without ambition, shares a strong plot strand with the courtesan Saeeda Bai, with whom he is besotted.

The Khans of Brahmpur are an old and prestigious Muslim family guided by the Nawab Sahib of Baitar, a widower and a close friend of Mahesh Kapoor despite their religious differences. His brother has chosen to live in Pakistan, leaving his wife, the Begum Abida Khan, behind to bedevil the Hindu authorities. The Nawab has a married daughter, Zaidab, and two talented sons, a doctor, Imtiaz, and a lawyer, Firoz, whose close friendship with Maan Kapoor leads to near tragedy for both.

The Chatterjis, of Ballygunge Circular Road, Calcutta, are cut from a different social cloth. Mr. Justice Chatterji sits on the Calcutta High Court and with his wife entertains splendidly. He studies Sanskrit classics and looks at his family with a realistic eye. He sees right through his pretentious son-in-law, Arun Kapoor, judging him "a needlessly aggressive man and a rank snob." The oldest Chatterji son, Amit, studied at Oxford and Lincoln's Inn and writes poetry; the next son, Dipankar, moons over the mystical but can be clever and practical when seriousness is demanded; and the youngest son, Tapan, has but a slight supporting role in the Chatterji family comedy. Meenakshi, Arun Mehra's selfish wife, cuckolds her husband with his best friend, and she and

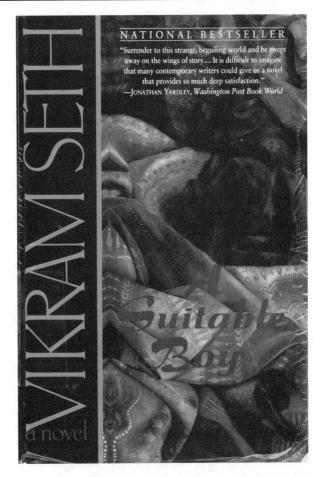

Front cover for a 1994 U.S. paperback edition of Seth's 1993 novel—1,474 pages long in this edition—which follows the interconnected lives of four Indian families in the early 1950s (Richland County Public Library)

her younger sister, Kakoli, are bright, amoral creatures always spouting impromptu rhymes. They are altogether too sophisticated for Rupa Mehra.

The interaction of this large cast of characters produces a work of great richness. Its diversity of incident; its firm grounding in the events of the postindependence history of India; its many completely believable—and mostly likable—characters from all levels of Indian society; and its detailed portrayal of Indian culture combine to produce a Victorian novel in the best sense of that genre. Seth's linear account of his world utilizes no manipulation of time or point of view, nor any deflating irony. His warm depiction of the mathematical prodigy, Bhaskar, adds a great deal to the family drama, especially as he is taken up by Dr. Durrani and when he is rescued from the Pul Mela tragedy by Kabir. Finally, Seth's tone toward such admirable individuals as Rupa Mehra, Mahesh Kapoor, and Haresh Khanna seeks to reassure readers they are in a world that makes moral sense at least part of the time.

A Suitable Boy was introduced by an extensive publicity campaign, but its length was criticized by some. Richard Jenkyns, for instance, writing in the *New Republic* (14 June 1993), called it only "a decent, unremarkable, second-rate novel," but Pico Iyer, in *TLS: The Times Literary Supplement* (19 March 1993), found Seth's "counter-Rushdie epic" all "readable and true," and Anita Desai (*New York Review*, 27 May 1993) praised its "density and richness." In her overview of Seth's work, Pandurang noted that *A Suitable Boy* has "often been evaluated on the basis of its 'un-Rushdie-like' techniques, and Seth has faced sharp criticism for rejecting the multiple forms of postmodernism and its accompanying complexities of utterance, choosing instead a coherent, straightforward and linear narrative." Pandurang summed up the debate over the contrasting visions of Rushdie and Seth and responded with insight to the accusation by Desai and others that Seth's characters are disappointingly flat: "Seth's methods of character delineation must be considered in the context of his fictional credo of social realism. If there is little room for detailed psychological analysis, this is because Seth invests his characters with great realism of detail with the intention of using them to identify and develop a wide array of social-related themes." *A Suitable Boy* won both the Commonwealth Writers Prize for best book overall and the W. H. Smith Literary Award.

In *An Equal Music* (the title derives from one of Donne's sermons), Seth writes another love story, developing it in a rich context derived from Western classical music. Seth's first-person narrator, Michael Holme, lives in London and plays second violin for the Maggiore Quartet. Michael grew up in Rochdale, in northern England, and attended the Royal Northern College of Music in Manchester. Michael's violin is a Tononi, generously on indefinite loan to him from Mrs. Formby, a kind neighbor in Rochdale who appreciates his talent. Michael is in his mid thirties, restless and haunted by two ghosts. Carl Käll, his former teacher at the Musikhochschule in Vienna, is now old and unwell in Sweden. Michael's natural difficulty with authority figures led to a personality clash with the demanding Käll, "that stubborn magician, brutal and full of suffocating energy"; and when Michael "came apart" at a concert, "It was because he had said I would fail, and I could see him in the audience and knew he willed me to." The other ghost is Julia McNicholl, the fellow student whom he loved in Vienna and whom he hurt when he abandoned her and Vienna after his disastrous concert. Ten years later he still regrets the rashness that took Julia out of his life.

The other members of the quartet are Helen, their viola player; Helen's elder brother, Piers, first violinist; and Billy, their cellist and composer. One

Dust jacket for the U.S. edition of Seth's 1999 novel, in which a violinist reunites with his former lover, a fellow musician who has lost her ability to hear (Richland County Public Library)

evening they play a program of Joseph Haydn, Wolfgang Amadeus Mozart, and Ludwig van Beethoven at Wigmore Hall, and as Michael leaves he is stunned to be greeted by Julia. She is now married to a banker from Boston—James Hansen—and has a young son, Luke. Their meetings inevitably turn into a renewal of their romance (otherwise, Michael says, "how self-congratulatory, how false, how agonizing, how comfortless" their relationship would have been), and Michael is shocked to learn that Julia, who still plays the piano, has gone deaf. At this point, their romance merges with the career of the Maggiore Quartet, who receive a prestigious contract to record Johann Sebastian Bach's *Die Kunst der Fuge* (The Art of the Fugue) and have an important concert coming up in Vienna.

The Vienna concert, at the Musikverein, has crucial consequences. First, Julia informs Michael that Piers, not knowing of her deafness or her affair with Michael, has invited Julia to join them in playing Franz Schubert's *Trout Quintet*. Michael is overjoyed at the news—and delighted that Piers asks him to take his place with the violin in the performance—but the group's first rehearsal leads to puzzlement about some aspects of Julia's playing, and Michael has to tell them the truth about her hearing. They eventually decide that Julia can perform well if she has a strong bass sound to lead her, and the performance goes off well even though their triumph is almost sullied by Michael's nervous collapse between the *Trout* and the concluding string quintet.

From Vienna the quartet goes on to Venice, with Julia accompanying Michael. Their interlude is tender and loving until Michael reads an affectionate fax that Julia has sent her husband, and when in bed that night he bites her shoulder hard and cruelly mocks her words to James, she is badly hurt. They manage a reconciliation of sorts, but Julia leaves the next day. Back in London, Michael accepts James's invitation to a party for Julia, but James's coolness toward him reveals that he knows of their affair. When Michael visits his father and his Aunt Joan at Rochdale for Christmas, Mrs. Formby tells him that she is going to leave the Tononi to her nephew. The final blow, though, comes when Michael learns that Julia has scheduled a performance of *Die Kunst der Fuge,* and with that discovery Michael quits the quartet.

When Mrs. Formby dies, however, she leaves the Tononi to Michael, and in his relief he stops patronizing prostitutes and settles into working with his students. Another Christmas passes, and Michael goes to Wigmore Hall to hear Julia play *Die Kunst der Fuge,* rushing out at the interval to walk the streets in the rain. The last paragraph of *An Equal Music* spells out Seth's declaration in his author's note that "Music to me is dearer even than speech": "Music, such music, is a sufficient gift. Why ask for happiness; why hope not to grieve? It is enough, it is to be blessed enough, to live from day to day and to hear such music—not too much, or the soul could not sustain it—from time to time."

An Equal Music has occasioned less critical commentary than Seth's first two novels, and much of what has been written centers around Seth's accomplishment in writing about Western music. For most Western readers the intricate web of musical references in *A Suitable Boy* will defeat full appreciation, but with Bach and Schubert these same readers will feel more comfortable. Seth's broad sensibility clearly encompasses the cultures of both the East and the West, and in what may be the best judgment on Seth as an international writer, Pandurang quotes Namita Gokhale's judgment from *The Times of India* (4 May 1999) that Seth should be seen as "a citizen of the world in the best sense. . . . His genius should be evaluated in his control over his material, and in creating a credible world-in-itself which he can co-habit and explore." *An Equal Music* won the EMMA (BT Ethnic and Multicultural Media Award) for best book or novel.

Interviews:

Dilip Bobb and Vincent Digirolamo, "I Am Looking Forward to Non-entityhood," *India Today,* 15 June 1986, pp. 152–155;

"An Interview with Vikram Seth," *Bold Type* (May 1999) <www.randomhouse.com/boldtype/0599/seth/interview.html>;

Jay Currie and Michèle Denis, "Hearing a Different Music," *January Magazine* (June 1999) <www.jan-mag.com/profiles/vseth.html>;

Akash Kapur, "The Seth Variations," *Atlantic Unbound* (23 June 1999) <theatlantic.com/unbound/interviews/ba990623.htm>.

References:

Albert Borgmann, *Crossing the Postmodern Divide* (Chicago: University of Chicago Press, 1992);

John Harlow, "The Moor Battles the Suitable Boy for Literary Crown," *Times of India,* 4 March 1999, p. 14;

Ashok K. Jha, "Vikram Seth: *The Golden Gate* and Other Writings," in *Recent Indian Fiction,* edited by R. S. Pathak (New Delhi: Prestige, 1994);

Feroza Jussawalla, "Chiffon Saris: The Plight of Asian Immigrants in the New World," *Massachusetts Review,* 29, no. 4 (1988): 583–595;

Himanshu Mohapatra, "Riches of India: Reading Vikram Seth's *A Suitable Boy,*" in *The Postmodern English Indian Novel: Interrogating the 1980s and 1990s,* edited by Viney Kripal (New Delhi: Allied, 1996), pp. 41–48;

Rukmani Bhaya Nair, "Gender, Genre, and Generative Grammar: Deconstructing the Matrimonial Column," in *Language, Text and Context: Essays in Stylistics,* edited by Michael J. Toolan (London & New York: Routledge, 1992), pp. 227–254;

Leeia Lakshmi Narayen, "The Golden Bridge Is Falling Down, Falling Down, Falling Down: A Study of Vikram Seth's *The Golden Gate,*" in *Commonwealth Literature,* volume 1 of *Critical Responses* (New Delhi: Sterling, 1993);

Mala Pandurang, *Vikram Seth: Multiple Locations, Multiple Affiliations* (Jaipur & New Delhi: Rawat, 2001);

Z. N. Patil, "The Image of America in Vikram Seth's *The Golden Gate,*" *Commonwealth Review,* 4 (1992–1993): 2, 21–29;

Marjorie Perloff, "Homeland Ho! Silicon Valley Pushkin," *American Poetry Review* (November–December 1986): 37–46;

Khushwant Singh, "California Dreaming," *Illustrated Weekly of India* (20 July 1986): 52–53.

Bapsi Sidhwa

(11 August 1939 –   )

Niaz Zaman
University of Dhaka

BOOKS: *The Crow Eaters* (Lahore: Ilmi Press, 1978; London: Cape, 1980; New York: St. Martin's Press, 1981);

The Bride (London: Cape, 1983; New York: St. Martin's Press, 1983); republished as *The Pakistani Bride* (New Delhi: Penguin, 1990);

Ice-Candy-Man (London: Heinemann, 1988); republished as *Cracking India* (Minneapolis: Milkweed, 1991);

An American Brat (Minneapolis: Milkweed, 1993; New Delhi & London: Penguin, 1994);

The Bapsi Sidhwa Omnibus (Karachi: Oxford University Press, 2001)—comprises *The Crow Eaters, The Bride, Ice-Candy-Man,* and *An American Brat.*

Edition: *The Crow Eaters* (Minneapolis: Milkweed, 1992).

PRODUCED SCRIPT: *Earth,* adapted by Sidhwa and Deepa Mehta from *Ice-Candy-Man,* motion picture, Cracking the Earth Films, 1998.

OTHER: "Defend Yourself Against Me," in *Colours of a New Day: Writing for South Africa,* edited by Sarah Lefanu and Stephen Hayward (London: Lawrence & Wishart, 1990; New York: Pantheon, 1990), pp. 361–383;

"The Spouse and the Preacher," in *Her Mother's Ashes, and Other Stories by South Asian Women in Canada and the United States,* edited by Nurjehan Aziz (Toronto: Tsar, 1994), pp. 12–25;

"Highway to the Black Mountain," in *Without A Guide: Contemporary Women's Travel Adventures,* edited by Katherine Govier (St. Paul, Minn.: Hungry Mind, 1994; London: Pandora, 1996);

"Why Do I Write?" in *The Novels of Bapsi Sidhwa,* edited by R. K. Dhawan and Novy Kapadia (Delhi: Prestige, 1996), pp. 27–34;

"Reading: A Private Obsession," in *The Most Wonderful Books: Writers on Discovering the Pleasures of Reading,* edited by Michael Dorris and Emilie Buchwald (Minneapolis: Milkweed, 1997);

Bapsi Sidhwa (from the dust jacket for the U.S. edition of The Bride, *1983; Richland County Public Library)*

"A Selective Memory for History," in *To Mend the World: Women Reflect on 9/11,* edited by Marjorie Agosín and Betty Jean Craige (Buffalo, N.Y.: White Pine Press, 2002);

Beloved City: Writings on Lahore, edited by Sidhwa (Karachi: Oxford University Press, 2005); published as *City of Sin and Splendour: Writings on Lahore* (New Delhi: Penguin, 2005).

SELECTED PERIODICAL PUBLICATION–
UNCOLLECTED: "Third World, Our World," *Massachusetts Review* (Winter 1988–1989): 703–706.

Bapsi Sidhwa is a Parsi writer from Pakistan, now settled in the United States. Since 1978 she has published four novels and several short stories. In three of her novels Sidhwa has written about her own community, helping to bring the small, little-known Parsi people into the literary limelight. Her writings are rooted in a deep political-historical consciousness, manifested particularly when she writes about the partition of the Indian subcontinent in 1947. Sidhwa also has a strong sense of humor that she uses both to amuse and to palliate grim facts about politics or religion. Though Sidhwa does not call herself a feminist, three of her novels have female protagonists, as do all her short stories.

Parsis or Parsees are a small religious minority, numbering about 150,000 worldwide. They are descendants of Persian Zoroastrians, followers of the Iranian prophet Zoroaster or Zarathustra, who migrated to India between the eighth and ninth centuries during the Arab invasion of Persia. The Persian refugees first settled at Kathiawar, but then moved to Gujarat. According to Parsi lore, they were allowed to settle in Gujarat by its ruler on the conditions that they learn Gujarati and not try to convert people to their faith. In the seventeenth century, Bombay (now Mumbai) came under the control of the East India Company, and the Parsis started to settle there. They were an industrious community and helped to build the city into a center of trade and industry. Since the late twentieth century there has been a Parsi diaspora, but Mumbai still remains the center of Parsi life.

There are also some Parsis in Pakistan, mainly in Karachi and a few in Lahore. At the time of the partition, there were about three hundred Parsis in Lahore. Sidhwa was born Bapsy Bhandara in Karachi on 11 August 1939 to Tehmina and Peshotan Bhandara. Her father was a businessman who acquired the Murree Brewery after the partition of India; she has two brothers who are businessmen as well. Her grandmother named her Bapsy, mistakenly thinking it was an English name; Sidhwa changed the spelling to "Bapsi," thinking it looked more respectable, in 1978 when she published her first book. Young Bapsy was brought up mainly in Lahore, with occasional visits to Karachi, where her maternal grandparents lived. Karachi was more cosmopolitan at the time than Lahore and, though smaller than Bombay, had a more sizable Parsi community.

An attack of polio kept Bapsy at home for much of her childhood. Between operations she attended school sporadically, two or three months at a time. When she was about eleven, she spent one year in Karachi, studying at Mama Parsi Girls High School, founded by her maternal grandfather. Despite the frequent absences caused by her illness, the experience was enjoyable and helped her to have friends of her own age. Most of the time, however, she was tutored at home. One of her tutors was an Anglo-Indian neighbor, Mrs. Penherow, who also introduced her to the world of books by giving her a copy of Louisa May Alcott's *Little Women* (1868–1869) on her eleventh birthday. This gift sent Sidhwa into what she calls, in "Reading: A Private Obsession" (1997), "an orgy of reading." Apart from Alcott, she read Charlotte Brönte's *Jane Eyre* (1847) and Emily Brönte's *Wuthering Heights* (1847). Earlier, like other Pakistani children of the affluent, English-speaking class, she had read Enid Blyton's adventure stories as well as Johann Rudolf Wyss's *The Swiss Family Robinson* (1812–1813) and Daniel Defoe's *Robinson Crusoe* (1719). She sat for the matriculation or school-leaving examination privately and, as she had no aptitude for mathematics, was allowed to sit for art. She then went on to Kinnaird College for Women, Lahore, from which she graduated with a B.A. in psychology and ethics in 1957.

In 1958, when she was nineteen, Bapsy Bhandara married Gustad Kermani, an Irani Zoroastrian whose grandparents had migrated to India more recently than the Parsi community to which Bhandara belonged. The couple lived in Bombay, where they had two children, a son and a daughter. The marriage did not last, and Bapsy Kermani returned to Lahore with her daughter. She had to leave her son behind with his father. In 1963 she married Noshir Sidhwa, son of Rustam Sidhwa, who had taken an active part in the nationalist movement and served as a minister in Jawaharlal Nehru's cabinet in India. Bapsy Sidhwa had one daughter by this marriage. In 1975 Kermani died, and Sidhwa's son, then aged sixteen, was returned to his mother.

Back in Lahore, Sidhwa settled into the routine of a quieter, but still leisurely, life. Bombay was the center of Parsi life with its Parsi priests, its Parsi women in their distinctive saris, and its Towers of Silence, where Parsi corpses were laid out to be devoured by vultures. In Lahore, the Parsis were a small minority, and Sidhwa was thrown into the larger Punjabi milieu. Despite the scar of her divorce and the loss of her son, she was caught up in the social whirl. She attended to domestic duties (which meant mainly giving orders to trained servants) and performed the social obligations that were part of the life of the Indian and Pakistani upper class. In an interview with Jugnu Mohsin in *The Friday Times* (20–26 July 1989), Sidhwa noted how she "abhorred those coffee parties." Her reading—and then her writing—gave her a new purpose in life.

A visit to the Karakoram mountains in northern Pakistan changed Sidhwa the housewife into a writer. The tribal regions of Pakistan have their own feudal laws of fierce loyalties and violent enmities. Guns are a way of life. In these regions the concept of honor is fiercely guarded, and violators are punished brutally. This fact was brought home to Sidhwa in the starkest fashion when, at the remote army camp where she and her husband were staying—partly described in *The Bride* (1983)—she heard about a young bride who had run away. The young woman was decapitated, and her body was flung into a mountain stream. That incident horrified Sidhwa, who sought to assuage her sorrow and register her outrage in writing. In many of her interviews, as well as in "Highway to the Black Mountain" (1994), she talks about the incident that inspired her book. To Feroza Jussawalla, for example, in *Interviews with Writers of the Post-Colonial World* (1990), she described how she initially started writing a short story about the girl. The story lengthened and turned into a novel, which was later published as *The Bride*. Her novel of protest was, however, not published until after the success of *The Crow Eaters* (1978) in England in 1980.

While *The Bride* remained unpublished, Sidhwa went on to write a book that was quite different from her first one. This time she chose the Lahore-based Parsi community of businessmen with which she was familiar. In this book, unlike her first and subsequent ones, Sidhwa has a male protagonist: *The Crow Eaters* is the story of Faredoon Junglewalla (Freddy for short), who migrates to Lahore with his wife, Putli, and mother-in-law, Jerbanoo, toward the end of the nineteenth century. The book describes how Freddy rises in the business world—often by shady means. It also describes his relations with his family: his wife, his mother-in-law, and his sons. In the descriptions of Freddy's relationship with his wife, Sidhwa brings in the feminist issues that inspire all her writings.

The relationship between husband and wife is a loving one. Nevertheless, Freddy is undoubtedly master of the house. Sidhwa shows how women like Putli (the name means "doll" or "puppet") accept their subordinate position. Even when Freddy, under the influence of Western ways, wants her to walk beside him, he has to keep his arm firmly around her waist. Later, Putli is shown reprimanding her daughter-in-law when the young woman walks ahead of her husband. Putli even enjoys the period of seclusion that the uncleanness of menstruation imposes on her: though the writer uses the term "banishment" for this seclusion, Putli does not resent it. Perhaps, in the midst of the many demands

that were made on women, Sidhwa suggests, these intervals were the only times women could get some rest.

Though united by the character of Freddy, the book, as Makarand R. Paranjape notes in "The Early Novels of Bapsi Sidhwa" (included in *The Novels of Bapsi Sidhwa*, 1996), has "a somewhat loose, episodic structure." The middle sections of the novel, dealing with Freddy's relationships with his sons, are serious and tragic. Soli, his eldest son, dies, and Freddy is alienated from Yazdi, his second son, because the thoughtful, poetic young man falls in love with the wrong girl. When Freddy learns that Yazdi is in love with an Anglo-Indian girl, he is furious. He believes all Anglo-Indians are immoral. His prejudices are proved right when he visits Hira Mandi (the red-light district of Lahore) with his English acquaintance, Mr. Allen. There he realizes that one of the dancers, whom he had thought to be Kashmiri, is the girl that his son is in love with. He proves that she is a prostitute by having her sent to his room and sleeping with her. The girl fades out of the story, and Yazdi leaves home, rejecting his father.

By and large, however, *The Crow Eaters* is a comic book. Part of the humor may be owing to Sidhwa's reading of V. S. Naipaul's *A House for Mr. Biswas* (1961) at the time she was writing the novel—a point she mentioned in conversation with Jussawalla. A lot of the comedy is the result of Sidhwa's own sense of humor, which she seems to have inherited from her mother but which was also, as Sidhwa suggests in "Why Do I Write?" (1996), part of the "quintessentially Parsi ethos." As Sidhwa observes, this rich humor "just tumbled out, barrelling through everything that stood in its path, just as Freddy Junglewalla's boisterous mother-in-law bulldozes her way through the novel." The comic note is struck early in the book in the verbal sparring matches between Freddy and Jerbanoo and in his attempts throughout the book to get rid of her. In "Chronicling Women's Lives Beyond the Towers of Silence" (1996), Niaz Zaman shows how Sidhwa also puts humor to good use in portraying the little-known Parsi community and conveying some of its more startling customs.

Freddy's rise, as most critics note, is by dubious means. Freddy takes cuts, pays bribes, and attempts to burn down the house with his mother-in-law inside, hoping thus not only to get rid of the old woman but also to get the insurance money. His scheme succeeds partially: he gets the money, but his mother-in-law does not die in the fire. She is brought down in a basket from the burning house and becomes an instant celebrity. Despite Sidhwa's dependence on the male voice in this novel, Zaman suggests in "Bapsi Sidhwa: Search for

Identity" (1994) that Sidhwa was always conscious of her feminine identity. For example, the mother-in-law, whom Freddy had tried so hard to get rid of, proves tougher than her son-in-law, who ultimately dies of an unnamed feverish illness in old age.

Zaman points out in "Chronicling Women's Lives Beyond the Towers of Silence" that as a Pakistani and a Parsi, Sidhwa assumed a dual role. In *The Bride* she had attempted to be wholly Pakistani, writing about the Muslim community—even as she possessed the perspective of an outsider. In *The Crow Eaters* she described her own Parsi community as part of the larger Pakistani-Punjabi milieu of Lahore. As Alamgir Hashmi noted in "*The Crow Eaters*: A Noteworthy Novel" (included in *The Novels of Bapsi Sidhwa*), Sidhwa is a writer with roots in Lahore and succeeds in evoking the life of the city as it probably was in the first half of the twentieth century. It is, however, more than "local colour" that Sidhwa provides. As Robert L. Ross says in "The Search for Community in Bapsi Sidhwa's Novels" (included in *The Novels of Bapsi Sidhwa*), Sidhwa's three early novels "are firmly grounded in Pakistan" and provide a Pakistani angle on political and historical issues.

The Crow Eaters ends just before the partition, suggesting the importance of that date. In "'A Passion for History and for Truth Telling': The Early Novels of Bapsi Sidhwa" (included in *The Novels of Bapsi Sidhwa*), Ralph J. Crane stresses the political perspective of *The Crow Eaters*. Crane suggests that, by showing that Englishmen accepted bribes or visited Hira Mandi, Sidhwa critiques the British rulers.

The Parsis are a business community as much at home in Pakistan as in India. Freddy makes this point quite clear when he observes that his community is outside politics. Freddy—like Sidhwa herself—was outside the "two-nation theory" (the idea that Hindus and Muslims could not live together in the same state) that led to the partition of India and the creation of Pakistan. Her Parsi background gives Sidhwa—as it gives Freddy—a critical, neutral perspective. Freddy's dying words to the people gathered around him is to assure them that they will be safe despite the bickering and divisions that are tearing the land: "We will stay where we are . . . let Hindus, Muslims, Sikhs or whoever rule. What does it matter? The sun will continue to rise—and the sun continue to set—in their arses. . . ."

The Crow Eaters might have remained unpublished but for Sidhwa's meeting with Javed Iqbal, son of the poet-philosopher Mohammad Iqbal, who urged her to publish the work. Accordingly, she self-published the book at Ilmi Press. Once the book was in print, it attracted some attention. Sidhwa sent the book to a friend, who sent it to an agent in England. Finally, the

Cover for a 1992 U.S. paperback edition of Sidhwa's first published novel (1978), which depicts a shady businessman's relationships with his wife, mother-in-law, and sons (Thomas Cooper Library, University of South Carolina)

book was brought out by Jonathan Cape in London in 1980. Despite its success abroad, the book was a mixed success in Pakistan. As Sidhwa told David Montenegro in a 1989 interview, there was a bomb threat at the book launching. The Parsis were upset because they thought that she was making fun of them in the title of the book and had divulged secrets that damaged the image of their community. Though there was praise for Sidhwa in the Pakistani press, Lahore academics were critical of her bawdy language, which they felt was far removed from what they expected a refined woman to use.

The international recognition that Sidhwa got, slow though it was, brought her in 1983 the chance to visit the United States to conduct a fiction-writing workshop at St. Thomas University in Houston, Texas. This job was followed by a novel-writing workshop at

Rice University, Houston. *The Bride* was also finally published in 1983.

The Bride is a novel with a purpose. As R. K. Dhawan and Novy Kapadia note in *The Novels of Bapsi Sidhwa,* Sidhwa has "a proselytizing role" in this novel, criticizing "unjust traditions." Though *The Bride* essentially condemns tribal mores, Sidhwa also uses the novel to comment on Pakistani society where strict codes of purdah and honor continue to prevail. The feminist and political concerns of this novel also inform almost all of Sidhwa's later writing.

When Sidhwa wrote *The Bride,* she was writing, as most of her critics have pointed out, in a vacuum. Indo-Pakistani author Zulfikar Ghose was in self-exile, and most Pakistani writers in English were relegated to literary pages of weekend newspapers or magazines. Apart from her readings in English and American writers, there were no Pakistani or Indian writers to whom she could relate. Salman Rushdie had not yet published *Midnight's Children* (1981). Sidhwa's anger at the condition of women in tribal areas in particular and in Pakistan in general therefore combined with the realization that she had to begin at the beginning, and that she had to set the context before she could begin the story.

Writing in English and unsure of her audience, without a literary tradition, Sidhwa starts the story of *The Bride* not with the incident that inspired her to write it, but with a depiction of Pakistan. Her anxiety to provide a context for her novel leads to a divided focus, as does the episodic structure of much of her writing. Tariq Rahman, for example, observes that in the novel there is too much action that diverts attention from the characters. Paranjape also refers to the "lack of unity" in the novel, which "tells several almost independent stories."

Partly as a Parsi who needs to establish her political identity, partly as a Third-World author writing in a foreign language for a foreign audience, Sidhwa uses her writing to explain her culture to audiences unfamiliar with it. As she points out in "Third World, Our World" (1988–1989), "I have no identity outside my culture, which is a curious mix of the Punjabi and Pakistani cultures. I am not a writer unless I voice the aspirations, humor, travails and reality of the only people I know well." Sidhwa's Pakistani identity is reflected in the historical consciousness that, as Crane notes, is evidenced in her first three novels, each of which, directly or indirectly, is concerned with the partition of the Indian subcontinent and the creation of the independent states of India and Pakistan. Thus *The Bride,* which was inspired by violence against women, begins some years before the partition and describes briefly the communal tensions during this period and the displacement that resulted because of the partition. Only subse-

quently does it come to the story of the girl who broke the tribal code of honor and was punished for it.

The Bride begins with the ten-year-old Qasim marrying the fifteen-year-old Afshan, in a marriage arranged by their elders. Qasim's growing into puberty and his marital relations with Afshan over the next few years are narrated briefly, though there are some vivid descriptions and telling details, until Afshan and their three children die of smallpox. Qasim then leaves the hills for the plains town of Jullunder. But then the subcontinent is divided, and Jullunder is made part of India. Qasim has to leave, because he is a Muslim and because he has killed a Hindu who he felt had insulted him over his bathroom habits. The train that Qasim is on is attacked by Sikhs, but he manages to escape. Among the survivors is also a little girl who has lost her parents. Qasim does not want the responsibility of the child, but the child clings to him, mistaking him for her father. Gradually he softens. She reminds him of his daughter, and he names her Zaitoon after the daughter he had lost.

In the next few chapters Sidhwa describes the life of Qasim and Zaitoon in Lahore. Part of this narrative focuses on the adolescent girl growing up in a repressed milieu, while part of it critiques the different forms of corruption in the newly created state. Qasim's new friend Nikka is shown making a fortune for himself by playing upon the cupidity of high officials. The chapters on Lahore also include a trip to Hira Mandi, where Nikka and Qasim take some officials to witness a dance.

The plot then abruptly switches to Qasim's decision to marry Zaitoon to Sakhi, a distant nephew. At this point, Sidhwa brings in a parallel subplot involving another bride, the American Carol, who is visiting the hills with Farukh, her Pakistani husband. Carol is bored and has an affair with Mushtaq, a young army major with whom the couple are staying. Carol sees Zaitoon briefly, as does Mushtaq's driver, Ashiq. The look that Ashiq gives the young woman is not lost on the jealous Sakhi, who beats his bride. Not brought up in the hills, Zaitoon rebels and runs away. Two men come upon the young woman and rape her. Seeing the dazed woman and knowing that her husband will kill her if he finds her, Mushtaq rescues Zaitoon. The novel ends on a positive note, indicating that perhaps Ashiq will whisk the young woman away to his mountain hideout and keep her safe.

Sidhwa told Montenegro and Jussawalla that she had originally planned to end the book with Zaitoon's death, but then changed her mind and allowed Zaitoon to live. However, Sidhwa includes a vignette that reflects the incident of the tribal woman who had inspired her story. Carol comes across the head of a dead woman floating in the river. Though the woman is not Zaitoon, the incident allows Sidhwa, through Carol, to protest against unjust laws and violence directed against women. Sidhwa suggests that these primitive codes of honor are applicable not just to tribal society but also to Pakistani society in general. Though Carol appears the privileged outsider, Paranjape notes that Carol too is oppressed and exploited.

As Fawzia Afzal-Khan points out, despite the pessimism of the story, Zaitoon's escape from the tribal community with its rigid codes is "a challenge" to patriarchal culture. Though women are still treated like objects, Sidhwa shows that women can and must strive to escape their fate. Thus, Sidhwa stresses how women must exercise what Mohammad Iqbal called *khudi* or inner strength, to escape from the coils of their fate. As Ross notes in "*The Bride:* The Treatment of Women" (included in *The Novels of Bapsi Sidhwa*), by altering the original story, Sidhwa was sending a message to women that "they must rebel no matter the consequences." This realization also gives Carol the courage to admit that she too must escape—but not through a meaningless affair.

In 1985 Sidhwa was an assistant professor in the creative-writing program at the University of Houston. In 1986 she was a Bunting Fellow at Radcliffe/Harvard. Thus, when she came to write her third novel, *Ice-Candy-Man* (1988; published in the United States as *Cracking India*, 1991), Sidhwa was surer of herself, her audience, and her material. She was also, as Zaman notes in "Bapsi Sidhwa: Search for Identity," more conscious of her triple identity: "Pakistani, Parsi, and female."

Ice-Candy-Man is told through the eyes of a Parsi girl, Lenny. Though, like the writer, Lenny has had a bout of polio and has had to undergo several operations, Sidhwa insists that the character is not a self-portrait. The narrative is about Lenny's comprehension of the turbulent events during the partition of the Indian subcontinent into India and Pakistan. Most of the narrative centers upon what happens to her beloved Ayah, the maid who looks after her. When the story begins, Ayah is surrounded by many admirers, Hindu and Muslim. Among them is the character Lenny calls "Ice-candy-man," a seller of treats. As the partition nears, and the breakup of the Indian subcontinent becomes imminent, Muslims and Hindus become enemies. In an attempt to save themselves, some Hindus convert to Christianity, others to Islam. Some Hindus leave Lahore. Ayah is Hindu, but she assumes that as a member of a Parsi household she will be safe. Ice-candy-man, who has not received any special favors from her, arrives with a group and abducts her. The narrative follows Ayah to Hira Mandi, where Ice-

candy-man has ensconced her, and then goes on to describe her rescue and subsequent departure for India.

In her review of the novel in the *New Statesman* (26 February 1988), Marianne Wiggins roundly criticized *Ice-Candy-Man,* suggesting that "much of Sidhwa's trouble in telling this tale lies in her choice of narrative voice," and noting that "As character fails, so does any sense of the politics of the time–so does any sense of place." (Wiggins also compared Sidhwa unfavorably to Rushdie throughout the review, while failing to disclose that she was Rushdie's new wife; she later attributed the unethical diatribe to Rushdie.) Crane, however, suggests that Sidhwa's choice of narrator is appropriate: "the atrocities of 1947 are best seen through the innocent naive eyes of a child, who has no Hindu, Muslim, or Sikh ax to grind." In his introduction to *The Bapsi Sidhwa Omnibus* (2001), Aamer Hussain also approves of Sidhwa's choice of narrator, declaring that "the point of view that Bapsi adopts is one of the novel's most successful ploys," and pointing out that through "strategically placed flashbacks," readers are given a "double–dialogic–perspective."

Several critics have commented on the inaccurate historical details of *Ice-Candy-Man*. Crane, for example, points out that Mahatma Gandhi's march to Dandi Beach in protest over the tax on salt took place in 1930 and not in the early months of 1947, and that Gandhi did not visit Lahore during 1947. However, as he also stresses, these details are "tricks of memory . . . received truths," which "become part of the ethos of the age." As Sidhwa herself suggested in an August 2002 letter to Zaman, "A writer of fiction has the poetic licence to bend dates to arrive at the larger atmospheric truth."

The Parsis were neutral throughout the communal fighting that accompanied the partition. Nevertheless, as a sensitive writer, Sidhwa shows how violence affects everybody. Many critics have noted, however, that Sidhwa looks at the partition from the Pakistani perspective. Sidhwa uses Lenny to comment on the favoritism that attended the cutting up of the land. Thus, she emphasizes that areas were allotted to India that, on the rationale of the division of Muslim areas falling to Pakistan and Hindu areas to India, should have come to Pakistan. This attempt on Sidhwa's part to correct the Indian perspective also extends to the way that Pakistan's first head of state, Mohammad Ali Jinnah, has been treated by Indians and British alike: "And today, in films of Gandhi's and Mountbatten's lives, in books by British and Indian scholars, Jinnah, who for a decade was known as the ambassador of Hindu-Muslim unity, is caricatured and portrayed as a monster."

The novel also examines a girl's sexual awakening as well as the greater vulnerability of women, espe-

*Dust jacket for the American edition of Sidhwa's 1983 novel, inspired
by a story she heard about a young Pakistani bride who was
decapitated as punishment for running away
(Richland County Public Library)*

cially during turbulent times. Sexuality in a society
where sex is not openly talked about and where young
men and women do not even hold hands in public is,
Sidhwa suggests, almost an explosive force. Sidhwa
shows that, young as she is, Lenny vaguely understands the sexual power that Ayah has over the men
who flock around her—a power that during the communal disturbances results in Ayah's abduction. In earlier
times Ayah could dole out her favors. The communal
riots reverse the equation, giving the Muslim Ice-candy-
man brute power.

The sexuality that the little girl experiences is not
just vicarious. There is a male cousin who peeps into
the bathroom whenever he can and corners her to
show her his penis. Though in *The Bride,* Sidhwa suggests that there are possibilities of romance, in *Ice-Candy-
Man* there are no romances. The sexual games that
Cousin plays have no effect on Lenny. The story of
Ayah does not have a happy ending. Though Ayah

says to Godmother that Ice-candy-man does not mis-
treat her after the initial abduction and rape, she does
not want to stay with him. When Ayah departs for
India, Ice-candy-man follows her, but there has been no
softening in Ayah's attitude toward the man who
abducted her. In this novel too there is a young bride;
but there is no possibility of happiness for the lively,
fun-loving Papoo, the sweeper's daughter, when she is
married to a pockmarked dwarf twice her age. Drugged
with opium, she is propped up for the ceremony conducted by the mission padre.

In *Ice-Candy-Man,* Sidhwa critiques not only sexual
repression and the norms of purdah but also the position of women during conflicts. Stories of the partition
in the west and north were full of accounts of women
being stripped and forced to march naked through the
streets, of women raped and mutilated before being
killed. In *Ice-Candy-Man,* Sidhwa unfolds all the horrors
that partition novels describe. Apart from Ayah, who is
abducted and raped, there is Hamida, a Muslim refugee
from India, who has suffered a similar fate. Sidhwa also
portrays the large-scale violence that accompanied the
division of the Indian subcontinent: there is a train massacre; women have their breasts chopped off; and an
entire village is sacked, the women raped and killed.
Except for Ayah's abduction, however, these killings
and rapes are not depicted directly: Ice-candy-man
describes the scene at the railway station, while Ranna,
who miraculously escaped, tells of the massacre and
rape of the village.

Despite Sidhwa's portrayal of the violence against
women in *Ice-Candy-Man,* she also stresses their strength.
Though they may often be victims, women are also
saviors and heroes. Thus, Lenny's mother—a shadowy
figure who hovers on the edges of Lenny's consciousness most of the time—smuggles rationed petrol to her
Hindu and Sikh friends to help them escape Lahore.
Godmother rebukes Ice-candy-man for his abduction of
Ayah and his pimping. Godmother also helps Ayah
escape from Hira Mandi. The strength of Sidhwa's
women is a point emphasized by both Afzal-Khan and
Ross. Afzal-Khan notes that all those who display moral
strength in *Ice-Candy-Man* are women. She points out
that though Sidhwa still depicts women as little more
than objects of history, she has moved away from seeing women solely as victims and makes them "emotional pillars of strength who can, through the power of
compassion, effect good for others."

Unlike Afzal-Khan, Ross suggests that men also
suffer in Sidhwa's work. Particularly, in *Ice-Candy-Man,*
men are humiliated and killed. Hari, the Hindu servant
who wears a dhoti, is also the butt of a humiliating
game. The dhoti is a flimsy garment, often threatening
to expose the wearer's genitals. When the narrative

begins, the teasing is in fun—though always charged with sexual overtones. As communal tensions grow, the game is no longer about teasing. One day the dhoti does come off, and the cowering man's genitals are revealed in all their smallness. The man's humiliation is a foreshadowing of Ayah's humiliation as well as a vivid reminder of how men's religious affiliations were often verified during Hindu-Muslim conflicts in the Indian subcontinent.

Sidhwa focuses on the vulnerability of women in conflict even more starkly in the short story "Defend Yourself Against Me" (1990), which builds upon the Ranna episode in *Ice-Candy-Man*. Unlike *Ice-Candy-Man*, however, the short story is set in the United States, where Sidhwa was spending more time. This story also introduces the diaspora theme that became the focus of Sidhwa's fourth novel, *An American Brat* (1993). "Defend Yourself Against Me" thus forms a bridge from the theme of the partition—which has in direct or indirect ways affected all Sidhwa's novels—to the "new immigrant" theme, which Sidhwa shares with Bharati Mukherjee and Anita Desai.

"Defend Yourself Against Me" is set in Houston and is narrated by Mrs. Jacobs, a Christian from Lahore. Mrs. Jacobs is invited to a party attended by people from the South Asian community, Pakistanis and Indians. There she meets a man named Sikander Khan, whom she realizes she had met years before in Lahore, when he and his mother had moved next door. The young Sikander suffered a deep scar, the effect of a wound he received during the violence of the Hindu-Muslim riots, and his mother, Ammijee, was raped and brutalized. Mrs. Jacobs recounts how the now elderly Ammijee has never forgotten that incident. Nor, it appears, have some Sikh friends of Sikander's who, hearing of what was done to the old woman, ask forgiveness for their fathers' sins when they encounter Ammijee at a dinner party Sikander throws for her. Initially it appears that the old woman will never soften toward them, but Ammijee tells the men that she forgives them—as she forgave their fathers, because without forgiveness she could not have continued living. As Zaman notes in "Bapsi Sidhwa: Search for Identity," Sidhwa seems to suggest that while one cannot forget the trauma of the past, it is necessary to forgive. In "American, Pakistani, or Indian: Nationalism and Ethnicity in Bharati Mukherjee's 'The Management of Grief' and Bapsi Sidhwa's 'Defend Yourself Against Me'" (1999), Zaman further points out that while Mukherjee focuses on the new immigrant theme, Sidhwa's story stresses that Indians and Pakistanis can meet as friends and confront the past only on neutral ground such as in the United States.

Meanwhile, Sidhwa was working on her fourth novel. By this time she had won several prestigious awards at home and abroad. In addition to her teaching assignments in the United States, she had, in 1991, been a visiting scholar at the Rockefeller Center in Bellagio, Italy. That same year she received the Sitara-i-Imtiaz, Pakistan's highest national honor in the arts, as well as the National Award for English Literature, given by the Pakistani Academy of Letters. *Ice-Candy-Man* also won the Literaturepreis in Germany that year.

In 1993 Sidhwa received the Lila Wallace-Reader's Digest Award of $105,000. The money gave her some time to do what she wanted. She decided to work with the Asia Society to provide a forum for Pakistanis, Indians, and Bangladeshis to meet and be friends. During the three years that she worked closely with the Asia Society, she arranged talks in Houston for prominent academics, writers, and human-rights activists from South Asia.

When *An American Brat* was published in 1993, Sidhwa was an internationally recognized author. Her other three novels had been published initially in Pakistan or England, but *An American Brat* was published first in the United States. She was now both American and Pakistani. However, she is also Parsi, and in her own migration experience as well as in the Parsi diaspora she found her latest theme. Her fourth novel combined her Parsi-Pakistani background with her American experience.

Set initially in Lahore and then in the United States, the novel narrates how Feroza Ginwalla, a descendant of Freddy from *The Crow Eaters,* becomes "an American brat." The time is the late 1970s; the military dictator Ziaul Huq is in power, and Islamic fundamentalism is growing in Pakistan. Feroza, though a Parsi, is affected by the fundamentalist fervor. Alarmed at the Islamic trends in Pakistan and the effect they are having on Feroza, the girl's mother, Zareen Ginwalla, packs off her daughter to the United States, where the girl's uncle, Manek, is studying at the Massachusetts Institute of Technology. Six years older than Feroza, Manek becomes her friend and mentor and introduces her to life in America. Though repelled by some of her American experiences, Feroza succumbs to America's charms and decides to stay on as a student.

Feroza learns to speak like Americans, to flirt, to drink, and also to smoke, which—for a Parsi, for whom fire is a symbol of purity—is an act of desecration. She discovers sexual freedom, having affairs first with a young Indian and then with David Press, a Jew. By providing detailed descriptions of Jewish rituals, Sidhwa introduces her Pakistani audience to a way of life that would, in most cases, be unfamiliar. Different though these rituals are, Sidhwa suggests that all religions are

Dust jacket for the U.S. edition of Sidhwa's 1993 novel, in which a young Parsi woman visits her uncle in the United States, starts adopting American ways, and dates a Jewish man, much to the dismay of her mother (Richland County Public Library)

The novel also focuses on the wider effect of the Parsi diaspora on the small community. Through Zareen, Sidhwa questions the strictures that are placed on Parsi women. Parsi men can marry outside their faith and still remain Parsi and bring up their children in their faith, but Parsi women who marry non-Parsis—"nons," as they are called—are excommunicated. In a rapidly changing world where girls like Feroza increasingly find themselves outside their own culture, Sidhwa stresses that Parsis cannot continue to ignore present realities.

American reviewers spoke highly of the book because of its immigrant theme. In her review of the book in *The Washington Post* (16 December 1993), Edit Villareal pointed out that for women born in restrictive societies, "immigration may be the only way to come of age." Adam L. Penenberg, in *The New York Times Book Review* (16 January 1994), called the novel "a sensitive portrayal of how modern America appears to a new arrival." Carol Fleming Lumpkin, in "A Pakistani's View of America: Cynical, Brazen–and Promising," in the *Houston Chronicle* (7 January 1994), described the book as "a paean to freedom." South Asian writers, however, were less quick to praise the book. In "Coming to America," in *Fanfare* (7 November 1993), Parul Kapur pointed out that the chapters that deal with Pakistan are "bustling," whereas the chapters on America "drone on." In "The Americanization of Bapsi Sidhwa" (1994), Zaman suggests that while the American experience allowed Sidhwa to expand her canvas by dealing with the South Asian diaspora, the book lacks the "blend of cynicism, sympathy and wry humour" that marks *The Crow Eaters* and *Ice-Candy Man*.

Since the publication of *An American Brat*, Sidhwa has published several short stories—partly drawn from her earlier writings, such as "The Sweeper's Daughter" (*Ice-Candy-Man*) and "Don't Date a Non" (*An American Brat*), as well as "The Spouse and the Preacher" (1994), "The Trouble Easers," and "Sehrabai's Story." She also worked on the script of *Ice-Candy-Man*, which was made into a motion picture by Deepa Mehta titled *Earth* in 1998. (Sidhwa herself played the adult Lenny in the movie.) *The Crow Eaters* is also scheduled to be made into a movie, again by Mehta, and Sidhwa is working on the script. She is also working on a dramatization of *An American Brat*, titled "Feroza Among the Farangees."

Until the mid 1990s, Sidhwa was conscious of her dual identity as a Pakistani citizen and an American resident—unlike Mukherjee, who prided herself on being an immigrant in the tradition of the early Puritans. For example, in a letter to Zaman dated 21 October 1994, Sidhwa said, " I don't know if I can call myself an immigrant because I divide my time between both countries." In *An American Brat* this dichotomy is expressed

basically alike. Feroza is invited to a Sabbath meal, and though the details are different—the men wear yarmulkes, and there is a kiddush cup with sweet wine as well as braided bread—she ponders the similarity underlying the differences: "Breaking bread, sharing salt. . . . they belonged also to the Parsee, Christian, and Muslim traditions of Pakistan."

Though Feroza sees the similarities, her mother is alarmed and rushes to America to make it plain to Feroza and David that the two cultures are not just different but ultimately incompatible. Moreover, as Zareen explains, Feroza would be cut off from her religion if she married outside her faith: she would never be allowed to enter the Parsi places of worship or attend the funeral rites of her parents. Zareen regrets having allowed Feroza to come to America: "You've become an American brat." Feroza's relationship with David fades, but she also realizes that she has changed too much in America to ever go back to Pakistan.

by Feroza's remaining in the United States while Zareen goes back to Pakistan. Sidhwa became an American citizen in 1992. However, she explains that borders are porous, and identities are fluid. She is more than just a Pakistani American. In "A Selective Memory for History" (2002), she defines herself and where she stood in 2001: "I have been, at various times, a citizen of Pakistan and India, and now I am an American. As one for whom national borders are becoming blurred and matters of citizenship disconcertingly fluid, I feel I belong to these countries simultaneously rather than sequentially: and whatever happens in them resonates for me as a writer."

In his introduction to *The Bapsi Sidhwa Omnibus,* Hussain notes Sidhwa's significance by pointing out that *The Crow Eaters* was published in 1978, three years before Rushdie's *Midnight's Children,* which is usually considered to have changed South Asian writing in English. Thus, Hussain stresses that Sidhwa, rather than Rushdie, signaled the "coming-of-age of South Asian fiction in English."

Even as Bapsi Sidhwa joins the writers of the diaspora, she stands out for her threefold contribution: to Parsi literature, to Pakistani writing in English, and to South Asian fiction in English. Parsis were a mysterious, little-known minority until Sidhwa made them the subject of her novels. Similarly, Pakistani writing in English was a category that did not exist abroad. In the twenty-first century, thanks to Sidhwa, it is not just the Parsi writer who has a literary tradition in English but also Pakistani fiction. Paradoxically, even as Sidhwa speaks of the blurring of boundaries and joins the rank of immigrant American writers, her Pakistani lineage will continue to define her in America as her Parsi heritage does in Pakistan.

Interviews:

David Montenegro, "Bapsi Sidhwa," in his *Points of Departure: International Writers on Writing and Politics* (Ann Arbor: University of Michigan Press, 1989), pp. 26–51;

Feroza Jussawalla and Reed Way Dasenbrock, eds., *Interviews with Writers of the Post-Colonial World* (Jackson: University Press of Mississippi, 1990).

References:

Fawzia Afzal-Khan, "Women in History," in *International Literature in English: Essays on Major Writers,* edited by Robert L. Ross (New York: Garland, 1991), pp. 271–281;

R. K. Dhawan and Novy Kapadia, eds., *The Novels of Bapsi Sidhwa* (Delhi: Prestige, 1996);

Tariq Rahman, *A History of Pakistani Literature in English* (Lahore: Vanguard, 1991);

Mohammed Yasin, "Bapsi Sidhwa—from Housewife to Fiction Writer," *Pakistan Times,* 27 April 1990, p. 4;

Niaz Zaman, "American, Pakistani or Indian? Nationalism and Ethnicity in Bharati Mukherjee's 'The Management of Grief' and Bapsi Sidhwa's 'Defend Yourself Against Me,'" *Spectrum: Journal of the Department of English,* University of Dhaka, 2 (1999): 17–33;

Zaman, "The Americanization of Bapsi Sidhwa," *Bangladesh Journal of American Studies,* 7–8 (1994): 197–212;

Zaman, "Bapsi Sidhwa: Search for Identity," in *Infinite Variety: Women in Society and Literature,* edited by Firdous Azim and Zaman (Dhaka: University Press, 1994), pp. 202–222;

Zaman, "Chronicling Women's Lives Beyond the Towers of Silence," *Dhaka University Studies,* 53 (June 1996): 1–20;

Zaman, "Images of Purdah in Bapsi Sidhwa's Novels," in *Margins of Erasure: Purdah in the Subcontinental Novel in English,* edited by Jasbir Jain and Amina Amin (New Delhi: Sterling, 1995), pp. 156–173.

Khushwant Singh

(2 February 1915 –   )

Aali Areefur Rehman
Rajshahi University

BOOKS: *The Mark of Vishnu and Other Stories* (London: Saturn Press, 1950);

The Sikhs (New York: Macmillan / London: Allen & Unwin, 1953);

Train to Pakistan (London: Chatto & Windus, 1956); published as *Mano Majra* (New York: Grove, 1956);

The Unending Trail (New Delhi: Rajkamal, 1957);

The Voice of God and Other Stories (Bombay: Jaico, 1957);

I Shall Not Hear the Nightingale (New York: Grove, 1959; London: Calder, 1959);

The Sikhs Today: Their Religion, History, Culture, Customs and Way of Life (Bombay: Orient Longman, 1959; revised, 1964; revised edition, New Delhi: Sangam, 1976);

The Fall of the Kingdom of the Punjab (Bombay: Orient Longman, 1962);

Ranjit Singh: Maharajah of the Punjab (London: Allen & Unwin, 1962);

A History of the Sikhs 1469–1964, 2 volumes (volume 1, Princeton: Princeton University Press, 1963; volume 2, Delhi: Oxford University Press / London: Oxford University Press, 1963; revised edition, Bombay: Orient Longman, 1967);

Not Wanted in Pakistan (New Delhi: Rajkamal, 1965);

Ghadar, 1915: India's First Armed Revolution, by Singh and Satindra Singh (New Delhi: R & K Publishing House, 1966);

Homage to Guru Gobind Singh, by Singh and Suneet Veer Singh (Bombay: Jaico, 1966);

A Bride for the Sahib and Other Stories (New Delhi: Hind Pocket Books, 1967);

Shri Ram: A Biography, by Singh and Arun Joshi (Bombay: Asia, 1968; London: Asia, 1968; New York: Asia, 1968);

Khushwant Singh's India: A Mirror for Its Monsters and Monstrosities (Bombay: India Book House, 1969);

Black Jasmine (Bombay: Jaico, 1971);

Khushwant Singh's View of India, edited by Rahul Singh (Bombay: India Book House, 1974);

Khushwant Singh (AFP/Getty Images)

Khushwant Singh on War and Peace in India, Pakistan, and Bangladesh, edited by Mala Singh (New Delhi: Hind Pocket Books, 1976);

Good People, Bad People, edited by Rahul Singh (New Delhi: Orient, 1977);

Khushwant Singh's India without Humbug, edited by Rahul Singh (Bombay: India Book House, 1977);

Around the World with Khushwant Singh, edited by Rahul Singh (New Delhi: Orient, 1978);

Indira Gandhi Returns! (New Delhi: Vision, 1979);

Khushwant Singh's Editor's Page, edited by Rahul Singh (Bombay: India Book House, 1981);

We Indians (New Delhi: Orient, 1982);

Delhi: A Portrait (Delhi & Oxford: Oxford University Press, 1983);

The Sikhs, text by Singh, photographs by Raghu Rai (Varanasi: Lustre, 1984);

Tragedy of Punjab: Operation Blue Star and After, by Singh and Kuldip Nayar (New Delhi: Vision, 1984);

Many Faces of Communalism, by Singh and Bipan Chandra (Chandigarh: Centre for Research in Rural and Industrial Development, 1985);

Malicious Gossip, edited by Rohini Singh (New Delhi: Konark Publishers, 1987);

Delhi, Agra, Jaipur, text by Singh, photographs by Gopi Gajwani (New Delhi: Himalayan, 1990);

Delhi: A Novel (New Delhi: Penguin, 1990);

India: An Introduction (New Delhi: Vision, 1990);

Kalighat to Calcutta (Calcutta: Manjushree Foundation / New Delhi: Lustre, 1990);

Nature Watch (New Delhi: Lustre, 1990);

More Malicious Gossip, edited by Rohini Singh (Delhi: Konark Publishers, 1991);

Need for a New Religion in India and Other Essays, edited by Rohini Singh (New Delhi: UBSPD, 1991);

My Bleeding Punjab (New Delhi & London: UBSPD, 1992);

Women and Men in My Life (New Delhi: UBSPD, 1995);

How the Sikhs Lost Their Kingdom (New Delhi: UBSPD, 1996);

Khushwant Singh's JokeBook III (New Delhi: Orient, 1997);

The Company of Women (New Delhi & New York: Penguin, 1999; New Delhi: Viking / London: Penguin, 1999);

Khushwant Singh's Big Book of Malice (New Delhi & New York: Penguin, 2000);

Khushwant Singh's Big Fat Joke Book (New Delhi & New York: Penguin in association with Vision, 2000);

Khushwant Singh's Book of Unforgettable Women, edited by Mala Dayal (New Delhi & New York: Penguin, 2000);

Notes on the Great Indian Circus (New Delhi & New York: Penguin, 2001);

Sights and Sounds of the World, edited by N. Krishnamurthy (New Delhi: Books Today, 2001);

Khushwant Singh on Women, Love & Lust, compiled by Krishnamurthy (New Delhi: Books Today, 2002);

Truth, Love and a Little Malice: An Autobiography (New Delhi & New York: Viking in association with Ravi Dayal, 2002);

The End of India (New Delhi: Penguin, 2003);

Gods and Godmen of India (New Delhi: HarperCollins, 2003);

Burial at Sea (New Delhi & New York: Penguin, 2004);

Paradise and Other Stories (New Delhi & New York: Penguin, Viking in association with Ravi Dayal, 2004).

Collections: *Collected Short Stories of Khushwant Singh* (Delhi: Ravi Dayal, 1989);

Sex, Scotch and Scholarship: Selected Writings, edited by Rohini Singh (New Delhi: UBSPD, 1992);

Not a Nice Man to Know: The Best of Khushwant Singh, edited by Nandini Mehta (New Delhi & Harmondsworth, U.K.: Viking, 1993);

Collected Novels (Delhi & London: Penguin, 1996).

OTHER: *A Note on G. V. Desani's "All about H. Hatterr" and "Hali,"* edited by Singh and Peter Russel (London & Amsterdam: Szeben, 1952);

Land of the Five Rivers, edited by Singh and Jaya Thadani (Bombay: Jaico, 1965);

Sita Ram Kohli, *Sunset of the Sikh Empire,* edited by Singh (Bombay: Orient Longman, 1967);

N. Gerald Barrier, *The Sikhs and Their Literature (A Guide to Tracts, Books, and Periodicals, 1849–1919),* introduction by Singh (Delhi: Nanohar, 1970);

I Believe, edited by Singh (Delhi: Hind Pocket Books, 1971);

Love and Friendship, edited by Singh (New Delhi: Sterling, 1973);

William Godolphin Osborne, *The Court and Camp of Runjeet Singh,* introduction by Singh (Karachi: Oxford University Press, 1973);

Kailash Chander Gulati, *Akalis Past and Present,* foreword by Singh (New Delhi: Ashajanak, 1974);

Mario de Miranda, *Laugh It Off: A Collection of Cartoons,* introduction by Singh (Bombay: India Book House, 1974);

Stories from India, edited by Singh and Qurrutalain Hyder (New Delhi: Sterling, 1974);

Henry Montgomery Lawrence, *Adventures of an Officer in the Service of Runjeet Singh,* introduction by Singh (Karachi & New York: Oxford University Press, 1975);

Gurus, Godmen and Good People, edited by Singh (Bombay: Orient Longman, 1975);

Altaf Alfroid David, *Sweet and Sour,* foreword by Singh (Delhi: Sunrise, 1975);

Manmohan Singh, *A Dome of Many-Coloured Glass: 25 Essays on Life, War and Poetry,* foreword by Singh (Delhi: Kalyani, 1976);

Khalid Latif Gauba, *Pakistan Today,* introduction by Singh (Bombay: Thackers, 1977);

T. S. Sodhi, *Educational Concepts of Guru Nanak in Sidh Goshti,* foreword by Singh (Ludhiana: Mukand, 1980);

Anthology of Modern Urdu Poetry, foreword by Singh, edited and translated by Baidar Bakht and Kathleen Jaeger (Delhi: Educational Publishing House, 1984);

Noel Q. King, *Perspectives on the Sikh Tradition,* foreword by Singh (Chandigarh: Siddharth, 1986);

Harminder Kaur, *Blue Star over Amritsar,* introduction by Singh (Delhi: Ajanta, 1990);

Mrinal Pande, *The Subject Is Woman,* foreword by Singh (New Delhi: Sanchar Publishing House, 1991);

Rafiq Zakaria, *Iqbal: The Poet and the Politician,* introduction by Singh (New Delhi & New York: Viking, 1993);

Uncertain Liaisons: Sex, Strife and Togetherness in Urban India, edited by Singh and Shobha Dé (New Delhi & London: Viking, 1993);

A Dream Turns Seventy Five: The Modern School, 1920–1995, edited by Singh and Syeda Saiyidain Hameed (New Delhi: Allied, 1995);

Osho, *Life's Mysteries: An Introduction to the Teachings of Osho,* foreword by Singh (New Delhi & New York: Penguin, 1995);

Satish Gujral, *A Brush with Life: An Autobiography,* edited, with a foreword, by Singh (New Delhi: Penguin Books India, 1997);

Delhi, introduction by Singh, photographs by Gopi Gajwani, edited by Kishore Singh (New Delhi: Crest, 2000);

Khushwant Singh Selects Best Indian Short Stories, edited by Singh (New Delhi: Books Today, 2001, 2003);

City Improbable: An Anthology of Writings on Delhi, edited, with an introduction, by Singh (New Delhi & New York: Viking, 2001).

TRANSLATIONS: *Jupji: The Sikh Morning Prayer* (London: Probsthain, 1959); *Selections from Sacred Writings of the Sikhs,* translated by Trilochan Singh and Khushwant Singh (London: Allen & Unwin, 1960);

Mirza Mohammad Hadi Ruswa, *Umrao Jan Ada: Courtesan of Lucknow,* translated by Singh and M. A. Husaini (Bombay: Orient Longman, 1961);

Amrita Pritam, *The Skeleton and Other Writings* (Bombay: Jaico, 1964);

Rajinder Singh Bedi, *I Take This Woman* (New Delhi: Hind Pocket Books, 1967);

Guru Nanak, *Hymns of Guru Nanak* (Bombay: Orient Longman, 1969);

Amrita Pritam, *Selected Poems,* translated by Singh and others, edited by Pritish Nandy (Calcutta: Dialogue Publications, 1970);

Satindra Singh, *Dreams in Debris: A Collection of Punjabi Short Stories* (Bombay: Jaico, 1972);

K. S. Duggal, *Come Back, My Master and Other Stories* (New Delhi: Ben, 1978);

Mohammad Iqbal, *Shikwa and Jawab-I-Shikwa: Complaint and Answer: Iqbal's Dialogue with Allah* (New Delhi & Oxford: Oxford University Press, 1981);

Sheikh Mohammad Abdullah, *Flames of the Chinar: An Autobiography,* abridged and translated by Singh (New Delhi & New York: Viking Penguin, 1993);

Rehras = Evensong: The Sikh Evening Prayer, translated by Singh and Reema Anand (New Delhi & New York: Viking, 2002).

One of the earliest of the Indian writers in English who came to notice after the subcontinent gained independence from Britain in 1947 and was partitioned into the two separate countries of India and Pakistan, Khushwant Singh is a lawyer by training and became a diplomat by accident. He gave up both professions to make writing his chosen career. Beginning as a writer of short fiction in his mid thirties, he went on, over the next fifty years of his life, to become an historian, a biographer, a translator, a leading journalist, and a man of letters. Though best known in India for his journalism, he is the author as well of four collections of short stories and four novels that have earned him a permanent place in the canon of Indian writing in English.

Singh was born 2 February 1915 into a Sikh family in the village of Hadali in the Sargodha district (now in Pakistan) of the province of Punjab, one of the five children of his father, Sobha Singh, and mother, Veeran Bai. His grandfather, Sujan Singh, had become prosperous in the early years of the century as the owner of a construction business in which his father eventually became a partner. When the British government announced in 1911 the shifting of the Indian capital from Calcutta to Delhi and the construction of a new city there to be designed by Edward Lutyens and Herbert Baker, Sujan Singh and Sobha Singh, lured by the prospect of lucrative building contracts, moved to Delhi from the Punjab. Father and son were eventually awarded some of the largest contracts when the construction of New Delhi actually began after World War I. Sobha Singh, especially, is remembered as the builder of some of the most impressive landmarks of New Delhi. Having bought large tracts of land in and around New Delhi, he became one of the largest landowners of the city and was eventually knighted.

With his parents away in Delhi, Khushwant Singh spent the first five years of his life in his native Hadali in the care of his grandmother. When he was about five years old, however, he was brought by his parents to Delhi and sent, with his elder brother, to Modern School, an institution that his father had helped found that year. Khushwant Singh remained in this school until 1930 and eventually did his intermediate schooling (high school) at the prestigious St.

Stephen's College in 1932. He went next to Government College, Lahore, in the Punjab, as an undergraduate. During his first summer holidays there he also enrolled, on an impulse, as a music and arts student at Shantiniketan, the rural university in Bengal founded by Nobel laureate Rabindranath Tagore, but Singh left soon after without taking a qualification. Graduating with a B.A. from Government College in 1934, he went on to King's College, London, and then, as a law student, to the Inner Temple, from where he qualified as a barrister in 1939. He returned that year to India to marry Kaval Malik, daughter of Sir Teja Singh Malik, who had been chief engineer of the Central Public Works Department during the building of New Delhi and from whom Sir Sobha Singh had received many of his construction contracts. The marriage, which produced a son, Rahul, and a daughter, Mala, lasted until his wife's death from Alzheimer's disease in December 2001 at the age of eighty-five. Soon after his marriage, he took his bride off to Lahore to begin practicing law there. His practice, never prosperous even though he stuck to it for eight years, ended permanently in 1947 when the city of Lahore was awarded to Pakistan, and he was forced to return to Delhi. He entered instead the Indian Foreign Service and was posted as information officer to the Indian High Commission in London. In 1948 he was transferred to a similar post in Ottawa, Canada, from where he returned a year later to London as press attaché.

His first book of short fiction (and first publication of note) appeared while he was still a diplomat. *The Mark of Vishnu and Other Stories* was published by the Saturn Press of London in 1950; it included some stories that had appeared earlier in journals and magazines. Though neither a critical nor a financial success, the collection is in many ways representative of Khushwant Singh's later work in the genre. The settings are Indian, both rural and urban, though some of the protagonists are not, and the themes he pursues are characteristic: the ironies inherent in human behavior that result in comic reversals, the pomposities and ridiculous postures of Anglicized Indians, the conflict between old native ways and learned (but only skin-deep) modern innovations. "The Rape" and "Kusum" are of this kind, as are "Karma," "The Butterfly," and "The Great Difference." The title story, "The Mark of Vishnu," demonstrates in multiple ironies the conflict between the old India of religion and superstition and the Western-educated but uncomprehendingly materialistic India of modern times. Not all of the contents of the volume are properly classifiable as stories. Some are really journalistic essays, such as the personal and whimsical "Posthumous," in which the author imagines himself witnessing the reactions of his friends and relatives to

Title page for Singh's 1956 novel, published in England as Train to Pakistan, *about civil strife in the Punjab following the partition of the subcontinent in August 1947 (University of Kentucky Library)*

the news of his sudden death. "Portrait of a Lady" is a slightly fictionalized account of his memories of the grandmother with whom he had lived as a child in Hadali.

Following the publication of *The Mark of Vishnu,* he resigned his position, since he found diplomatic life uncongenial, and, having sent his family home, he stayed on in England for some time to devote himself to writing some of the books that he published in the next few years. Back in India before the end of 1950, he soon joined the External Service of All India Radio in Delhi as a producer of English programs, where one of his colleagues was Nirad C. Chaudhuri, soon to become well known as the author of *The Autobiography of an Unknown Indian* (1951). Uncongenial as diplomatic life may have been in London and Ottawa, it had allowed Singh time not only to write fiction but also to

I Shall Not Hear The Nightingale

Khushwant Singh

Grove Press, Inc. • *New York*

Title page for Singh's 1959 novel, about a well-to-do landowner in the Punjab whose son is arrested as a nationalist terrorist during Mohandas Karamchand Gandhi's Quit India movement in 1942 (Joyner Library, East Carolina University)

research Sikh history, a subject that has remained one of his abiding interests. His next publication was *The Sikhs* (1953), the first of a succession of books on Sikh history, politics, and religion that he published throughout his career. A year after the publication of this volume he left India once again, for Paris this time, to become a member of the staff at the Department of Mass Communications at UNESCO headquarters, where he remained until 1956.

In 1956 *Train to Pakistan* (published as *Mano Majra* in the United States), the novel for which he is best known, appeared. Having begun it in England, he had entered the manuscript after his return home in a Grove Press competition for fiction from India, where it had won first prize. Though it did not sell well initially, it was critically well received and reviewed favorably, though briefly, in major literary journals in England

and the United States, including the *Times Literary Supplement* (16 August 1956). Since then, it has been translated into several languages and has remained constantly in print, in India as well as abroad.

Set in the Punjab in the period immediately after the partition of the subcontinent in August 1947, *Train to Pakistan* deals with the civil strife that accompanied partition in that province. The novel opens against the backdrop of communal violence in northern India, where Sikh and Hindu communities are pitted against the Muslim community. Both sides blame each other for the violence, but, as the narrator explicitly states, both are equally guilty and equally the victims. The only "remaining oases of peace" amid this carnage are small, remote villages on the frontier. Mano Majra, where the entire action of the novel takes place, is one such tiny village; it is inhabited mainly by Sikh and Muslim peasants who have lived together peacefully for generations. As the novel opens, a robbery is committed in the house of the local moneylender, the only Hindu in the village, and he is murdered. Though carried out by a gang of outsiders, the crime is blamed on Juggut Singh, the most notorious of the villagers, who is in love with a Muslim girl, Nooran, daughter of the imam of the village mosque. The local subinspector of police immediately arrests Juggut Singh on suspicion and, for good measure, also arrests Iqbal, a communist political worker whose religious and political identity cannot be clearly established, even though Iqbal had arrived in Mano Majra only on the morning after the murder. The subinspector reports his actions to Hukum Chand, a debauched magistrate who has been sent to this rural area to oversee law and order, although he spends most of his time with a young Muslim prostitute from a nearby town.

Despite the robbery, nothing happens in the village until a train from Pakistan pulls in at the station carrying the corpses of Hindus and Sikhs massacred on their way to India. This event makes the Muslims and Sikhs of Mano Majra even more suspicious of each other until animosities are laid to rest at a village assembly in the house of the headman, where it is decided that the Muslims must leave the village until it is safe for them to come back. The Muslims, including Nooran and her father, are thereupon evacuated to a refugee camp. The morning after the Muslims' evacuation, the villagers see scores of mutilated human bodies being carried downriver in the monsoon-swollen waters of the river Sutlej, indicating a massacre somewhere upriver in Pakistan. That evening a small, armed group of Sikh strangers come to Mano Majra and browbeat some of the villagers into joining an ambush of a trainload of Muslims the next evening in revenge for massacres of Sikhs in Pakistan. The headman protests feebly that this train will have Mano Majra Muslims on it, but the strangers brush his words aside. Hukum Chand, the magistrate, informed of the rumors of the planned massacre and wishing to prevent it, on a hunch frees both Juggut Singh and Iqbal from jail. On being freed, Iqbal and Juggut react in different ways. A "tense, economical novel, thoroughly true to the events and the people in the story," as William Walsh calls it in *Indian Literature in English, Train to Pakistan* superbly and movingly evokes the horrors of partition and re-creates imaginatively one of the most horrible and blood-stained episodes in the modern history of the subcontinent. It is deservedly described as the best Indian novel in English on partition.

On his return from Paris, Khushwant Singh was once again out of a job but was soon invited to edit *Yojana,* a weekly government journal. He remained in this position until 1958. His second collection of short fiction, *The Voice of God and Other Stories,* was published in India in 1957 while he was editor of *Yojana.* The title story of this collection is a typical Khushwant Singh cameo-narrative, a brief satire on the politics of contemporary India that shows a rural election being won by the richest and most obviously corrupt candidate instead of the poor but sincere man of the people. The title, as the last sentence of the story makes explicit, is a sardonic reference to the Latin tag *vox populi, vox dei* (the voice of the people, the voice of god). Other stories in the volume—for example, "The Fawn," "The Insurance Agent," and "Death Comes to Daulat Ram"—vary in tone, style, and theme. "Man, How the Government of India Run!" details humorously a day in the work-shunning lives of low-paid clerks of the Indian bureaucracy. Another significant publication of this time was a translation of *Jupji: The Sikh Morning Prayer* from the original Gurmukhi form of Punjabi, a work that Singh had begun years earlier in London but which was not published until 1959.

I Shall Not Hear the Nightingale, Singh's second novel, also appeared in 1959. It is set, like *Train to Pakistan,* in the Punjab countryside, but the action takes place between April 1942 and April 1943, some five years before that of the earlier novel. This period covers Mohandas Karamchand Gandhi's tumultuous Quit India movement against the British. The principal event that the narrative turns upon is the arrest of Sher Singh, son of Buta Singh, on suspicion of being a member of a terrorist gang of nationalists that has murdered a village elder who was also a police informer. Buta Singh is a well-to-do landholder who has been made a magistrate by the authorities and honored by them for his unswerving and demonstrative loyalty to the British Raj. The arrest of his son on suspicion of treason and murder is a terrible blow to him personally and, he

fears, to his standing with the government, represented locally by John Taylor, the deputy commissioner of the district. Taylor, out of his regard for Buta Singh, offers Singh's son a pardon, but only if Sher Singh will turn informer and reveal the name of the other members of the terrorist group. The narrative thereafter focuses upon the effect of Sher Singh's imprisonment on the whole family, on Buta Singh himself, and upon Sher's oversexed young wife, Champak, who begins an affair with Madan Lal, Sher's best friend and accomplice. At the center of the novel, however, is Sher Singh's mother, Sabhrai. On Buta Singh's refusal to visit his son in jail and persuade him to accept Taylor's offer, Sabhrai decides to go instead, but she spends a night first in the gurdwara praying for herself and her son and reading the scriptures in hope of guidance. During her visit to the jail, her son asks her what guidance the guru had granted her in her prayers. She answers that the guru had said that her son had done wrong, but if he were to reveal the names of his friends to the police, he would be doing a greater wrong. But Sabhrai, after forcing a moral choice upon her son, falls ill of a fatal sickness. She will not, as she tells Sher Singh before her death—using the lyrical image in which her son had earlier justified all his actions to her—hear the nightingale in an independent India. The novel explores personal relationships within the thematic context of loyalty, faith, and betrayal, but also portrays the morally troublous relationship between the British colonizers and their Indian subjects, somewhat in the manner of E. M. Forster's *A Passage to India* (1924). Though still in print, *I Shall Not Hear the Nightingale* has never been numbered among Khushwant Singh's best fiction, and most critics have declared it a failure. In *Contemporary Novelists,* Warren French, for example, finds it "wooden" and its ironies "heavy-handed." Commentary on the novel, nevertheless, has not failed to notice its redeeming feature: the sensitively drawn character of Sabhrai, who, according to K. R. Srinivasa Iyengar in *Indian Writing in English,* in the moral murkiness of the narrative, shines with "the radiance of Faith" and, according to M. K. Naik in *A History of Indian English Literature,* "wins our respect."

A grant from the Rockefeller Foundation led Singh to his next work, a definitive history of the Sikhs, which drew on his earlier book, *The Sikhs.* Research for this project took him to England, Canada, the United States, Japan, Singapore, Hong Kong, and Burma—all of them countries and regions where Sikhs had settled as immigrants or that had figured in their history. Princeton University Press eventually published the resulting work in 1963 as the first volume of *A History of the Sikhs, 1469–1964.* The same year London publishers Allen and Unwin brought out *Ranjit Singh: Maharajah of the*

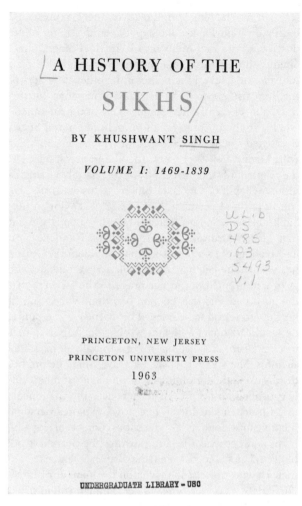

A HISTORY OF THE

SIKHS

BY KHUSHWANT SINGH

VOLUME I: 1469-1839

PRINCETON, NEW JERSEY

PRINCETON UNIVERSITY PRESS

1963

Title page for the first volume of the two-volume history that helped establish Singh's reputation as the preeminent English-language historian of the Sikhs (Thomas Cooper Library, University of South Carolina)

Punjab. Meanwhile, Orient Longman had already published in India two other books on the same subject: *The Sikhs Today: Their Religion, History, Culture, Customs and Way of Life* (1959) and *The Fall of the Kingdom of the Punjab* (1962). Oxford University Press, London, published the second volume of *The History of the Sikhs* in 1966. These books, especially the *History of the Sikhs,* established Singh's reputation as the first Sikh historian in English of his people. These works have remained, to a greater extent than his fiction or his journalism, among the literary achievements of which he is proudest. Though not a particularly religious man (indeed he has gloried in his unorthodoxy and been vilified by extremists among his community for his impious lifestyle), he has regarded them—as the Latin phrase *Opus Exegi* (the work is done) at the end of the second volume of the *History* testifies—as his life's work.

The critical success of these books also brought him temporary academic appointments in the United States. The first of these works took him to the University of Rochester, New York, in 1965. Two years later he accepted an invitation to teach at Princeton University on comparative religion in the department of philosophy. Next, he lectured on Indian religions and contemporary Indian history at the East-West Center of the University of Hawaii. In 1969 he spent another three months at Swarthmore College in Pennsylvania teaching Indian religions and contemporary politics. In between these appointments, his third book of short fiction, *A Bride for the Sahib and Other Stories,* was published in India in 1967.

While he was at Swarthmore in the spring of 1969, Singh was offered the editorship of the Bombay-based magazine *Illustrated Weekly of India.* On his return to India, he accepted the position, even though taking it meant moving to Bombay. The magazine, a colonial-era publication, had once chronicled the life of upper-crust Anglo-India. After independence, under Indian editorship, it had remained a staid, society journal that documented art and culture and had begun to see a falling circulation. During Khushwant Singh's nine-year stewardship, it was transformed into a brash, popular magazine. As he wrote in what was meant to be a valedictory column, the *Illustrated Weekly of India,* once "a four-wheeled victoria taking well-draped ladies out to eat the Indian air," had become under him "a noisy, rumbustious, jet-propelled vehicle of information, controversy and amusement" (*Not a Nice Man to Know: The Best of Khushwant Singh* [1993]). Its older clientele protested the change, but the circulation soared soon from 65,000 to 400,000. An example of the kind of material that he admitted to its pages was "The Bottom Pincher," one of his naughtier stories, which he had originally published in a *London Magazine* short-fiction collection of 1973. Under his editorship the magazine also began championing unpopular causes and highlighted the plight of Indian Muslims, a community that he felt was often wrongly accused of disloyalty to the country, especially at times of conflict and tension with neighboring Muslim Pakistan, such as the war in 1971 over Bangladesh. He also went out of his way to recruit Muslim writers such as novelist Qurrutalain Hyder and journalist M. J. Akbar. His relations with leaders of his own community improved while he was in Bombay. Despite his unorthodoxy and his often-repeated professions of agnosticism, his books on Sikhism and translations of scriptural texts had given him stature among his coreligionists, and he was given assignments to lecture on Sikhism in Europe and East Africa as well as within India itself. In the midst of all this activity, he found time to put together his fourth collection of short stories, *Black Jasmine,* which was published in Bombay in 1971. His rising stature as a man of letters was reflected in the award to him, in 1974, of one of India's highest civilian honors, the Padma Bhushan.

Under his editorship, the *Illustrated Weekly of India* survived the crisis of the state of emergency that was proclaimed in 1975 by Indira Gandhi, the prime minister of the time, when she suspended the constitution, assumed dictatorial powers and put the Indian press, hitherto one of the freest in Asia, under censorship. Though essentially a partisan of Indira Gandhi, Khushwant Singh ceased publication of the magazine for three weeks in protest against censorship before being forced to resume. His actions angered the government, but his good relations with Indira Gandhi were not overtly affected. The crunch for his editorship came, however, after a new government was elected in 1977, with Morarji Desai as prime minister. In the national political confrontations of the next two years Singh continued to support Indira Gandhi and her son Sanjay, even going so far as to publish in 1979 *Indira Gandhi Returns!* a pamphlet predicting her imminent return to power. This publication soured his relations with the current government, as well as the owners of the magazine, and resulted in his dismissal from the *Illustrated Weekly of India* that year and his return to Delhi after almost a decade in Bombay.

The period that he spent in Bombay as editor of the weekly had made him one of India's best-known journalists. His editorials were read throughout the country, giving him the reputation that he still retains, of outspokenness and of a man who had no patience with humbug, prejudice, or prudery in any form. Books by him, too, continued to appear throughout these years. Some of these were collections of his journalism edited by his son and daughter; some were collaborative productions, and others were translations. Among the most prominent of his translations of the period is a rendition into English of the Urdu poet Mohammad Iqbal's long poem *Shikwa and Jawab-I-Shikwa: Complaint and Answer: Iqbal's Dialogue with Allah* (1981). Extracts from the latter were reprinted, and drew praise, even in Pakistan, where Iqbal is revered as the national poet.

Soon after his return to Delhi in 1979 he was offered, through the influence of his Gandhi family connections, the editorship of a small newspaper, *The National Herald.* With the intention of remaining in journalism as long as he could, he accepted this offer as well as, a year later, the editorship of a magazine called *New Delhi.* After the return to power of Indira Gandhi in January 1980, he was nominated to a seat in the Rajya Sabha, Upper House of the Indian Parliament, and was also made editor of *The Hindustan Times,* one of Delhi's largest and most popular newspapers. Unlike his posi-

tion at the *Illustrated Weekly,* however, Singh's editorial independence at *The Hindustan Times* was circumscribed by the tight control maintained over it by its owner, K. K. Birla, a member of the family that runs one of India's biggest corporate groups. Singh's three-year-long editorship of *The Hindustan Times,* therefore, left little personal imprint upon the paper, except for his weekly column titled "With Malice towards One and All," which, like his Editor's Page in the *Illustrated Weekly,* became extremely popular. It continued to run even after he left the *Times* in 1983 and still retains it status as India's most widely read and syndicated English column.

His tenure as a nominated member of parliament, ending in 1986, ran longer than his editorship and through some of the gravest crises in the history of post-Independence India. The Rajya Sabha is little more than a debating chamber–real power is the preserve of the lower house, the Lok Sabha–but its membership is typically divided along party lines. Having been nominated by the new government, Singh was initially a Gandhi partisan, but a little more than two years into his tenure, a militant secessionist movement began in his native Punjab over which he eventually found himself at odds with the government. The armed movement, led by Sant Bhindranwale, a fiercely anti-Indian Sikh cleric, climaxed in June 1984 when the Indian government ordered Operation Blue Star, a military assault on the holiest of Sikh shrines, the Golden Temple at Amritsar, which Bhindranwale had been using as his fortified headquarters. Bhindranwale and most of his followers were killed, and the temple, including its holiest part, the Akal Takht, sustained extensive damage that outraged Sikhs everywhere. Even though he had repeatedly denounced Bhindranwale and the separatist movement and been denounced in turn by the separatists and threatened with death, Singh shared the general Sikh sense of outrage and shock at the army action on the temple; in protest, he immediately and personally returned to the Indian president the Padma Bhushan that he had been awarded ten years before. Henceforward, his speeches in parliament were increasingly critical of Indira Gandhi and her government.

The military action of June 1984, however, led to even more violent and tragic events for the Sikh community and for India. Only a few months later, in October 1984, Indira Gandhi was assassinated in New Delhi by two of her Sikh bodyguards. The event not only plunged the country into a political crisis but also triggered ugly civil riots, in which Hindu mobs, often led by local politicians, targeted Delhi's Sikh community in a display of bloodletting and pillage that left more than two thousand men, women, and children dead. Although Singh shared the terror, pain, and sense of

*Truth, Love and a
Little Malice:
An Autobiography*

KHUSHWANT SINGH

VIKING

in association with

RAVI DAYAL Publisher

*Title page for Singh's 2002 autobiography, which was ready for publication
in 1996 but was held up during litigation brought by Sanjay
Gandhi's widow, whose expulsion from the home of her
mother-in-law, Indira Gandhi, is depicted in the book
(Smith College Library)*

injustice of his community during and after the riots, at the same time he mourned Indira Gandhi's violent and untimely death, despite his recent attempts to distance himself politically from her. His reactions to and reflections on the events of 1984 are scattered throughout his journalism and appear as commentary in some of his later books of fiction as well. *Tragedy of Punjab: Operation Blue Star and After* (1984) deals with the storming of the Golden Temple, while *My Bleeding Punjab* (1992) deals with the continuing strife in that province that did not end until the mid 1990s.

Though he did not publish any significant fiction during the 1980s, taken up as he was with journalism and politics, Singh had not given up the writing of it. His next major work, *Delhi: A Novel,* appeared in 1990, an historical narrative based upon painstaking research.

It had been twenty years in the making, for he had been working on it off and on since his dismissal from the *Illustrated Weekly.* Panoramic and much longer than either of his previous novels, it comes close to being the "vast . . . magnum opus" it was advertised as by his publishers. The protagonist of the main first-person narrative is a middle-aged Sikh journalist, a bachelor man-about-town and reprobate, and the larger part of the novel depicts the life he leads amid the landscape of his native Delhi. Contemporary Delhi, its modern precincts as well as the landmarks of its ancient ruins and monuments, is evoked in sharp detail, as are the different classes of its inhabitants, ranging from the foreign diplomats of New Delhi to the *hijda* (or hermaphrodite) prostitutes of its more disreputable districts, one of which is the protagonist's mistress. Its status as an historical novel rests upon the digressions that interrupt the main narrative to tell the personal stories of a variety of individuals—men and women, fictional and historical, emperors and peasants, saints and sinners—drawn from the most significant periods of Delhi's history between the thirteenth and twentieth centuries. The greater part of the history covered in the inset stories is thus the Muslim and British periods, from the reign of the medieval Sultan Balban to the assassination of Gandhi just after independence.

The attitude, tone, and style of all the different narrators through most of the novel is vintage Singh; the work includes a great deal of irony and much bawdy matter; moreover, no community treated comes off as superior in morals or conduct to any other. The unnamed protagonist of the main narrative is obviously a persona of the author; his love for his *hijda* mistress, Bhagmati, and the bonds that tie him to her, are similar to his love for Delhi. Indeed, the hermaphrodite Bhagmati functions as his metaphor for the city: whore and mistress, neither male nor female, neither Hindu nor Muslim nor Sikh (or, conversely, all of these together at the same time), she is compounded of the same qualities as Delhi itself. The novel, cast in the kind of comic mode made famous by Salman Rushdie in *Midnight's Children* (1981), nevertheless ends darkly with the killing of the protagonist's old Sikh servant, Budh Singh, during the riots that accompanied the assassination of Indira Gandhi in 1984. As the protagonist watches from the windows of his apartment, the young hooligans who kill Budh Singh in the courtyard of a neighboring Gurdwara shout the Sikh battle cry—*Bole So Nihal! Sat Sri Akal!*—in derision over his dead body. The scene suggests that the cycles of violence that made and remade Delhi in the past still have not come to an end.

Between 1990 and 1997, books by Singh, some of them provocatively titled, continued to make the bestseller lists in India. In addition, an award-winning movie version of *Train to Pakistan* appeared in 1997, directed by Pamela Rooks. During this time, Singh translated from Punjabi and Urdu and edited and collaborated with others in the production of a variety of publications while continuing to write his weekly column for *The Hindustan Times*. Among the best-known books of this period are *Sex, Scotch and Scholarship: Selected Writings* (1992), *Uncertain Liaisons: Sex, Strife and Togetherness in Urban India* (edited with Shobha Dé, 1993), the collection *Not a Nice Man to Know: The Best of Khushwant Singh,* and *Women and Men in My Life* (1995). The last named aroused some indignation because of the unflattering portrayal it included of some of Singh's contemporaries and acquaintances. Even more indignation arose when his fourth novel, *The Company of Women,* was published by Viking in 1999. It came close to being proscribed as pornography, and indeed the novel is little more than that. It begins as a third-person narrative of the unhappy marriage and sexual adventures of one Mohun Kumar, but it switches midway to the first person when the protagonist decides that his friend, Khushwant Singh, does not know him well enough to write a novel about him. He therefore takes over the narrative and relates his past, his initiation into sex by one of his classmates at Princeton, his return to India, and his immense success in business and subsequent unfortunate marriage, on the failure of which he conceives the idea of advertising for paid sexual partners who will live with him as his guests. The rest of the novel describes in detail the variety of women he hires and his couplings with them. Ultimately, carrying unsafe sexual practices too far, he contracts AIDS, and, as the narrative reverts to the third person in the end, commits suicide to avoid the inevitable lingering death and shame that the disease brings. *The Company of Women* was a commercial success in India, but many reviewers greeted it with distaste and sometimes amusement.

A more substantial work, *Truth, Love and a Little Malice: An Autobiography* had actually been ready for the press in 1996. Its publication, however, was held up by a court case instituted against it by Maneka Gandhi, widow of Sanjay Gandhi, who objected to certain passages in it that were printed in advance of publication in the magazine *India Today:* they dealt with her expulsion from the home of her mother-in-law, Indira Gandhi, after the two quarreled bitterly. The case dragged on in the courts but was eventually settled in Singh's favor, and the book appeared in 2002 with some revisions that brought it up to date. The autobiography, more than four hundred pages in the hardcover edition, gives an account of Singh's long life (he was eighty-seven when it was published) from his early years in Hadali to the death of his wife in 2001. Inevitably, the account includes lacunas, and though full of intimate descriptions and his customary frank opinions of people, places, and events, it is a little short on dates. Nevertheless, as the reminiscences of one of the most colorful and interesting personalities in Indian letters today, it is both enjoyable reading and an important literary source for critics of his work.

Khushwant Singh's career has spanned more than half a century of continuous writing. Though he has never achieved, as he himself has acknowledged on many occasions, the front rank of Indian writing in English, he has been a presence on the literary scene of his country for most of the post-Independence period of its history—a period that he has chronicled, commented incisively upon, and enlivened in his fiction, journalism, history, translations, and autobiography. Having outlived his older contemporaries, such as R. K. Narayan and N. C. Chaudhuri, he still continues to be what he has often been called, both enfant terrible and Grand Old Man of Indian letters.

References:

Warren French, "Khushwant Singh," in *Contemporary Novelists,* fourth edition, edited by D. L. Kirkpatrick (London & Chicago: St. James Press, 1986);

K. R. Srinivasa Iyengar, *Indian Writing in English* (New Delhi: Sterling, 1962; revised and enlarged, 1985);

M. K. Naik, *A History of Indian English Literature* (Delhi: Sahitya Akademi, 1982);

William Walsh, *Indian Literature in English* (London: Longman, 1990).

Ambalavaner Sivanandan

(1923 -)

Ruvani Ranasinha
Brunel University

BOOKS: *A Different Hunger: Writings on Black Resistance* (London: Pluto, 1982);

Asian and Afro-Caribbean Struggles in Britain (London: Institute of Race Relations, 1986);

Communities of Resistance: Writings on Black Struggles for Socialism (London: Verso, 1990);

Black America: The Street and the Campus (London: Institute of Race Relations, 1993);

When Memory Dies (London: Arcadia, 1997; New Delhi & London: Penguin, 1998);

Race & Class, by Sivanandan and Hazel Waters (2000);

Where the Dance Is: Stories from Two Worlds and Three (London: Arcadia, 2000).

OTHER: "Alien Gods," in *Colour, Culture and Consciousness: Immigrant Intellectuals in Britain,* edited by B. Parckh (London: Allen & Unwin, 1974);

Europe: Variations on a Theme of Racism, edited by Sivanandan (London: Institute of Race Relations, 1991);

The New Conquistadors, edited by Sivanandan and Eqbal Ahmad (London: Institute of Race Relations, 1992);

Liz Fekete and Frances Webber, *Inside Racist Europe,* introduction by Sivanandan (London: Institute of Race Relations, 1994).

SELECTED PERIODICAL PUBLICATIONS– UNCOLLECTED: "White Racism & Black," *Encounter,* 31, no. 1 (1968): 95–96;

Skin: A One-Act Play, Race Today, 4, no. 7 (July 1972);

"The Liberation of the Black Intellectual," *Race and Class,* 18, no. 2 (1977): 329–343;

"Imperialism and Disorganic Development in the Silicon Age," *Race and Class,* 21, no. 2 (1979): 1–26;

"All That Melts into Air Is Solid: The Hokum of New Times," *Race and Class,* 31, no. 3 (1990);

"European Commentary. Racism, the Road from Germany," *Race and Class,* 34, no. 3 (1993): 67–73;

"Race against Time," *New Statesman and Society,* 15 October 1993, p. 16;

Ambalavaner Sivanandan (photograph by Jane Brown; from the cover for Where the Dance Is, *2000; Jean and Alexander Heard Library, Vanderbilt University)*

"La Trahison des clercs," *New Statesman and Society,* 14 July 1995, pp. 20–21;

"Globalism and the Left," *Race and Class,* 40, nos. 2–3 (1998–1999): 5–19.

Since the 1960s, Ambalavaner Sivanandan, a radical left-wing ideologue and activist as well as director of London's Institute of Race Relations (IRR), has exemplified a tradition of critical dissent. He belongs to the first generation of Sri Lanka's Tamil minority displaced from Sri Lanka after the anti-Tamil riots of 1958. He left Sri Lanka because of the hostility against its Tamil citizens but arrived in Britain in the context of heightened racial intolerance exacerbated by postwar immigration, and in the immediate aftermath of the antiblack violence of Notting Hill, London. He describes this move as a "double baptism of fire–Sinhalese-Tamil riots there, white-black riots here." Coming from a minority group in Sri Lanka helps explain Sivanandan's trenchant critiques of racism and his interest in the difficulties that postcolonial societies such as Sri Lanka and multicultural societies such as Britain have in the evolution of pluralistic social formations. Sensitive to the hegemonic, repressive aspects of nationalism, his work questions and instructively problematizes prevailing representations of the dominant majority in both countries and traces shared trends between racism in Britain and communalism in Sri Lanka.

Sivanandan was born in 1923 in a rural area in the northern part of Sri Lanka. His grandfather was a tenant farmer and his father a postmaster. Sivanandan describes how his peasant background gave him a "sense of poverty." Moving to urban Colombo in order to obtain an English education, necessary for social and economic mobility, he experienced in his childhood the contradictions of his world. Although a Hindu, he was educated at a Roman Catholic school, St. Joseph's College. He received a privileged education while living in a slum area of Colombo with an uncle who worked for the railways. Sivanandan analyzes his experience in explicitly class terms. His colonial education, according to *Communities of Resistance: Writings on Black Struggles for Socialism* (1990), enabled him to escape poverty but alienated him from the village life:

> There was a searing gap between me and my contemporaries, which was painful because I wanted so much to belong to the village. And then again there was the other side of me–the one that wanted to belong to Colombo and my English school and my pukka friends. I remember most acutely my sense of betrayal when I disowned my favorite aunt when she came to visit me in school, because she was shabby and unshod, and I made out to my school-friends that she was some sort of family servant.

From 1942 to 1946 he read economics and politics at the University of Ceylon in Colombo in pre-independent Sri Lanka (then Ceylon). He emphasizes in *Communities of Resistance* that at this time his affiliation was with "the progressive, anti-colonial, subaltern aspects of British culture, [and] not [its] dominant aspects." Also in this work, he refers to the left-wing lectures he attended at the University of Ceylon, given by teachers who had studied at the London School of Economics: "They had absorbed some of the British Left traditions [Harold Laski, Maurice Dobb, and Joan Robinson] and became the conduits through which those traditions passed on to us." He recalls the profound influence of "the writings of such people as Hobbes and Locke, Rousseau, Owen and Proudhon and Fourier and finally, Marx." Many of Sivanandan's Sri Lankan lecturers were members of the Lanka Sama Samaja Party (LSSP). The LSSP was one of the three most successful Trotskyite or Internationalist Socialist movements in the world. From its foundation in 1935 until its expulsion from the Fourth International (because it joined a coalition government led by the Sri Lanka Freedom Party) in 1964, it played a decisive role in Sri Lankan politics. It mobilized militant trade unions, strikes, and anticolonial demonstrations and at first fought the contentious "Sinhala Only" state language issue. Before succumbing to communalism, it constituted the main opposition to the postindependence governments.

As a result, he observes in *Communities of Resistance*, "politics was not just what we learnt as part of our degree syllabus but also those activities we took part in outside university hours when we went to public meetings, or attended various LSSP study groups and societies." His political consciousness developed in Sri Lanka during its move toward independence in 1948, the rise of the Left, and then its decline.

Sivanandan's involvement with the LSSP as a student in Sri Lanka explains his involvement with international socialism on his arrival in Britain. It provided a natural context for him to join. In this way he was able to revisit the multicultural progressive political traditions of his own country.

He left the university in 1946 and taught English to children of disadvantaged plantation workers for two years. After he married Bernadette Wijewickrema in 1950, to support his new family and later three children, he became an executive officer at a bank, where he became involved in union politics. When the country was fragmented by communal tensions, he left Sri Lanka in 1958. These intersections of race and class inflect his polemical and creative analyses of his adopted and home countries.

In interviews Sivanandan emphasizes the shock of leaving Sri Lanka and having to start life anew at the age of thirty-five. He made Britain his home as a political exile and threw himself into the cause of the marginalized. When he arrived in England he could find work only as a tea boy in a library in Kingsbury, where he studied library science in the evenings. As a chartered librarian, he joined the Colonial Office Library and

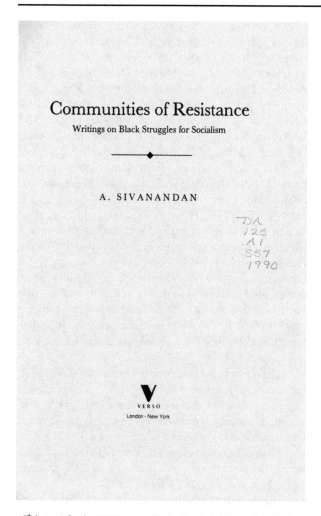

Communities of Resistance
Writings on Black Struggles for Socialism

◆

A. SIVANANDAN

*DA
125
.A1
S57
1990*

V
VERSO
London · New York

*Title page for the 1990 essay collection in which Sivanandan recounts
his impoverished upbringing in Ceylon, now Sri Lanka (Thomas
Cooper Library, University of South Carolina)*

nal with Hazel Waters. Sage Publications publishes the journal quarterly on behalf of the Institute of Race Relations.

Sivanandan has written and lectured extensively on Black British politics and Marxist internationalism, focusing on several countries, including Britain, Sri Lanka, the United States, and South Africa. Sivanandan's polemics are collected in two volumes of essays, *A Different Hunger: Writings on Black Resistance* (1982) and *Communities of Resistance*. These influential collections historicize the black communities of Britain and document their campaigns against racism. In them he has produced a provocative critique of the ways in which the dominant structures of the host society oppress and undermine the emancipatory struggles of black socialist politics, basing his criticism upon his view of institutionalized racism and domestic neocolonialism. He has long maintained that racial oppression cannot be dissociated from class exploitation, thus developing a link already forged by C. L. R. James and W. E. B. Du Bois.

Working in the tradition of the anticolonialist socialism of Frantz Fanon and within the contexts of the antiracist socialist and Black Nationalist movements of Britain and the United States in the 1960s and 1970s, he showed his determination to fight against the injustice, disempowerment, and racism experienced by the working-class black communities of Britain. Sivanandan initiated a series of IRR research pamphlets and antiracist educational publications, and supported not only a range of black self-help movements, such as Black Unity and Freedom Party, but also projects documenting black deaths in police custody. With Sivanandan at the helm, the IRR became identified as a radical black political institution. From the start he demanded equality, seeking neither acceptance nor approval from the host community.

Sivanandan's outspoken personality and commitment inspired generations of antiracist socialists, as the many contributions to the special *Race & Class* (2000) issue in his honor bear witness. His negotiation of his identity is played out in terms of an international socialism, not aligned to any particular racial identity or geographical location. He situates himself within a larger social struggle. He draws on Marxism as a way of interpreting the world in order to change it. His self-representation is assertively third-worldist, rather than Sri Lankan. His particular focus on the ways in which the exploitation of minorities and immigrants is linked to the global economy has influenced a range of activists worldwide.

Sivanandan's immersion in working-class politics in Sri Lanka and Britain, which inform his fictional narrative, sets him apart from many writers. Consumed by activism for many decades, he turned to fiction late in

finally the Institute of Race Relations in London in 1964, then directed by Philip Mason. Sivanandan's family followed him to the United Kingdom, although he and Bernadette divorced in 1968. Their three children remained with him. In 1970 Sivanandan married fellow activist Jenny Bourne.

In 1972 a staff-led rebellion transformed the IRR. Previously a forum aimed at exploiting third-world resources, it became the first antiracist, antiimperialist think tank in Britain. In 1972 he became the new director of the institute and reoriented the IRR toward black militancy. He re-launched the institute's journal, *Race,* as *Race and Class: A Journal for Black and Third World Liberation* in 1974 to reflect its new emphasis on issues of racism, the legacies of imperialism, and the organization's wider, sustained commitment to supporting third-world socialist struggles worldwide. Sivanandan edits this long-running, international multidisciplinary jour-

his life. He published his first novel toward the end of his career, renegotiating the relationship between aesthetics and politics—perhaps to reinstate the importance of the native subject and decolonizing narratives. Recalling fragments of the history of his country for more than fifteen years, he published his first compelling, disturbing part novel part memoir, *When Memory Dies,* in 1997. After forty years of antiracist activism in Britain he wrote this first novel, according to an interview with the author, as an attempt to "make a contribution to my own country."

This self-consciously collective history of Tamils in Sri Lanka tells the story of three generations of a Jaffna Tamil family in three sections: the first is about Sahadevan (the second son of a postal worker from a "bone-dry village in the north of Ceylon," who, like Sivanandan, was sent at a young age to Colombo to live with a relative and attend a Catholic school); the second is about his son, Rajan, the narrator; and the third is about Rajan's adopted Sinhalese son, Vijay. This trigenerational structure is partly designed to rewrite the past and counter colonial and neocolonial interpretations. The title of the novel and the dialogue between the generations signal the enterprise of historical reclamation dramatized through the contrasting perspectives of a range of characters. For instance, Sahadevan's anticolonial education begins with meeting Sinhalese railwayman and union militant S. W. and his wife, Prema. In *When Memory Dies,* S. W. foregrounds the importance of recovering and reclaiming histories to counter British versions: "There were rebellions going on all the time. . . . But your history books wouldn't tell you that, would they? After all, they are written by the English. Soon no one will know the history of our country." But Sivanandan's main concern is with the continued rewriting of the nation's past by Sinhala and Tamil nationalists. The emphasis of the novel on interethnic friendship, class solidarity, and intermarriage suggests that the two communities are not inevitably mutually incompatible, antagonistic, and hostile. This position is articulated in Rajan's reflections from exile in England: he left Sri Lanka after his Sinhalese wife, Lali, mistaken for a Tamil, was raped and killed by Sinhalese thugs during the anti-Tamil pogrom. His expression of past amity is poignant in view of the juxtaposition of present violent atrocities:

> I thought I lived in a world where there was no communal hatred or conflict, where we didn't kill each other just because we spoke different languages. It is not even that we had so much in common, Sinhalese and Tamils, Buddhists and Hindus, or that we derived from the same racial branch of the tree of man. We were one people. We sang each other's songs as our own, ate each other's food, talked each other's talk,

Paperback cover for the British edition of Sivanandan's autobiographical 1997 novel, about three generations of a Tamil family and their experiences with ethnic and political strife in Ceylon (Richland County Public Library)

worshipped each other's Gods. Even when we lived our particular lives, they always touched on those around us, and theirs on ours.

This re-creation of past peaceful culturally different coexistence is an important part of the argument of the book—to counter representations (especially in the Western press) of the current crisis as endemic or as an "ethnic" or "religious" war between Hindus and Buddhists. It shifts the debate from intrinsic differences to wider questions of power sharing and social relations.

This incident also points to a weakness in the text. Gender issues, such as sectarian rape, are raised as part of his political project. Sivanandan's emphasis is less upon that communal violence is fought on the site of women's bodies and more on the impact of the rape on the deceased rape victim's husband. Lali fulfils her function and then cannot be accommodated in the nar-

Front cover for Sivanandan's collection of short stories (2000) about the dislocation and loss experienced by English and Sri Lankan characters from varied backgrounds (Jean and Alexander Heard Library, Vanderbilt University)

rative. Sivanandan's concern is not female interiority, subjectivity, agency, or the questioning of prescribed gender roles. Even his assertive, independent female characters–such as Mrs. Bandara, Meena, and Manel–are not the subjects of his novel, but remain in and constitute its background, frequently described in erotic terms and functioning as exotic backdrop.

When Memory Dies foregrounds not feminist but native politics and working-class self-organization and resistance to British rule in the 1920s, in the form of uprisings and mutinies, rather than the elite's contribution to the nationalist struggle. S. W. reminds Sahadevan of the sacrifices made by the strike leaders and the ordinary people "who suffered a lot of hardship in helping the strikers. It is their sacrifices that made things better for the rest of us."

The novel charts the various forms of resistance adopted by the Left and then dramatizes how Sri Lanka's revolutionary Left became fissured by com-

munal interests, and ends with the institutionalizing of Sinhala Buddhist hegemony and the beginning of separatist violence in the early 1980s. The failures of Sri Lanka's Left are voiced through the critical perspective of Dr. Lal. On the Sri Lanka Freedom Party's "Sinhala Only" Language Act of 1956, he comments that " . . . socialism is dead . . . we'll no longer be fighting injustice but each other." He observes that his old party's talk of "working class unity is sullied with communalism." He goes on to prophesy that "this combination of religion and race will finish class politics forever." The emphasis on the oppressions faced by Sri Lanka's Tamil minority gives Sivanandan's work contemporary relevance and urgency.

Sivanandan's broadly realist novel shows a commitment to naturalism; at the same time, his novel, recounted by Rajan from London, makes thematic the writing and the fictionalizing of history. While the style of this novel is not Salman Rushdie's magic realism, it presents the theme of the recuperation of history as a method of fictionalizing experience, subject to the selective truth and inevitable distortions of personal memory. Such poststructural conceptions of history suggest Sivanandan's text shares an interesting intertextual relationship with the younger writer Rushdie's influential *Midnight's Children* (1981). This suggestion is particularly significant because, in other ways, Sivanandan and Rushdie can be seen as products of a generational divide in British intellectual culture between traditional Marxism and postmodernism. Sivanandan's moving and sensitive work was well received in both Britain and Sri Lanka and was awarded the Commonwealth Writers First Book Award (Eurasia region) in 1998 and the Sagittarius Prize in 1999. In 2005 he received the arts honor of Kala Keerchi from the president of Sri Lanka for the novel.

His subsequent collection of short stories, *Where the Dance Is: Stories from Two Worlds and Three* (2000), further explores the themes of loss and dislocation that he had treated in *When Memory Dies*. These stories, written over a period of time, unveil the frailties and susceptibilities of a cross section of characters ranging from a psychiatric patient in an asylum in Sri Lanka to an actress in Hampstead. Although the English and Sri Lankan characters that people Sivanandan's narratives are differentiated in terms of race and class, these vignettes are animated by the drama of universal human passions and personal relationships.

Sivanandan's emphasis on the interconnection of race and class constituted a major step toward a revision of leftist politics in Britain. His focus on the dangers of privileging race over class is perhaps overdetermined by his being a victim of a Sri Lankan political crisis in which issues of race undermined class solidarity. In Britain in the 1980s, Sivanandan particularly condemned the move away from class politics and the breakdown of class alliances between Asian and African and Caribbean communities that, according to *Communities of Resistance,* fragmented "community into classes." In "Fighting our Fundamentalisms" he suggests that "multiculturalism and subsequently ethnicism have fragmented Black politics" and "negated Black political culture."

A close reading of *When Memory Dies* reveals that Ambalavaner Sivanandan's theoretical articulations of the relations between race and class in Britain are embodied in his fictional treatment of their dynamics in Sri Lanka and provide him with analogies for analyzing the stratification of power in his novel on Sri Lanka. His perceptions of the race and class dynamics in Sri Lanka both feed into and are reinforced by his immersion in black British socialist politics.

Interviews:

Quintin Hoare and Malcom Imrie, "The Heart is Where the Battle Is: An Interview with the Author," in *Communities of Resistance: Writings on Black Struggles for Socialism* (London: Verso, 1990), pp. 1–16;

CARF, "Fighting our Fundamentalisms: An Interview with A. Sivanandan," *Race and Class,* 36, no. 3 (1995): 73–81;

Kwesi Owusu, "The Struggle for Radical Black Culture," in *Black British Culture,* edited by Owusu (London: Routledge, 1999), pp. 416–424;

Ruvani Ranasinha, Personal interview with Ambalavaner Sivanandan, 12 April 1999.

References:

Colin Prescod and Hazel Waters, eds., *A World to Win: Essays in Honour of Sivanandan, Race and Class,* 41, nos. 1–2 (1999);

Regi Siriwardena, "When Memory Dies," *Nethra,* 1, no. 2 (1997): 74–81.

Rabindranath Tagore

(7 May 1861 – 7 August 1941)

Fakrul Alam
University of Dhaka

SELECTED BOOKS IN ENGLISH: *Gitanjali (Song Offerings),* introduction by William Butler Yeats (London: Printed at the Chiswick Press for the India Society, 1912; Boston: International Pocket Library, 1912; London: Macmillan, 1913);

Glimpses of Bengal Life: Being Short Stories from the Bengali of Rabindranath Tagore, translated by Rajani Ranjan Sen (Madras: G. A. Natesan, 1913);

The Gardener (London: Macmillan, 1913; New York: Macmillan, 1913);

Sadhana: The Realisation of Life (London: Macmillan, 1913; New York: Macmillan, 1913; Calcutta: Macmillan, 1920);

The Crescent Moon: Child-Poems (London: Macmillan, 1913; New York: Macmillan, 1913);

Chitra: A Play in One Act (London: India Society, 1913; London: Macmillan, 1914; New York: Macmillan, 1914);

The King of the Dark Chamber (London: Macmillan, 1914; New York: Macmillan, 1914);

The Post Office: A Play, translated by Devabrata Mukerjea, preface by Yeats (Churchtown, Ireland: Cuala Press, 1914; London: Macmillan, 1914; New York: Macmillan, 1914);

Fruit-Gathering (London: Macmillan, 1916; New York: Macmillan, 1916; Calcutta: Macmillan of India, 1916);

The Hungry Stones and Other Stories, translated by Tagore, C. F. Andrews, Edward J. Thompson, Panna Lal Basu, Prabhat Kumar Mukerji, and the Sister Nivedita (London: Macmillan, 1916; New York: Macmillan, 1916);

Stray Birds (New York & Toronto: Macmillan, 1916; London: Macmillan, 1917);

My Reminiscences, translated by Surendranath Tagore (New York: Macmillan, 1917); republished as *Reminiscences* (London: Macmillan, 1917);

Sacrifice and Other Plays (London: Macmillan, 1917; New York: Macmillan, 1917);

Rabindranath Tagore (Library of Congress)

The Cycle of Spring, translated by Andrews and Nishikanta Sen, translation revised by Tagore (London: Macmillan, 1917; New York: Macmillan, 1917);

Nationalism (London: Macmillan, 1917; New York: Macmillan, 1917);

Personality: Lectures Delivered in America (London: Macmillan, 1917; New York: Macmillan, 1917);

Lover's Gift and Crossing (London: Macmillan, 1918; New York: Macmillan, 1918);

Mashi and Other Stories, translated by various writers (London: Macmillan, 1918; New York: Macmillan, 1918);

Stories from Tagore (New York: Macmillan, 1918; Calcutta: Macmillan, 1945);

The Parrot's Training, translated by Tagore (Calcutta: Simla, Thacker, Spink, 1918); translated by Debjani Chatterjee (London: Tagore Centre U.K., 1993);

The Home and the World, translated by Surendranath Tagore, translation revised by Rabindranath Tagore (London: Macmillan, 1919; New York: Macmillan, 1919);

The Fugitive (London: Macmillan, 1921; New York: Macmillan, 1921);

Greater India (Madras: S. Ganesan, 1921);

The Wreck (London: Macmillan, 1921; London: Macmillan, 1921);

Thought Relics (New York: Macmillan, 1921); enlarged as *Thoughts from Tagore* (London: Macmillan, 1929);

Creative Unity (London: Macmillan, 1922; New York: Macmillan, 1922);

Poems from Tagore, edited by C. F. Andrews (Calcutta: Macmillan, 1923);

The Curse at Farewell, translated by Thompson (London: Harrap, 1924);

Gora, translated by Tagore, translation revised by Surendranath Tagore (London: Macmillan, 1924; Madras: Macmillan of India, 1968);

Talks in China: Lectures Delivered in April and May, 1924 (Calcutta: Visva-Bharati Book-Shop, 1925);

Red Oleanders: A Drama in One Act (London: Macmillan, 1925; Madras: Macmillan India, 1961);

Broken Ties and Other Stories (London: Macmillan, 1925);

Lectures and Addresses, edited by Anthony X. Soares (London: Macmillan, 1928; Calcutta: Macmillan India, 1970);

Fireflies (New York: Macmillan, 1928);

The Tagore Birthday Book: Selected from the English Works of Rabindranath Tagore, edited by Andrews (London: Macmillan, 1928; New Delhi: Rupa, 2002);

The Religion of Man: Being the Hibbert Lectures for 1930 (London: Allen & Unwin, 1931);

The Child (London: Allen & Unwin, 1931);

The Golden Boat, translated by Bhabani Bhattacharya (London: Allen & Unwin, 1932; Bombay: Jaico, 1955);

Mahatmaji & the Depressed Humanity (Calcutta: Visva-Bharati Bookshop, 1932);

Crisis in Civilization: A Message on Completing His Eighty Years, translated by Kshitis Roy and Krishna R. Kripalini (Santiniketan: Santiniketan Press, 1941);

Four Chapters, translated by Surendranath Tagore from Rabindranath Tagore's novel *Char adhyaya* (Calcutta: Visva-Bharati, 1950);

Binodini: A Novel, translated by Kripalani from Tagore's novel *Chokher bali* (New Delhi: Sahitya Akademi, 1959; revised edition, New Delhi: Sahitya Akademi, 1968);

Wings of Death: The Last Poems of Rabindranath Tagore, translated by Aurobindo Bose (London: Murray, 1960).

Editions and Collections: *Collected Poems and Plays of Rabindranath Tagore,* edited by Amiya Chakravarty, C. F. Andrews, and Ernest Rhys (London: Macmillan, 1936; New York: Macmillan, 1937);

A Tagore Reader, edited by Amiya Chakravarty (New York: Macmillan / Boston: Beacon, 1953; London: Macmillan, 1961);

Towards Universal Man (Bombay & New York: Asia Publishing House, 1961; London: Asia Publishing House, 1961);

The Housewarming and Other Selected Writings, translated by Chakravarty, Mary Lago, and Tarun Gupta, edited by Chakravarty (New York: American Library, 1965);

Selected Poems, translated by William Radice (Harmondsworth, U.K.: Penguin / New York: Viking Penguin, 1985; revised, 1987);

I Won't Let You Go: Selected Poems, translated by Ketaki Kushari Dyson (Newcastle upon Tyne, U.K.: Bloodaxe, 1991; New Delhi: UBS Publishers' Distributors, 1992);

Selected Short Stories, translated by Lago and Krishna Dutta (London: Macmillan, 1991; Calcutta: Rupa, 1991);

Selected Short Stories, translated by Radice (London & New York: Penguin, 1991; revised, 1994);

Nationalism, introduction by E. P. Thompson (Calcutta: Rupa, 1992);

Quartet, translated by Kaiser Haq (Oxford, U.K.: Heinemann, 1993);

The English Writings of Rabindranath Tagore, 3 volumes, edited by Sisir Kumar Das (New Delhi: Sahitya Akademi, 1994–1996);

The Post Office, translated by Dutta and Andrew Robinson (New York: St. Martin's Press, 1996);

The Post Office, translated by Radice, set as a play within a play by Jill Parvin (London: Tagore Centre U.K., 1996);

Rabindranath Tagore: An Anthology, edited by Dutta and Robinson (London: Picador, 1997);

Particles, Jottings, Sparks: The Collected Brief Poems of Rabindranath Tagore, translated by Radice (New Delhi: HarperCollins, 2000; London: Angel, 2001);

Selected Short Stories, edited by Sukanta Chaudhuri, Sankha Ghosh, and Tapobrata Ghosh (New Delhi & Oxford: Oxford University Press, 2001);

Selected Writings on Literature and Language, edited by Chaudhuri, Das, and Sankha Ghosh (New Delhi & New York: Oxford University Press, 2001);

Final Poems, edited and translated by Wendy Barker and Saranindanath Tagore (New York: Braziller, 2001);

Selected Writings for Children, edited by Chaudhuri and Sankha Ghosh (New Delhi & New York: Oxford University Press, 2002; Oxford: Oxford University Press, 2002);

Show Yourself to My Soul: A New Translation of Gitanjali, translated by Brother James (James Talarovic) (Notre Dame, Ind.: Sorrin, 2002);

Selected Poems, edited by Chaudhuri and Sankha Ghosh (New Delhi & Oxford: Oxford University Press, 2004).

PLAY PRODUCTION: *The Post Office,* translated by Devabrata Mukhopaddya, Dublin, Abbey Theatre, 1913.

OTHER: Ratan Devi and Ananda Coomaraswamy, eds., *Thirty Songs from the Panjab and Kashmir,* foreword by Tagore (London: The Authors, 1913);

Kabir, *One Hundred Poems of Kabir,* translated by Tagore and Evelyn Underhill (London: India Society, 1914); republished as *Songs of Kabir* (New York: Macmillan, 1915).

Rabindranath Tagore did not write primarily in English but in Bengali; nevertheless, his English writings are voluminous. They consist mostly of the many speeches and lectures that he delivered in English and of his translations of his own poems and plays, but in the West his translations of his works were long viewed as original compositions. Tagore's claim to a preeminent position as a South Asian writer in English was assured when he received the Nobel Prize in literature in 1913 for his collection of prose poems, *Gitanjali (Song Offerings)* (1912), which was published in England with an introduction by the poet William Butler Yeats. But when that volume appeared, Tagore was fifty-two years old and had been publishing poetry in Bengali since adolescence; his fame as a Bengali writer had resulted in the call for a representative English selection of his work. Near the end of his career, in 1936, *Collected Poems and Plays of Rabindranath Tagore* was published; for many years afterward it was the best-known English-language book by an Indian writer available in the West. Since nowhere in this volume is there any indication that it consists almost entirely of translated works, Tagore's reputation as an Indian writing in English persisted.

Tagore was born in Calcutta (known since 2001 as Kolkata) on 7 May 1861, the fourteenth of fifteen children of the philosopher, religious reformer, landowner, and businessman Devendranath Tagore and Sarada Devi Tagore. His grandfather, Dwarkanath Tagore, a wealthy businessman and flamboyant personality who had led the movement for reform and modernization in Bengal and was an early advocate of English education in India, had sent Tagore's father to the Anglo-Hindu school run by the reformer Raja Rammohan Roy and to Hindu College, an institution set up by the British in 1817. That both Dwarkanath Tagore and Roy died in England indicates the close connection between leading Bengali reformers of the time and Britain, which the reformers saw not only as a colonizing power but also as a source of Enlightenment values. Devendranath Tagore remained in Bengal, where he revived his father's business and nurtured the reformist Brahmo Samaj (Theistic Church) sect founded by Roy.

Rabindranath Tagore was, thus, born into a family that was prominent in Calcutta not only because of its wealth but also because of its cultural and spiritual affiliations. Their home in Jorasanko, north of Calcutta, was a center of musical, literary, and theatrical events. Tagore's mind was formed by that rich cultural atmosphere and by his own reading, rather than by the various schools to which he was sent; he felt constricted by their teaching methods and preferred to study with family members and private tutors. Unlike some other leading Bengali authors, who tried to write in English before deciding that they could express themselves adequately only in their mother tongue, Tagore published his first poem in Bengali when he was thirteen; his first collection of poems in the language came out in 1878.

Tagore's father sent him to England in September 1878 to get an education that would prepare him for an administrative post in the Indian Civil Service. He began his studies at a school in Brighton and continued them at University College London but abandoned them and returned to India in February 1880. The songs and poems he wrote on his return show that he had absorbed Western musical styles, as well as the works of the English Romantics and eminent Victorian poets and dramatists. His poems and plays creatively mingled Eastern and Western traditions to strike a new note in Bengali literature. In 1882 he and his brother Jyotirindranath helped establish Sarasvat Samaj, a kind of academy of Bengali letters, which became Bangiya Sahitya Parishat ten years later. On 9 December 1883 he married ten-year-old Mrinalini Devi. The couple had a daughter, Madhurilata (also known as Bela); a son, Rathindranath; a daughter, Renuka; another daughter,

Mira; and a second son, Samindranath. In 1884 Tagore became the secretary of Adi Brahmo Samaj, a religious society.

During the next two decades Tagore consolidated his reputation as a Bengali man of letters. In addition to poems, he wrote songs, short stories, plays, essays, and literary criticism. Constantly reinventing himself artistically and introducing new genres and styles to Bengali literature, he began as a late-Romantic aesthete and soon turned to social and political criticism in realistic verse and then to meditative religious poetry. He is widely acknowledged as one of the founders of the modern Bengali language.

In 1890 Tagore spent a few months in England, returning home to become active in nationalist and anti-British agitation and religious reform. That same year his father turned over to him the management of family estates in eastern Bengal (today Bangladesh), a responsibility that he took seriously and discharged efficiently. In 1891 he founded the literary journal *Sadhana,* and in 1894 he became vice president of the Academy of Bengali Letters. Between 1895 and 1902 he cofounded several businesses in Calcutta and Kushtia. On 22 December 1901 he started an experimental school at Santiniketan in a remote area of Bengal; later he set up a weaving school at Kushtia and an agricultural cooperative bank at Patisar. His wife died on 23 November 1902, his daughter Renuka in September 1903, and his father on 19 January 1905. His son Samindranath died of cholera in November 1907.

A public reception in Calcutta on 12 January 1912 confirmed Tagore's standing as a leading Bengali writer. Up to this time he had not done any work in English, but some of his Indian admirers who lived in England had translated his short fiction and verse and had extolled their virtues in a bid to introduce his achievement to the West. The British art critic Ananda Coomaraswamy, who had been born in Ceylon (today Sri Lanka), had also translated a handful of Tagore's poems in the *Modern Review.* Many Europeans at the time were becoming interested in the mystical traditions of the East, and Tagore received letters from some Bengali admirers in England, inviting him to meet the English literati and acquaint them with his work. He booked passage for London on a ship that was departing in March 1912; but the day before he was to leave Calcutta, he fell ill and was forced to postpone his trip. While convalescing in Shelidah, he translated some of his poems into English prose so that he could circulate them in England. He sailed for England in June, continuing to work on his translations en route. When he reached London, he had completed a collection of 103 prose poems. The painter William Rothenstein, a friend of the Tagore family, sent a copy of the manu-

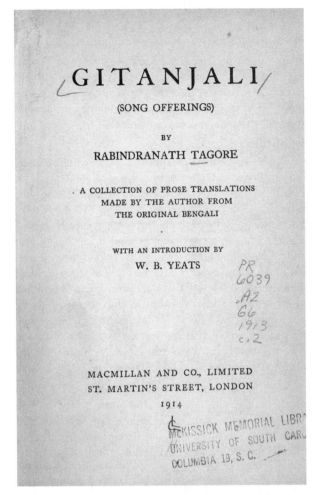

Title page for Tagore's first book in English, originally published in a limited edition in 1913 (Thomas Cooper Library, University of South Carolina)

script to Yeats. Tagore read the pieces at a literary evening at Rothenstein's home on 30 June; among the writers who attended were Yeats, Ernest Rhys, and Ezra Pound. The reading was a great success and was followed by other readings and receptions.

In October 1912 Tagore sailed for the United States to visit his son, who was graduating from the University of Illinois. In November the India Society of London published a limited edition of his collection of translations as *Gitanjali (Song Offerings),* with a pencil sketch of the author by Rothenstein and an introduction in which Yeats recorded that the poems had "moved" him so much that he obsessively carried them everywhere, stirred by their lyrical beauty and spirit. The poems are devotional songs addressed to God; though mystical, they make abundant use of imagery from nature. Even in the English prose versions the poems strike a meditative note and have a haunting, melodic tone. The qualities that endeared the collection to Western readers are summed up by the comments of the Swedish poet Verner von Heidenstam, who played a key role in the Nobel Committee's choice of Tagore for the 1913 prize in literature: "The intense and loving piety that permeates his every thought and feeling, the purity of heart, the noble and natural sublimity of his style, all combine to create a whole that has a deep and rare spiritual beauty."

The 750 copies of the India Society edition sold out quickly, and Rothenstein persuaded the Macmillan firm to publish the book under its imprint. Reviewing the volume in the *Fortnightly Review* in October 1912, Pound said that he found in the poems "pure Hellenic" phrases, "poetic pieties" that reminded him of Dante, and a "sense of a saner stillness" that came from nature itself. An anonymous reviewer for *The Times Literary Supplement* (*TLS*) wrote that the poems had a "harmony of emotion and idea" lacking in contemporary European writing and added: "That divorce of religion and philosophy which prevails among us is a sign of our failure in both. . . . As we read his pieces we seem to be reading the psalms of a David in our time."

Pound persuaded Harriet Monroe to publish six of the poems in the American journal *Poetry,* and Tagore visited Monroe in Chicago in January 1913. He lectured on metaphysics at the Unity Club in Urbana, Illinois; on ancient Indian civilization at the University of Chicago; and on the problem of evil at the Unitarian Hall in Chicago. He also gave lectures at the Philosophical Club and the Divinity Club at Harvard University. He returned to England in April and to India in October. In the latter month a second volume of his verse, *The Gardener,* was published in England. Dedicated to Yeats, it consists of prose translations of eighty-five poems Tagore had written over a period of several years. They are not as religious in tone as the poems in *Gitanjali* but are more concerned with romantic love and other human emotions. Tagore abridged and even paraphrased the original poems in the process of rendering them in English. Reviews of the volume were mixed.

Sadhana: The Realisation of Life, a collection of eight lectures Tagore had given in the United States between October 1912 and April 1913, was published by Macmillan in London in October 1913. Dealing with issues such as the relation of the individual to the universe, the problem of evil, and the revelation of the infinite, they embody the philosophy underlying the *Gitanjali* poems; perhaps for this reason, they were received enthusiastically. They thus contributed to Tagore's image in the West as a prophet and mystic who combined love of God with a belief in the essential divinity of humanity. Among the most popular of Tagore's English works, *Sadhana* was reprinted eight times in England within a year of its original publication.

The success of *Gitanjali* and the consequent demand for his works in English led Tagore to bring out *The Crescent Moon: Child-Poems* in November 1913. Most of the forty poems in this collection deal with childhood as seen from a variety of angles. But the speed with which the poems were rendered into English led the anonymous reviewer for *TLS* to describe the poems as "more childish than childlike," although the reviewer for *The Nation* (30 November 1916) saw in the book "a vision of childhood which is only paralleled in our literature by the work of William Blake."

Tagore published one other book in English in 1913: *Chitra: A Play in One Act*, translated from a Bengali play that he had written many years earlier. But as was increasingly the case with his verse translations, the English work is a truncated form of the Bengali version, which is a delightful lyrical celebration of spring based on a story from the Indian epic *The Mahabharata.* Responses to the English work were muted, and *Chitra* did not add to Tagore's reputation in the West.

Tagore was at his school in Santiniketan when he learned on 14 November 1913 that he had been awarded the Nobel Prize in literature for that year; he was the thirteenth writer, and the first Asian, to receive the honor. The award transformed his life: demand for his works in English increased substantially, and he became the center of attention wherever he went; he acquired almost mythical status both in India and in the West and drew attention to Indian writing in English in a way that was unprecedented.

A consequence of the demand for Tagore's work fueled by the Nobel Prize was the publication in 1916 of *Fruit-Gathering,* a collection of poems that he had translated from a recent volume of his Bengali verse. One of the poems, "The Trumpet," had been published in *The Times* of London on 26 November 1914 with a headnote that indicates that Tagore's verse was still appreciated in England:

> The author of this poem, Mr. Rabindranath Tagore, is the famous Indian poet, whose lyrics, plays and essays have brought in recent years a new delight to lovers of English literature. Mr. Tagore, who is personally not unknown in the country, himself translates many of his works from the original into English; and his command of our language has done much to make the West acquainted with the finest Indian thought.

Like *Gitanjali, Fruit-Gathering* is essentially religious in orientation, although it also includes some narrative poems about historical figures and some long philosophical poems. The English versions, however, fail to retain the sublimity of the spiritual verse or the distinctive qualities of the narrative and meditative poems in Bengali.

Nevertheless, Tagore's international reputation was still on the rise. On 3 June 1915 he was knighted by the British government, and in May 1916 he undertook his fourth foreign trip in response to invitations to give readings and lectures in Japan, Canada, and the United States. Biographer Krishna R. Kripalani suggests that the idea for his next book in English, *Stray Birds* (1916), a collection of epigrams and short verses, came from the many occasions on the trip when women asked him to write a few lines in autograph books or on fans. Many of these pieces, some of which may have been influenced by Japanese haiku, seem to have been written in English and can, therefore, be seen as original works in the language.

On the Japanese portion of the trip Tagore spoke out against the aggressive nationalism he saw in the country. In lectures such as "The Nation" and "The Spirit of Japan" he criticized Japanese expansionist policies and warned against blind imitation of Western imperialism, reminding his audiences in the latter talk that "True Modernism is freedom of mind, not slavery of taste. It is independence of thought and action, not tutelage under European schoolmasters." In Seattle in September 1916 Tagore continued to critique what he saw as a disturbing worldwide phenomenon in the lecture "The Cult of Nationalism." He also spoke out on the evils of materialism.

The lectures Tagore gave on his 1916 tour were collected in two books in 1917. *Nationalism* is based on lectures he gave in Japan and in the United States and is dedicated to C. F. Andrews, an English missionary who was one of his closest associates at his school in Santiniketan. While Tagore's criticism of the virulent nationalism he had witnessed in Japan and America was widely denounced in those countries at the time, *Nationalism* has proved to be one of his most enduring works in English and is still cited in discussions of the subject. The English historian E. P. Thompson observes in his introduction to a 1992 edition of the work that the lectures, written in the shadow of World War I, link nationalism with "the self-destructive tendency of the organized modern nation." In their biography, *Rabindranath Tagore: The Myriad-Minded Man* (2000), Krishna Dutta and Andrew Robinson describe the book as an "indictment of power politics and commercialism." The other book published in 1917, *Personality: Lectures Delivered in America,* is also dedicated to Andrews. It is a collection of six of the lectures he gave on his American tour: "What Is Art," "The World of Personality," "The Second Birth," "My School," "Meditation," and "Women."

Cover for the U.S. edition of Tagore's translations of his poems about childhood, published in 1913 (Thomas Cooper Library, University of South Carolina)

In 1918 Tagore published *Lover's Gift and Crossing,* a volume of religious poems in English based on poems and songs he had written in Bengali over the last few years. The translations continue to deteriorate in quality; some are no more than partial English paraphrases of the originals. The volume did not attract a great deal of attention.

In December 1918 Tagore laid the cornerstone for Visva-Bharati, a university that replaced his school in Santiniketan. He conceived Visva-Bharati as an "international center of humanistic studies" where scholars and artists from all over the world could meet, do research, teach, and create. The institution also had a practical side, as evidenced by the Departments of Village Reconstruction and Rural Development. Leonard Elmhirst, a young Englishman who had a degree in agriculture from Cornell University, became an important associate in this venture. In 1919 Tagore founded the literary journal *Santiniketan Patra,* which began publication in April.

On 13 April 1919 British troops killed nearly four hundred Indians and wounded more than a thousand

Frontispiece and title page for the U.S. edition of a collection of poems that Tagore translated from a recent volume of his Bengali verse
(Thomas Cooper Library, University of South Carolina)

at Jallianwalah Bagh in the Punjab in what became known as the Amritsar Massacre. In response, Tagore resigned his knighthood on 30 May in a letter to the viceroy of India. One of the most famous letters in Indian English prose, it testifies to the eloquence of which he was capable in English: "The time has come when badges of honor make our shame glaring in the incongruous context of humiliation, and I for my part wish to stand, shorn of all special distinctions, by the side of those of my countrymen who for their so-called insignificance are liable to suffer a degradation not fit for human beings." At the same time, Tagore spoke out against Mohandas Karamchand Gandhi's campaign of passive resistance to British rule in India, since he believed that this tactic should not be used as a weapon until Indians understood the principles underlying it. Tagore and Gandhi were, however, united in their opposition to British rule, and they maintained a warm relationship over the years.

Tagore's novel *The Home and the World* (1919) is the story of a romantic triangle: the idealistic landowner Nikhil's wife, Bimala, is attracted to her husband's seductive college friend, Sandip, an activist in the nationalist cause. Based on the tensions and ambivalence created in many educated Bengalis by the Swadeshi (Nationalist) movement of 1905 and the terrorist violence that followed, it depicts a society changing rapidly because of the introduction of Western ideas. It is a moral work that is implicitly critical of violence as a tool of emancipation; it is also a daring work that treats women's attempts to break out of the confines of the home and enter the wider world. The mood of the novel is somber; Dutta and Robinson place it "among Tagore's darkest works." Nevertheless, it is one of Tagore's most popular novels, and its reputation has been boosted by Satyajit Ray's 1984 movie version.

Tagore's need for funds to sustain and expand his university led to his fifth foreign tour in May 1920. His reception by the English was much less enthusiastic than it had been on his earlier trips: he had recently spurned the country by resigning his knighthood in such a dramatic fashion, and he persisted in criticizing

British rule in India at every opportunity. On the Continent, however, where his works had been translated into various languages by eminent writers such as André Gide, he was feted by the literati in Paris, Strasbourg, Geneva, Hamburg, Copenhagen, Stockholm, Berlin, Munich, Vienna, and Prague. In the United States, as in England, his reception was not as warm as it had been on his previous visits. He traveled again to Britain and the Continent before returning to India in July 1921.

In 1921 Tagore published *The Fugitive,* which includes his prose "translations" not only of his own poems but also of seventeen religious poems by other Bengali mystical writers. Like his other translations of his own work after *Gitanjali,* the verses rendered into English in *The Fugitive* fail to do justice to the emotional intensity or the craft he displays in the Bengali originals. Most of the poems are religious in tone and spirit, but the reader will find it difficult to trace the borders between the sacred and the secular: in Tagore's verse the beloved can be either God or a woman. *The Fugitive* also includes five short plays based on Indian myths.

Also in 1921 Tagore published *Thought Relics,* a collection of 109 brief devotional essays. Some of them originated in Bengali pieces he had written earlier and had translated during his 1920 voyage to England. Many, however, are original works and testify to Tagore's status as one of the earliest Indian writers of English prose of high quality. In number 16, for example, he writes feelingly and sensitively of the human quest for the infinite:

> We are like the stray line of a poem, which ever feels that it rhymes with another line and must find it, or miss its own fulfillment. The quest of the unattained is the great impulse in man which brings forth all his best creations. Man seems deeply to be aware of a separation at the root of his being; he tries to be led across it to a union; and somehow he knows that it is love which can lead him to a love which is final.

The volume did not attract much attention in England or America, indicating that Tagore was no longer the literary phenomenon in the English-speaking West that he had once been. (Even so, Macmillan commissioned Andrews to publish an edition of the book in 1929 that included eighty-nine more pieces and was retitled *Thoughts from Tagore.*)

Although Tagore's stay in America was, on the whole, a disappointment for him, he did give at least two significant lectures there. In "The Meeting of the East and the West," given at a reception organized by the Discussion Guild and the Indian Society on 1 December 1930 at Carnegie Hall in New York City, he remembered the aspect of the West that had stirred him

and his fellow Indians in the nineteenth century: "the ideal of the freedom of man, freedom of self-expression for all races and all countries." Cherishing the period in Indian history when East and West came together, he lamented the "terrible menace" of power that he sees in "the conflagration of war and misery" in the contemporary West. In the other lecture, "The Poet's Religion," delivered at the Brooklyn Civic forum, Tagore declared that "the faith in God, in the reality of the ideal of perfection, has built up all that is great in the human world" and that when "the faith of the infinite reality of Perfection" fails to ignite, materialism destroys all values and stifles creativity.

As early as 1921 Tagore appears to have realized the disservice he had done to himself by rushing volume after volume of his translations into print to meet the demand for his work in English-speaking countries. He wrote to his admirer Edward J. Thompson on 2 February: "I know I am misrepresenting myself as a poet to the western readers. But when I began this career of falsifying my own coins I did it in play. Now I am becoming frightened of its enormity and I am willing to make a confession of my misdeeds and withdraw into my original vocation as a mere Bengali poet."

"The Poet's Religion" is the inaugural essay in Tagore's 1922 book in English, *Creative Unity.* The other essays are "The Creative Ideal," "The Religion of the Forest," "An Indian Folk Religion," "East and West," "The Modern Age," "The Spirit of Freedom," "The Nation," "Woman and Home," and "An Eastern University." "The Spirit of Freedom" is a letter that he wrote in New York urging Indians to avoid the "spirit of the machine" in the civilization of the West as well as the repressive nature of contemporary Indian civilization. In these essays Tagore articulates his ideas in English prose with clarity and conviction.

For the rest of the decade Tagore did not publish much in English, although collections of his letters in English to Andrews and collections of his lectures abroad came out from time to time in India and in the West. Much of his energy in these years was devoted to building and raising funds for Visva-Bharati and responding to speaking invitations at home and abroad. In 1922 he traveled to Ceylon, and in 1924 he spent several months in China and Japan. In September 1924 he sailed for Peru to attend the ceremonies celebrating the centenary of Peruvian independence, but he fell ill en route and spent three months recuperating in the home of the Argentine publisher and writer Victorio Ocampo in Buenos Aires. Returning home via Italy, he arrived in India in February 1925. In 1926 he returned to Italy as the guest of the Fascist dictator Benito Mussolini. From Italy he traveled to Switzerland, where the writer Romain Rolland showed him statements in the

Tagore reading to students in 1925 (Time & Life Pictures/Getty Images)

Italian press depicting him as sympathetic to Mussolini. In response, Tagore published a letter in the *Manchester Guardian* (5 August 1926) protesting the distortion of his views and expressing his aversion to Fascism. He went on to England, Austria, Norway, Sweden, Germany, Hungary, Bulgaria, Greece, and Egypt before returning to India in December 1926. In July 1927 he traveled to southeast Asia and in May 1928 to Ceylon. In 1928 he published an English work, *Fireflies;* like *Stray Birds,* it consists of epigrammatic verse.

In 1929 Tagore visited Canada, the United States, and Japan, returning to Calcutta in July. In March 1930 he departed for England; en route he stopped in Paris, where friends and admirers celebrated his sixty-ninth birthday. The main reason for his visit to England was to deliver the Hibbert Lectures at the University of Oxford in May. The subject of the lectures was "the idea of the humanity of our God, or the divinity of Man the Eternal." They offered his English audience an insight into the faith that underlay Tagore's verse: "For it is evident that my religion is a poet's religion. . . . Its touch comes to me through the same unseen and trackless channel as does the inspira-

tion of my songs." The lectures were well attended and earned glowing reviews, the *Manchester Guardian* commenting on 27 May that "the personality of the poet as he spoke with the sunshine falling on his white head and lighting up his beautiful face made comparatively easy even his most difficult thoughts." The lectures were published in 1931 as *The Religion of Man.* Reprinted many times, the book ranks with *Nationalism* as one of his most enduring works in English. Going beyond institutionalized religion and drawing lovingly on the rural religious traditions of Bengal, Tagore discourses on reality, the world of the spirit, and the nature of prophecy and of the artist. But Tagore's humanism is the quality that most impresses the reader: "We can never go beyond man in all that we know and feel."

Tagore traveled from England to Germany in July. Moved by the performance of the Passion Play in Oberammergau, he wrote his only long poem in English, *The Child* (1931), in the course of a single night. Combining biblical allusions with Hindu traditions, the poem alludes to Christ's coming and to Gandhi's travails as "a man of Faith" in a world where people seem

Tagore with Albert Einstein in the 1920s (Hulton Archive/Getty Images)

to have lost their way. The poem did not attract much critical attention.

Tagore went on from Germany to Switzerland, Russia, and the United States. On 25 November 1930 a banquet was held in his honor in New York City. He met President Herbert Hoover, lectured to thousands at Carnegie Hall, and was honored by a dance performance given at the Broadway Theater by Ruth St. Dennis to help him raise funds for Visva-Bharati. He returned home in January 1931. To commemorate his seventieth birthday that year, admirers from all over the world sent messages and tributes that were compiled as *The Golden Book of Tagore*. Remembering "the incomparable purity" of *Gitanjali,* which he had translated into French in 1913, Gide observed that "through the war and beyond all our political and confessional dissensions, this fixed star has continued to shine and pour on the world a tranquil light of love, confidence, and peace." The British philosopher Bertrand Russell wrote: "He has contributed as much as any man living to the most important work of our time, namely, the promotion of understanding between different races. Of what he has done for India it is not for me to speak, but of what he has done for Europe and America in the way of softening of prejudices and the removal of misconceptions I can speak, and I know that on this account he is worthy of the highest honor." Despite becoming disillusioned with Tagore's translations in the 1920s, Yeats declared that "of recent years, I have found wisdom and beauty, or both, in your prose—*The*

Home and the World, your short stories, and your *Reminiscences.*" (It should be noted that both *The Home and the World* and *Reminiscences* [1917] were translated into English not by Tagore but by his nephew, and some of his short stories were translated by others.) The American philosopher Will Durant noted that "something of the ancient idealism of the East has been poured into our blood by the wine and music of your verse, by the example and majesty of your life." The physicist Albert Einstein resorted to almost biblical cadences to praise the Indian poet and sage: "Thou hast served mankind all through a long and fruitful life, spreading everywhere a gentle and free thought in a manner such as the Seers of thy people have proclaimed as the ideal."

In the 1930s Tagore became absorbed in painting, and his creative energies were devoted to this medium, as well as to composing songs, verse, and fiction in Bengali. Others took on the task of translating his works into English. His only significant work in English to appear during the decade was the 1936 *Collected Poems and Plays of Rabindranath Tagore.* On 21 October 1935 he wrote a long letter to Thomas Sturge Moore, one of his earliest admirers and the man who had nominated him for the Nobel Prize, in which he described translations as "acrobatic tricks" that "in most cases" constitute "treason against the majesty of the original." He went on to declare that he ought not to have dared to intrude into the "realm of glory" of English verse with "offerings" that he had polished "hastily" to "a foreign shine" by "assumed gestures."

Tagore with the art historian Ananda Coomaraswamy in the early 1930s (photograph by Doña Luisa Coomaraswamy;
Coomaraswamy Family Collection, Princeton University Research Collections; from Roger Lipsey,
Coomaraswamy: His Life and Work, *1977; Richland County Public Library)*

He noted that he had done "injustice" to himself and had abased himself by "clamoring for one's immediate due in wrong times and out of the way places." He added that his realization of the futility of his bid to represent himself in English had led him to instruct his admirer, the Bengali poet Amiya Chakravarty, at that time a student at Oxford, "not to participate in perpetuating my offence of transgression by arranging a collected edition of my own translations" that Macmillan was planning. He was convinced that "casual visitors must not overstay their welcome" and must know when it is time "for them to leave the stage, withdrawing themselves from a too prolonged stare of the critical footlight."

And yet, Tagore allowed Chakravarty to compile the *Collected Poems and Plays* with the help of Andrews and Rhys. When the work was published, Tagore wrote to Rhys and Macmillan expressing his satisfaction, seemingly having forgotten the qualms he had had about such a volume.

The *Collected Poems and Plays of Rabindranath Tagore* remained in print for decades, giving English-speaking readers of successive generations an impression of Tagore's achievement. But Dutta and Robinson argue that the collection was "disastrous" in the long-term impact it had on his reputation. Since there is no editorial commentary, readers are not informed that they are being offered translations from the Bengali or that some of the translations are not by Tagore but by others. Furthermore, of the translations done by Tagore, those of works after *Gitanjali* are not of high quality. Amazingly, works Tagore had written in English, such as *Fireflies* and *The Child,* are not included. Finally, the poems chosen are mainly those that represent him as a mystic poet; thus, the selections do not represent the full range of his work.

According to Dutta and Robinson, Tagore's reputation in the English-speaking world, already declining in the decades following the publication of *Gitanjali,* "took a nose-dive" with the publication of *The Collected*

Poems and Plays, even though the work aroused "minimal interest" from critics at the time. They note, for example, that the author Graham Greene wrote in his introduction to R. K. Narayan's novel *The Bachelor of Arts* (1937): "As for Rabindranath Tagore, I cannot believe that anyone but Mr. Yeats"—who had included Tagore in *The Oxford Book of Modern Verse* (1936)—"can still take his poems very seriously."

But Dutta and Robinson point out that "while Tagore's literary stock among English writers was extremely low, his personal reputation was Olympian." They cite a reviewer of a 1939 Tagore biography who characterized Tagore as "the most famous of living poets," one whose "renown is worldwide." Further evidence of Tagore's enduring reputation as a literary figure was the honorary D.Litt. conferred on him by the University of Oxford in July 1940. In his speech at the event, Sir Maurice Gwyer, the chief justice of India, called Tagore "the myriad-minded poet and writer, the musician famous in his art, the philosopher proven both in word and deed, the fervent upholder of learning and sound doctrine, the ardent defender of public liberties, one who by the sanctity of his life and character has won for himself the praise of all mankind." Tagore was too frail to travel to Oxford to receive the degree, and he fell seriously ill in September. He died on 7 August 1941.

Although Bengali was always Tagore's preferred language for his creative work, the quantity of his English writings is substantial: the three-volume edition of *The English Writings of Rabindranath Tagore* (1994–1996), edited by Sisir Kumar Das, runs to more than two thousand folio pages. The two standard literary histories of Indian writing in English, by K. R. Srinivasa Iyengar (1962) and M. K. Naik (1982), devote considerable space to him. Srinivasa Iyengar comments: "He belongs unquestionably to Bengali literature, but he belongs to Indo-Anglian literature too." Naik notes that "Tagore presents a case of literary bilingualism which is perhaps without parallel in literary history" and insists that his English verse must be evaluated on its own merits. Treating it thus, he considers the religious poems of *Gitanjali* and the love poems of *The Gardener* far superior to the later collections. He believes, however, that the verse epigrams of *Stray Birds* and *Fireflies* have been unjustly neglected. He finds Tagore's "verse in English essentially lyrical in quality" and points out that it deals with "the elemental subjects of all lyrical poetry— God, Nature, Love, the Child, Life and death." Tagore brings to his English lyrical works, Naik says, "the born poet's simplicity, sensuousness and passion," although they are steeped in the "Indian ethos" and touched with the spirit of the Hindu holy book, the Upanishads. According to Naik, Tagore's English prose shows him to be "an internationalist and humanist preaching the gospel

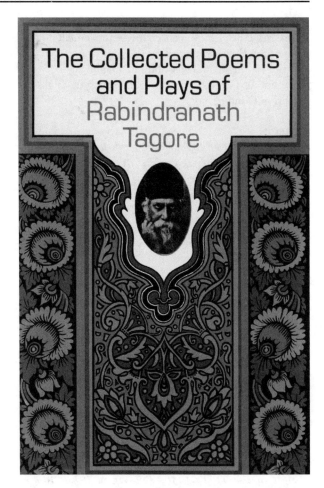

Dust jacket for the U.S. edition (1937) of the 1936 volume of English versions of some of Tagore's Bengali works, translated by himself and others (Richland County Public Library)

of universal harmony between Man and man, Man and nature, and Man and the Divine." For Naik, "Tagore's prose is remarkable less for qualities of precision and logical argumentation than for its frequent spells of impassioned, semi-poetic utterance." Finally, Naik says that Tagore's plays suffer the most in his English translations because he subjected them to "rigorous condensation," though at their best they are comparable to "the modern imaginative drama of W. B. Yeats and Maurice Maeterlinck."

The current generation of South Asian writers in English appears largely unwilling to acknowledge Rabindranath Tagore as a forerunner. But the poet Nissim Ezekiel thought that he was too important a figure to be passed over, saying in a 1980 lecture that "any educated Indian today and for a long time to come who has not had the profoundest possible experience of Tagore has missed a crucial element in the shaping of modern Indian culture." And in his introduction to selections from Tagore's writings in *The Picador Book of Modern Indian Literature*

(1961), the novelist Amit Chaudhuri considers Tagore's efforts as crucial in Indian culture's movement toward modernity. Perhaps, then, Tagore's importance is that he not only brought Indian writing in English to the world stage but also brought South Asian writing in English to the brink of modernity.

Letters:

Glimpses of Bengal: Selected from the Letters of Sir Rabindranath Tagore, 1885–1895 (London: Macmillan, 1921; Calcutta: Macmillan, 1960);

Letters from Abroad (Madras: S. Ganesan, 1924);

Letters to a Friend, edited by C. F. Andrews (London: Allen & Unwin, 1928);

Letters from Russia, translated by Sasadhar Sinha (Calcutta: Visva-Bharati, 1960);

Imperfect Encounter: Letters of William Rothenstein and Rabindranath Tagore, 1911–1941, edited by Mary M. Lago (Cambridge, Mass.: Harvard University Press, 1972);

Glimpses of Bengal: Selected Letters, translated by Krishna Dutta and Andrew Robinson (London: Papermac, 1991);

A Rich Harvest: The Complete Tagore/Elmhirst Correspondence and Other Writings, edited by Kissoonsingh Hazareesingh (Stanley, Rose-Hill, Mauritius: Editions de l'océan Indien, 1992);

Selected Letters, edited by Dutta and Robinson (Cambridge: Cambridge University Press, 1997);

Poets to a Poet, 1912–1940: Letters from Robert Bridges, Ernest Rhys, W. B. Yeats, Thomas Sturge Moore, R. C. Trevelyan and Ezra Pound to Rabindranath Tagore, edited by Bikash Chakravarty (Calcutta: Visva-Bharati, 1998);

The Geddes–Tagore Correspondence, edited by Bashabi Fraser (Edinburgh: Edinburgh Review, 2002);

A Difficult Friendship: Letters of Edward Thompson and Rabindranath Tagore 1913–1940, edited by Uma Das Gupta (New Delhi: Oxford University Press, 2003).

Bibliographies:

Dar al-Kutub al-Misriyah, *Rabindranath Tagore: A Bibliographical List Issued on the Occasion of His Centenary Celebration* (Cairo: National Library Press, 1961);

Katherine Henn, *Rabindranath Tagore: A Bibliography* (Metuchen, N.J. & London: Scarecrow Press / Philadelphia: American Theological Library Association, 1985).

Biographies:

Ernest Rhys, *Rabindranath Tagore: A Biographical Study* (London: Macmillan, 1915; New York: Macmillan, 1915);

Edward J. Thompson, *Rabindranath Tagore: His Life and Work* (Calcutta: Association Press / London: Oxford University Press, 1921); revised as *Rabindranath Tagore: Poet and Dramatist* (London: Oxford University Press, 1948);

Vincenc Lesný, *Rabindranath Tagore: His Personality and Work,* translated by Guy McKeever Phillips, foreword by C. F. Andrews (London: Allen & Unwin, 1939);

Mohinimohan Bhattacharya, *Rabindranath Tagore: Poet and Thinker* (Allahabad: Kitab Mahal, 1961);

Krishna R. Kripalani, *Rabindranath Tagore: A Biography* (New York: Oxford University Press, 1962; London: Oxford University Press, 1962; revised edition, Calcutta: Visva-Bharati, 1980);

Gangadhara Devarava Khanolakara, *The Lute and the Plough: A Life of Rabindranath Tagore* (Bombay: Book Centre, 1963);

Hiranmay Banerjee, *Rabindranath Tagore* (New Delhi: Publications Division, Ministry of Information and Broadcasting, Government of India, 1971);

Probhat Kumar Mukherji, *Life of Tagore,* translated by Sisirkumar Ghosh (New Delhi: Indian Book Co., 1975; Thompson, Conn.: InterCulture Associates, 1975);

Buddhadeva Bose, *Tagore: Portrait of a Poet* (Calcutta: Papyrus, 1994);

Krishna Dutta and Andrew Robinson, *Rabindranath Tagore: The Myriad-Minded Man* (Calcutta: Rupa, 2000);

Uma Das Gupta, *Rabindranath Tagore: A Biography* (Delhi & Oxford: Oxford University Press, 2004).

References:

Beena Agarwal, *The Plays of Rabindra Nath Tagore: A Thematic Study* (New Delhi: Satyam, 2003);

R. S. Agarwala, *Aesthetic Consciousness of Tagore* (Calcutta: Abhishek Agarwal, 1996);

B. K. Ahluwalia and Shashi Ahluwalia, *Tagore and Gandhi: The Tagore-Gandhi Controversy* (New Delhi: Pankaj, 1981);

Mulk Raj Anand, *Homage to Tagore* (Lahore: Sangram, 1946);

Anand, *The Humanism of Rabindranath Tagore: Three Lectures* (Aurangabad: Marathwada University, 1979);

Anand, *Poet-Painter: Paintings by Rabindranath Tagore* (New Delhi: Abhinav, 1985);

Anand, *The Volcano: Some Comments on the Development of Rabindranath Tagore's Aesthetic Theories and Art Practice* (Baroda: Maharaja Sayajirao University of Baroda, 1967);

Alex Aronson, *Rabindranath Tagore: A Celebration of His Life and Work* (Oxford: Museum of Modern Art, 1986);

Aronson, *Rabindranath through Western Eyes* (Allahabad: Kitabistan, 1943);

Aronson and Krishna R. Kripalani, eds., *Rolland and Tagore* (Calcutta: Visva-Bharati, 1945);

David W. Atkinson, *Gandhi and Tagore: Visionaries of Modern India* (Hong Kong: Asian Research Service, 1989);

Abu Sayeed Ayyub, *Modernism and Tagore,* translated by Amitava Ray (New Delhi: Sahitya Akademi, 1995);

Ayyub, *Tagore's Quest* (Calcutta: Papyrus, 1980);

Asoke K. Bagchi, *Rabindranath Tagore and His Medical World* (Delhi: Konark, 2000);

Srikumar Banerji, *Phases of Tagore's Poetry,* Tagore Memorial Lectures, 1968–1969 (Mysore: Prasaranga, University of Mysore, 1973);

Sudhansu Bimal Barua, *Studies in Tagore and Buddhist Culture* (Calcutta: Sahitya Samsad, 1991);

Kakoli Basak, *Rabindranath Tagore, a Humanist* (New Delhi: Classical Publishing Company, 1991);

Sankar Basu, *Chekhov and Tagore: A Comparative Study of Their Short Stories* (New Delhi: Sterling, 1985);

K. S. Bharathi, *The Political Thought of Rabindranath Tagore* (New Delhi: Concept, 1998);

Vivek Ranjan Bhattacharya, *Relevance of Tagore* (New Delhi: Metropolitan, 1979);

Bhattacharya, *Tagore: The Citizen of the World* (Delhi: Metropolitan, 1961);

Bhattacharya, *Tagore's Vision of a Global Family* (New Delhi: Enkay, 1987);

Abinash Chandra Bose, *Three Mystic Poets: A Study of W. B. Yeats, A.E., and Rabindranath Tagore* (Kolhapur: School and College Bookstall, 1945; Folcroft, Pa.: Folcroft Press, 1970);

Buddhadeva Bose, *An Acre of Green Grass: A Review of Modern Bengali Literature* (Calcutta: Papyrus, 1948), pp. 13–25;

Somendranath Bose, ed., *Tagore Studies 1970* (Calcutta: Tagore Research Institute, 1970);

Mohit Chakrabarti, *Philosophy of Education of Rabindranath Tagore: A Critical Evaluation* (New Delhi: Atlantic, 1988);

Chakrabarti, *Rabindranath Tagore: A Miscellany* (New Delhi: Kanishka, 2003);

Chakrabarti, *Rabindranath Tagore: A Quest* (New Delhi: Gyan, 1995);

Chakrabarti, *Rabindranath Tagore: Diverse Dimensions* (New Delhi: Atlantic, 1990);

Chakrabarti, *Tagore and Education for Social Change* (New Delhi: Gyan, 1993);

Santosh Chakrabarti, *Studies in Tagore: Critical Essays* (New Delhi: Atlantic, 2004);

Bishweshwar Chakraverty, *Tagore, the Dramatist: A Critical Study* (Delhi: B.R. Publishing Corporation, 2000);

Byomkesh Chandra Chakravorty, *Rabindranath Tagore: His Mind and Art. Tagore's Contribution to English Literature* (New Delhi: Young India Publications, 1971);

Bhabatosh Chatterjee, *Rabindranath Tagore and Modern Sensibility* (Delhi: Oxford University Press, 1996);

Ramananda Chatterjee, ed., *The Golden Book of Tagore: A Homage to Rabindranath Tagore from India and the World in Celebration of His Seventieth Birthday* (Calcutta: The Golden Book Committee, 1931);

Amit Chaudhuri, *The Picador Book of Modern Indian Literature* (London: Picador, 1961), p. xviii;

Bhudeb Chaudhuri and K. G. Subramanyan, eds., *Rabindranath Tagore and the Challenges of Today* (Shimla: Indian Institute of Advanced Study, 1988);

B. M. Chauduri, ed., *Homage to Rabindranath Tagore: In Commemoration of the Birth Centenary of Rabindranath Tagore* (Kharagpur: Tagore Centenary Celebrations Committee, Indian Institute of Technology, 1961);

Luciano Colussi, *Universality in Tagore: Souvenir of a Symposium on Rabindranath Tagore* (Calcutta: Nitika/Don Bosco, 1991);

P. K. Datta, ed., *Rabindranath Tagore's* The Home and the World: *A Critical Companion* (Delhi: Permanent Black, 2003); republished as *Tagore's* Home and the World: *Modern Essays in Criticism* (London: Anthem, 2003);

Bimalendu Dutta, ed., *Tagore in Abroad: From the Pages of the* Modern Review, *August 1912–July 1934* (Calcutta: Papyrus, 2001);

Nissim Ezekiel, *Selected Prose* (Delhi: Oxford University Press, 1992);

Sisirkumar Ghose, *The Later Poems of Tagore* (London: Asia Publishing House, 1961; New York: Asia Publishing House, 1961);

Verinder Grover, ed., *Rabindranath Tagore,* Political Thinkers of Modern India, no. 25 (New Delhi: Deep & Deep, 1993);

Stephen N. Hay, *Asian Ideas of East and West: Tagore and His Critics in Japan, China, and India* (Cambridge, Mass.: Harvard University Press, 1970);

Patrick Colm Hogan and Lalita Pandit, eds., *Rabindranath Tagore: Universality and Tradition* (Madison, N.J.: Fairleigh Dickinson University Press / London: Associated University Presses, 2003);

Manindranath Jana, *Education for Life: Tagore and Modern Thinkers* (Calcutta: Firma KLM, 1984);

Kalyan Kundu, Sakti Bhattacharya, and Kalyan Sircar, eds., *Rabindranath and the British Press, 1912–1941* (London: Tagore Centre UK, 1990); republished as *Imagining Tagore: Rabindranath and the British Press, 1912–1941* (Calcutta: Shishu Sahitya Samsad, 2000);

Mary M. Lago, *Rabindranath Tagore* (Boston: Twayne, 1976);

Lago and Ronald Warwick, eds., *Rabindranath Tagore: Perspectives in Time. International Tagore Conference: Selected Papers* (Basingstoke, U.K.: Macmillan, 1989);

Roger Lipsey, *Coomaraswamy: His Life and Work* (Princeton: Princeton University Press, 1977);

Ray Monk and Andrew Robinson, eds., *Rabindranath Tagore: A Celebration of His Life and Work* (London: Tagore Festival Committee, 1986);

Sujit Mukherjee, *Passage to America: The Reception of Rabindranath Tagore in the United States, 1912–1941* (Calcutta: Bookland, 1964);

B. C. Mukherji, *Vedanta and Tagore* (New Delhi: M.D. Publications, 1994);

Dhurjati Prasad Mukherji, *Tagore: A Study* (Bombay: Padma, 1944);

Anupam Ratan Shankar Nagar, *Mysticism in Tagore's Poetry* (Bareilly: Prakash Book Depot, 1995);

M. K. Naik, *A History of Indian English Literature* (New Delhi: Sahitya Akademi, 1982), pp. 58–66, 79–81, 101–103;

Vishwanath S. Naravane, *An Introduction to Rabindranath Tagore* (Delhi: Macmillan India, 1977; Columbia, Mo.: South Asia Books, 1978);

Joseph T. O'Connell and others, eds., *Presenting Tagore's Heritage in Canada* (Toronto: Rabindranath Tagore Lectureship Foundation, 1989);

D. K. Pabby and Alpana Neogy, eds., *Rabindranath Tagore's* The Home and the World: *New Dimensions* (New Delhi: Asia Book Club, 2001);

Ratan Parimoo, ed., *Rabindranath Tagore: Collection of Essays* (New Delhi: Lalit Kala Akademi, 1989);

Sarvepalli Radhakrishnan, *The Philosophy of Rabindranath Tagore* (London: Macmillan, 1918);

G. V. Raj, *Tagore, the Novelist* (New Delhi: Sterling, 1983);

Mohit K. Ray, ed., *Studies on Rabindranath Tagore,* 2 volumes (New Delhi: Atlantic, 2004);

T. R. Sharma, ed., *Essays on Rabindranath Tagore: In Honour of D. M. Gupta* (Ghaziabad: Vimal Prakashan, 1987);

Sharma, ed., *Perspectives on Rabindranath Tagore,* Indo-English Writers, no. 7 (Ghaziabad: Vimal Prakashan, 1986);

Rita D. Sil, ed., *Profile of Rabindranath Tagore in World Literature* (New Delhi: Khama, 2000);

K. R. Srinivasa Iyengar, *Indian Writing in English* (New Delhi: Sterling, 1985), pp. 99–143;

Srinivasa Iyengar, *Rabindranath Tagore: A Critical Introduction* (New Delhi: Sterling, 1985; London: Oriental University Press, 1986);

Ira G. Zepp Jr., ed., *Rabindranath Tagore: American Interpretations* (Calcutta: Writers Workshop, 1981).

Papers:

Rabindranath Tagore's papers are at the University of London Library and in Rabindra Bhavan, Santiniketan.

Checklist of Further Readings

Ariel (1972–).

Ayyappa Paniker, K. *Indian English Literature since Independence.* New Delhi: Indian Association for English Studies, 1991.

Baumgardner, Robert J., ed. *The English Language in Pakistan.* Karachi & Oxford: Oxford University Press, 1993.

Behl, Aditya, and David Nicholls, eds. *The Penguin New Writing in India,* revised edition. New Delhi & London: Penguin, 1994.

Bharucha, Nilufar E., and Vrinda Nabar, eds. *Mapping Cultural Spaces: Postcolonial Indian Literature in English. Essays in Honor of Nissim Ezekiel.* New Delhi: Vision, 1998.

Blamires, Harry, ed. *A Guide to Twentieth-Century Literature in English.* London: Methuen, 1983.

Boehmer, Elleke. *Colonial and Postcolonial Literature: Migrant Metaphors.* Oxford & New York: Oxford University Press, 1995.

Chaudhuri, Amit, ed. *The Picador Book of Modern Indian Literature.* London: Picador, 2001.

De Mel, Neloufer, ed. *Essays in Sri Lankan Poetry in English.* Colombo: English Association of Sri Lanka, 1995.

De Souza, Eunice, ed. *Nine Indian Women Poets: An Anthology.* New Delhi & Oxford: Oxford University Press, 1997.

Dharwadker, Vinay, and A. K. Ramanujan, eds. *The Oxford Anthology of Modern Indian Poetry.* New Delhi & Oxford: Oxford University Press, 1994.

Goonetilleke, D. C. R. A., ed. *Modern Sri Lankan Poetry: An Anthology.* Delhi: Sri Satguru, 1987.

Goonetilleke, ed. *Modern Sri Lankan Stories: An Anthology.* Delhi: Sri Satguru, 1986.

Goonetilleke, ed. *Sri Lankan Literature in English: A 50th Independence Anniversary Anthology.* Colombo: Department of Cultural Affairs, Sri Lanka, 1998.

Gupta, R. S., and Kapil Kapoor, eds. *English in India: Issues and Problems.* Delhi: Academic Foundation, 1991.

Haq, Kaiser, ed. *Contemporary Indian Poetry.* Columbus: Ohio State University Press, 1990.

Hashmi, Alamgir, ed. *Pakistani Literature: The Contemporary Writers,* second edition. Islamabad: Gulmohar, 1987.

Jayasuriya, Wilfred. *Sri Lanka's Modern English Literature: A Case Study in Literary Theory.* New Delhi: Navrang, 1994.

Joshi, Svati, ed. *Rethinking English: Essays in Literature, Language, History.* Delhi & Oxford: Oxford University Press, 1994.

Journal of Commonwealth Literature (1965–).

Jussawalla, Adil J., ed. *New Writing in India.* Harmondsworth, U.K.: Penguin, 1974.

Jussawalla, Feroza F. *Family Quarrels: Towards a Criticism of Indian Writing in English.* American University Studies, Series IV: English Language and Literature, volume 17. New York: Peter Lang, 1985.

Kachru, Braj B. *The Indianization of English: The English Language in India.* Delhi & New York: Oxford University Press, 1983.

King, Bruce. *Modern Indian Poetry in English,* revised edition. New Delhi & Oxford: Oxford University Press, 2001.

King, ed. *The Commonwealth Novel since 1960.* London: Macmillan, 1991.

King, ed. *Literatures of the World in English.* London: Routledge & Kegan Paul, 1974.

Lal, Malashri. *The Law of the Threshold: Women Writers in Indian English.* Shimla: Indian Institute of Advanced Study, 1995.

Lal, Alamgir Hashmi, and Victor J. Ramraj, eds. *Post Independence Voices in South Asian Writings.* Delhi: Doaba, 2001.

Lal, P., ed. *Modern Indian Poetry in English: An Anthology and a Credo.* Calcutta: Writers Workshop, 1969.

McCutchion, David. *Indian Writing in English: Critical Essays.* Calcutta: Writers Workshop, 1969.

Mehrotra, Arvind Krishna, ed. *History of Indian Literature in English.* New York: Columbia University Press, 2003.

Mehrotra, ed. *The Oxford India Anthology of Twelve Modern Indian Poets.* Delhi & Oxford: Oxford University Press, 1992.

Mukherjee, Meenakshi. *The Perishable Empire: Essays on Indian Writing in English.* New Delhi & New York: Oxford University Press, 2000.

Mukherjee. *The Twice-Born Fiction: Themes and Techniques of the Indian Novel in English,* second edition. New Delhi: Arnold-Heinemann, 1974.

Naik, M. K. *Dimensions of Indian English Literature.* New Delhi: Sterling, 1984.

Naik. *A History of Indian English Literature.* New Delhi: Sahitya Akademi, 1982.

Naik and Shyamala Narayan. *Indian English Literature, 1980–2000: A Critical Survey.* Delhi: Pencraft International, 2001.

Naik, S. K. Desai, and G. S. Amur, eds. *Critical Essays on Indian Writing in English Presented to Armando Menezes,* revised and enlarged edition. Dharwar: Karnatak University, 1972.

Nanavati, U. M., and Prafulla C. Kar, eds. *Rethinking Indian English Literature.* Delhi: Pencraft International, 2000.

Narasimhaiah, C. D. *The Swan and the Eagle: Essays on Indian English Literature,* third edition, revised and enlarged. New Delhi: Vision, 1999.

Narasimhaiah, ed. *Makers of Indian English Literature.* New Delhi: Pencraft International, 2000.

Navasilu: Journal of the English Association and the Association for Commonwealth Literature and Language Studies (1976–).

New Ceylon Writing, 1–4 (1970, 1973, 1977, 1984).

New Lankan Review, 1–8 (1983–1990).

Oaten, Edward Farley. *A Sketch of Anglo-Indian Literature.* London: Kegan Paul, Trench, Trübner, 1908.

Parthasarathy, R., ed. *Ten Twentieth-Century Indian Poets.* Delhi & New York: Oxford University Press, 1976.

Pathak, R. S., ed. *Recent Indian Fiction.* New Delhi: Prestige, 1994.

Perry, John Oliver. *Absent Authority: Issues in Contemporary Indian English Criticism.* New Delhi: Sterling, 1992.

Prasad, Amar Nath, ed. *Indian Women Novelists in English.* New Delhi: Atlantic, 2001.

Prasad, G. V. J. *Continuities in Indian English Poetry: Nation Language Form.* Delhi: Pencraft International, 1999.

Press, John, ed. *Commonwealth Literature: Unity and Diversity in a Commonwealth Culture. Extracts from the Proceedings of a Conference Held at Bodington Hall, Leeds 9–12 September 1964 under the Auspices of the University of Leeds.* London: Heinemann, 1965.

Rahman, Tariq. *A History of Pakistani Literature in English.* Lahore: Vanguard, 1991.

Rahman. *Language and Politics in Pakistan.* Karachi & Oxford: Oxford University Press, 1996.

Rao, P. Mallikarjuna, and M. Rajeshwar, eds. *Indian Fiction in English.* New Delhi: Atlantic, 1999.

Rushdie, Salman, and Elizabeth West, eds. *The Vintage Book of Indian Writing, 1947–1997.* London: Vintage, 1997.

Satchidanandan, K. *Indian Literature: Positions and Propositions.* Delhi: Pencraft International, 1999.

Seymour-Smith, Martin. *Macmillan Guide to Modern World Literature,* third edition. London: Macmillan, 1985. Republished as *The New Guide to Modern World Literature.* New York: P. Bedrick, 1985.

Shamsie, Muneeza, ed. *A Dragonfly in the Sun: An Anthology of Pakistani Writing in English*. Oxford: Oxford University Press, 1997.

Singh, Ram Sewak, and Charu Sheel Singh, eds. *Spectrum History of Indian Literature in English*. New Delhi: Atlantic, 1997.

Sodhi, Meena. *Indian English Writing: The Autobiographical Mode*. Creative New Literatures, no. 35. New Delhi: Creative, 1999.

Srinivasa Iyengar, K. R. *Indian Writing in English,* revised edition. New Delhi: Sterling, 1985.

Walsh, William. *Commonwealth Literature*. London & New York: Oxford University Press, 1973.

Walsh. *Indian Literature in English*. London: Longman, 1990.

Walsh, ed. *Readings in Commonwealth Literature*. Oxford: Clarendon Press, 1973.

Wijesinha, Rajiva. *Breaking Bounds: Essays on Sri Lankan Writing in English*. Belihuloya, Sri Lanka: Sabaragamuwa University Press, 1998.

Wijesinha, ed. *An Anthology of Contemporary Sri Lankan Poetry in English*. Colombo: British Council/English Association of Sri Lanka, 1988.

Williams, H. M. *Indo-Anglian Literature 1800–1970: A Survey*. Madras: Orient Longman, 1976; Columbia, Mo.: South Asia, 1977.

World Literature Written in English (1971–2004).

Zaman, Niaz, and others, eds. *Other Englishes: Essays on Commonwealth Writing*. Dhaka: University Press, 1991.

Contributors

Satish C. Aikant . . . . *H.N.B. Garhwal University*

Fakrul Alam . . . . *University of Dhaka*

Nilufer E. Bharucha . . . . *University of Mumbai*

Radha Chakravarty . . . . *Gargi College, University of Delhi*

Ralph J. Crane . . . . *University of Tasmania*

Frank Day . . . . *Clemson University*

Christel R. Devadawson . . . . *University of Delhi*

Anthony R. Guneratne . . . . *Florida Atlantic University*

Felicity Hand . . . . *Universitat Autònoma de Barcelona*

Kaiser Haq . . . . *University of Dhaka*

Farhad B. Idris . . . . *Frostburg State University*

Syed Manzoorul Islam . . . . *University of Dhaka*

Chelva Kanaganayakam . . . . *University of Toronto*

Rezaul Karim . . . . *Humber College*

Somdatta Mandal . . . . *Visva-Bharati University*

Shyamala A. Narayan . . . . *Jamia Millia Islamia University*

Lawrence Needham . . . . *Lakeland Community College*

Mala Pandurang . . . . *Dr. B. M. N. College*

Premila Paul . . . . *American College, Madurai*

Murari Prasad . . . . *Sana'a University*

Tariq Rahman . . . . *Quaid-i-Azam University*

Sridhar Rajeswaran . . . .

Ruvani Ranasinha . . . . *Brunel University*

E. Nageswara Rao . . . . *Osmania University*

Aali Areefur Rehman . . . . *Rajshahi University*

Manju Sampat . . . . *University of Mumbai*

Krishna Sen . . . . *University of Calcutta*

Ashis Sengupta . . . . *University of North Bengal*

Sukhbir Singh . . . . *Osmania University*

Rebecca Sultana . . . . *McMaster University*

Kamal D. Verma . . . . *University of Pittsburgh at Johnstown*

Niaz Zaman . . . . *University of Dhaka*

Cumulative Index

Dictionary of Literary Biography, Volumes 1-323
Dictionary of Literary Biography Yearbook, 1980-2002
Dictionary of Literary Biography Documentary Series, Volumes 1-19
Concise Dictionary of American Literary Biography, Volumes 1-7
Concise Dictionary of British Literary Biography, Volumes 1-8
Concise Dictionary of World Literary Biography, Volumes 1-4

Cumulative Index

DLB before number: *Dictionary of Literary Biography,* Volumes 1-323
Y before number: *Dictionary of Literary Biography Yearbook,* 1980-2002
DS before number: *Dictionary of Literary Biography Documentary Series,* Volumes 1-19
CDALB before number: *Concise Dictionary of American Literary Biography,* Volumes 1-7
CDBLB before number: *Concise Dictionary of British Literary Biography,* Volumes 1-8
CDWLB before number: *Concise Dictionary of World Literary Biography,* Volumes 1-4

Colden, Cadwallader
1688-1776 . . . . .DLB-24, 30, 270

Colden, Jane 1724-1766 . . . . DLB-200

Cole, Barry 1936- DLB-14

Cole, George Watson 1850-1939 . . . . DLB-140

Colegate, Isabel 1931- DLB-14, 231

Coleman, Emily Holmes 1899-1974 . . . . . . DLB-4

Coleman, Wanda 1946- DLB-130

Coleridge, Hartley 1796-1849 . . . . DLB-96

Coleridge, Mary 1861-1907 . . . . DLB-19, 98

Coleridge, Samuel Taylor
1772-1834 . . . . DLB-93, 107; CDBLB-3

Coleridge, Sara 1802-1852 . . . . DLB-199

Colet, John 1467-1519 . . . . DLB-132

Colette 1873-1954 . . . . DLB-65

Colette, Sidonie Gabrielle (see Colette)

Colinas, Antonio 1946- DLB-134

Coll, Joseph Clement 1881-1921 . . . . DLB-188

A Century of Poetry, a Lifetime of Collecting:
J. M. Edelstein's Collection of
Twentieth-Century American Poetry Y-02

Collier, John 1901-1980 . . . . .DLB-77, 255

Collier, John Payne 1789-1883 . . . . DLB-184

Collier, Mary 1690-1762 . . . . DLB-95

Collier, Robert J. 1876-1918 . . . . DLB-91

P. F. Collier [publishing house] DLB-49

Collin and Small DLB-49

Collingwood, R. G. 1889-1943 . . . . DLB-262

Collingwood, W. G. 1854-1932 . . . . DLB-149

Collins, An floruit circa 1653 . . . . DLB-131

Collins, Anthony 1676-1729 . . . . DLB-252

Collins, Merle 1950- DLB-157

Collins, Michael 1964- DLB-267

Collins, Michael (see Lynds, Dennis)

Collins, Mortimer 1827-1876 . . . . DLB-21, 35

Collins, Tom (see Furphy, Joseph)

Collins, Wilkie
1824-1889 . . . . . . DLB-18, 70, 159; CDBLB-4

"The Unknown Public" (1858)
[excerpt] DLB-57

The Wilkie Collins Society Y-98

Collins, William 1721-1759 . . . . DLB-109

Isaac Collins [publishing house] DLB-49

William Collins, Sons and Company DLB-154

Collis, Maurice 1889-1973 . . . . DLB-195

Collyer, Mary 1716?-1763? DLB-39

Colman, Benjamin 1673-1747 . . . . DLB-24

Colman, George, the Elder 1732-1794 . . . . DLB-89

Colman, George, the Younger
1762-1836 . . . . DLB-89

S. Colman [publishing house] DLB-49

Colombo, John Robert 1936- DLB-53

Colonial Literature DLB-307

Colquhoun, Patrick 1745-1820 . . . . DLB-158

Colter, Cyrus 1910-2002 . . . . DLB-33

Colum, Padraic 1881-1972 . . . . DLB-19

The Columbia History of the American Novel
A Symposium on Y-92

Columbus, Christopher 1451-1506 . . . . . DLB-318

Columella fl. first century A.D. DLB-211

Colvin, Sir Sidney 1845-1927 . . . . DLB-149

Colwin, Laurie 1944-1992 . . . . . . .DLB-218; Y-80

Comden, Betty 1915- and
Green, Adolph 1918-2002 . . . . . . DLB-44, 265

Comi, Girolamo 1890-1968 . . . . DLB-114

Comisso, Giovanni 1895-1969 . . . . DLB-264

Commager, Henry Steele 1902-1998 . . . . . DLB-17

Commynes, Philippe de
circa 1447-1511 . . . . DLB-208

Compton, D. G. 1930- DLB-261

Compton-Burnett, Ivy 1884?-1969 . . . . . . DLB-36

Conan, Laure (Félicité Angers)
1845-1924 . . . . DLB-99

Concord, Massachusetts
Concord History and Life DLB-223

Concord: Literary History
of a Town DLB-223

The Old Manse, by Hawthorne DLB-223

The Thoreauvian Pilgrimage: The
Structure of an American Cult . . DLB-223

Concrete Poetry DLB-307

Conde, Carmen 1901-1996 . . . . DLB-108

Condillac, Etienne Bonnot de
1714-1780 . . . . DLB-313

Condorcet, Marie-Jean-Antoine-Nicolas Caritat,
marquis de 1743-1794 . . . . DLB-313

"The Tenth Stage" DLB-314

Congreve, William
1670-1729 . . . . DLB-39, 84; CDBLB-2

Preface to *Incognita* (1692) DLB-39

W. B. Conkey Company DLB-49

Conlon, Evelyn 1952- DLB-319

Conn, Stewart 1936- DLB-233

Connell, Evan S., Jr. 1924- DLB-2; Y-81

Connelly, Marc 1890-1980 . . . . .DLB-7; Y-80

Connolly, Cyril 1903-1974 . . . . DLB-98

Connolly, James B. 1868-1957 . . . . DLB-78

Connor, Ralph (Charles William Gordon)
1860-1937 . . . . DLB-92

Connor, Tony 1930- DLB-40

Conquest, Robert 1917- DLB-27

Conrad, Joseph
1857-1924 . . . . DLB-10, 34, 98, 156; CDBLB-5

John Conrad and Company DLB-49

Conroy, Jack 1899-1990 . . . . Y-81

A Tribute [to Nelson Algren] Y-81

Conroy, Pat 1945- DLB-6

Considine, Bob 1906-1975 . . . . DLB-241

Consolo, Vincenzo 1933- DLB-196

Constable, Henry 1562-1613 . . . . DLB-136

Archibald Constable and Company DLB-154

Constable and Company Limited DLB-112

Constant, Benjamin 1767-1830 . . . . DLB-119

Constant de Rebecque, Henri-Benjamin de
(see Constant, Benjamin)

Constantine, David 1944- DLB-40

Constantine, Murray (see Burdekin, Katharine)

Constantin-Weyer, Maurice 1881-1964 . . . DLB-92

Contempo (magazine)
Contempo Caravan:
Kites in a Windstorm Y-85

The Continental Publishing Company DLB-49

A Conversation between William Riggan
and Janette Turner Hospital Y-02

Conversations with Editors Y-95

Conway, Anne 1631-1679 . . . . DLB-252

Conway, Moncure Daniel
1832-1907 . . . . DLB-1, 223

Cook, Ebenezer circa 1667-circa 1732 . . . . DLB-24

Cook, Edward Tyas 1857-1919 . . . . DLB-149

Cook, Eliza 1818-1889 . . . . DLB-199

Cook, George Cram 1873-1924 . . . . DLB-266

Cook, Michael 1933-1994 . . . . DLB-53

David C. Cook Publishing Company DLB-49

Cooke, George Willis 1848-1923 . . . . DLB-71

Cooke, John Esten 1830-1886 . . . . DLB-3, 248

Cooke, Philip Pendleton
1816-1850 . . . . DLB-3, 59, 248

Cooke, Rose Terry 1827-1892 . . . . . . .DLB-12, 74

Increase Cooke and Company DLB-49

Cook-Lynn, Elizabeth 1930- DLB-175

Coolbrith, Ina 1841-1928 . . . . DLB-54, 186

Cooley, Peter 1940- DLB-105

"Into the Mirror" DLB-105

Coolidge, Clark 1939- DLB-193

Coolidge, Susan
(see Woolsey, Sarah Chauncy)

George Coolidge [publishing house] DLB-49

Coomaraswamy, Ananda 1877-1947 . . . . DLB-323

Cooper, Anna Julia 1858-1964 . . . . DLB-221

Cooper, Edith Emma 1862-1913 . . . . DLB-240

Cooper, Giles 1918-1966 . . . . DLB-13

Cooper, J. California 19??- DLB-212

Cooper, James Fenimore
1789-1851 . . . . DLB-3, 183, 250; CDALB-2

The Bicentennial of James Fenimore Cooper:
An International Celebration Y-89

The James Fenimore Cooper Society Y-01

Cooper, Kent 1880-1965 . . . . DLB-29

Cooper, Susan 1935- DLB-161, 261

Cooper, Susan Fenimore 1813-1894 . . . . . DLB-239

William Cooper [publishing house] DLB-170

J. Coote [publishing house] DLB-154

Coover, Robert 1932- DLB-2, 227; Y-81

Tribute to Donald Barthelme Y-89

Tribute to Theodor Seuss Geisel Y-91

Copeland and Day DLB-49

Ćopić, Branko 1915-1984 . . . . DLB-181

Copland, Robert 1470?-1548 . . . . DLB-136

Coppard, A. E. 1878-1957 . . . . DLB-162

K

Nelson, William Rockhill 1841-1915 . . . . . DLB-23

Nemerov, Howard 1920-1991 . . . . .DLB-5, 6; Y-83

Németh, László 1901-1975 . . . . DLB-215

Nepos circa 100 B.C.-post 27 B.C. DLB-211

Néris, Salomėja 1904-1945 . . DLB-220; CDWLB-4

Neruda, Pablo 1904-1973 . . . . DLB-283

Nerval, Gérard de 1808-1855 . . . . DLB-217

Nervo, Amado 1870-1919 . . . . DLB-290

Nesbit, E. 1858-1924 . . . . .DLB-141, 153, 178

Ness, Evaline 1911-1986 . . . . DLB-61

Nestroy, Johann 1801-1862 . . . . DLB-133

Nettleship, R. L. 1846-1892 . . . . DLB-262

Neugeboren, Jay 1938- DLB-28

Neukirch, Benjamin 1655-1729 . . . . DLB-168

Neumann, Alfred 1895-1952 . . . . DLB-56

Neumann, Ferenc (see Molnár, Ferenc)

Neumark, Georg 1621-1681 . . . . DLB-164

Neumeister, Erdmann 1671-1756 . . . . DLB-168

Nevins, Allan 1890-1971 . . . . .DLB-17; DS-17

Nevinson, Henry Woodd 1856-1941 . . . . DLB-135

The New American Library DLB-46

New Directions Publishing Corporation. . . DLB-46

The New Monthly Magazine 1814-1884 . . . . DLB-110

New York Times Book Review Y-82

John Newbery [publishing house] DLB-154

Newbolt, Henry 1862-1938 . . . . DLB-19

Newbound, Bernard Slade (see Slade, Bernard)

Newby, Eric 1919- DLB-204

Newby, P. H. 1918-1997 . . . . DLB-15

Thomas Cautley Newby
 [publishing house] DLB-106

Newcomb, Charles King 1820-1894 . . . DLB-1, 223

Newell, Peter 1862-1924 . . . . DLB-42

Newell, Robert Henry 1836-1901 . . . . DLB-11

Newhouse, Samuel I. 1895-1979 . . . . DLB-127

Newman, Cecil Earl 1903-1976 . . . . DLB-127

Newman, David 1937- DLB-44

Newman, Frances 1883-1928 . . . . .Y-80

Newman, Francis William 1805-1897 . . . . DLB-190

Newman, G. F. 1946- DLB-310

Newman, John Henry
 1801-1890 . . . . DLB-18, 32, 55

Mark Newman [publishing house] DLB-49

Newmarch, Rosa Harriet 1857-1940 . . . . . DLB-240

George Newnes Limited DLB-112

Newsome, Effie Lee 1885-1979 . . . . DLB-76

Newton, A. Edward 1864-1940 . . . . DLB-140

Newton, Sir Isaac 1642-1727 . . . . DLB-252

Nexø, Martin Andersen 1869-1954 . . . . . DLB-214

Nezval, Vítěslav
 1900-1958 . . . . DLB-215; CDWLB-4

Ngugi wa Thiong'o
 1938- DLB-125; CDWLB-3

Niatum, Duane 1938- DLB-175

The *Nibelungenlied* and the *Klage*
 circa 1200 . . . . DLB-138

Nichol, B. P. 1944-1988 . . . . DLB-53

Nicholas of Cusa 1401-1464 . . . . DLB-115

Nichols, Ann 1891?-1966 . . . . DLB-249

Nichols, Beverly 1898-1983 . . . . DLB-191

Nichols, Dudley 1895-1960 . . . . DLB-26

Nichols, Grace 1950- DLB-157

Nichols, John 1940- Y-82

Nichols, Mary Sargeant (Neal) Gove
 1810-1884 . . . . DLB-1, 243

Nichols, Peter 1927- DLB-13, 245

Nichols, Roy F. 1896-1973 . . . . DLB-17

Nichols, Ruth 1948- DLB-60

Nicholson, Edward Williams Byron
 1849-1912 . . . . DLB-184

Nicholson, Geoff 1953- DLB-271

Nicholson, Norman 1914-1987 . . . . DLB-27

Nicholson, William 1872-1949 . . . . DLB-141

Ní Chuilleanáin, Eiléan 1942- DLB-40

Nicol, Eric 1919- DLB-68

Nicolai, Friedrich 1733-1811 . . . . DLB-97

Nicolas de Clamanges circa 1363-1437. . . DLB-208

Nicolay, John G. 1832-1901 and
 Hay, John 1838-1905 . . . . DLB-47

Nicole, Pierre 1625-1695 . . . . DLB-268

Nicolson, Adela Florence Cory (see Hope, Laurence)

Nicolson, Harold 1886-1968. . . . . . .DLB-100, 149

 "The Practice of Biography," in
 *The English Sense of Humour and
 Other Essays* DLB-149

Nicolson, Nigel 1917-2004 . . . . DLB-155

Ní Dhuibhne, Éilís 1954- DLB-319

Niebuhr, Reinhold 1892-1971 . . . . .DLB-17; DS-17

Niedecker, Lorine 1903-1970 . . . . DLB-48

Nieman, Lucius W. 1857-1935 . . . . DLB-25

Nietzsche, Friedrich
 1844-1900 . . . . DLB-129; CDWLB-2

 Mencken and Nietzsche: An Unpublished
 Excerpt from H. L. Mencken's *My Life
 as Author and Editor* Y-93

Nievo, Stanislao 1928- DLB-196

Niggli, Josefina 1910-1983 . . . . .Y-80

Nightingale, Florence 1820-1910 . . . . DLB-166

Nijō, Lady (Nakano-in Masatada no Musume)
 1258-after 1306 . . . . DLB-203

Nijō Yoshimoto 1320-1388 . . . . DLB-203

Nikitin, Ivan Savvich 1824-1861 . . . . .DLB-277

Nikitin, Nikolai Nikolaevich 1895-1963 . . .DLB-272

Nikolev, Nikolai Petrovich 1758-1815 . . . DLB-150

Niles, Hezekiah 1777-1839 . . . . DLB-43

Nims, John Frederick 1913-1999 . . . . DLB-5

 Tribute to Nancy Hale Y-88

Nin, Anaïs 1903-1977 . . . . DLB-2, 4, 152

Nína Björk Árnadóttir 1941-2000 . . . . . . DLB-293

Niño, Raúl 1961- DLB-209

Nissenson, Hugh 1933- DLB-28

Niven, Frederick John 1878-1944 . . . . DLB-92

Niven, Larry 1938- DLB-8

Nixon, Howard M. 1909-1983 . . . . DLB-201

Nizan, Paul 1905-1940 . . . . DLB-72

Njegoš, Petar II Petrović
 1813-1851 . . . . .DLB-147; CDWLB-4

Nkosi, Lewis 1936- DLB-157, 225

Noah, Mordecai M. 1785-1851 . . . . DLB-250

Noailles, Anna de 1876-1933 . . . . DLB-258

Nobel Peace Prize
 The Nobel Prize and Literary Politics Y-88

 Elie Wiesel Y-86

Nobel Prize in Literature
 Joseph Brodsky .Y-87

 Camilo José Cela Y-89

 Dario Fo Y-97

 Gabriel García Márquez. Y-82

 William Golding Y-83

 Nadine Gordimer. Y-91

 Günter Grass Y-99

 Seamus Heaney .Y-95

 Imre Kertész Y-02

 Najīb Mahfūz Y-88

 Toni Morrison. .Y-93

 V. S. Naipaul Y-01

 Kenzaburō Ōe .Y-94

 Octavio Paz Y-90

 José Saramago .Y-98

 Jaroslav Seifert .Y-84

 Claude Simon Y-85

 Wole Soyinka Y-86

 Wisława Szymborska. Y-96

 Derek Walcott .Y-92

 Gao Xingjian Y-00

Nobre, António 1867-1900 . . . . DLB-287

Nodier, Charles 1780-1844 . . . . DLB-119

Noël, Marie (Marie Mélanie Rouget)
 1883-1967 . . . . DLB-258

Noel, Roden 1834-1894 . . . . DLB-35

Nogami Yaeko 1885-1985 . . . . DLB-180

Nogo, Rajko Petrov 1945- DLB-181

Nolan, William F. 1928- DLB-8

 Tribute to Raymond Chandler Y-88

Noland, C. F. M. 1810?-1858 . . . . DLB-11

Noma Hiroshi 1915-1991 . . . . DLB-182

Nonesuch Press DLB-112

Creative Nonfiction Y-02

Nonni (Jón Stefán Sveinsson or Svensson)
 1857-1944. . . . . DLB-293

Noon, Jeff 1957- DLB-267

Noonan, Robert Phillipe (see Tressell, Robert)

Noonday Press DLB-46

Noone, John 1936- DLB-14

Nora, Eugenio de 1923- DLB-134

Nordan, Lewis 1939- DLB-234

Nordbrandt, Henrik 1945- DLB-214

Nordhoff, Charles 1887-1947 . . . . DLB-9

Norén, Lars 1944- DLB-257